Bhagavad Gītā

In the Light of Kashmir Shaivism

WITH ORIGINAL VIDEO

Revealed by
Swami Lakshmanjoo

John Hughes, Editor

Lakshmanjoo Academy

Published by:

Lakshmanjoo Academy

First printing 2013

Printed in the United States of America

For information, address:
Lakshmanjoo Academy
http://www.lakshmanjooacademy.org

ISBN 978-0-9816228-7-3 (paperback)
ISBN 978-0-9816228-1-1 (hardcover)

This pursuit is dedicated to Swamiji

to whom I owe everything.

Contents

Guide to Pronunciation		vii
Preface		ix
Acknowledgements		xvii
Author		xix
Bhagavad Gītā		
Introduction		1
Chapter One		13
Chapter Two	Part 1	33
	Part 2	55
	Part 3	81
Chapter Three	Part 1	105
	Part 2	131
Chapter Four	Part 1	153
	Part 2	173
	Part 3	193
Chapter Five	Part 1	213
	Part 2	233
Chapter Six	Part 1	251
	Part 2	267
	Part 3	287
Chapter Seven		311
Chapter Eight		343
Chapter Nine		375

Chapter Ten		401
Chapter Eleven		431
Chapter Twelve		467
Chapter Thirteen		483
Chapter Fourteen		513
Chapter Fifteen		533
Chapter Sixteen		557
Chapter Seventeen		575
Chapter Eighteen	Part 1	605
	Part 2	635
Bibliography		671
Index		673
Instructions to download audio		688

Guide to Pronounciation

The following English words exemplify the pronunciation of selected Sanskṛit vowels and consonants. The Romanized Sanskṛit vowel or consonant is first listed and then an English word is given to aid you in its proper pronunciation.

a	as	a in ***A***merica.
ā	as	a in f***a***ther.
i	as	i in f***i***ll, l***i***ly.
ī	as	i in pol***i***ce.
u	as	u in f***u***ll.
ū	as	u in r***u***de.
ṛi	as	ri in mer***ri***ly.
ṛī	as	ri in ma***ri***ne.
e	as	e in pr***e***y.
ai	as	ai in ***ai***sle.
o	as	o in st***o***ne.
au	as	ou in h***ou***se
ś	as	s in ***s***ure.
ṣ	as	sh in ***sh***un, bu***sh***
s	as	s in ***s***aint, ***s***un

Preface

Kashmir Shaivism is a magnificently profound yet practical theology, which teaches the radical unity of God and creation. Kashmir Shaivism emphasizes the importance of an intellectual comprehension of its philosophy and cosmology as well as a direct realization of its truth. According to this system, truth cannot be grasped by the intellect alone; truth must finally be apprehended through direct experience. On account of its emphasis on praxis, Kashmir Shaivism has relied heavily upon its oral tradition, which, through an unbroken line of masters and disciples, has preserved and passed along the secrets and subtleties of its impeccably detailed path towards Self-realization.

Swami Lakshmanjoo embodies the teaching and experience of Kashmir Shaivism. He has a profound intellectual and spiritual understanding of this great tradition, which is made evident in all of his recorded lectures. Swamiji was an extraordinary man who dedicated his whole life to the study and practice of Kashmir Shaivism. He was a selfless devotee of Lord Śiva and his life was marked by the continual remembrance and celebration of the Divine.

Swamiji's manner of teaching is traditional and inspiring. His lectures are always given through the medium of scripture. The verses he explains are in Sanskrit, the traditional philosophical and liturgical language of India. In all of his lectures, Swamiji chants the Sanskrit verses before translating and illuminating their meaning. His command of the Sanskrit language and his ability to explain the most difficult and esoteric concepts with simplicity and eloquence earned him an honorary degree – Dr. of Letters – from the Sampurnanand Sanskrit University in Varanasi (Benares) in 1965. This award was instigated by the eminent scholar Mahāmahopadyāya Pandit Gopinath Kaviraj, principal of the Sanskrit University.

Swamiji became interested in learning Sanskrit as a young boy. One day he overheard his father reciting verses from Utpaladeva's *Śivastotrāvalī*. Swamiji was enchanted with the sound of these verses and asked his father to explain their meaning. His father admitted that he did not actually understand Sanskrit and was therefore unable to provide Swamiji with the meaning of the verses. Burning with the desire to know the meaning of these verses, Swamiji requested his father to find him a reputable teacher who could teach him Sanskrit. Pleased by this request, his father found him a reputable teacher and Swamiji began his study of Sanskrit.

Swamiji learned Sanskrit in the traditional fashion by first reciting and memorizing the 3,959 rules of Sanskrit grammar, which were composed by the great Sanskrit grammarian, Pāṇini, in his masterwork, the *Aṣṭādhyāyī*. Swamiji then began to study the language from the Kashmir Shaiva point of view. In doing so, he came to understand that every Sanskrit letter represented a particular element of the universe, and the entire body of the Sanskrit alphabet represented the kingdom of God. With a deep understanding of the fundamentals of the language, the constant guidance of his master, Swami Mahatabkak, and through his own contemplative experience, Swamiji was able to comprehend the meaning of every Kashmiri Shaivite scripture that he came across.

Swamiji was extremely well-read. He was well-informed in Eastern and Western religious and philosophical traditions. Swamiji would freely draw upon other texts and commentaries to further clarify, expand, and substantiate his lectures. He could recall any text by simply remembering the first few words of a verse. His mind was so clear and focused that he held countless verses in his active memory, and he could draw on them as needed. I once asked him if he ever forgot a verse. He replied, "if I see or read anything, I remember it."

Bhagavad Gītā

The *Bhagavad Gītā* is one of the most celebrated and revered scriptures of India, if not the entire world. The *Bhagavad Gītā* is understood to contain 700 verses. The unique version found in Kashmir, however, contains 716 verses. These additional sixteen verses are accepted by Abhinavagupta and are included in his forthcoming commentary on the *Bhagavad Gītā*.

In 1933, at the age of twenty-six, Swamiji published Abhinavagupta's commentary of the *Bhagavad Gītā*, the *Gītārtha Saṁgraha* (*The Essence of the Lord's Song*). In the dedication at the end of this publication, Swamiji wrote the following *ślokas*, which are paraphrased here:

सांख्ययोगादिशास्त्रज्ञः पाणिनीये कृतश्रमः
शिवार्करश्मिसंपातव्याकोशहृदयाम्बुजः ।
महामाहेश्वरः श्रीमान्राजानकमहेश्वरः
शैवशास्त्रगुरुः स मे वाग्पुष्पैरस्तु पूजितः ॥

sāṁkhyayogādiśāstrajñaḥ pāṇinīye kṛtaśramaḥ /
śivārkaraśmisaṁpātavyākośahṛdayāmbujaḥ //
mahāmāheśvaraḥ śrīmānrājānakamaheśvaraḥ /
śaivaśāstraguruḥ sa me vāgpuṣpairastu pūjitaḥ //

My Sanskrit guru was fully informed in the understanding of Sāṁkhya and all Yoga śāstra. He had undergone the study of Pāṇinī's grammar (*āṣṭadhyayi*) and his heart-lotus had bloomed by the *tīvra śaktipāta* of Parabhairava; he was devoted to Parabhairava. To him, Rājānaka Maheśvaraḥ Rāzdan, I give thanks wholeheartedly.

शिवभक्त्यमृतास्वादात्तृणीकृतरसान्तरः
राजानलक्ष्मणाभिख्यः सुधीर्नारायणात्मजः ।
हृदन्तर्वर्त्तिना साक्षाच्छ्रीरामेण प्रचोदितः
प्राकाश्यमनयद् गीताव्याख्यामभिनवोदिताम् ॥

[śivabhakty]amṛtāsvādāttṛṇīkṛtarasāntaraḥ /
rājānalakṣmaṇābhikhyaḥ sudhīrnārāyaṇātmajaḥ //
hṛdantarvarttinā sākṣācchrīrāmeṇa pracoditaḥ /
prākāśyamanayad gītāvyākhyāmabhinavoditām //

By tasting the nectar of *śiva bhakti* (devotion to Lord Śiva), I lost all craving for sensual enjoyments. I was a scholar and the son of Nārāyaṇa Dass, and in my heart was residing my grandmaster, Swami Rām.[1] And it was Swami Rām who had put this kind of request or behavior into my intellect. So I have published and revealed this *gītā vyākhyām*, the commentary of the Bhagavad Gītā, which is commentated upon by Abhinavagupta himself.

It was my great fortune that in 1972, Swami Lakshmanjoo accepted me as his student. I moved from the USA to Kashmir where my family would spend the better part of two decades living beside this great master. By the grace of God, I was able to fulfill my commitment to record Swamiji's English lectures on Kashmir Shaivism. This resulted in over 600 hours of recorded lectures.

We were so very fortunate that Swamiji was able to give us lectures in English. Throughout these discourses, he made the

1 In 1911, Maharaja Pratap Singh established the Archaeological and Research Department of Kashmir, whose purpose it was to gather and preserve the sacred scriptures of Kashmir Shaivism which had almost disappeared over the past five centuries. These sacred texts were to be published under the banner of the Kashmir Series of Texts and Studies (*KSTS*). This enterprise was borne out of a single request from the great Shaiva master Swami Rām (1850-1915), whom the Maharaja Pratap Singh held in highest esteem.

As a result of this work, almost all of the important texts of the Kashmir Shaiva tradition were readily available to Swami Lakshmanjoo when the time was ripe for him to begin his studies. Interestingly, Abhinavagupta's *Gītārtha Saṁgraha* had not been included in the Kashmir Series. It is almost two decades after his passing that Swami Rām appeared to Swamiji and requested him to edit and publish Abhinavagupta's *Bhagavad Gītā* in order to ensure its preservation.

This present publication, based on Swamiji's renewed revelation, represents the complete fulfillment of Swami Rām's humble request, made more than a century ago.

Shaivite philosophy and ancient Hindu myths vibrate with life and profound meaning. He never spoke as if he were talking about something separate or remote from his own experience. Rather, his words vibrated with the very fiber of his own life and reality, revealing the secrets of an ancient philosophy and in so doing, the greatness of the preceptor who imparted it.

In 1988, my wife Denise and I, along with our children, Shanna and Viresh, traveled to Nepal to spend a month with Swamiji. At that time, he brought with him a series of specially selected sacred verses, which he wanted us to learn to recite. The entire month was filled with his explanations of the deeper meaning of these verses, coupled with our attempts to learn to chant them. There was no time to be wasted.

Two years later, in the early Spring of 1990, we again traveled to Nepal to spend a month with Swamiji. We had no idea what to expect. We knew that Swamiji wouldn't waste time with idle talk–he never did. He would want to spend as much time as possible teaching and sharing with us his vast understanding of the spiritual and intellectual aspects of Kashmir Shaivism.

As expected, when we arrived, Swamiji informed us that he was eager to get to work. He wanted to teach us his new revelation of the Kashmiri recension of the *Bhagavad Gītā.* This would be Swamiji's last translation of Abhinavagupta's commentary on *Bhagavad Gītā*, having published a light commentary on Abhinavagupta's original in Sanskrit in 1933,[2] his first English translation in 1978,[3] a Hindi translation and commentary published in 1986,[4] and Kashmiri translations between

---

2 *Bhagavadgītārthasaṁgraha: Śrimad Bhagavad Gītā with the commentary of Mahāmāheśvara Rājānaka Abhinavagupta*, ed. Pandit Lakshman Raina Brahmachari (Swami Laksmanjoo), Kashmir Pratap Steam Press, Srinagar, 1933.

3 Swami Lakshmanjoo, Abhinavagupta's *Bhagavad Gītā*, original audio recording (1978), Universal Shaiva Fellowship archive, Los Angeles.

4 *Bhagavadgītārthasaṁgraha* of Abhinavagupta: Hindi translation by Swami Lakshmanjoo, Ishwar Ashram Srinagar 1986, published by Sagar Press, Srinagar, Kashmir.

1960 and 1980.[5]

This new revelation was, however, exceedingly important as it was given through the lens of Swamiji's immersion in the state of Universal God Consciousness. He said that after completing this translation of *Bhagavad Gītā*, he would reveal Abhinavagupta's *Paramārthasāra* (*Essence of the Highest Reality*). He again emphasized that these were new revelations, different from any that he had given before. We were ready to begin.

I brought a portable video recorder to record Swamiji's lectures in Nepal. The quality of the recorder was consumer-grade, which was all that I could afford at that time. In spite of the fact that we had no special lighting and experienced an irritating, intermittent, and unresolvable audio problem, by Swamiji's blessings, we were able to record and preserve all of his revelations of these two texts, a total of thirty-six hours.

The present video study set contains Swamiji's complete revelation of the eighteen chapters of the Kashmiri recension of the *Bhagavad Gītā*. The transcript follows Swamiji's words exactly, with minimal edits and additions for clarity. In many places, we have also added footnotes, the majority of which are from Swamiji's first English translation of the *Bhagavad Gītā*, which was recorded twenty-two years earlier in 1978.

The footnotes also contain extracts from Swamiji's original audio recordings of Abhinavagupta's *Tantrāloka*, *Bodhapañcadaśika*, *Paramārthasāra*, *Parātriśikā Laghuvṛtti* and *Parātriśikā Vivaraṇa*, Utpaladeva's *Śivastotrāvalī*, Vasugupta's *Śiva Sūtra Vimarśini* and *Spanda Kārikā*, Kṣemarāja's *Spanda Saṁdoha* and *Parāprāveśikā*, Bhaṭṭanārāyaṇa's *Stava Cintāmaṇi*, the *Vijñāna Bhairava*, and *Kashmir Shaivism–The Secret Supreme*. Unless otherwise indicated, all footnotes are extracts from Swamiji's original audio recordings, taken from the Universal Shaiva Fellowship archive.

In the *Bhagavad Gītā*, Lord Kṛṣṇa, God incarnate, instructs his disciple Arjuna about the world and the nature of life. Why is our mind torn by conflicting duties and loyalties? What is the

5 Swamiji often translated selected verses from the Bhagavad Gītā in his Kashmiri Lectures which were recorded by John Hughes between 1972 and 1985. These Kashmiri recordings have been archived by the Ishwar Ashram Trust in India.

main purpose of our life? How are we to be freed from the pain and suffering we experience living in this world?

Swami Lakshmanjoo answers these questions by unveiling the heretofore hidden meanings contained within the *Bhagavad Gītā*. Swamiji tells us, "the freedom from all our miseries, as Abhinavagupta boldly declares, can neither be obtained through the renunciation of the world, nor by hatred towards this world, but by experiencing the presence of God everywhere."

May Swamiji's blessings shine upon you!

John Hughes
Lakshmanjoo Academy
Culver City, California
April 9, 2013

Acknowledgements

First of all I would like to thank those who made the success of this project possible, our team of editors, Viresh Hughes, Denise Hughes and George van den Barselaar. These editors meticulously scoured the transcript adding additions and corrections to aid the reader and incorporating numerous anno-tations quoting Swamiji speaking on the same subject elsewhere. Leanne von Stolzenheim who carefully examined the manuscript for errors and offered her valuable suggestions for corrections and additions. Claudia Dose our art director who, using her considerable talents, is responsible for the artwork in our project including the look and feel of the DVD, its menus, structure and interface. Michael Van Winkle our audio engineer who employed a number of tricks and techniques to polish, clarify, and enhance the original audio. They all proved to be invaluable in the preparation of these videos and the accompanying annotated transcript for publication.

I want to thank Dr. Yajneshwar Shastri and his wife Dr. Sunanda Shastri, both renowned Sanskrit scholars, for their invaluable help in checking the Sanskrit verses.

Swami Lakshmanjoo

Swami Lakshmanjoo

The Author

Swami Lakshmanjoo was born in Srinagar, Kashmir on May 9, 1907. He was the most recent and the greatest of the saints and masters of the tradition of Kashmir Shaivism. Having a deep understanding of the philosophy and practices of Kashmir Shaivism, he was like a splendid and shining rare jewel. From early childhood he spent his life studying and practicing the teachings of this unique sacred tradition. Because of his intellectual power and strength of awareness, he realized both spiritually and intellectually the reality of its thought.

Being born with a photographic memory, learning was always easy for him. In addition to complete knowledge of Kashmir Shaivism, he had a vast knowledge of the traditional religious and philosophical schools and texts of India. When translating or teaching he would freely draw on other texts to clarify, expand, and substantiate his teaching. He could recall an entire text by simply remembering the first few words of a verse.

In time, his reputation as a learned philosopher and spiritual adept spread. Spiritual leaders and scholars journeyed from all over the world to receive his blessings and to ask him questions about various aspects of Kashmir Shaiva philosophy. He gained renown as a devotee of Lord Shiva and as a master of the non-dual tradition of Kashmir Shaivism.

Throughout his life, Swamiji taught his disciples and devotees the ways of devotion and awareness. He shunned fame and recognition and did not seek his own glory. He knew Kashmir Shaivism was the most precious jewel and that, by God's grace, those who desired to understand would be attracted to its teachings. His earnest wish was for Kashmir Shaivism to be preserved and made available to all humankind.

In 1990, in Nepal, during his explanation of the sixth chapter of the Bhagavad Gītā, Swamiji gave a rare glimpse into the fullness and glory of his own experience:

DVD 6.3 (42:01)

"I was smoothly going on with my practice and abruptly *śaktipāta* [grace] came and threw all its force in me. It was *tīvra tīvra* (super-supreme) *śaktipāta*. And then it happened and I was newborn. I became so great. I don't mean to boast but this is what happened. I was newly reborn. And, because I had to become Bhairava, I had to experience all of the states of yoga. And it happened, everything happened. I had all experiences; and *cidānanda* also, *jagadānanda*[6] also. Everything happened. You can't imagine the ways of *śaktipāta*."

On the 27th of September 1991, Swami Lakshmanjoo left his physical body and attained the great liberation.

---

6. *Cidānanda* and *jagadānanda* are the final stages of the seven states of *tūrya*, also known as the seven states of *ānanda* (bliss). See *Kashmir Shaivism, The Secret Supreme*, (16.113-115).

Swami Lakshmanjoo

INTRODUCTION

SWAMIJI: This is the *Bhagavad Gītā*, which is commentated upon by Abhinavagupta.

DVD 1 (00:07)

य एष विततस्फुरद्विविधभावचक्रात्मकः
परस्परविभेदवान्विषयतामुपागच्छति ।
यदेकमयभावनावशात एत्यभेदान्वयं
स शंभुरशिवापहो जयति बोधभासां निधिः ॥१॥

ya eṣa vitatasphuradvividhabhāvacakrātmakaḥ
parasparavibhedavānviṣayatāmupāgacchati /
yadekamayabhāvanāvaśata etyabhedānvayaṁ
śa śaṁbhuraśivāpaho jayati bodhabhāsāṁ nidhiḥ //1

First, [Abhinavagupta], before starting to commentate on the *Bhagavad Gītā*, he first pays [respect to and] sings the glory of Lord Śiva.

Sa śaṁbhur jayati, glory be to that Lord Śiva who is *bodha bhāsāṁ nidhiḥ*, who is the treasure of only knowledge, who is the treasure of knowledge. Who?

JOHN: Lord Śiva.

SWAMIJI: Lord Śiva. And what are the qualifications of Lord Śiva?

Ya eṣa vitata sphurad vividha bhāva cakra ātmakaṁ. That Lord Śiva who has . . . whose glory is spread in each and every object of this world. *Vividha bhāva cakra ātmaka*, all [of] this objective world is His glory.

Paraspara vibhedavān viṣayatām upāgacchati. And although He is one with His own divine nature, how does He experience the varieties of His glory in duality? Because, for instance, this *chappal* (sandals), this *chappal* is His glory, a sock is His glory, this rod is His glory; but actually this rod, *chappal*, and everything, is [the glory of] His own nature. But how does He experience this variety also?

He experiences this variety also without [experiencing] His glory. Although it is His glory, but He experiences it separately: "this is a *chappal*," "this is a wire," "this is a . . . " He does not ignore that [variety] also because this also is the glory of His own nature, i.e., differentiatedly exposed Lord Śiva.

Undifferentiatedly exposed Lord Śiva cannot be spoken. You can't describe it, you can't explain it at that time [of experiencing it] because it is the explaining power, it is not explained. It cannot be the object of being explained. You cannot explain Lord Śiva. You can explain Lord Śiva when Lord Śiva has become varieties, in various forms of His own glory. Then you can experience, "this is Denise, this is Viresh, this is a rod, this is that, and this is this." And at that moment, He cannot explain His nature. In which moment? When it is un-manifested.

It is not manifested [and] it is manifested. In one way it is manifested when it is explained and in another way, in the real way, it is not manifested and it can't be explained–it is for [Lord Śiva] to experience. He experiences the experiencer. He does not experience the experienced. [The experience of the] experienced is only, it comes only, when it is in varieties, when it has gone a bit down, [i.e., when Lord Śiva] has descended from His real nature.

Do you understand?

Yadeka maya bhāvanā, and even then also, at that moment also, when He is, He wants to withdraw at the same time . . . for instance, [when] I experience it (i.e., differentiatedness), if He has *śaktipāta* (grace), if He puts *śaktipāta* in force, in process, then at that very moment, I can rise again. When there is no *śaktipāta*, I won't rise; I will just roam in this differentiated world. And that too is the glory of God.

Let that Lord Śiva be glorified here and hereafter. Here and hereafter. "Here" means in the differentiated world; "hereafter" means in undifferentiated Being. This is [Abhinavagupta singing Lord Śiva's] glory, first.[1] And now he starts his commentary.

---

1 "Glory be to Lord Siva who destroys all distress, and tortures

---

(*aśivāpaho*, all tortures are destroyed by Him). And He is the treasure of *prakāśa* and *vimarśa*, *bodhabhāsāṁ nidhiḥ* (*nidhiḥ* means treasure). He is the treasure of *prakāśa* and *vimarśa*.* Let that Lord Śiva be glorified." Swami Lakshmanjoo, *Bhagavad Gītā*, original audio recording, 1978 (Universal Shaiva Fellowship archive).

* "*Prakāśa* is the state of Śiva. *Vimarśa* is the state of *śakti*. . . . This whole objective world shines because of that *prakāśa*. *Prakāśa* is the force by which force this whole universe shines." Swami Lakshmanjoo, *Tantrāloka* 3.1 (1973).

"*Prakāśa* is the seat of that God consciousness. *Prakāśa* is the blissful state [of Śiva] and that you will have through *vimarśa*." Swami Lakshmanjoo, Abhinavagupta's *Dehasthadevatācakrastotram* (1980).

"*Vimarśa* is the flow of the universe, *vimarśa* is the creation of the universe, and *prakāśa* is the state of Śiva. . . . Universe cannot remain without Śiva; Śiva cannot remain without the universe–they are both together." Swami Lakshmanjoo, *Parātriśikā Vivaraṇa* (1982-85).

"*Prakāśa* is the subjective state of consciousness; *vimarśa* is when you realize this subjective state. When you perceive it, it becomes an object; when you perceive yourself, when you perceive your nature, that is object. It is not an object just as you see a pot or a jug. It is not that way an object. It is object of Śiva." Swami Lakshmanjoo, *Tantrāloka*, 6.247 (1974).

"In this world of Shaivite philosophy, it is admitted that Lord Śiva is *prakāśātmā*, [He] is filled with light; [He] is only light, embodiment of light. And that light is not light just like the light of the sun or moon or fire. It is some other light. Because, *prakaśāśca vimarśa svabhāvaḥ*, it is light with consciousness. And that light with consciousness is the nature of Lord Śiva, is the nature of that supreme consciousness, i.e., *vimarśa*, light with consciousness. What is consciousness? The consciousness of light is not only consciousness, pure consciousness. It is just to understand that, "I am the creator of everything, I am the protector of everything, and I am the destroyer of everything." Just to know that, is consciousness. If this consciousness would not be attached with that light of consciousness, *anīśvaro jaḍaśca prasajyeta*, then we would have to admit that the light of sun is also Lord Śiva, the light of moon is also Lord Śiva, and the light of fire is also Lord Śiva. But that is not [the case]. And this *vimarśa*, this consciousness, is nominated in various names. It is called *cit* (consciousness), *caitanyam* (*caitanyam* means the strength of consciousness), *svarasoditā parāvāk* (and supreme word is another name of that), *svātantryam* (perfect independence), *paramātmano mukhyam aiśvaryaṁ* (the predominent glory of supreme Śiva is its name), *kartṛtvam* (power of acting), *sphurattā* (power of existing), *sāra* (complete essence of everything), *hṛdayam* (heart, universal heart), *spanda* (universal movement). These are names which are attributed to this consciousness in *tantras*." Swami Lakshmanjoo, *Parāprāveśikā* by Kṣemarāja (1980).

"There are two positions of Śiva. One is *prakāśa* and another is *vimarśa*; one is *bindu* and another is *nāda*.* *Bindu* [corresponds] to *prakāśa*, *nāda* [corresponds] to *vimarśa*. When *bindu* is there, He is in full bliss. When He understands [i.e., is aware of] that full bliss, there is *nāda*. That is *nāda*. When He feels this blissful state as His own nature, that is *prakāśa*. When He feels that blissful state is My glory, that is *vimarśa*. When He feels that this blissful state is My being, that is Śiva. When He believes that this is My glory, that is *śakti*. The cycle of glory is residing in *śakti*, and the cycle of *prakāśa* is residing in Śiva. Both are in one. That is indicated by *visarga* in Śiva, i.e., [the vowel] *aḥ*. So, *vimarśa śakti* is supreme *parā parameśvarī* attributed to *svātantrya śakti*. It is the intensity of independence of the *svātantrya* of Bhairava, i.e., this *vimarśa śakti*." Swami Lakshmanjoo, *Parātriśikā Vivaraṇa* (1982-85). See footnote 77 for an explanation of *svātantrya śakti*.

* "*Bindu* is the residence of *nāda*; *bindu* is the resting state of *nāda*." Swami Lakshmanjoo, *Tantrāloka* 6.158a (1974).

"*Nāda* is perception of God consciousness, perception." Ibid., *Tantrāloka* 15.435 (1981).

"Announcing in this universe that there is nothing else than My own consciousness, that is *nāda*." Ibid., *Tantrāloka* 4.175 (1973).

"JOHN: So, from Vedantic point of view–because they have only *prakāśa*–from our point of view, there is no way they can perceive *prakāśa* . . .

SWAMIJI: No [affirmative].

JOHN: . . . if they don't have *vimarśa*?

SWAMIJI: There must be *vimarśa*. Without *vimarśa*, you can't be carried to *prakāśa*. How can *prakāśa* be experienced without *vimarśa*?

JOHN: What would you say the best understanding of the word *vimarśa* is in English? The best understanding of the word. Awareness is the best understanding?

SWAMIJI: Awareness is, yes. Awareness is *vimarśa*. You see, the chain-like maintenance of consciousness is awareness. Chain-like maintenance of consciousness is awareness."

Swami Lakshmanjoo, Abhinavagupta's *Dehasthadevatācakra-stotram* (1980).

DVD 1 (07:15)

द्वैपायनेन मुनिना यदिदं व्यधायि
शास्त्रं सहस्रशतसंमितमत्र मोक्षः ।
प्राधान्यतः फलतया प्रथितस्तदन्य-
धर्मादि तस्य परिपोषयितुं प्रगीतम् ॥२॥

dvaipāyanena muninā yadidaṁ vyadhāyi
śāstraṁ sahasraśatasaṁmitamatra mokṣaḥ /
prādhānyataḥ phalatayā prathitastadanya-
dharmādi tasya paripoṣayituṁ pragītam //2//

Dvaipāyanena muninā. The *śāstra* (scripture) of *Mahābhārata śāstra*, which is penned down by Kṛṣṇadvaipāyana, i.e., Vyāsa, which is exactly one *lakh* of *ślokas* (one [hundred] thousand *ślokas* is *Mahābhārata*), in this *Mahābhārata*, in the whole *Mahābhārata*, *mokṣaḥ prādhānyataḥ phalatayā prathitastad*, the definition is of *mokṣa*, of liberation, i.e., how you can liberate, how you can be liberated from repeated births and deaths (*saṁsāra*). It is explained that, it is . . . *mokṣa* is explained in these one hundred thousand verses. The main *phala*, the main fruit of this *śāstra* is *mokṣa*. And there are some other aspects also explained in the *Mahābhārata*–that is *dharma*, *artha*, and *kāma*.

Dharma means good deeds, i.e., you should do good deeds–that is *dharma*. *Artha* means you should raise money. *Kāma* means you should think of . . . you should desire for good things to have. [But *kāma*] is not for [the sake of] those good things. *Dharma* is, you should do good deeds just for the sake of *mokṣa*, just for the sake of experiencing the nature of God. You should collect money, you should raise money for the experience of knowing God. And you should desire to have so many possessions just for God's sake, just for experiencing God.

Dharma, *artha*, and *kāma* are meant for God. *Dharma*, *artha*, and *kāma* are not meant for worldly objects, i.e., to get involved in this worldly *tamasha* (commotion). Money is not for . . . the raising of money is not meant for getting involved in worldly . . .

DENISE: Affairs.

SWAMIJI: . . . worldly affairs. *Dharma* and . . . *artha* means money, *dharma* means good deeds, and *kāma* means the desire for having some best things in your possession. These best things must be . . . all these three are meant for *mokṣa*, for realizing the truth of your own nature. They are not meant for worldly affairs.[2]

But what is *mokṣa*? What is liberation?

[Abhinavagupta] explains what is liberation. What you can understand, what is liberation? Wherefrom you have to get liberated?

DVD 1 (12:00)

मोक्षश्च नाम सकलाप्रविभागरूपे
सर्वज्ञसर्वकरणादिशुभस्वभावे ।
आकाङ्क्षया विरहिते भगवत्यधीशे
नित्योदिते लय इयान्प्रथितः समासात् ॥३॥

mokṣaśca nāma sakalāpravibhāgarūpe
sarvajñasarvakaraṇādiśubhasvabhāve /
ākāṅkṣayā virahite bhagavatyadhīśe
nityodite laya iyānprathitaḥ samāsāt //3//

Mokṣa is, in brief words, *mokṣa* (liberation) is, in brief words, explained in these one hundred thousand *ślokas*.

What is *mokṣa*?

Adhīśe bhagavati. Adhīśe, who is the Lord of Lords (*bhagavati*

---

2 "[Abhinavagupta] says, *dharmādi tasya paripoṣayituṁ pragītam. Dharmādi*, in these three sections, *dharma*, *artha*, and *kāma*, are explained in *Mahābhārata* just to strengthen the enthusiasm for liberation, [for] getting liberation. Because when you do your duty (*dharma*)–you look after Viresh, you look after John, you look after everyone–your mind is diverted from that point to liberation; you want liberation. And money, you can earn money, earn money, earn money, and a thief comes and steals it, and you are distressed, and you think of liberation. And *kāma*, you are giving whole strength to sexual enjoyment but still you are not satisfied, and you are diverted towards liberation. These three conducts do not mean [that you are] to reside there in these three sections. It means that you have to get out from these three and get yourself liberated. So in *Mahābhārata*, these three are explained, but for the sake of liberation." *Bhagavad Gītā* (1978).

Bhairava, *pūrṇa* Bhairava). [Liberation is] *laya*, to get absorbed in that; to get absorbed in the Lord of Lords is *mokṣa*.

It is *prathitaḥ samāsāt*, in brief words, it is explained that *mokṣa* is that [condition of that Being] who is *nityodite*, who is always eternal, who is eternal, *adhīśe*, who is the Lord of Lords, who is *ākāṅkṣayā virahite*, who has no desire at all for anything, and who is filled, who is filled with, glorified with, all-knowledge and all-action, and all-will (*icchā*, *jñāna*, and *kriyā*[3]), who is filled with that, and *sakala apravibhāga rūpe*, and who is one with the whole universe, that is *mokṣa*.

DVD 1 (14:03)

यद्यप्यन्यप्रसङ्गेषु मोक्षो नामात्र गीयते ।
तथापि भगवद्गीताः सम्यक्तत्प्राप्तिदायिकाः ॥४॥

yadyapyanyaprasaṅgeṣu mokṣo nāmātra gīyate /
tathāpi bhagavadgītāḥ samyaktatprāptidāyikāḥ //4//

Although *anyaprasaṅgeṣu,* in other chapters also of the *Mahābhārata*, *mokṣa* (liberation) is defined, *mokṣa* is explained, but still then this chapter of the *Bhagavad Gītā*, which is existing in the *Mahābhārata* (the *Bhagavad Gītā* [consists] of eighteen chapters, this *Bhagavad Gītā*), in predominance, *mokṣa* is explained in the *Bhagavad Gītā*. Although *mokṣa* is explained in all of those one hundred thousand *ślokas* [of the *Mahābhārata*], but in the real sense, *mokṣa* is explained in the *Bhagavad Gītā* only.

Another *śloka*.

DVD 1 (15:13)

तास्वन्यैः प्राक्तनैर्व्याख्याः कृता यद्यपि भूयसा ।
न्याय्यस्तथाप्युद्यमो मे तद्गूढार्थप्रकाशकः ॥५॥

tāsvanyaiḥ prāktanairvyākhyāḥ kṛtā yadyapi bhūyasā /
nyāyyastathāpyudyamo me tadgūḍhārthaprakāśakaḥ //5//

---

3 *Icchā* means will, *jñāna* means knowledge, and *kriyā* means action. [*Editor's note*]

Although he says there are so many commentaries laid down, written down, by all of those old so-called masters, so-called these . . .

Masters?

JOHN: Masters?

DENISE: Scholars.

SWAMIJI: . . . scholars, but still then my effort is also needed. Because my effort is not for explaining the word-by-word translation of the *Bhagavad Gītā*. My effort is to explain the essence of the *Bhagavad Gītā*, which is the cream of the *Bhagavad Gītā*. And it is *gūḍhārtha*, where nobody has touched, that point which has not been touched so far by all of those commentators.

DVD 1 (16:32)

भट्टेन्दुराजादाम्नाय विविच्य च चिरं धिया ।
कृतोऽभिनवगुप्तेन सोऽयं गीतार्थसंग्रहः ॥ ६ ॥

bhaṭṭendurājādāmnāya vivicya ca ciraṁ dhiyā /
kṛto'bhinavaguptena so'yaṁ gītārthasaṁgrahaḥ //6//

This knowledge I got from Bhaṭṭendurāja; Bhaṭṭendurāja was my master for this. He taught me what is the essence of the *Bhagavad Gītā*. He says here, "he was my *guru* of the *Bhagavad Gītā*."

Whose *guru*?

DENISE: Abhinavagupta's.

SWAMIJI: Abhinavagupta's *guru*.

Bhaṭṭendurājādāmnāya, I have got knowledge of the *Bhagavad Gītā* from Bhaṭṭendurāja. And afterwards, *vivicya ca ciraṁ dhiyā*, then I have meditated upon what he has taught me. And afterwards, by the grace of Lord Śiva, I have experienced the reality of Bhaṭṭendurāja, which he has told me. That Bhaṭṭendurāja's teaching has come in vivid form.

JOHN: Vivid clarity.

SWAMIJI: Clarity, I have got its experience in *samādhi*.

Kṛto'bhinavaguptena so'yaṁ gītārtha saṁgrahaḥ, Abhinavagupta writes down the *gītārtha saṁgrahaḥ*, *Bhagavad Gītā Saṁgrahaḥ*, the essence of the *Bhagavad Gītā*, i.e., what is the *Bhagavad Gītā*.

DVD 1 (18:10)

vidyāvidyātmanordvayorabhibhāvyābhibhāvakātmakatvaṁ pradarśayituṁ prathamādhyāyaprastāvaḥ /

First *adhyāya*, the first chapter of the *Bhagavad Gītā*, it is nothing; it is . . . he says, in the first chapter . . .

There are actually how many chapters?

JOHN: Eighteen chapters.

SWAMIJI: Eighteen chapters.

You have got assimilating power. It is my good luck.

There are . . . Kauravas and Pāṇḍavās are not actually Kauravas and Pāṇḍavās. Kauravas and Pāṇḍavās are *vidyāpuruṣa* and *avidyāpuruṣa*. *Vidyāpuruṣa* means good thoughts; *avidyāpuruṣa* means bad thoughts. Bad thoughts are fighting with good thoughts.

Sometimes you want to kill somebody [and then] another party comes (the opposite party) and says, "no, you should not kill. Don't kill. Don't be so cruel."

So this is a tug [of war]. This is a tug [of war] going on between *vidyāpuruṣa* and *avidyāpuruṣa*. In the daily routine of life, you'll [feel] inside this war, tug of war, between good actions and bad actions. You want to do good actions and at the same time you want to do bad actions. They are . . .

DENISE: Fighting.

SWAMIJI: . . . fighting with each other. In that way you should find out which is the good action. You should do according to the good actions. If you are really . . . if you have got the fragrance of *śaktipāta* (grace), if you are scented with *śaktipāta*, scented . . . what is scented? If *śaktipāta* is . . .

JOHN: Perfumed with.

SWAMIJI: What?

JOHN: Perfumed with.

DENISE: Sprayed.

JOHN: Perfumed with.

SWAMIJI: What?

JOHN: Sprayed with the perfume, with the scent of *śaktipāta*.

DENISE: Touched by *śaktipāta*.

SWAMIJI: Yes. Then you will do good deeds. You have conquered that bad-deeds *walla* (party), [i.e., *avidyāpuruṣa*].

DVD 1 (21:19)

nahyanutpannavidyāleśāvakāśa upadeśabhājanam; [comm.]

Upadeśa (instruction) cannot be done if you are not fit for that. If you are not fit for that, [if] you are involved in your own ways of your daily routine of life, [then] you are *not* fit for the *Bhagavad Gītā*, to hear my commentary of the *Bhagavad Gītā*. You are only fit when you have got this capacity to conquer bad actions in the daily routine of your life.

This is the *Bhagavad Gītā's* commentary of Abhinavagupta.

nāpi nirmūlitasamastāvidyāprapañcaḥ [comm.]

If you are already placed in God consciousness, for [you] also the *Bhagavad Gītā* is not needed. For he who is all-knowledge, who is exactly residing in the state of Bhairava, for him the *Bhagavad Gītā* is not needed. The *Bhagavad Gītā* is needed only for that person who has got . . .

DENISE: Touch of *śaktipāta*.

SWAMIJI: . . . touch of *śaktipāta* (grace) and who conquers the . . .

DENISE: Bad thoughts.

SWAMIJI: . . . bad thoughts.

So there must be some doubt. If there is some doubt, then for him, this *Bhagavad Gītā* is meant, i.e., [one] who is doubtful, who wants to remove his doubts.

[For that person] who says ignorantly, "I have understood the *Bhagavad Gītā*," for him, this commentary of my *Bhagavad Gītā* is not meant. This commentary is meant only for him who has got doubts, who will ask his master, "O my master, I don't know what is good and what is bad, please teach me!" For him, my *Bhagavad Gītā* is meant.

For him who is always with thorns, who says, "I want to understand what is your theory," for him there is no place for *Bhagavad Gītā*.

If he says, "I want to know the exact thing," he is fit for that [knowledge of the *Bhagavad Gītā*].

[One] who has come with knowledge, with knowledge of his own, he is not fit for my *Bhagavad Gītā*.

So, *deva* and *asura sṛṣṭi* is *vidya āvidyāmayi*; *vidyāpuruṣa* and *avidyāpuruṣa* are the creation of *devapuruṣa* (gods) and *anya-puruṣa* (demons).[4]

Jñānaṁ ca pradhānaṁ. Here, [in the *Bhagavad Gītā*], knowledge is predominant, action is not predominant. Action is . . . you have to do action *with* knowledge. You have not to do . . . you have to do action with knowledge. Knowledge is not to be done with action. You have to act with knowledge. If you do something, you must be aware of what you are doing. So knowledge is predominant here in this *Bhagavad Gītā*.

You can't say that knowledge and action are just opposite to each other, that they have one weight. Knowledge has got more weight than action. You have to act with knowledge. You have not to know with action.

Do you understand?

DENISE: Yes.

SWAMIJI: In this way I, [Abhinavagupta], will explain to readers the heart of Vyāsa from time to time.

4 "Right persons and wrong persons, the creation of these two classes is "with knowledge (*vidyāpuruṣa*)" and "without knowledge (*avidyā-puruṣa*)." The class of right persons is with knowledge [viz., the Pāṇḍavās]; the class of wrong persons is without knowledge, i.e., ignorant [viz., the Kauravas]." *Bhagavad Gītā* (1978).

Chapter 1

This is . . . Dhṛtarāṣṭra asks Sañjaya (Dhṛtarāṣṭra was the ancestor of Kauravas and Pāṇḍavās–Dhṛtarāṣṭra[5]), Dhṛtarāṣṭra asks Sañjaya:

DVD 1 (27:34)

धृतराष्ट्र उवाच

dhṛtarāṣṭra uvāca

धर्मक्षेत्रे कुरुक्षेत्रे सर्वक्षत्रसमागमे ।
मामकाः पाण्डवाश्चैव किमकुर्वत संजय ॥ १ ॥

dharmakṣetre kurukṣetre sarvakṣatrasamāgame /
māmakāḥ pāṇḍavāścaiva kimakurvata sañjaya //1//

O Sañjaya, in *dharmakṣetra*, where there was *sarva kṣatra samāgame*[6], where there was a fight [between] both parties, the fight of *vidyāpuruṣa* and the fight of *avidyāpuruṣa*, i.e., what I have already explained to you beforehand, . . .

[Abhinavagupta] has put this reading of the *Bhagavad Gītā* in another way, which is not found in other [commentaries of the] *Bhagavad Gītā*. The reading of the *Bhagavad Gītā* is different in his [commentary].

---

5 The blind Kuru king who was the father of the Kauravas and the uncle of the Pāṇḍavās. [*Editor's note*]

6 "*Sarva kṣatra samāgame*, where there was the union of all kṣatriyas (warriors). . . . [Abhinavagupta] explains the word *kṣatra*. *Kṣatra* means *kṣaderhiṁsārthatvāt*. *Kṣader hiṁsāyam* is that verbal root from which verbal root this *kṣatra* has [been] derived. [The verbal root] *kṣad* means *hiṁsā*; *hiṁsā* means just hurting."
Bhagavad Gītā (1978).

. . . *sarva kṣatra samāgame, kurukṣetra* was . . . *kurukṣetra* is that *kurūnāṁ karaṇānāṁ kṣetraṁ. Kurukṣetra* does not mean Kurukṣetra, which is in Delhi, where there was fight, the battle of Kauravas and Pāṇḍavās. Actually, *kurukṣetra* means the *kṣetra* (field) of the organs; all of the organs of one's own self, *they* fight with each other.[7]

DVD 1 (29:40)

ayaṁ sa paramo dharmo yadyogenātmadarśanam [comm.] [quoted from the *Yājñavalkya Smṛti*]

It is *dharmakṣetra. Dharmakṣetra* means the *kṣetra* of *dharma*, the battlefield of *dharma*, the battlefield of purity; the battlefield of purity, not the battlefield of impurity.

As this, at present, this is the battlefield of impurity; they [i.e., the warriors] dash down everything here in this battlefield. But actually the battlefield is that where good deeds are conquering bad deeds–bad deeds are subsided and good deeds are shining–that is the battlefield. And this is that field . . . in that field you experience the glory of Parabhairava.[8]

7 "*Karaṇānāṁ yatkṣetraṁ*, the field of organs, where there is a field of organs, where organs are held, organs take place, that is body. *Kṣetram* means *anugrāhakam* [which] means bliss-bestowers. Actually, these organs of senses bestow bliss if they are handled properly. If these organs are handled properly, they bestow bliss. If they are not handled properly, they bestow grief, sadness. *Ata eva sāṁsārikadharmāṇāṁ sarveṣāṁ kṣetraṁ*. So, it is the field of all actions because all actions rise from this body." Ibid.

8 "Now, the qualification of Parabhairava is described by Abhinavagupta. . . . *Bārupam*, who is *bārupam*, who is *prakāśa*, who is filled with *prakāśa* (the light of consciousness), who is *pari pūrṇam*, who is *pūrṇam* (full), *svātmani viśrāntito mahānandam*, who is residing in His own way, and is filled with *ānanda*, bliss, blissful state.

Bārūpaṁ pari pūrnaṁ is [He] who is *cit*, who is the embodiment of *cit śakti* (energy of consciousness). *Svātmani viśrāntito mahānandam*, when He resides in His *cit śakti*, He becomes filled with *ānanda* (bliss).

"*Icchā-saṁvit-karaṇair, icchā nirbharitam*, He is also filled with *icchā śakti*, *saṁvit*, *jñāna śakti*, and *karaṇair, kriyā śakti*. *Icchā* means energy of will, *saṁvit* means energy of knowledge, and *karaṇair* means the energy of action. He is filled with these three energies.

"So he is filled with *cit śakti*, *ānanda śakti*, *icchā śakti*, *jñāna śakti* [viz., *saṁvit*], and *kriyā śakti* [viz., *karaṇair*]. And exclusively, He is

Yat yogena ātma darśanam, all *dharmas*, all activities, where all activities end, and there is only *mokṣa* (*mokṣa* means only liberation from all these [things] that are happening outside), and for this [i.e., *mokṣa*] you have got this body. The body is meant for that liberation. The body is not meant for dashing down each other.[9] So,

rāgavairāgyakrodhakṣamāprabhṛtīnāṁ samāgamo yatra

In this *kurukṣetra*, *rāga* (attachment) is fighting with *vairāgya* (detachment), *krodha* (wrath) is fighting with its opposite (*śānti*, peace), good is fighting with bad actions. So this is the war, which is going on all the twenty-four hours, everywhere, in one's own body–*rāga*, *vairāgya*, *krodha*, *kṣamā*. And when you have got wrath (*krodha*), you want to dash [someone] down; and there is *kṣamā*[10] [telling you], "no, be peaceful, don't be so rash, don't take such fast steps, just think."

Rāga vairāgya; *rāga* is fighting with *vairāgya*, *krodha* is fighting with *kṣamā*, and all other [such opposing feelings fight with one another].

DVD 1 (33:00)

tasmin sthitā ye māmakāḥ–avidyāpuruṣocitā avidyāmayāḥ

---

ananta-śakti-paripūrṇam, He is not only filled with [these] five energies, He has got numberless *śaktis*. *Ananta-śakti-paripūrṇam*, He is filled with all energies, which are offshoots of these five energies.

"*Sarva vikalpa vihīnaṁ*, who is *sarva vikalpa vihīnaṁ*, all varieties of thoughts have taken their end there. *Śuddhaṁ*, who is clean, *śāntaṁ*, who is appeased, *layodaya-vihīnam*, who has rise and fall, and who is absent from rise and fall. He neither rises nor falls down.

"And that *para tattvaṁ*, that supreme state of God consciousness, supreme state of Parabhairava, *tasmin*, in that, *śivatattvaṁ*, *tasmin sivādidharāntaṁ jagat viśvam*, *ṣaṭtriṁ-śadātma*, all this universe, which is from *pṛthivī* to *śiva tattva*, it is existing in that *para tattva*."

Swami Lakshmanjoo, *Paramārthasāra* (1990).

9 "The real and only pure action is that action by which action you can perceive, you can experience God consciousness. And, for explaining God consciousness, this also is meant, the same body is meant. For experiencing all worldly activities, this *kṣetra* is meant. This body will do that thing also. And this body will do, side-by-side, it will make you fit to recognize the state of God consciousness." *Bhagavad Gītā* (1978).

10 Forebearance or patience. [*Editor's note*]

saṅkalpāḥ / pāṇḍavāḥ–śuddhavidyāpuruṣocitā vidyātmānaḥ [comm.]

[Dhṛtarāṣṭra]: O Sañjaya, and in that field there was the collection of *māmakāḥ*, [my sons, the Kauravas, which] means *avidyāpuruṣo citā saṅkalpāḥ*; *avidyāpuruṣa* [means] Kauravas and Pāṇḍavas means *śuddhavidyā puruṣocitā vidyātmānaḥ*, *śuddha*, good [pure] people.[11]

te kimakurvata–kaiḥ khalu ke jitā iti yāvat /

Māmakāḥ means . . .

. . . *mameti kāyatīti māmakaḥ avidyāpuruṣaḥ / pāṇḍuḥ śuddhaḥ* //[end of comm. for verse 1]

Pāṇḍuḥ means white; the Pāṇḍavās were innocent. Kauravas were filled with prejudice.

This is the 2nd verse:

Sañjaya says, "O Dhṛtarāṣṭra . . .

DVD 1 (34:05)

सञ्जय उवाच

sañjaya uvāca

द्रष्ट्वा तु पाण्डवानीकं व्यूढं दुर्योधनस्तदा ।
आचार्यमुपसङ्गम्य राजा वचनमब्रवीत् ॥२॥

dṛṣṭvā tu pāṇḍavānīkaṁ vyūḍhaṁ duryodhanastadā /
ācāryamupasaṅgamya rājā vacanamabravīt //2//

11 "My sons means *avidyāpuruṣocitā avidyāmayāḥ saṅkalpāḥ*, e.g., "this is mine, this is mine, this is mine, this is mine, this is mine"–this is *māmaka*. This is what is called Kauravas. So these are these [egoistic] thoughts. . . . *Śuddhavidyā puruśocitā vidyātmānaḥ, saṅkalpāḥ*, these thoughts pertaining to experience the state of God consciousness, thoughts pertaining to meditation, all these, these are Pāṇḍavās." *Bhagavad Gītā* (1978).

When, in the battlefield of *kurukṣetra* . . .

Duryodhana was the chief, the head of the Kauravas. These troops of Kauravas were on one side and the troops of Pāṇḍavās were on another side.

. . . when Duryodhana saw *pāṇḍavānīkaṁ* (*ānīkaṁ* means *sena*, the troops of the Pāṇḍavās), which was *vyūḍhaṁ*, which was protected by Duryodhana, *rāja* (king) Duryodhana, *ācāryam upasaṅgame*, he went to Droṇācārya (Droṇācārya was his master, Duryodhana) and *vacanam abravīti*, he asked him one question:

DVD 1 (35:20)

पश्यैतां पाण्डुपुत्राणामाचार्य महतीं चमुम् ।
व्यूढां द्रुपदपुत्रेण तव शिष्येण धीमता ॥३॥

paśyaitāṁ pāṇḍuputrāṇāmācārya mahatīṁ camūm /
vyūḍhāṁ drupadaputreṇa tava śiṣyeṇa dhīmatā //3//

[Duryodhana]: O Droṇācārya! See these big troops of Pāṇḍavās, kindly look upon these troops, which is protected by Drupadarāja (the son of Drupada), who was your *śiṣya*, he was your disciple. He has protected the troops of Pāṇḍavās.

I will explain to you who are the warriors [among] these Pāṇḍavās.

DVD 1 (36:25)

अत्र शूरा महेष्वासा भीमार्जुनसमा युधि ।
युयुधानो विराटश्च द्रुपदश्च महारथः ॥४॥
धृष्टकेतुश्चेकितानः काशिराजश्च वीर्यवान् ।
पुरुजित्कुन्तिभोजश्च शैव्यश्च नरपुङ्गवः ॥५॥

atra śūrā maheṣvāsā bhīmārjunasamā yudhi /
yuyudhāno virāṭaśca drupadaśca mahārathaḥ //4//
dhṛṣṭaketuścekitānaḥ kāśirājaśca vīryavān /
purujitkuntibhojaśca śaivyaśca narapuṅgavaḥ //5//

They are just like warriors, just like Bhīma and Arjuna. They are no less than Arjuna. They are no less than Bhīma.[12]

Yuyudhāna, Virāṭa–these are the names of these [Pāṇḍava] warriors–Drupadaśca, Dhṛṣṭaketu, Cekitānaḥ, Kāśirāja. They are *vīryavān*, having great power. And Bhūriśravā and Kuntibhoja, these are the names of those [Pāṇḍavā] troops.

DVD 1 (37:00)

युधामन्युश्च विक्रान्त उत्तमौजाश्च वीर्यवान् ।
सौभद्रो द्रौपदेयाश्च सर्व एव महारथाः ॥६॥

yudhāmanyuśca vikrānta uttamaujāśca vīryavān /
saubhadro draupadeyāśca sarva eva mahārathāḥ //6//

Yudhāmanyu (King Yudhāmanyu) and Saubhadrā (Saubhadrā means Abhimanyu[13])–these are great warriors in Pāṇḍavās–all are *mahārathāḥ*, all are capable of shooting ten thousand people at a time with these "anti-aircraft guns."[14]

[Duryodhana]: Now our troops, I want to explain our troops, which are of Kauravas.

DVD 1 (37:51)

अस्माकं तु विशिष्टा ये तान्निबोध द्विजोत्तम ।
नायका मम सैन्यस्य संज्ञार्थं तान्ब्रवीमि ते ॥७॥

asmākaṁ tu viśiṣṭā ye tānnibodha dvijottama /
nāyakā mama sainyasya sañjñārthaṁ tānbravīmi te //7//

Now I am explaining to you, which are our troops.

DVD 1 (38:06)

सैन्ये महति ये सर्वे नेतारः शूरसंमताः ।
भवान्भीष्मश्च कर्णश्च कृपः शल्यो जयद्रथः ॥८॥

12 The second of the Pāṇḍava brothers who is renowned for his unparalleled strength. [*Editor's note*]

13 Abhimanyu is the son of Subhadrā. [*Editor's note*]

14 Swamiji is referring to the formidable weaponry that is wielded by the Pāṇḍavās. [*Editor's note*]

अश्वत्थामा विकर्णश्च सौमदत्तिश्च वीर्यवान् ।
अन्ये च बहवः शूरा मदर्थे त्यक्तजीविताः ॥९॥
नानाशस्त्रप्रहरणा नानायुद्धविशारदाः ।

sainye mahati ye sarve netāraḥ śūrasaṁmatāḥ /
bhavānbhīṣmaśca karṇaśca kṛpaḥ śalyo jayadrathaḥ //8//
aśvatthāmā vikarṇaśca saumadattiśca vīryavān /
anye ca bahavaḥ śūrā madarthe tyatkajīvitāḥ //9//
nānāśastrapraharaṇā nānāyuddhaviśāradāḥ /

First, you are the first one. O Dhṛtarāṣṭra, you are the first one. Bhīṣma, Bhīṣma is [second], Karṇa, Kṛpacarya, Śalya, Jayadratha, Aṣhotama, Vikarna, Saumadatti, and there are many others who are ready to sacrifice their lives for victory.

Now there is the 10th *śloka*.

DVD 1 (38:51)

अपर्याप्तं तदस्माकं बलं भीमाभिरक्षितम् ।
पार्याप्तं त्विदमेतेषां बलं भीष्माभिरक्षितम् ॥१०॥

aparyāptaṁ tadasmākaṁ balaṁ bhīmābhirakṣitam /
paryāptaṁ tvidameteśāṁ balaṁ bhīṣmābhirakṣitam //10//

bhīmasenābhirakṣitaṁ pāṇḍavīyaṁ balam asmākam aparyāptam – jetumaśakyam, [comm.]

The troops of Pāṇḍavās, which are protected by Bhīmasena (Bhīma's army), *asmākam aparyāptam*, we cannot conquer them (*jetumaśakyam*, we cannot conquer them). We will fail, we will die.

idaṁ tu bhīṣmābhirakṣitam balamasmākaṁ saṁbandhi eteṣāṁ — pāṇḍavānāṁ paryāptaṁ — [comm.]

Our troops, [it] seems that our troops will be killed by the Pāṇḍavās, the troops of Pāṇḍavās.

Then 11th *śloka*:

DVD 1 (39:50)

अयनेषु च सर्वेषु यथाभागमवस्थिताः ॥ ११ ॥

ayaneṣu ca sarveṣu yathābhāgamavasthitāḥ //11//

Then, they announced in that battlefield: "You have to take care of Bhīṣma! Bhīṣma is our *guru*, i.e., the *guru* of Pāṇḍavās and the *guru* of Kauravas. You have to see that Bhīṣma is protected–nobody should kill Bhīṣma!"[15]

भीष्ममेवाभिरक्षन्तु भवन्तः सर्व एव हि ।
तस्य सञ्जनयन् हर्षं कुरुवृद्धः पितामहः ॥ १२ ॥
सिंहनादं विनद्योच्चैः शङ्खं दध्मौ प्रतापवान् ।

bhīṣmamevābhirakṣantu bhavantaḥ sarva eva hi /
tasya sañjanayan harṣaṁ kuruvṛddhaḥ pitāmahaḥ //12//
siṁhanādaṁ vinadyoccaiḥ śaṅkhaṁ dadhmau pratāpavān /

Then, Bhīṣma *pitāmahaḥ*, when he was glorified by both parties, he said, "no, I'll be safe." He thought [this] to himself.
Then he announced with Siṁhanāda by *śaṅkha*,[16] those . . .
DENISE: Conch shells.
SWAMIJI: Yes.

DVD 1 (41:12)

ततः शङ्खाश्च भीर्यश्च पणवानकगोमुखाः ।
सहसैवाभिहन्यन्त स शब्दस्तुमुलोऽभवत् ॥ १३ ॥

tataḥ śaṅkhāśca bhīryaśca paṇavānakagomukhāḥ /
sahasaivābhihanyanta sa śabdastumulo'bhavat //13//

15 Bhīṣma is the grand uncle of both the Pāṇḍavās and Kauravas. [*Editor's note*]
16 Siṁhanāda is the name of Bhīṣma's *śaṅkha* (conch shell). [*Editor's note*]

Then, these [conch] shells were making so much noise from the side of the Pāṇḍavās and from the side of the Kauravas. And its noise became *tumulo* (*tumulo* means unbearable). It was a furious, roaring [sound].

Then . . .

ततः श्वेतैर्हयैर्युक्ते महति स्यन्दने स्थितौ ॥ १४ ॥

[tataḥ] śvetairhayairyutke mahati syandane sthitau //14//

. . . then there was one chariot (*ratha*), with seven white ponies carrying that *ratha*. And . . .

माधवः पाणडवश्चैव दिव्यौ शङ्खौ प्रदध्मतुः ।
पाञ्चजन्यं हृषीकेशो देवदत्तं धनञ्जयः ॥ १५ ॥

mādhavaḥ paṇḍavaścaiva divyau śaṅkhau pradadhmatuḥ /
pāñcajanyaṁ hṛṣīkeśo devadattaṁ dhanañjayaḥ //15//
[not recited]

. . . *mādhavaḥ paṇḍavaścaiva*, in that [chariot] was seated *mādhavaḥ*, [which] means Lord Kṛṣṇa, and *paṇḍavaḥ*, [which] means Arjuna.

Divyau śaṅkhau pradadhmatuḥ, they also . . .

DENISE: Blew?

SWAMIJI: . . . blew those *śaṅkhas* (conch shells).

Pāñcajanyaṁ hṛṣīkeśa. Hṛṣīkeśa (Lord Kṛṣṇa) blew Pāñcajanya (the name [of His conch shell] was Pāñcajanya). *Devadattaṁ.* Devadatta was another *śaṅkha*, which started to blow; [it was blown by] Dhanañjayaḥ (Arjuna).

पौण्ड्रं दध्मौ महाशङ्खं भीमकर्मा वृकोदरः ।

pauṇḍraṁ dadhmau mahāśaṅkhaṁ bhīmakarmā vṛkodaraḥ /

[Bhīma] blew that Pauṇḍraṁ *śaṅkha.*

अनन्तविजयं राजा कुन्तीपुत्रो युधिष्ठिरः ॥१६॥

anantavijayaṁ rājā kuntīputro yudhiṣṭhiraḥ //16//

Yudhiṣṭhiraḥ blew Anantavijay.

नकुलः सहदेवश्च सुघोषमणिपुष्पकौ ।

nakulaḥ sahadevaśca sughoṣamaṇipuṣpakau /

Sughoṣa and Maṇipuṣpaka were blown by Nakulaḥ and Sahadeva [respectively, and] all these five [Pāṇḍavā] brothers [blew their respective conch shells].

DVD 1 (43:40)

काश्यश्च परमेष्वासः शिखण्डी च महारथः ॥१७॥
धृष्टद्युम्नो विराटश्च सात्यकिश्चापराजितः ।
पाञ्चालश्च महेष्वासो द्रौपदेयाश्च पञ्च ये ॥१८॥
सौभद्रश्च महाबाहुः शङ्खान्दध्मुः पृथक्पृथक् ।
स घोषो धार्तराष्ट्राणां हृदयानि व्यदारयत् ॥१९॥

kāśyaśca parameṣvāsaḥ śikhaṇḍī ca mahārathaḥ //17//
dhṛṣṭadyumno virāṭaśca sātyakiścāparājitaḥ /
pāñcālaśca maheṣvāso draupadeyāśca pañca ye //18//
saubhadraśca mahābāhuḥ śaṅkhāndadhmuḥ pṛthakpṛthak
sa ghoṣo dhārtarāṣṭrāṇāṁ hṛdayāni vyadārayat //19//

And this noise pierced the hearts of all the Kauravas, this dreadful noise.

नभश्च पृथिवीं चैव तुमुलो व्यनुनादयन् ।

nabhaśca pṛthivīṁ caiva tumulo vyanunādayan /

And *akāśa* (heaven) and *pṛthvi* (earth) were trembling by that sound there in the battlefield.

अथ व्यवस्थितान्दृष्ट्वा धार्तराष्ट्रान्कपिध्वजः ।
प्रवृत्ते शस्त्रसंपाते धनुरुद्यम्य पाण्डवः ॥२०॥
हृषीकेशं तदा वाक्यमिदमाह महीपते ।

atha vyavasthitāndṛṣṭvā dhārtarāṣṭrānkapidhvajaḥ /
pravṛtte śastrasaṁpāte dhanurudyamya pāṇḍavaḥ //20//
hṛṣīkeśaṁ tadā vākyamidamāha mahīpate /

[Sañjaya]: Then they were about to start the war with each other. Then Arjuna took his bow and started, but as soon as . . . and he told . . . he asked his charioteer (that Lord Kṛṣna) to go a little bit forward [and Arjuna said], "I want to see with whom I have to fight. Please take this *ratha* (chariot) in between these two troops. I want to see who is going to fight with me and whom I have to kill. And I want to see why Dhṛtarāṣṭra has made them fight with us."

And [then, after seeing who he was to kill], his mind changed altogether in *karuṇa* (compassion). *Karuṇa* means he didn't want to kill them at all.

DENISE: He felt compassion, compassionate?

SWAMIJI: Compassionate.

DVD 1 (46:05)

अर्जुन उवाच

arjuna uvāca

सेनयोरुभयोर्मध्ये रथं स्थापय मेऽच्युत ॥२१॥
यावदेतान्निरीक्षेऽहं योद्धुकामानवस्थितान् ।

कैर्मया सह योद्धव्यमस्मिन् रणसमुद्यमे ॥२२॥
योत्स्यमानानवेक्षेऽहं य एतेऽत्र समागताः ।
धार्तराष्ट्रस्य दुर्बुद्धेर्युद्धे प्रियचिकीर्षवः ॥२३॥

senayorubhayormadhye rathaṁ sthāpaya me'cyuta //21//
yāvadetānnirīkṣe'haṁ yoddhukāmānavasthitān /
kairmayā saha yoddhavyamasmin raṇasamudyame //22//
yotsyamānānavekṣe'haṁ ya ete'tra samāgatāḥ /
dhārtarāṣṭraya durbuddheryuddhe priyacikīrṣavaḥ //23//

सञ्जय उवाच
sañjaya uvāca

एवमुक्तो हृषीकेशो गुडाकेशेन भारत ।
सेनयोरुभयोर्मध्ये स्थापयित्वा रथोत्तमम् ॥२४॥

evamukto hṛṣīkeśo guḍākeśena bhārata /
senayorubhayormadhye sthāpayitvā rathottamam //24//

[Sañjaya]: Then afterwards, when he asked his charioteer, Lord Kṛṣṇa, to go ahead and [Arjuna said], "I want to see with whom I have to fight," and [Lord Kṛṣṇa] placed that *ratha* in between these two troops.

भीष्मद्रोणप्रमुखतः सर्वेषां च महीक्षिताम् ।
उवाच पार्थ पश्यैतान्समवेतान्कुरूनिति ॥२५॥
तत्रापश्यत्स्थितान्पार्थः पितॄनथ पितामहान् ।

bhīṣmadroṇapramukhataḥ sarveṣāṁ ca mahīkṣitām /
uvāca partha paśyaitānsamavetānkurūniti //25//
tatrāpaśyatsthitānpārthaḥ pitṝnatha pitāmahān /

[Lord Kṛṣṇa] said, "*paśyaitān samavetān*, see, O Arjuna, see these Kauravas who are just opposite [you], and are about to fight with you." And there, what Arjuna experiences, sees?

आचार्यान्मातुलान्भ्रातॄन्पुत्रान्पौत्रान्सखींस्तथा ॥२६॥
श्वशुरान्सुहृदश्चैव सेनयोरुभयोरपि ॥२७॥
तान्समीक्ष्य स कौन्तेयः सर्वान्बन्धूनवस्थितान् ।

ācāryānmātulānbhrātṝnputrānpautrānsakhīṁstathā //26//
śvaśurānsuhṛdaścaiva senayorubhayorapi //27//
tānsamīkṣaya sa kaunteyaḥ sarvānbandhūnavasthitān /28a

He sees his *pitṝn*, his ancestors, his fathers, his grandfathers, his masters, his *mamas* (maternal uncles), his brothers, his sons, his sons' sons, and his *sakhīm* (*sakhīm* means his friends), *śvaśurān*, his . . . *śvaśurān* means that *śvaśu*.

Śvaśurān means . . .

VIRESH: Uncle?

SWAMIJI: What? *Acku*?

JOHN: Uncle?

SWAMIJI: No, *śvaśurān* means father-in-laws.

. . . *śvaśurān suhṛdaścaiva,* and fast friends. And when he saw that all of these are my own, . . .

कृपया परयाविष्टः सीदमानोऽब्रवीदिदम् ॥२८॥

kṛpayā parayāviṣṭaḥ sīdamāno'bravīdidaṁ //28//

. . . then he was sighing and he said these words to Lord Kṛṣṇa:

DVD 1 (48:13)

अर्जुन उवाच

arjuna uvāca

दृष्ट्वेमास्वजनानकृष्ण युयुत्सूनसमवस्थितान् ।
सीदन्ति मम गात्राणि मुखं च परिशुष्यति ॥२९॥

dṛṣṭvamānsvajanānkṛṣṇa yuyutsūnsamavasthitān /
sīdanti mama gātrāṇi mukhaṁ ca pariśuṣyati //29//

As soon as I see and look at these, my own kith and kin, my [whole] body is trembling with grief.

DVD 1 (48:39)

वेपथुश्च शरीरे मे रोमहर्षश्च जायते ।
गाणडीवं स्रंसते हस्तात्त्वक्चैव परिदह्यते ॥३०॥

vepathuśca śarīre me romaharṣaśca jāyate /
gāṇḍīvaṁ sramsate hastāttvakcaiva paridahyate //30//

Vepathuśca śarīre me, my body cannot exist; my body cannot stand. I want to sit down and lie down. My *mukhaṁ ca pariśuṣyati*, my . . .

It is not exactly Shaivism, but I have to translate this also.

. . . my mouth is dry, I want some water to drink. I cannot speak. I cannot talk. *Gāṇḍīvaṁ sramsate,* this bow and arrow has dropped down on the ground, I cannot, I cannot fight with them. *Tvakcaiva paridahyate,* this body has caught fire, the fire of grief; *tvakcaiva paridahyate,* my body is filled with grief.

And symptoms [i.e., omens] also I see, terrifying, very bad signs. I see there are eagles and . . . *ahhhhhhh*! [Like] all those that were there in our ashram.[17]

JONATHAN: Owls.

SWAMIJI: Yes.

JOHN: What?

SWAMIJI: Owls.

17 Here, Swamiji is referring to the owls which would frequent his ashram during the military occupation in Kashmir. [*Editor's note*]

DVD 1 (50:16)

न च शक्नोम्यवस्थातुं भ्रमतीव च मे मनः ।
निमित्तानि चा पश्यामि विपरीतानि केशव ॥३१॥
न च श्रेयोऽनुपश्यामि हत्वा स्वजनमाहवे ।
न काङ्क्षे विजयं कृष्ण न च राज्यं सुखानि च ॥३२॥

na ca śaknomyavasthātuṁ bhramatīva ca me manaḥ /
nimittāni ca paśyāmi viparītāni keśava //31//
na ca śreyo'nupaśyāmi hatvā svajanamāhave /
na kāṅkṣe vijayaṁ kṛṣṇa na ca rājyaṁ sukhāni ca //32//
[not recited]

[Arjuna]: *Na ca śreya anupaśyāmi hatvā.* I don't think I'll find any peace after killing my own kith and kin. I don't want *rājya*, I don't want a kingdom. Let them conquer me. *Na kāṅkṣe vijayaṁ kṛṣṇa*, I don't want a kingdom. I don't want any peace.

DVD 1 (50:52)

किं नो राज्येन गोविन्द किं भोगैर्जीवितेन वा ।

kiṁ no rājyena govinda kiṁ bhogairjīvitena vā /

What shall I do? If I become king, whom [will] I rule? The ruled ones [i.e., the citizens] will be dead. There is no fun; there is no meaning in my ruling alone here. What shall I do here? I will also die with them.

येषामर्थे कङ्क्षितं नो राज्यं भोगाः सुखानि च ॥३३॥

yeṣāmarthe kāṅkṣitaṁ no rājyaṁ bhogāḥ sukhāni ca //33//

For *them* I was thinking of becoming king and . . . but when they will all die, what shall I do afterwards?

DVD 1 (51:34)

त इमेऽवस्थिता युद्धे प्राणांस्त्यक्त्वा धनानि च ।
आचार्याः पितरः पुत्रास्तथैव च पितामहाः ॥३४॥
मातुलाः श्वशुराः पौत्राः स्यालाः संबन्धिनस्तथा ।

ta ime'vasthitā yuddhe prāṇaṁstyaktvā dhanāni ca /
ācāryāḥ pitaraḥ putrāstathaiva ca pitāmahāḥ //34//
mātulāḥ śvaśurāḥ pautrāḥ syālāḥ sambandhinastathā /

[Arjuna]: They are my masters (*ācāryas*), they are *pitra* (fathers), *putra's* (sons), *pitāmahāḥ* (grandfathers), *mamas* (maternal uncles), these *śvaśurāḥ* (*śvaśurāḥ* means . . .

I forget . . . *śvaśurāḥ* means?

JOHN: Father in laws.

SWAMIJI: . . . father in laws), *pautrāḥ* (grand sons), *syālāḥ* (*syālāḥ* means *hahra*,[18] brother in laws).

एतान्न हन्तुमिच्छामि घ्नतोऽपि मधुसूदन ॥३५॥

etānna hantumicchāmi ghnato'pi madhusūdana //35//

If they kill me, it [will be] peaceful for me! Let them kill me.

अपि त्रैलोक्यराज्यस्य हेतोः किमु महीकृते ।

api trailokyarājyasya hetoḥ kimu mahīkṛte /

[Even] if I have to win the kingdom of the three *lokas*[19], *kimu mahīkṛte*, [I still wouldn't fight against them]. What to speak of one kingdom of this mortal *pṛthvī* [earth]?

36th *śloka*:

18 Kashmiri.

19 Earth, sky, and heaven.

DVD 1 (52:40)

निहत्य धार्तराष्ट्रान्नः का प्रीतिः स्याज्जनार्दन ॥३६॥

nihatya dhārtarāṣṭrānnaḥ kā prītiḥ syājjanārdana //36//

[Arjuna]: Hey Janārdana, hey Lord Kṛṣṇa! When we will kill the Kauravas, what *sukha,* what peace will we have? We won't get any peace. On the contrary, . . .

पापमेवाश्रयेदस्मान् हत्वैतानाततायिनः ।

pāpamevāśrayedasmān hatvaitānātatāyinaḥ /

. . . we will be sinful! When I will die, I will be sinful; I will be sentenced to hells there. [People will say], "what have you done with your own kith and kin? You have killed them for nothing."

तस्मान्नार्हा वयं हन्तुं धार्तराष्ट्रान्स्वबान्धवान् ॥३७॥

tasmānnārhā vayaṁ hantuṁ dhārtarāṣṭrānsvabāndhavān 37

We are not fit [for this war]. I cannot fight with them.

It is not Shaivism; it is the *Bhagavad Gītā*.[20]

---

20 Swamiji illustrates the difference between the philosophies of the *Bhagavad Gītā* and Kashmir Shaivism:

"The *Bhagavad Gītā* teaches, with great respect, you have to do *utkrānti* i.e., you have to get out from this body. At the time of death it is done. When you are about to leave this physical body, you have to meditate on the center of two eyebrows, and breathe in and out, breathe in and out–at the time of death–breathe in and out and focus your breath in between two eyebrows and leave this physical frame. Then what happens next? You rise in God consciousness after death. You throw this body away and you are united with God consciousness. This is explained in *Bhagavad Gītā* with great respect.

"But, in our Shaivism, it is just a play, play of world. This is a worldly play. He has done nothing, he has achieved nothing, and he can achieve nothing by this. *Proktā sā sāra śāstreṣu bhogopāyatayūditā.* It

|| Here ends the 1st chapter of the *Bhagavad Gītā* ||

[Note: Swamiji did not recite or translate verses 38 to 47.][21]

---

is *bhoga upāya*. Because, in the *Bhagavad Gītā*, it is said:

> *sarvadvārāṇi saṁyamya mano hṛdi nirudhya ca /*
> *murdhnyādhāyātmanaḥ prāṇamāsthito yogadhāraṇām //*
> [*Bhagavad Gītā*, 8.12]

"*Sarvadvārāṇi saṁyamya*, all doors of your senses you must squeeze, you must close, you must withdraw from senses at the time of death. *Mano hṛdi nirudhya ca*, you must focus your mind in your heart. *Murdhnyādhāyātmanaḥ prāṇam*, you should take your breath in *sahasrara* and just exhibit your nature in this kind of *yoga dhāraṇa* (contemplation) as long as your body is thrown away. As long as this body, when this body is being thrown, then you rise in that God consciousness. This is said in the *Bhagavad Gītā*.

"It is absolutely wrong! This kind of teaching that is found in the *Bhagavad Gītā* is absolutely incorrect. *Sāra śāstras* does not recognize this kind of *dhāraṇa*. *Sāra śāstras* says, "why to go, where to go? [What is the purpose of] going and leaving this body aside and getting up? What is up and what is down? Down below is Lord Śiva; up is Lord Śiva. Why to go? Wherefrom to go? So this is only just an ignorant play; play in the field of ignorance. Now he puts that [quote] of Lord Śiva is *Sāra śāstras*, [which] he has addressed to Pārvatī:

> *yadi sarvagato devo vadotkramya kva yāsyati //TĀ 33//*
> *athāsarvagatastarhi ghaṭatulyastadā bhavet /*

"If Lord Śiva is everywhere, then this body is also Lord Śiva! Why should you leave this body and go in high level? What is there? *Athāsarvagata*, if Lord Śiva is not everywhere, [if] he is only in seventh world, not in other worlds, Lord Śiva is not existing in other worlds, other inferior worlds, *ghaṭata*, then he is a pot [i.e., an inert object], then he is just like us. Then he should be kicked out." Swami Lakshmanjoo, *Tantrāloka* 14.32 (1980).

21 [Arjuna addresses Lord Kṛṣṇa]:

Verses 38-39: "They don't observe that this is a sin to destroy our dynasty of Kauravas and Pāṇḍavās . . . but we observe it! [So] we must walk out from this sinful act because we see that . . . this whole dynasty of ours will get ruined."

Verses 40-41: "[And] when our dynasty will be ruined, what will happen? *Kulakṣaye praṇaśyanti kuladharma*, all those *dharmas*, all those pious activities, pure activities, will get ruined . . . and only *adharma* (sinful activities) will shine altogether everywhere. And when we are ruined, wrong things will appear; *kula striyaḥ* means all respected ladies will [become corrupt]."

Verse 42: "And by [that corruption], the production of people will be *varṇa saṅkara*, [there will be] the mixing of castes. And those *saṅkaras*, those boys and girls, will become the cause of hell. Everybody will go to hell. And when they go to hell, their ancestors who have died, they will also be carried to hell."

Verses 43-44: "And their *śrāddha vadha* [ceremonies for the deceased] will be useless [when performed] by those people. I have heard from my masters and elders that when all *dharmas*, all purity, all-pious actions have [been] ruined, then all people will be sentenced to hell (*narake niyatam vāso*). So there is no fun in killing them."

Verse 45: "[Now Arjuna thinks to himself], "*aho vata mahatpāpaṁ*, this is great torture, crises, that we are bent upon doing this great sin . . . that we are bent upon killing our kith and kin just for the sake of our own comfort. This is a great sin."

Verse 46: "So I have concluded . . . *yadi māmapratīkāram*, I won't touch any weapon . . . and these Kauravas will dash me down and kill me. *Tanme kṣemataram,* that will be a peaceful state for me. I will welcome that."

Verse 47: "[Sañjaya tells king Dhṛtarāṣtra what happens next]: "After addressing this way to Lord Kṛṣṇa, Arjuna moved to the back of this *ratha* [chariot] . . . and he kept all his weapons on the seat, *śokasaṁ,* and began to think deeply with grief."
Bhagavad Gītā (1978).

[Abhinavagupta's concluding *śloka* for Chapter One]: "What a *yogi* has to do in this war, in this battlefield? Which battlefield? The battlefield of senses, i.e., good fighting with bad, right fighting with wrong, pride fighting with humility, humility fighting with pride (all the opposites are fighting every now and then). This fight does not persist only in waking state, this fight persists in dreaming state also. Everywhere you find this fight. You have to observe this fight going on in your own brain, in your own mind. What a *yogi* must do there? He says, *vidyāvidyo bhayāghāta saṁghaṭṭa vivaśīkṛtaḥ yuktā dvayamapi.* If there is *yukti*, if there is a way, the avenue is only *dvayam api tyaktā*, don't think of right, don't think of wrong, be relaxed in your own nature, just enjoy this fight, just witness it. You have to witness it only,

don't get entangled in right and wrong, just witness this war. Then you will get rid of this war [and] there will be neither right nor wrong."
Swami Lakshmanjoo, *Bhagavad Gītā* in a Nutshell (1978).

Chapter 2 Part 1

SWAMIJI: [Sañjaya] has already said that when Arjuna was fed up with seeing all of his kith and kin who were to be killed and he changed his seat and sat in the back of that chariot and he placed his bow and arrow on the seat and *bas* [Swamiji puts his head in his hands in resignation]. He was *bas*, residing in his own nature [thinking of] what to do.[22]

Now, it is second discourse.

DVD 2.1 (00:48)

अथ द्वितीयोऽध्यायः

[atha] dvitīyo'dhyāyaḥ

सञ्जय उवाच

sañjaya uvāca

तं तथा कृपयाविष्टमस्त्रुपूर्णाकुलेक्षणम् ।
सीदमानमिदं वाक्यमुवाच मधुसूदनः ॥ १ ॥

taṁ tathā kṛpayāviṣṭamasrupūrṇākulekṣaṇam /
sīdamānamidaṁ vākyamuvāca madhusūdanaḥ //1//

[Sañjaya]: Arjuna who was *kṛpayāviṣṭam*, who was filled, whose all-consciousness was filled with *kṛpā* (*kṛpā* means [compassion], i.e., not to kill those kith and kin), *asrupūrṇākulekṣaṇam*, his eyes were filled with tears and he was not in his own wits–he was seated in the backseat of the chariot–to whom, *sīdamānam*, he who was always [i.e., completely] sunk in deep

22 Swamiji uses the hindi word "*bas*" often throughout the text, which means "enough" or "that is all." [*Editor's note*]

thoughts of grief, *madhusūdan*, Lord Kṛṣṇa placed these words before him:

DVD 2.1 (02:03)

श्रीभगवानुवाच

śrī bhagavān uvāca

कुतस्त्वा कश्मलमिदं विषमे समुपस्थितम् ।

kutastvā kaśmalamidaṁ viṣame samupasthitam /

Where did you get this *kaśmalam* (*kaśmalam* means this darkness of your soul)? Your soul is filled with darkness and there is no need to [be overcome by] that darkness at this critical moment, because war is going on just now.

अनार्यजुष्टमस्वर्ग्यमकीर्तिकरमर्जुन ॥२॥

anāryajuṣṭam asvargyamakīrtikaramarjuna //2//

[For] those who are wise like you, it does not befit you [to have] this kind of attitude. *Asvargyam*, it won't take you to heaven, and you will be defamed altogether! People will say, "he escaped from this battlefield because of his threat." Nobody will say that, "he had produced that *kṛpa*, that compassion for us." Everybody will say, "because of the threat [i.e., fear], he has . . ."

JONATHAN: Run away.

SWAMIJI: Yes.

This way, Lord Kṛṣṇa inserts knowledge into the consciousness of Arjuna in [terms of] worldly affairs first, i.e., that the world does not accept this kind of escape from critical times.

Kramāttu jñānaṁ kariṣyatīti [comm.]. He will insert real knowledge [into Arjuna] by and by, not abruptly, because [Arjuna] was fed up with [this situation that arose] abruptly, i.e., what he had to face [in fighting against] all of his kith and kin.

klaivyādibhirnirbhartsanamabhidadhadharme tava

dharmābhimāno'yam [comm.]

It is really *adharma*; it is not vice.
Vice is *dharma*?
JOHN: Duty is *dharma*. Vice is *adharma*.
SWAMIJI: Vice is *adharma*.
[Lord Kṛṣṇa]: In vice (*adharma*), you have the misunderstanding that it is *dharma*. Vice is not *dharma*. You are doing vice; you are owning vice at this critical moment. It is all wrong and nonsense. It does not suit you, Arjuna.

DVD 2.1 (05:26)

मा क्लैव्यं गच्छ कौन्तेय नैतत्त्वय्युपपद्यते ।

mā klaivyaṁ gaccha kaunteya naitattvayyupapadyate /

Don't be squeezed like this, like a coward. You are just like a coward! You don't want to fight with them.

क्षुद्रं हृदयदौर्बल्यं त्यक्त्वोत्तिष्ठ परंतप ॥३॥

kṣudraṁ hṛdayadaurbalyaṁ tyaktvottiṣṭha paraṁtapa //3

This is *kṣudraṁ*, it is hollow; it has no substance inside. *Hṛdaya daurbalyaṁ*, it is only the weakness of your heart. Leave it aside! *Uttiṣṭha paraṁtapa*, stand up and fight with them!

अर्जुन उवाच
arjuna uvāca

Now, Arjuna says to Him in answer:

DVD 2.1 (06:09)

कथं भीष्ममहं संख्ये द्रोणं च मधुसूदन ।
इषुभिः प्रतियोत्स्यामि पूजार्हावरिसूदन ॥४॥

kathaṁ bhīṣmamahaṁ saṁkhye droṇaṁ ca madhusūdana /
iṣubhiḥ pratiyotsyāmi pūjārhāvarisūdana //4//

O Lord, how can I face Bhīṣma, who is my master and kill him? And Droṇācārya who is my *guru*? How will I face them with arrows and bows and kill them who are *pūjarhau*? They are adorable to me, I have to adore them. On the contrary, how can I kill them?

Another *śloka* he says, Arjuna to Lord Kṛṣṇa:

DVD 2.1 (07:00)

गुरूनहत्वा हि महानुभावा-
ञ्छ्रेयश्चर्तुं भैक्षमपीह लोके ।
न त्वर्थकामस्तु गुरून्निहत्य
भुञ्जीय भोगान् रुधिरप्रदिग्धान् ॥५॥

gurūnahatvā hi mahānubhāvāñ-
chreyaścartuṁ bhaikṣamapīha loke /
na tvarthakāmastu gurūnnihatya
bhuñjīya bhogānrudhirapradhigdhān //5//

Gurūna hi mahānubhāvāñ gurūn. Those revered masters, how can I [kill them]? It is better for me not to kill those revered masters. I won't kill them! I won't face them and kill them. It is better for me to go from door to door and beg for alms–it is better for me–but not to kill my masters.

Arthakāmastu gurūn, although my masters are *arthakāma,* they want wealth, they want kingdom–I know that! O Lord Kṛṣṇa, I know that they have got greed, my masters and my kith and kin, they have got greed. But for me, it does not suit.[23] How can I take [the produce] from the fields, where the *shali* (rice) will grow, and [wherefrom] this production will grow afterwards, after killing them? There will be all-bloodshed everywhere and from blood-soaked [fields], they will grow. What?

JONATHAN: Rice.

23 That is, to obtain this wealth and kingdom by killing his kith and kin does not suit him. [*Editor's note*]

SWAMIJI: Rice will grow bloodsoaked from their blood. How can I eat that? It is not advisable for me to eat [that blood-soaked rice]. It is better for me to beg from door to door and live like a *sañyasin*, but I won't kill them.

In this *śloka*, [Abhinavagupta] says there is *karma viśeṣānu sandhānaṁ* and *phala viśeṣānu sandhānaṁ*, what action we are doing and what fruit we will get from it. *Karma viśeṣānu sandhānaṁ* is to kill revered masters. *Phal* will be (i.e., the fruit) to eat [the produce that will grow] from their bloodshed; [the blood-soaked] produce/production, that will be the fruit of [killing the revered masters]. [For Arjuna], it is absolutely . . . both are nonsense [i.e., unacceptable].

DVD 2.1 (10:12)

नैतद्विद्मः कतरन्नो गरीयो
यद्वा जयेम यदि वा नो जयेयुः ।
यानेव हत्वा न जिजीविषाम-
स्ते नः स्थिताः प्रमुखे धार्तराष्ट्राः ॥६॥

naitadvidmaḥ kataranno garīyo
yadvā jayema yadi vā no jayeyuḥ /
yāneva hatvā na jijīviṣāma -
ste naḥ sthitāḥ pramukhe dhārtarāṣṭrāḥ //6//
[not recited]

[Arjuna]: And also I don't know, *naitadvidmaḥ kataranno garī-[yaḥ]*, this also I don't know who will win. After [fighting in the] battlefield, who will win?

Yadvā jayema yadi vā no jayeyuḥ, is it so that we will conquer [them] in the battlefield or they will conquer [us] in the battlefield, they will conquer us?

Yāneva hatvā, if at all I will kill them, after killing them, *na jijīviṣāma*, I won't like to live afterwards. How can I live afterwards when I kill all of my kith and kin?

Te naḥ sthitāḥ pramukhe, and they are facing me for fighting.

DVD 2.1 (11:26)

कार्पण्यदोषोपहतस्वभावः
पृच्छामि त्वां धर्मसंमूढचेताः ।
यच्छ्रेयः स्यान्निश्चितं ब्रूहि तन्मे
शिष्यस्तेऽहं शाधि मां त्वां प्रपन्नम् ॥७॥

kārpaṇyadoṣopahatasvabhāvaḥ
pṛcchāmi tvāṁ dharmasammūḍhacetāḥ /
yacchreyaḥ syānniścitaṁ brūhi tanme
śiṣyaste' haṁ śādhi māṁ tvāṁ prapannam //7//

[Arjuna]: *Kārpaṇya doṣopahata svabhāvaḥ*, my nature is absolutely stuck; it is covered with the burden of grief. I don't see any way out of this grief. So I ask You, O Lord Kṛṣṇa, I ask You, tell me what I should do?

It seems that he has not ignored [the fact] that He is my master. Who? Arjuna has not ignored that He is my master. Who? Lord Kṛṣṇa. So he asks Lord Kṛṣṇa, "tell me what I should do, because my consciousness is subsided all-round. I cannot see any way out of it."

Yat śreyaḥ syāt, whatever is good for me, and You [keep it] in your mind, think over it, and tell me what should I do. *Śiṣyaste 'haṁ*, I am Your disciple!

Now he becomes His disciple. Who? Arjuna is disciple of Kṛṣṇa.

Śādhi māṁ, give me orders of what I should do. *Tvāṁ prapannam*, I have prostrated before Thy feet. And at the same time, I have this courage to tell You.

DVD 2.1 (13:36)

नहि प्रपश्यामि ममापनुद्या-
द्यः शोकमुच्छोषणमिन्द्रियाणाम् ।
अवाप्य भूमावसपत्नमृद्धं
राज्यं सुराणामपि चाधिपत्यम् ॥८॥

nahi prapaśyāmi mamāpanudyād-
yaḥ śokamucchoṣaṇamindrayāṇām /
avāpya bhūmāvasapatnamṛddhaṁ
rājyaṁ suraṇāmapi cādhipatyam //8//

[Arjuna]: I don't see *mama apanudyāt*, this *śoka* (this grief), which has made a [deep recess] in my heart–the grief of this [question of] what will happen next–I don't see its way out. This grief will remain for eternity in my heart. And this grief is *uccho-ṣaṇam indrayāṇām,* it will squeeze all of my organs by and by and I will die. I will die. In the end, I will die [from this grief]. I think–it seems to me–that I will die, and I will die just like a dog in the street. Although *avāpya bhūmau,* although I achieve the kingdom, the kingdom of this world of Kauravas and Pāṇḍavās, I achieve the kingdom, [but] after achieving that kingdom, what to speak of this kingdom of the Kauravas and Pāṇḍavās? If I achieve *suraṇāmapi cādhipatyam,* the kingdom of gods also in heaven, even then my grief will persist and it will just finish me.

DVD 2.1 (15:45)

सञ्जय उवाच

sañjaya uvāca

एवमुक्त्वा हृषीकेशं गुडाकेशः परन्तप ।
न योत्स्यामीति गोविन्दमुक्त्वातूष्णीं बभूव ह ॥९॥

evamuktvā hṛṣīkeśaṁ guḍākeśaḥ parantapa /
na yotsyāmīti govindamuktvā tūṣṇīṁ babhūva ha //9//

This way–Sañjaya says to Dhṛtarāṣṭra–this way, when Arjuna spoke with Lord Kṛṣṇa, afterwards he made this final decision: "I have taken this final decision, *na yotsyāmīti*, I won't fight!" After speaking these words, *tūṣṇīṁ babhūva ha* [Swamiji puts his head in his hands], then he stopped talking and he was, *bas*, he closed his eyes and didn't say a word afterwards.

Then what happened?

DVD 2.1 (17:18)

तमुवाच हृषीकेशः प्रहसन्निव भारत ।

tamuvāca hṛṣīkeśaḥ prahasanniva bhārata /

Hṛṣīkeśaḥ means Lord Kṛṣṇa. In reply to that, He laughed at him. Laughed at whom? Arjuna.

सेनयोरुभयोर्मध्ये सीदमानमिदं वचः ॥१०॥

senayorubhayormadhye sīdamānamidaṁ vacaḥ //10//

And He spoke these words to [Arjuna] who was filled with grief all-round.

ata[24] *ubhayorapi jñānājñānayormadhyagaḥ śrībhagavatānuśiṣyate* [comm.]

What is right and what is wrong? He was in a fix to decide what is right and what is wrong for me. It seems so by his talk. By whose talk?

DENISE: By Arjuna's.

SWAMIJI: Arjuna's. He was in a fix to know what is right and what is wrong. In this scale of right and wrong, he couldn't decide what is right and what is wrong for me.

Śrībhagavatānuśiṣyate, Lord Kṛṣṇa *ānuśiṣyate*, He puts [Arjuna] to task now.

श्रीभगवानुवाच

śrī bhagavān uvāca

Bhagavān means Lord Kṛṣṇa addresses this to Arjuna:

DVD 2.1 (18:55)

त्वं मानुष्येणोपहतान्तरात्मा

24 Swamiji says *tatra*. [*Editor's note*]

विषादमोहाभिभवाद्विसंज्ञः ।
कृपागृहीतः समवेक्ष्य बन्धू-
नभिप्रपन्नान्मुखमन्तकस्य ॥११॥

tvaṁ mānuṣyeṇopahatāntarātmā
viṣādamohābhibhavādvisaṁjñaḥ /
kṛpāgṛhītaḥ samavekṣya bandhūn-
abhiprapannānmukhamantakasya //11//

[Lord Kṛṣṇa]: You are actually . . . your internal consciousness is subsided by being limited, which is very disgraceful for you. *Mānuṣyeṇa,* by this limitation of being, you are just like worldly people; you are just like worldly people, just like a worldly widowed woman [who is] filled with grief. It does not suit you. *Mānuṣyeṇa*, this [grief is] *mānuṣyeṇa* (this is *mānuṣyeṇa*, the limitation of being a limited being), and by that, *upahatāntar-ātmā*, your inner God Consciousness is subsided. You have killed [your] inner God consciousness, which you have ignored at this time.

Viṣāda mohābhi bhavād, and *viṣāda* (*viṣāda* means grief; *moha* means ignorance), grief and ignorance, *ābhibhavād*, they have conquered you. Grief and ignorance have conquered you. *Visaṁjñaḥ*, your consciousness is *visaṁjñaḥ* (*visaṁjñaḥ* [means] *khatam*, [finished]), your consciousness is not living now. You are finished. *Kṛpāgṛhītaḥ*, and you want to save those people (*kṛpā-gṛhītaḥ*). Which people? *Samavekṣya bandhūn*, your kith and kin; [by] seeing your kith and kin in front of you in this battlefield, *kṛpā* has pervaded your heart (*kṛpā* means having compassion that I won't kill them).

Whom? *Abhi prapannān mukhamantakasya*, they have . . . [they] who have entered in the mouth of the lord of death beforehand. They have [already] entered! [Even] if you don't kill them, they have [already] entered! I have killed them.

Who says?

JOHN: Kṛṣṇa.

SWAMIJI: Kṛṣṇa.

I have killed them. And for those [who] are already killed (I have already killed them!), it is not worthwhile for you not to [kill them] . . . not to just . . . just be your . . . keep some respect for yourself. Just shoot them. [Understand that] before shooting them, they [have already been] killed. I have killed them. They have gone in the belly of the lord of death beforehand.

mānuṣyam–manuṣyabhāvaḥ [comm.]

Mānuṣyam means *manuṣyabhāvaḥ* (limitation), which is not creditable for such a person who is My disciple. It is disgraceful for you.

anta[ka]mukhaṁ svayamete praviṣṭā

They are [already] digested in the belly of the lord of death. They are gone.

iti tava ko bādhaḥ // [end of comm., vs. 11]

What to you? You also keep your respect and kill them. They are already killed! If you don't kill them, [still] they are killed. I have killed them.

DVD 2.1 (23:11)

Śocitumaśakyaṁ kalevaraṁ– . . . [comm.]

अशोच्याननुशोचंस्त्वं प्राज्ञवन्नाभिभाषसे ।
गतासूनगतासूंश्च नानुशोचन्ति पण्डिताः ॥१२॥

aśocyānanuśocaṁstvaṁ prājñavannābhibhāṣase /
gatāsūnagatāsūṁśca nānuśocanti paṇḍitāḥ //12//

[Lord Kṛṣṇa]: *Aśocyān anuśocaṁstvaṁ*, you grieve when it is not worthwhile to grieve. *Prākṣavannābhibhāṣase*, you do not talk just like a sane person. I think you are mad! Lord Kṛṣṇa says [this] to Arjuna.

Gatāsūn agatāsūṁśca, those who are dead, those who are not yet born . . . when somebody is born, you should [Swamiji demonstrates by pounding his chest].

DENISE: Pound your chest?

SWAMIJI: Pound your chest. Because he is born and he will die now. What will you do?

JONATHAN: Grieve.

SWAMIJI: Then you should do that way also.

JONATHAN: So you should grieve when someone is born?

SWAMIJI: And you should grieve also . . . if you grieve when somebody is dead, why do you keep quiet when somebody is born [laughs]? Why don't you pound your chest at that time [and grieve] that he will now die! This is not wise behavior for you. It does not suit you.

Na kaścit gatāsuḥ mṛtaḥ, agatāsuḥ jīvanvā śocyo'sti [comm.]. [One] who is dead, or *agatāsuḥ*, who has not yet come into this world, there is no place [i.e., nothing] to grieve upon.

It will be clarified.

Ātmā tāvad avināśī. Ātmā, the soul, is *avināśī*, it never dies. The soul who has taken the position of the body, inside–inside, that God who is God consciousness inside your body–He is always life-full.

Nānāśarīreṣu saṁcarataḥ kāsya śocyatā. If he passes from one body to another body, why should we pound our heads? If he travels from one body to another body, from that body to another body, there is no place to pound your heads.

If you pound your heads even then, then *evaṁ hi yauvanādāvapi śocyatā bhavet*, then you should pound your heads when one is born. Well and good. After fifteen years of age, he is grown up, [then] you should pound your head at that time [because] he has got change. Then, he has got pain, headache, toothache, so you should pound your head at that time.

It is not worthwhile! How much grief will you possess?

It is not worthwhile to grieve on the soul, which is passing from one body to another body. If it is so, then, when you change your clothes and they are torn–you throw them off [and] you wear some other clothes–and these clothes, for these [torn] clothes, do you weep?

Why don't you weep? You should weep for those clothes [and lament], "I have thrown these."

Do you understand what He means?

This is the way of *samsāra*.[25]

---

25 That is, transmigration is the condition of *samsāra*. [*Editor's note*]

This is 12th finished.

Now, *evam arthadvayam āha*, this is clarified [by Abhinavagupta] in the [next] two *ślokas*, 13th and 14th.

DVD 2.1 (28:05)

नह्येवाहं जातु नासं न त्वं नेमे जनाधिपाः ।
नचैव न भविष्यामः सर्वे वयमितः परम् ॥ १३ ॥

naḥyevāhāṁ jātu nāsaṁ na tvaṁ neme janādhipāḥ /
na caiva na bhaviṣyāmaḥ sarve vayamitaḥ param //13//

[Lord Kṛṣṇa]: Do you think I was not born beforehand? I was born [beforehand]! Do you think that you were not born beforehand? You were born in this world! *Neme janādhipāḥ*, these kings and queens of your kith and kin who are against you, ready to fight with you, [do you think] they were not born beforehand? They were born! Now they have come in another body. *Na caiva na bhaviṣyāmaḥ*, do you think that they won't come again? They will come again. If they die, they will come again. Not only them! You also will come again. I will also come again in another incarnation to set the whole thing right.

God also incarnates His body from time to time.

DVD 2.1 (29:11)

देहिनोऽस्मिन्यथा देहे कौमारं यौवनं जरा ।
तथा देहान्तरप्राप्तिर्धीरस्तत्र न मुह्यति ॥ १४ ॥

dehino'sminyathā dehe kaumāraṁ yauvanaṁ jarā /
tathā dehāntaraprāptirdhīrastatra na muhyati //14//

[Lord Kṛṣṇa]: *Dehina*, one who has possessed a body, just as he [passes through] childhood, youth, and old age–he passes from childhood to youth, from youth to old age, from old age [and] "*bhaaaa*" [laughs], he becomes invalid, he is always invalid afterwards, and afterwards, "*ahhhh*," *bas,* he is finished [laughs]–in the same way, *dehāntaraprāpti*, we have to pass on from one body to another body. *Dhīrastatra na muhyati*, that [person] who is *dhīr*, who is bold, he is never moved by these things [that] are going on in this world.

Ahaṁ hi naiva nāsam (the commentary of this). Was I not [existing] beforehand also? I was! In the same way, *tvam amī ca rājānaḥ*, you and these kings, your kith and kin there, they were also [existing beforehand].

Ākārāntare ca sati yadi śocyatā, if they change their bodies [and] change their formations, is it worthwhile for you to grieve? [If it is], *tarhi kaumārāt yauvanāvāptau kimiti na śocyate*, when you pass from childhood to youth, why don't you pound your head [and cry out], "what has happened to me?"

Because sometimes you will see gray hairs also [growing on your head], then you should pound your head over it [laughs]: "My youth, where has my youth gone? It is finished! What shall I do? I will just die!"

Yo dhīraḥ, [the one] who is bold, *sa na śocati*, he does not accept grief to come into his mind. And boldness is possessed by that person–*dhairyam ca etat śarīre'pi yasyāsthā nāsti, tena sukaram* [comm.]–boldness is possessed by that person who does not care for life and death, who is always fine, always residing in God consciousness. How will he die? He is always living eternally! So it is good for him, it suits him. [Lord Kṛṣṇa tells Arjuna:] "Be like that! Be like Me!"

Now He is addressing Arjuna.

Now the commentary, the text of another *śloka*; [introductory] text of 15th *śloka*.

DVD 2.1 (33:10)

adhīrāstu mātrāśabdavācyairarthairye kṛtāḥ sparśā
indriyadvāreṇātmanā saṁbandhāḥ, tatkṛtā yāḥ
śītoṣṇasukhaduḥkhādyāvasthā anityāḥ, tāsvapi śocanti /

[Abhinavagupta]: Those who are not bold, they weep at the time when they feel cold, when they feel hot, when they feel headache–they cry, they cry, "I have got headache!"[26]

26 "Those who are not possessing the heroic state of life, do you know what they do? They repent not only for the change of their bodies. When their money is gone, they repent, and when their money comes, they become joyful. But this is the incorrect way of understanding. You should not be joyful at the time by attaining this money and all these

When a dentist operated on my tooth and it was so painful, but I enjoyed it. I said, "oh, it is fine, but you should not [stop]. Go on, go on doing [it], I enjoy it, I enjoy this pain. It is wonderful!" I was laughing.
JONATHAN: Swamiji was saying . . . he said, "oh it hurts, but it's so sweet."

SWAMIJI: So,

DVD 2.1 (34:27)

मात्रास्पर्शास्तु कौन्तेय शीतोष्णसुखदुःखदाः ।
आगमापायिनोऽनित्यास्तांस्तितिक्षस्व भारत ॥१५॥

mātrāsparśāstu kaunteya śītoṣṇasukhaduḥkhadāḥ /
āgamāpāyino'nityāstāmstitikṣasva bhārata //15//

[Lord Kṛṣṇa says], you should tolerate these *sparśa mātrās* [sensations], which are the cause of your organs in the body.[27] They give pain, they give pleasure, they give joy, they give happiness, they give grief, they give [all of these sensations], but you should tolerate that! Without tolerance, there is no way out. If you don't tolerate, you will make others weep. They will also weep. They will say, "our child is dying. What shall I do?"

16th [*śloka*] now.

---

facilities, and you should not be sad when these possessions are taken away from you. You should remain the same. But that sameness is possessed only by those persons who have a heroic state of mind." *Bhagavad Gītā* (1978).

27 "[Abhinavagupta says], this happiness, pain, pleasure, sorrow, sadness, ups and downs of this life–they are connected with body. They are not connected with your soul. It is *mātrābhiḥ sparśa. Mātrā* means they have got organic connection. They have not connection with soul. . . . Nothing is destroyed, nothing is created. Creation and destruction is seen but it is not existing. Someone gets birth, someone is born, someone is dead; it is seen [but] nothing is born, nothing is dead. Let [you] tolerate them, you should tolerate them in this life. You must have that courage to tolerate them. That is the way how you will possess the heroic state of life." Ibid.

DVD 2.1 (35:22)

यं हि ना व्यथयन्त्येते पुरुषं पुरुषर्षभ ।
समदुःखसुखं धीरं सोऽमृतत्वाय कल्पते ॥ १६ ॥

yaṁ hi na vyathayantyete puruṣaṁ puruṣarṣabha /
samaduḥkhasukhaṁ dhīraṁ so'mṛtatvāya kalpate //16//

[Lord Kṛṣṇa]: And that *puruṣa*, on the contrary, that person who is *dhīr*, who is bold, to him, they [i.e., *sparśa mātrās*] don't give any alteration of position. He remains the same in pain and pleasure. That person is really fit to get liberation and enter into the Bhairava state of Parabhairava. He will actually . . . he is fit to get the state of Bhairava, Parabhairava.

Who?

DENISE: The one who is the same in pleasure and pain.

SWAMIJI: Yes.

Now, this commentary . . . this is logic, should we do it or leave this chapter?

JOHN: We should do it only if it will benefit us from the point of view of our writing.

SWAMIJI: Yes.

Nāsato . . . 17th now, 17th *śloka*.

DVD 2.1 (37:10)

नासतो विद्यते भावो नाभावो विद्यते सतः ।
उभयोरपि दृष्टोऽन्तस्त्वनयोस्तत्त्वदर्शिभिः ॥ १७ ॥

nāsato vidyate bhāvo nābhāvo vidyate sataḥ /
ubhayorapi dṛṣṭo'ntastvanayostattvadarśibhiḥ //17//

[Lord Kṛṣṇa]: *Nāsato vidyate bhāva*, that which is not existing, that will never exist. That which is not existing, that will never exist. It is a rule. That which is not existing will never exist.

Āsato, that which is not existing, what is that?

Nityavināśinaḥ śarīrasya [comm.]. This *śarīra*, this body, which is going on, it has got *sthūla vināśinaḥ* and *sūkṣma vināśinaḥ* (subtle death and gross death). The body has actually subtle death and gross death.

As long as there is body, it has got subtle death. Subtle death [takes place] from one minute to another minute. If you have come into a body, you are born, from that very moment there is death of that body. That is subtle death. It appears to those who can know [i.e., perceive] that there is [subtle] death. That is *sūkṣma vināśinaḥ,* subtle death. Subtle death [is, for example], one person is born and he is dying, he is dying, he is dying, he is dying, he is dying. He is dying from one minute to another minute, he is dying. He is not that [same] person, he does not remain that person [whom] he was one minute earlier. And in the second minute . . . [in] the third minute, he is not that same person he was in the second minute. In the fourth [minute], he is not that person which was in the third minute. He is dying. He is dying from time to time, from one minute . . . not even one minute–even one second! One second passes, each second he dies in the course [of his life] and his whole life of one hundred years span goes . . . goes [on] like this.

So there is subtle death.

DVD 2.1 (40:22)

अविनाशि तु तद्विद्धि येन सर्वमिदं ततम् ।
विनाशमव्ययस्यास्य न कश्चित्कर्तुमर्हति ॥१८॥
अन्तवन्त इमे देहा नित्यस्योक्ताः शरीरिणः ।
विनाशिनोऽप्रमेयस्य तस्माद्युध्यस्व भारत ॥१९॥

avināśi tu tadviddhi yena sarvamidaṁ tatam /
vināśamavyayasyāsya na kaścitkartumarhati //18//
antavanta ime dehā nityasyoktāḥ śarīriṇaḥ /
vināśino 'prameyasya tasmādyūddhyasva bhārata //19//
[not recited]

[Abhinavagupta]: Now, how will you come to know that there was subtle death?

For instance, you have a sister. You have seen that sister at the age of seventeen years, when she was seventeen years old. Afterwards you didn't get time to see her for about twenty-four years.

When you see her [after twenty-four years], you will see her anew. You will see that she has already changed. She has got wrinkles and she has [become older]. She is not that sister [you had seen twenty-four years ago].

Do you understand what I mean?

He says that. It is a subtle death. And this subtle death goes on up to the [final] death time. And *nirupākhyatākāle* [comm.], when this body is burned, cremated or buried–when there is actual death–then that is [called] gross death. That is what he says.

No other commentator has explained these two kinds of death in the *Bhagavad Gītā*. No commentator.

DENISE: They only see the gross death?

SWAMIJI: Yes.

DENISE: Not the subtle decaying body.

SWAMIJI: Yes.

Nirupākhyatākāle sthūlavināśayoginaḥ, when he becomes *nirupākhya*, *nirupākhya* means when there is no . . .[28]

For instance, [after] my father died, there is no name of his [remaining]; there is not name now. One who dies and he is cremated or buried or whatever it is, but he is not . . . [his body] has no [existence afterwards]. But according to Shaivism, he is also existing [after death]; he is also existing in memory. In memory also he is also existing.

> *ante purāṇatāṁ dṛṣṭvā pratikṣaṇaṁ navatvahānir anumīyate* / [comm.]

When [you] see that person after forty-five years, you can well calculate that she or he has changed from each and every second. She has changed her body each and every second for all this span of time. It is *anumāna* (inference). You can calculate it. It is very easy to calculate at that time. *Ante purāṇatāṁ dṛṣṭvā pratikṣaṇaṁ navatvahānir anumīyate.*

In the *Mahābhārata*, Vyāsa also has said this, Vyāsa also has

28 "*Nirupākhya* means only in photos you will see him or her, nowhere else in this world. Why? Because when that body is decomposed, that is in fire or in graveyard or anywhere, then you won't find that body existing in this world afterwards. In photos only, that is only art, [but] you can't talk to these [images]." *Bhagavad Gītā* (1978).

quoted this:

kalānāṁ pṛthagarthānāṁ pratibhedaḥ kṣaṇe kṣaṇe /
vartate sarvabhāveṣu saukṣmyāttu na vibhāvyate //

Pṛthagarthānāṁ kalānāṁ rūpabhedaḥ. Rūpabhedaḥ pratikṣaṇaṁ anumīyate, it is calculated by those who experience this, that *rūpa bhedaḥ*, [the changes of formation], is going on in the body. From one second to another second, there is change, there is change, and afterwards . . . that is *sūkṣma vināśa* (subtle death). And there is *sthūla vināśa* (gross death) at the time of death.[29]

20th *śloka*:

DVD 2.1 (44:59)

य एनं वेत्ति हन्तारं यश्चैनं मन्यते हतम् ।
उभौ तौ न विजानीतो नायं हन्ति न हन्यते ॥२०॥

ya enaṁ vetti hantāraṁ yaścainaṁ manyate hatam /
ubhau tau na vijānīto nāyaṁ hanti na hanyate //20//

[Lord Kṛṣṇa]: That person who believes that he is the killer, [that] *ātma* (the soul) is the killer, *ātma* has killed . . . for instance, I am Arjuna [who says], "my *ātma*, my soul has killed these kith and kins." *Yaścainaṁ manyate hatam*, and that person who believes that these [people] are dead now, I have killed them, they are dead, they have fallen down, *ubhau tau na vijānīto*, those persons do not understand what has happened.

29 "*Dehā antavanto vināśinaśca* [comm.]. So, these bodies are decaying and ending. *Ātmā tu nityaḥ*, the soul is eternal because *yato aprayameyaḥ*, it cannot come in the clutches of limitation. *Prameyasya tu jaḍasya pariñāmitvaṁ*. The *prameya* (the object), that which is limited, can be changed, can come in the clutches of change. *Na tvajaḍasya cidekarūpasya*. *Ajaḍa cidekarūpasya* is never changing, that is *ātmā* (the soul). *Svābhāvāntarāyogāt*, because his existence does not change. *Evaṁ dehā*, in the same way, *dehā nityamantvantaḥ*, in the same way, thus in conclusion, *deha* (these bodies) are always decaying and ending. *Iti śocitum aśakyāḥ*, so you cannot repent, it is beyond your power to repent on this body." Ibid.

Because *nāyaṁ hanti na hanyate,* this *ātma* never kills anybody and never is being killed by anybody. This *ātma* is always eternal. [The soul] never kills anybody and he is never killed by anybody.

Do you understand?

This is what He says in this *śloka*.

DVD 2.1 (46:21)

न जायते म्रियते वा कदाचि–
न्नायं भूत्वा भविता वा न भूयः ।
अजो नित्यः शाश्वतोऽयं पुराणो
न हन्यते हन्यमाने शरीरे ॥२१॥

na jāyate mriyate vā kadācin-
nāyaṁ bhūtvā bhavitā vā na bhūyaḥ /
ajo nityaḥ śāśvato'yaṁ purāṇo
na hanyate hanyamāne śarīre //21//

[Lord Kṛṣṇa]: This soul, which has come into the body as an incarnation (in each and every body there is an incarnation of the soul), he has come into this body as an *avatār* does, but [it is a] misfortune for that person who does not understand this. It is a misfortune for that person who does not understand that I am an incarnation. [A person ought to think], "I have come [in this body] to elevate this whole universe." Being the elevator, He wants to make others get themselves elevated.

Do you understand?

No, for instance, I have come into this body. Actually, whoever has come into this body, he wants to make you understand that you are Parabhairava, you are one with Bhairava. There is nothing less than Bhairava [existing] in you also–in anybody! In a feeble person also, he is also Parabhairava. He has come into this body to elevate the whole universe.

This you cannot understand very easily.

This is the cream of Shaivism!

Anybody who is . . . Viresh is here. He is the incarnation of

Lord.[30] This is the essence of *Bhagavad Gītā*, which is not exposed by any commentator in this world.

[Lord Kṛṣṇa]: *Na jāyate*, [the soul] is not born; *mriyate vā kadācit*, he does not die. *Nāyaṁ bhūtvā*, when he is born, *bhavitā vā na bhūyaḥ*, do you think that he will not be born again? He will be born again. *Ajaḥ*, he is without birth, he is without death. *Nityaḥ*, he is eternal. *Śāśvato'yaṁ*, he is ancient. The soul is ancient. *Na hanyate hanyamāne śarīre*, when this body falls [down] absolutely dead, he is not dead, he is alive there. He does not disappear.

This is the Shaivite philosophy.

Vedāvināśinaṁ nityaṁ . . . 22nd *śloka* now.

DVD 2.1 (50:18)

वेदाविनाशिनं नित्यं य एनमजमव्ययम् ।
कथं स पुरुषः पार्थ हन्यते हन्ति वा कथम् ॥२२॥

vedāvināśinaṁ nityaṁ ya enamajamavyayam /
kathaṁ sa puruṣaḥ pārtha hanyate hanti vā kathaṁ //22//

[Lord Kṛṣṇa]: *Vedāvināśinaṁ nityaṁ ya enam ajamavyayam.*

How beautiful are these *ślokas*.

Veda, one who understands [that] *enam*, this soul, *avināśinaṁ*, [is] eternal–who understands that this soul is eternal–*ajam*, he is not born, *avyayam*, he is not [going] to die, *kathaṁ sa puruṣaḥ pārtha*, O Arjuna, how [will] that *puruṣa*[31] kills and how [is it possible that] that *puruṣa* will be killed by anybody? He is always eternal. He is the person who is to be understood.

DVD 2.1 (51:39)

वासांसि जीर्णानि यथा विहाय
नवानि गृह्णाति नरोऽपराणि ।
तथा शरीराणि विहाय जीर्णा–

30 Swamiji uses Viresh as an example to convey the fact that everyone is an incarnation of the Lord. [*Editor's note*]

31 That person who understands the qualifications of the soul. [*Editor's note*]

न्यन्यानि संयाति नवानि देही ॥२३॥

vāsāṁsi jīrṇāni yathā vihāya
navāni gṛhṇāti naro'parāṇi /
tatha śarīrāṇi vihāya jīrṇā-
nyanyani saṁyāti navāni dehī //23//

[Lord Kṛṣṇa]: *Jīrṇāni vāsāṁsi. Nara*, just as *nara* (anybody), *jīrṇāni vāsāṁsi*, those torn clothes, *vihāya*, he discards them, he throws them off, *navāni aparāṇi*, and he wears another stock of new clothes, in the same way, *jīrṇāni śarīrāṇi*, those who [have] invalid bodies, in the same way, invalid bodies they throw away and get in a good body again. What is there in that? Why should you weep?

yathā vastrācchāditastadvastranāśe samucitavas-trāntarāvṛto na vinaśyati, evamātmā dehāntarāvṛtaḥ [comm.]

Just in one line, [Abhinavagupta] has described the [entire] explanation of this *śloka*.

Yathā, just as, *vastrāt chādita*, one who is covered with some clothes, *samucita vastrāntar āvṛto*, and he throws those clothes away and possesses another lot of clothes, *na vinaśyati*, he does not die, he does not die [by doing] that. Does he die at that time?

In the same way, *ātmā dehāntar āvṛtaḥ*, this soul, when he leaves the body and gets another body, he does not die, he is always eternal!

Chapter 2 Part 2

In the same way, *ātmā dehāntar āvṛtaḥ*, this soul, when he leaves the body and gets another body, he does not die, he is always eternal!

Why? *Nainaṁ chin* . . . another *śloka*:

DVD 2.2 (00:16)

नैनं छिन्दन्ति शस्त्राणि नैनं दहति पावकः ।
न चैनं क्लेदयन्त्यापो न शोषयति मारुतः ॥२४॥
अच्छेद्योऽयमदाह्योऽयमक्लेद्योऽशोष्य एव च ।
नित्यः सर्वगतः स्थाणुरचलोऽयं सनातनः ॥२५॥
अव्यक्तोऽयमचिन्त्योऽयमविकार्योऽयमुच्यते ।
तस्मादेवं विदित्वैनं नानुशोचितुमार्हसि ॥२६॥

nainaṁ chindanti śastrāṇi nainaṁ dahati pāvakaḥ /
na cainaṁ kledayantyāpo na śoṣayati mārutaḥ //24//
acchedyo'yamadāhyo'yamakledyo'śoṣya eva ca /
nityaḥ sarvagataḥ sthāṇuracalo'yaṁ sanātanaḥ //25//
avyakto'yamacintyo'yamavikāryo'yamucyate /
tasmādevaṁ viditvainaṁ nānuśocitumārhasi //26//

[Lord Kṛṣṇa]: *Nainaṁ chindanti śastrāṇi.* These weapons, they cannot cut this *ātma* into pieces. [Even] if you cut the body into pieces, *ātma* cannot be cut by these hatchets and saws and whatever it is. *Nainaṁ dahati pāvakaḥ.* Fire cannot burn it; fire cannot burn this *ātma. Na cainaṁ kledayantyāpa*, when we leave a body in water, it swells, it becomes very big. In the same way, *ātma* cannot become big. *Na śoṣayati mārutaḥ*, *vayu* (wind) cannot dry it. *Acchedyo'yam*, it [cannot be] cut. *Adāhyo'yam*, it [cannot be] burned. *Akledyo*, it [cannot become swollen]. *Aśoṣya eva ca*, it is not to be grieved upon.

[The soul is] eternal, all-pervading, *sthāṇur* (*sthāṇur* means without any change, changeless), *acala*, he does not move from his reality of God consciousness, *sanātana*, and it is absolutely eternal.

It is more than one thousand years old and more than one *lakh* (100,000) years old–more than that. You can't imagine how old [the soul] is and how young he is. He is the oldest being ever we have [existing] in this world. So we are lucky to have that great Lord, the oldest one. And nobody can kill it; nobody can do it any harm.

He is older than the oldest. Whatever you can imagine, it is older than that. *Sanātana*, and it is always one and changeless.

So you must possess that kind of wisdom so that you become also one with that. Because everybody has the right to get that, possess that . . .

Possess that what?

DENISE: Awareness of their *ātma*?

SWAMIJI: Awareness not!

. . . possess that Being. Not awareness, it is not only awareness.

DENISE: But everybody has that opportunity . . .

SWAMIJI: Everybody has.

DENISE: . . . they just ignore it.

SWAMIJI: Yes.

DENISE: I mean to possess it, to have that.

SWAMIJI: But they are ignorant because they are ignorant. They don't know. They are misguided. They are misguided by their own limitation.

DENISE: So it's knowledge.

SWAMIJI: It is full knowledge! They have got capacity of full knowledge, which they have ignored because of their ignorance.

Everybody is possessing that full knowledge.

DVD 2.2 (04:50)

अथवैनं नित्यजातं नित्यं वा मन्यसे मृतम् ।
तथापि त्वं महाबाहो नैनं शोचितुमार्हसि ॥२७॥

athavainaṁ nityajātaṁ nityaṁ vā manyase mṛtam /
tathāpi tvaṁ mahābāho nainaṁ śocitumārhasi //27//
[not recited]

So this way, if you think this way, why should you give place for grief? Where is the place for grief to come? Why should grief be allowed? You should not allow any grief [and lament], "what shall I do? What shall I . . . ?" [O Arjuna], go on and kill them! They won't be killed.[32]

There is one alternate process [that] I will explain to you, O Arjuna.

This is in the 28th *śloka.*

DVD 2.2 (05:40)

जातस्य हि ध्रुवो मृत्युर्ध्रुवं जन्म मृतस्य च ।
तस्मादपरिहार्येऽर्थे न त्वं शोचितुमर्हसि ॥२८॥

jātasya hi dhruvo mṛtyurdhruvaṁ janma mṛtasya ca /
tasmādaparihārye'rthe na tvaṁ śocitumarhasi //28//

One who has been born, he has to die. And one who is dead, he has to be born, i.e., he will be born again. So you can't change this chain of the world. You can't change this chain of the world. Why should you allow grief in your consciousness? Remain quite happy.

No, if that person who is born, he has to die. Well and good. Then the one who is dead, he has to be born. Why should you pound your heads for nothing [laughs]? It will happen. Still it will happen. If you pound your head, it will happen. If you don't pound your head, [it will happen]. If you laugh . . .

Utpaladeva has said [in his] *Śivastotrāvali*, 16th chapter:

jaiyanto'pi hasantyete jitā api hasanti ca /
bhavadbhaktisudhāpānamattāḥ ke'pyeva ye prabho //16.3//

32 "O Arjuna, if you think this soul is always dying and always getting birth, still then, why should you repent? You can't change this wheel, this circle, by repenting on this." *Bhagavad Gītā* (1978).

Jaiyanto'pi hasantyete, if they conquer [others], they laugh; if they are conquered by others, they laugh. This is the way of Your devotees, O Lord. Your devotees are such [that] when they are conquered by people, they laugh; when they conquer others, they laugh. Why should they allow any grief to remain in their consciousness? They laugh in both ways.

This is *Utpalastotrāvali* [i.e., Utpaladeva's *Śivastotrāvali*].

Jaiyanto'pi hasantyete jitā api hasanti ca. If you tell them, "you are defeated in this world," they laugh. If you tell them, "you have conquered," they laugh [laughs]. They laugh in both ways. They are always fine.

Another *śloka*, the 29th of this chapter.

DVD 2.2 (08:25)

अव्यक्तादीनि भूतानि व्यक्तमध्यानि भारत ।
अव्यक्तनिधनान्येव तत्र का परिदेवना ॥२९॥

avyaktādīni bhūtāni vyaktamadhyāni bhārata /
avyaktanidhanānyeva tatra kā paridevanā //29//

[Lord Kṛṣṇa]: Now Arjuna, I will tell you another secret of Shaivism, the reality (I mean, not Shaivism, reality).

Avyaktādīni bhūtāni, these souls were, in the beginning, they were not, they were not . . . they were in the background (*avyaktā*). *Avyaktā* means they were not being created . . .

JOHN: Manifested.

SWAMIJI: . . . they were not manifested. *Vyakta madhyāni bhārata*, and in the middle span of this world, they have appeared.

Before your birth, you were nowhere. If you see, if you go to the depth of this, [you will discover] that before your birth, you were nowhere. And when you appeared, when you were born, up to the point of death (after all, you have to leave this body after death; after one thousand years you may die, but you have to die), in this span of time, this is actually one way of your being.

Āvyakta nidhanānyeva, when you die, you are again nowhere to be seen after death. *Tatra kā paridevanā*, [when] should you pound your head? You should pound your head when you have got *vikāra* (*vikāra* means from your birth up to your death). You should pound your head for this period, not the origin of this. Origin is nowhere.

Do you understand?

Originally you were not at all existing and in the end you are not at all existing. In the middle you were existing. And it was a false notion that you were existing [in this middle period]. It was just change. Where should you weep? You should weep in this [middle] course. She is born and she will die; go on beating your head [laughs].

Actually, *ātma* is *nitya* (eternal); he is neither born nor he dies.

But who can realize this *ātma*?

He says in the 30th *śloka* of this chapter:

DVD 2.2 (12:21)

आश्चर्यवत्पश्यति कश्चिदेन-
माश्चर्यवद्वदति तथैनमन्यः ।
आश्चर्यवच्चैनमन्यः शृणोति
श्रुत्वाप्येनं वेद न चैव कश्चित् ॥३०॥

āścaryavatpaśyati kaścadenam-
āścaryavadvadati tathainamanyaḥ /
āścaryavaccainamanyaḥ śṛṇoti
śrutvāpyenaṁ veda na caiva kaścit //30//

At least one in one million persons, somebody who is fortunate, he experiences this state of being of Bhairava in his own way. As Parabhairava . . . for instance, how have I become Parabhairava?

DENISE: You always were Parabhairava.

SWAMIJI: You were always Parabhairava also! Why don't you become Parabhairava? You can't deny it, Parabhairava is everywhere. You can't deny that you are Parabhairava.

So even [out of] thousands and millions of people, somebody who is fortunate, he experiences the state of Parabhairava.

JOHN: Why only one?

SWAMIJI: Huh?

DENISE: *Śaktipāta*, isn't it?

SWAMIJI: *Śaktipāta–tīvra tīvra śaktipāta.*[33] When *tīvra tīvra śaktipāta* comes, *bas*! He makes you anew; you are born anew.

JOHN: Why so few?

SWAMIJI: Why so few? There is only one! There is only one pervading in each and every corner of the world. It is all one. But you have forgotten that; you have forgotten your nature.

JOHN: But why does He reveal himself only in one?

SWAMIJI: It is your own play . . . it is your own play. When you withdraw this play, you'll become the same. It is your will that you don't want to reside in . . .

JONATHAN: How do we withdraw that play?

SWAMIJI: Huh?

JONATHAN: How do we do that? How do we withdraw that play?

SWAMIJI: Why should you withdraw [laughs]? Why should you withdraw? As long as you don't withdraw, don't withdraw. It won't go anywhere.

DENISE: How do you withdraw? How? How?

SWAMIJI: It is there [clapping hands, laughing].

DENISE: There must be a way . . . I don't think there's a way. If *śaktipāta* comes from above, then how can we do anything? Doesn't it come from above?

SWAMIJI: It comes from the bottom also. It comes from the bottom also, not above only. He is not above only in the one hundred and eighteenth world. He is in the bottom also. He is in the center also. He is everywhere; *śaktipāta* is everywhere.

DVD 2.2 (15:45)

So, *āścaryavat paśyati kaścadenam. Kaścad*, in one thousand millions, some fortunate person understands and realizes the [reality] of his nature–Parabhairava.

---

33 "The first and highest level of grace is called *tīvra tīvra śaktipāta. Tīvra tīvra śaktipāta* means "super-supreme-grace." When Lord Śiva bestows super-supreme-grace on anyone, then that person becomes perfectly Self-recognized. He knows his real nature completely and in perfection." Swami Lakshmanjoo, *Kashmir Shaivism–The Secret Supreme* 10.66 (Universal Shaiva Fellowship, Los Angeles, 1985-2003).

Aścaryavad vadati tathainam anyaḥ. In the same way, that person who has realized it, he explains [to others] that I have understood [it in] this way. He explains this to his kith and kin [and to] his fast friend, he explains this, and that person (his fast friend) cannot understand it. He cannot understand what he is barking. *Āścaryavat cainam anyaḥ śṛṇoti*. The other person [to] whom he reveals the nature of his being, he is also astonished. He says, "what is he doing? What is he talking [about]? I think he is mad!" *Śrutvāpyenaṁ veda na caiva kaścit*. By merely hearing [him], nobody can understand him.

JONATHAN: But you also said, Swamiji, that your master can give rise to you just by explaining something. Isn't that true? You said by hearing, if your master tells you something at the correct time, then that person will get rise.

SWAMIJI: Actually, masters are disciples. Really, masters are disciples! When there is a disciple, then there is a master. Without a disciple, there won't be a master. Master cannot exist without a disciple. When there is *pakka* (first class) disciple, then there is master. Otherwise [not].

This is the theory of our Shaivism that, when you are initiated by your real master, and when you have grasped his philosophy, then you'll see him always in [your] dreams. Each and every night, you will see him near [your] pillow; near [your] pillow you will see him.

This is the one indication.

And the time will come, you will see me near [your] pillow, when you understand this theory of mine. Then you should come to know that you have become mine, you have become myself.

But there is no distance [between master and disciple]. Distance is just twinkling, twinkling, twinkling . . . what is it?

JOHN: Twinkling of the eye?

SWAMIJI: Yes.

Twinkling of the eye, *bas*! It is not this much distance [Swamiji demonstrates by pressing his thumb and index finger together]. *Bas*. There is no distance, just vibration. It is vibration. There is no breath, there is nothing, there is just vibration.

However, you can't understand it at this critical moment.

Let us leave it to Abhinavagupta.

When it is understood, you'll not know, you won't say that you have understood. When you have understood, actually understood, you won't say, "I have understood."

DENISE: What will you say, nothing?

SWAMIJI:

DVD 2.2 (20:18)

avijñātaṁ vijānatāṁ vijñātaṁ avijānatāṁ //[34]

Those who say, "I have understood the reality of Parabhairava," they have not understood. Those who say, "I have not understood the reality of Parabhairava," they have actually understood.

For instance, if you just plunge, jump into water, and take hold of those bushes on the shore, and those bushes also are uprooted and you fall down and there is no way out . . . when you have lost all confidence, then you are . . . some, another incarnation comes and takes you up. That is *śaktipāta*, when you have lost all hope.

Draupadi, when she was, she was . . .

DENISE: Disrobed.[35]

SWAMIJI: . . . disrobed, as long as she was holding [onto her sari with her teeth], she was calling Lord Kṛṣṇa, "come and help me," but at the same time, she was holding [onto her] sari with . . .

JONATHAN: Her mouth.

SWAMIJI: But He didn't come. He said "no, she has [still] got faith that [she can] hide [herself]." Then, when she lost all courage [to hold on], she [let go of her sari], and *then* Lord Kṛṣṇa appeared and gave [her a] tremendous [supply] of *dhotis* (cloth) [so that] she would never be undressed. And it was a miracle.

There, that was the real time of *śaktipāta.*

JOHN: So there must be unconditional surrender.

SWAMIJI: Unconditional surrender, *bas*! When there is unconditional surrender, *bas*, you are one with the Lord. There is not this much difference between you and Parabhairava. Parabhairava is you and you are Parabhairava. Or, in brief words, there is only one Parabhairava.

---

34 *Kena Upaniṣad*, 2.3.

35 The wife of the five Pāṇḍavā brothers. After being shamefully gambled away by Yudhiṣṭhira to the Kauravas, Duryodhana's brother, Dushasana, attempted to disrobe her. [*Editor's note*]

DVD 2.2 (23:39)

देही नित्यमवध्योऽयं देहे सर्वस्य भारत ।
तस्मात्सर्वाणि भूतानि न त्वं शोचितुमर्हसि ॥३१॥

dehī nityamavadhyo'yaṁ dehe sarvasya bhārata /
tasmātsarvāṇi bhūtāni na tvaṁ śocitumarhasi //31//

[Lord Kṛṣṇa]: *Dehī*. *Dehī* means [the one] who has occupied the body. The *ātma*, the soul who has occupied the body (no matter if this body is held by ignorant people or [by those who are] filled with knowledge–those people), this body holder does not vanish at all. In the same way, all individuals are like that; [some are] elevated and [others are] not-elevated.

Why should you then accept grief for your Self? Your Self is always imperishable.

If you think . . . another *śloka*. If you think, "what is your duty?"

DVD 2.2 (25:17)

स्वधर्ममपि चावेक्ष्य न विकम्पितुमर्हसि ।
धर्म्याद्धि युद्धाच्छ्रेयोऽन्यत्क्षत्रियस्य न विद्यते ॥३२॥

svadharmamapi cāvekṣya na vikampitumarhasi /
dharmyāddhi yuddhācchreyo'nyatkṣatriyasya na vidyate //32

[Lord Kṛṣṇa]: You, [O Arjuna], are a kṣatriya, you are a warrior. If you look at your duty, what is your duty, you are a warrior. So you should not get [caught] in a fix, "why should I [fight]?" Your work is to fight, you are a warrior, you are not a brahmin. For a kṣatriya, your [only] duty is to mix with [i.e., engage in] war, so that everybody is calmed down.

If you go to this depth also [and ask], "after death, what will happen [to me]? If I am killed in this war, in this battlefield, if I am killed or if I win [and conquer my] kith and kin . . . "

DVD 2.2 (26:46)

यदृच्छया चोपपन्नं स्वर्गद्वारमपावृतम् ।

सुकृतात्क्षत्रियाः पार्थ लभन्ते युद्धमीदृशम् ॥३३॥

yadṛcchayā copapannaṁ svargadvāramapāvṛtam /
sukṛtātkṣatriyāḥ pārtha labhante yuddhamīdṛśam //33//
[not recited in full]

[Lord Kṛṣṇa]: Automatically, *svarga dvāram*, heaven is waiting for you. If you die [in battle], you will just rise in heaven. If you win, you will be the king of this whole area. It is a great boon that you have got this golden opportunity to fight. [In] both ways, you [will succeed]. If you are killed, you will go to heaven; if you are not killed, you will be the king, you will . . .

DENISE: Rule.

SWAMIJI: . . . you will rule nicely.

And this theory I told you: [those Kṣatriyas] who are not filled with the knowledge of Bhairava, *bodha-bhairava*[36], who are just worldly people, [even] for those worldly people it is best to fight. Either be killed and go to heaven or win and be the ruler of this whole area.

And what to speak of that person who is my disciple and [in] whom I insert the knowledge of Parabhairava, the supreme Bhairava?

Yadbhayāt . . . 34th *śloka.*

yadbhayāt bhavān yuddhāt nivarteta, [comm. intro 34]

[Abhinavagupta]: If at all you think that, "I will walk out, I won't fight with them . . ."

tadeva śataśākhamupanipatiṣyati bhavata [*ityāha*]

. . . you will have to fight. It is destined that you have to fight. You cannot walk out from this. You are caught, you have to fight. It is My will that you will fight. If you don't fight, what will happen?

34th *śloka*:

---

36 *Bodha-bhairava* is the the awareness of Bhairava consciousness, i.e., universal God consciousness. [*Editor's note*]

DVD 2.2 (29:37)

अथ चेत्त्वमिमं धर्म्यं सङ्ग्रामं न करिष्यसि ।
ततः स्वधर्मं कीर्तिं च हित्वा पापमवाप्स्यसि ॥३४॥

atha cettvamimaṁ dharmyaṁ saṅgrāmaṁ na kariṣyasi /
tataḥ svadharmaṁ kīrtiṁ ca hitvā pāpamavāpsyasi //34//

[Lord Kṛṣṇa]: If at all you won't fight . . . for instance, for two minutes, say that you won't fight, then everybody will give you bad names [and say] that, "he wants to quit from this [war] because of threat [i.e., fear]."

JONATHAN: He is a coward.

SWAMIJI: "He is a coward." And nobody will say what is the *truth* in your mind, i.e., that you don't want to kill your kith and kin. Nobody will say that. Everybody will say that, "he is a coward and he does not want to fight." So you will be defamed before your kith and kin.

DVD 2.2 (30:55)

अकीर्तिं चापि भूतानि कथयिष्यन्ति तेऽव्ययाम् ।
संभावितस्य चाकीर्तिर्मरणादतिरिच्यते ॥३५॥

akīrtiṁ cāpi bhūtāni kathayiṣyanti te'vyayām /
sambhāvitasya cākīrtirmaraṇādatiricyate //35//
[not recited in full]

Sambhāvita, they were afraid of you; always they have been afraid of you because they thought that, "Arjuna is supported by Lord Kṛṣṇa and he will kill us!" And [if you don't fight], afterwards they will think that, "he is a coward, he was not that type [i.e., a courageous warrior]." And it is better for you to die and take poison and finish your body [if you don't fight].

भयाद्रणादुपरतं मंस्यन्ते त्वां महारथाः ।
येषां च त्वं बहुमतो भूत्वा यास्यसि लाघवम् ॥३६॥

bhayādraṇāduparataṁ mansyante tvām mahārathāḥ /
yeṣāṁ ca tvaṁ bahumato bhūtvā yāsyasi lāghavam //36//
[not recited or translated][37]

DVD 2.2 (31:34)

अवाच्यवादांश्च बहून्वदिष्यन्ति तवाहिताः ।
निन्दन्तस्तव सामर्थ्यं ततो दुःखतरं नु किम् ॥ ३७ ॥

avācyavādāmśca bahūnvadiṣyanti tavāhitāḥ /
nindantastava sāmarthyaṁ tato duḥkhataraṁ nu kim //37//

[Lord Kṛṣṇa]: Many amongst your kith and kin–if you don't fight with them–*avācyavādāmśca bahūnvadiṣyanti*, they will say . . . they will only think that, "you have been a coward and you are afraid of fighting with us." And they will know that you have no *sāmarthya,* you have no power; you are powerless. *Tato duḥkhataraṁ nu kim*. Tell me what will happen next for you, which is unbearable pain for you? [This pain and disrespect] will remain for your dynasty afterwards.

[They will say], "oh, that was . . . he was very cowardly! He ran away from the battlefield." Nobody will think that, "he had compassion for us." Nobody will think that.

हतो वा प्राप्स्यसि स्वर्गं जित्वा वा भोक्ष्यसे महीम् ।
तस्मादुत्तिष्ठ कौन्तेय युद्धाय कृतनिश्चयः ॥ ३८ ॥

hato vā prāpsyasi svargaṁ jitvā vā bhokṣyase mahīm /
tasmāduttiṣṭha kaunteya yuddhāya kṛtaniścayaḥ //38//
[not recited]

37 "And these warriors, which are in front of you, ready to fight with you, they will think *bhayādaraṇāduparatam,* he has walked out from this battlefield just from fear. . . . not because he had . . . compassion and pity for us. They will never think like that . . . they won't have any respect for you in the future. So you will become shallow (*lāghavam*)." *Bhagavad Gītā* (1978).

So fight! And if you at all die, you will be sentenced to heaven. If you don't die, you will win and you will be king.

DVD 2.2 (33:25)

सुखदुःखे समे कृत्वा लाभालाभौ जयाजयौ ।
ततो युद्धाय युज्यस्व नैवं पापमवाप्स्यसि ॥३९॥

sukhaduḥkhe same kṛtvā lābhālābhau jayājayau /
tato yuddhāya yujyasva naivaṁ pāpamavāpsyasi //39//

Now, I will tell you some trick of knowledge (knowledge of Parabhairava) because you are My disciple.

Lord Kṛṣṇa says to him: *sukha* and *duḥkha* (pleasure and pain), *lābha* and [*alābha*] (gain and loss), victory and defeat, think [of these] in the same way, in the same manner. If there is victory, that is okay; if there is not victory, that is okay. If there is *sukha* (pleasure), okay. If there is pain, okay, don't mind.

Tato yuddhāya yujyaso, then you [can] go on fighting. *Naivaṁ pāpam avāpsyasi,* then there will be no *sparśa* (touch) of any *papa* (of any sin, sinful act). No sinful act will have courage [i.e., ability] to stand before you (against you), because you are Bhairava then.

DVD 2.2 (34:52)

एषा तेऽभिहिता सांख्ये बुद्धिर्योगे त्विमां शृणु ।
बुद्ध्या युक्तो यया पार्थ कर्मबन्धं प्रहास्यसि ॥४०॥

eṣā te'bhihitā sāṅkhye buddhiryoge tvimāṁ śṛṇu /
buddhyā yukto yayā pārtha karmabandhaṁ prahāsyasi //40//

[Lord Kṛṣṇa]: This is knowledge, which I have placed before you; it is the knowledge of complete *jñāna* (knowledge) of yourself. All bondage of your actions, whatever actions you do in this life will have no effect at all. They won't bear any fruit, good or bad. You will be just free from your actions. Your actions will have no power to subside your consciousness. Your consciousness will be clear throughout.

These actions actually are *jaḍa*, they are innate or . . .

JOHN: Non-living, inanimate, *jaḍa*.

SWAMIJI: *Jaḍa,* yes.

They are . . . actions are *jaḍa* (inert). How can actions work before [i.e., have an effect upon] an active person who is *cetana*, who is conscious? [If] you are always conscious, actions, which are *jaḍa*, they will have no effect on you; they'll bear nothing [i.e., no fruit]. If you kill the whole world, you won't be caught.

Only there is one thing: *yāsa nāham krito bhāva*, you should not keep it in your mind that, "I have done this."

[Instead] say, "this was to happen. It has been done. I have not done it! It is the way of *prakṛti* that it is being done. I have nothing to do with this. I am absolutely free from this . . .

DENISE: Action.

SWAMIJI: . . . action." [In this way], if he kills this whole universe, he has not [actually] killed [anybody] and he won't be caught.[38] He is just like Bhairava.

DVD 2.2 (37:46)

नेहातिक्रमनाशोऽस्ति प्रत्यवायो न विद्यते ।
स्वल्पमप्यस्य धर्मस्य त्रायते महतो भयात् ॥४१॥

nehātikramanāśo'sti pratyavāyo na vidyate /
svalpamapyasya dharmasya trāyate mahato bhayāt //41//
[not recited]

And this kind of knowledge, if you possess this kind of knowledge of being supreme, [and remain] far above your actions–[because] actions are *jaḍa*, actions have no voice before you–there will be no fear for you at all in this world.

asyāṁ buddhau atikrameṇa–aparādhena pramādena nāśo na bhavati–pramādasyābhāvāt / [comm.]

38 "So, binding is done by your own self, by thinking, e.g., if you think you have done a very bad thing. But this action of bad thing won't bind you. This thinking will bind you." *Bhagavad Gītā* (1978).

Because there is no *pramāda.*[39] If you are aware of God consciousness, what will actions do? Action has no . . .

JOHN: No life, no consciousness.

SWAMIJI: . . . no life, no consciousness.

yathā ca parimītena śrīkhaṇḍakaṇena jvālāyamāno'pi tailakaṭāhaḥ sadyaḥ śītībhavati; [comm.]

So this kind of knowledge of truth, it is just like this: for instance, you put a big frying pan . . .

You know those big . . .

JOHN: *Kray.*

SWAMIJI: *Kray*, big *kray* (frying pan).

. . . and you put mustard oil in it, fill it, and it is so bubbling (very hot), and if you have got *śrikhandakaṇena,* if you put two or three drops of that actual . . .

That *śrikhandakaṇena* means that real sandal[wood] oil. Not [that] sandal[wood] oil which is . . . some sandalwood is touch [impure?] sandalwood from which oil is produced. That is not . . . that won't work. Real sandalwood, where there are snakes around it–that is [real] sandalwood.

. . . [with] that sandalwood oil, two or three drops you pour in that . . .

DENISE: Oil.

SWAMIJI: . . . in that oil, burning oil, [then] you can dip your arm into it and it won't burn [because that oil] will become so cold at once.

Just like that, if you have got the knowledge of God consciousness, then actions will have no existence; actions will have no power to work out [i.e., bear any fruit]. [Your] actions will be dead–all your actions.

So be like that!

evamanayā svalpayāpi yogabuddhyā mahābhayam saṁsārarūpam vinaśyati [comm.]

[Abhinavagupta]: The great threat of the world and repeated births and deaths, these threats [are] vanished altogether, for good.

39 Lack of awareness.

DVD 2.2 (41:33)

व्यवसायात्मिका बुद्धिरेकैव कुरुनन्दन ।
बहुशाखा ह्यनन्ताश्च बुद्धयोऽव्यवसायिनाम् ॥४२॥

vyavasāyātmikā buddhirekaiva kurunandana /
bahuśākhā hyanantāśca buddhayo'vyavasāyinām //42//

[Lord Kṛṣṇa]: O Arjuna, this knowledge of *vyavasāi* (*vyavasāi* means knowledge of truth, i.e., knowledge of being supreme and one with God), this is only one. This knowledge is only one. And others, they have got many branches; other knowledge, i.e., of worldly knowledge, they have got many branches, and it has no end. So possess that one knowledge, supreme knowledge, then everything will be okay.

यामिमां पुष्पितां वाचं प्रवदन्त्यविपश्चितः ।
वेदवादपराः पार्थ नान्यदस्तीतिवादिनः ॥४३॥
कामात्मानः स्वर्गपरा जन्मकर्मफलेप्सवः ।
क्रियाविशेषबहुला भोगैश्वर्यगतीः प्रति ॥४४॥
भोगैश्वर्यप्रसक्तानां तयापहृतचेतसाम् ।
व्यवसायात्मिका बुद्धिः समाधौ न विधीयते ॥४५॥

yāmimāṁ puṣpitāṁ vācaṁ pravadantyavipaścitaḥ /
vedavādaparāḥ pārtha nānyadastītivādinaḥ //43//
kāmātmānaḥ svargaparā janmakarmaphalepsavaḥ /
kriyāviśeṣabahulā bhogaiśvaryagatīḥ prati //44//
[verses not recited or translated][40]

40 Verse 43: "Some philosophers are *vedavādaparā*, they believe in the sayings of *Vedas,* and they say, 'you have to act for the sake of achievement of heaven; you will get heaven in the end and you will be peaceful.' This is the thought which is possessed by Vedāntins. But those philosophers . . . are *avipaścita*, they are not realized souls. Because they say there is only heaven to be achieved. . . . [According to them], beyond

bhogaiśvaryaprasaktānāṁ tayāpahṛtacetasām /
vyavasāyātmikā buddhiḥ samādhau na viddhīyate //45//
[not recited]

DVD 2.2 (42:33)

[Lord Kṛṣṇa]: There are some people who like to remain away from God by their own will. By the sweet will of God, there are some people who don't want to remain with God. They want to remain away, away from God. And it is His sweet will.

Because they want to enjoy worldly . . .

JOHN: Pleasures.

SWAMIJI: . . . to get involved in worldly matters. This is also His will. They want to live in this world to enjoy worldly pleasures and afterwards they want to go up to heaven; [their desire is] not to get liberated from repeated births and deaths. It is their will. This is also the grace of God for them because they don't want the grace of God. They want to live in this world away from God consciousness.

Those people are not fit for *samādhi*; those people are not fit for *samādhi* by the grace of God. So they don't maintain *samādhi* at all; they don't like *samādhi*. Why should they like? Although they know there is God, but they are not *api na samādhi yogyāḥ,* they are not fit for *samādhi*; they are not fit for achieving the reality of God consciousness.

So for you, as you are My own soul, you are inseparable from My soul, O Arjuna, I give you *aśarvad* (blessings), I bestow *aśarvad* to you.

---

heaven, there is nothing to be achieved."

Verse 44: "And they are *kāmātmānaḥ,* they are given to enjoyment of the world. *Svargaparā,* they are bent upon having achievement of heaven. *Janma karma phalepsavaḥ,* and they think that the reality of life is to get birth and do actions and enjoy world of senses. If you enjoy fully the world of senses here, still that enjoyment won't become complete unless you get entry in heaven also. . . . This is what they say [but] really they are ignorant persons. They don't know what the actual reality is. Reality of life is just awareness of God consciousness. *Triyāviśeṣabahulā,* so they adopt various actions in this world, *bhogaiśvaryagatīḥ prati,* just for the sake of enjoyment and sovereignty."

Bhagavad Gītā (1978).

DVD 2.2 (45:24)

त्रैगुण्यविषया वेदा निस्त्रैगुण्यो भवार्जुन ।

traiguṇyaviṣayā vedā [nistraiguṇyo bhavārjuna] /

Vedas, all the four *Vedas*, they are not away from *sattvaguṇa*, *rajoguṇa*, and *tamoguṇa*. *Sattvaguṇa*, *rajoguṇa*, and *tamoguṇa* are existing in the *Vedas*. You [must] possess [the knowledge of the] *Vedas*, but not with [i.e., under the influence of] the *guṇas*. You [must] remain away from the three *guṇas*.[41]

निर्द्वन्द्वो नित्यसत्त्वस्थो निर्योगक्षेम अत्मवान् ॥४६॥

nirdvandvo nityasattvastho niryogakṣema ātmavān //46//

You [should] remain fixed, focused, in your own God consciousness always, then you are a real Vedāntist.

Vedas means *śāstras*.

Vedas are for those people who are above the three *guṇas*. The *Vedas* direct them towards God consciousness.

JOHN: The *Vedas*?

SWAMIJI: Yes, *Vedas*. The *Vedas* mean all *śāstras*.

DVD 2.2 (46:52)

यावानर्थ उदपाने सर्वतः संप्लुतोदके ।
तावान्सर्वेषु वेदेषु ब्राह्मणस्य विजानतः ॥४७॥

yāvānartha udapāne sarvataḥ saṁplutodake /
tāvānsarveṣu vedeṣu brāhmaṇasya vijānataḥ / /47//
[not translated][42]

---

41 "These *Vedas* are *traiguṇyaviṣayā*, because of *triguṇas* they bind. They will bind you because of three *guṇas*. If you put these three *guṇas* away from the hymns of *Vedas*, they won't bind you, they will just liberate you." Ibid.

42 "Any thirsty person can quench his thirst in *udapāne*, in just a small spring. And the same quenching of thirst will remain in that scale when he gets water from a great vast ocean. . . . In the same way,

[Abhinavagupta]: The person who is focused in his own *dharma*, in his own duty, just as you have to do, *parimitādapi veda bhāṣitāt kāryam* [comm.], as you are [standing] before me, whatever I tell you, this is *Veda*, this is *Veda* for you. Books are not *Veda*. The *Vedas* are something you learn from your master. Those are the *Vedas*.

DVD 2.2 (47:46)

कर्मण्यस्त्वधिकारस्ते मा फलेषु कदाचन ।
मा कर्मफलहेतुर्भूर्मा ते सङ्गोऽस्त्वकर्मणि ॥४८॥

karmaṇyastvadhikāraste mā phaleṣu kadācana /
mā karmaphalaheturbhūrmā te saṅgo'stvakarmaṇi //48//

[Lord Kṛṣṇa]: You do your actions, *karmaṇyastvadhikāraste*, you always do your actions. Don't be idle; don't remain idle. But don't desire for any fruit from your actions. Go on doing whatever you like to do, you go on doing it, [just] don't crave for its action, i.e., don't crave for its fruit. And don't be attached to [your] actions.

When you do your work and you don't ask for its fruit, that is knowledge; that is [how] real Bhairava knowledge will come.

yadaprārthyamānam phalaṁ tat jñānam [comm.]

[Abhinavagupta]: When you don't ask for any fruit from your actions, that is knowledge; knowledge will be at your disposal.

---

sarveṣu vedeṣu brāhmaṇasya vijānataḥ, if you go through all the four *Vedas* and that thirst of ignorance will be removed, in the same way, this thirst of ignorance will be removed from *brāhmaṇasya vijānataḥ*, the one who is a God realized person. From a God realized person, he will quench that thirst also. So he has nothing to worry for *Vedas*. He will go to realized soul and *bas*, get satisfaction, and his thirst will be no more existing. Otherwise, if he won't get a realized soul's companionship, then he has to go through all the *Vedas*, which means a lifetime. *Vedas* are so many . . . *Vedas* are vast. So, it is better for a *sādhaka* (aspirant) to go to a master and get the aimed object [i.e., liberation] at once, in one sip." Ibid.

Knowledge means knowledge of Parabhairava.

If you think, how will knowledge of Parabhairava come also if you don't ask for anything, that is your ghost making a nest in your heart that [makes you say], "I won't act."[43]

You have to act. You [must] do actions and don't ask for its fruit. Don't be attached to any of your actions.

DVD 2.2 (49:45)

योगस्थः कुरु कर्माणि सङ्गं त्यक्त्वा धनञ्जय ।
सिद्ध्यसिद्ध्योः समो भूत्वा समत्वं योग उच्यते ॥४९॥

yogasthaḥ kuru karmāṇi saṅgaṁ tyaktvā dhanañjaya /
siddhyasiddhyoḥ samo bhūtvā samatvaṁ yoga ucyate //49//

[Lord Kṛṣṇa]: If you get fruits [from your actions], well and good; if you don't get fruit, well and good. Be the same. Be the same in the fruit bearing [of *karma*]. Whatever fruit [your action] bears, be peaceful in your own nature.[44]

43 "In the background of your mind, there is tendency of not doing actions. . . . You want to discard all your actions. . . . just for the sake of not doing actions, sluggishness. That is *gāḍha graha rūpa* . . . the ghost of not doing actions has caught you in his own clutches, *mithyājñāna-svarūpaḥ*, and it is absolutely wrong understanding. This kind of thought should be avoided from your mind." Ibid.

44 "Dhanañjaya, O Arjuna, do your actions already established in *yoga*, i.e., actions and remembering God at the same time. Do your actions and remember God at the same time.

JOHN: Remembering God means here?

SWAMIJI: Watch your breath [while] doing all actions. *Saṇgaṁ tyaktvā*, and attachment won't come there. You will be detached from all actions. *Yogīs* have realized this and experienced this: when they do all actions and watch each and every breath . . . the impressions of those actions do not remain. When he goes into dreaming state, those [impressions of] things which he has done in the daytime, he won't dream those. He will dream God consciousness at that time. He will dream that he will be doing his *yoga abhyāsa* (practice of *yoga*). So this is the *only* way how to get rid of the entanglement of actions. Do your actions [and] think of God. While doing actions, you should remember God. Remembering God is just . . . watch your breath!" Ibid.

यस्य सर्वे समारम्भा निराशीर्बन्धनास्त्विह ।
त्यागे यस्य हुतं सर्वं स त्यागी स च बुद्धिमान् ॥५०॥

yasya sarve samārambhā nirāśīrbandhanāstviha /
tyāge yasya hutaṁ sarvaṁ sa tyāgī sa ca buddhimān //50//

You must have *tyāga* (renunciation). Renunciation does not mean to leave all worldly activities and go to the forest and dense woods and perform penance. That is not renunciation. Renun-

---

"And at the same time, when you watch your breath, if you watch your breath without resting your awareness in *pramiti bhāva**, it is useless." Swami Lakshmanjoo, *Tantrāloka* 11.72 (1979).

* "[*Pramiti bhāva* is] objectless-subjective state. It is residing in only pure subjective consciousness. It has nothing to do with object. When there is objective state also attached to subjective state, that is not *pramiti bhāva*, that is *pramātṛ bhāva*. And when that objective state is connected with cognitive state, that is *pramāṇa bhāva*. When that objective state is completely pure objective state, that is *prameya bhāva*. And *pramiti bhava* is complete subjective consciousness without the slightest touch and traces of this object. In the long run, everything resides in *pramiti bhāva*; *pramiti bhāva* is the life of all the three. This is pure consciousness. . . . And that *pramiti bhāva* is absolutely one with *svātantrya śakti* . . . it is one with Lord Śiva." Ibid., 11.72-73a.

"In fact, this *pramiti bhāva* is the real source of understanding anything. Whatever you see, it must touch the state of *pramiti bhāva* otherwise you won't understand it. For instance, you see [an object]; you'll only know [that object] when this sensation of [that object already] resides in *pramiti bhāva*, i.e., in that super state of subjective consciousness. And super state of subjective consciousness is not differentiated. From that undifferentiated point of *pramiti bhāva*, the differentiated flow of *pramātṛ bhāva* and *pramāṇa bhāva* flow out." Ibid., 11.62.

"For instance, when you are [giving a lecture while] reading your book, your consciousness is *with* object. When you are giving lecture without a book, without any support, your consciousness is *without* object, it flows out . . . this is the state of *pramiti bhāva*." Ibid., 6.180.

"It is *nirvikalpa*, it is thoughtless state. And in that thoughtless state, it must reside otherwise it is not known; it will be unknown for . . . eternity." Ibid., 11.68-69. See footnote 61 for an explanation of *nirvikalpa*.

ciation is whatever you do, whatever action you do, don't care for its fruit. "It may bear fruit or it may not bear fruit, [in either case], I will act!"

[Swamiji accidentally catches the microphone cable]
It is finished?

DVD 2.2 (51:14)

दूरेण ह्यवरं कर्म बुद्धियोगाद्धनञ्जय ।
बुद्धौ शरणमन्विच्छ कृपणाः फलहेतवः ॥५१॥

dūreṇa hyavaraṁ karma buddhiyogāddhanañjaya /
buddhau śaraṇamanviccha kṛpaṇāḥ phalahetavaḥ //51//

buddhiyogātkila hetoravaraṁ–duṣṭaphalaṁ riktaṁ karma dūrībhavati / atastādṛśyāṁ buddhau śaraṇamanviccha–prārthayasva, yena sā buddhirlabhyate [comm.]

[Abhinavagupta]: You should crave for that *buddhi,* that knowledge.[45]

DVD 2.2 (51:40)

बुद्धियुक्तो जहातीमे उमे सुकृतदुष्कृते ।
तस्माद्योगाय युज्यस्व योगः कर्मसु कौशलम् ॥५२॥

buddhiyukto jahātīme ubhe sukṛtaduṣkṛte /
tasmādyogāya yujyasva yogaḥ karmasu kauśalam //52//
[not recited]

[Lord Kṛṣṇa]: The possessor of that great supreme knowledge, *jahātīme ubhe sukṛtaduṣkṛte*, if he does good actions, those good actions won't bear fruit for him. If he does bad actions, those bad

45 "*Buddhiyogātkila hetur.* Before the *buddhi yoga*, before the *yoga* of intellectual *yoga*, *avaraṁ duṣṭaphalaṁ riktaṁ karma*, that action which is attached with bearing its fruit is far away from that *buddhi yoga. Atastādṛśyāṁ buddhau śaraṇamanviccha prārthayasva,* so you should crave and search for that intellectual *yoga* . . . by which you'll achieve that kind of understanding." *Bhagavad Gītā* (1978).

actions won't bear fruit for him. He will be a *yogi*. *Yogi* means [one] who is melted and attached to God consciousness for good–that is all! This is the greatest trick in this life to get the state of Bhairava automatically. It is automatic Bhairava; automatic Bhairava [occurs] without doing anything.

And those fortunate persons who have maintained this trick in all of their actions and non-actions, they are focused in that supreme God consciousness where they are placed in the supreme state of Bhairava, and they become one with Parabhairava.

कर्मजं बुद्धियुक्ता हि फलं त्यक्त्वा मनीषिणः ।
जन्मबन्धविनिर्मुक्ताः पदं गच्छन्त्यनामयम् ॥५३॥
यदा ते मोहकलिलं बुद्धिर्व्यतितरिष्यति ।

karmajaṁ buddhiyuktā hi phalaṁ tyaktvā manīṣiṇaḥ /
janmabandhavinirmuktāḥ padaṁ gacchantyanāmayam //53
yadā te mohakalilaṁ buddhirvyatitariṣyati /
[not recited or translated][46]

तदा गन्तासि निर्वेदं श्रोतव्यस्य श्रुतस्य च ॥५४॥

tadā gantāsi nirvedaṁ śrotavyasya śrutasya ca //54//
[not recited]

46 Verse 53: "*Manīṣiṇaḥ*, those who are always aware of God consciousness, they are attached because they are attached with *buddhi* (i.e., *jñāna yoga*, intellectual *yoga*). *Karmajaṁ phalaṁ tyaktvā*, after shattering down, after removing [desire for] all the fruits of their actions, *janma bandha vinirmuktāḥ,* they are liberated from the entanglement in the wheel of repeated births and deaths. *Padaṁ gacchantyanāmayaṁ*, and they reach that state of Self which is *anāmayaṁ,* where there is no *āmaya*, [which] means *roga* [disease]; where there is no pain, where there is no sadness. They achieve that state of God consciousness which is filled with absolute bliss."

Verse 54a: "When that time will come . . . your intellect will cross the ocean of your congestion of ignorance [*mohakalilaṁ*]." *Bhagavad Gītā* (1978).

DVD 2.2 (53:21)

When this happens to you, by the grace of God, and by the grace of your master, then you will lose interest in hearing good lessons from your master. You will lose interest in that. You won't like to hear from anybody [who wants] to teach you. Because you are already taught; you are already filled with knowledge. This you will lose, i.e., interest in hearing some good lessons from your great masters. That you will lose. You won't have that interest afterwards because you will be focused in your own nature. Why should you hear [lessons] from others? You are hearing your own voice, always.

Do you understand?

JOHN: You don't need to have any outside help because you already have all that you need.

SWAMIJI: [Lord Kṛṣṇa]: You'll have *vairāgya* (detachment). *Śrotavyasya śrutasya ca*, whatever you have read in the past and whatever you had in your mind to read in the future, both things vanish altogether from your mind. You will ignore what you have read in the past and you don't crave anything to derive from others any . . .

DENISE: Lessons.

SWAMIJI: . . . any lessons. Then you are likely to get focused in the state of Bhairava where there is nothing to be done.

JOHN: Wouldn't you already be focused in that state?

SWAMIJI: Huh?

JOHN: If you don't need any outside help, aren't you already in that state?

SWAMIJI: What?

JOHN: You said, "then you would be likely to get that state." But if you don't need outside help, aren't you already in that state?

SWAMIJI: You are already in that state. You are already in that state. There is no need to get outside things to fill your consciousness.

श्रुतिविप्रतिपन्ना ते यदा स्थास्यति निश्चिता ।
समाधावचला बुद्धिस्तदा योगमवाप्स्यसि ॥५५॥

śrutivipratipannā te yadā sthāsyati niścitā /
samādhāvacalā buddhistadā yogamavāpsyasi //55//
[not recited or translated][47]

47 "[Then], at the time of your doing meditation, you won't get opposite thoughts to destroy the way of meditation. For instance, you are doing such and such meditation described by your master, and you have read so many books at the same time, and you think of those points also of books at the time of your meditation, then you lose the charm of your meditation. This is not the way of meditating.

"The way of meditating is just to do it according to the sayings of your master. Don't add another departmental information from books to your meditation, e.g., that this [particular] kind of meditation is not written in such and such book . . . and in that book, this [particular] way is described. The fruit of your meditation will be nothing, it will be useless. Because your *buddhi* is *śruti vipratipannā*, your will is destroyed. The position of your intellect is destroyed by various information from other departments, i.e., from books.

"*Yadā sthāsyati niścatā samādhāvacalā buddhi*, when you do your meditation one-pointedly according to the sayings of your master only, don't think of other departments at that time, e.g., [another] *yogi* has said like this . . . should I do that or should I do this? Such and such master has said like this. What should I do? So you lose the charm of your meditation.

"When you don't lose this charm of meditation and you meditate according to the sayings of your master only and *tadā yogamavāpsyasi*, then you will get the entry of *yoga* in its real sense."
Bhagavad Gītā (1978).

Chapter 2 Part 3

अर्जुन उवाच

arjuna uvāca

Now Arjuna puts a question before his master, Lord Kṛṣṇa.

sthita prajñasya kā bhāṣā . . .

This is the 56th *śloka*.

DVD 2.3 (00:21)

स्थितप्रज्ञस्य का भाषा समाधिस्थस्य केशव ।
स्थिरधीः किं प्रभाषेत किमासीत व्रजेच्च किम् ॥५६॥

sthita prajñasya kā bhāṣā samādhisthasya keśava /
sthiradhīḥ kiṁ prabhāṣeta kimāsīta vrajecca kim //56//

Who is *sthita prajña*, i.e., whose God consciousness is established, already established in his own nature and who is established in *samādhi*? In "*samādhi*" means who is established in the state of Parabhairava. *Sthiradhīḥ kiṁ prabhāṣeta,* how does he act in the outside world? How does he talk? How does he sit? What does he *do* afterwards? *Vrajecca kim*, where does he go? These are my questions before you, O Lord Kṛṣṇa.

[Abhinavagupta]: *Samādhisthasya yogina*. That *yogi* who is already focused in his *samādhi*, *kim pravṛttinimittaṁ*, what does he do after that? After achieving the state of Parabhairava, what does he do afterwards in the remaining period of his life?

bhaṣyate yena nimittena śabdairartha iti kṛtvā yoginaḥ,
sthitaprajñaśabdaḥ kim rūḍhyāvācako'nvarthayā vā [comm.]

[The question is whether or not] his God consciousness is established (*sthitaprajña*). It is [to be investigated] if it is *rūḍhi* or *anvartha*. *Rūḍhi* means, for instance, there is a cook; if he does not cook food and, at that time, you call him a cook. [*Anvartha* means], if at the time he is cooking, you call him cook.

For instance, Oṁ Prakash is your cook.

JOHN: Viṣṇu.

SWAMIJI: Viṣṇu! Viṣṇu!

He is your cook. But he is a cook . . . actually he is a cook when he is cooking. When he is sleeping, he cannot be a cook. He is a sleeping man then. Is it like that, that you call [i.e., nominate] one who is established in God consciousness or [is he one] who is just resting? At the time of resting, he is not established in God consciousness. How can you say that he is established in God consciousness? [You must investigate] if it is *rūḍhi* or *sārthaka*?[48] [If he is resting and you call him *sthitaprajña*, then] it must be *rūḍhi*.

He must be always established in God consciousness. Just like the cook who cooks food day and night altogether, then he is a cook. The actual cook is he who cooks day and night. When he sleeps, then he is a sleeping person; he is not a cook at that time.

JOHN: So, an enlightened person must be one who always has enlightenment, not just glimpses.

SWAMIJI: No, he must not be . . . he must be established in . . .

DENISE: In all states.

SWAMIJI: . . . in all states.

In that way, you should understand the person who is established in God consciousness. He must be established in God consciousness while talking, while walking, while doing, while [doing everything]; he must [always] be in God consciousness. It must be that all of his actions are filled with God consciousness. That way [i.e., when all of his actions are *not* filled with God consciousness], it is *rūḍhi*, it is not *anvartha*. *Anvartha* means just as you [call someone a cook when they are actually cooking]. *Rūḍhi* is only when you call him always cook [even] if he is not in the process of cooking; still you call him a cook, e.g., Viṣṇu, Viṣṇu

48 That is, if the nomination is merely a conventional word (*rūḍhi*) or if it carries actual meaning (*sārthaka* or *anvartha*). [*Editor's note*]

Digambhar. That way, [*sthitaprajña*] is not that. So, in each and every action, he must be there. He must not be away from God consciousness at all, in any case. While breathing, while laughing, while hearing, while touching, while sneezing, while . . .

JOHN: Sleeping.

SWAMIJI: . . . sleeping–always he must be there. That is the reality of His being.

Where does he go? How does he act? And where does he go in the end? These questions are respectively answered by Lord Kṛṣṇa in the following *ślokas*.

श्रीभगवानुवाच

śrī bhagavān uvāca

Lord Kṛṣṇa gives the answers to these four questions.

DVD 2.3 (06:20)

प्रजहाति यदा कामान्सर्वान्पार्थ मनोगतान् ।
आत्मन्येवात्मना तुष्टः स्थितप्रज्ञस्तदोच्यते ॥५७॥

prajahāti yadā kāmānsarvānpartha manogatān /
ātmanyevātmanā tuṣṭaḥ sthitaprajñastadocyate //57//

Sthita prajña, his *prajña* (wisdom) is established then when all desires and thoughts he leaves aside and remains always in God consciousness–then he is *sthita prajña.* This is the answer to the first question.

DVD 2.3 (07:13)

दुःखेष्वनुद्विग्नमनाः सुखेषु विगतस्पृहः ।
वीतरागभयक्रोधः स्थिरधीर्मुनिरुच्यते ॥५८॥

duḥkheṣvanudvignamanāḥ sukheṣu vigataspṛhaḥ /
vītarāgabhayakrodhaḥ sthiradhīrmunirucyate //58//

At the time of [experiencing] tides of pain, when they come to him, when tides of pain come to him, there he is not changed; he does not get shaken [even] by furious pain. And on the contrary, he does not crave for pleasures. He is absolutely away form *rāga* (*rāga* means attachment, *bhaya* means threat, *krodha* means wrath), these are already gone from him forever. *Sthiradhīr munir ucyate,* that is the real existence of God consciousness [for one] who is established in God consciousness.

DVD 2.3 (08:41)

यः सर्वत्रानभिस्नेहस्तत्तत्प्राप्य शुभाशुभम् ।
नाभिनन्दति न द्वेष्टि तस्य प्रज्ञा प्रतिष्ठिता ॥५९॥

yaḥ sarvatrānabhisnehastattatprāpya śubhāśubhaṁ /
nābhinandati na dveṣṭi tasya prajñā pratiṣṭhitā //59//

[Lord Kṛṣṇa]: *Yaḥ sarvatrānabhisneha*, [for one] who is not changed, who is always *anabhisnehah*, without any attachment, *tattatprāpya śubhāśubhaṁ*, if he gets good news, [if] good news has come, [he would say]:

"Hello, what is the news?"

"Your son has died."

"Okay."

He is okay.

"What is the news?"

"Your son is married."

"Okay."

In both ways, he is okay; he does not get moved by this.

Yaḥ sarvatrānabhisneha, he has no attachment because he says, "that is also God consciousness, that is also God consciousness." Where will he go? If he is dead, where will he go? He is there.

JOHN: But Sir, my experience is that you feel compassion for people and so, when something [bad] happens, you feel some pinch in your heart because of that compassion.

SWAMIJI: Huh?

JOHN: Compassion is also there. If a person feels compassion, that causes him to feel some sadness or some . . .

SWAMIJI: No, [this is meant] for those persons who are established in Bhairava state.

JONATHAN: Don't they still feel some compassion?

SWAMIJI: Huh?

JONATHAN: Someone who is established in Bhairava state, don't they still feel compassion?

SWAMIJI: They have got compassion for Bhairava state. They are really fond of Bhairava state. They are not fond of other states, which have no substance.

JOHN: But you're established in Bhairava state and you feel compassion.

SWAMIJI: No, in real sense, compassion does not mean that. Because this Bhairava state is above these limitations. It does not mean . . .

For instance, I have got compassion . . . compassion is there in supreme Bhairava, that anybody who comes at His feet, he will always be saved from bad happenings. He will be saved altogether. There is no . . .

JOHN: Question about that.

SWAMIJI: . . . there is no question about that.[49]

But at the same time, they are invalid to him. Value is only meant for being established in Bhairava state.

JONATHAN: But it's hard to understand.

SWAMIJI: It's hard to understand, because when Lord Kṛṣṇa appeared in a huge form [i.e., *viśvarūpa*] before Arjuna,[50] Lord Kṛṣṇa says:

ṛte'pi tvā nabhaviṣyanti sarve / *BG* 11.33

All will die except for you and your kith and kin. Your kith and kin won't die. Your kith and kin whom you love, whom you have got internal love for, they will live. The others will die. This kind of compassion He has.

Do you understand?

JOHN: Those who take refuge in Him, He saves those.

SWAMIJI: Yes, they are saved. They are saved because it is His choice, His will. [It is] not that He wants them to live. They live

---

49 In the early part of Swamiji's life, he witnessed a plane crash in Jammu. In the aftermath of that incident, Swamiji was so moved with compassion that he prayed to Lord Śiva that, "in the future, his devotees should be saved from any such bad happenings." [*Editor's note*]

50 See eleventh chapter of the *Bhagavad Gītā*.

because they have taken refuge in Him.

You have understood?

JOHNATHAN: Yes, I think.

SWAMIJI: No [laughs].

But it has no value; it has no value to him. Valuation only is in being in God consciousness always.[51]

JONATHAN: But from a personal point of view, I've seen you, and I've never ever experienced such compassion in anybody. From your side, the compassion that we see in you, and the love that you give to everybody, I've never experienced in anybody.

SWAMIJI: I don't love . . . I love everybody but I don't love [laughs]; actually, I don't love them at all. And by that love of mine, they are saved. They don't get any trouble in their lifetime.

JOHN: What does it mean when you say, "I love"?

Because what Jonathan is saying is true. You are the essence of compassion. We experience that nobody has compassion like we have experienced that you have.

SWAMIJI: That is right.

JOHN: But at the same time, you say you don't have compassion, you don't have love.

SWAMIJI: Because Lord Kṛṣṇa also tells Arjuna that, "those whom you internally wish good, they will be saved. Not others. Others will be destroyed. If in the background of your [mind], you

---

51 "You have to become a ray of Lord Siva. That ray of Lord Siva you will become only when you maintain qualities of a *Brāhmaṇa*. Brahmin qualities are always nice, always full of compassion, love, fear from bad actings. You must not do such an act by which you trouble others. I think Christ was a *brāhmaṇa* [because] he had all these qualities. Had he not?" Swami Lakshmanjoo, *Tantrāloka* 15.519 (1981).

"When it is realized, then there will be no difference; you won't feel any difference in being compassionate and in the absence of compassion. . . . He transcends these limited boundaries of dualistic ways of thought; he transcends [duality] at the time of [realizing supreme] knowledge. He comes out from these narrow boundaries. . . . It is the course for beginners to tread, that there must be morals, there must be character, there must be everything–it is for us. Not when you realize it. When you realize it in a complete way, then this is Shaivism. Then you come to the point of Shaivism afterwards. Then, at that moment, right and wrong has nothing to do. But till then, we have to follow all the rules and regulation of *śāstras* (scripture), till then."
Swami Lakshmanjoo, *Bodhapañcadaśikā* (1980).

think that your kith and kin with whom you are fighting, you know that they are frauds–those [people] won't survive. But those who are not frauds, who are well-wishers of you, they will live, they will live along with you."

śubhāśubhaprāptau tasyāhlādatāpau na bhavataḥ [comm.]

[Abhinavagupta]: If something good happens or something bad happens, he is not changed, his consciousness is not changed, he remains the same, unmoved.

DVD 2.3 (15:54)

यदा संहरते चायं कूर्मोऽङ्गनीव सर्वतः ।
इन्द्रियाणीन्द्रियार्थेभ्यः स्थिरप्रज्ञस्तदोच्यते ॥६०॥

yadā samharate cāyaṁ kūrmo'ṅgānīva sarvataḥ /
indriyāṇīndriyārthebhyaḥ sthiraprajñastadocyate //60//

[Lord Kṛṣṇa]: Whenever he withdraws all of his thoughts from the varieties of outward pleasures and pains, when he withdraws that, at the time when he withdraws all of those activities just like a tortoise, when . . .

You know tortoise?

Tortoise has got that cover over it.

JONATHAN: Shell.

SWAMIJI: Yes, shell.

. . . then he goes for . . . he comes underneath [its shell] and [then he] goes for eating something and whenever he finds there is something bad happening, he comes again and sits inside [its shell]. In the same way, when you see that . . .

In the past, there were some saints who were just jumping [because] they didn't like to see the world. They didn't like *māyā*. But this kind of action is not shining in that state [that is held by one] who is established in the Parabhairava state for good. These are just nominal states of being.

Why should he get fear? Why should he get afraid of anything in this world? If this whole universe is his own expansion, why should he get afraid of that?

One who gets afraid, he is a Vedānti, he is a *pakka* Vedānti, *chor.*[52] He is not recognized by the man who is established in the Parabhairava state; he does not recognize him.

So,

DVD 2.3 (19:00)

na cāsya pācakavadyogarūḍhitvam; [comm.]

[Abhinavagupta]: *Pācaka* means cook. Like a cook, he is not a *yogi* [viz., *anvartha*] and *rūḍhi*, both. The one who is established always in God consciousness is a *yogi.* [He is] not just like a [part-time] cook. He is [truly] a cook when he is [like a full-time] *yogi*; when he is not [like a full-time] *yogi*, then he is not [truly] a cook, he is sleeping. When he sleeps, he is not [like a full-time] *yogi*. Who? [The part-time] cook.

Yogi means [one whose *yoga* practice] is mixed in that work of cooking, when he cooks, frying everything–that [way], he is [properly called] a *yogi*. When [a cook] is not a *yogi,* at that time [when he is not cooking], he is sleeping or he is washing utensils–he is not a cook at that time. Like that, the one established in God consciousness is not [like a part-time cook]. He is always there. He is always . . .

How does he do that?

–indriyārthebhyaḥ prabhṛti indriyāṇi ātmani saṁharate– [comm.]

Right from internal [I-]consciousness up to external this-consciousness, he sees in the right form [i.e., correctly] that external consciousness and internal consciousness are not separate from each other–they are all Bhairava. So he mixes everything in Bhairava state. That is the reality of his being. He is never away from that.

So, [a *yogi*] is not supposed [to be] like [a part-time] cook.

The one who is *tapasvi*, one who is given to penance, why is *sthira prajña śabda* (establishment in God consciousness) not attached to [i.e., held by] him? For that, He says:

52 *Pakka* means sure or confirmed and *chor* means a thief. Vedāntin's are considered "thieves" insofar as they deny the reality of the objective world (i.e., *māyā*) and thereby deprive God of His own glory. [*Editor's note*]

DVD 2.3 (22:09)

विषया विनिवर्तन्ते निराहारस्य देहिनः ।
रसवर्जं रसोऽप्यस्य परं दृष्ट्वा निवर्तते ॥६१॥

viṣayā vinivartante nirāhārasya dehinaḥ /
rasavarjaṁ ras'opyasya paraṁ dṛṣṭvā nivartate //61//

[Lord Kṛṣṇa]: *Nirāhārasya*, when [the *tapasvi*] does not take anything, he does not eat anything, when he is fasting, at that time for him there is no choice to eat something. There is no choice . . . the one who has no vigor, the one who has lost vigor, he has no choice to enjoy worldly enjoyments.

For instance, one who is fed up with his body [because] his body is always aching, and he is fasting, he has no appetite, his appetite is gone for good, and who does not even digest water, for him, there is no *viṣayā* (attachment for worldly enjoyments). If somebody comes [to visit] him [and says], "let us go and see a picture," he won't [want to] see a picture. He is fed up with all of these things because he has no choice [i.e., desire]. But when by and by vitamins are inserted in his body and he gets [strength] again, those cravings for worldly pleasures appear again. This is an example.

In the same way, the one who is established in God consciousness, the one who is established in Parabhairava state, for him, he will never come to this limitation. If he is already placed in the limited world, still in spite of being placed in the limited world, he does not move from his unlimited Being. He is always there.

So this *rasa* (taste for worldly enjoyments) does not vanish [until] that point when Bhairava state is achieved.[53] *Paraṁ*

---

53 "But at the time, when you feed him with things, with precious and sweet things, this enjoyment will grow again altogether in his mind. So it is *rasavarjaṁ*, the *rasa*, the root is there. Root is not dead. Root of enjoying the world is not dead; only their senses have no power to enjoy. *Raso'pyasya paraṁ,* and the root will only be dead when he realizes the nature of God consciousness . . . the *yogi* who has realized the nature of God consciousness, all curiosity for enjoying world, worldly senses, worldly enjoyments have vanished altogether along with their roots. . . .

dṛṣṭvā, when he realizes that supreme . . . what is supreme? Bhairava state.

When he realizes the supreme [state of Bhairava], *bas*, he has no choice [i.e., desires] afterwards in this world. In this world also he sees the glamour of his own nature.

DVD 2.3 (25:54)

यत्तस्यापि कि कौन्तेय पुरुषस्य विपश्चितः ।
इन्द्रियाणि प्रमाथीनि हरन्ति प्रसभं मनः ॥६२॥

yattasyāpi hi kaunteya puruṣasya vipaścitaḥ /
indriyāṇi pramāthīni haranti prasabhaṁ manaḥ //62//

[Lord Kṛṣṇa]: *Tasyāpi*, that *tapasvi*, one who is *tapasvi*, one who is absorbed in that austerity, penance, although he has knowledge, knowledge of God consciousness, but *indriyāṇi pramāthīni*, his organs are looting him; *haranti prasabhaṁ manaḥ*, and his *mana*, his mind is [susceptible to becoming] focused in worldly pleasures, at once.

So *tapasya* (the penance), by penance you cannot be established in the state of Parabhairava, by penance. Penance won't help.[54]

Yattasya (*yattasya* means *sayatnasyāpi*), the one who is adopting *yoga* of God consciousness, for him also at the time of practicing *mana eva jetavyam,* he must be conscious to overcome the power of his mind." *Bhagavad Gītā* (1978).

54 "*Tapasvi*, the one who is adopting that penance, for him, *viṣaya tyāga eva*, when he abandons *viṣayas* (the world of senses), he is detached from world of senses, [but] by detachment of world of senses, he is attached to world of senses on the contrary. Why? *Dhyatva hi ti tyajante,* because while living, abandoning this world of senses, they think that I have abandoned this and this . . . and while thinking [about] abandoning this and this, they are having [in their mind], they are holding that [which they have tried to abandon]. . . . So this is the difference between that *tapasvi* and *yogi*. *Yogi* has no impression of enjoying, enjoyment, and *tapasvi* has [impressions] in the background." Ibid.

DVD 2.3 (27:17)

तानि संयम्य मनसा युक्त आसीत मत्परः ।
वशे हि यस्येन्द्रियाणि तस्य प्रज्ञा प्रतिष्ठिता ॥६३॥

tāni saṁyamya manasā yukta āsīta matparaḥ /
vaśe hi yasyendriyāṇi tasya prajñā pratiṣṭhitā //63//

This is a trick, i.e., how you become focused in the Parabhairava state. By awareness!

Not by weeping, not by laughing, not by possessing grief. Parabhairava state is a trick. When you lose interest in things other than Parabhairava state. That is the Parabhairava state . . .

That cannot be observed through penance; [acts of] penance are not successful there.[55]

DVD 2.3 (28:32)

ध्यायतो विषयान्पुंसः सङ्गस्तेषूपजायते ।
सङ्गात्संजायते कामः कामात्क्रोधोऽभिजायते ॥६४॥
क्रोधाद्भवति संमोहः संमोहात्स्मृतिविभ्रमः ।
स्मृतिभ्रंशाट्बुद्धिनाशो बुद्धिनाशात्प्रणश्यति ॥६५॥

55 ". . . the one who has already controlled all those organs and he is established in adopting the *abhyāsa* of God consciousness, *vaśe hi yasyendriyāṇi*, and all his organs are under his control, have come under his control, *tasya prajñā pratiṣṭhitā*, he is really a realized soul. *Ya evaṁ manasā indriyāṇi niyamayati* [comm.], he has to control all these organs through mind, not through not acting [viz., *tapasya*]. He must act through organs, but he must control those organs through mind, not through actions. So actions have nothing to do with that. You can act, but control through mind. That is awareness, God [consciousness] . . . *Na tu apravṛttyā*, [by] not not doing, [by] not ignoring all the actions, *sa eva sthiraprajña*, he is *sthira prajña,* he is established in *yoga. Sa ca matpara evāsīta*, for him, this is My order that he should always remain in the sphere of God consciousness, in the awareness of God consciousness. *Māmeva cidātmānam parameśvaraṁ abhyasyet*, so he must do practice to find out Me, again and again, again and again. Otherwise he will be dragged again and again towards other objects." Ibid.

dhyāyato viṣayānpumsaḥ saṅgasteṣūpajāyate /
saṅgātsañjāyate kāmaḥ kāmātkrodho 'bhijāyate //64//
krodhādbhavati sammohaḥ sammohātsmṛtivibhramaḥ /
smṛtibhramśāṭbuddhināśo buddhināśātpraṇaśyati //65//

Anybody who is thinking of . . . one who is meditating upon God consciousness, [he goes] on meditating, meditating, and at the same time he thinks, "this meditation of God consciousness is very sweet." And this is one thought, this is temptation, temptation is there, it is *māyā*. And this thought focuses him to things other than Parabhairava.

And afterwards, [the mind] goes [to another similar thought]; this [initial] *saṁskāra* (impression) gives move to [i.e., creates] another *saṁskāra*, [then] another *saṁskāra*, and he is on the inferior plane of the world.

JOHN: The *saṁskāra* that, "this meditation is sweet"?

SWAMIJI: Not meditation. He is dragged away from God consciousness by and by. This is *māyā*. You must be so alert and so . . . you can't remain idle. Meditation you have to do with vigor, with alertness. If alertness is a bit lessened, [God consciousness is] gone! It will carry you to the ordinary course of being. You become just like dogs in the street. There is no God consciousness.

So this is a trick. This is a trick when there is *śaktipāta*. When there is *śaktipāta,* you become focused.

> *Kṣiptam, mūdham, vikṣiptam, ekāgram, niruddham*–these are the states of mind. The states of mind are five: *kṣipta, vikṣipta, mūdha, ekāgra, niruddha.*[56]

> *Kṣipta* is for *yogi*–these [states of mind] are for *yogis*–*kṣipta* is, [for example], "*om namaḥ śivāya, om namaḥ śivāya, om namaḥ śivāya, om namaḥ śivāya,* I had been there, I will go to some other shop tomorrow, *om namaḥ śivāya, om namaḥ śivāya, om namaḥ śivāya,* O Denise is a very good disciple of mine, *om namaḥ śivāya, om namaḥ śivāya, om namaḥ*

56 These are the five states that a *yogi* experiences while engaged in contemplative practice, which are explained in classical *yoga* texts. [*Editor's note*]

śivāya." Like that, he is dragged [away from one-pointedness]. It is called *kṣipta*; this is the nature of *kṣipta*. This is the first *yoga*, the first start of *yoga*. At that time [when these intervening thoughts arise], you should not allow [your mind] to think other things that are similar to these. It may be similar. Do you know "similar"?

And there is another [stage of *yoga*]: *vikṣiptam*. *Vikṣiptam* is, "*om namaḥ śivāya, om namaḥ śivāya, om namaḥ śivāya, om namaḥ śivāya*–what are you doing?[57]–*om namaḥ śivāya, om namaḥ śivāya, om namaḥ śivāya, om namaḥ śivāya*, I have to go there, no, *om namaḥ śivāya, om namaḥ śivāya.*" Just at once you . . .
JONATHAN: Become aware.
SWAMIJI: No sooner has it taken a step outside, you . . .
JONATHAN: You pull it back.
SWAMIJI: . . . you pull it back at once. That is *vikṣiptam*.

If you do it like this, then there is the third state, that *ekāgra*. *Ekāgra* means: "*om namaḥ śivāya, om namaḥ śivāya, om namaḥ śivāya, om namaḥ śivāya, om namaḥ śivāya,*" and go on [reciting], "*om namaḥ śivāya*, and [yawning], *om namaḥ śivāya, om namaḥ śivāya, om namaḥ śivāya*, [scratching], *om namaḥ śivāya, om namaḥ śivāya, om namaḥ śivāya.*" This is *ekāgra*. But these things [i.e., yawning, scratching, etc.] happen. These things, they destroy your one-pointedness.

Then it is *nirūddha*. At once [you recite], "*om namaḥ śivāya, om namaḥ śivāya, om namaḥ śivāya, om namaḥ śivāya, om namaḥ śivāya, om namaḥ śivāya,*" then it goes on in one chain.

[Lord Kṛṣṇa] says in that [*śloka*]:

yatroparamate cittaṁ niruddhaṁ yogasevanāt /
yatra caivātmanātmānaṁ paśyannātmani tuṣyati //BG 6.21

57 Swamiji is asking someone in the audience what they are doing. [*Editor's note*]

[Lord Kṛṣṇa]: *Yatroparamate cittaṁ niruddhaṁ yogasevanāt.* At that time when, by *yogābhyāsa*, [the *yogi*] reaches the state of *niruddha*, the fifth state of *yoga*–what happens then?

Yatra caivātmanātmānaṁ paśyannātmani tuṣyati, where he realizes his own nature and he is enjoying the super-consciousness of that nature.

sukhamātyantikaṁ yattadbuddhigrāhyamatīndriyam
vetti yatra na caivāyaṁ sthitaścalati tattvataḥ //BG 6.22

Sukhamātyantikaṁ yattad, and the glamour of that *sukham* (*sukham* means godly . . .

JOHN: Pleasure.

SWAMIJI: Not pleasure, you can't say pleasure.

JOHN: Super-pleasure?

SWAMIJI: Yes.

. . . *buddhigrahyam*, it is *buddhigrāhyam*.[58] You can only calculate it with intellect, not with the body. *Atīndriyam,* it is beyond, that *sukha* [joy] is beyond the cycle of organs. Organs cannot experience that *ānanda* (that bliss). And once he is established in that, *na calati tattvataḥ,* he is not moved at all; [even] for one second also, he is not moved from that [bliss].

JONATHAN: But to achieve that state you have to have that *śaktipāta*, isn't it?

SWAMIJI: *Śaktipāta* means you have to maintain your vigor, you have to maintain your will. There must be firm will. That is *śaktipāta*. *Śaktipāta* is not derived from other sources. You have got *śaktipāta*, you have got the power of *śaktipāta*, i.e., to have it. You [must] possess it with vigor, with force, because you have got that power.

But you don't like it [laughs]!

You don't like it and you go on meeting others and everything and . . .

58 "Patañjalī describes this intellect as *ṛtaṁbharā**, it is filled with . . . *ṛtaṁ* means truth. It is truth, true joy, it is not adjusted joy. Adjusted joy takes its position in the contact of two and this is not adjusted joy. This is automatic joy." Swami Lakshmanjoo, Special Verses on Practice.

* *yoga eva yogasyopāyaḥ / ṛtambharā tatra prajñā / /* Patañjalī's *Yoga Sūtras,* 1.48.

[Verses 66 to 70 were not recited or translated but Swamiji gave a general explanation in his commentary above. For his complete translations of these verses, see footnote below.][59]

DVD 2.3 (37:16)

रागद्वेषविमुक्तैस्तु विषयानिन्द्रियैश्चरन् ।
आत्मवश्यैर्विधेयात्मा प्रसादमधिगच्छति ॥६६॥
प्रसादे सर्वदुःखानां हानिरस्योपजायते ।
प्रसन्नचेतसो ह्याशु बुद्धिः पर्यवतिष्ठते ॥६७॥
नास्ति बुद्धिरयुक्तस्य न चायुक्तस्य भावना ।
न चाभावयतः शान्तिरशान्तस्य कुतः सुखम् ॥६८॥
इन्द्रियाणां हि चरतां यन्मनोऽनुविधीयते ।
तदस्य हरति प्रज्ञां वायुर्नावमिवाम्भसि ॥६९॥
तस्माद्यस्य महाबाहो निगृहीतानि सर्वतः ।
इन्द्रियाणीन्द्रियार्थेभ्यस्तस्य प्रज्ञा प्रतिष्ठिता ॥७०॥

59 Verse 66: "The aspirant who goes on tasting those pleasures of the senses, but with those organs which are absolutely free from attachment and hatred, which are absolutely under his control, he enters in the state of absolute purity."

Verse 67: "And when his mind becomes purified, all pains of the world take their end altogether, and his intellect gets established in his God consciousness."

Verse 68: "The one who is not alert, his intellect is wavering, and he has no love for this practice, when he has no love for his practice, how can he get peace? How can he get that blissful state?"

Verse 69: "When you love your practice, *bas*, you will do it. It is not in the hands of God. It is in your hands. Create love for God!" What happens when you don't have the way of love? Then your mind follows the activities of your organs without any argument, and your awareness is carried away from your control just like a boat is carried away by a storm."

Verse 70: "That man whose knowledge and intellect is established fully, the flow of his sense organs are controlled, he is established in his nature of alertness, and he has realized his nature." *Bhagavad Gītā*.

rāgadveṣavimuktaistu viṣayānindriyaiścaran /
ātmavaśyairvidheyātmā prasādamadhigacchati //66//
prasāde sarvaduḥkhānāṁ hānirasyopajāyate /
prasannacetaso hyāśu buddhiḥ paryavatiṣṭhate //67//
nāsti buddhirayuktasya na cāyukrasya bhāvanā /
na cābhāvayataḥ śāntiraśāntasya kutaḥ sukham //68//
indriyāṇāṁ hi caratāṁ yanmano 'nuvidhīyate /
tadasya harati prajñāṁ vāyurnāvamivāmbhasi //69//
tasmādyasya mahābāho nigṛhītāni sarvataḥ /
indriyāṇīndriyārthebhyastasya prajñā pratiṣṭhitā //70//

Now this is the 70th *śloka* finished.

JONATHAN: Can I just ask one question? What causes that change? You said you possess that *śaktipāta*, that power, but you don't like it, you just go to these other things. What makes that change, when you suddenly are not worried about these things and you dive into that?

SWAMIJI: When *śaktipāta* comes from within. From within! *Śaktipāta* does not come from without. It is not [from] without.

JONATHAN: It is there already.

SWAMIJI: It is there. Because when God is united with limited God, [this is possible only because] limited God is not separate from unlimited God.

yogī ca sarvavyavahārān kurvāṇo'pi . . . [comm.]

[Abhinavagupta]: That *yogi*, although he does each and every activity of the world–he [goes] to the pictures, he [goes to see] everybody, he [goes] to the cinema and sightseeing and everything, whatever we do–*lokottaraḥ*, but he is above [those activities], he is supreme.

And Lord Kṛṣṇa places before Arjuna his real state of life, real state of being, who is established in Parabhairava.

DVD 2.3 (39:05)

या निशा सर्वभूतानां तस्यां जागर्ति संयमी ।
यस्यां जाग्रति भूतानि सा रात्रिः पश्यतो मुनेः ॥७१॥

yā niśā sarvabhūtānāṁ tasyām jāgarti saṁyamī /
yasyāṁ jāgrati bhūtāni sā rātriḥ paśyato muneḥ //71//

Yā niśā sarvabhūtānāṁ . . . yā sarveṣāṁ bhūtānāṁ niśā [comm.]. That which is night for everybody–what is night? *Mohanī māyā*, the span of *māyā.*[60]–*tasyāṁ munirjāgarti*, the *yogi*, in that ["night" of] *māyā*, he is aware, he remains aware.

Yasyā ca daśāyāṁ loko jāgarti, and in which state *loko jāgarti*, ordinary people remain aware–what is that? *Nānāvidhāṁ ceṣṭāṁ kurute*, they do all of the activities of the world–*sā muneḥ rātriḥ*, for this state of *yogi*, [the worldly state of being] is night for him. Because *yato'sau vyavahāraṁ pratyabuddhaḥ,* he does not understand what is *vyavahāra* (*vyavahāra* means worldly activities).

In other words, it will be clarified. Abhinavagupta says, *etad-uktaṁ bhavati*, I will clarify this more vividly.

Yeyaṁ māyā khalu, this *māyā,* which is placed here in this world, *tasyā mohakatvaṁ* [*nāma*] *rūpaṁ sukhatantratā-bhāsanaṁ ca* [comm.], it has got two wings of . . . two aspects. It subsides your God consciousness–this is one activity of *māyā*. And another activity, at the same time attached to that activity, is *sukha tantratābhāsanaṁ*, it produces the formation of happiness, joy. And an ordinary person ignores [i.e., is ignorant of] that *mohakatva*, that being away from God consciousness, the absence of God consciousness. One phase is absence of God consciousness–of *māyā*–and another phase is to give . . .

DENISE: Happiness and joy.

SWAMIJI: . . . happiness, joy. And ordinary people ignore [i.e., are ignorant of] that *māyā* and they focus themselves in [worldly] joy. And on the contrary, the one who is a *yogi*, he always sees and observes that there is *mohakatva,* there is a threat that it [i.e., the affections of *māyā*] will take him away from God consciousness. And that joyfulness [conferred by *māyā*], he does not respect; he does not respect that joy, which it shows, i.e., the joy [that] worldly people respect.

DENISE: *Yogi*?

60 "*Māyā* means unawareness, loss of consciousness, loss of awareness, loss of alertness. *Yā niśā*, that is *niśā*, when you lose your awareness, that is night. [Worldly people] sleep there. They don't do any remedy for it, to get rid of that night." *Bhagavad Gītā* (1978).

SWAMIJI: The *yogi* does not respect that joy.

Tastadīyaṁ mohakatvaṁ tadunmūlanāya paśyati, that *mohakatva,* the absence of God consciousness, the *yogi* puts force in the absence of God consciousness so that God consciousness is always appearing vividly to him. *Sukhatantratāṁ tu nādriyte,* this [worldly] joy, he does not respect; he does not respect that joy, the pleasure of joy.

How does he act then?

It is nearly ending. 72nd *śloka*.

DVD 2.3 (44:12)

आपूर्यमाणमचलप्रतिष्ठं
समुद्रमापः प्रविशन्ति यद्वत् ।
तद्वत्कामा यं प्रविशन्ति सर्वे
स शान्तिमाप्नोति न कामकामी ॥७२॥

āpūryamāṇamacalapratiṣṭhaṁ
samudramāpaḥ praviśanti yadvat /
tadvatkāmā yaṁ praviśanti sarve
sa śāntimāpnoti na kāmakāmī //72//

[Lord Kṛṣṇa]: Just like *āpa*, varieties of all rivers, just like the varieties of all rivers, the flows of all rivers, *praviśanti*, in the end, *praviśanti*, gets entry in the ocean, in the ocean who is *āpūryamāṇam*, who is always filled with these streams and all varieties of rivers. *Acala pratiṣṭhaṁ*, it does not change its being. What? Ocean. Ocean is the same. *Pratiṣṭhaṁ*, he is always established in his own nature just like all streams and all rivers enter [the ocean] and they are calmed down there.

In the same way, the real person [i.e., the *yogi*] who is established in God consciousness, all thoughts with force come to him, get entry in him, and they are calmed down. There they are calmed down, they become established in one-pointedness. In the same way, all thoughts and all desires get entry in that person and they are calmed down; they become *nirvikalpa*.[61] In the same

61 "The state of God consciousness . . . *kāla adi paricchedā abhāva*,

there is no limitation of time, there is no limitation of space, there is no limitation of form. It is formless. There is no difference [found] in the state of God consciousness, e.g., there is no difference between specks and hankie. Specks and hankie are the same . . . in *nirvikalpa* state . . . there is only throbbing of this[-ness]." Swami Lakshmanjoo, *Parātriśikā Vivaraṇa* (1982-85).

"[For example, in] some peacock painting, *citra vijñāna*, there are differentiated things, there are so many various colors in that painting. But we don't perceive those various colors one by one. What do we then perceive? We perceive, "this is a peacock." That is Lord Śiva! The totality, that is *nirvikalpa*. These variations of those colors is *savikalpa*." Ibid.

"When you say *idam* (e.g., "this is such and such a thing, this is a book, this is a pot") . . . this is just directing you to limitation only, not unlimited thing. . . . When you perceive some particular object, it means the other objects are not included there, so it is limited. . . . Where there is limitation, that is *vikalpa*, it is not *nirvikalpa*. *Nirvikalpa* is that state where there is unlimited surface of understanding." Ibid.

"In reality . . . everything, whatever exists, it is in *nirvikalpa* state [where] you can't define anything . . . you can define only in the *vikalpa* state, in the cycle of *vikalpa*, e.g., when you say "this is specks cover." But it is not specks cover in real sense, i.e., in the state of God consciousness. It is just *nirvikalpa*, you can't say what it is . . . but it is! *Saṁketādismaraṇam*, when you understand, "this is mine, O, this was in my house, and this is mine," this memory takes place in the *vikalpa* state, not *nirvikalpa* state; and that *vikalpa* state cannot [exist] without *anubhavam*, i.e., *nirvikalpa* state." Ibid.

"*Nirvikalpa* is the cause of all *vikalpas*; undifferentiated state is the cause of all *vikalpas* . . . it is not something foreign [to *vikalpas*], it is their life." Ibid.

"When that [absolute] consciousness descends in the cycle of differentiatedness (*bhedasāratālabdhatayā*), then *artha bhāvaṁ kuryat*, then "this is right, this is wrong, this is pot, this is that and this is that," this kind of [discriminating] activity takes place. Otherwise, in the state of absolute consciousness, there is no [discriminating] activity at all; it is one with God consciousness. But these *vikalpas*, these differentiated aspects of life cannot exist without coming out from that *nirvikalpa bhāva*." Ibid.

"The first flow of [perception], it is *nirvikalpa* (without impression). . . . That is *prathama anusaṁdhāna*, the first movement of realization. That is *nirvikalpa*, that is the reality of God. . . . it is just *aham* (I-ness), it is not *idam* (this-ness). First there is some sensation, after that sensation you come to this [realization] that, "this is a pot, this is a jug, this is tape recorder." This is the next step from that point of God consciousness, state of God consciousness. Otherwise, there is only sensation, vibration, some vibration of coming out. You don't come out first. It is only the vibrating force that makes you to go outside." Ibid.

"*Vikalpas* will be attributed afterwards, after [they are] established in *nirvikalpa* state. So *nirvikalpa* state is the life of the object. For instance, I want to see Denise. Before that, I see only a phantom figure of Denise, and before that I see only seeing force, and before that I see only myself, and that is *nirvikalpa*." Swami Lakshmanjoo, *Tantrāloka* 1.179 (1972).

"This happens in each and every activity of your daily life . . . in each and every perception, you have to start from that first throb [of *nirvikalpa*]." Swami Lakshmanjoo, *Parātriśikā Vivaraṇa* (1982-85).

"When I begin to deliver lectures with the help of a book, it is *savikalpa* knowledge. When I deliver lectures . . . without the help of [books], without keeping [books] in from of me . . . that is *nirvikalpa*, that knowledge is *nirvikalpa*. . . . It is only residing in the oneness of God consciousness because there is no need of getting help from books, from other sources." Ibid.

"It is *dharmi* (the holder of all aspects). The holder of all aspects is Lord Śiva; all aspects of present, past, future." Ibid.

"Memory exists through *nirvikalpa*, otherwise memory would not exist at all." Ibid.

"How that past knowledge is united in this present knowledge? That is *antarāla*, that is the gap, the gap [between] these two (present and that past) . . . these two knowledges of present and past were absolutely separate from each other, so how could they be united [in memory]? There is only one way to unite them, i.e., by this *nirvikalpa* state, which is always there in the gap; and that *antarāla*, the state in-between the two objects, it is *saṁvit ātmakameva*, it is just consciousness, that is God consciousness." Ibid.

"You can't practice on *nirvikalpa*. You have to practice just after that . . . when it is [just about] to become *savikalpa*. That is *prathama ābhasa*, *prathamā prasara*, the first flow outside. At that first flow, you have to watch. You can't watch [*nirvikalpa*], because it is not watched, it is the watcher. . . . You can't watch the watcher, you can't see the seer." Ibid.

"In the same way, you have to contemplate on each and every element of the universe. . . . When your *saṁvitti* [consciousness] observes this earth element (*pṛthvī*), in the beginning it is *nirvikalpa*, in the end it is *savikalpa*; and after it has ended in *savikalpa* state, way, God consciousness, [the one] who is established in that God consciousness, he is always peaceful. He is not hankering after worldly pleasures afterwards.

He will enjoy worldly pleasures. Why should he not?

JONATHAN: But he doesn't hanker after them.

SWAMIJI: He does not hanker. If he enjoys, well and good; if he does not enjoy, he does not pound his head.

JONATHAN: And if pain comes then he also enjoys that.

SWAMIJI: Yes.

JONATHAN: He enjoys everything.

SWAMIJI: Next *śloka*.

DVD 2.3 (47:16)

विहाय कामान्यः सर्वान्पुमांश्चरति निःस्पृहः ।
निर्ममो निरहङ्कारः स शन्तिमधिगच्छति ॥७३॥

vihāya kāmānyaḥ sarvānpumāmścarati nihaspṛhaḥ /
nirmamo nirahaṅkāraḥ sa śāntimadhigacchati //73//

[Lord Kṛṣṇa]: In the same way, that fortunate person who is established in Parabhairava state and [for whom] *sarvān kāmānyaḥ vihāya*, all desires have disappeared in his mind for good, *carati*, and he roams, he walks, he goes for a walk; like Bhairava, he goes for a walk without any change in his nature. *Niraṅkāraḥ*, he has no ego; *nirmamaḥ*, he does not have attachment for anybody; *sa śāntimadhigacchati*, he really is focused in that peaceful state of Parabhairava.

---

take it back to *nirvikalpa saṁvitti*. This is to be done in *śāmbhava* state. So it will rest in the *nirvikalpa* state in the end. It has come out from *nirvikalpa saṁvitti*, it resides in *nirvikalpa saṁvitti*, it is to be carried to *nirvikalpa saṁvitti*." Swami Lakshmanjoo, *Tantrāloka* 3.279 (1973).

"You have to rise to *nirvikalpa* state through *vikalpa* in *āṇavopāya* and *śāktopāya*. But in *śāmbhavopāya*, you have not to rise [with *vikalpa*]. You have to get establishment in an instant with awareness, with awareness of *śāmbhava* state. And that is the real *samāveśa* (absorption)." *Tantrāloka* 1.179 (1972).

See footnote 126 for an explanation of the *upāyas*.

DVD 2.3 (48:48)

एषा ब्राह्मी स्थितिः पार्थ नैनां प्राप्य विमुह्यति ।

eṣā brāhmī sthitiḥ pārtha naināṁ prāpya vimuhyati /

O Arjuna, this is the reality of God consciousness, which I have placed before you.

स्थित्वास्यामन्तकालेऽपि ब्रह्म निर्वाणमृच्छति ॥७४॥

sthitvāsyāmantakāle'pi brahma nirvāṇamṛcchati //74//

No matter if you achieve this state at the time of death also, there is no fear, you will become one with Bhairava. There are some fortunate persons who become one with Bhairava at the time of death also. And most fortunate persons become [one with Bhairava] in their lifetime also. They are the most fortunate! And fortunate persons are also those who become . . .

[Swamiji addresses someone in the audience]

I think at the time of death you'll become fortunate.
I am fortunate already.
This is now the conclusion of this second discourse . . .

अत्र संग्रहश्लोकः
atra saṅgraha ślokaḥ

. . . by Abhinavagupta.

DVD 2.3 (50:01)

अहो नु चेतसश्चित्रा गतिस्त्यागेन यत्किल ।
आरोहत्येव विषयाञ्छ्रयंस्तांस्तु परित्यजेत् ॥२॥

aho nu cetasaścitrā gatistyāgena yatkila /
ārohatyeva viṣayāñchrayaṁtāṁstu parityajet //2//

|| Concluding *śloka* of 2nd chapter ||

The state of one's mind is very rare [i.e., difficult] to understand; you cannot understand the state of your mind. The one who shuns the world, one who shuns the worldly activities, he possesses it. The one who possesses it, he shuns it. This is the trick!

JOHN: Say that again.

SWAMIJI: The one who shuns this world, worldly activities, he possesses it. [He says], "I have left my wife, I have left my child, I have gone, I am *sanyāsi*, I am . . ." and he catches them again by thinking. By thinking, always thinking, "I had one chair that I have shunned; I had a sofa set in my house, that I have shunned; I have television set, that I have shunned; I am *sanyāsi* now." And he catches hold of everything.

DENISE: He misses those things.

JOHN: By thinking about them.

SWAMIJI: No, he possesses it. He possesses it in his mind. In mind he possesses everything by shunning. So you cannot understand the ways of your mind. One who shuns it, he possesses it. One who possesses it, he shuns it [and says], "I am in this world, I have nothing, I have shunned it." *Śrayaṁstāṁstu parityajet*, this is the conclusion of 2nd chapter of the *Bhagavad Gītā*. Now it is over.

Now there is 3rd chapter of the *Bhagavad Gītā*.

In this way you had not been taught beforehand.[62]

62 Swamiji is referring to his first English translation of the *Bhagavad Gītā* that he gave in 1978. In saying, "this way you had not been taught before," he is emphasizing that this second translation (1990) is a new revelation of Abhinvagupta's *Bhagavad Gītā*. [*Editor's note*]

Chapter 3 Part 1

अर्जुन उवाच

arjuna uvāca

Arjuna places his question before his master, Lord Kṛṣṇa.

DVD 3.1 (0:11)

ज्यायसी चेत्कर्मणस्ते मता बुद्धिर्जनार्दन ।
तत्किं कर्मणि घोरे मां नियोजयसि केशव ॥ १ ॥

jāyasī cetkarmaṇaste matā buddhirjanārdana /
tatkiṁ karmaṇi ghore māṁ niyojayasi keśava //1//

O Keśava, O Lord Kṛṣṇa, if You have . . .

O Janārdana! Janārdana means [He] who gives trouble to those people who are not virtuous–that is Janārdana. So he is called Janārdana (i.e., Lord Kṛṣṇa). He gives trouble to those people.

. . . if, [as] You have said already, that knowledge is more [i.e., greater] than action (knowledge is valid, knowledge is better than action), why should You insert [i.e., advise] action for me? Because action is troublesome. I have to kill those [Kauravas] and what . . . if I practice only knowledge–You told me that knowledge is greater than action–why [then] should You insert [i.e., advise] me in activities? I don't want to act because these are very troublesome actions, i.e., to fight with people and all those . . .

DVD 3.1 (2:09)

व्यामिश्रेणेव वाक्येन बुद्धिं मोहयसीव मे ।
तदेकं वद निश्चित्य येन श्रेयोऽहमाप्नुयाम् ॥ २ ॥

vyāmiśreṇeva vākyena buddhiṁ mohayasīva me /
tadekaṁ vada niścitya yena śreyo'hamāpnuyām //2//

[Arjuna]: You have placed before me two opposite things: action and knowledge. But You should decide what is good for me, action or knowledge. Don't say that action is also needed and knowledge is also needed. These two things are equally opposite. What should I do . . . tell me only one thing, which is worthwhile to do. Only knowledge would be better, i.e., to think that, "all is Lord Śiva", *bas*, that is all. I have not to act. I have not to take [i.e., lead] troops and everything. You decide with Yourself so that I will remain peaceful here and hereafter.

You have already related to me [i.e., told me about] action and knowledge. *Tatra na dvayoḥ prādhānyaṁ yuktam* [comm.]. Though, amongst these two, one can be inferior and the other can be superior. Both cannot be superior, i.e., that knowledge is superior and action is [also] superior. The superior [one] is knowledge. That You have already said in the end of the 2nd chapter, that knowledge is great, greater than action. Why should You insert [i.e., advise] me into activity?

Tatbalena kṣapaṇīyatvaṁ yadi karmaṇāṁ. Holding the strength of knowledge, if all actions are to be thrown out, thrown aside (viz., *buddhiyukto jahātīme*)–he refers to the [*śloka*] which Lord Kṛṣṇa already told him at the end of the 2nd chapter [verse 52]–*mūlata eva tat karmaṇā kim prayojanam*, why should I do any action at all? This is what I mean.

श्रीभगवांस्तूत्तरं ददाति
śrī bhagavāṁstūttaraṁ dadāti

Now Śrī Bhagavān, Lord Kṛṣṇa, places before him its answer.

DVD 3.1 (5:19)

लोकेऽस्मिन्द्विविधा निष्ठा पुरा प्रोक्ता मयानघ ।
ज्ञानयोगेन सांख्यानां कर्मयोगेन योगिनाम् ॥ ३ ॥

loke'smindvividhā niṣṭhā purā proktā mayānagha /
jñānayogena sāṁkhyānāṁ karmayogena yoginām //3//

In this world, I have, in My previous lives, from times immemorial, from ancient times, I have placed [i.e., revealed] here in this world, in My previous lives, I have already explained it, that there are two predominant ways: *jñānayogena sāṁkhyānāṁ*, those who are blessed with knowledge, for them, knowledge is good, and those who are blessed with actions, for them, action is good. Both are predominant. You can't say that action is not predominant [or] knowledge is only predominant. It cannot be.

Loke eṣā dvayī gatiḥ prasiddhā [comm.]. This is absolutely . . . there are two pathways for achieving salvation in the end. *Sāṁkhyānāṁ jñānaṁ pradhānaṁ*, those who are *sāṁkhyās*, who are always sentenced in God consciousness, for them there is knowledge. And *yogināṁ*, those who are *karma yogīs*, who have got *yoga* in action, who observe *yoga* in action.

What is *yoga* in action?

While walking you are dissolved in Lord Śiva's state; while talking, while doing, while kissing, while doing *bakwas* (nonsense), while going to the cinema, you are always sentenced in that God consciousness while acting. Those are *karma yogīs*.

On the contrary, *karma yogīs* are better than *jñāna yogīs* [viz., *sāṁkhyās*] because *jñāna yogīs* cannot remain always in *jñāna yoga*. After all, they have to go to the bathroom, they have to urinate. That is *karma* (action). While urinating they must not be kept away from God consciousness. While going to bathroom, they must not be kept away from God consciousness.

So, this *yoga* in action is very predominant. And it works, it works always. And that does not work always, i.e., *jñāna yoga* does not work always. *Jñāna yoga* works only in your *pūja* room. You can't remain in your *pūja* room for all the twenty-four hours. Afterwards you have to come down and have a walk, have a talk, have a *gupshup* (idle conversation). So you should be . . . it is more important to do *gupshup* and be sentenced to God consciousness at the same time.

Mayā tu sā ekaiva niṣṭhoktā jñānakriyamayatvātsaṁ vittattvasyeti [comm.]. I have, in My [past] lives, related in the past, that this is only one pathway. Because the pathway is of knowledge and the pathway is of action. And in these two pathways, the pathway of action works continuously whereas the pathway of knowledge does not work continuously. It stops at times; from time to time, it stops. You have to stop this pathway of [knowledge].

Do you understand?

DENISE: Yes.

SWAMIJI: *na karmaṇāmanārambhāt . . .*

It will be cleared in these [next] two *ślokas*, 4th and 5th.

DVD 3.1 (10:21)

न कर्मणामनारम्भान्नैष्कर्म्यं पुरुषोऽश्नुते ।
न च संन्यसनादेव सिद्धिं समधिगच्छति ॥४॥

na karmaṇāmanārambhānnaiṣkarmyaṁ puruṣo'śnute //
na ca sannyasanādeva siddhiṁ samadhigacchati //4//

[Lord Kṛṣṇa]: *Na karmaṇāmanārambhāt.* If you just discard [i.e., cease] doing any action, [still] you cannot remain inactive; even then you cannot remain [completely] inactive. If you just [try to] discard all actions, but still then you cannot remain inactive. Why?

In [your] mind you will do some acting, you will think, you will do something or another thing in your mind, in your intellect, or in the ego. Or you will do yawning, or you will sleep, you will do something. Without doing . . . you cannot remain just like a dead body. *Naiṣkarmi* is where there is nothing to be done. *Naiṣkarma* is not possible. *Naiṣkarma* means being inactive for all times. It is not possible, it cannot be [achieved], it does not succeed.

Na ca sannyasanādeva siddhiṁ samadhigacchati. Just [by ceasing] all activities, you cannot get entry in God consciousness in its real sense.

DVD 3.1 (12:03)

नहि कश्चित्क्षणमपि जातु तिष्ठत्यकर्मकृत् ।
कार्यते ह्यवशः कर्म सर्वः प्रकृतिजैर्गुणैः ॥५॥

nahi kaścitkṣaṇamapi jātu tiṣṭhatyakarmakṛt /
kāryate hyavaśaḥ karma sarvaḥ prakṛtijairguṇaiḥ //5//

Nobody in this world can remain without any action. Some action or any action he will do. If he does not do it in movement, still he will do [action] in his mind, still he will act with ego, still he will do something inside.

Kāryate hyavaśaḥ karma sarvaḥ prakṛti. It is necessary that everybody works according to their nature. They will do something. If they do not do any action through body, [then] through mind they will do [action].

Jñānaṁ kramaṇā rahitaṁ na bhavati, karma ca kauśalopetaṁ jñānarahitaṁ na bhavati [comm.]. *Jñāna* cannot remain without actions, and actions cannot remain without knowledge. Actions and knowledge are interdependent. *Ityekameva vastu jñānakarmaṇī*, it is only one element (i.e., *jñāna* and *karma*).

It is well said in Shaivite philosophies:

> *na kriyārahitaṁ jñānaṁ na jñānarahitā kriyā /*
> *jñānakriyāviniṣpanna ācāryaḥ paśupāśahā //*

Action cannot remain without knowledge and knowledge cannot remain without action. So, the master who is efficient in activity and knowledge, both of these simultaneously, he can elevate the whole universe. He alone is capable of elevating the whole universe.

Do you understand?

Tasmājjhānāntarvarti karmāparihāri [comm.]. *Karma* (action), which is residing in the center of knowledge, you cannot avoid it. You cannot avoid it. It is impossible to avoid that *karma* (action).

Yataḥ paravaśa eva kāyavāṅmanasāṁ parispandāt [comm.]. *Paravaśa eva* means dependently. He will be dependent to do something. Without doing something he won't remain [alive]. He won't live.

Still he will breathe! If he does not do anything, still he will breathe. If he does not do anything, [still] he will think. If he does not do anything, he will sleep and go into the dreaming state, and do activities there (e.g., rides and walks, ride on pathways) in dreaming state. He will do something.

DENISE: So that's action too?

SWAMIJI: Yes, actions are predominant everywhere.

Now, if you say that, "no, I want to remain like this, with eyes closed, *bas*!" [You] don't move your body [and say] that, "I want to remain like this." If you say that, I, [Lord Kṛṣṇa], have got the answer to that.

DVD 3.1 (16:07)

कर्मेन्द्रियाणि संयम्य य आस्ते मनसा स्मरन् ।
इन्द्रियार्थान्विमूढत्मा मूढाचारः स उच्यते ॥६॥

karmendriyāṇi samyamya ya āste manasā smaran /
indriyārthānvimūḍhātmā mūḍhācāraḥ sa ucyate //6//

Karmendriyāṇi, all organs of action, one who will squeeze all of his organs of action, his own organs and *ya āste,* who just sits, *manasā smaran*, through mind, what will he do? *Indriyārthān,* through mind he will be thinking, he will go here and there, and his disciples will think, "our master is in *samādhi.*" [But] sometimes he goes to sleep.

Who?

DENISE: The master.

SWAMIJI: Their master who is just idly sitting for meditation. This meditation is fraud! This meditation does not work.

Indriyārthān, he goes here and there through his mind. *Mūḍhācāraḥ sa ucyate. Mūḍhācāraḥ*, he is a fraud and he is not a good master. He is [more] wretched than an ordinary person. An ordinary person who works day and night in the garden and goes on digging the ground and everything, that person is far better than that *yogi* who sits like this [Swamiji sits straight].

Right?

yastvindriyāṇi manasā . . .

Now, who is the best one? The best *yogi* is that person . . .

DVD 3.1 (18:09)

यस्त्विन्द्रियाणि मनसा नियम्यारभतेऽर्जुन ।
कर्मेन्द्रियैः कर्मयोगमसक्तः स विशिष्यते ॥७॥

yastvindriyāṇi manasā niyamyārabhate'rjuna /
karmendriyaiḥ karmayogamasaktaḥ sa viśiṣyate //7//

The one who is always walking, talking, and fully aware of God consciousness while walking, while talking, while doing *gup-shup* (idle conversation), and seeing, shaking hands, *karmen-driyaiḥ karma yogam asaktaḥ*, without being attached to all of these. He sees . . . he [walks] on the pathway for a change, but he does not know where he went and wherefrom he returned. Because, it is just like *rathyaṁ grāmaṇe tṛṇaparṇādivat.* When you walk on the roadside, you will see [objects] on the roadside here and there. When you go in motorcar, in motorcar ride, you see leaves and everything on the right side and on the left side of your car, but those impressions of leaves do not remain in your mind; it is just *nirvikalpa.*[63]

Like that you should act in this world.

DVD 3.1 (19:54)

नियतं कुरु कर्म त्वं कर्म ज्यायो ह्यकर्मणः ।
शरीरयात्रापि च ते न प्रसिद्ध्येदकर्मणः ॥८॥

niyataṁ kuru karma tvaṁ karma jyāyo hyakaramaṇaḥ /
śarīrayātrāpi ca te na prasiddhyedakarmaṇaḥ //8//

[Lord Kṛṣṇa]: So you should do action, always do action with God consciousness. *Karma jyāyo hyakarmaṇaḥ. Karma* is, action is very superior, most superior, more superior than discarding actions. *Śarīrayātrāpi ca te. Śarīrayātrā* means this bodily existence also is dependent to *karma.* Without *karma*, bodily existence . . . the body won't exist, the body won't live, it will be shattered to pieces.

DVD 3.1 (20:55)

यज्ञार्थात्कर्मणोऽन्यत्र लोकोऽयं कर्मबन्धनः ।
तदर्थं कर्म कौन्तेय मुक्तसङ्गः समाचर ॥९॥

63 See footnote 61 for an explanation of *nirvikalpa*.

yajñārthātkarmaṇo'nyatra loko'yaṁ karmabandhanaḥ /
tadarthaṁ karma kaunteya muktasaṅgaḥ samācara //9//

O Arjuna, you should do actions, *yajñārthāt*, you should do actions, leave actions in God consciousness, *bas*! Don't crave for its fruit, [then] all your actions will bear no fruit. And when they bear no fruit, what is remaining in the background of fruit? The knowledge of Parabhairava. The supreme Bhairava state will shine automatically.

JOHN: What does it mean [when] he says it won't bear fruit, these actions will bear no fruit? I mean, it bears some fruit . . . what does it mean?

SWAMIJI: No, these actions will bear fruit [only] when you ask for them, when you ask for fruits. When you do actions and remain in God consciousness, always be introverted and do all actions, then there will be no fruit from that. And that fruit will be, automatically, the knowledge of Parabhairava.

JOHN: So what is it when some fruit comes? I mean in other words, you do something and some result comes from that. That is not the same kind of fruit?

SWAMIJI: No, that fruit should not come, that is the wrong way of action.

JOHN: No, I agree with that, but . . .

SWAMIJI: Wrong way of action is to pray for this *karma* (action), e.g., "this *karma* (action) should be successful. Any *karma*, any action which I do, it must be successful, it must remain successful, it must not remain undone, it must have some fruit. It is worthwhile to have some fruit from my actions."

This you should not have!

As long as you have this idea, this desire that, "I want some good action from this fruit [i.e., some good fruit from this action]," you are away from God consciousness.

You go on doing your work, you go on serving Viresh wholeheartedly [and feel], "it is my duty to serve Viresh. Viresh is my own self [so] I must serve him, I must see that he is alright." But his attachment you should not have. If you don't have his attachment, Viresh will be fine and you will also be fine. You will be sentenced in God consciousness at that time. This is how we work in action.

DENISE: If I don't have attachment to him?

SWAMIJI: Huh?

DENISE: If I serve him, I take care of him, but I don't have attachment to him.

SWAMIJI: No, don't have attachment. See that it is your duty because, "I am mother. I have been made, placed, on the post of mother-ship. I am mother and he is my son. So this is my duty to serve him. It is my duty to see that he is alright." *Bas*! That is all. And he will be alright, you will be alright. This is how we act.

There must not be attachment to any action.

As long as you do this job [with attachment], you remain away from God consciousness.

JOHN: So, in other words, when you pray for example, you should pray just for prayer sake, not for getting some fruit from that prayer.

SWAMIJI: *Yadaprārthyamānaṁ phalaṁ tat jñānam* [comm. from 2:48]. [Abhinavagupta] has said in his commentary of the *Bhagavad Gītā*, *"yat aprārthyamānaṁ phalaṁ."* That which is not asked, that fruit from your actions, which is not asked, which is not craved for, that is knowledge, that is Parabhairava knowledge. Parabhairava knowledge will come automatically there, it will shine.

This is the cream of Shaivism. It is renewed Shaivism. For this purpose I came to tell you this secret.

DVD 3.1 (26:07)

सहयज्ञाः प्रजाः सृष्ट्वा पुरोवाच प्रजापतिः ।
अनेन प्रसविष्यध्वमेष वोऽस्त्विष्टकामधुक् ॥१०॥

sahayajñāḥ prajāḥ sṛṣṭvā purovāca prajāpatiḥ /
anena prasaviṣyadhvameṣa vo'stviṣṭakāmadhuk //10//

Prajāpati means Brahmā. It is translated by all commentators of the *Bhagavad Gītā* [that] Prajāpati means Brahmā. They commentated upon Prajāpati as Brahmā, who is the creator of this whole universe–not protector, nor destroyer, nor concealer, nor revealer.

JONATHAN: Just creator.

SWAMIJI: Creator.

But he has translated this, Abhinavagupta has translated Prajāpati [to] mean *paramātma*, Parabhairava. Prajāpati means *paramātma*, Parabhairava.

Prajāḥ sahaiva karmabhiḥ sasarja [comm.]. He created this whole universe, right from *pṛthvī* (earth) to *śāntātīta kalā.*[64] He created this whole universe–this is *prajāḥ. Sahaiva karmabhiḥ sasarja*, He created [this universe] with actions. Lord Śiva created all of this stuff [out] of His glamour, His outside glamour. This is His glamour, outside glamour . . .

What is outside glamour?

DENISE: His creation.

SWAMIJI: His creation, whatever He has created. It is His outside glamour, stuff. He created this stuff with actions. Only He made this discrimination with actions, *uktaṁ ca tena*, and then while creating this stuff, He told them, He instructed [the people whom He created]:

> *prajānāṁ karmabhya eva prasavaḥ santānaḥ, etānyeva ceṣṭaṁ saṁsāraṁ mokṣaṁ vā dāsyanti* / [comm.]

All of these actions, whatever you do, will give you liberation and will give you enjoyment of the world. Enjoyment of the world they will give you when you have attachment for whatever you do. And whatever you do, [if] you have no attachment, then [your actions] will liberate you and fix [i.e., establish] you in My nature, in the Parabhairava state. You will become Parabhairava then.

Do you understand?

JOHN: If you do action with attachment, then you get joy. If you do actions without attachment to its fruits, then you get the enlightened state.

SWAMIJI: Yes.

> *yatra yeṣāṁ mokṣaprādhānyaṁ taireva viṣayāḥ*
> [comm. intro to *śloka* 11]

64 "The fifth and last enclosure [of creation] is known as *śāntātīta kalā*. Here you will only find the existence of *Śiva tattva*." *Kashmir Shaivism–The Secret Supreme* 2.12.

But the discretion is here, [as] related by Vyāsa in the *Mahābhārata* in this chapter of the *Bhagavad Gītā*, that when actions divert you, sentence you to *mokṣa* (liberation, Parabhairava state), those [aspirants] are a likely fit for the enjoyments of the world. *They* should enjoy the world. Other persons who have not the capacity [to attain] *mokṣa*, they should not be allowed to touch anything in this world. All of these enjoyments are best to [be] possessed by those who are worthy of the Bhairava state; [worldly] enjoyments must be enjoyed by those people.

Which people?

DENISE: That are in the Parabhairava state.

SWAMIJI: Parabhairava state. Others should not be allowed to touch this enjoyment. They are not worthy. They should be kept aloof [and told], "no, you have no right to eat, you have no right to talk, you have no right to think, you have no right to think about anything. All rights are reserved by Parabhairava."

Food is for Parabhairava! That person who is likely to go into the Parabhairava state, food is meant for him. [Food is meant for one] who is likely [to have the] enjoyment of one thousand . . . [who is capable of] captivating the whole universal ladies, he is capable [i.e., worthy] of that. Others have no right to touch any lady. Those have got . . . those are free. They can do anything, whatever [they choose]; any nonsense they can do. And sensible act is also prohibited for those who are not capable. They cannot do sensible [actions] also, what to speak of . . .

DENISE: Insensible [actions].

SWAMIJI: Yes [laughter].

Nobody has commentated upon this verse of the *Bhagavad Gītā* [in this manner] other than Abhinavagupta.

DVD 3.1 (32:53)

देवान्भावयतानेन ते देवा भावयन्तु वः ।
परस्परं भावयन्तः श्रेयः परमवाप्स्यथ ॥११॥

devānbhāvayatānena te devā bhavayantu vaḥ /
parasparaṁ bhāvayantaḥ śreyaḥ paramavāpsyatha //11//

[Abhinavagupta]: *Deva* (*deva* does not mean gods; you have not to satisfy gods). *Deva* means *krīḍanaśīlā indriya vrittayaḥ* [comm.], your own organs, your own organs are gods. *Karaṇeśvaryo devatā*, these organs, your bodily organs are all *devas*. *Rahasya śāstra prasiddhāḥ,* they are nominated in *Rahasya Śāstra* (Shaivite books): *tā anena karmaṇā tarpayata*, your organs you should feed by these *karmas* (actions), by giving them good food, good taste, good enjoyment, *ghee*, *paratha*, *pulau* (fried rice), everything, whatever fine [substance] you can get for them, for your own organs. Feed them with many delicious things. Give them delicious food.

This is . . . I wanted to, I craved to tell you.[65]

Tṛptāśca styastā, when your organs are *tṛptā* (*tṛptā* means satisfied with these enjoyments), *vo–yuṣmān ātmana eva svarūpamātrocitān bhāvayantu,* they will give you *apavarga,* they will make you reside in the real state of Parabhairava. After this enjoyment, when you feed your organs with delicious foods in the Parabhairava state, when feeding is over, then you will rest. Just at the time of rest, you will have trance in Parabhairava state, at once! [Your organs] will give you this fruit because *svātmasthitiyogyatvāt*, you become fit to reside in Parabhairava [state] at that time.

evam-anavaratam̐
vyutthānasamādhi[*samaya*]*paramparāyām* [comm.]

So in *vyutthāna*[66] you have to feed them. When you are out of Parabhairava state, you have to feed them. Whom? Your organs. And just after feeding [them], you will remain in the Parabhairava state–that is the fruit.

But [Abhinavagupta] says, "it is worthwhile only for those who are likely to go into the state of Parabhairava; these delicious things are meant for those persons. These delicious things are not meant for worldly people who will waste it."

65 Swamiji is talking to John and Denise Hughes, saying that he was craving to tell them his new revelation on this *Bhagavad Gītā*. [*Editor's note*]

66 *Vyutthāna* means the field of worldly activity. [*Editor's note*]

11th *śloka* is finished. *Bas*!

> *na kevalamitthamapavarge yāvatsiddhilābhe'pyayaṁ mārga* [comm. intro to 12th *śloka*]

This was done [i.e., explained] for those who reside in Bhairava state. They have the right to take delicious things.

Those who are not fit for focusing their thoughts on Parabhairava state, for them also it is essential. If they take . . . in fact, there is no need to feed them at all. Now, if you do feed them, still they should make the good purpose of that. If they are fed in ordinary way [i.e., with ordinary food such as] *channa dhal* or *masoor dhal* or whatever it is (i.e., not delicious food), [or] if they take some sweet food, for those also it is essential to take good purpose of this [act of eating]. If they take food, they should thank God and be grateful to Him [because] they have been blessed by this food also, which they didn't deserve. But for that also, they should be grateful to God.

Otherwise they are thieves [if] they get food from Parabhairava and don't utilize it in a good way. They should also take good chance [i.e., opportunity] of reciting the *mantra* of Parabhairava from a distance. They should also do some *sādhana* after taking their food.[67] After taking their food, they are bound [i.e., obliged] to do some *sādhana* [after] bestowing them some food. Otherwise they have no right to take food.

DVD 3.1 (39:37)

इष्टान्कामान्हि वो देवा दास्यन्ते यज्ञभाविताः ।
तैर्दत्तानप्रदायैभ्यो यो भुङ्क्ते स्तेन एव सः ॥१२॥

iṣṭānkāmānhi vo devā dāsyante yajñabhāvitāḥ /
tairdattānapradāyaibhyo yo bhuṅkte stena eva saḥ //12//

67 Swamiji advised that after taking food, it is a good practice to sit quietly and reflect on the cycle of nature in relation to what you have eaten. For instance, the seasons, the rain, the sunshine, the moon, the seeds, the soil, the time it took to grow, the cultivating, cooking and preparation, etc. In all, everything up to the food arriving on your plate. [*Editor's note*]

Otherwise, when these *indriyas* (these organs) are fed with good things [or] nearly good things, they get those things from Bhairava. But for that sake also, they should be thankful to Bhairava and make good purpose of [doing] *sādhana*, some *sādhana*.

Maybe it is not that *sādhana* to that extent [like] what we do already in Shaivism, but they should still do some thanks to God. They should remember God. Maybe from distance, but they should remember [Him]. If they don't remember [God], then they are thieves. They are snatching things away from God and not . . .

DENISE: Not thanking him.

SWAMIJI: . . . not thanking him.

DVD 3.1 (41:09)

यज्ञशिष्टाशिनः सन्तो मुच्यन्ते सर्वकिल्विषैः ।
भुञ्जते ते त्वघं पापा ये पचन्त्यात्मकारणात् ॥१३॥

yajñaśiṣṭā śinaḥ santo mucyante sarvakilviṣaiḥ /
bhuñjate te tvaghaṁ pāpā ye pacantyātmakāraṇāt //13//

Those great saints, they take this [food while] they perform this *yajña* (this is a kind of a *havan*, i.e., to do *svāhā* (offerings) to organs, [giving] delicious food to organs). [In this way], they are freed from all sins and bad actions. And on the contrary, those who only take good food and in return they don't thank them, they don't think of them, they are eating just sinful things.[68] They are sinners. They are one kind of thief. They are snatching

68 ". . . with awareness, you have to serve organs. Give them whatever they need, and in return, they will push you back in God consciousness. The actual joy of God consciousness, which you have momentarily, which you have got momentarily, *bas*, for a little bit. That is the *yajñaśiṣṭā*. But don't strive to enhance that by yourself. Don't strive to increase that by yourself . . . you can't increase it. You can increase it only by serving your senses in right way. When you serve your senses in right way, they will push you back in God consciousness. By this way, it becomes stronger and stronger, and in the end it is strongest. When it is strongest, you are one with God. That is the real state of *jīvan mukta*." *Bhagavad Gītā* (1978).

things from God and not behaving [towards] them [i.e., their senses] properly in return.[69]

Now the 14th and 15th *ślokas*.

DVD 3.1 (43:01)

अन्नाद्भवन्ति भूतानि पर्जन्यादन्नसंभवः ।
यज्ञाद्भवति पर्जन्यो यज्ञः कर्मसमुद्भवः ॥१४॥
कर्म ब्रह्मोद्भवं विद्धि ब्रह्माक्षरसमुद्भवम् ।
तस्मात्सर्वगतं ब्रह्म नित्यं यज्ञे प्रतिष्ठितम् ॥१५॥

annādbhavanti bhūtāni parjanyādannasambhavaḥ /
yajñādbhavati parjanyo yajñaḥ karmasamudbhavaḥ //14//
karma brahmodbhavaṁ viddhi brahmākṣarasamudbhavam
tasmātsarvagataṁ brahma nityaṁ yajñe pratiṣṭhitam //15//

Now, Abhinavagupta has commentated upon these two *ślokas* in a unique way. All other commentators have translated these two *ślokas* [in the following way]:

Annādbhavanti bhūtāni. Anna means food (*anna* means whatever is produced, the production from fields). By that, *bhavanti bhūtāni,* people are created, people are soaked [with food] and they get life. *Parjanyādannasambhavaḥ*, but *anna* is produced by rains, occasional rains. Occasional rain [falls] on the fields and the [plants] are produced and they produce that production–say *moong dhal* and *śali* (rice)–but rain comes only when you perform *havan*. It is said in *śāstras* that unless we perform *havan* rain does not come. By performing *havan*, rain comes (*yajñāt bhavati parjanyo*).

Yajñaḥ karma samudbhavaḥ. And *yajñaḥ* (*havan*) is produced by *karmas,* good actions. When you produce *sāmagri* (offerings) for *havan* [with] *til* (sesame), *sarśap* (oil), *ghee*, all those [things]

69 "*Bhuñjate te tvaghaṁ pāpā*. Those people who think that they have snatched this joy from these senses and they take hold of that, it does not remain. So that is not *yajña śeṣa*, [the actual joy of God consciousness]; that is not *yajña śeṣa*. They are not eating *yajña śeṣa*, they are not using *yajña śeṣa*. They are using sin, they are eating sin there." Ibid.

you offer it in *havan*, then *varśa* (rain) comes and production is produced in the fields.

Karma brahmodbhavaṁ viddhi. That *karma* is produced by *brahma*. It is translated by other commentators in this way.

Brahmākṣarasamuddhavaḥ. *Brahma* is produced by *akṣara*. *Akṣara* means [the one] who is always established in the upper world–that Anantabhaṭṭāraka.[70]

Tasmātsarvagataṁ brahma nityaṁ yajñe pratiṣṭhitam. So *yajña* is the foundation of all sources of beings. In this way, everybody has commentated upon these two *ślokas*.

Now see the unique meaning of Abhinavagupta.

You write down! You write down with pencil.

There is *anna* (*anna* is first); *anna* is food (first number). *Annādbhavanti bhūtāni*. *Bhūtāni* means these souls, which are born.

JONATHAN: These what?

DENISE: Souls.

JONATHAN: Souls.

SWAMIJI: Yes. This is second.

And that *parjanyāt annasambhavaḥ*. *Parjan* is another one, the third. *Parjan* means . . .

JOHN: *Parjan*?

SWAMIJI: *Parjan* means *megha*.

JOHN: *Megha*. *Parjan* means?

SWAMIJI: The clouds and rain. *Parjan* means rain and clouds (*megha*).

What is it? Is it third?

JOHN: Yes.

---

70 "There are two Anantabhaṭṭāraka's. One is that Anantabhaṭṭāraka [who] is individual Anantabhaṭṭāraka, which is functioning in the lower [field from *māyā* to *pṛthvī*], and this is universal Anantabhaṭṭāraka [who is functioning from *śakti tattva* to *śuddhavidya tattva*]." Swami Lakshmanjoo, *Tantrāloka* 6.173 (1974).

"Anantabhaṭṭāraka [also known as Aghoranātha] is PA to Lord Śiva, i.e., just assistant, [personal] assistant *rudra* of Lord Śiva. He assists Lord Śiva in inferior creation. He is Lord, he is Śiva. He is Śiva but he is called Anantabhaṭṭāraka. But he functions only in inferior creation, i.e., in creation, protection, and destruction. And in revealing and concealing, Lord Śiva handles Himself." Ibid., 9.143-144 (1977).

SWAMIJI: And that *yajñādbhavati parjanyo. Yajña* is the fourth. And *yajñaḥ karma samudbhavaḥ. Karma* is the fourth.

JOHN: Fifth.

SWAMIJI: Huh? Fifth?

JOHN: Yes: food, souls, clouds, sacrifice (*annād, bhūtāni, parjan*, and *yajña*).

SWAMIJI: How many?

JOHN: That is four.

SWAMIJI: Four.

JOHN: And *karma*?

SWAMIJI: *Karma* you have done, fourth?

JOHN: Is *karma* part of *yajña*?

SWAMIJI: Yes. *Karma brahmodbhavaṁ viddhi.* It is from *brahma*; *karma* is produced by *brahma*. *Brahma* is fifth. *Brahma akṣara samudbhavam. Brahma* is produced by *akṣara.*

JOHN: *Brahma* is produced by which?

SWAMIJI: *Akṣara*, who is unperishable, *akṣara.*[71] So *brahma* is always residing . . . [it is *brahma*] who is established on *yajña.*

Now these six, Abhinavagupta translates in his own unique way.[72]

Annāt. Anna, what is *anna*?

avibhāgabhogyasvabhāvāt
kathañcinmāyāvidyākālādyanekāparaparyāyāt [comm.]

Aparaparyāyāt. Anna is not actually eatable food. *Avibhāga bhogya svabhāvāt. Bhogya* means . . .

na bhogyaṁ vyatiriktaṁ hi bhoktustvatto vibhāvyate /[73]

. . . *bhogya* is whatever is eatable [but] eatable thing cannot be separated from *bhoktā* (the eater, enjoyer). One is *bhogya* (what is eaten), another is eating (*bhoga*), [another] one is the eater

71 "The supreme blissful state of consciousness is *akṣara.*" *Bhagavad Gītā* (1978).

72 In Swamiji's earlier translation the six are: *anna*, *parjan*, *yajña*, *karma*, *brahma,* and *akṣara*. Each is produced by the next, i.e., food by rain, rain by *havan*, *havan* by action, action by *brahma*, and *brahma* by Anantabhaṭṭāraka. [*Editor's note*]

73 *Bhagavad Gītā,* 4.26.

(*bhoktā*).

Do you understand?

JOHN: Eater, eating, and eatable.

SWAMIJI: There are three aspects. This [food] is edible–this is food, it is edible–it is *bhogya*. *Bhoktā* is [the one] who is eating it. And then there is the process of eating (*bhoga*). So there are three aspects in this aspect [of food]; in these triple aspects, there are three things: one is *prameya*, another is *pramāṇa*, and the third is *pramātṛ*–subject, object and . . .

JOHN: Means of knowing, *pramāṇa*

SWAMIJI: . . . *pramāṇa* (cognition).

Na bhogyaṁ vyatiriktaṁ hi bhoktustvatto. Bhogya cannot be separated; you cannot see *bhogya* separated from *bhoktā*. When there is no *bhoktā* (enjoyer, knower), how will *bhogya* (enjoyed, known) exist? *Bhogya* cannot exist [by itself]. *Bhogya* is only [existing] when *bhoktā* is there. Object (*bhogya*) lives and shines only when there is a subject (*bhoktā*). The produced thing is that which comes from the producer. If it is produced, who has produced it?

DENISE: The producer.

SWAMIJI: Producer. So there must be the producer first and then [something is capable of being] produced. How can produced become [an existent] without a producer? How can it exist without a producer?

So, *bhoga* is enjoying, *bhogya* is enjoyed, *bhoktā* is enjoyer. These three aspects are always shining everywhere, in each and [every perception].

For instance, there is a *thali* (plate), in front of Viresh there is a *thali*, and in that *thali* there are so many things, curds and everything–it is *bhogya*.

Who is *bhoktā*?

It cannot remain . . . a *thali* cannot eat the *thali*. The *thali* can only exist when Viresh is there to eat it. Viresh also cannot eat it until there is an eating process, i.e., when he has got arms and hands and he throws [the food] into his mouth. So these three aspects are in each and every *bhoga* (act of enjoyment).

DVD 3.1 (54:10)

avibhāgabhogyasvabhāvāt kathañcinmāyāvidyākālādy-
anekāparaparyāyāt [*bhūtāni vicitrāṇi bhavanti* /

taccānnaṁ parjanyāt āvicchinnasaṁvitsvabhāvādātmanaḥ bhoktṛtantrātmalābhatvādbhogyatāyāḥ] / [comm.]

Avibhāga bhogya svabhāvāt ātmanaḥ. So *avibhāga bhogya svabhāvāt ātmanaḥ* means *māyā*, *kalā*, *vidyā*, *rāga*, *kāla*, *niyati*, all of these one hundred and eighteen worlds are *bhogya* (food), right from *māyā* to *pṛthvī tattva* (earth), which are inseparable from *bhoktā* (the enjoyer).[74]

That is [what Abhinavagupta] says: *kathañcit māyā vidyā kāla ādi anekāparaparyāyāt*. All of these *bhūtāni vicitrāṇi bhavanti* are varieties of men, people, and souls. *Tat ca annaṁ*, [and] that *anna*, [which is produced by] *parjanyāt* (*parjanyāt* (rain) means *āvicchinna saṁvit svabhāvāda atmanaḥ bhoktṛ tantrātma lābhatvāt bhogya tāyāḥ*). *Āvicchinna saṁvit svabhāvāt*, [one] who is knowledge, who is one with knowledge . . .[75]

---

74 "Abhinavagupta's meaning [for] *anna* is not food, *anna* is *bhogya*. *Bhogya* means with which we [i.e., the enjoyers] are connected. And this *bhogya* is this object. This object is . . . it appears in all the *tattvas* from earth to *māyā*. From earth to *māyā*, all this is *bhogya*, it is your object, it is with which you are concerned. That is *anna*." *Bhagavad Gītā* (1978).

75 "From that *anna* is produced *bhūtāni*, all these individuals. All these individuals exist, they are established, they get establishment by this *anna*, by the contact of this, all this collective cycle of *tattvas*, from *pṛthvi* to *māyā*. That *anna*, *parjanyād-anna-saṁbhavaḥ*, that *anna* (that *bhogya*), that objective world produces the state of *parjanya*. The word meaning of *parjanya* [literally] means rain. Here it does not mean rain. *Parjanya* means the way how we taste this universe, taste these five senses. Five senses are connected with all these elements from earth to *māyā*. How we taste it, how we get entangled with it, that is *bhogya kriya*. This is *bhogya* (*bhogya* means [that] which is to be tasted). *Bhogya kriya* is how to taste it, the way how we taste it. That is through organs, through senses, through mind, we taste it through that cycle. That is *parjanya*.

"*Yajñādbhavati parjanya*, but *parjanya* is produced by *yajña*. *Yajña* is *bhoktā*, limited *pramāta*, limited knower, limited actor; whosoever is limited is called *yajña*. And *yajña* is produced by *karma*. *Karma* means *kriyā svātantrya*, freedom in action. Because there must be freedom in action when you do something with senses or *śabda* (sound), *sparśa* (touch), *rūpa* (form), *rasa* (taste), *gandha* (smell). There must be that freedom [and] that capacity is *kriyā svātantrya*. But that *kriyā svā-*

Because that knowledge, when there is no knowledge [of the] known, when known things [e.g., food], when there is no knowledge [of it], how can you eat it? How can the eater eat [food] without knowledge [of it]? Because, if the eater has no knowledge [of food], why does he put that [food] in his mouth? Why doesn't he put it into his ear [laughter]? He has got that knowledge and knowledge has got that . . . there is knower also. So three aspects are moving everywhere.

Now, these three aspects are found in *bhoga* (enjoyment). This is the three-fold manifestation of *bhoga.* The first threefold manifestation is the manifestation of *bhoga* and the next threefold manifestation is the manifestation of *mokṣa.*

JOHN: *Mokṣa*?

SWAMIJI: *Mokṣa.* He will [explain *mokṣa*] in the second *śloka.*

DVD 3.1 (57:08)

कर्म ब्रह्मोद्भवं विद्धि ब्रह्माक्षरसमुद्भवम् ।
तस्मात्सर्वगतं ब्रह्म नित्यं यज्ञे प्रतिष्ठितम् ॥ १५ ॥

karma brahmodbhavaṁ viddhi brahmākṣarasamudbhavam
tasmātsarvagataṁ brahma nityaṁ yajñe pratiṣṭhitam //15//

Karma, *brahma*, and *akṣara* are the three aspects, which are in *mokṣa*. That is internal.

JOHN: So the first three, *anna* (food), *bhutani* (souls), and *parjanya* (rain) are both *bhoktā* (the enjoyer)?

SWAMIJI: *Bhogya*.[76]

JOHN: And these *yajña* or *karma*, *brahma*, and *akṣara* are all part of *mokṣa*.

SWAMIJI: *Mokṣa*.

arātrayasandhānād- . . . mokṣamvyavahārati

Aviccinna saṁvit svabhāvād ātmanaḥ (earlier comm.)

---

tantrya is not that *svātantrya*, that supreme *svātantrya*. That is *kriyā svātantrya,* which is being attached, which is attached with that *bhogya kriyā*." Ibid.

76 The objects of enjoyment, from *māyā* to *pṛthvī*. [*Editor's note*]

sa ca parjanyo —

That *parjanya* is from *bhoktā*, because *bhoktā* is always involved in *bhogakriyā* (*bhogakriyā* means in eating, the process of eating). *Bhogakriyā* is only possible when there is *svātantrya śakti*.[77]

---

77 "*Karma brahmodbhavaṁ viddhi*. That *kriyā svātantrya*, that freedom of doing action, *brahmodbhavaṁ viddhi*, is produced by *brahma*. *Brahma* is *anavaccchinnā svātantrya*. *Anavaccchinnāsvātantrya* is where from all these sparks of freedom rise. That is *anavacchinnā svātantrya*. But that too is unlimited, but still it has got some limitation in that *brahma*, *kriyā svātantrya*. And that *brahma ākṣara samudbhavam*, that *kriya svātantrya* is produced by *akṣara*, *akṣara* means unlimited blissful consciousness. So unlimited blissful consciousness is the source of all this cycle." *Bhagavad Gītā* (1978).

"This *svatantratā*, this being independent, the state of independence is attributed only to Lord Śiva." Swami Lakshmanjoo, *Tantrāloka* 9.9a (1977).

"*Svātantrya śakti* is His free will. Whatever He wishes, that is *svātantrya śakti*. *Svātantrya śakti* is the germ of all His five energies. He has got five energies: *cit śakti* (energy of consciousness), *ānanda śakti* (energy of bliss), [*īcchā śakti*], energy of will, [*jñāna śakti*], energy of knowledge, and [*kriyā śakti*], energy of action. All these five energies of God consciousness are produced by His *svātantrya śakti* of freedom, His free power. That is called *svātantrya śakti*. *Svātantrya śakti* produces these five energies of Lord Śiva. And *cit śakti* is actually based on His nature, *ānanda śakti* is based on his *śakti*, on his *Pārvatī*, *īcchā śakti* is based in *Sādaśiva*, and *jñāna śakti* (the energy of knowledge) is based on *Īśvara*, and the energy of *kriyā* is based of *Śuddhāvidya*. All these five pure states of Lord Śiva are one with Lord Śiva. *Cit śakti* indicates Lord Śiva's actual position. *Ānanda śakti* indicates Lord Śiva's position of *śakti*. And *icchā śakti* indicates Lord Śiva's position of *Sādaśiva*. And *jñāna śakti* indicates his position in *Īśvara*. And *Śuddhāvidya* is fifth position. All these five positions are filled with God consciousness. Below that is the scale of *māyā*, illusion; that will go from *māya* to earth." Swami Lakshmanjoo, *Special Verses on Practice*, original audio/DVD (1988).

"The outside [i.e., the external, differentiated] existence of *svātantrya* is *māyā*." Swami Lakshmanjoo, *Parātriśikā Vivaraṇa* (1982-85)

"*Svātantrya śakti* and *māyā* are one. *Svātantrya śakti* is that state of energy which can produce the power of going down and coming up again. And *māyā* is not like that. *Māyā* will give you strength of coming down and then no ability of going up. Then you cannot go up again. This is the state of *māyā*. And all these three *malas* [see footnote 504] reside in *māyā śākti*, not *svātantrya śakti,* although *svātantrya śakti* and *māyā śakti* are one. *Māyā śakti* is that energy, universal energy, which is owned by individual being, individual soul. The same energy, when it is owned by universal being, is called *svātantrya śakti*." Swami Lakshmanjoo, *Kashmir Shaivism–The Secret Supreme* 7.47.

"Definition of *svātantrya* is, freedom in action and freedom in knowledge. When you know with your freedom, when you act with your freedom. When you know and you don't succeed in that knowledge, there is not *svātantrya*; when there is not *svātantrya*, it is not really knowledge. When there is not *svātantrya*, it is not really action. The action of individuals is just like that. Individuals know, they know something (you can't say that they don't know anything), they know something, but that knowledge has not *svātantrya*. And they act also, they do something, but that doing also has not *svātantrya*. So without *svātantrya*, doing and knowing has no value. When there is *svātantrya*, it is fully valued." Swami Lakshmanjoo, *Parātriśikā Vivaraṇa* (1982-85).

"His state of *svātantrya śakti* is *eṣaṇavidikriyātmakam*, is the essence of will, essence of knowledge, and essence of action. And although it is the essence of will, knowledge, and action, this state of *svātantrya śakti* is *anavacchinnam* (*anavacchinnam* is unlimited), unlimited in its *prakāśa* and in its *vimarśa*. *Prakāśa* is unlimited there, *vimarśa* is unlimited there. What can we understand by this? The unlimitation of *prakāśa* and *vimarśa* is when you catch hold of *prakāśa*, the next moment it will appear as *vimarśa*, next moment it will appear as *prakāśa*, again *vimarśa*, again *prakāśa*, again *vimarśa*. So *vimarśa* and *prakāśa* are diluted with each other, that is *anavacchinnam*. *Prakāśa* cannot remain without *vimarśa* and *vimarśa* cannot remain without *prakāśa*. *Prakāśa* is *vikalpa*, *vimarśa* is *svātantrya*; *svātantrya* and *vikalpa*, both are functioning there in unlimited way." Swami Lakshmanjoo, *Tantrāloka* 15.349 (1981).

See footnote 1 for an explanation of *prakāśa* and *vimarśa*.

"That essence of *svātantrya* is *anavacchinna* (beyond limitation), all-round beyond limitation; there is no such limit found in that state. *Vicchinna camatkāra maya viśrāntyā* and this limited state of being is also found there. [Lord Śiva] is unlimited, but limited cycle of God consciousness is also found there. So it is both limited and unlimited. That being who is limited only, he is not true. That being who is unlimited only, he is not true. Why? Because he is limited. The being *tat ca svātantryam – aviccinnam api anavacchinnānanta-svātantrya-pūrṇa-samucchalan-maheśvara-bhāva-paramātma-brahma-saṁsparśavaśāt* /. . .

And the last abode of that *mokṣa* is *param ātma brahma*–Parabhairava *bhāva* (state). And then it goes to *akṣara*. *Akṣarāt* means *praśāntāśeṣaiśvaryataraṅgātsaṁvinmātrāt*, when there is only the state of Parabhairava remaining in the end.

So, [the second set of] three aspects are supplying *mokṣa* and the first three aspects are supplying *bhoga*.

Evaṁ pravar . . . the 16th *śloka*.

DVD 3.1 (59:29)

एवं प्रवर्तितं चक्रं नानुवर्तयतीह यः ।
अघायुरिन्द्रियारामो मोघं पार्थ स जीवति ॥१६॥

evaṁ pravartitaṁ cakraṁ nānuvartayatīha yaḥ /
aghāyurindriyārāmo moghaṁ pārtha sa jīvati //16//

[Lord Kṛṣṇa]: And this wheel, this *cakra*, which is already existing in this world to manifest the drama of *bhoga* and to manifest the drama of *mokṣa* (threefold is the manifestation of the drama of *bhoga* and another threefold is the manifestation of the drama of *mokṣa*), and that person who does not follow this kind of treatment, which is already in process, *moghaṁ pārtha sa jīvati*, his life has no meaning. That person's life has *no* meaning.

Because *yataḥ sa indriyeṣu-eva rama-te nātmani* [comm.], because he is residing only in his own section of organs. He does not go above that.

---

who is unlimited is not true because he is unlimited only [and] not limited. That fullness of God consciousness is found [in one] who is limited and at the same time unlimited also. That is the fullness of God consciousness; fullness of God consciousness is where nothing is excluded. Whatever is excluded, it is also one with that. That is fullness of God consciousness." Swami Lakshmanjoo, *Parātriśikā Vivaraṇa* (1982-85).

DVD 3.1 (1:00:58)

यश्चात्मरतिरेव स्यादात्मतृप्तश्च मानवः ।
आत्मन्येव च सन्तुष्टस्तस्य कार्यं न विद्यते ॥१७॥

yaścātmaratireva syādātmatṛptaśca mānavaḥ /
ātmanyeva ca santuṣṭastasya kāryaṁ na vidyate //17//

And that person who is, on the contrary, *ātma ratireva*, who is focused in his own nature of Parabhairava, and *ātma tṛptaśca,* who is satisfied with Parabhairava, *ātmanyeva ca,* who is actually resting in the Parabhairava state, *tasya kāryaṁ na vidyate,* he has nothing to do in this world. Whatever he does, he does for the sake of play, for the sake of just play. He has no particular thing to be done. Whatever was to be done, he has done that. He has conquered the whole universe.

DVD 3.1 (1:01:57)

नैव तस्य कृतेनार्थो नाकृतेनेह कश्चन ।
न चास्य सर्वभूतेषु कश्चिदर्थव्यपाश्रयः ॥१८॥

naiva tasya kṛtenārtho nākṛteneha kaścana /
na cāsya sarvabhuteṣu kaścidarthavyapāśrayaḥ //18//

If he does [some action], there is no meaning in that, i.e., his doing. If he does not do anything, there is no meaning in that [either]. And he is not dependent to anything in this world.

DVD 3.1 (1:02:34)

कर्मणैव हि संसिद्धिमास्थिता जनकादयः ।
लोकसंग्रहमेवापि संपश्यन्कर्तुमर्हसि ॥१९॥

karmaṇaiva hi saṁsiddhimāsthitā janakādayaḥ /
lokasaṁgrahamevāpi saṁpaśyankartumarhasi //19//

Now, if you say that you are Parabhairava, you don't need to do work, to do action in this world, but you should do, still you should do action. You must not mislead those who are ignorant persons. On the contrary, you must try to behave in *pūja*. Do *pūja* with them.

"Yes, we will do *pūja*, come along!" Have a gathering and go on doing *havan*.

So, it is for the sake of the world, not for him. He does not need to join this *pūja*. But for the sake of ignorant people, he should act like that.

If he does not act, then he should . . . it is his choice if he does not [want to do uplifting actions], but then he should remain out of society. As long as he is placed [i.e., living] in society, he has to act according to society's [wellbeing].

"Come along and we will do *pūja* of the Śiva *liṅga*!" And [he forms a] gathering and [they] do *pūja*. "Internally," [he feels], "I don't need to do Śiva *pūja*," but he *has* to do it.

Chapter 3 Part 2

यद्यदाचरति श्रेष्ठस्तत्तदेवेतरो जनः ।
स यत्प्रमाणं कुरुते लोकस्तदनुवर्तते ॥२०॥

yadyadācarati śreṣṭhastattadevetaro janaḥ /
sa yatpramāṇaṁ kurute lokastadanuvartate //20//

[Lord Kṛṣṇa]: *Śreṣṭha.* The person who is actually established in God consciousness (Parabhairava state), he is *śreṣṭha.* Everybody recognizes him as great, a very highly great person. Whatever he does, people take the copy of his doing. If he does *utpattang* (*utpattang* means if he goes and becomes debauched in the presence of [people])–secretly he can become debauched, there is no fear for him–but in the presence of the world, as long as he is placed in society, he has to work out [i.e., behave] for the sake of society's well-being. He has to work out and maintain good behavior in their presence.

DENISE: Or else they will try to imitate him.

SWAMIJI: Yes.

JONATHAN: He must give a good example.

SWAMIJI: Yes.

Sa yat pramāṇaṁ kurute, whatever he does, *lokas tat anuvartate,* all others will follow his deeds.

[Lord Kṛṣṇa]: "Take My example, O Arjuna, take My example!"

DVD 3.2 (2:11)

न मे पार्थास्ति कर्तव्यं त्रिषु लोकेषु किंचन ।

na me pārthāsti kartavyaṁ triṣu lokeṣu kiñcana /

"O Arjuna, I have nothing to do. I am full. I am always shining in My own nature of Parabhairava state. I have nothing to do."

नानवाप्तमवाप्तव्यं प्रवर्तेऽथ च कर्मणि ॥२१॥

nānavāptamavāptavyaṁ pravarte'tha ca karmaṇi //21//

What for [i.e., for what purpose] I have to do good things? Whatever good I had to obtain, I have obtained already that good. *Pravarte'tha ca karmaṇi*, still I do good *karmas* (actions) for the sake of worldly people so that they are not misled.

DVD 3.2 (2:38)

यदि ह्यहं न वर्तेयं जातु कर्मण्यतन्द्रितः ।
मम वर्त्मानुवर्तेरन्मनुष्याः पार्थ सर्वशः ॥२२॥

yadi hyahaṁ na varteyaṁ jātu karmaṇyatandritaḥ /
mama vartmānuvartante manuṣyāḥ pārtha sarvaśaḥ //22//

It is *vartaṇte*; it is not *varteran*.

If I won't act in actions (good actions) and avoid bad actions in the presence of public, *mama vartmānu varteran manuṣyāḥ,* then all-round, all of the people will copy My actions. Then what will happen next?

DVD 3.2 (3:28)

उत्सीदेयुरिमे लोका न कुर्यां कर्म चेदहम् ।
संकरस्य च कर्ता स्यामुपहन्यामिमाः प्रजाः ॥२३॥

utsīdeyurime lokā na kuryā karma jedaham /
saṅkarasya ca kartā syāmupahanyāmimāḥ prajāḥ //23//

I'll be forced to kill them. I will be forced to sentence them to hell. *Saṅkarasya ca kartā syām*, and I will do bad actions, *upahanyāmimāḥ prajāḥ,* and I will be forced to sentence them to heavy hells so that they don't come out from that.

DVD 3.2 (4:08)

तस्मादसक्तः सततं कार्यं कर्म समाचर ।
असक्तो ह्याचरन्कर्म परमाप्नोति पूरुषः ॥२४॥

tasmādasaktaḥ satataṁ kāryaṁ karma samācara /
asakto hyācarankarma paramāpnoti pūruṣaḥ //24//

So, taking this into your consideration, O Arjuna, you should do all actions in this world before public without being attached to those actions. Internally you should be detached [from] those actions, which you are doing. [Even though] internally you are laughing at those actions (e.g., putting flowers on the Śiva *liṅga* and [reciting], "*dhūpam samarpayāmi namaḥ, gandham, tilakam samarpayāmi namah, puṣpam samarpayāmi namaḥ, naivedyam,*" all of this. Actually it is nonsense for him but in public you should not [disclose] that. You should copy them. You should encourage them to do this. Otherwise they will be, in both ways, fallen down. They [will] have no courage to catch hold of that state of Parabhairava and still they would be of some treatment [i.e., benefit] if they would do some *pūja* or good actions.

DVD 3.2 (5:46)

सक्ताः कर्मण्यविद्वांसो यथा कुर्वन्ति भारत ।
कुर्याद्विद्वांस्तथासक्तश्चिकीर्षुर्लोकसंग्रहम् ॥२५॥

saktāḥ kramaṇyavidvāmso yathā kurvanti bhārata /
kuryādvidvāmstathāsaktaścikīrṣurlokasaṅgraham //25//

prāptaprāpaṇīyasya paripūrṇamanaso'pi karmapravṛttau lokānugrahaḥ prayojanam [comm.]

Prāptaprāpaṇīyasya, what was to be gained, what was to be achieved–[the one] who has achieved that–*paripūrṇa manaso'pi*, whose mind is fully appeased all-round, *karma pravṛttau*, for him to do actions, *lokānugrahaḥ prayojanam*, there is only need [for him] to help people, i.e., those who are ignorant.

Ityatra, in this way, Srī Bhagavān (Lord Kṛṣṇa) puts His own example [and says], "look at Me, how I serve people like this. I do all *pūja* and everything. Whatever everybody has to do, I enjoy [doing it with] them."

> When Indra showered [heavy] thunders [and rains on] Gokul, in the country of Lord Kṛṣṇa, and all of those citizens of Vrindavan and Gokul [were in a fix what to do] and [Lord Kṛṣṇa] held up Mount Govardhan in His hands [to shelter them from the thunder and rain] and told all of those citizens to [help] hold it up with sticks. [He said], "because it is very heavy, so you help Me hold it up with sticks."
>
> Then they were holding it, all those citizens of Govardhan–[Lord Kṛṣṇa] was also holding it–and then they thought that Lord Kṛṣṇa is tired now. Lord Kṛṣṇa is tired now by holding this [so] they implored Lord Kṛṣṇa, "O Lord Kṛṣṇa, *kinnosi*, You are tired, *munjiśāyanam*, You [should] leave this, don't hold it [any longer], *vipraṁobhayam*, we will hold it now, we will hold it now for You. And [Lord Kṛṣṇa] laughed, but He continued to hold it. He laughed. In response, He laughed only but he continued to hold [up the mountain].
>
> But when they insisted, "no, leave it, leave it, You are tired," *śitilabuja*, [Lord Kṛṣṇa] only just kept it a little bit lower. *Paribhoga nividatā-bhāvaśukha,* then there was crack [in the arms] of all those citizens–they were just broken at once. Then He laughed and kept on lifting it. *Kopeṣuhasān harī jāyate*, and He was smiling and holding it and He was so glorified.

In the same way, he has all others do work and join him.

Ityatra bhagavān-ātamānam-eva dṛṣṭāntīkaroti [comm.]. [Abhinavagupta] gives his own examples.

Kiṁca viditavedyaḥ karma cet tyajet, if he shuns altogether all good actions, that [person] who is focused and established in the Parabhairava state, if he at all [does not perform] good actions in the presence of people, *tat-lokanāṁ durbheda evaika-prasiddha-pakṣaśithilitāsthā-bandhatvena-aprarūḍhi-lakṣaṇo jāyate,* then all [those people] will be dashed down. You can't know what will happen to them. They'll simply be focused in [i.e., sentenced to] hell.

Yataḥ karmavāsanām ca na moktuṁ śaknuvanti. The *vāsanā*, the impressions of *karma*, the impressions of *māyā*, the impressions of kith and kin, they can't leave [i.e., transcend]. They have no capacity to leave these impressions of kith and kin [because] they have got attachment, they have got love, they have got *māyā* all-round. *Māyā* has enwrapped them in their own circle.

Jñānadhārāṁ ca nāśrayitum. That Parabhairava state they cannot touch, they cannot even think of Parabhairava state. They don't know, they will only imagine that Parabhairava state [and say], "our Lord Kṛṣṇa is residing in Parabhairava state." They don't know what is Parabhairava state. They only say to people, "He is our Parabhairava" [while] actually not knowing what is Parabhairava, actually. They announce in public that, "our Lord Kṛṣṇa is residing in Parabhairava state!" If someone asks them what is Parabhairava state, they don't know.

Once Mahātma Gandhi had gone to tour in some village (an ignored village). When Mahātma Gandhi asked them, "who is your king, who is your ruler?" They told him, "some ruler must be ruling us. There must be some ruler who rules us."

DENISE: But they didn't know who it was.

SWAMIJI: They didn't know who was ruling them.

In the same way, those who are ignorant persons, they say, "there is some Parabhairava; our Lord Kṛṣṇa is residing in the Parabhairava state," without knowing what Parabhairava actually is.

Yataste na samyagjñānena pūtāḥ; ato buddherbhedanaṁ–vicālanaṁ teṣāṁ paramo'nartha, because they are not purified with the knowledge of Bhairava–those people, ordinary people. So, to discard [i.e., discourage] their nature [i.e., desire] of [performing] their own *pūja*, of their own way of circle [i.e., life-style], is nearly killing them–it is just ruining them. So you should not tell them to elevate their intellectual knowledge. They should remain in that intellectual knowledge, which they have already possessed, and you should support them.

JOHN: Not grace them.

SWAMIJI: Huh?

JOHN: Not raise them?

SWAMIJI: No, not raise them. They cannot rise. How can they rise? They have no such capacity to rise.

DVD 3.2 (15:50)

न बुद्धिभेदं जनयेदज्ञानां कर्मसङ्गिनाम् ।
जोषयेत्सर्वकर्माणि विद्वान्युक्तः समाचरन् ॥२६॥

na buddhibhedaṁ janayedajñānāṁ karmasaṅginām /
joṣayetsarvakarmāṇi vidvānyuktaḥ samācaran //26//

[Lord Kṛṣṇa]: *Buddhibhedaṁ, ajñānāṁ,* [those] who are ignorant, *karma saṅginām,* who are attached to their own limited circle of work, you should cooperate with them. You should not tell them that they are treading on the wrong [path]. *Joṣayet sarva karmāṇi,* you should encourage them to do all those good actions. And in their presence, you should also do these good actions.

DVD 3.2 (16:46)

प्रकृतेः क्रियमाणानि गुणैः कर्माणि भागशः ।
अहंकारविमूढात्मा कर्ताहमिति मन्यते ॥२७॥
तत्त्ववित्तु महाबाहो गुणकर्मविभागयोः ।
गुणा गुणार्थे वर्तन्ते इति मत्वा न सज्जते ॥२८॥

prakṛteḥ kriyamāṇāni guṇaiḥ karmāṇi bhāgaśaḥ /
ahaṅkāravimūḍhātmā kartāhamiti manyate //27//
tattvavittu mahābāho guṇakarmavibhāgayoḥ /
guṇā guṇārthe vartante iti matvā na sajjate //28//

There is only one difference between an ignorant person and that person who is residing in the Parabhairava state. [The one] who has got ego and who is residing in the limited cycle of limitation, he always thinks that, "I have done this, I have done this." And the others who are residing in God consciousness, they say, "although I have done this, I have not done this. I am not the doer. The doers are the inferior cycles of organs. I am not the doer." This is the difference between the one who is residing in the Parabhairava state and the other one who is residing in his limited cycle of being.

प्रकृतेर्गुणसंमूढाः सज्जन्ते गुणकर्मसु ।
नानकृत्स्नविदो मन्दान्कृत्स्नविन्न विचालयेत् ॥२९॥

prakṛterguṇasaṁmūḍhāḥ sajjante guṇakarmasu /
tānakṛtsnavido mandānkṛtsnavinna vicālayet //29//
[not translated][78]

So you should do one thing, if you ask Me, Arjuna:

DVD 3.2 (18:46)

मयि सर्वाणि कर्माणि संन्यस्याध्यात्मचेतसा ।
निराशीर्निर्ममो भूत्वा युध्यस्व विगतज्वरः ॥३०॥

mayi sarvāṇi karmāṇi saṁanyasyādhyātmacetasā /
nirāśīrnirmamo bhūtvā yuddhyasva vigatajvaraḥ //30//

Mayi sarvāṇi karmāṇi. Surrender all of your actions, all your deeds, to Me, who is your master. *Adhyātma cetasā*, focus your mind on Parabhairava state. *Nirāśīr*, don't think [about] your kith and kin; don't be a well-wisher of your kith and kin. *Nirmamo*, don't [attribute] I-ness and my-ness [to] your kith and kin.

"I-ness" and "my-ness" you know?

[To feel that], "these are mine." [This is] I-ness and my-ness.

Yuddhyasva vigata jvaraḥ. Just go on fighting, go on fighting in your own way and you'll become *jīvan mukta*.[79]

78 "They are played by *prakṛti*, so they are attached to all the senses; and they [may try to] do *karmas* (actions) according to *śāstras*. And the one who is elevated should not tell them that you are on the wrong path." *Bhagavad Gītā* (1978).

79 Liberated while embodied. [*Editor's note*]

DVD 3.2 (19:43)

ये मे मतमिदं नित्यमनुवर्तन्ति मानवाः ।
श्रद्धावन्तोऽनसूयन्तो मुच्यन्ते सर्वकर्मभिः ॥ ३१ ॥

ye me matamidaṁ nityamanuvartanti mānavāḥ /
śraddhāvanto'nasūyanto mucyante sarvakarmabhiḥ //31//

Those fortunate persons who act according to this theory of Mine, and they have got full faith in Me, *anasūyanta*, and who do not get attached or detached [to or] from anybody . . .

For instance, you are attached to your own cycle [and] you are detached from other cycles–it is natural.

But don't be like that!

. . . *mucyante sarva karmabhiḥ*, they also are liberated from all good actions and bad actions. They also become Bhairava in the end, i.e., those who have not these two cycles [of attachment and detachment] in tug [with one another].

DVD 3.2 (21:10)

ये त्वेतदभ्यसूयन्तो नानुवर्तन्ति मे मतम् ।
सर्वज्ञानविमूढांस्तान्विद्धि नष्टानचेतसः ॥ ३२ ॥
सदृशं चेष्टते स्वस्याः प्रकृतेर्ज्ञानवानपि ।
प्रकृतिं यान्ति भूतानि निग्रहः किं करिष्यति ॥ ३३ ॥

ye tvetadabhyasūyanto nānuvartanti me matam /
sarvajñānavimūḍhāṁstānviddhi naṣṭānacetasaḥ //32//

sadṛśāṁ ceṣṭate svasyāḥ prakṛterjñānavānapi /
prakṛtiṁ yānti bhūtāni nigrahaḥ kiṁ kariṣyati //33//
[not translated][80]

80 "According to the position of your bodily structure, you act according to your *prakṛti*. You should not say that it is wrong. It is according to the nature of your bodily structure [that] you do like this. *Prakṛtiṁ yānti bhūtāni*. So you should understand that this is *prakṛti* [and] this *prakṛti* has nothing to do with me. I am separate from this.
Nigrahaḥ kiṁ kariṣyati. You cannot stop it; *nigrahaḥ kiṁ kariṣyati*, you

Etasmiṁ jñāne ye na śraddhālava [comm.]. In this Bhairava state of knowledge, [those] who do not digest it, *aviratam̐ janma-maraṇādi-bhayabhāvitatvāt,* in the future they [are subject to the] threat of getting involved in the repeated cycle of births and deaths after their death.

DVD 3.2 (22:22)

इन्द्रियस्येन्द्रियस्यार्थे रागद्वेषौ व्यवस्थितौ ।
तयोर्न वशमागच्छेत्तौ ह्यस्य परिपन्थिनौ ॥३४॥
श्रेयान्स्वधर्मो विगुणः परधर्मात्स्वनुष्ठितात् ।
स्वधर्मे निधनं श्रेयः परधर्मोदयादपि ॥३५॥

indriyasyendriyasyārthe rāgadveṣau vyavasthitau /
tayorna vaśamāgacchettau hyasya paripanthinau //34//
śreyānsvadharmo viguṇaḥ paradharmātsvanuṣṭhitāt /
svadharme nidhanaṁ śreyaḥ paradharmodayādapi //35//

Indriyasi indriyasyārthe. Take [for instance] your organs, O Arjuna! *Indriyasyārthe*, for it's *bhoga*, to feed your organs, *rāga-dveṣau vyavasthitau*, it is essential that there will be *rāga* and *dveṣa*; there will be attachment and there will be detachment. There will be attachment for those who are your kith and kin; there will be detachment for those who are not your kith and kin. *Tayorna vaśamāgacchet,* you should not come into their grip–*rāga* and *dveṣa,* of attachment and detachment–you should not come into their possession. *Tau hyasya paripanthinau,* they are absolutely . . .

DENISE: Misleading?

SWAMIJI: . . . misleading, and they are *śatru* (*śatru* means enemies), they are your enemies of God consciousness; they will spoil the treasure of your God consciousness. They will never allow you to rise in the cycle of God consciousness.

So it is better to reside in your own nature and it is better for you to die in your own nature, i.e., your nature of Parabhairava state.

---

can never stop that." *Bhagavad Gītā* (1978).

Now Arjuna puts a question:

DVD 3.2 (24:44)

अथ केन प्रयुक्तोऽयं पापं चरति पूरुषः ।
अनिच्छमानोऽपि बलादाक्रम्येव नियोजितः ॥ ३६ ॥

atha kena prayukto'yaṁ pāpaṁ carati pūruṣaḥ /
anicchamāno'pi balādākramyeva niyojitaḥ //36//

Now, I have got this question: I think I have found in my own consciousness [that] there are two aspects in one's own body. I have understood that there are two aspects in one's own body. Who has understood? Arjuna. Arjuna says I have understood that there are two aspects: one is saying, "do this," and another one says, "don't do this, it is bad." Who says "don't" and who says "yes"?

And afterwards it happens, *anichamāno'pi balād*, without willing to do [something bad], I go on, I thrust into doing it [anyway]. Then after doing that, I repent, "what have I done?"

Who are these aspects? I have not understood who they are. There are two parties inside of me. One gives me encouragement to do [some action] and another party encourages me not to do [that action]. And in the long run, I do it, I commit that [action]. But after committing that [action], I repent, "why have I done this?"

Who is that person who has committed this and thrown me in this position?

Pāpaṁ pāpatayā vidannapi. If *pāpa*, a sinful act–I already know that a sinful act is already a sinful act [and that I] should not do it–somebody asks me to do it [saying], "do it. What is it to you? Do it. For your pleasure, do it!" And some other party comes and he says, "no, don't do it, it is bad."

Who is [making] this trouble?

Atrottaraṁ'satyapi svadharme hṛdisthe āgantukāvaraṇakṛto 'yaṁ viplavaḥ, na tu tadabhāvakṛtaḥ [comm.]. And the answer for that [question], Lord Kṛṣṇa places before him, before Arjuna.

Now Lord Kṛṣṇa answers Arjuna.

DVD 3.2 (27:55)

काम एष क्रोध एष रजोगुणसमुद्भवः ।
महाशनो महापाप्मा विद्ध्येनमिह वैरिणम् ॥३७॥

kāma eṣa krodha eṣa rajoguṇasamuddhavaḥ /
mahāśano mahāpāpmā viddhyenamiha vairiṇam //37//

It is just *kāma* (*kāma* is desire) and *krodha* (wrath). For instance, you have got *kāma* (*kāma* means desire), you want to have [some] thing. When you don't get it, you struggle to [obtain it]. After great struggling and spending so much money–this is the [outcome of] desire for doing that, achieving that [object of desire]–when it does not take place, then wrath (*krodha*) encircles [you]. You don't want to talk to anybody afterwards if it does not happen.

There was one prostitute; her name was Madhāllasa. Madhāllasa, she was the greatest prostitute. She was [well]-known and her fees were tremendous fees. In the meantime, Śukadeva, Vyāsa's son, was passing on the roadside. He was going somewhere but he was tired. He was tired, he was *brahmachari*, he was filled with the Bhairava state of being.
Who?
JONATHAN: Vyāsa's son.
SWAMIJI: Vyāsa's son. Vyāsa means who was . . .
JOHN: Compiler of this *Gīta*.
SWAMIJI: *Mahābhārata*.
He was walking, he was just [passing by]. He had no desire for sex at all, from his very childhood. He didn't know what sex was and he didn't know anything about sexual intercourse. He had no knowledge of that. He was above that. He was residing in his own way in God consciousness. And he was a *brahmachari*, he was brilliant, he was shining just like Lord Śiva, and he was walking on the roadside. And this poor girl thought, "he wants to come to me."
Who?
DENISE: Vyāsa's son.

SWAMIJI: Vyāsa's son, Sukadeva.
And she directed him from her window on the [side of the] market to come. He said, "all right, all right I'll come." He didn't know what for he was called. And she lost interest in all of her friends, at once, as soon as he stepped into her bedroom.
Who?
JONATHAN: Vyāsa's son.
SWAMIJI: Śukadeva.
And [with] whatever best bedding she had possessed [after] all of these years of doing this job, she decorated her bed for him to lie down. He stepped into that room and laid down, flat. He was tired. Then she wanted to press [i.e., massage] his legs. She pressed his legs with great reverence, with great love. She said, "he is my real friend. I don't want any money from him. It is only this blissful state that I have received from him." Then she pressed him for about one hour and a half and in the meantime any friend who came to see her with fees [saw that] she had locked from the inside all of the doors and windows.
Who?
DENISE: She.
SWAMIJI: She had locked [her doors and windows from the] inside, and she didn't allow anybody to come inside. She wanted him only.
He said, "I want to go, I want to go now."
She said, "Where?"
He said, "Just here."
She thought that he is going to urinate or something and he will again return.
Then she opened the window and saw him passing, passing, and passing and passing until he disappeared altogether. He didn't return afterwards at all and it took her [a long time to fall asleep]. It was eleven at night [when he left] and up to three or four a.m. in the morning, she was *bas*, thinking of him. And he didn't return. When he didn't return, then she went to sleep. As soon as she slept she went into a trance and became Parabhairava, she became one with Parabhairava. Then she was called the greatest *devī* residing in Parabhairava state. This was his grace.

So this is the grace, i.e., how He showers grace to [both] worthy and nonworthy. Everybody has the right to occupy that great state of wealth, the Parabhairava state.

For the aspirant of truth, [these two] should be avoided: *kāma* is desire and *krodha* (wrath). [Anger arises] when [your desire] is not fulfilled. You get annoyed.

Now Arjuna places his question for this.

DVD 3.2 (35:49)

भवत्येष कथं कृष्ण कथं चैव विवर्धते ।
किमात्मकः किमाचारस्तन्ममाचक्ष्व पृच्छतः ॥३८॥

bhavatyeṣā katham kṛṣṇa katham caiva vivardhate /
kimātmakaḥ kimācārastanmamācakṣva pṛcchataḥ //38//

O Lord Kṛṣṇa, how does it appear–this *kāma* and *krodha*? *Katham caiva vivardhate*, how does it rise? *Kimātmaka*, what is the nature of this enemy? *Kimācāra*, what is the activity of this enemy? Please explain it to me so that I understand who is this enemy inside of our consciousness. *Asya cotpattau kimkāranam*, how does it appear? How does it rise in one's own mind? *Vardhane ca ko hetuḥ*, how does it increase day by day? *Svarūpam cāsya kīdṛk*, what is the nature of [its] formation? How does it get formed? When [they] take a position and [are] established in one's own body, how does he act then? *Iti praśnāḥ*, these are my questions. Please clear these questions for me.

श्रीभगवानुवाच

śrī bhagavān uvāca

Now Śrī Bhagavān (Lord Kṛṣṇa) places its answer.

DVD 3.2 (37:37)

एष सूक्ष्मः परः शत्रुर्देहिनामिन्द्रियैः सह ।
सुखतन्त्र इवसीनो मोहयन्पार्थ तिष्ठति ॥३९॥

eṣa sūkṣmaḥ paraḥ śatrurdehināmindriyaiḥ saha /
sukhatantra ivāsīno mohayanpārtha tiṣṭhati //39//

This is the supreme enemy (*śatru*) of the aspirant of truth, *dehinām*, [for] one who has a body, one who has maintained a body, one who is existing in a body. *Indriyaiḥ saha*, along with the classification of all of his organs, it is established in one corner of his intellect, *sukhatantra ivāsīno,* and creates *sukhābhāsa.*[81] Actually it is not *sukha,* it is not pleasure, but it gives this temptation of pleasure, [that] there will be pleasure. In fact, [this enemy] is depriving you of God consciousness and keeps you absolutely away from its nature.

This is a very subtle enemy. *Atha*, when it rises, you cannot mark how it rose in your intellect. It rises unknowingly. Secretly it rises.

DVD 3.2 (39:26)

कामक्रोधमयो घोरः स्तम्भहर्षसमुद्भवः ।
अहंकारोऽभिमानात्मा दुस्तरः पापकर्मभिः ॥४०॥

kāmakrodhamayo dhoraḥ stambhaharṣasamudbhavaḥ /
ahaṁkāro'bhimānātmā dustaraḥ pāpakarmabhiḥ //40//

Stambhaharṣa samudbhavaḥ, and it gets strength by *stambha* and *harṣa. Stambha* means *kulādyabhimānaḥ*, [to think that], "I am such and such a person." *Harṣa* means *aham īdṛśaḥ*, "I am very great!" These [manifestations of the] ego are there.

ata evāḥ – ahaṁkāra iti
[comm. intro to 41st *śloka*]

It is only due to ego. Ego gives its rise day by day–increases. How does it [affect] him?

DVD 3.2 (40:11)

हर्षमस्य निवर्त्यैष शोकमस्य ददाति च ।
भयं चास्य करोत्येष मोहयंस्तु मुहुर्मुहुः ॥४१॥

81 The appearance of pleasure. [*Editor's note*]

harṣamasya nivartyaiṣa śokamasya dadāti ca /
bhayaṁ cāsya karotyeṣa mohayamstu muhurmuhuḥ //41//

All of his joy, [this enemy] extracts at once. All joy is gone in him by this. This is the [enemy's] activity inside the one [in whom] it appears. *Śokamasya dadāti ca*, it gives him grief. In place of *harṣa*, in place of joy, it gives him grief. Joy is extracted and grief is produced by [this enemy]. *Bhayaṁ cāsya karotyeṣa*, and there is the threat that, "I may die, that something bad will happen to me." *Mohayamstu muhurmuhuḥ*, and it keeps him away from God consciousness. It keeps him away from the touch of God. This is the nature [of the enemy].

Ata eva ca garvādvardhate'bhimānasvabhāvaḥ [comm.]. It is *garu* (*garu* means ego). *Sukhabuddhiprakāreṇa ca jāyate*, by producing some vision of pleasure, [the ego] gives rise [to the enemy] inside.

Iti trayaḥ praśnāḥ parihṛtāḥ, these three questions were answered altogether.

DVD 3.2 (41:50)

स एष कलुषी क्षुद्रश्छिद्रप्रेक्षी धनञ्जय ।
रजःप्रवृत्तो मोहात्मा मनुष्याणामुपद्रवः ॥४२॥

sa eṣa kaluṣī kṣudraśchidraprekṣī dhanañjaya /
rajaḥpravṛtto mohātmā manuṣyāṇāmupadravaḥ //42//

O Dhanañjaya, O Arjuna! This enemy is *kaluṣī* (*kaluṣī* means a very dirty enemy). *Kṣudra, kṣudra* means it has no substance at all; it is *kṣudra* [which] means inside it is hollow.

What is hollow?

JONATHAN: Hollow.

SWAMIJI: Hollow.

Chidraprekṣī, [the enemy] only watches [to find] where is the leakage, by which leakage I will enter and destroy all of his future blissful fruits in *ihaloka*, in this life and hereafter (*paraloka*). [The enemy] watches [for] those leakages, by which leakage [it] will enter into his consciousness and destroy his God consciousness altogether. *Rajaḥ pravṛtto*, and it is strengthened by *rajoguṇa. Rajoguṇa* gives its strength. *Mohātmā*, it is just *mohātmā*; *mohātmā* [means] its nature is to ignore God altogether, for good. *Manuṣyāṇāmupadravaḥ*, it is really *upadrava* (*upadrava* means torture), torture for everybody.

Sa eṣa cchidrāṇi prekṣate [comm.]. [The enemy] watches [for] the leakage by which leakage [it] will enter and destroy his whole status of wellbeing.

Amunā cchidreṇāsyehalokaparalokau nāśayāmi. [The enemy says], "by this leakage I will destroy [his] *sukha* (pleasure) of this life and hereafter. I will destroy [all of] his peace of mind, here and hereafter."

Tathā ca mokṣa dharmeṣu. It is *mokṣa dharmeṣu*. In *Mahābhārata*, it is said:

> *yatkrodhano yajate yaddadāti*
> *yadvā tapastapyate yajjuhoti /*
> *vaivasvatastaddharate'sya sarvaṁ*
> *moghaḥ śramo bhavati krodhanasya //*

Yatkrodhana [means] that person who is the embodiment of wrath (it is said in the *Mahābhārata*), *yajate*, whatever he offers in *havan*, whatever *havan* he does, *yat dadāti*, whatever alms he gives to people [who are] needful, *yadvā tapastapyate*, whatever penance he undergoes for some long period (*tapasya*), *yat juhoti*, whatever *āhuti* (oblations) he offers in *havan*, *vaivasvatastaddharate'sya sarvaṁ*, *vaivasvata*, Lord Śiva withdraws everything from [one who is overcome by wrath]. All of the fruit of these *tapasyas* is withdrawn by Lord Śiva.

So, the one who is embodiment of *krodha* . . .

JOHN: *Krodha* takes you away.

SWAMIJI: Takes away all of your glory. All of your glory is lost by *krodha* (wrath).

JONATHAN: Even if you are fully established in that?

SWAMIJI: Yes.

JONATHAN: And it still takes it away?

SWAMIJI: It does not take it away, but it [becomes] subsided. It is subsided for the time being.

Now 43rd [*śloka*]:

DVD 3.2 (46:52)

धूमेनाव्रियते वह्निर्यथादर्शो मलेन च ।
यथोल्वेनावृतो गर्भस्तथानेनायमावृतः ॥४३॥

dhūmenāvriyate vahniryathādarśo malena ca /
yatholvenāvṛto garbhastathānenāyamāvṛtaḥ //43//

[Lord Kṛṣṇa]: Just as the shining flames of fire are covered by smoke and *yatha adarśaḥ malena ca,* just as a mirror is covered with dust over it and you cannot see your shape (i.e., reflection) at all in that mirror, *yatholvenāvṛto garbha*, just as this *garbha* (the womb), [within which] that child is *āvṛta*, is covered with that covering of the womb, *tatha anena ayamāvṛtaḥ*, in the same way, *anena*, this *krodha* also covers this God consciousness. It is gone. It does not show its effect. It is there but it does not show its effect [i.e., glory].

DVD 3.2 (48:34)

आवृतं ज्ञानमेतेन ज्ञानिनो नित्यवैरिणा ।
कामरूपेणा कौन्तेय दुष्पूरेणानलेन च ॥४४॥

āvṛtaṁ jñānametena jñānino nityavairiṇā /
kāmarūpeṇa kaunteya duṣpūreṇānalena ca //44//

This is *nitya vairiṇā*, the eternal enemy of *jñāni*. *Jñāni* means [one] who is filled with Bhairava knowledge. This *kāma* or *krodha* is the eternal enemy of *jñāni*, and who has *jñānam etena āvṛtaṁ*, *jñāna* is covered by [this enemy]. *Duṣpūreṇānalena ca*, and this is *duṣpūreṇa analena ca,* just as in fire, whatever you throw [into it], whatever you offer [into it], it burns, it burns, it burns everything burns. [Likewise], there is no end of this *kāma* (desire).

Najatukāma kāmanāṁ upabhogena śameti.[82] For instance, if you want to go to cinema, if you want to go for [having] some pleasure, if you want to [watch] the TV, you will [want to] see TV always; you won't [want to] remain without seeing TV. You will

82 *Viṣṇudharmaśāstra.*

never be filled; your hunger [will never be satiated].

In the same way, just as fire, whatever you throw into it, the fire gives more flames, more flames, it [increases] in power., and the more you keep it without giving it [more fuel], then [the fire] subsides. Then it is calmed and it becomes one with the ashes, and [finally] there is no fire. The fire subsides altogether.

DVD 3.2 (51:17)

इन्द्रियाणि मनो बुद्धिरस्याधिष्ठानमुच्यते ।
एतैर्विमोहयत्येष ज्ञानमावृत्य देहिनम् ॥४५॥

indriyāṇi mano buddhirasyādhiṣṭhānamucyate /
etairvimohayatyeṣa jñānamāvṛtya dehinam //45//

This is the 45th *śloka*.

It's seat, I will tell you what is its seat–the enemy, *kāma* and *krodha*–where this enemy is seated in one's body.

These three: organs, mind, and intellect are its seat in one's body.[83] *Etair vimohayatyeṣa*, by [their establishment in] these three, *kāma* and *krodha vimohayatyeṣa*, destroys the God consciousness of *ātma* (the soul) and keeps him away from the knowledge of God consciousness.

Ādau indriyeṣu satsu tiṣṭhati [comm.]. First it steps into organs. For instance, *yathā cakṣuṣā śatrur dṛṣṭa*, just [as] when you see your enemy with your eyes, you lose your temper at once. When you see an enemy, you can't remain [calm] and you lose your temper at once.

Do you understand?

DENISE: Yes, you start to breathe heavily. Your heart beats harder.

SWAMIJI: You breathe heavily and [think], "I want to quit [i.e., leave] that place at once. Because I would kill that enemy but if I have not the power to kill him, still I want to quit from that place. I don't want to stand there at all." So, it appears in the organs first.

Yathā cakṣuṣā śatrurdṛṣṭa indriyapradeśe eva krodhamāt-

83 "Ego has become victim of this, he is crushed by this." *Bhagavad Gītā* (1978).

mano janayati [comm.]. First, [this anger] gives shape [i.e., arises] in *indriyas* (organs). *Tato manasi*, then it treads in the mind [where thoughts arise regarding] what to do, what is the remedy to get rid of this enemy. *Tato buddhau*, then it passes in the intellect, [which discerns] what is to be decided for him [to do], e.g., if he has no power to kill [his enemy] because [the enemy] is also powerful; he won't let him kill [him easily]. *Etad-dvāreṇa mohaṁ janayan jñānaṁ nāśayati.* So [his] God consciousness is subsided, it is shattered to pieces. There is no hope for maintaining God consciousness at all for him. God consciousness is shattered to pieces by this enemy.[84]

Asya nivāraṇe upāyamāha, now I will tell you how to get rid of this enemy.

DVD 3.2 (55:39)

तस्मात्त्वमिन्द्रियाण्यादौ नियम्य भरतर्षभ ।
पाप्मानं प्रजहीह्येनं ज्ञानविज्ञाननाशनम् ॥४६॥

tasmāttvamindriyāṇyādau niyamya bharatarṣabha /
pāpmānaṁ prajahīhyenaṁ jñānavijñānanāśanam //46//

Tasmāt ādau indriyāṇi niyamya [comm.]. Whenever you see your enemy with your eyes, just quit [from that place] and sit in your bedroom. Lock [the door from the] inside and get [your anger] subsided. Don't say a word to him. This is the best way of getting rid of this enemy.

If you stay there, something bad will happen. You will lose consciousness [and yell], "*haaa*!" Your lips will tremble and you will dash down your father, you will dash down your mother, you will dash down your kith and kin. And you will slap them and you will be furious just [like a] wild beast [moving] all-around in your house. So it is better for you to quit and lock yourself inside.

And it is *jñāna* and *vijñāna*, [the enemy] destroys *jñāna* and *vijñāna*. *Jñāna* means God consciousness; *vijñāna* means the trick of achieving God consciousness. The trick of achieving God consciousness and God consciousness, both are destroyed by this

84 "The more you are indulging with *kāma* and *krodha*, [the more] you are kept away from God consciousness." Ibid.

enemy. *Ataḥ pāpmānaṁ krodhaṁ tyaja*. So you must abandon [*kāma* and *krodha*] for good.[85]

This is the essence of this [verse].

Atra yuktiṁ śloka dvayenāha. Now, [Lord Kṛṣṇa] places two *ślokas* [that explain] how to get rid of this enemy.

DVD 3.2 (58:14)

इन्द्रियाणि पराण्याहुरिन्द्रियेभ्यः परं मनः ।
मनसस्तु परा बुद्धिर्यो बुद्धेः परतस्तु सः ॥४७॥
एवं बुद्धेः परं बुद्ध्वा संस्तभ्यात्मानमात्मना ।
जहि शत्रुं महाबाहो कामरूपं दुरासदम् ॥४८॥

indriyāṇi parāṇyāhurindriyebhyaḥ paraṁ manaḥ /
manasastu parā buddhiryo buddheḥ paratastu saḥ //47//
evaṁ buddheḥ paraṁ buddhā saṁstabhyātmānamātmanā /
jahi śatruṁ mahābāho kāmarūpaṁ durāsadam //48//

Just think [to] yourself, *indriyāṇi parāṇyāhur*, "these are organs, which see this enemy, but these organs are not mine." *Indriyāṇi parāṇyāhur indriyebhyaḥ paraṁ manaḥ*. And *mana* (mind) has nothing to do with *indriyās*; the mind is separate from organs. And the intellect is absolutely separate from the mind. *Yo buddheḥ paratastu saḥ*, and my nature, my *ātma*, is absolutely separate from all of these three. So, my soul is above these three. Why should I come into their grip, i.e., *indriyas* (organs), *mana* (mind), and intellect (*buddhi*)?

Jahi śatruṁ, [so] kill this enemy, O Arjuna, which is *kāma rūpaṁ durāsadam*, which is not conquered by anybody in this world [i.e., which is difficult to conquer].

Evamindriya-utpannena krodhena kathaṁ manaso buddher-ātmano vā kṣobhaḥ iti paryālocayedi . . . [comm.]. You should think over it: how *ātma* can be moved by the activity of these three organs?

Which organs?

85 "For instance, your eyes are open and you see a beautiful girl. Temptation is produced in your mind. No, don't allow any temptation there, *bas,* ignore that. This is what you have to do." Ibid.

DENISE: Mind, intellect, and organs.

SWAMIJI: Yes.

[Abhinavagupta]: *Rahasyavidāṁ tvayamāśayaḥ.* Some elevated souls commentated upon these *ślokas* in this way where I have no objection, where I have sympathy. *Buddheryaḥ paratra vartate paro'haṁkāraḥ.* That is, above *buddhi*, there is universal-I; above *buddhi*, there is universal-I. Before [the existence of *buddhi* exists the] universal-I [who knows], "I am *kāma,* I am *krodha*, I am everything, I am everything. What [difference does it make] to me? I am everything! What can only *krodha* do or *kāma* do to me? I will be unmoved." So it is universality.

This is Abhinavagupta's favorite procedure.

Do you understand?

Para ahaṁkāra, supreme universal *aham* (universal-I), universal-I consciousness is beyond that. In universal-I consciousness, this is also digested in one corner.

DENISE: *Kāma* and *krodha.*

SWAMIJI: *Kāma* (desire) and *krodha* (wrath) is nothing. *Kāma* and *krodha* is just one ray of that [universal-I]. For instance, there is a big ocean, there are tides, there are bubbles, like this, [*kāma* and *krodha*] are one bubble. How will one bubble agitate this ocean? It can't be agitated. It is [only one] bubble. What can one bubble do? So you should be above that. You should remain above that in universal God consciousness.

That way also there is no fear of *kāma* and *krodha.*

अत्र संग्रहश्लोकः

atra saṇgraha ślokaḥ

This is the conclusion of this chapter.

DVD 3.2 (1:03:16)

धनानि दारान्देहं च योऽन्यत्वेनाधिगच्छति ।
किं नाम तस्य कुर्वन्ति क्रोधाद्याश्चित्तविभ्रमाः ॥३॥

dhanāni dārāndehaṁ ca yo'nyatvenādhigacchati /
kiṁ nāma tasya kurvanti krodhādyāścittavibhramāḥ //3//

|| Concluding *śloka* of 3rd chapter ||

My property, my wife, my body, my kith and kin–I am not my body, I am not my bank balance, I am not my child, I am not my brothers, I am not my father, I am not my husband, I am not my wife–I am separate and above these! *Kiṁ nāma tasya kurvanti krodhādyā citta vibhramāḥ*, how can *krodha* or *kāma* rise there in universality, in universal God consciousness? This is the conclusion.

Here ends the 3rd chapter of the *Bhagavad Gītā*.

Chapter 4 Part 1

श्रीभगवानुवाच

śrī bhagavān uvāca

The fourth discourse.

DVD 4.1 (00:04)

एवं विवस्वते योगं प्रोक्तवानहमव्ययम् ।
विवस्वान्मनवे प्राह मनुरिक्ष्वाकवेऽब्रवीत् ॥१॥
एवं परम्पराप्राप्तमिमं राजर्षयो विदुः ।
स कालेनैव महता योगो नष्टः परन्तप ॥२॥

evaṁ vivasvate yogaṁ proktavānahamavyayaṁ /
vivasvānmanave prāha manurikṣvākave'bravīt //1//
evaṁ paramparāprāptamimaṁ rājarṣayo viduḥ /
sa kālenaiva mahatā yogo naṣṭaḥ parantapa //2//

Evaṁ, this way, *aham*, I (I means Lord Kṛṣṇa is speaking), *evaṁ avyayaṁ yogaṁ*, this *yoga*, this *karma yoga*, I was, in My last period of time, *vivasvate proktavān,* Vivasvate, I was explaining this *yoga* to Vivasvate (Vivasvate means the sun, sun . . . I mean the sun, Vivasvān). I explained this *yoga* to Vivasvān (Vivasvān means this *sūrya*) when he was . . . many, many, numberless centuries beforehand. I spoke this, I explained this *yoga* to Vivasvān.

Vivasvān manave prāha, and Vivasvān passed on this [knowledge of] *yoga* to Manuprajāpati. *Manurikṣvākave'bravīt*, Manuprajāpati explained it to Ikṣvāku King. *Evaṁ param parā-prāptam*, in this way it was passed on, from time to time, *imaṁ*, this *yoga*, *rājarṣayo viduh*, [to] *rājarṣi.*

Rājarṣi means those *ṛṣis* (saints) who were kings, Kṣatriya (warrior) *ṛṣis*. Because *rājarṣi* means the one who has the power of force to make you believe [something]. As when there is military rule, by miltary force you [are forced] to accept [their dictates]. In the same way, those *ṛṣis* who were monarchs, they understood this *yoga*.

Then, after many centuries passed on, this *yoga* was finished. Nobody knew this *yoga*. *Etacca guru-paramparayā prāptam-api* [comm.]. This *yoga* was passed on from one master to another master, that master to another master, *adyatve naṣṭaṁ*, and now it is finished. Now, nobody knows this *yoga*.

Ityanena bhagavānasya jñānasya durlabhatāṁ gauravaṁ ca pradarśayati. Lord Kṛṣṇa speaks to Arjuna, that this knowledge is very ancient knowledge and it is very important knowledge.

DVD 4.1 (04:12)

स एवायं मया तेऽद्य योगः प्रोक्तः पुरातनः ।

sa evāyaṁ mayā te'dya yogaḥ proktaḥ purātanaḥ /3a

That *yoga* I have explained to you now, at this time, at this moment. Today, I have explained to you the same *yoga*, which I had in the past told to all of those *devas* and *ṛṣis* and *brahmaṛṣis*.

Why have I told you?

Who are you?

What qualifications do you have?

भक्तोऽसि मे सखा चेति रहस्यमेतदुत्तमम् ॥३॥

bhakto'si me sakhā ceti rahasyametaduttamam //3//

Bhakto'si me, you are My devotee. *Sakhā ca,* you are My friend also. You are My devotee and you are My friend, both. *Etat uttamam rahasyam,* this supreme secret I have explained to you.

Now Abhinavagupta commentates upon these two things: you are my "devotee" and you are my "friend".

Friendship does not count, devotion counts. As a disciple, disciple must have . . . the weight is in devotion, weight is not put in friendship. Friendship is only vague. [Lord Kṛṣṇa says], "if you were [only] My friend, I would not have explained [this secret] to you at all. [But] you are [also] My devotee. *Bhakto'si me sakhā ceti*, you are My devotee and friend; *tvaṁ bhakto matparamaḥ*, you are My devotee (*paramaḥ* means supreme), *sakhā ca*, and you are My friend also."

"Also" means *ca śabdenā*; "also", by this [word] "also," *ānvācaya ucyate–ānvācaya*, it is Pāṇini's grammar; the ruling of Pāṇini's grammar, it is called *ānvācaya–ānvācaya* means when [something] is not predominant. For instance, "*bhikṣāmaṭa gāṁcānaya*"[86]–this is explained in Pāṇini's grammar as an example–when *guru* says, *guru* asks his disciple, "O disciple, go and collect alms for us from door to door. You beg, you collect things (eatable things) from door to door–go on. Because we have to eat food, we have to cook food. Get wood from the forest, get rice, get *dhal*, get *channa*, get everything . . . all utensils [with] which we will cook here and eat. And at the same time, if you find our cow who is grazing in the fields–because there was not so much congestion of people; all [land] was open [so the cow] was grazing on grass)–if you find the cow, you should *also* collect her to the *ashram*." That is *ānvācaya*–it is not important! Importance is [placed upon] collecting food and everything. [Retrieving the cow] is not important.

In the same way, [Lord Kṛṣṇa tells Arjuna], "you are My devotee–that is important! Not as friendship. I would not have explained to you the real secrets of Shaivism [if you were only My friend]."

Do you understand?

Evaṁ bhaktiratra guruṁ prati pradhānaṁ, na sakhitvamapīti [comm.]. This friendship does not count. Devotion counts.

Arjuno bhagavatsvarūpaṁ jānannapi. This Arjuna (this Abhinavagupta says), *arjuna bhagavat svarūpaṁ jānannapi*, although he [already] knows the state of Lord Kṛṣṇa, *loke sphuṭīkartu pṛcchati*, just to throw light in the world, he asks [the following question] just to . . .

JONATHAN: Uplift other people.

SWAMIJI: Yes.

86 Jayaditya's *Kāśikāvṛttī*. 2.2.29, a commentary on Pāṇini's grammar. [*Editor's note*]

DVD 4.1 (09:28)

अर्जुन उवाच

arjuna uvāca

अपरं भवतो जन्म परं जन्म विवस्वतः ।
कथमेवं विजानीयां त्वमादौ प्रोक्तवनिति ॥४॥

aparaṁ bhavato janma paraṁ janma vivasvataḥ /
kathamevaṁ vijānīyāṁ tvamādau proktavāniti //4//

O Lord Kṛṣṇa, *aparaṁ bhavato janma*, You were born now, You were born anew in this period. *Paraṁ janma vivasvataḥ*, Vivasvān was born long ago, so many centuries ago. *Katham evaṁ vijānīyāṁ*, how can I understand [i.e., believe] that You were explaining this *yoga* to him? You were not there. How were You there and explaining this *yoga* to him? But I was not [there], so I [cannot] know about that.

श्रीभगवानुवाच

śrī bhagavān uvāca

Now Śrī Bhagavān places the answer before Arjuna.

DVD 4.1 (10:28)

बहूनि मे व्यतीतानि जन्मानि तव चार्जुन ।
तान्यहं वेद सर्वाणि न त्वं वेत्थ परन्तप ॥५॥

bahūni me vyatītāni janmāni tava cārjuna /
tānyahaṁ veda sarvāṇi na tvaṁ vettha parantapa //5//

This is the 5th *śloka*.

Bahūni me vyatītāni janmāni tava cārjunam. I have passed [through] so many lives and you have also passed [through] so many lives. *Tānyahaṁ veda sarvāṇi*, all those previous lives of

Mine, Myself, I know [each of them] one by one, *na tvaṁ vettha parantapa,* but you don't know, you have forgotten. You have forgotten your previous lives. You were also born in previous lives, numberless times.

DVD 4.1 (11:20)

अजोऽपि सन्नव्ययात्मा भूतानामीश्वरोऽपि सन् ।
प्रकृतिं स्वामधिष्ठाय संभवाम्यात्ममायया ॥ ६ ॥

ajo'pi sannavyayātmā bhūtānāmīśvaro'pi san /
prakṛtiṁ svāmadhiṣṭāya saṁbhavāmyātmamāyayā //6//

Ajo'pi san, if I am not . . . if I am unborn, I am never born; *avyayātmā*, I am imperishable, I don't die at all; *bhūtānām īśvaro'pi san,* if I am the Lord of Lords of everybody; *prakṛtiṁ svāmadhiṣṭhāya*, My *prakṛti*, My nature, I hold My nature within My Self; *saṁbhavāmi ātmamāyayā,* I am born by the *svātantrya śakti* of My free will–I get birth. When I am born, I will make you understand when I take My birth in this world, again and again.

DVD 4.1 (12:36)

यदा यदा हि धर्मस्य ग्लानिर्भवति भारत ।
अभ्युत्थानमधर्मस्य तदात्मांशं सृजाम्यहम् ॥ ७ ॥

yadā yadā hi dharmasya glānirbhavati bhārata /
abhyutthānamadharmasya tadātmāṁśaṁ sṛjāmyaham //7//

O Arjuna, from time to time when *dharmasya glānirbhavati*, all *dharma* (all duty), which was to be held up by people who are created in this world, [when] they neglect their duty, *abhyutthānam adharmasya*, and they create this "*utphathām tamasha*", i.e., they kill each other and they fight and they become demons and *tat ātmāṁśaṁ sṛjāmyaham*, at that time I create My one ray, one ray to destroy all the devils in this world.

Śrībhagavānkila . . . this is Abhinavagupta's commentary. *Śrībhagavānkila pūrṇaṣāḍ-guṇyatvāt*, Lord Kṛṣṇa is *pūrṇa ṣāḍ guṇyatvāt,* He has six aspects: *sarvajñatā*, *tṛptiḥ*, *anādibodha*, *svatantratā*, *nityamaluptaśaktiḥ*, *ananta śaktiśca ṣaḍāhur aṅgāni maheṣvara*. These are six aspects of Lord Śiva.

Sarvajñatā (all-knowledge), *tṛtpti* (always full, no appetite *tṛtpti*), *anādibodha* (knowledge, eternal knowledge, which has no end, which has no beginning, which has no span of time; *anādi-bodha*, and knowledge which is *anādi*, which is beginningless and endless and span-less), *svatantratā*, He is always *svatantrā* (absolutely independent), *alupta śakti*, and His energy does not get exhausted by utilizing it. If He utilizes His energy, His energy does not become weakened. These are the six great aspects of Lord Kṛṣṇa.[87]

So the 7th *śloka* is finished.

[Lord Kṛṣṇa]: "What for I create My ray here in this world?"

DVD 4.1 (15:40)

परित्राणाय साधूनां विनाशाय च दुष्कृताम् ।
धर्मसंस्थापनार्थाय संभवामि युगे युगे ॥८॥

paritrāṇāya sādhūnāṁ vināśāya ca duṣkṛtām /
dharmasamsthāpanārthāya saṁbhavāmi yuge yuge //8//

To protect those who are saints here and to destroy those who are sinners. For that [reason], I appear *yuge yuge*, from one *yuga* (age) to another *yuga*, from that *yuga* to another *yuga*, I appear again and again.

Dharma samsthāpanārthāya, to see that *dharma* (*sanātana*

87 "Lord Kṛṣṇa creates his *aṁśa,* His one spark, one *aṁśa* of His consciousness in this universe, although He is *pūrṇaṣāḍguṇyatvāt*, He has got six great qualities. . . . Although He possesses these six great qualities, and *śarīra saṁparkamātra rahito'pi*, He is not touched with the contact of body. He is never touched with the contact of body. He will never maintain body; He is bodiless. But, *sthiti kāritatvāt-kātiṇkatayā*, because of His greatness and because of His pity for others, He creates Himself, His nature in body. He puts Himself in body just for elevating mankind. It is why He has [said] *aṁśa* (ray); He creates only one spark of that being, of His being. He does not create the whole consciousness, body of His consciousness. It is only one tiny particle." *Bhagavad Gītā* (1978).

dharma, the ancient *dharma*), the ancient duty is established properly in this world.

DVD 4.1 (16:32)

जन्म कर्म च मे दिव्यमेवं यो वेत्ति तत्त्वतः ।
त्यक्त्वा देहं पुनर्जन्म नैति मामेति सोऽर्जुन ॥९॥

janma karma ca me divyamevaṁ yo vetti tattvataḥ /
tyaktvā dehaṁ punarjanma naiti māmeti so'rjuna //9//

Anybody who realizes that My being born and My activities are all divine–My birth is divine and My activities are divine–whoever realizes this divinity of Mine in [My] action and in My birth, no matter if he is a limited soul, but he will also get dissolved in My Being at the end of his life. *Māmeti so'rjuna,* and he becomes one with Me.

Ata evāsya janma divyaṁ [comm.]. [Lord Kṛṣṇa] has got divine birth because *ātmamāyayā yogaprajñayā svasvātantryśaktyā ārabdhaṁ*, He creates that birth not by theory of *karmas*, not as the fruit of His old *karmas*. No, it is fruit of His *svātantrya śakti*. By His free will He creates His birth. *Na karmabhiḥ,* it is not by past actions. "I have no past actions. *Karmāpi divyaṁ*, My actions are also divine. Because, *phaladāna asamarthatvāt*, My actions have no fruit, they bear no fruit. This is just play. My actions are play, playful, and they bear no fruit."

Yaścaivam etattattvaṁ veti, anybody who concentrates upon My such body with such divine activity and divine birth, *so'vaśyaṁ bhagavad-vāsudeva-tattvaṁ jānāti*, he will also become one with My divinity. No matter if he is a limited soul, he will become unlimited.

10th [*śloka*]:

DVD 4.1 (19:22)

वीतरागभयक्रोधा मन्मया मद्यपाश्रयाः ।
बहवो ज्ञानतपसा पूता मद्भावमागताः ॥१०॥

vītarāgabhayakrodhā manmayā madvyapāśrayāḥ /
bahavo jñānatapasā pūtā madbhāvamāgatāḥ //10//

You cannot imagine how many people have entered in My state of Bhairava. *Vītarāga bhaya krodhā*, after having discarded their attachment, discarded their fear, discarded their wrath, *manmayā* and they have sentenced their minds towards Me only, *madvyapāśrayāḥ*, and they are residing on My support.

And in the same way, *bahava*, you cannot imagine how many people, *jñānatapasā pūtā,* that are purified by their knowledge and their austerities. *Madbhāvamāgatāḥ*, they have entered in My universal Being and become Bhairava.

Tathā ca-evaṁ vidantaḥ manmayatvāt-paripūrṇecchatvāt krodhādirahitā niṣphalaṁ karma karaṇīyaṁ kurvāṇā bahavo matsvarūpam-avāptāḥ [comm]. In the same way, numberless people have become united with My Being.

Next [*śloka*]:

DVD 4.1 (20:51)

ये यथा मां प्रपद्यन्ते तांस्तथैव भजाम्यहम् ।
मम वर्त्मानुवर्तन्ते मनुष्याः पार्थ सर्वशः ॥ ११ ॥

ye yathā māṁ prapadyante tāṁstathaiva bhajāmyaham /
mama vartmānuvartante manuṣyāḥ pārtha sarvaśāḥ //11//

Those people who take refuge in Me, *tāṁstathaiva bhajāmyaham,* I support them in that way, in which way they take refuge in Me. If they want money, I give them money. If they want kith and kin, I give them kith and kin. If they want to support their family members, I bestow that to them. If they want nothing, if they want only Me, I am at their disposal; I am always with them then.

Mama vartmānu vartante manuṣyāḥ pārtha sarvaśāḥ. Everybody is following My tradition. It is not a tradition only [for one] who is following [the path] to become Bhagavān Bhairava Himself. There are many who like to feed people, who like to construct temples, who like to make pathways, who like to support their children, who like to support their wives, support their masters, support their elders, support their husbands–I do that.[88] So, [in this way], everybody is fine, everybody is peaceful in this world.

Evameva madīyaṁ mārgaṁ manmayā amanmayāśca sarve evānuvartante [comm]. All are treading on My path. Those who are away from My path, they are [also] treading on My path. Those who are on the right path, they [too] are treading on My path.

Do you understand?

This is the theory of Abhinavagupta.

Nahi jyotiṣṭomādir-anyo mārgaḥ, when you perform *havan* for the sake of achieving a seat in heaven or for the sake of achieving a seat on the throne of becoming a universal king, that also is My *mārga* (path), that also is My seat. *Madīyaiva sā tathecchā,* it is My will. I have created all thrones; all thrones within and without. "Within" means in My body; "without" means . . .

DENISE: Outside My body.

SWAMIJI: . . . outside My body.[89]

Vakṣyate hi, Lord Kṛṣṇa will say onwards, "*cāturvarṇyaṁ mayā sṛṣṭam*, I have created four *varṇas* (castes): brahmin, kṣatriya, vaiśyas, and śūdra. I have created *brāhmaṇas* (one section), kṣatriyas (another section), vaiśyas (third section), and śūdras (fourth section). But all are Hindus. If they are Mohammedans, those are also Hindus. If they are Christians, they are also Hindus."

DVD 4.1 (25:12)

काङ्क्षन्तः कर्मणां सिद्धिं यजन्त इह देवताः ।
क्षिप्रं हि मानुषे लोके सिद्धिर्भवति कर्मजा ॥ १२ ॥

kāṅkṣantaḥ karmaṇāṁ siddhiṁ yajanta iha devatāḥ /
kṣipraṁ hi mānuṣe loke siddhirbhavati karmajā //12//

---

88 "I am the handler of each and every action in this universe." *Bhagavad Gītā* (1978).

89 "Outside means in worldly activity." Swami Lakshmanjoo, *Śivastotrāvalī*.

"Whatever exists inside God consciousness, that exists outside also, not another element. Only that element exists. Whatever exists inside God consciousness, that is outside. It is not a foreign element in this world." Swami Lakshmanjoo, *Spanda Saṁdoha* (1981).

In this *mānuṣa loka*, where the human body is being born . . .

This is *mānuṣa loka*, where *martyas* are born. You know, human beings. Human beings are the source of rising again or the source of falling down. This is the center. This is the chief center for falling down or rising upwards.[90]

JOHN: Human being.

SWAMIJI: Human, yes, this . . .

JOHN: Body.

SWAMIJI: Yes.

That is exceptional when crows also rise.

JONATHAN: But it is possible.

SWAMIJI: It is also possible. But [the human condition] is the center, the center of growing and decaying. You can rise and you can fall, whatever is your wish, you can do that. But this is the center to grow and this is the center to fall.

Mānuṣa eva loke bhogāpavargalakṣaṇā siddhirnānyatra. In this *loka*, you can have *bhoga* and you can have *mokṣa* also. You can have enjoyment (*bhoga*) and you can have liberation (*mokṣa*) also, for good. [*Mokṣa* is] becoming one with Bhairava.

DVD 4.1 (27:14)

चातुर्वर्ण्यं मया सृष्टं गुणकर्मविभागतः ।
तस्य कर्तारमपि मां विद्ध्यकर्तारमव्ययम् ॥१३॥

cāturvarṇyaṁ mayā sṛṣṭaṁ guṇakarmavibhāgataḥ /
tasya kartāramapi māṁ viddhyakartāramavyayam //13//

[Lord Kṛṣṇa]: I have created four *varṇas*, four classes. I have not created four classes by birth. If you are born in England as a European and you have got qualities of a brahmin, you are a brahmin.[91] *Guṇa karma vighāgataḥ,* your actions and your quali-

90 "When you are created as a human being–not bird, not cow, or beast, or anything else–when you get entry in *manuṣya loka* (*manuṣa loka* means this body, human body), then there is hope for rise. So this is golden opportunity for each and every human being to rise." *Bhagavad Gītā* (1978).

91 "Whenever a brahmin is there, you will feel compassion in him,

fications are predominant, not your birth. If you are by birth English, it does not matter. Qualifications matter. If you are by birth English and in qualification you do the deeds of a brahmin, [then] you are a brahmin. If you have got the qualities of brahmin, you are a brahmin because you have qualifications, not by birth.[92] By birth it has no value.

Do you understand?

So, I am creator and destroyer [of the *varṇas*] also.

DVD 4.1 (28:53)

न मां कर्माणि लिम्पन्ति न मे कामः फलेष्वपि ।
इति मां योऽभिजानाति कर्मभिर्न स बध्यते ॥१४॥

na māṁ karmāṇi limpanti na me kāmaḥ phaleṣvapi /
iti māṁ yo'bhijānāti karmabhirna sa badhyate //14//

That person who believes in God and who has no desire, if he acts, it bears no fruit for him. If he desires, there is actually no desire for him. He has no desire. In this way, [the one] who understands . . . and these aspects are realized in Me, in Bhairava, he also becomes Bhairava in the end, i.e., [the one] who realizes this. Because it is touchwood. Whenever you think of Bhairava, you become Bhairava. "*Wurwurwurwur*," you become Bhairava.

It gives you an electrical shock and you are finished. You leave

---

you'll feel absence of hatred in him, you'll feel friendship in him, friendly attitude in him; everything you will find, all good qualities in him. So by those good qualities you must confirm that he is a brahmin." Swami Lakshmanjoo, *Tantrāloka* 15.511 (1981).

ābhayaṁ sarvabhūtemyaḥ sarveṣāmabhayaṁ yataḥ /
sarvabhūtātmabhūto yastaṁ devā brāhmaṇam viduḥ //
[Quote from *Mahābharata*]

"Brahmin is that person who gives *ābhaya* to everybody, who removes fear from people. *Sarvabhūtātmabhūto yaḥ taṁ devā brāhmaṇam. devas* (gods) call him a brahmin." Ibid., 15.513.

92 "*Guṇakarmavibhāgataḥ*, the qualifications of a *brāhmaṇa* is considered according to qualities and actions." *Bhagavad Gītā* (1978).

this limited body and possessions and everything [else]– you are finished, you become Bhairava. In the end, after enjoying the welfare of your kith and kin and everything, afterwards you get sentenced in the supreme state of Parabhairava.

JONATHAN: At that time of death?

SWAMIJI: Yes, at the time of death.

Because this body is to be thrown in the end.

But for Parabhairava, this body, he may throw it or he may close it, close it, this chapter. His body is not cremated; his body is not buried.

JONATHAN: Just disappears.

SWAMIJI: Yes, it disappears [laughs] in vacuum.

This is Abhinavagupta's theory. Sir, have you understood? I think you understand things day by day, more and more vividly.

JONATHAN: But you tell us so clearly.

SWAMIJI: What?

JONATHAN: You tell us so clearly, in such a simple way.

SWAMIJI: Thank you.

Mama kila kathamākāśakalpasya. I am just like a vacuum.[93] How can limited actions leave impressions in My body, in My Being? Because I am just a vacuum, I am a vacuum; I have no space, I have no time, I have no formation. If I think of anything, then I am there. If I think of anything absurd, I am there. If I think of *kālāgnirudra*, I am there. If I think of *śāntātītakalā*, I am there. [Actually] there is no vacuum, there is no space, there is no time, there is no formation. I am just everywhere [laughs].

How wonderful it is!

Ityanena jñānaprakāreṇ yo bhagavantamevāśrayate. [The one] who takes the refuge of Lord Bhairava, *sarvatra sarvadā ānandaghanaṁ parameśvarameva*, [and realizes that] everywhere there is only the expansion of Parameśvara, this is the manifestation of Bhairava everywhere (everywhere, and anywhere, and nowhere; in nowhere also, everywhere also, anywhere also, and somewhere also) . . .

DENISE: That covers it all.

SWAMIJI: Yes, all . . . all is pervaded by Him.

93 "How can actions get any contact with Me, with My mind? Because *ākāśakalpasya*, I am just like ether, vacuum. Why is His being just like *ākāśa*? Because there is no desire in Lord Kṛṣṇa." Ibid.

JONATHAN: And nowhere.

SWAMIJI: And nowhere also. And no-no-nothing-nothing-nothing, numberless-nothings also. If there is something left, and there also, and nowhere also.

. . . *tasya kim karmabhir bandhaḥ*, how can these feeble actions entangle him?

DENISE: Which feeble actions?

SWAMIJI: These small petty things. He is actually everywhere; everywhere, nowhere, anywhere, somewhere, even negation of whichwhere [laughs].

DVD 4.1 (34:42)

एवं ज्ञात्वा कृतं कर्म पूर्वैरपि मुमुक्षुभिः ।
कुरु कर्मैव तस्मात्त्वं पूर्वैः पूर्वतरं कृतम् ॥ १५ ॥

evaṁ jñātvā kṛtaṁ karma pūrvairapi mumukṣubhiḥ /
kuru karmaiva tasmāttvaṁ pūrvaiḥ pūrvataraṁ kṛtam //15//

Tasmādanyā buddhyā pavitrīkṛtastvamapi karmāṇi–avaśya-kartavyā ni kuru [comm.]. So, by holding this knowledge of Mine, O Arjuna, you should also possess this knowledge of Mine and you should fight with them. Go on fighting and destroy them. [Actually] they won't be destroyed. It is just your play of your manifestation.

DVD 4.1 (35:18)

किं कर्म किमकर्मेति कवयोऽप्यत्र मोहिताः ।
तत्ते कर्म प्रवक्ष्यामि यज्ज्ञात्वा मोक्ष्यसेऽशुभात् ॥ १६ ॥
कर्मणो ह्यपि बोद्धव्यं बोद्धव्यं च विकर्मणः ।
अकर्मणश्च बोद्धव्यं गहना कर्मणो गतिः ॥ १७ ॥

kiṁ karma kimakarmeti kavayo'pyatra mohitāḥ /
tatte karma pravakṣyāmi yajjñātvā mokṣyase'śubhāt //16//
karmaṇo hyapi boddhavyaṁ boddhavyaṁ ca vikarmaṇaḥ /
akarmaṇaśca boddhavyaṁ gahanā karmaṇo gatiḥ //17//

What is good action and what is bad action? Even great souls, realized souls, cannot understand what is good action and what is [bad action]. They cannot discriminate what is good and what is bad. Even realized souls also cannot understand the theory of *karmas*; the theory of good *karmas* and the theory of bad *karmas,* what is good and what is bad. *Tatte karma pravakṣyāmi,* I will tell you that way of action, *yajjñātvā*, by which knowledge–not by doing, only you have to know what is the action, what is good action and what is bad action, you have to know that–*mokṣyase aśubhāt*, you will become one with Bhairava, you will be embraced by Bhairava.[94]

Karmaṇo hyapi boddhavyaṁ boddhavyaṁ ca vikarmaṇaḥ. Good actions also are understandable.[95] *Vikarmaṇaḥ. Vikarma* means those actions which are not actually bad actions and which are not good also (*vikarmaṇa*). For instance, there is *billy*, there is a cat, there is a rat. There is a cat and there is a rat. This cat jumps upon the rat. What should we do? Should we kill the rat or should we kill the cat? To save the rat should we kill the cat? Or to save the cat should we kill the rat? What should we do? So you are in a fix to understand what is good there. What should we do in this circumstance?

In which circumstance?

DENISE: When the cat is about to kill the rat.

SWAMIJI: Or, there is a tiger and he is amidst cows, hundreds of cows. What should we do? Should we kill the tiger or let him take one-by-one these cows and kill them?

DENISE: We should kill the tiger.

SWAMIJI: Huh?

DENISE: We should kill the tiger!

JONATHAN: But that's also his nature.

SWAMIJI: But when you kill the tiger, he will say, "aaaaah-hhh," and he will die. It is bad. It is very painful for him. Who?

JOHN: This tiger.

SWAMIJI: For the tiger it is painful.

94 "I will tell you that kind of action, by knowing that action, you will be delivered from *aśubha*, delivered from sadness, pain." Ibid.

95 "But by which action, what fruit you get, you cannot understand. If you do right action, it will bear some bad fruit. If you do wrong action, it will bear some good fruit. You can't understand the ways and fruits of these actions." Ibid.

DENISE: Then we should ignore it and let happen what happens.

SWAMIJI: [laughs] You can't say that. You can't say what is to be [done]. That is *vikarma*. *Akarma* (non-action) is . . .

JONATHAN: So there's no correct answer for that.

SWAMIJI: There is no correct answer. Nobody can understand what is good, what is bad, what is to be done, which *karma* is to be kept in view.

Gahanā karmaṇo gatiḥ, you can't say how *karmas* take place in this world. So this is . . . combined everything, all [of] this is the drama of Parabhairava.

[Lord Kṛṣṇa]: "Let the drama go on, let the drama go forward. Kill these kith and kin of yours, O Arjuna! Why are you waiting? Why are you waiting in the backseat? Come forward and kill them!"

Whom?

JOHN: Kith and kin.

SWAMIJI: *Tathāhi hiṁsraprāṇivadhe prajopatāpābhāvaḥ* [comm.]. There is a cobra and he kills everybody, whoever passes that way. He kills [them] by just smelling [them], *bas*, finished! That person is gone who passes by [the cobra's] hole; he is just [Swamiji imitates a cobra breathing], *bas*, finished.

So you should kill the cobra. Kill the cobra and all will remain fine. But that too is also bad. When the cobra is killed, what will happen to him? He will just die, just like *sratasrat*–he will die.

JONATHAN: But don't you sometimes have to do something bad to get good *karma*?

SWAMIJI: Huh?

JONATHAN: Didn't you say once [that] sometimes you have to do some bad action to get good *karma*?

SWAMIJI: But actually, what is good and what is bad, you cannot understand.

JONATHAN: It's not for us to decide.

SWAMIJI: Yes.

Akaraṇe'pi ca śubhāśubhaṁ karmāsti. [Even] if you do nothing, if you sit idle, that way also you [may be] killing others in dreams.[96]

---

96 "If you don't do any action, there also you will find good fruit and bad fruit. Because in mind, you will do some action. If you don't do with

So, this [*karmic*] theory you cannot understand.
So, He say's what is the conclusion of that.
Karmaṇyakarma yaḥ paśyatya. . . the 18th *śloka*.

DVD 4.1 (42:33)

कर्मण्यकर्म यः पश्यत्यकर्माणि च कर्म यः ।
स बुद्धिमान्मनुष्येषु स चोक्तः कृत्स्नकर्मकृत् ॥१८॥

karmaṇyakarma yaḥ paśyatyakarmaṇi ca karma yaḥ /
sa buddhimānmanuṣyeṣu sa coktaḥ kṛtsnakarmakṛt //18//

When you do something, when somebody does something [and they think], "I have done this mischief. [But] I should not repent. If I am well established in my Bhairava state, I will do some work and I will think that, 'I have not done it. These are the classes of organs, they have done it. I have nothing to do with this. I have not done it! My organs are [doing it], I have nothing to do with organs. Organs are not mine. Organs are of this body.'"

"I am not this body, this body is not mine . . ."

"I am not this body or the organs of this body. [If] they have done something wrong, what have I to do with this? I have not done anything wrong. I am established in my own way."

And the one who sees that Viresh has done this work, [he should think], "this is not Viresh's [doing], this is my doing. I have done this!" Because, taking into view, having in view, the universal point of view . . .

The universal point of view is, "whatever you are doing, it is my doing [and] whatever I am doing, it is not my doing, it is other's doing, it is my organs doing. Whatever you're doing, it is my doing because I am universal!"

Right?

. . .this way, I am doing [everything] everywhere [and] I am not doing anything.

---

your organs, with your limbs, in mind, through mind, you will do actions; good actions and bad actions [through] thoughts. Unless there is knowledge of God consciousness, you cannot avoid actions altogether. Mind will act. If you don't do actions, mind will act automatically. So, in this way, [even] elevated souls cannot understand what is good action and what is bad action." Ibid.

Parakṛteṣu ātmakṛtatvaṁ jānāti [comm.]. [If] somebody is working and digging the ground of garden, I will think, "I am digging this garden, he is not digging".

Right [laughs]?

So, when I am everywhere, I am digging [that garden]. This is my digging.

JOHN: Everybody should think this way.

SWAMIJI: Everybody does not [think] this way. He will think, "I am doing this," [when doing some action]. So he is bound, so he is caught. He is caught in the clutches of *māyā*.

JOHN: But everybody *should* think this way.

SWAMIJI: Everybody should think [this way], then *māyā* won't exist; *māyā* will fail to exist.

DENISE: That's a kind of meditation, right?

SWAMIJI: That is *real* meditation in action, in action.

Not in . . . like this. In that, there is this fraud action, this fraud meditation. If you sit [erect], this is fraud. Because, internally he is roaming here and there and doing nothing.

Right!

JONATHAN: So, can I ask you a question on a practical level?

Is that why you enjoy so much to watch people working? Is that why you enjoy, in *ashram*. Some days you say . . .

SWAMIJI: Yes. I say, I watch. Because I am doing . . . I am doing it!

JONATHAN: When I say, "there is nothing to do," you say, "it doesn't matter, just do something, anything." And you sit. Swamiji just sits and watches all the time.

DENISE: And then at the end of the day he is tired and he says, "I have done so much work today."

SWAMIJI: [laughs]

JONATHAN: And he did.

DENISE: Yeah.

SWAMIJI: *Karmaṇyakarma yaḥ paśyat . . . ātmakarmaṇi*, in your own work, whatever you do yourself, you [should] say, "it is done by others." *Akarmaṇi*, what is not done by yourself, you [should] think that, "it is done by me." He is actually a great soul who thinks like that. *Sa coktaḥ kṛtsna*, and he has done everything. He has done everything and he has done nothing. He has actually, in the end, done everything, and he has actually done nothing. He has done everything because he is God; he has done nothing because he doesn't get any fruit from that *karma*.

Sa eva sarvasya madhye buddhimān [comm.], he is actually a realized soul. *Kārtsnyena–sākalyena-asau karma karoti*, he does whatever is being done in this universe, from *kālāgnirudra* to *śāntātītakalā*,[97] [and thinks], "it is [all] my doing or it is not my doing at all."

Ato 'sya kena karmaṇā phalaṁ dīyatām. What fruit will it produce? His *karma* won't produce any fruit! [The only] fruit is his being always established in the Parabhairava state.

Ataḥ sarvameva karoti na kiṁcidvā karoti. He does everything. In one way he does everything, in another way he does not do anything.

Iti-upaniṣat, this is the secret of Shaivism. It is [the commentary of] Abhinavagupta. This is the secret. You must hide it, you must not expose this secret.[98]

DVD 4.1 (48:55)

यस्य सर्वे समारम्भाः कामसंकल्पवर्जिताः ।
ज्ञानाग्निदग्धकर्माणं तमाहुः पण्डितं बुधाः ॥१९॥

yasya sarve samārambhāḥ
kāmasaṅkalpavarjitāḥ /
jñānāgnidagdhakarmāṇaṁ
tamāhuḥ paṇḍitaṁ budhāḥ //19//

All of your activities, to whom all activites are *nirāśīr bandhanaḥ*, whatever action he does, he does not think that, "may this dream come true; for which I am doing this work, may this dream come true." This is *āśīrvād* (blessing) for that *karma*. That you should not do. You should not put your *āśīrvād* for that *karma*. All *karmas*!

Tyāge yasya hutaṁ sarvaṁ. "I have done this, I am watching Viresh, I am watching John, I am watching Jonathan, I am watching Denise, and they do work, and I am watching." Like

---

97 "From *kālāgnirudra* to *śāntātītakalā*" means from the lowest point of creation to the highest point of creation. [*Editor's note*]

98 "By keeping it secret, it remains precious and it is in its full strength." Swami Lakshmanjoo, *Tantrāloka* 3.65 (1973).

this, I [feel that I] have done it. I have done it but I have no connection with [those actions]. I have done it. I have done everything. I think I have done it because I don't pray for it, I don't give *āśīrvād* to it. I don't believe that this will be successful. I don't believe that this will not be successful.

DENISE: You don't go that far. You just stay in the action and watch the action.

SWAMIJI: Yes. *Satyāgisacabuddhimāna,* he has renounced everything and he is really a realized soul and no one else. That is me.

Where is that *śloka*?

Yes, this, 19th *śloka*.

Chapter 4 Part 2

त्यक्त्वा कर्मफलासङ्गं नित्यतृप्तो निराश्रयः ।
कर्मण्यभिप्रवृत्तोऽपि नैव किञ्चित्करोति सः ॥२०॥

tyaktvā karmaphalāsaṅgaṁ nityatṛpto nirāśrayaḥ /
karmaṇyabhipravṛtto'pi naiva kiñcitkaroti saḥ //20//

Karma phalāsaṅgaṁ tyaktvā, if you do your work but you don't ask for its fruit, *nitya tṛpta,* because as you are always *tṛpta* (satisfied), you don't need any gain in doing [some action and] you don't have any loss in not doing [some action]. When this is so, then you are always full. *Nirāśrayaḥ,* you are supportless; you don't want anybodys support for you to stand on or to live on or to die on. You don't want anybody's support. *Karmaṇyabhipra-vṛtto'pi,* if you do work, *naiva kiñcitkaroti,* actually you don't do any work. So [*karma*] does not bear any fruit for you.

Ābhimukhyena (*abhipravṛtto'pi* means *ābhimukhyena pravṛtto 'pi*), if you do each and every action of the world, but as you have no attachment for [the fruits], then you have done nothing.

DVD 4.2 (01:45)

निराशीर्यतचित्तात्मा त्यक्तसर्वपरिग्रहः ।
शारीरं केवलं कर्म कुर्वन्नाप्नोति किल्बिषम् ॥२१॥

nirāśīryatacittātmā tyaktasarvaparigrahaḥ /
śārīraṁ kevalaṁ karma kurvannāpnoti kilviṣam //21//

Nirāśīr, when you don't appreciate your activities, that these activities will bear some fruit, *yata cittātmā,* your mind and intellect are always one-pointed, one-pointedly controlled in your own nature, which is situated in your own state of Parabhairava.

Tyakta sarva parigrahaḥ, all bindings you have crossed. You have crossed for good all bindings that [make you feel], "this I have to do [or] this I have not to do."

If you do [some action], well and good. If you don't do [that action], well and good. Why should you have bindings? As long as there are bindings, they will entangle you and push you in limitations. When there are no bindings, then you are not . . . you are away from limitations. You are all-round free.

Śārīraṁ kevalaṁ karma, only you have to do *karma* (action) . . . for instance, you have to wake up in the morning, have a *hubble-bubble* (smoke),[99] then go for a walk, then take a cup of tea (bed tea), then go for a walk, then have a shower-bath, then have *gupshup* (gossip). These are the things that you have to do, nothing else. You have not to concentrate on anything. You have not to think of God. Who is God other than you? You are yourself [God]! Whatever you have to do, it is God's doing.

That is *śārīraṁ kevalaṁ karma. Kevalaṁ* means *saṅgrahitam*, you are detached. You are detached. Whatever you do, you are detached from each and every activity of yours. *Kurvannāpnoti kilviṣam,* then you won't get entangled in your activities. You are free and *jīvan mukta*.

That is *indriya vyāpārātmakaṁ karma* [comm.]. *Indriya vyāpārātmaka*, you can do yawning or scratch your body, you can do like this, you can laugh, you can do like this [Swamiji demonstrates]. Whatever you do, this [activity] is natural. What then? You are established in God consciousness in each and every respect because *yat-mano-buddhibhyāṁ na tathānur-añjitam*, [your] intellect and mind does not get involved in your activities. In these activities, when [your] intellect and mind does not get involved as the mind [and intellect] in the activity of others, on the contrary, *are* involved–[their] mind and [intellect are involved in their] activities–in this way, you are not doing [anything].

Yadṛcchālābhasantuṣṭo . . . 22nd [*śloka*]:

DVD 4.2 (5:33)

यदृच्छालाभसन्तुष्टो द्वन्द्वातीतो विमत्सरः ।
समः सिद्धावसिद्धौ च कृत्वापि न निबध्यते ॥२२॥

99 Swamiji did not smoke. He mentions smoking here in terms of what may be a part of your daily routine. [*Editor's note*]

yadṛcchālābhasantuṣṭo dvandvātīto vimatsaraḥ /
samaḥ siddhāvasiddhau ca kṛtvāpi na nibadhyate //22//

[Lord Kṛṣṇa]: *Yadṛcchālābhasantuṣṭaḥ*, whatever comes in front of you, you [should] remain satisfied with that. If anybody comes [to you and] he says, "I have to ask you a question," [you should] hear his question and reply to it. That is it. [If he says], "I have to give you some money," [you should reply], "yes, you keep it [with me]." You don't deny it. [Or, he may say], "I want some money from you, Sir." [You should say], "yes, take it." That is *yadṛcchālābhasantuṣṭo.*

Dvandvātīto (*dvandva* means, e.g., "O, I am cold. I want a *kongri* (fire pot)." No matter if you are shivering with cold, what then? You [should] enjoy that coldness and shivering. You [should] behave in such a way that you will get entry in God consciousness by this cold, this cold wave in your limbs. *Vimatsaraḥ,* you don't hate anything, when you don't hate anything.

Samaḥ siddhāvasiddhau ca, when it is fruitful, when your activities are fruitful, good. When your activities do not bear any fruit [and] you say, "*hai, hey,*" [but] nothing has happened to [you]. Then it is alright. Then you remain in your own way of glamour. *Kṛtvāpi,* if you do activities of this world, *na nibaddhyate,* you have not done anything. You are doing nothing. You are only established in the state of Parabhairava.

Karmakartari prayogaḥ [comm.]. *Kṛtvāpi*, Abhinavagupta says *kṛtvāpi*, if he does activity, if he conducts activity, any activity, that activity cannot entangle him. Activities are in real sense . . . it is *karma,* it is object. Object cannot entangle the subjective being. *Karma* is *jaḍa*; action is *jaḍa* (inert, insentient). The *jaḍa* action cannot entangle the *cetana* (sentient) actor.

When does it happen on the contrary?

When the actor is entangled in his own [activity], when [his mind and intellect] are involved in action, he is entangled then. Otherwise there is no possibility of *jaḍa* action to bind the actor, *pramāta*. So, *svayameva hyātmā ātmānaṁ badhnāti phalavāsanākāluṣyam-upādadāna,* when he searches for fruit for his actions, whatever he has done, [when] he searches fruit for that [action], then he is bound. He'll be bound by that action.

Anyathā jaḍānāṁ karmaṇāṁ bandhane svātantryaṁ na tathā.

Jaḍa (inert) actions cannot [actually] entangle *ātma* who is always free, everywhere free.

DVD 4.2 (9:54)

गतसङ्गस्य मुक्तस्य ज्ञानावस्थितचेतसः ।
यज्ञायारभतः कर्म समग्रं प्रविलीयते ॥२३॥

gatasaṅgasya muktasya jñānāvasthitacetasaḥ /
yajñāyārabhataḥ karma samagraṁ pravilīyate //23//

Gatasaṅgasya, [the one] who is not attached to anything in this world, *muktasya*, who is absolutely *mukta* (*mukta* means absolutely liberated from all bindings), *jñānāvasthita-cetasaḥ*, and whose mind and intellect are focused in supreme knowledge of Bhairava, that is *jñānāvasthita cetasaḥ*.

Yajñāyārabhataḥ (*yajñāya* is singular for *yajña*), it is singular, but [Abhinavagupta] says it is, according to Pāṇini's grammar, *yajña*, although it is singular [in this verse], it is only one *yajña*, it is [actually] *jātayajña*,[100] these are *yajñas*, many, many *yajñas*. So there are so many *yajñas*.

Yajñāḥ. *Yajñāḥ* means *vakṣyamāṇalakṣaṇāḥ* [comm.], which will be explained in these [following] *ślokas*, which all other commentators have [understood] this as singular, *yajñāya*. And they have commentated upon it in a singular way, that *yajña* is only one. But Abhinavagupta says *yajñas* are many.

JONATHAN: What is the meaning of that?

SWAMIJI: *Yajña* means offering. This is offering to God. Whatever you do, you have to offer it to God, in various ways, not in one way only. If it was only to offer in one way then it [would be] according to the commentary of other commentators. But Abhinavagupta says it is, according to my theory, that this *yajña* is a collective form of *yajña*s, it is not only singular. There are so many *yajñas,* there are so many offerings, which [one] has to do, which he is doing in this world.

---

100 *Jāti* means 'class,' 'universal,' '*genus*.' So '*jāta yajña*' means that the word '*yajñā*,' though singular in this verse, refers to all *yajñās* just as the word 'tree' refers to all types of trees. [*Editor's note*]

Yajñāḥ [is] *vakṣyamāṇalakṣaṇāḥ*.[101] These *yajñas* will be explained in the following *ślokas* here.

Yajñāyetyuktam;–tatsvarūpaṁ sāmānyaṁ tāvadāha [comm.]. First He explains what is *yajña*, what is the typical meaning of *yajña*.

DVD 4.2 (13:08)

ब्रह्मार्पणं ब्रह्म हविर्ब्रह्माग्नौ ब्रह्मणा हुतम् ।
ब्रह्मैव तेन गन्तव्यं ब्रह्मकर्मसमाधिना ॥२४॥

brahmārpaṇaṁ brahma havir-
brahmāgnau brahmaṇā hutam /
brahmaiva tena gantavyaṁ
brahmakarmasamādhinā //24//

Other commentators have [commentated]: *brahmārpaṇaṁ*, you offer it to supreme Brahman. Whenever you put a *thali* in front of you, you take *achamana* (water); just after *yajña*, you take *achamana*. Don't you take *achamana*? When you perform *yajña* of our master, when there is time of taking food, Shamlal[102] [and I], we put some water in our palms and recite this *śloka*:

brahmārpaṇaṁ brahma havir-
brahmāgnau brahmaṇā hutam /
brahmaiva tena gantavyaṁ
brahmakarmasamādhinā //24//

Brahmārpaṇaṁ, whatever I take is offered to Lord Śiva. Whatever I have to offer is for Lord Śiva. Whatever I offer is itself Lord Śiva. I have to offer Lord Śiva *in* Lord Śiva. *Brahmārpaṇaṁ brahma havir brahmāgnau*. I have to offer this food to my body, to my stomach. What is the stomach? Stomach is Lord Śiva. I am offering this food to Lord Śiva in my stomach. In stomach also is the residence of Lord Śiva. *Brahmārpaṇaṁ brahma havir brahmāgnau brahmaṇā hutam*. And then offering, the act of

101 "It is not *upalakṣaṇa* [metaphor]. It is *jāti*, *jāta*. *Jāta* means class." *Bhagavad Gītā* (1978).
102 Swamiji's priest.

offering is also Lord Siva. [The one] who offers [and] the offering itself is the play and drama of Lord Śiva. This is *brahma karma samādhi. Brahma karma samādhi* means whatever you do, it is only *brahma;* everywhere [there is only] *brahma* [Lord Śiva].

Somānanda also has said:

asmadrūpa samāviṣṭaḥ svātmanātma nivāraṇe /
śivaḥ karotu nijayā namaḥ śaktyā tatātmane //[103]

Asmadrūpa samāviṣṭaḥ, I have to bow. Who is 'I'? *Asmadrūpa samāviṣṭaḥ*, that is Śiva. Śiva has to bow. [To] whom Śiva has to bow? *Asmadrūpa samāviṣṭaḥ svātmana,* myself, I am bowing to Śiva [who is] myself. Who is myself? Śiva. *Asmadrūpa samāviṣṭaḥ,* Śiva. *Ātma nivāraṇe,* for removing obstacles. What are obstacles? Śiva! Obstacles also are Śiva. For removing Śiva away. Which Śiva?

JOHN: Obstacles.

SWAMIJI: Obstacles. Obstacles are Śiva. We have to remove that Śiva. For removal of that Śiva, I am doing *prānam* to Śiva, i.e., myself, for removal of these obstacles; *śivaḥ karotu,* let Śiva do *prānam* [to Himself]. *Tatātmane,* who is universal Śiva, in the end he will become universal Śiva. That is, he will take the seat of Parabhairava in the end, where everything is everything [*sarvasarvātmakam*].

Obstacles are Śiva, everything is Śiva, that is Śiva, [the one] who does this is Śiva, by whom it is done . . . the way how he does *prānam* is Śiva, to whom he does *prānam* is Śiva, by whom he does *prānam* is Śiva, for the sake of whom he does *prānam* is Śiva, for destroying the obstacles which are Śiva. To destroy those obstacles, he does *prānam* [to Śiva]. And in the end, he does *prānam* and resides in *tatātmane* (*tatātmane* means [that] which is everywhere Śiva). That is the Parabhairava state.

That is *brahmārpaṇaṁ brahma havir brahmāgnau brahmaṇā hutam*. This is *brahma karma samādhi*; this is *samādhi* of *brahma karma*. This way, no other commentator has commentated upon [this verse] like this as Abhinavagupta has done.

JOHN: What verse is that, Sir?

103 *Sivadṛṣti*, 1.1.

SWAMIJI:

brahmārpaṇaṁ brahma havir-
brahmāgnau brahmaṇā hutam /
brahmaiva tena gantavyaṁ
brahmakarmasamādhinā //24//

This is the verse.

JOHN: What number?

SWAMIJI: 24th *śloka*.

Brahmārpaṇaṁ (he commentates upon [this verse] word-by-word now, Abhinavagupta), *brahmārpaṇaṁ* means *brahmaṇi arpaṇaṁ*, it is to be offered to *brahma*, in *brahma*. This offering is to be offered in *brahma*.

What is that? *Brahmaṇi arpaṇaṁ*.

Tata eva pravṛttasya punastatraivān [*upraveśanaṁ yasya tat*]. [The substance (*dravya*) to be offered[104]] has come out from [Lord Śiva] and it has to reside in the same place. It has come out from [Lord Śiva] in a separated [i.e., differentiated] form and it has to be offered, i.e., sent back [to Lord Śiva]. That is *brahmārpaṇaṁ*.

Now *brahma haviḥ*. *Brahma* means *bṛhatvāt brahma katvāt brahma*. From the grammarian point of view, the meaning of *brahma* is "one who is broad and one who [spreads] broadness everywhere." The one who spreads broadness everywhere and the one who is Himself broad, He is *brahma* (*bṛhatvāt brahma katvāt brahma*).

You should go into the depth of this.

So this is *viśvātmakaṁ*, this whole universe, this whole universe is broad and it is rising, it is rising; day by day it is rising. Day by day it is spreading more and more in span.

DENISE: It's becoming larger and larger?

SWAMIJI: Huh?

DENISE: It's becoming bigger and bigger?

SWAMIJI: Bigger and bigger, day by day, by production, by

104 "What are those things? Those things are *śabda*, *sparśa*, *rūpa*, *rasa*, and *gandha*. Whatever you hear, whatever you smell, or taste, or touch, all these things, these are *dravyas*. And you have to adopt now, *yajña*. And this *yajña* is nominated by Abhinavagupta as *dravya yajña*. Others have not explained it as *dravya yajña*. It is only Abhinavagupta who has put that it is *dravya yajña*." *Bhagavad Gītā* (1978).

creation. It is created; in various forms it is created.

Havistat, this whole universe is *haviḥ*, it is offering in *brahma*. That is *brahma haviḥ*.[105]

Now *brahmāgnau*, into the fire of *brahma*; you have to put this offering into the fire of Brahman. That is another word in this *śloka*, *brahmāgnau* (in the fire of *brahma*).

What is the fire of *brahma*?

Brahmaṇi means *paramabodhe praśānte'gnau*. *Paramabodhe*, the supreme state of Bhairava, which is *praśānte agnau*, the fire which is an appeased fire, where there are no flames (*śānta*, an appeased fire). You have to put that offering [i.e., *haviḥ*, this whole universe] into that [appeased fire of Bhairava].

DENISE: That offering into what?

SWAMIJI: Appeased fire; fire which is not burning. When you put offering [in that appeased fire], you will become appeased, without any thoughts, one-pointedness everywhere, God consciousness everywhere. So you become appeased and you stay in your well-being.

JOHN: That's appeased fire?

SWAMIJI: Appeased fire, appeased fire, where there are no flames.

When fire is . . .

DENISE: Raging?

SWAMIJI: No.

. . . when fire is very soft and cold, [but] not so cold, [not] shivering cold, [it is] tolerable cold, when you enjoy this coldness.

Do you understand?

Coldness means . . .

JOHN: We are calling this "fire" because it consumes these offerings.

DENISE: Cooling?

SWAMIJI: No. It is cold fire. Cold fire means when once you get a dip in this fire, you get appeased [and you experience the] blissful state of your being where there is neither cold nor heat, nor shivering cold. It is only just an absolutely blissful state of being (*ānanda*).

105 "Whatever is done in this universe, that is *haviḥ*. *Haviḥ* means offerings, [which are] *śabda*, *sparśa*, *rūpa*, *rasa*, and *gandha*. All these five senses. This is one with *brahma*, so this is *haviḥ*." Ibid.

JOHN: And we are calling it "fire" because it is into that that we offer all our fruits and everything.

SWAMIJI: Yes, yes.

Brahmaṇā hutam. Brahmaṇā, brahmaṇā means . . . *brahma* means *karma. Brahmaṇā* means *yenakena citkarmaṇā*, by seeing, by touching, by hearing, by drinking, by talking, by walking–that is *brahma. Brahmaṇā* means *yenakena citkarma*, in each and every action of your daily routine of life. *Brahmaṇā* means *yenakena citkarma*, *brahma* means the activity of all [of your] actions. *Tena . . . brahma karma samādhinā*, this is *brahma karma samādhi*, this is the *samādhi* which is appeased, which is achieved, obtained by *brahma karma.* This is *brahma karma.*

Offer . . . what do you offer? This is *brahma.* In which you offer, it is *brahma.* By which you offer, it is *brahma. Brahma* means Parabhairava state.

Brahmaiva tena gantavyaṁ. Only *brahma* is available there. This is called *brahma karma samādhi.*

JOHN: So this is that, this is that *samādhi* where by in all activities you offer all perceptions, all experiences into the fire of your own being.

SWAMIJI: Parabhairava, yes.

JONATHAN: But you have to be in the Parabhairava state to be able to do that, don't you?

SWAMIJI: Huh?

JONATHAN: You have to already be in Parabhairava state to be able to do that, to realize that.

SWAMIJI: No, no, no! You can do it! You are really Parabhairava!

JONATHAN: So anyone can do that.

SWAMIJI: Anyone can do it. Anyone can do it, who is capable of doing it.

JONATHAN: But how do you become capable to do it?

SWAMIJI: As I have become! I was also an ordinary being playing with you before four years, before five years or six years [ago]. I was also like you.

Aparimitaparipūrṇamadātmakayajñasvarūpavedinastu [commentary.]. Those blessed souls who have got this knowledge, i.e., what is the real meaning of *yajña*, as we have already explained in the commentary of '*brahmārpaṇaṁ brahmāhaviḥ . . .*,' this general explanation of *yajña*, *kathaṁ parimitaphalalavalām-paṭyabhāgino bhaveyuriti*, [those blessed souls] will never accept limited fruit from this kind of *yajña*. This is universal *yajña*.

Ityanena ślokena vakṣyamāṇaiśca ślokaiḥ. In this first general *śloka* of *yajña*, and *vakṣyamāṇaiśca ślokaiḥ*, and there are some more *yajñas*, which are to be explained in these following *ślokas* of this chapter, *parama rahasyam-upanibaddham*, there is the essence of the secret; [it] is existing [in these *ślokas*].

Taccāsmābhirmitabuddhibhirapi. "That secret," Abhinavagupta says to himself, "*mitabuddhibhirapi*, if I am not fit to explain this secret, if I am not capable of explaining this secret . . ."

See, Abhinavagupta says when he had [his] first life . . .

DENISE: First what?

SWAMIJI: When he was first born in this universe. When he wrote the *Tantrāloka* and all of the other things, all of the other commentaries.

. . . Abhinavagupta says, "if I am not capable of explaining this secret, *mitabuddhibhirapi*, [it is] because my intellect [was] not so vast as *my* intellect is vast now," i.e., in another *janma* (lifetime) of Abhinavagupta. Because I had to take another incarnation; from Abhinavagupta, I am produced.[106]

Don't you understand?

So, *mitabuddhi*, "as I had [a limited] intellect [and] as I [now have] expansion of my intellect, and *yathā-gurvāmnāyaṁ*, as I had received the instruction of my masters and ancestors (great masters)–that I have explained–but [I am] sorry [to say], *mukha saṁpradāya krama mantareṇa*, unless you go to master, unless [the master] talks to readers, [unless] he gives instructions to readers of [my] commentary on the *Bhagavad Gītā*, [unless the master] gives instructions to readers who will read this commentary, sorry, it is too much for you to understand. You can't understand it. You readers cannot understand it unless you have got *mukha saṁpradāya*.[107] Unless this *saṁpradāya* comes

106 Swamiji is referring to himself having taken another incarnation as Abhinavagupta. [*Editor's note*]

107 "When you have not *mukhasaṁpadāya*, when you have not understood the trick [of] how to do these actions from your master's lips, those who have not understood, *naitat nabhaścitramiva cittmu-pārohati*, it won't be established in your mind. You can't understand

direct from Parabhairava to you, *then* you can understand it. Otherwise you will never understand it. [Without *mukha saṁpradāya*], this [commentary] will be just as [insignificant as if] you are dreaming. You won't understand it. Sorry to keep you so depressed by my [words, but] I am talking in real sense."

It won't get digested in your consciousness because your consciousness is very gross. It needs subtle consciousness and subtle consciousness will only rise when you will go to great, experienced masters, and derive those thoughts from the *śaktipāta* of your masters. Then you can understand it. Otherwise you cannot understand it. So you have to go and search [for those] great masters–that is through *śaktipāta.* Only *śaktipāta* can arrange for your master. *Śaktipāta* will arrange for a master to throw light on this for you, in your consciousness.

Understand?

Thank you.

Iti na vaymupālambhanīyāḥ. So you should not speak amongst yourselves. You readers should not speak amongst yourselves that, "this commentary is *utphatān* (unintelligible) commentary, you cannot understand it properly." [Don't say], "he is just barking. It is madness. He has [written] madness with his pen here. You can't understand it. [It] is just useless talk. It is a waste of time!" You should not say that. It is a sin for you! You should not give us bad names. Parabhairava will kill you; otherwise Parabhairava will kill you. If you don't understand it, it is your fault! It is not my fault!

Atra haviṣo'gneḥ karaṇānāṁ ca srugādīnāṁ kriyāyāśca brahmaviśeṣaṇatvam-iti kaiścid-ūktaṁ. In these *ślokas*, *kaiścit*, by other commentators who have commentated upon these *yajñas*, they have said: *brahmārpaṇaṁ brahma havir brahmāgnau . . . brahmārpaṇaṁ*, the fire is *brahma*; *brahma haviḥ*, this *sāmagri* is *brahma*.

What *sāmagri*?

DENISE: Which you are offering.

SWAMIJI: What you are offering.

---

this way of thinking. You will say that, "no, I am doing this, how can it reach God? It won't reach there." So it won't touch their brain when there is not *mukha saṁpadāya. Mukha saṁpadāya* is the penetration from that sound which has come out from the lips of the master–that trick." *Bhagavad Gītā* (1978).

Brahmārpaṇaṁ brahma havir . . . brahmāgnau, this fire is *brahma*; this *ahūti* (oblation) is *brahma*; *brahmaṇā hutam*, and this priest is *brahma*. Like this, they have commentated upon it like this in these *ślokas*. *Tadupekṣyameva*, you should [make an] about turn to these commentaries of other commentators. Because, *teṣāṁ rahasya krame'kṣuṇṇatvāt*, this super-most secret they have not understood. And they will never understand that supreme secret of Shaivism. They will never understand. They have not the capacity; they have not such capacity that they will understand this. So leave that commentary to dogs.

Which commentary?

JONATHAN: The other one's.

SWAMIJI: Other commentaries.

Now the 25th *śloka*.

DVD 4.2 (36:20)

दैवमेवापरे यज्ञं योगिनः पर्युपासते ।
ब्रह्माग्नावपरे यज्ञं यज्ञेनैवोपजुह्वति ॥२५॥

daivamevāpare yajñaṁ yoginaḥ paryupāsate /
brahmāgnāvapare yajñaṁ yajñenaivopajuhvati //25//

Brahma is supreme; the wonder of wonders. This is the wonderful state of this wonderful world. The wonderful state of this wonderful world is the Parabhairava state, which Abhinavagupta had to come again to explain it in it's real sense.

daivamevāpare yajñaṁ yoginaḥ paryupāsate /
brahmāgnāvapare yajñaṁ yajñenaivopajuhvati //25//

Daiva yajña means the *yajña* pertaining to *devas* (gods).

Who are gods?

Not those, which are residing in heavens. Gods are one's own organs. One's own organs are gods.

What is *daiva yajña* then?

Pertaining to one's own organs.

What is *nijanijaviṣayagṛhaṇalakṣaṇaḥ* [comm.]? To see with eyes, to hear with [ears], to smell [with nose], to touch with skin, to taste with [tongue], and like that. This is a kind of *yajña*.

Nijanija viṣaya gṛhaṇa lakṣaṇaḥ, just eat, go on eating, go on tasting, go on smelling, go on touching, go on [doing] whatever you like–this is *daiva yajña*, this is the *yajña* pertaining to *devas*.[108] *Tameva parita upāsate*, some *yogīs* adopt this kind of *havan*.

What is that and what do they do in the end? What is the purpose of this kind of *yajña*?

That is *āmūlāt vimṛśanta svātmalābhaṁ labhante*, they find out what is the source of . . . where from this *yajña* is born. And that [source] is God consciousness. They go up to the root of organs, the activities of organs, and find out the state of Parabhairava there in the root of organs, in the root of the action of organs.

Ata eva te yoginaḥ, so they are called *yogīs*. Because *yoginaḥ* means–it is *matvarthīyaḥ* there–*yoginaḥ* means they are always *yogīs*.

Why are they always *yogīs*?

Not like that Vishnu Digambar, i.e., like cooks.[109]

Sarvāvasthāsu satatameva yogayuktatvat [comm.]. In each and every action, they are *yogīs*. In each and every action, they find out the reality of God consciousness in the activities of the organic field. *Nityayoge hi*, I am *matvarthīyaḥ*.[110]

According to Pāṇini's grammar, it is *matup*, i.e., [the word] *yoginaḥ* (*yogin śabda*) is *yogi* plus *matup* [i.e., the suffix '*in*']. *Matup* is a [suffix denoting possession]. The [*matup* suffix] is adopted according to the theory of the grammarian Pāṇini that [signifies that the root word to which this suffix is attached to] is for always. He is a *yogi* for always. He is not a *yogi* only when he adopts *yoga*. So his *yoga* is continuous, like in chain form.

Enameva ca viṣayagṛhaṇātmakaṁ yajñaṁ yajñenaiva–tenaiva lakṣhaṇena apare–pūrayitumaśakye brahmāgnau juhvati-iti kaiściddhākhyātam. This kind of translation is placed before

108 This is well explained in Abhinavagupta's *Dehasthadevatacakra stotra*.

109 See *Bhagavad Gītā,* 2.56 for a discussion of the *rūḍhi* and *anvartha* forms of nomination. [*Editor's note*]

110 "[The word] *yoginaḥ* is *matup pratyaya*, i.e., *yoginaḥ* is that *yogi* who is always *yogi*, who is not only *yogi* in the morning and in the evening. *Yogin* is *nitya yogi*, always residing in *yoga* practice." *Bhagavad Gītā* (1978).

some great souls of Shaivism.

Now I will tell you the cream that was placed in the heart of Vyāsa. Abhinavagupta says, "I know what is the background cream of Vyāsa for this *śloka*."

> *kecidyogayuktā santo daivaṁ–nānārūpendrādidevatoddeśe-naiva bāhyadravyamayaṁ yajñamupācaranti* / *taṁ ca kriyamāṇameva yajñaṁ kartavyamidamityeva buddhyā phalānapekṣayā apare–duṣpūre brahmāgnāvarpayanti–iti dravyayajñā api paraṁ brahma yānti* / [comm.]

Vyāsa's theory for this *yajña* is that it is *dravya yajñā*. It is *dravya yajñā*, i.e., it is *yajña* [performed with] *sāmagri* and everything . . . what you do outwardly. Outwardly *yajña* is also *yajña*. It is the *abhiprāya* (intention or meaning) of Vyāsa.

That was my [i.e., Abhinavagupta's] viewpoint, the first meaning of this *dravya yajñā*. And this is the view point of Vyāsa also. Vyāsa says *dravya yajñā*. *Dravya yajñā* is what we do [during] the *havan* of our master's *jag* or grandmaster's *jag*, [where] we do *havan* with *sāmagri*–it is [called] *dravya yajñā*. But there is only one trick to do that [*havan* properly]. That is, if you do that *havan*, you perform that *havan* for your master, don't ask for any reward from your master or grandmaster in [performing] this *havan*. Don't ask for a reward. Don't think that we'll get a reward. It is *kartavyamidamityeva buddhyā*, [think that], "it is my duty to offer without [receiving] any reward from [my master or grandmaster]. It is my duty [and I do it only] for duty's sake." This kind of *dravya yajña* is also valuable. So that *havan* also we perform. At least I perform [*havan*] without [asking for a] reward from my masters.

Yato vakṣhyate, because [Lord Kṛṣṇa] will, onwards in this chapter, He will say in the end of the [30th] *śloka*, "*sarve'pyete yajñavido*, all of these [performers of external and internal *yajñas*] are performing *yajñas* in the real sense. *Yajñakṣa-pitakalmaṣāḥ*, by [performing both of those *yajñas*], all of their gaps are filled. All of their gaps, which remain by asking for [the *yajña's*] fruit and by asking for its rewards–that is gap. They don't leave any gap by not asking [for its fruit]. No gap remains. No leakage remains there."

Do you understand?

Bas! Now 26th *śloka*.

DVD 4.2 (46:24)

श्रोत्रादीनीन्द्रियाण्यन्ये संयमाग्निषु जुह्वति ।
शब्दादीन्विषयानन्य इन्द्रियाग्निषु जुह्वति ॥२६॥

śrotrādīnīndriyāṇyanye saṁyamāgniṣu juhvati /
śabdādīnviṣayānanya indriyāgniṣu juhvati //26//

This is another kind of *yajña*.

Anye, some *yogīs*, *anye tu saṁyamāgniṣvindriyāṇīti* [comm.], *saṁyama* (*saṁyama* means the controlling center) . . .[111]

What is controlling center?

That is when there is one-pointedness of center; center of one-pointedness.

What is the center of one-pointedness?

Your mind! Your mind is the center of one-pointedness and unfortunately we have made this mind the center of thoughts, the center of varieties of thoughts, varieties of desires, on the contrary. And it is the wrong notion for centering your mind.

Actually your mind is the center of what?

One-pointedness. Mind is actually created by Lord Śiva for maintaining one-pointedness. Mind has got its capacity to remain in one-pointedness, just like *niruddha* in *samādhi*. Not *kṣipta, vikṣipta mūdha*, *ekāgra*.[112]

What is that?

This is the [fifth state of *yoga*].

What is [fifth]?

JONATHAN: One just keeps one-pointedness.

SWAMIJI: *Niruddha*, when it is automatic; automatically [all thoughts] have stopped. Mind has *that* capacity. And on the

---

111 "*Saṁyama* means *manaḥ*, mind, *tasya ye'gnayaḥ*, *saṁyamāgni*, the fire of mind. When one does not allowed them to go ahead towards their objects. So they sentence their organs in their mind. When you see some beautiful girl, it burns your thought. That fire appears in your mind, you want to pursue that, towards that object. But you have not to do that. You have to control it." *Bhagavad Gītā* (1978).

112 Swamiji explained the five states of mind (*kṣipta*, *vikṣipta*, *mūdha*, *ekāgra*, and *niruddha*) in *Bhagavad Gītā*, 2.65 commentary.

contrary, those people who are ignorant and who are misled by their so called masters, they go on roaming from one point to another point, from one point to another point, and they are scattered, always scattered, and they find nothing out of mind [i.e., mind's capacity to remain one-pointed]. Otherwise the mind has the power for un-minding in such a way that one becomes Bhairava at once, there and then, without any span of journey. He has not to pass from one point to another point. As soon as he remains in that one-pointedness, *bas*, he goes inside.

I think you have understood it.

Thank you.

Tasya ye'agnayaḥ, agnayaḥ. Agni means *pratipannabhāvabhavanārūpā abhilāṣaploṣakā visphūliṅgāḥ*, the sparks, which destroy and burn altogether to ashes all thoughts, all varieties of thoughts. *Ata eva te tapoyajñāḥ*, this is called *tapo yajña*, this is called the *yajña* of penance. Penance means one-pointedness.

And some *yogīs*, *jñānapradīpiteṣu phaladāhakeṣvindriyāgniṣu viṣayān-arpayanti*, there are some *yogīs* who offer [*viṣaya's*].[113] For instance, I have to do something, I have to eat–that is *viṣaya*. I have to eat food, I have to hear sound, I have to smell something, I have to touch something. What am I going to do there? [Abhinavagupta answers] that.

This is another way of *havan*.

Bhoga vāsanānirāsāyaiva bhogānabhilaṣanti.[114]

Tāstṛptāḥ svātmanaḥ pūrṇaṁ. This is Abhinavagupta's *śloka* for this. *Tāstṛpta . . .* in *Tantrāloka*.

tāstṛptāḥ svātmanaḥ pūrṇaṁ hṛdayaikāntaśāyinam /
cidvyomabhairavaṁ devamabhedenādhiśerate // TĀ 3.264[115]

Tāstṛptā, when all of these organs are satisfied by eating,

---

113 *Viṣayas* are the objects of the senses. [*Editor's note*]

114 "*Bhoga vāsanānirāsāyaiva bhogān abhilaṣantī*, you must enjoy the world of senses not for the sake of enjoyment, but for the sake of getting freedom from that curiosity. So that curiosity of enjoying, that does not remain there. So it is just to subside curiosity. For subsiding curiosity, they enjoy. This is also *tapasvī* from Shaiva viewpoint." *Bhagavad Gītā* (1978).

115 This verse from the *Tantrāloka* does not appear in Abhinavagupta's commentary of the *Bhagavad Gītā*. [*Editor's note*]

drinking, smelling, touching, then *hṛdayaikānta śāyinam*, *cit vyoma bhairavaṁ devaṁ*, *bas*, they don't hanker after doing it again and again. They go and get entry into the depth of God consciousness, for good. Like this [Swamiji gives a practical demonstration of how to eat with awareness and get entry inside].

Do you understand?

JOHN: I am trying.

SWAMIJI: [laughs] Yes, try. This is the way of how we do everything in this world. This is *havan*.

JOHN: That sensation carries you?

SWAMIJI: Yes, carries you to God consciousness.

Tathā ca mayaiva laghvyāṁ prakriyāyāmuktam, Abhinavagupta says, "I have, in a small booklet, I have noted down this *śloka*. You should read it." He has written that down [in his commentary]:

na bhogyaṁ vyatiriktaṁ hi bhoktustvatto vibhāvyate /
eṣa eva hi bhogo yattādātmyaṁ bhoktṛbhogyayoḥ //

Na bhogyaṁ vyatiriktaṁ hi. *Bhogyaṁ* means what is to be eaten, what is to be touched, what is to be smelled, what is to be spoken, what is to be heard, what is to be embraced–that is *bhogyaṁ*.

Now *bhogyaṁ vyatiriktaṁ hi*, that *bhogya* . . .

For instance, *bhogya* is [when] I see a beautiful lady in front of me, [she] is not to be touched. Don't touch [her]! [The *yogi*] can touch [her, but] as soon as [the *yogi*] touches [her, the *yogi*] will go into Bhairava state. At once, [the *yogi*] will go into Bhairava state. [*Yogi*] will fly into Bhairava state at once.

JOHN: Like your master would do when he would see a pretty girl sitting in front of him.

SWAMIJI: [When he would see a] pretty girl, then he would go into *samādhi*.

Eṣa eva, this is tasting the nectar of every object.

What is tasting nectar?

Tādātmyaṁ boktṛ bhogyayoḥ, when they are unified, both are unified with each other.

Which both?

JONATHAN: Your vision and . . .

SWAMIJI: *Bhokta* and *bhogya*, taster and tasted. Tasted is the object, taster is the subject. [When] taster and tasted become one, this is real *bhoga* (enjoyment).[116]

It is not hankering after . . . [it is not] to spoil that girl with kisses and everything. Don't spoil [her]; don't go that way. What is in that flesh? Just see the beauty of that girl and rush inside.[117]

Do you understand?

This is the way how we produce the glamour of God consciousness.

JOHN: Is this what we mean by *sahṛdayam*?

SWAMIJI: *Sahṛdayam*, yes, *sahṛdayam*. Yes, this is [*sa*] *hṛdayatā.*[118]

'loka sahṛdaye prasiddhyati'

This is real heart. This is the real activity of one's own heart. Heart, this is heart. This is not heart to hanker after objects. [When] you unite the object with your subjective consciousness, that is *sahṛdayatā.*

JONATHAN: But to do that you have to be totally one-pointed, isn't it?

SWAMIJI: What one-pointed?

---

116 "This *bhogya*, that which is to be enjoyed, it is not separate from God consciousness. Actually, if you see, if you analyze this, i.e., what is this that is to be enjoyed, it is not separate from God, it is not separate from enjoyer. Enjoyer is God. *Eṣa eva hi bhogoyat*, so enjoying that enjoyment is just to focus that which is enjoyable; focus that [which is] enjoyable towards that enjoyer so that you direct that enjoyable object towards enjoyer, the real *pramātṛ bhava* [i.e., *pramiti bhava*]. . . . this is *śāktopāya*." *Bhagavad Gītā* (1978).

See footnote 126 for an explanation of the *upāyas* (the means).

See also the later part of footnote 44 for an explanation of *pramiti bhāva*.

117 "So at the time when you embrace a girl, you should get entry in God consciousness, at that time. If you don't get entry, you are not meant for this technique (this way is not meant for those who are treading on *āṇavopāya* technique). You have to do penance then, *bas,* deprive." *Bhagavad Gītā* (1978).

118 "That is, they are with heart, they are attached with heart." Swami Lakshmanjoo, *Parātriśikā Vivaraṇa* (1982-85).

JONATHAN: If you are looking at that object you have to be totally one-pointed to unite with that, otherwise you are off here and there?

SWAMIJI: Yes. So you have understood it, to some extent.

JOHN: So is this why our Shaivism puts more emphasis on music and plays and drama?

SWAMIJI: Everything, everything, don't leave [out] anything in this world.

Play with that kite also, as much as you can. Do and enjoy it!

VIRESH: Until it breaks!

SWAMIJI: [laughs]

JONATHAN: But then you should enjoy that also.

SWAMIJI: Yes.

DENISE: He did.

SWAMIJI: You enjoyed . . . you enjoyed, you were quite happy. You told that kite, "all right, *adieu*, good bye." God bless you!

Chapter 4 Part 3

DVD 4.3 (00:00)

Spande'pi, in *Spanda śāstra* also (the author of *Spanda* is Vasugupta; Vasugupta is the author of *Spanda śāstra*), in *Spanda* also it is said:

bhoktaiva bhogyabhāvena
sadā sarvatra saṁsthitaḥ //2:4

It is *bhoktā* who has become *bhogya*. *Bhoktā* (the knower) has become the known; known is not separate from the knower. This is the manifestation of the knower that known is known. Known is known. The known is known [only because it] is the manifestation of the knower. Otherwise, if the manifestation of the knower would not [be accepted as the cause of the known], then the known could *not* be known. It would remain unknown. What?

JOHN: Known.

SWAMIJI: Known would remain unknown to everybody.

JONATHAN: So you have to have both. You have to have known and knower.

SWAMIJI: [laughs] Yes.

JOHN: But which one comes first?

SWAMIJI: No, no. Knower. It is the act, it is the manifestation of the knower. It is [owing to] the manifestation of the knower that known has taken place. It is not both.

JOHN: So you have *pramātṛ* and then *pramāṇa* and then . . .

SWAMIJI: And *prameya*.

JOHN: . . . *prameya*. So *pramāṇa* and *prameya* are knowing and perceiving.[119]

SWAMIJI: *Pramāṇa* and *prameya* are the manifestations of the knower (*pramātṛ*).

---

119 *Pramātṛ* is the subject (the knower), *pramāṇa* is the means of knowing (cognition), and *prameya* is the object (the known). [*Editor's note*]

JOHN: Of known.
SWAMIJI: Knower! Knower!
JOHN: Knower.
SWAMIJI: Yes.
JONATHAN: So without the knower, nothing can exist.
SWAMIJI: No [affirmative], without knower. Knower is the hero, the hero in this drama–the predominant hero.

Sarvāṇīndriyakarmāṇi . . . 27th and 28th *śloka* now.

DVD 4.3 (02:29)

सर्वाणीन्द्रियकर्माणि प्राणकर्माणि चापरे ।
आत्मसंयमयोगाग्नौ जह्वति ज्ञानदीपिते ॥२७॥

sarvāṇīndriyakarmāṇi prāṇakarmāṇi cāpare /
ātmasaṁyamayogāgnau jahvati jñānadīpite //27//

Sarvāṇ īndriya karmāṇi, all activities of organs . . .

indriya-vyāpārān-mānasān mukhanāsikā-nirgamana-mūtrādy-adhonayanādīn-vāyavīyāṁśca ātmano–manasaḥ saṁyamahetau yoganāmnyaikāgrayavahnau samyak jñānaparidīpite pūrayitavye niveśayanti [comm.]

All activities of organs . . . some *yogīs* are there [who] adopt this kind of *havan*. What is that? *Indriya-vyāpārān*, all activities of [their] organs, *mukha nāsikānirgam*, breathing, touching, smelling, urinating, singing, seeing, hearing–whatever [organic activity] it is–all of these activities, where do they offer it? They offer into that Bhairava *agni* (fire).[120] In clear words, he clarifies this:

gṛhyamāṇaṁ viṣyaṁ saṁkalpyamānaṁ vā tadekāgratayaiva parityaktānyavyā-pāratayā buddhyā gṛhṇantīti tātparyam [comm.]

120 "All those actions of organs and actions of breath are offered in the fire of *ātma saṁyama*. *Saṁyama* means one-pointedness of your own thought, which is lighted with knowledge (*jñāna dīpite*)." *Bhagavad Gītā* (1978).

Those *yogīs* accept all of these things as the glamour of one's own manifestation of Bhairava–all these [*indriya*] *vyāpārās* (organic activites). These are not dirty activities, i.e., going to the bathroom and throwing [out] whatever rubbish that you are throwing. You go on throwing it [out] but [know] that it is also the state of Bhairava. Think that you are residing in the Bhairava state [while performing all of these activities].

And our Grandmaster used to go to the latrine and after coming from the latrine, returning from the latrine–our grandmaster Swami Ram–he would explain *ślokas* in a more glamourous way afterwards, when he came out from the bathroom.

DENISE: He had divine experiences in the bathroom.

SWAMIJI: [laughs] Yes. This is that.

JOHN: Everything is divine.

SWAMIJI: Everything is divine. Nothing is impure and nothing is pure.

JONATHAN: Can I ask one thing? What is memory, i.e., when you remember something? Is that also an object?

SWAMIJI: Memory is the unification of the past with the present. The unification of the past with the present is memory. Memory is of the past and you remember that in the present. So you have united this. You have united 1998th year with 1997th year. You have united that by memory.

DVD 4.3 (06:57)

द्रव्ययज्ञास्तपोयज्ञा योगयज्ञास्तथापरे ।
स्वाध्यायज्ञानयज्ञाश्च यतयः संशितव्रताः ॥२८॥

dravyayajñāstapoyajñā yogayajñāstathāpare /
svādhyāyajñānayajñāśca yatayaḥ saṁśitavratāh //28//

evaṁ dravyayajñastapoyajño yogayajñaścoktalakṣaṇāḥ /
[comm. intro to the 29th śloka]

Dravyayajña, *tapoyajño*, *yogayajña* are already defined. Now *svādhyāya yajña* and *jñāna yajña* are yet to be explained.

What is *svādhyāya*? *Svādhyāya* means to give lectures on Shaivism–that is *svādhyāya*. And there is *jñāna yajña* also. [These] two *yajñas* are left [to be explained].

And [Abhinavagupta] derives [i.e., explains the essence of] this [next] *śloka* of the *Bhagavad Gītā*, which is totally ignored by all other commentators. It is a unique translation that he has done–Abhinavagupta.

DVD 4.3 (08:12)

अपाने जुह्वति प्राणं प्राणोऽपानं तथापरे ।
प्राणापानगती रुद्धा प्राणायामपरायणाः ॥२९॥

apāne juhvati prāṇaṁ prāṇe'pānaṁ tathāpare /
prāṇāpānagatī ruddhvā prāṇāyāmaparāyaṇāḥ //29//

Great souls breathe [out] with *apāna*, that *nāda*. They throw [their] breath [out] and that breath is [inhaled] by the disciple. [The great soul] throws his breath out [Swamiji breathes out loudly] and that is [inhaled] by the disciple, inside. By this, initiation is being done. The disciple becomes one with the master. This is *svādhyāya yajña*; this is how to teach your disciple.

You have not to teach your disciple with words, with explanations. You have to teach him with breath. You breathe in his . . .

What is *prāna*?

. . . *apāna* (*apāna* means [the disciple] has to breathe in and [the master] has to breathe out; the master has to breathe out into the breath of the disciple and he is initiated. *Prāṇāpānagatī ruddhvā*, and they are united with each other. *Prāṇāyāma parāyaṇāḥ*, *prāṇāyāma* is actually in its proper state. This is the real *prāṇāyāma*.

This is called *svādhyāya yajña. Svādhyāya yajña* means to teach, to teach him what is the secret of Shaivism. You cannot teach him with words–the secret of Shaivism. [Rather], you have to teach him with breath. You breathe into him and he is taught, he knows everything. This is *svādhyāya yajña*.

Have you understood it?

JONATHAN: I can understand it a little bit. But does that person, this disciple, have to be risen before that can happen, or can he do that with any disciple?

SWAMIJI: Huh?

JONATHAN: Can the master do that to any disciple if he wishes?

SWAMIJI: Not any disciple, but [one] who has got *śaktipāta*. There must be *śaktipāta* also. There must be the will of Parabhairava. Unless there is the will of Parabhairava, this kind of teaching won't be successful.

apāne juhvati prāṇaṁ prāṇe'pānaṁ tathāpare /
prāṇāpānagatī ruddhvā prāṇāyāmaparāyaṇāḥ //29//

This is *prāṇāyāma*. This is the real *prāṇāyāma*.

JOHN: Breathing into disciple.

SWAMIJI: Breathing into the disciples' consciousness and putting back the limited consciousness of the disciple into the unlimited consciousness of the master. That is teaching him. So they become the same just like one candle lights another candle; there is no difference between [the light of] the two candles. They shine with glamour; both candles [shine] in the same glamour. *Śiṣya* (disciple) is also just like master; master is also just like *śiṣya*. There is not [even the slightest] difference also. This much difference does not remain between these two [Swamiji demonstrates this by pressing his thumb and index finger together]. This is the real *svādhyāya* [*yajña*].

This kind of teaching remains undone yet, and this way, I have to teach people.

DVD 4.3 (13:44)

अपरे नियताहाराः प्राणान्प्राणेषु जुह्वति ।
सर्वेऽप्येते यज्ञविदो यज्ञक्षपितकल्मषाः ॥३०॥

apare niyatāhārāḥ prāṇān prāṇeṣu juhvati /
sarve'pyete yajñavido yajñakṣapitakalmaṣāḥ //30//

Some *yogīs* are . . .

ete evoktavyāpāraparišīlanāvaśa-paripūritasvātma-śiṣyātma-manorathāḥ dve'pyete gatī nirudhyāhāraṁ viṣayabhogātmakaṁ niyamya prāṇān–sakala-cittavṛttyudayān prāṇeṣu–paranirānanda-ullāseṣu juhvati / [comm.]

Apare niyatāhārāḥ, some *gurus* and *śiṣyas* remain *niyatāhārā*, they don't take much food. They take very little food.[121]

Prāṇān prāṇeṣu juhvati, they go inside; both the [master] and *śiṣya* (disciple) enter into the six stages of *prāṇa vṛtti*: *parāṇanda*, *nirānanda*, *brahmānanda*, *cidānanda*, [*mahānanda*], and *jagadānanda*. All of these six states of *ānanda* are derived by this [*niyatāhārā*].[122] So both become topmost great *yogīs*. They don't eat food or anything. They eat just one *chammach* (spoonful) [of food] and that is all.

Sarve'pyete yajñavido, all of these masters and disciples are clever in knowing what is a real *havan*. *Yajña kṣapita kalmaṣaḥ,* and by [performing] these kinds of *havan*, all their dots [i.e., imperfections] and leakages are finished. They remain complete and full.

DVD 4.3 (16:45)

यज्ञशिष्टामृतभुजो यान्ति ब्रह्म सनातनम् ।
नायं लोकोऽस्त्ययज्ञस्य कुतोऽन्यः कुरुसत्तम ॥३१॥

yajñaśiṣṭāmṛtabhujo yānti brahma sanātanam /
nāyaṁ loko'styayajñasya kuto'nyaḥ kurusattama //31//

---

121 "[Other commentators say] there are some *yogīs* who do not eat, drink, and [take] nothing, they just fast. *Prāṇān prāṇeṣu juhvati*, they, what do they do? They breathe, and that is their diet. They just starve. This is the way they have commentated, other commentators. But this is not the real technique of Abhinavagupta. And this is not the real technique of Vyāsa, who has written these *ślokas*. Vyāsa was a Shaivite, actually Shaivite." *Bhagavad Gītā* (1978).

122 "*Apare*, there are some *yogīs* who are *niyatāhārāḥ*, whose *āhārāḥ*, [which] means enjoyment, is *niyata* (*niyata* is one-pointed)." Ibid.

See also *Kashmir Shaivism–The Secret Supreme*, chapter 17.

Yajña śiṣṭām . . . yajña śiṣṭa amṛta bhujo yānti brahma sanātanam. Those people who perform this kind of *yajña,* which is already explained in these previous verses, what fruit remains? That is *yajña śeṣa. Yajña śeṣa* means when *yajña* is performed, then there is *naivedya* afterwards; afterwards you distribute *praśād* to everybody.[123] After *yajña* is performed, you distribute *praśād* to everybody. What [kind of] *praśād* is being distributed after doing these kinds of *yajñas*?

That is *yajña śeṣa*; that is *amṛta* (nectar).

Yānti brahma sanātanam, they achieve the *sanātanam. Sanātanam* means eternal and very old, and very young, and everlasting, i.e., *brahma,* Parabhairava. They reside absolutely for good in that Parabhairava state. Although they walk, they talk, they do all *gupshup* in this world, they are just like Parabhairava.

JOHN: What is *gupshup*?

SWAMIJI: Huh?

JONATHAN: Chit-chat, just talking, just gossiping.

SWAMIJI: That doesn't bind them. They can do anything in this world, any nonsense; any nonsense habits [that they may] have, that is divine. That is glamor!

What should I do for you?

JONATHAN: Can I ask one question about this initiation through breathing?

SWAMIJI: Yes.

JONATHAN: When that happens from master to disciple, does that disciple feel that immediately or is that . . .

SWAMIJI: Immediately, there and then! It is just an electric shock, electric light–shock.

JONATHAN: It's not bit by bit?

SWAMIJI: No, no it is not step-by-step.

JONATHAN: Just the whole thing in one go?

SWAMIJI: I told you, just [as] you light one candle with another candle. It does not take time.

---

123 The *naivedya* offerings, which include edible substances, are blessed by the deity during the performance of the *yajña*, after which the remnants (*śeṣa, praśād*) are distributed to everyone as a blessing. [*Editor's note*]

bhujaṅgavat garala saṁkrama . . .[124]

When there is cobra, [its] poison becomes poisonous [to the one who is bitten]. There is no difference between *bhujaṅga* (cobra) and the one who is touched with [the venom of the] *bhujaṅga*. [The victim] also becomes a *bhujaṅga* [by that venom]. When object and subject are united–subject is master, object is disciple–when they are united, they become one. They are both the same.

Atra ca vyākhyāntarāṇī ṭīkākāraiḥ pradarśitāni [comm.]. In these stanzas of *Bhagavad Gītā*, commentators other than myself have done their own . . . they have tried to understand this. But why should I nominate those commentators to you?

If you have got *śaktipāta*, you can yourself know what is the difference between those commentaries and my commentary. You will find the difference and you will know what is what.

Why should I nominate those [other commentators]? Because they have also, in their own way, tried to explain it [but] they could not succeed. They have not succeeded. Who?

JOHN: Those other commentators.

DENISE: Other commentators of that verse.

DVD 4.3 (22:36)

एवं बहुविधा यज्ञा वितता ब्रह्मणो मुखे ।
कर्मजान्विद्धि तान्सर्वानेवं ज्ञात्वा विमोक्ष्यसे ॥३२॥

evam bahuvidhā yajñā vitatā brahmaṇo mukhe /
karmajānviddhi tānsarvān-evaṁ jñātvā vimokṣyase //32//[125]

श्रेयान्द्रव्यमयाद्यज्ञाज्ज्ञानयाज्ञः परन्तप ।

---

124 See also Swami Lakshmanjoo, *Special Verses on Practice*, 76 (1988).

125 "In this way, O Arjuna, there are so many ways of *yajñas*, which are explained by the Lord Himself or in the *Vedas*, in *śāstras*. *Karma jānviddhi tānsarvān*, all those *yajñas* are meant [to be performed] in the active world, not in inaction. Whatever you have to do, you have to act in each and every technique of these *yajñas*. You have to act." *Bhagavad Gītā* (1978).

सर्वं कर्माखिलं पार्थ ज्ञाने परिसमाप्यते ॥३३॥

śreyāndravyamayādyajñājjñānayajñah parantapa /
sarvaṁ karmākhilaṁ pārtha jñāne parisamāpyate //33//

SWAMIJI: *Śreyān dravyamayāt yajñāt jñāna yajñah parantapa*. It is better, O Arjuna . . . I [will] freely tell you the real truth of *yajña–dravyayajñā, tapoyajñā, yogayajña, svādhyāya-yajña*–whatever *yajñas* I have explained here. All of these *yajñas* are subsided [i.e., superceded] by *jñāna yajña*. *Jñāna yajña* means when you [attain] the eternal state of Parabhairava–that is *jñāna yajña*. And *jñāna yajña* is the end of all *yajñas*.

Then there is nothing to be done afterwards. You are divine, you will become divine, you have become divine, you were divine, and you will be divine.

JOHN: *Anupāya.*

SWAMIJI: *Anupāya* or *upāya*. *Upāya* also.[126]

---

126 "[Lord Siva's] energies are the means; [His] energies have become the *upāyas*. For instance, energy of His will . . . is explained as *śāmbhavopāya*. Energy of knowledge is *śāktopāya*. And energy of action is *āṇavopāya*. Energy of action is breathing exercises, reciting *mantras*, reciting *ślokas* (hymns), and *pūjā* (worship). All these are in action, in the world of action. So, all these things are included in *āṇavopāya*. And they will carry you to the state of Lord Śiva. And [the energy of] knowledge, this is *śāktopāya*. Perceiving, middle-ing, centering, all these are in the world of *śāktopāya*. They will also carry you to the state of Lord Śiva. And [the energy of] will is the first start of each and every action. That is *śāmbhavopāya*. That will carry you to Śiva's state." Swami Lakshmanjoo, *Tantrāloka* 1.70 (1972).

"Thoughtlessness is called *śāmbhavopāya*, one-pointedness is called *śāktopāya*, concentration on *mantra* and breathing and all these things are called *āṇavopāya*. *Anupāya* is above these. *Anupāya* is no *upāya*. In *anupāya*, *sādhaka* has only to observe that nothing is to be done, be as you are. If you are talking, go on talking; if you are sitting, go on sitting, don't do anything. This is called *anupāya*." Swami Lakshmanjoo, *Kashmir Shaivism – The Secret Supreme* 5.40.

"[*Anupāya*] is no *upāya* because *upāyas* end there. In *krama mudrā*, all *upāyas* end. There is nothing to be done, it [just] happens, it is automatic from above. This is the processless process." Swami

JOHN: The state of *jagadānanda*?[127]
SWAMIJI: Exactly like that, but more than that.

DVD 4.3 (24:35)

तद्विद्धि प्रणिपातेन परिप्रश्नेन सेवया ।
उपदेक्ष्यन्ति ते ज्ञानं ज्ञानिनस्तत्त्वदर्शिनः ॥३४॥

tadviddhi praṇipātena paripraśnena sevayā /
upadekṣyanti te jñānaṁ jñāninastattvadarśinaḥ //34//

[Lord Kṛṣṇa]: That knowledge you will understand by bowing before them [i.e., the learned masters], *paripraśnena*, by placing questions before them, by *sevayā*, by serving them. Then, *te*, you will become *jñānina*, [one of] those who are glamourous with real knowledge of God consciousness. *Tattva darśinaḥ,* those who have the real observation of Parabhairava state, they will *upadekṣyanti* (*upadekṣyanti* means they will show you the reality of God consciousness).

Now he commentates upon these words in another way.

Tat ca jñānaṁ [comm.]. That knowledge of Parabhairava [can be attained by] *praṇipātena* (*praṇipātena* means by bowing your head before your masters; this is the [literal] meaning of this

---

Lakshmanjoo, *Tantrāloka* 5.59 (1974). See footnote 139 for an explanation of *krama mudrā*.

"But the aspirant must know, you must note that, that all of these *upāyas* lead you to one transcendental consciousness state. Of course, *āṇavopyāya* will carry you in a long way, *śāktopāya* [is a] shorter way, and shortest way is *śāmbhavopāya*." Swami Lakshmanjoo, *Kashmir Shaivism–The Secret Supreme*, original audio recording (1972).

127 Lit. rejoicing the world. "*Jagadānanda* is *anākhyā*, where God consciousness is not felt [because] it is your nature, it becomes your nature. . . . This is the real *samādhi* when you get entry in *jagadānanda* . . . when *jagadānanda* is well established, then you have to find out *jagadānanda* in the very action of the outward world." Swami Lakshmanjoo, *Tantrāloka* 5.52-61 (1974).

"That is the *svātantrya*, that is *kartṛtvaṁ*, and that is *īśvaratā*, that is everything. When you see outside situated inside, and inside situated outside, that is the reality of Lord Śiva. The real state of *jagadānanda* is that." Ibid., 6.238 (1974).

[word], *praṇipātena*). "*Jai!*" This is not the way of *praṇipātena*, this is not *praṇipātena*. This is just fraud.

What?

JOHN: Bowing your head before your master.

SWAMIJI: *Praṇipātena* means . . . what is the meaning of *praṇipātena* then?

This *bhaktyā*, with attachment, when you have got devotion for that, when you have devotion for that knowledge, that knowledge will come to you when you have devotion for that knowledge. That is [the meaning of] bowing your head before your master (*praṇipāta*).

na pādapatanam bhaktir vyāpinā paramātmanam
bhaktir bhāva padarthanaṁ tadeki bhāva bhāvanam

> *Pāda patanam na bhaktir*, this is not *bhakti* (devotion), this is not the sign of *bhakti* [when] you go and catch hold of your masters feet and do like this [Swamiji rubs his fingers over his eyes]. This is not *bhakti*. *Vyāpinā paramātmana*, that *param-ātmana* is all-knowing, all-knowledge, and everywhere omni-present. He knows whatever is happening in one's own mind. This is not *bhakti*.
>
> Then what is *bhakti*?
>
> *Bhaktir bhāva padarthanam tadekybhāva bhāvanam*. *Bhakti* is when you see that each and every object is the glamour of [your] own consciousness–that is *bhakti*. You should do that *bhakti*. You should not do this *bhakti*, i.e., show [respect through external prostrations]. This is fraud. "*Jai!*" All disciples come before me and say, "*Jai!*" This is all fraud, nonsense.
>
> Have you understood?
>
> *Bhaktir bhāva padarthanam tadeki bhāva bhāvanam,* all of these varieties of universal objectivity, when this universal objectivity, [when] all objects are found [to be] one with Parabhairava, that is *bhakti*.

And *upadekṣyanti te jñānaṁ*. *Upadekṣyanti*, [masters] will initiate you. But initiation does not mean initiation. When you are initiated, the initiated [person] is not initiated.

What is initiated?

Upadeṣa.[128] *Upadeṣa* means to get God consciousness and keep it before you. *Upa* means to get nearer and nearer in God consciousness and keep [it] at your disposal. That is *upadeṣa.*

JOHN: Keep God consciousness at your disposal?

SWAMIJI: God consciousness [is kept] at your disposal–that is *upadeṣa. Upa* means near to your consciousness. To carry God consciousness near to your consciousness–that is *upadeṣa. Upadeṣa* is not [merely reciting], "*om klīṁ bhairavāya namah, om klīṁ bhairavāya namah,*" i.e., what [masters] say in [the devotee's] ear [during initiation]. That *upadeṣa* is not *upadeṣa.* It is all fraud.

I also do that [laughs] to everybody: "*oṁ klīm . . . oṁ juṁ saḥ amriteśvara bhairavāya namah,*" [and tell them], "you must go on reciting this [*mantra*]."

This is fraud! What will happen to them [by reciting] this, "*oṁ juṁ saḥ amriteśvara*?" And there are some people who like it; who go on doing it [saying], "I have no [reservations], I will do that." I am doing that to people [i.e., initating them with *mantra*]. And I know that they are fraud. They are finished. They are placed away from God consciousness.

DENISE: By reciting those *mantras*?

SWAMIJI: Yes [laughs]. *Mantra* recitation is not really recitation. [Actual] *mantra* recitation is just keeping at your disposal the real state of Bhairava.[129] That is *upadeṣa.*

---

128 The literal meaning of *upadeṣa* is instruction or initiation. [*Editor's note*]

129 SWAMIJI: Any thought will take you to the state of God consciousness, but there must be one thought and this first fresh thought, like that, in all cycles of thought.

JOHN: Then why do we use *mantras*? If any thought will carry you, why use special thoughts?

SWAMIJI: Special thoughts (i.e., *mantras*) only we produce in the beginning in disciples. Afterwards, when they have developed this strength of awareness of *pramiti bhāva** . . . [then] you can give rise to any thought, any disgusted thought. . . . Thought becomes *mantra.* Because in each and every word, there is the residence of God consciousness; God consciousness is residing in each and every action, each and every word. . . . In the beginning, we [prescribe] *mantras* just to create faith in the devotee that, "I am reciting *mantra* of God!" Swami Lakshmanjoo, *Tantrāloka* 11.81 (1979).

What else shall I tell you about this?

I don't think I have anything else to say.

Tat ca jñānaṁ praṇipātena means . . . *praṇipāt* means not [mere recitation of *mantra* and external prostrations]; *praṇipāt* means *bhaktyā*, by devotion. *Paripraśnena* means to ask, to put question before your master. That is *ūhāpoha tarka vitarkādibhiḥ*, to find out the truth in your own consciousness, to think over it yourself. *Sevayā* does not mean that you will cook food for him.

For whom?

DENISE: Your master.

SWAMIJI: Your master.

It is not *seva* (service). *Sevayā* means *abhyāsena*, when you try to stay in that [state of] God consciousness–that is *seva*.

Yata evaṁbhūtasya tava jñānino. Jñānino means those who are *jñānis*, those who are filled with God consciousness.

Who are those?

Those masters, [which are] your own organs!

Jñānino–nijā eva . . . indriyaviśeṣāḥ, your own organs are your masters; they will direct you towards God consciousness. Those are your masters. "Master" [does not mean] to find out a master in a gross [i.e., external] way. Your masters are your own organs.

This is the cream of Shaivism derived by Abhinavagupta in his commentary on the *Bhagavad Gītā–'indriya viśeṣāḥ.'*

Tattvam upasamīpe dekṣyanti, they will *upadekṣyanti* (*upadekṣyanti* means [that your organs] will carry that God consciousness near to you). What is that? *Prāpayiṣyanti*, so that you will reside in that state.

It is said in Patañjalī's *Yoga Sutra* also:

yoga eva yogasyopāyaḥ /
ṛtambharā tatra prajñā //1.48

Yoga is *upāya*, i.e., *yoga* is the meaning of *yoga*. *Yoga* can be achieved by *yoga*. *Yoga* has no other means without *yoga*.

[When] limited soul is united with unlimited soul, unlimited being, that is *yoga*. *Yoga* means *yujaryoge* (union).

Anye jñāninaḥ puruṣāḥ:–iti vyākhyāyamān. Other commen-

* See the later part of footnote 44 for an explanation of *pramiti bhāva*.

tators who have translated this verse of the *Bhagavad Gītā* (because this was spoken, this has come from the lips of Lord Kṛṣṇa to Arjuna), "that you should hear [this knowledge] from great masters. O Arjuna, you should hear, you should know that from masters. They will explain to you the reality of what is right and what is wrong."

If it were correct that Arjuna was deputed by Lord Kṛṣṇa to go to masters [to obtain this knowledge], but Lord Kṛṣṇa was speaking to him, Himself, [telling Arjuna] to go to masters.

[To] whom else [Arjuna] has to go?

Lord Kṛṣṇa was there.

So it is just a joke! Master means your own consciousness. You have to insert all of your force in your own consciousness, then you will find it out. Don't try to catch Me. I have nothing to do with this. It is your own business to have it.

Yajjñātvā na punar . . . now this is the 35th *śloka*.

DVD 4.3 (38:24)

यज्ज्ञात्वा न पुनर्मोहमेवं यास्यसि पाण्डव ।
येन भूतान्यशेषेण द्रक्ष्यस्यात्मन्यथो मयि ॥ ३५ ॥

yajjñātvā na punarmohamevaṁ yāsyasi pāṇḍava /
yena bhūtānyaśeṣeṇa drakṣyasyātmanyatho mayi //35//

By that knowledge . . . when you achieve that knowledge of God consciousness by your own effort of that, [in] your own way. That you have to find out by yourself.[130]

---

130 "O Arjuna, and when you once understand that knowledge of awareness from those masters (organs, purified organs), *na punar mohamevaṁ yāsyasi pāṇḍava*, then you won't get any delusion, never. You will never be the victim of delusion, ignorance. *Yena bhūtān-yaśeṣeṇa drakṣyasyātmanyatho mayi*, you will unify, you will see all this world established in God consciousness and God consciousness established in world. World and God consciousness will be united to you in your awareness. There will be no difference between world and God consciousness. *Ātmani mayi-matsvarūpatāṁ prāpte* [comm.], and you will be sentenced to your own nature which is Mine, which is the nature of Mine. That individual nature is the nature of universality. Universal nature and individual nature will become one by the

Kṛṣṇamurti was also [correct] in this way–in some way or another way–when he used to tell people, "you have to find out for yourself what is right and what is wrong. You have not to ask your master. You are your master." He would speak these things to the public.

DVD 4.3 (39:43)

अपि चेदसि पापेभ्यः सर्वेभ्यः पापकृत्तमः ।
सर्वं ज्ञानप्लवेनैव वृजिनं सन्तरिष्यसि ॥ ३६ ॥
यथैधांसि समिद्धोऽग्निर्भस्मसात्क्रियतेऽर्जुन ।
ज्ञानाग्निः सर्वकर्माणि भस्मसात्कुरुते तथा ॥ ३७ ॥
नहि ज्ञानेन सदृशं पवित्रमिह विद्यते ।
तत्स्वयं योगसंसिद्धः कालेनात्मनि विन्दति ॥ ३८ ॥
श्रद्धावांल्लभते ज्ञानं तत्परः संयतेन्द्रियः ।
ज्ञानं लब्ध्वा परां शान्तिमचिरेणाधिगच्छति ॥ ३९ ॥
अज्ञश्चाश्रद्दधानश्च संशयात्मा विनश्यति ।
नायं लोकोऽस्ति न परो न सुखं संशयात्मनः ॥ ४० ॥

api cedasi pāpebhyaḥ sarvebhyaḥ pāpakṛttamaḥ /
sarvaṁ jñānaplavenaiva vṛjinaṁ santariṣyasi //36//
yathaidhāṁsi samiddho'gnirbhasmasātkriyate'rjuna /
jñānāgniḥ sarvakarmāṇi bhasmasātkurute tathā //37//
nahi jñānena sadṛśaṁ pavitramiha vidyate /
tatsvayaṁ yogasaṁsiddhaḥ kālenātmani vindati //38//
śraddhāvāṁllabhate jñānaṁ tatparaḥ saṁyatendriyaḥ /
jñānaṁ labdhvā parāṁ śāntimacireṇādhigacchati //39//
ajñaścāśraddadhānaśca saṁśayātmā vinaśyati /

---

achievement of that kind of knowledge. *Atmani-iti sāmānādhikaraṇyam*. It is *sāmānādhikaraṇya*, they are residing in one point, i.e., these two states of self. One state of self is individual self and the other state of self is universal self. Universal self is united with individual self. So it is only one, one soul. You may call it universal, you may call it individual; individual is also universal." *Bhagavad Gītā* (1978).

nāyaṁ loko'sti na paro na sukhaṁ saṁśayātmanaḥ //40//

36th, 37th, 38th, 39th and 40th *śloka*. This is collective; it is *kulakam*. *Kulakam* means [these verses have] only one connection with each other.[131]

samiddho'bhyāsajātapratipattidārḍhyabandhena jñānāgnirbhavati yathā tathā prayatanīyam [comm.]

The fire of Parabhairava knowledge should be *samiddha*, should be put to fire, should be put to glamor in flames (*samiddha*). *Samiddha* means put to fire, so that this fire of Parabhairava knowledge catches flames [and spreads] all-round. That way, *prayatanīyam*, you have to work out, you have to work out wholeheartedly so that [the fire of Parabhairava knowledge] catches fire all-round, so that it leaves not [even] one *tinka* anywhere without this fire [Swamiji presses his thumb and forefinger together to show the negation of space]. All is burned in that [fire]; all becomes one with that.[132] *Tathā prayatanīyam*, in that way you should [tighten] your belts and work out so that it catches fire all-round. *Tathā prayatanīyam*, in one way or another way, you have to work out. You have to work out with all

131 These *ślokas* will collectively explain the meaning of *akhilaṁ* from the phrase "*sarvaṁ karma akhilaṁ,*" which appears in verse 4.33. Swamiji previously explained: "Where the kingdom of *jñāna yajña* shines, at that point all these *yajñas* end. They have no importance there; only importance is attributed to *jñāna yajña* only." Abhinavagupta further explains in his commentary for verse 4.35. Swamiji translates: "*sarvaṁ karmākhilaṁ*, all knowledge, all action will end, will take its end. Nothing will be left to know, nothing will be left to do. Everything is done, everything is known then. And to clarify this point, [Abhinavagupta] clarifies this point in these *ślokas* and says, adds, *prathama ślokena-adharmo 'pi naśyati,* all actions–and not [specific] actions–good actions and bad actions also, *adharmas* and *dharmas*, both take its end. Neither *dharma* remains; [neither] good actions nor bad actions. Bad actions become glorified with awareness (i.e., *jñāna yajña*); good actions become glorified with awareness. Everything is divine then." Ibid.

132 "This fire of knowledge, fire of awareness must be lit, must be lit in such a way that it becomes universal fire [and] it burns all the impurity of individuality." Ibid.

of your might, [use] all of your might. And don't think of any other thing to be done in this world.

Pavitraṁ hi jñānasamaṁ nāsti, there is nothing purer than Parabhairava knowledge; there is no other element purer than this. This is the purest element.

What is the purest element?

DENISE: Parabhairava.

SWAMIJI: The knowledge of Parabhairava, being Parabhairava. Because everybody has the right to become Parabhairava.

Anyasya saṁvṛddhyā pavitratvaṁ na vastuta. All other things are purified by *saṁskāra*, by white-washing, by spraying of scent–they become purer. This *saṁvṛddhi, saṁvṛddhyā* means [purification] by other elements. But it is not natural purity. Natural purity comes only in the Parabhairava state. All other things, which are other than Parabhairava–which are not actually [other than Parabhairava because] nothing is left without Parabhairava, but as long as [the state of Parabhairava] is not known, it seems to be that it is separated from Parabhairava–for those separated Parabhairava states, you have to keep, you have to adopt some other element to keep them pure. But it is not natural purity. Natural purity is found only in the Parabhairava state. That is what he says.

Pavitratāṁ cāsya svayaṁ jñāsyati suprabudhatāyām. This purity he will know, the one who is blessed with *śaktipāta, tīvra śaktipāta*, he will himself know how he has become the purest element, the purest one in this world.

> *atra ca śraddhāgamastatpara vyāpāratvaṁ jhagityeva āstikatvādasaṁśayatve sati utpadyate* / [comm.]

For this, you need only to believe it. Just belief (*śraddhā*) will make you fit to rise in Parabhairava state–only belief. If you adopt belief, *full* belief in this that, "I am [in the] Parabhairava state, I am one with Parabhairava," you will become Parabhairava. No matter if you are playing with a kite, you will become Parabhairava. Only belief will insert you, belief will push you there. There is no other element [other than belief to make one fit to rise in Parabhairava state]. [Even if] you will do like this [Swamiji pounds his chest], by this you can't [rise in Parabhairava state]! It does not work.[133]

sakalādhyāyavisphārito'rthaḥ ślokadvayena saṁkṣipyate — [*comm. intro. to* 41st *śloka*]

This 4th chapter, the subject of this 4th chapter, all of this 4th chapter, is concluded in two *ślokas* in the end by Lord Kṛṣṇa.

DVD 4.3 (47:45)

योगासंन्यस्तकर्माणं ज्ञानसंछिन्नसंशयम् ।
आत्मवन्तं न कर्माणि निबध्नन्ति धनञ्जय ॥४१॥

yogasaṁnyastakarmāṇaṁ jñānasañchinnasaṁśayam /
ātmavantaṁ na karmāṇi nibadhnanti dhanañjaya //41//

O Arjuna, *yoga saṁnyasta karmāṇaṁ*, [one] who has kept away all of the worldly activities by *yoga*, by unification with Parabhairava, *jñāna sañchinna saṁśayam*, and whose all doubts have been shattered by the knowledge of Parabhairava, *ātmavantaṁ*, who has possessed the real state of Parabhairava (*ātmavantaṁ*, who has possessed [his own nature]),[134] *karmāṇi nibadhnanti*, then no activity–whatever he does in this world–no activity will have any fruit for him. The fruit will be only the state of Parabhairava for him, altogether, everywhere.

133 "In your brain, in your mind, in your organs, in your field of organs, you have to put faith. *Jhagityeva āstikatvāt asaṁśayatve sati utpadyate*, and that faith will rise only when you have surrendered everything to that awareness. Don't put your understanding there. If you put your understanding, if you attribute your own understanding, e.g., "from my point of view, this is not right; from Mahesh's point of view, this is not right . . . " don't put all these impure vibrations in it. Go on doing it, go on doing your meditation and you will rise to that kingdom of purity. . . . *Tasmādasaṁśayavatā gurvāgamadṛte na bhāvyaṁ saṁsyasya sarvanāśaktvāt*. You should doubt everything else with the exception of master and his technique for you. Only those two should be excluded from doubt. In all other things you should put doubt . . . because all other things are doubtful." Ibid.

134 In his previous translation, Swamiji translated *ātmavantaṁ* as "owning one's own nature." [*Editor's note*]

If he shoots anybody, the fruit will be the residence in Parabhairava. If he does good things, the fruit will be the residence in Parabhairava. If he kicks a football, the fruit will be the residence in Parabhairava. Everywhere he will become Parabhairava.

What else he could have?

There is another *śloka*. There is the second [concluding] *śloka*.

DVD 4.3 (49:34)

तस्मादज्ञानसंभूतं हृत्स्थं ज्ञानासिनात्मनः ।
छित्वैवं संशयं योगमातिष्ठोत्तिष्ठ भारत ॥४२॥

tasmādajñānasambhūtaṁ hṛtsthaṁ jñānāsinātmanaḥ /
chitvaivaṁ saṁśayaṁ yogamātiṣṭhottiṣṭha bhārata //42//

Tasmāt, so, *ajñāna sambhūtaṁ . . . samśayaṁ,* the doubt, which you have created by ignorance, and which has made a place to live in your heart, that doubt,[135] *ātmananaḥ jñānāsinā*, by your own knowledge (Parabhairava knowledge), is *asi* (*asi* means a hatchet), this doubt, *chitva*, you cut it into pieces. *Yogamātiṣṭha*, be united with Parabhairava state. *Uttiṣṭha bhārata*, fight with them and finish them! Whom?

JONATHAN: Doubts.

SWAMIJI: Yes, Kauravas [laughs]. No, Kauravas. The Pāṇḍavās [should] go on fighting with them.

Saṁśayaṁ chitvā yogaṁ [comm.]. *Yogaṁ* means *yogaṁ karma kauśalam*, the trick in actions, this is a trick in actions.[136] *Tataśca uttiṣṭha* (*uttiṣṭha* means stand up), stand up and come in the front seat of this chariot. *Tvam . . . vyāpāraṁ kartavyatāmātreṇa kuru*, do this job and finish this whole *tamasha* (drama).

Iti śivam, this is the welfare of Parabhairava, Śiva.

135 "The doubt which is established in your heart that [tells you], "if I kill Kauravas, it will be sin; if I don't protect my own kith and kin [i.e., the Kauravas], it will be sin," this is your doubt." *Bhagavad Gītā* (1978).

136 "So, you must do actions according to your own way, but only when you keep aside all your doubts. Keep away all your doubts and centralize yourself in meditation, and then you do your actions, good or bad. There is no question of being accused or being sinner afterwards." Ibid.

अत्र संग्रहश्लोकः
atra saṁgraha ślokaḥ

Now, [Abhinavagupta's] conclusion of this.

DVD 4.3 (51:51)

विधत्ते कर्म यत्किञ्चिदक्षेच्छामात्रपूर्वकम् ।
तेनैव शुभभाजः स्युस्तृप्ताः करणदेवताः ॥४॥

vidhatte karma yatkiñcidakṣecchāmātrapūrvakaṁ /
tenaiva śubhabhājaḥ syustṛptāḥ karaṇadevatāḥ //4//

॥ Concluding *śloka* of 4th chapter ॥

Whatever a man does, whatever activity, whatever action a man does, any individual does, according to the ways of his own organs, according to the desires of his own organs, *tenaiva śubhabhājaḥ syuḥ,* by that, to fulfill the desire of his own organs, he will become seated in the state of supreme Parabhairava.[137]

137 "Whatever action you do according to the way of your organs, that action will become divine only when there is awareness. Go on doing your actions according to the nature of your organs, go on doing that. Go to movies, go to any disgusting thing you can do, but [do it] with awareness. When you are watching your breath, everything will be divine. *Tenaiva śubhabhājaḥ syustṛptāḥ karaṇa devatāḥ.* Your organs will just carry you towards that center of God consciousness." Ibid.

Chapter 5 Part 1

Now 5th [chapter].

अर्जुना उवाच

arjuna uvāca

Arjuna asks a question before Lord Kṛṣṇa:

DVD 5.1 (00:18)

संन्यासं कर्मणां कृष्ण पुनर्योगं च शंससि ।
यश्छ्रेयानेतयोरेकस्तं मे ब्रूहि विनिश्चितम् ॥ १ ॥

saṁnyāsaṁ karmaṇāṁ kṛṣṇa punaryogaṁ ca śaṁsasi /
yaśchreyānetayorekastaṁ me brūhi viniścitam //1//

First you told me *karma saṁnyās–saṁnyāsam karmaṇāṁ–karma saṁnyās*, all *karmas* are to be shattered, and then you say *punaryogaṁ*, *karma yoga* is also important. *Yat śreyānetayorekaḥ,* please tell me after finding out, should I indulge in *karma yoga* or *karma saṁnyās*? Have I to abandon all activities or I have to do *karma yoga*?

Karma yoga means *yoga* in action.

Saṁnyāsaḥ pradhānaṁ, *punaryoga*, first you say *karma saṁnyās* is very essential, then you say *karma yoga* is also very essential. What should I do [among] these two things?

श्रीभगवानुवाच

srī bhagavān uvāca

Srī Bhagavān, Lord Kṛṣṇa, places the answer of this.

DVD 5.1 (01:52)

संन्यासः कर्मयोगश्च निःश्रेयसकरावुभौ ।
तयोस्तु कर्मसंन्यासात्कर्मयोगो विशिष्यते ॥२॥

saṁnyāsaḥ karmayogaśca niḥśreyasakarāvubhau /
tayostu karmasaṁnyāsātkarmayogo viśiṣyate //2//

Karma saṁnyās and *karma yoga*, *niḥśreyasakarāvubhau*, both direct you towards the state of supreme Bhairava. But even then, *karma saṁnyāsāt,* abandoning all *karmas* . . . *karma yoga*, *yoga* in action is most essential. *Karma yoga* works, *karma yoga* works and *karma saṁnyāsa* does not work always.

Karma saṁnyās, *saṁnyāsaḥ karma ca–nātraiko'bhihitaḥ* [comm.]. These are not two things. *Karma saṁnyās* and *karma yoga* are not two things.

Apitu, then what?

Ubhau saṁmilitau niḥśreyasaṁ dattaḥ, *karma yoga* must be also attached and *karma saṁnyās* must be also attached, then you will be likely to achieve the real state of God consciousness. *Yogena vinā saṁnyāso na saṁbhavatī*, if there is not *karma yoga, karma saṁnyās* is not possible. *Iti yogasya viśeṣaḥ*, *karma yoga* is essential, *karma yoga* is first and then *karma saṁnyās.* After indulging in *karma yoga*, then you will abandon all *karmas* [automatically].

Karma yoga is essential because when you are doing all of the activities of [the world, you] indulge [while remaining in] God consciousness–it works! When you remain only in God consciousness and do nothing, you do no actions, then there is the possibility of falling down from that God consciousness. God consciousness will not remain for always. It will remain for always [only] then when you are in action, when you are going here and there and everywhere.

Iti yogasya viśeṣaḥ, *karma yoga* is essential. *Karma yoga* is essential first and then *karma saṁnyāsa* will take place.

DVD 5.1 (05:03)

ज्ञेयः स नित्यसंन्यासी यो न द्वेष्टि न काङ्क्षति ।
निर्द्वन्द्वो हि महाबाहो सुखं बन्धाद्विमुच्यते ॥ ३ ॥

jñeyaḥ sa nityasaṁnyāsī yo na dveṣṭi na kāṅkṣati /
nirdvandvo hi mahābāho sukhaṁ bandhādvimucyate //3//

[Lord Kṛṣṇa]: *Jñeyaḥ sa nityasaṁnyāsī yo na dveṣṭi na kāṅkṣati*. He is *saṁnyās*, he has done *karma saṁnyās*, *yo na dveṣṭi na kāṅkṣati*, who does not desire and does not discard [anything].

Discarding and desire are both interdependent. When you discard [something] then desire remains in the background. When you indulge in work, then there is no desire, you are free from all desires.

Nirdvandvo hi mahābāho, he becomes *nirdvandva*, without the impressions of good and bad. *Sukham bandhāt vimucyate*, and he is, luckily he is sentenced to the state of Bhairava without doing anything, without entering. Without entering he enters there by *yoga*, by *karma yoga*, if he does all activities and remains in God consciousness. Only remaining in God consciousness does not work, you will come down. One day you will come down from that and you will be thrown out from that God consciousness.

JOHN: So that . . . so only remaining in God consciousness means just being in *nimīlana samādhi*[138] without . . .

---

138 "*Unmīlana samādhi* is experienced in *turyātita* and *nimīlana samādhi* is experienced in *turya*. This is the difference between *turya* and *turyātīta*. *Nimīlana samādhi* means absorption of universal consciousness; when universal consciousness is absorbed in your nature, that is *turya*. When universal consciousness is expanded everywhere, that is *turyātīta*." Swami Lakshmanjoo, *Tantrāloka* 10.288 (1978).

"*Turya* is the supreme (*parā*) energy of Lord Śiva, *suṣupti* is *parāpara* energy (medium energy) of Lord Śiva, and *jāgrat* and *svapna* (wakefulness and dreaming state) are inferior (*apara*) energies of Lord Śiva. So this is the way of understanding these three states." Ibid., 10.271-278.

"In the differentiated state of *jāgrat* (wakefulness), in the differentiated state of *svapna* (dreaming), and in the differentiated state of *suṣupti* (dreamless sleep), the expansive state of *turya* takes place to

SWAMIJI: Without activities.

JOHN: . . . without activity.

SWAMIJI: Yes.

JOHN: You need *krama mudrā*, you need to have that . . .

SWAMIJI: It is not *krama mudrā*. It is beyond that *krama mudrā*.[139]

---

him. . . . So for him, *jāgrat* is as good as *turya*, *svapna* is as good as *turya*, and *suṣupti* too is as good as *turya*. So there is no differentiation between this world and *samādhi*." Swami Lakshmanjoo, *Śiva Sūtras Vimarśinī,* 1.7, original audio recording (1975). See also Swami Lakshmanjoo, *Spanda Kārika* 1.3 (1981).

"This state of *turya* is all-active because this state of *turya* operates *jāgrat*, operates *svapna*, operates *suṣupti*. These three states are operated by *turya*. . . . And it is *anāmayā*, without any sickness; there is no trouble. If there is trouble in *jāgrat* and *svapna*, then it is connected with *jāgrat* [and *svapna*], it is not connected with *turya*. *Turya* is without trouble, there is no trouble. If you are once situated, established, in *turya* state, [then] in *jāgrat avastha* you will find always bliss, in *svapna* you will find bliss, and in *suṣupti* also you will be blissful." Swami Lakshmanjoo, *Tantrāloka* 10.271-278 (1978).

"This state of *turya* is *rūpakatvāt udāsīnāt cyuteyaṁ*, it is beyond *rūpa*, beyond the individual surface of consciousness. And it has gone beyond the level of ignoring the universal energies [as in *suṣupti*]. . . . Universal energies are existing there but in another coating; the coating is divine in *turya*. *Pūrṇatūnmukhyī daśā*, it is towards the fullness of God consciousness; [*turya*] is situated towards the fullness of God consciousness. It is not the fullness of God consciousness. It is situated *towards* the fullness of God consciousness." Ibid., 10.271-278.

"This *turya* you will find in *pramiti bhāva*." Ibid., 10.265. See footnote 44 for an explanation of *pramiti bhāva*.

"The difference between *turya* and *turyātīta* is, in *turya* you find in *samādhi* that this whole universe is existing there in the seed form, germ. The strength, the energy, of universal existence is existing there . . . but here he has [yet] to come out [into activity]. In *turyātīta*, he comes out in action and feels universal consciousness. This is the difference between *turya* and *turyātīta*. So, *turyātīta* is just like *jagadānanda* and *turya* is *cidānanda*." Ibid., 10.288.

139 "*Krama mudrā* is the process to get entry in *jagadānanda*. This is automatic process; it does not come by functioning it. You can't function it. . . . *Krama mudrā* is no *mudrā*; *krama mudrā* is automatic. . . . Just to observe that state of *samādhi* in [external world] also. When it is not so clearly found outside, go again in *samādhi* and pull it out with that

samādhi and see in external world again. And again and again, again and again, you have to [experience] this way of *krama mudrā* until [you get] entry in *jagadānanda*. When *jagadānanda* takes place, then everthing is divine, no *krama mudrā*." Ibid., 3.263-264 (1973).

"And this movement of going in and out and vice versa takes the position by the force of *samāveśa**, not by the effort of the *yogi* . . . [moving from] outside and inside is just to get this understanding that outside and inside are not different aspects, just only one. The one who experiences this state of *samāveśa*, that *yogi* experiences that this whole universe melts into nothingness in that great ether (great void) of God consciousness. . . . Then, when he strives to come out from that state, it is very difficult for him to come out. It is very difficult for us to go in and in the same way, for that *yogi*, it is very difficult to come out." *Self Realization in Kashmir Shaivism* – The oral teachings of Swami Lakshmanjoo, *The Secret Knowledge of Kuṇḍalinī*, 5.113-114, SUNY Press, Albany, 1994.

"After *krama mudrā* is over, it has functioned properly and you are established in *krama mudrā*, then you have to put *udyoga*, the rise of *udyoga* (will). By will you can get up from your *āsana* and try to step onwards for going outside in compound, or taking meals, or [whatever it may be]; you have to put that will, forced will. If you don't put that forced will, that *jagadānanda* . . . will vanish." Swami Lakshmanjoo, *Tantrāloka* 5.63 (1974).

"This is the connecting rod, *krama mudrā* is connecting rod, avenue. You can't get contact from *turya* to *turyātīta* unless *krama mudrā* is in between. *Krama mudrā* will carry you there." Ibid., 10.288 (1978).

* "For instance, you get the trace of a ghost, what the ghost does in your body? He enters in your body, puts your consciousness away from your body, and the kingdom of [the ghosts'] consciousness takes place in your body and you become yourself a ghost, e.g., you talk like the ghost. That is *samāveśa* of a ghost. In the same way, *samāveśa* of Lord Śiva takes place. When Lord Śiva enters in some soul, that limitation of that soul vanishes away and the unlimited state of conscious effulgence takes place in his soul; and he becomes Lord Śiva himself. That is *samāveśa*, that is real *bhajana* (worship), that is real *bhakti* (devotion)." Swami Lakshmanjoo, *Parātrīśikā Laghuvṛtti* (1982).

See also *Kashmir Shaivism–The Secret Supreme* 16.114.

DVD 5.1 (07:21)

सांख्ययोगौ पृथग्बालाः प्रवदन्ति न पण्डिताः ।

sāṅkhyayogau pṛthagbālāḥ pravadanti na paṇḍitāḥ /

"This is *karma saṁnyās* and this is *karma yoga*, these are separate!" *Bālāḥ pravadanti*, those who are ignorant people they think that these are two different elements; *karma saṁnyās* is one element and *karma yoga* is another element.

एकमप्यास्थितः सम्यगुभयोर्विन्दते फलम् ॥४॥

ekamapyāsthitaḥ samyagubhayorvindate phalam //4//

If you remain in one [then] you are established in both ways. *Karma yoga* cannot exist without *karma saṁnyāsa*; *karma saṁnyāsa* cannot work without *karma yoga*.

And predominant is *karma yoga*. By *karma yoga, karma saṁnyāsa* is also possible. But only by *karma saṁnyāsa, karma yoga* is not possible. With *karma yoga, karma saṁnyāsa* is also possible.

Because if you are always active in doing all of the things other than God consciousness [while remaining in God consciousness], then you are established in God consciousness there, permanently. So they are both interdependent. They are not two. It is only one, one element. And one element shines in *karma yoga* and *karma saṁnyāsa*; *karma saṁnyāsa* and *karma yoga* are one. You should not think that these are two different paths.

JOHN: So *karma yoga* is to establish yourself in God consciousness through action.

SWAMIJI: Through action, yes.

JOHN: And *karma saṁnyās* is to be in God consciousness . . .

SWAMIJI: Without action.

JOHN: . . . without action.

SWAMIJI: That does not work. That works only when you are active.

DVD 5.1 (09:32)

यत्सांख्यैः प्राप्यते स्थानं तद्योगैरनुगम्यते ।

एकं सांख्यं च योगं च यः पश्यति स पश्यति ॥५॥

yatsāṅkhyaiḥ prāpyate sthānaṁ tadyogairanugamyate /
ekaṁ sāṅkhyaṁ ca yogaṁ ca yaḥ paśyati sa paśyati //5//[140]

संन्यासस्तु महाबाहो दुःखमाप्तुमयोगतः
योगयुक्तो मुनिर्ब्रह्म न चिरेणाधिगच्छति ॥६॥

saṁnyāsastu mahābāho duḥkhamāptumayogataḥ /
yogayukto munirbrahma na cireṇādhigacchati //6//

Karma saṁnyāsa, O Mahābāho, O Arjuna, *karma saṁnyāsa* is not possible, it is very difficult to do *karma saṁnyāsa* without *karma yoga*. If *karma yoga* is not attached with *karma saṁnyāsa, karma saṁnyāsa* does not work. But *karma yoga yukta*, [one] who is *karma yogi*, who develops *yoga* in action, he is a *yogi* and *na cireṇa brahma gachati*, he rushes and is united in the supreme Parabhairava state in a few moments if he is established in *karma yoga*.

So *karma yoga* is the key, the master key of [achieving] *karma saṁnyāsa*. When you are established in *karma yoga,* you have abandoned all *karmas*, you are complete. *Karma saṁnyāsa* is very great but *karma saṁnyāsa* works only when there is *karma yoga*.

So it is only one path. You should not think, one should not think that these are two pathways, two directions. This is only one direction. *Karma saṁnyāsa* and *karma yoga* both work together. And luckily you will find the reality of the supreme state of Parabhairava in no time, in just one twinkling of the eye.

---

140 "That state which is obtained by abandoning actions, the same state is obtained by union of actions in *yoga*. So, that person who believes that *sāṁkhyā* [i.e., *karma saṁnyāsa*] and *yoga* [i.e., *karma yoga*] are actually one, he is the real seer, he has observed correctly. Otherwise, this is an incorrect observation to observe that *sāṁkhyā* is separate and *yoga* is separate. *Sāṁkhyā* and *yoga* must be united in one point. And that one-pointedness will be obtained by watching your breath in action. It is my interpretation." *Bhagavad Gītā* (1978).

See footnote 44 for a discussion of "watching your breath."

Saṁnyāsastu, but, but, but, (*tu* means but), but *saṁnyāsa*, but *karma saṁnyāsa*. "But" means it does not work: "but *karma saṁnyāsa*"–"but" (*tu*). The meaning of *tu* is "but". You know "but"? "But" means: "but this *karma saṁnyāsa* does not work, and *karma yoga*, yes, well and good." *Karma yoga* will direct you to *karma saṁnyāsa*; *karma saṁnyāsa* won't–it is "but", i.e., there is some difficulty.

One is right hand and [the other] is left hand. There must be right hand as *karma yoga* and left hand as *karma saṁnyāsa*. When there is right hand, the left hand is also in process. When there is only the left hand, the right hand is not in process and both fail–they don't work.

So this is the cream of Shaivism that you should work.

The proverb is: "work is worship . . . work is worship!"

To sit idle and, "*zzzz* (snore)", what is that?

Nothing comes out of it.

Yoga rahitasya saṁnyāsamāptuṁ duḥkhameva [comm.]. *Yoga rahitasya* means [one] who is deprived of *karma yoga*. For him, *karma saṁnyāsamāptuṁ duḥkhameva*, *karma saṁnyāsa* is not possible for him to achieve. *Prāgnītyā karmaṇāṁ duḥsaṁnyāsatvāt*, because we have already explained in previous chapters that *karma saṁnyāsa* is not possible by sitting in one corner in the *pūja* room and doing *pūja*–that won't work. That is fraud.

You should come out from [the *pūja* room and] open the door and come out in the field. In the field this works.[141]

141 "If you have not pointed out the point of God consciousness, you cannot abandon action. You can abandon actions only when you are sentenced to God consciousness, when your mind and intellect are focused to that point of God consciousness. And that focusing is not done in a sluggish way, it is done while doing all the activities of your daily life. So, without *yoga*, *saṁnyāsa* is not possible. And *saṁnyāsa* is not possible without *yoga*. *Karma saṁnyāsa*, abandoning of actions cannot take place without *yoga*; and because if you abandon all your actions and sit, still you will do something; you have not totally discarded all your actions. In mind, in intellect, in something, in breathing, you will do something. And if you are breathing, if you are talking, if you are walking, if you are going to movies, if you are doing any disgusted thing in this world, and at the same time you are concentrated on your point of that God consciousness, you are doing nothing. You have done nothing. You won't be blamed for any action.

The means of entering in God consciousness is His *Sakti*. The means of entering into God consciousness is not God. Through God you cannot enter into God consciousness. Through His *Śakti* you can enter into God consciousness. *Śakti* is the manifestation of the Lord. The manifestation of Parabhairava is the whole universe. *Through* the universe you can obtain God consciousness.

So, that is the reality of all religions, all knowledge, although all of these religions are just vague. These other religions do not work, but still they should know that they won't work; they won't work until they do some business [laughs]. They have to work.

Yogibhistu sulabhamevaitat–ityuktaṁ prāk, but *karma yogīs*, for *karma yogīs*, everything is possible.

DVD 5.1 (16:09)

योगयुक्तो विशुद्धात्मा विजितात्मा जितेन्द्रियः ।
सर्वभूतात्मभूतात्मा कुर्वन्नपि न लिप्यते ॥७॥

yogayukto viśuddhātmā vijitātmā jitendriyaḥ
sarvabhūtātmabhūtātmā kurvannapi na lipyate //7//

Yogayukta, [the one] who is established in *karma yoga*, *viśuddhātmā*, and whose mind is always pure, without any impressions, outside impressions [or] internal impressions . . .

Not [only] outside impressions. Outside impressions and internal impressions both exist in *karma saṁnyāsa*, and in *karma yoga,* outside impressions and internal impressions both vanish. This is the trick of *karma yoga.*

. . . *vijitātmā*, and he has conquered his mind, *jitendriyaḥ,* he has conquered all of his organs, *sarva bhūtātma bhūtātmā*, and he becomes one with the universe. *Kurvannapi*, although he does everything, *na lipyate*, he does not do anything.

Sa sarvapi kurvāṇo na lipyate [comm.]. If he does everything, he does not do anything. Because *karaṇa pratiṣedha arūḍhatvāt*, he always says, "I have done nothing." Although he does everything, he says, "no, I have not done anything."

You are just a liberated being, elevated. This is the theory of this *Bhagavad Gītā* here." *Bhagavad Gītā* (1978).

DVD 5.1 (17:45)

नैव किंचित्करोमीति युक्तो मन्येत तत्त्ववित् ।
पश्यञ्श‍ृण्वन्स्पृशञ्जिघ्रन्नश्नन्गच्छन्श्वसन्स्वपन् ॥८॥
प्रलपन्विसृजन्गृह्णन्नुन्मिषन्निमिषन्नपि ।
इन्द्रियाणीन्द्रियार्थेषु वर्तन्त इति धारयन् ॥९॥

naiva kiñcitkaromīte yukto manyeta tattvavit /
paśyañśṛṇvanspṛśañjighrannaśnangacchanśvasansvapan //8
pralapanvisṛjangṛhṇannunmiṣannimiṣannapi /
indriyāṇīnidriyārtheṣu vartanta iti dhārayan //9//

Naiva kiñcitkaromīti . . .
What *śloka*? Number 8th.
Naiva kiñcit karomīte, "I don't do anything." *Yukto* (*yukto* means *yogi*, *karma yogi*), *manyeta*, he believes that, "I don't do anything," *tattvavit*, because he is established in the supreme state of Bhairava. He [who] is established in the supreme state of Bhairava, he says, "although [I do] everything," he says, "I don't do anything." *Paśyan*, although he sees with eyes (*paśyan*), *śṛṇvan*, although he hears with ears (*śṛṇvan*), *spṛśan,* although he touches with this skin, (he touches, *spṛśan*), *jighran*, although he smells with nose, *aśnan*, although he eats with mouth, *gacchan*, although he walks with feet, *śvasan*, although he breathes, *svapan*, although he sleeps and snores, *pralapan*, although he cries, *visṛjan*, although he goes to bathroom and throws that stuff into toilet, *gṛhṇan*, although he holds with his hand anything, *unmiṣan nimiṣan api*, although he opens his eyes and closes his eyes, [in all of these actions], he says, "I don't do anything."

Indriyāṇīnidriyārtheṣu vartanta. [He says], "the organs are doing their own job, what have I have to do with them? I am separate; I am aloof from this organic *tamasha*. I am just the observer, I don't do anything."

DVD 5.1 (20:41)

ब्रह्मण्याधाय कर्माणि सङ्गं त्यक्त्वा करोति यः ।

लिप्यते न स पापेन पद्मपत्रमिवाम्भसा ॥१०॥

brahmaṇyādhāya karmāṇi saṅgaṁ tyaktvā karoti yaḥ /
lipyate na sa pāpena padmapatramivāmbhasā //10//

Pāpa means sin. Who is a sinner? The sinner is [one] who does anything and attributes [that action] to himself that, "I have done it." He is sinner. He'll be caught and he'll be shot.[142] If he has done good deeds and he says, "I have done good deeds," he'll be shot. If he has done bad deeds and he says, "I have done bad deeds," he'll be shot. He is a sinner; both are sinners. And on the contrary, the person who does everything and says, "I have done nothing," he is a *jīvan mukta*.

This is the trick of Shaivism.

Do everything and actually see that you don't do anything. If you do good deeds, you will be shot; if you do bad deeds, you will be shot, if you attribute it to yourself.

Right?

Thank you. You are assimilating my theory.

Ata eva darśanādīni, lipyate na sa pāpena [comm.]. This *pāpa*, this sin, does not touch him, and does not leave its impression in him [who does everything and understands, "I have done nothing"]. Just like the lotus leaf, although remaining in water for twenty-four hours, it [remains] without its touch, without its impressions. Those impressions do not touch that lotus leaf.

[Likewise], *ata eva darśanādīni kurvannapi*, although he sees, he touches, he smells, and he does everything, *asāvevam dhārayati*, he understands, not only [does he] understand ("understands" means *pratipattidārḍhyena niścinute*), he *believes*, actually he believes, "I have done nothing." He does not only [say this] for fun's sake; he does not [merely] say that, "I have not done anything," he actually *feels*, "I have done nothing."

Because that is fraud if you are pretending to be Parabhairava and say, "I do everything but I have not done anything," but internally . . .

DENISE: He feels he has done it.

SWAMIJI: . . . he feels he has done it–you are fraud. Then you

142 Swamiji is emphasizing the tremendous suffering inherent in claiming ownership over one's activities. [*Editor's note*]

are fraud. It must be in a natural way of understanding that you feel that.

That is *pratipattidārḍhyena niścinute*, he believes in his own nature, but he is responsible for speaking like this. If he speaks just to throw impression on his disciples [that], "I have done nothing," he will be shot dead by another demon. Because nothing is concealed there. In the state of Parabhairava, nothing is concealed. You cannot hide anything.

My servant in Ishber[143] would tell [me] when he dies–his name was Ramānji, he was my gardener–he said, "when I die, there they will [try to] catch me, [but] I will secretly hide somewhere where they won't touch me."

DENISE: Where death won't catch him.

SWAMIJI: Huh?

DENISE: Where who won't catch him, death?

SWAMIJI: No. There in another world after death.

I said, "you will be caught there also; they won't leave you."

Where can he hide? There is nothing to hide, you can't hide anything. Everything is vividly found there.

So you should not pretend. You should not pretend [by saying] that, "I am Bhairava!"

Tadeva brahmaṇi karmaṇāṁ samarpaṇam [comm.]. That is called, in other words, *brahmaṇi karmaṇāṁ samarpaṇam*, when you bestow all of your deeds into the supreme state of Bhairava. *Atra cihnamasya gatasaṁgatā*, the sign of this is *gatasaṁgatā*, he is not changed, he is unchangeable; he is always shining with joy.

> In Ramana Maharshi's *ashram* there was one *yogi*, he would say, "my *kuṇḍalinī* has risen." He would tell me, "my *kuṇḍalinī* has risen [but] oh, I have got pain here, I have pain here, I have got pain here. Oh! Oh! It is very terrible!" I told him, "*kuṇḍalinī* is not terrible. You have got some ghost that has entered in your brain. It is not *kuṇḍalinī*. You are painful; it is not painful. *Kuṇḍalinī* is *never* painful, it is filled with joy." He said, "no, I have got this whole area, it is vibrating and it is . . ."
>
> **DENISE:** Throbbing.

143 Swamiji is referring to his first *ashram* at upper Ishber.

SWAMIJI: " . . . throbbing and with pain, acute pain. I cannot exist [with this pain]." I said, "no, it is not *kuṇḍalinī*, it is some other ghost in you."
JONATHAN: This was another saint there? This was another person? Not Ramana Maharshi?
SWAMIJI: In Ramana Maharshi's hall, they were all practicing *yoga* before Ramana Maharshi and this [person] was . . . unfortunately he was seated just on my right side. When I was doing practice and he was also doing practice and he [told me that he saw that] Ramana Maharshi was speaking to me and he was fond of me to be there. And he told me that, "[you must be] an important person [to] Ramana Maharshi, so I will tell [you about] my own experience of *kuṇḍalinī.*" And he told me, "I have risen my *kuṇḍalinī* and it is all terrible here. I have got pain here and here and here [laughs]." I said to him, "It is not *kuṇḍalinī*, it is some serpent who has thrown some poison in you and you will die."
DENISE: What did he say? He still thought it was *kuṇḍalinī*?
SWAMIJI: He said, "no, no, no it is *kuṇḍalinī*. It is *kuṇḍalinī* which has risen in me!" I said, "no it is not! Ask Bhagavan, ask Ramana Maharshi." He said, "no, I won't ask, he will beat me."
DENISE: Swamiji, didn't Shri Ramana Maharishi mostly practice *karma saṁnyās*?
SWAMIJI: Huh?
DENISE: *Karma saṁnyās*.
SWAMIJI: No, *karma saṁnyās*, no. He used to tell them, "just find out who you are, *bas*! Just find out who you are, concentrate on 'I', that [Being] who is inside, who is talking, who is walking. Concentrate on that Being and you will find the truth." He said, "there is no need of any *mantra*."

DVD 5.1 (30:15)

कायेन मनसा बुद्ध्या केवलैरिन्द्रियैरपि ।
योगिनः कर्म कुर्वन्ति सङ्गं त्यक्त्वात्मसिद्धये ॥ ११ ॥

kāyena manasā buddhyā kevalairindriyairapi /
yoginaḥ karma kurvanti saṅgaṁ tyaktvātmasiddhaye //11//

There are *yogīs*, O Arjuna, with *kāyena* (with body), *manasā* (with mind), with *buddhyā* (intellect), *kevalair indriyairapi*, with [detachment to these] organs. *Yoginaḥ*, those *yogīs*, *karma kurvanti*, they do action, they do act, they don't sit idle. But only one thing, they have got that trick. That trick is *saṅgaṁ tyaktva,* they are not attached to any work, *ātma siddhaye*, because their *ātma*, their Self is illuminated. Their Self is ex . . .

DENISE: Expanded.

SWAMIJI: . . . expanded in the state of Parabhairava.

Next one, 12th *śloka*.

DVD 5.1 (31:30)

युक्तः कर्मफलं त्यक्त्वा शान्तिमाप्नोति नैष्ठिकीम् ।
अयुक्तः कामकारेण फले सक्तो निबध्यते ॥१२॥

yuktaḥ karmaphalaṁ tyaktvā śāntimāpnoti naiṣṭhikīm /
ayuktaḥ kāmakāreṇa phale sakto nibadhyate //12//

Yuktaḥ means *karma yogi* and *ayuktaḥ* means *karma saṁnyāsin* (*ayuktaḥ* means who is not a *yogi*, who abandons all activities, i.e., *karma saṁnyāsa)–karma saṁnyāsa* and *karma yoga.* He points out the difference between these two *yogas* separately. If you at all explain them separately, then what will happen? *Yuktaḥ, karma yogi*, what *karma yogi* does? *Karma phalaṁ tyaktvā śāntimāpnoti naiṣṭhikīm.* He is sentenced in God consciousness and the fruit of his *karmas* do not take place. He does not get any fruit from any *karma*, i.e., [one] who is a *karma yogi. Ayukta*, and [one] who is *karma saṁnyāsi*, who has left [all] activity, *kāmakāreṇa*, because the impressions are there, for him, the impressions remain life-long,[144] *phale sakto nibadhyate*, and he is caught [in the circle of his actions], and he is killed. He is

144 Later in the text, Swamiji clarifies that the impression of what the *karma saṁnyāsi* has given up remains throughout his life. [*Editor's note*]

shot dead afterwards.[145] So *karma saṁnyāsa* only does not work. There must be *karma yoga*. *Karma yoga* and *karma saṁnyāsa* are interdependent. *Karma saṁnyāsa* will work when there is *karma yoga*, and *karma yoga* will work when there is *karma saṁnyāsa*. It is only one path combined.

Naiṣṭhikīm means *apunarāvartinīm*; *naiṣṭhikīm* means *apunarāvartinīm*, when you don't return to this degraded field [i.e., *saṁsāra*].

DVD 5.1 (33:55)

सर्वकर्माणि मनसा संन्यस्यास्ते सुखं वशी ।
नवद्वारे पुरे देहे नैव कुर्वन्न कारयन् ॥१३॥

sarvakarmāṇi manasā saṁnyasyāste sukhaṁ vaśī /
navadvāre pure dehe naiva kurvanna kārayan //13//

Sarva karmāṇi manasā, all activities, *manasā*, through mind, who *saṁnyasya*, through mind he abandons [all activity], and *sukhaṁ,* and is established peacefully. *Vaśī*, [his field of organs, mind, intellect, and body is] controlled [by him] from all sides. *Navadvāre pure dehe*, in his body, which is just like . . . [his body] has got nine doors and windows, which are all of his organs–these windows and doors in his body–*naiva kurvanna*, in this body, he neither does anything nor [makes his organs do] anything, because he is inside.[146] He is [existing] in this body, [but] he is inside. What has he to do with doors and windows?

He can go into another house [i.e., body] and live there. So this *dvāra* (door) has nothing to do with [the *yogi*]; it has no attachment with that being who is a *karma yogi*. A *karma yogi* is absolutely away from that house, i.e., that body.

Yathā veśmāntargatasya puṁso na gṛhagatair jīrṇatvādi bhir-

145 Swamiji is again emphasizing the tremendous suffering inherent in claiming ownership over one's activities. [*Editor's note*]

146 "He acts, but through mind he does not act at all. Mind does not follow his actions. His mind is focused to God consciousness and he does everything. He does everything, anything absurd he does also. But he is not entangled in that action because he is away from that act. So he abandons all his actions through his mind, not through not acting." *Bhagavad Gītā* (1978).

yogaḥ [comm.]. Just as *yathā veśmāntargatasya puṁso*, anybody who has entered into some body or some house, *gṛha-gatair jīrṇatvādibhiryogaḥ*, if that house [or body] is rotten, [the dweller] does not get rotted.

Who?

DENISE: That person who owns that house.

SWAMIJI: The person who lives there.

Evaṁ mama, in the same way, [you should feel], "I am in this house, I am situated in the house [but] *cakṣurādicchidragavākṣanavakālaṅkṛta dehagehaga-tasya na taddharmayogaḥ*, I have nothing to do with this house. I can leave this house and enter into another house.

DVD 5.1 (36:49)

न कर्तृत्वं न कर्माणि लोकस्य सृजति प्रभुः ।
न कर्मफलसंयोगं स्वभावस्तु प्रवर्तते ॥१४॥

na kartṛtvaṁ na karmāṇi lokasya sṛjati prabhuḥ /
na karmaphalasaṁyogaṁ svabhāvastu pravartate //14//
[not translated][147]

Now, [Abhinavagupta commentates upon] this *śloka*, this is the 14th *śloka*.

147 "Lord Siva does not induce a person to do some act or to be an actor. Neither God induces a person to be an actor or be involved in actions, *na karma phala saṁyogaṁ*, or Lord does not induce him to get the fruit of his actions. *Svabhāvastu pravartate*, this is the nature of actions that they bear fruit. And at the time of bearing fruit, you must remain away from that. If, through the good actions of yours, of your organs, you are served a plate of cheese with *masala* and everything, and *ghee*, and butter and everything, you should not think it is sweet. You should taste it, but don't be involved in that taste. Because this is the fruit of your organs, not fruit of your *ātman,* of yourself. Because yourself is away from any action, he is above that action, but you just taste it though your organs. Don't think that it is tasty. Enjoy it, but still don't think it is tasty. Or that *laukī* [an Indian vegetable], which you tasted there on that day, we thought it was very bad, it had very bad taste. You should not think that, like that. [Eat it] and think that organs have [eaten] it." *Bhagavad Gītā* (1978).

Eṣa ātmā na kiṁcitkasyacitkaroti [comm.]. This *ātmā*, he does not do anything to anybody. *Pravṛttistvasya svabhāvamātraṁ na phalepsayā*, it is his nature to do [activity], but he does not ask any . . . he does not desire fruit from it, whatever he does.

tathāhi. saṁvedanātmano bhagavataḥ prakāśānanda-svātanatrya-paramārthasvabhāvasya svabhāva-mātrākṣipta-samasta-sṛṣṭi-sthiti-saṁhṛti-prabandhasya svasvabhāvānna manāgapyapāpo jātucit [comm.]

That *yogi* who is filled with *sṛṣṭi*, *sthiti*, *saṁhāra*, *pidāna*, and *anugrāha* (all of these five activities of his glamour[148]), he is never away from [these activities]. Sometimes he is doing creation, sometimes he is doing protection, sometimes he is doing destruction, sometimes he is concealing, and sometimes he is revealing. This is his nature.

JOHN: For the *yogi*?

SWAMIJI: For the *yogi*, yes, *karma yogi.*

JOHN: So what do these five acts mean for a *yogi*?

SWAMIJI: These are five energies. These five energies [are] his nature.

JOHN: So whatever he is doing. Either he is doing protection or he is doing creation . . .

SWAMIJI: Sometimes he is doing . . . in one way he is doing creation and in another way he is doing destruction at the same time.

JOHN: When you see one thing, you are creating that, and you are destroying the previous thing. Just like that.[149]

SWAMIJI: Yes.

Even then, *svasvabhāvāt na manāgapyapāpo jātucit*, but his nature of being established in Parabhairava state is unmoved. If [his nature] is working upon *sṛṣṭi*, it is unmoved; in *sthiti*, it is unmoved; *samhṛti*, *pidāna*, and *anugrāha*, in all of these five acts, [his nature] is unmoved. He is doing nothing.

JOHN: How do those two acts function for a *yogi* . . .

---

148 Creating, protecting, destroying, concealing, and revealing, respectively. [*Editor's note*]

149 The mechanics of these five acts are described exhaustively in Kṣemarāja's *Spanda Saṁdoha*. Swamiji's translation of this text will be published in the near future. [*Editor's note*]

SWAMIJI: Huh?

JOHN: . . . concealing and revealing? Concealing and revealing, those are the actual . . . ?

SWAMIJI: No, all the five.

JOHN: But how does a *yogi* . . . what does it mean to say a *yogi* "does" concealing and revealing?

SWAMIJI: Huh?

JOHN: What does it mean to say that the *yogi* . . . ?

SWAMIJI: No, it is His nature. It is His nature. These five acts, the five acts are the nature of Parabhairava.

JOHN: Parabhairava.

SWAMIJI: Yes, He creates, He protects, He destroys, He conceals, and He reveals.

DENISE: He conceals and reveals His own nature . . .

SWAMIJI: His own nature.

DENISE: . . . to Himself?

SWAMIJI: To Himself, yes.

If Parabhairava creates this whole world, what then? He has not [actually] "created" this whole world. It is His glamour.[150] If he has destroyed this whole world, what then? He is still in the Parabhairava state, in His own nature. And in both ways [i.e., creation and destruction], He is situated in His own nature. He is not away from His nature anywhere–never!

If he is always astray, he has gone astray, where will he go astray?

You know astray?

JONATHAN: Yes.

SWAMIJI: He who is *darbha-dhar*, who is going from one picture house to another picture house and from that picture house to another picture house.

What then?

JONATHAN: For him it doesn't matter.

SWAMIJI: For him it does not matter. For those who are very cautious, who are always holding the pious things, *they* are caught, they will be shot. Because they are afraid of impure thoughts; they [only] like pious thoughts [so] they will be shot

150 "It is not created as you create a child, outside. It is created *in* your own nature. That way, the creation of His universe takes place." Swami Lakshmanjoo, *Parāprāveśikā* by Kṣemarāja (1980).

dead.

JOHN: That's why Lord Śiva is *tamoguṇa.*

SWAMIJI: Huh?

No, not *tamoguṇa* [laughs]

JOHN: You told us once that Lord Śiva is in that lowest *guṇa* because nothing there obscures His nature. Those people who only want to be pious, they only want to be in *sattva guṇa* . . .

SWAMIJI: Those who want to be pious, they are fools. Those who want to be impure, they are also fools. Those who are pious and fools also, and are everywhere also, they are fine.

Whatever is discarded . . . when there is discarding and possessing, possessing and discarding, discarding and possessing, [both are] very sinful.

JOHN: Holding onto either one of those.

SWAMIJI: Yes.

You can [eat] pomegranate or you don't [eat] pomegranate, [either way is] well and good. You [eat] butter or you don't [eat] butter, well and good. But only [eating] butter and not [eating anything] other than butter, it is failure [laughs].

na kartṛtvaṁ na karmāṇi lokasya sṛjati prabhuḥ /
na karmaphalasaṁ yogaṁ svabhāvastu pravartate //14//

It is not *kartṛtva* or *karma*, neither objectivity [i.e., *karma*] nor subjectivity [i.e., *kartṛtva*]. These are one. Actually these are one. *Karma phalasaṁ yogaṁ*[151] is also the same. *Svabhāvastu pravartate*, it is the nature of God that you find everywhere.

Pravṛttisvasya svabhāvamātraṁ [comm.], this *pravṛtti* is his nature. It is not bad.[152] He can do this thing or he can not do this thing, it is all good. But [if] he will only do good things and he will not do bad things, this is bad; this will carry him to failure.

Why does he discard bad things and why does he possess good things? It is bad. Good things are there and bad things are there; in both ways this is the glamour of Parabhairava. Why should he discriminate these two?

Whatever is outside, that is inside. Whatever is inside, that is

151 The fruits of *karma* (activity). [*Editor's note*]

152 *Pravṛtti* "is the nature of the flow of organs and flow of intellect, mind, and body, that they act accordingly with their objects, with their meant objects." *Bhagavad Gītā* (1978).

outside. You should come to *this* understanding.

Tasmāt-cetanaḥ svatantraḥ parameśvara eva tathā tathā bhāti [comm.]. This *cetanaḥ parameśvara*, you will find *cetana*, all-consciousness, filled with all-consciousness. Parameśvara/ Parabhairava shines everywhere, in each and every way. *Iti na tad-vayatiriktaṁ kriyātatphalādikamiti siddhāntaḥ*, nothing is excluded there, everything is included. *Iti siddhāntaḥ*, this is the *siddhāntaḥ,* this is the topmost *siddhānta,* topmost philosophy of Parabhairava state–Shaivism.

Chapter 5 Part 2

Ata eva kriyātatphalayorabhāve vidhiphalasyāpi nādṛṣṭakṛtatā kācit [intro. comm.]. When *kriyā* (action) and its *phala* (fruit) are not separate from each other, *vidhi phalasyā* (*vidhi* means *karma*[153]), the fruit of your actions are not excluded [from the state of Parabhairava]. It is included. The fruit of *karma* is also included; the fruit of *karma* (i.e., the fruit of your actions), the fruit of . . . actual fruits.

Ityardhenābhidhāyārdhānterana saṁsāriṇaḥ prati tatsamarthanaṁ kartumāha. And on the contrary, he says, "what [about] those who are situated in worldly affairs? What have they got? What have they achieved [by their *karma* and its fruits]?"

DVD 5.2 (01:01)

नादत्ते कस्यचित्पापं न चैव सुकृतं विभुः ।
अज्ञानेनावृतं ज्ञानं तेन मुह्यन्ति जन्तवः ॥१५॥

nādatte kasyacitpāpaṁ na caiva sukṛtaṁ vibhu /
ajñānenāvṛtaṁ jñānaṁ tena muhyanti jantavaḥ //15//

This is 15th *śloka*.

Nādatte kasyacitpāpaṁ, he does not ask anybody to do [sinful] actions; he does not push anybody to do *sukṛtaṁ* (good actions). *Ajñānena avṛtaṁ jñānaṁ*, actually, knowledge is subsided by ignorance. By that ignorance everybody is *muhyanti* (*muhyanti* means they are mislead).

They are mislead [in thinking] that, "I have done this blunder, what will happen to me now?" [Or he thinks], "these are good actions that I have done, [so] I will be more happy now." In both ways, they are caught and they are shot.

153 "*Vidhi* means *prārabdha karma*." *Bhagavad Gītā* (1978).

DVD 5.2 (02:07)

ज्ञानेन तु तदज्ञानं येषां नाशितमात्मनः ।
तेषामादित्यवज्ज्ञानं प्रकाशयति तत्परम् ॥ १६ ॥

jñānena tu tadajñānaṁ yeṣāṁ nāśitamātmanaḥ /
teṣāmādityavajjñānaṁ prakāśayati tatparam //16//

But on the contrary, [those persons] whose ignorance is discarded by knowledge, to them, *ādityavat jñānaṁ prakāśayati tatparam*, that supreme knowledge of God consciousness shines in them always.

Jñānena tu ajñāne nāśite [comm.]. When *jñāna* subsides *ajñāna* (ignorance), *jñānasya svaprakāśatvaṁ svataḥ siddham*, *jñāna* shines everywhere for them. *Yathā ādityasya tamasi naṣṭe*, just like when the sun rises and all ignorance, all darkness, is nowhere to be found.

Vinivatritāyāṁ hi śaṅkāyām amṛtam amṛtakāryaṁ svayameva karoti. When all doubts are clarified, then this nectar works. Nectar means the state of Bhairava–it shines everywhere. And this nectar of the Parabhairava state is possible [only] to those, *tad gata buddhi manasāṁ*, who are always bent upon finding out the state of Bhairava in each and every respect. [Lord Kṛṣṇa] says:

DVD 5.2 (04:31)

तद्बुद्धयस्तदात्मानस्तन्निष्ठास्तत्परायणाः ।
गच्छन्त्यपुनरावृत्तिं ज्ञाननिर्धौतकल्मषाः ॥ १७ ॥

tadbuddhayastadātmānastanniṣṭhāstatparāyaṇāḥ /
gacchantyapunarāvṛttiṁ jñānanirdhautakalmaṣāḥ //17//

Tad buddhaya, whatever intellectual process they have, *tad ātmāna*, their mind is always diverted towards that God consciousness. *Tad niṣṭhā*, their position [i.e., attention] is also diverted towards God consciousness. *Tat parāyaṇāḥ*, they are bent upon finding out God consciousness. And *tad niṣṭhāḥ*, *tat parāyaṇāḥ*, and they are always bent upon holding [on to] it with all [of their] might. *Gacchantyapunarāvṛttiṁ*, they actually are sentenced to that supreme Parabhairava state where there is no hope to return [to ignorance]. They are always amidst that glamour of Parabhairava state. *Jñānanirdhauta-kalmaṣāḥ,* by that knowledge everything is washed. Whatever is and whatever is not, that is all washed. "Washed" means that [everything becomes] clarified [with the real knowledge of Parabhairava] and it has that whitewash of Parabhairava everywhere. Good, bad, disgusting, whatever it is, it is all divine.

DVD 5.2 (06:35)

स्मरन्तोऽपि मुहुस्त्वेतत्स्पृशन्तोऽपि स्वकर्मणि ।
सक्ता अपि न सज्जन्ति पङ्के रविकरा इव ॥१८॥

smaranto'pi muhustvetatspṛśanto'pi svakarmaṇī /
saktā api na sajjanti paṅke ravikarā iva //18//
[not recited or translated][154]

विद्याविनयसंपन्ने ब्राह्मणे गवि हस्तिनि ।
शुनि चैव श्वपाके च पण्डिताः समदर्शिनः ॥१९॥

vidyāvinayasaṁpanne brāhmaṇe gavi hastini /
śuni caiva śvapāke ca paṇḍitāḥ samadarśinaḥ //19//

Vidyāvinaya saṁpanne brāhmaṇe, in a brahmin . . .

Who is a brahmin?

[The one] who has got knowledge and who has got all qualifications.[155]

154 "Although they think [about] and they enjoy those worldly pleasures, and they are attached to those senses, [but] they are not attached, they are absolutely away from that, absolutely free from those actions. How? Just like the rays of sun, although they have sunk in mud, but they have nothing to do with mud; mud does not stick to them." *Bhagavad Gītā* (1978).

155 "*Vidyā vinaya saṁpanne*, who is filled with *vidyā* and *vinaya* (knowledge and humility). If there is knowledge and not humility, you

. . . in that brahmin; *gavi*, in a milking cow that produces milk for people; *hastini*, in an elephant; *śuni*, in dogs; *śvapāke ca*, in those who cut and kill dogs and eat its flesh; *paṇḍitāḥ samadarśinaḥ*, those [who are] actually established in the Parabhairava state see [all of these] in the same way. They don't see in a brahmin that the brahmin is pure; they don't see in a cow that she is *mātā*, [that] she is the mother of all living beings and producing milk for them; they don't see . . . those people do not see in dogs that they are impure; *śvapāke ca*, and those who eat the flesh of dogs, they don't see that they are brutes. They don't see like that. *Paṇḍitāḥ samadarśinaḥ*, those [who are] established in Bhairava state, they see them [and know that] they are created by Lord Śiva. They are fine. In their own way, they are fine.

But it does not mean that I will go and . . .

DENISE: Eat dogs.

SWAMIJI: . . . eat dogs.

No, but I have to see that this is the glamour of God also. [The person] who is established in Parabhairava state, he must see the glamour of God everywhere, in those people also. But he should not dine with them. He should see them, he must have the impression, the knowledge, that this is also His glamour and it is not bad. If somebody eats a fly, "ammm," it is the glamour of God. Why should you get angry?

DENISE: So we shouldn't judge anything.

SWAMIJI: No, it is His way of expanding His nature.

JONATHAN: So those people that eat dogs, they don't have any choice. That's their job in this lifetime.

SWAMIJI: Yes.

JONATHAN: So, as Denise said, we shouldn't make judgments on those people.

SWAMIJI: No [affirmative].

JONATHAN: That's their job.

SWAMIJI: Yes.

---

have knowledge and you think you are elevated, that is *abhimāna* (arrogance, ego). That won't do. You must have knowledge and humility. You must think that, "I don't know everything." Already you know everything, but you must realize that you don't know. You must feel that you don't know everything. . . . that is the nature of Brahman." Ibid.

Ata eva samaṁ paśyanti [comm.]. *Samaṁ paśyanti ata eva*, but you should not do those things. You should not do those things. But you should see that [everything] is the glamour of God.

JONATHAN: So also if you see someone with leprosy, who has leprosy . . .

SWAMIJI: Yes.

JONATHAN: . . . that is also God's wish.

SWAMIJI: Yes.

JONATHAN: Or if somebody gets killed in a plane crash, that is also His play, isn't it? They shouldn't be attached to that. They shouldn't grieve or anything?

SWAMIJI: No [affirmative].

In *Vijñāna Bhairava*, it is said . . . [Abhinavagupta] gives the example of a *Vijñāna Bhairava śloka* here in his commentary:

ciddharmā sarvadeheṣu viśeṣo nāsti kutracit /
ataśca tanmayaṁ sarvaṁ bhāvayanbhavajijjanaḥ //
[*Vijñāna Bhairava*, 100th *śloka*]

Ciddharmā sarvadeheṣu, the *cit dharmā*, the consciousness, the aspect of consciousness is found everywhere, *sarva deheṣu*, in each and every body. *Viśeṣo nāsti*, there is no difference at all from one to another. *Ataśca tanmayaṁ sarvaṁ bhāvayan,* you should feel that this is just the glamour of God consciousness. The person who feels like that, *bhavajit*, he has conquered this whole universe and he is established in Parabhairava state for always. *Tasya cetthaṁ saṁbhāvanā*, he feels like that, internally he feels like that.

DVD 5.2 (12:22)

न प्रहृष्येत्प्रियं प्राप्य नोद्विजेत्प्राप्य चाप्रियम् ।
स्थिरबुद्धिरसंमूढो ब्रह्मविद्ब्रह्मणि स्थितः ॥२०॥

na prahṛṣyetpriyaṁ prāpya nodvijetprāpya cāpriyam /

sthirabuddhirasaṁmūḍho brahmavidbrahmaṇi sthitaḥ //20[156]

Na prahṛṣyet priyaṁ prāpya. If he sees something good, he does not get excited. *Na prahṛṣyet priyaṁ prāpya*, whenever he sees something good or exciting, he does not get excited. *Nodvijet-prāpya cāpriyam*, when he sees something bad happening [and says] that, "I have lost my kith and kin. They [have been] shot dead in battlefield!"

"Alright," he thinks, "this was God's will."

DENISE: His organs also don't . . .

SWAMIJI: Huh?

DENISE: His organs don't change with the experience?

SWAMIJI: No.

Sthirabuddhir, his *buddhi* (intellect) is *sthira*, one-pointed, *asaṁ mūdha*, he never gets illusion, *brahmavit*, he is always filled with knowledge of supreme Bhairava, and *brahmaṇi sthitaḥ,* he is established in supreme *brahma*–that person.

DVD 5.2 (13:53)

बाह्यस्पर्शेष्वसक्तात्मा विन्दत्यात्मनि यत्सुखम् ।
स ब्रह्मयोगयुक्तात्मा सुखमव्ययमश्नुते ॥२१॥

bāhyasparśeṣvasaktātmā vindatyātmani yatsukham /
sa brahmayogayuktātmā sukhamavyayamaśnute //21//

Bāhya sparśeṣvasaktātmā. Bāhya sparśa means those which are outward sensual objects. In sensual objects, the one who is not attached to sensual objects . . .

It does not mean he does not utilize sensual objects. He can utilize sensual objects but [he] should not get *attached* to sensual objects. If it is possible, he can have [them]; if it is not possible, he won't care, he won't weep.

Do you understand?

It is [those] sensual objects. He is not attached to sensual objects. He can utilize sensual objects if it is possible. If it is not possible, he won't beat his head for the sake of having sensual

156 Swamiji recites "*brahmadarśanam,*" which does not appear in the text. [*Editor's note*]

objects. That is *asaktātmā*, he is not a slave to it. *Vindatyātmani yatsukham*, in both ways he is established in the glamour of his Parabhairava state. He is always enjoying, without and with. With this [sensual enjoyment] and without that; [both ways] he is fine, deliciously delicious.

Yes, truly speaking, you should believe me!

DENISE: Like the taste within his own self is so sweet . . .

SWAMIJI: Yes.

DENISE: . . . he doesn't need anything else. But he can take if he likes.

SWAMIJI: Yes, he can take.

DENISE: It won't affect his consciousness. It won't make things sweeter. He will be the same.

SWAMIJI: Yes. How wonderful is Shaivism!

Sa hyevaṁ manyate.[157] This is the 22nd *śloka* now.

DVD 5.2 (16:18)

ये हि संस्पर्शजा भोगा दुःखयोनय एव ते ।
आद्यन्तवन्तः कौन्तेय न तेषु रमते बुधः ॥२२॥

ye hi saṁsparśajā bhogā duḥkhayonaya eva te /
ādyantavantaḥ kaunteya na teṣu ramate budhaḥ //22//

He thinks, the person who is established in the Parabhairava state thinks within himself, *bāhyaviṣayajā bhogā* [comm.], "these *bhogās*, these enjoyments which are placed before me, they are fine, they are fine, I can have them, but I am not particular to have them. If they are there, let them be there. If they are not there, well and good I won't have them. *Ādyantavantaḥ kaunteya*, they are coming and going, this is just the drama of my own nature. *Na teṣu ramate budhaḥ*, I am not attached. I am not attached that, "I must have this!"

DENISE: You are not hankering after them.

SWAMIJI: Hankering, I am not hankering.

JONATHAN: Fine anyway.

SWAMIJI: I am fine in both ways.

157 "Whenever he is enjoying these pleasures of senses, he thinks:" *Bhagavad Gītā* (1978).

Next, the 23rd one.

DVD 5.2 (17:46)

शक्नोतीहैव यः सोढुं प्राक् शरीरविमोचनात् ।
कामक्रोधोद्भवं वेगं स योगी स सुखी मतः ॥२३॥

śaknotīhaiva yaḥ soḍhuṁ prāk śarīravimocanāt /
kāmakrodhodbhavaṁ vegaṁ sa yogī sa sukhī mataḥ //23//

That person who can tolerate the *vega* (impulse) of *kāma* and *krodha* (desire and wrath) in [their] lifetime; in their lifetime, [the one] who can subside this desire and wrath . . .[158]

These are very difficult to subside.

DVD 5.2 (18:30)

अन्तःसुखोऽन्तरारामस्तथान्तर्ज्योतिरेव यः ।
स पार्थ परमं [योगं] स्थानं ब्रह्मभूतोऽधिगच्छति ॥२

antaḥ sukho'ntarārāmastathāntarjyotireva yaḥ /
sa pārtha paramaṁ [yogaṁ]
sthānaṁ[159] *brahmabhūto'dhigacchati //24//*

Antaḥ sukha, [the one] who is established in the internal peaceful state of Parabhairava, *antarārāmaḥ*, and who is resting in that peaceful state of Parabhairava, *tathāntarjyotireva*, who is illuminated by the internal light of Parabhairava (*tatha antar jyotir*, that is *antar jyotir eva*), *sa pārtha paramaṁ sthānaṁ brahmabhūto'dhigacchati*, O Arjuna, he is always Parabhairava and he remains in the Parabhairava state; and he, in the end also, is dissolved in the Parabhairava state. No power on earth can take him out of that state.

Atastasya-antareva bāhyānapekṣhi sukham [comm.]. He has

158 "In this very lifetime, if only for one second you can subside this force, control this force [and say], "no, I won't do it," then there is great pleasure. Great pleasure will come forth and govern the position of your intellect and mind. You will become blissful for your whole life." Ibid.

159 Swamiji recites *sthanam* in place of *yogam*. [*Editor's note*]

got that glamour of Parabhairava within, it is not without. He does not see that *sukha* (joy) without. Without, he can see [joy] but [when he sees joy] without, he will see [joy] without and see it within. This outside *sukha,* he will find out within. He won't find [joy out] there. He won't find out *sukha* in Denise or in John or in Jonathan or in Viresh. He will find out [Swamiji points to himself], not in one's body, but inside. Not body, not inside body. It is inside.

Inside is outside and outside is inside [laughs]. It is nothing. Inside and outside is concerning body. When there is body, then inside is something else [i.e., distinguishable from the outside].

Inside is, for instance, [when] you keep your eyes wide open [Swamiji demonstrates Bhairava *mudrā*], [then] you are inside. This is inside! What?

DENISE: When you keep your eyes wide open?

SWAMIJI: This is inside. Not in body. In body, it is not inside.

DENISE: Inside where?

SWAMIJI: Inside consciousness. This is consciousness.

I will show you, I will show you what is inside.

Come [Swamiji motions to Viresh to come and stand by him while Swamiji opens his eyes wide].

Feel! Feel! What is this?

VIRESH: Tickling?

SWAMIJI: Something is going on inside. That is inside! That is it.

DENISE: What you feel inside.

SWAMIJI: Huh?

DENISE: What he feels inside when you tickle him?

SWAMIJI: It is not inside the body. It is inside consciousness.

JONATHAN: So, like when you have a sensation of pain, pain is in your consciousness, it's not a reality in skin.

SWAMIJI: No, it is not in skin.

JONATHAN: It is actually in your consciousness.

SWAMIJI: Like this [Swamiji again demonstrates]. It is not . . . [with] eyes open, you can see inside. This is inside. Where you feel that.

DENISE: It's inside my consciousness?

SWAMIJI: That sensation.

DENISE: Yes.

SWAMIJI: That is inside.

antaḥ sukho'ntarārāmas tathāntarjyotireva yaḥ /
sa pārtha paramaṁ [yogaṁ]
sthānam brahmabhūto'dhigacchati //24//

Antaḥ sukha, His glamour is inside; *antarārāma*, he is lying inside; *antarjyoti,* he is illuminated inside. *Sa pārtha paramaṁ sthānaṁ brahmabhūto'dhigacchati*. O Arjuna, he is united with that supreme state of Parabhairava after being Parabhairava.

Because nobody can enter Parabhairava; nobody can enter the Parabhairava state. Only Parabhairava can enter into Parabhairava state. When you are Parabhairava, then you are likely to merge into Parabhairava.

JOHN: But everybody is Parabhairava.

SWAMIJI: Everybody is not. Parabhairava only!

JOHN: But there is nothing besides Parabhairava.

SWAMIJI: Not everybody. No, only Parabhairava can go into Parabhairava.

JOHN: But is there something besides Parabhairava?

SWAMIJI: Huh?

JOHN: There is only Parabhairava.

SWAMIJI: No, that is *māyā*. That is *māyā*, which is beside Parabhairava; that is the *māyā* of Parabhairava. That too is Parabhairava. That too will become Parabhairava in the end when it becomes Parabhairava, when it becomes united with Parabhairava. But there is no entry [for] any other foreign element in Parabhairava.

JOHN: So he keeps that *māyā* separate?

SWAMIJI: Huh?

JOHN: Parabhairava keeps that *māyā* separate?

SWAMIJI: Separate.

JOHN: So, in some sense you can say it is stuck Parabhairava?

SWAMIJI: It is *śakti*. No, it is the glamour of His energy. It is the glamour of His energy.[160] Although these [manifestations of *māyā*] are also rays of Parabhairava, [they are] not separated from Parabhairava, but actual Parabhairava is that who is the real Parabhairava. Parabhairava is only allowed to get entry into

160 "*Māyā* is just the offshoot of *svātantrya śakti* of Lord Siva, [His] independent energy, for those who are elevated souls, *māyā* is just *svātantrya śakti* for them." Swami Lakshmanjoo, *Tantrāloka* 9.155 (1977).

the Parabhairava state.

Vyavahāre tu mūḍhatvamiva [comm.]. In *vyavahāra*, in the daily routine of worldly activities, he is ignorant. He does not find any interest in this.

DENISE: Who?

SWAMIJI: The one who is established in Parabhairava. If you tell him, "do you want curds (yogurt)?"

[He says], "all right, I'll take curds."

[He is] not like me [because I say that] I don't want that *phulgobi* (cauliflower) because it gives me a tickling sensation [laughs].

JONATHAN: And that 'nutri-nugget' (soy meal).

SWAMIJI: Yes, 'nutri-nugget' also.

DVD 5.2 (26:00)

लभन्ते ब्रह्मनिर्वाणमृषयः क्षीणकल्मषाः ।
छिन्नद्वैधा यतात्मानः सर्वभूतहिते रताः ॥२५॥

labhante brahmanirvāṇamṛṣayaḥ kṣīṇakalmaṣāḥ /
chinnadvaidhā yatātmānaḥ sarvabhūtahite ratāḥ //25//

Brahma nirvāṇa, brahma nirvāṇa is *mokṣa* (liberation) and that state of Parabhairava is obtained by *ṛṣis*.

Which *ṛṣis*?

Kṣīṇa kalmaṣāḥ, [those] whose all sins have disappeared. Sins are good actions and bad actions–these are sins. Sinful acts are good actions and bad actions–these are sinful acts. These are all sins. [They are] included in sinful acts.

What is a sinful act?

DENISE: Good and bad actions.

SWAMIJI: Yes.

DENISE: Or attachment to them?

SWAMIJI: Attachment or non-attachment, these are sinful actions.

Chinna dvaidhā, they have not *dvaidhā*, they have not two things in view. When two things do not appear to them, [neither] sinful acts nor good acts, they do not remain before them. *Sarva bhūta hite ratāḥ*, they are bent upon producing glamour everywhere in the world. They want to survive [i.e., spread Parabhairava's] glamour everywhere, in good and bad actions also.

But that takes time in them, to [experience] this expansion. It will take time. It may take one or two lives, or three lives, or four lives, or one hundred lives. One does not know.

It is for them to decide. Because if they want it, then they will get it; if they do not want, they won't get it. Because it is for them to decide.

Actually they don't want to have it, i.e., this state of Parabhairava. Those people who are away from Parabhairava, they don't want it. They don't want to have it, possess it.

DENISE: Why? Why don't they want to have it?

SWAMIJI: Because they don't have it. They don't want to have it. They want to go to school; they want to go [and do other things].

DENISE: They have other aspirations.

SWAMIJI: Yes.

DVD 5.2 (29:13)

कामक्रोधविमुक्तानां यतीनां यतचेतसाम् ।
सर्वतो ब्रह्मनिर्वाणं वर्तते विदितात्मनाम् ।२६॥

kāmakrodhavimuktānāṁ yatīnāṁ yatacetasām /
sarvato brahmanirvāṇaṁ vartate viditātmanām //26//

[Lord Kṛṣṇa]: *Kāma krodha vimuktānāṁ.* Those [who] are away from *kāma* (desire) and *krodha* (wrath), *yatīnāṁ*, who are always alert, *yatajetasām*, whose mind is focused in the Parabhairava state, *sarvato brahma nirvāṇaṁ vartate*, as such *viditātmanām*, who have understood the reality of Parabhairava, *sarvato brahma nirvāṇaṁ vartate*, for them, everywhere there is *brahma nirvāṇaṁ*; there is only the Parabhairava state everywhere dancing and glamorizing [everything] for them, inside and outside.

Teśāṁ sarvataḥ–sarvāsvavasthāsu brahmasattā pāramārthikī na nirodhakālam apekṣate [comm.]. For them, there is no hurry. They have not to wait for this *brahma sattā*, [the reality of God consciousness]. *Brahma sattā* is available in hand, always! If they go out for a walk, *brahma sattā* is there. If they sleep, *brahma sattā* is there. If they do nothing, *brahma sattā* is there.

If they do everything, *brahma sattā* is there.

It is available; it is always in hand for them. No matter if he does not have it, still it is there. If he does not have it, if he doesn't like it, still it is there. This is the glamour of *brahma sattā* itself. It is just throbbing. Once it has caught you, it will never leave you. *Bas*, you are gone for good.

JOHN: This wanting, you said that . . .

SWAMIJI: Wanting . . . there is not wanting.

JOHN: . . . people don't want, most people don't want.

SWAMIJI: Oh, yes! They don't want.

JOHN: So this wanting comes by His grace?

SWAMIJI: Wanting comes by His disgrace [laughs], by His *tirodhāna śakti* (concealing energy). It is His . . .

JOHN: When you have that urge to become Parabhairava, then that's His *anugrāha* (grace) then.

SWAMIJI: That is *anugrāha*, but . . .

JOHN: Not wanting . . .

SWAMIJI: Wanting . . . not wanting.

JOHN: . . . is covering, is *tirodhāna*.

SWAMIJI: Yes.

DVD 5.2 (32:04)

स्पर्शान्कृत्वा बहिर्बाह्यांश्चक्षुश्चैवान्तरे भ्रुवोः ।
प्राणापानौ समौ कृत्वा नासाभ्यन्तरचारिणौ ॥२७॥

sparśānkṛtvā bahirbāhyāṁścakṣuścaivāntare bhruvoḥ /
prāṇāpānau samau kṛtvā nāsābhyantaracāriṇau //27//

[Lord Kṛṣṇa]: *Sparśān kṛtvā bahir bāhyāṁ. Bāhyāṁ sparśān bahi kṛtvā*, those outside sensual objects, you should keep them outside. *Cakṣu caivāntare bhruvoḥ*, [your mind should be focused] in between the two eyebrows; you must feel the sensation inside, between two eyebrows. *Prāṇāpānau samau kṛtvā, nāsā abhyantara cāriṇau*, you should breathe out and breathe in, in *samatā*. *Samatā* means . . .

No, this is very important.

For instance, you breathe in and you breathe out. Not like [you normally do]. You have not to breathe in and out like that. You have to breathe in your own *nāsa* (inner consciousness).

For instance, you have to breathe like this and this; only this much [Swamiji demonstrates by showing the tiny distance between his thumb and index finger]. You have not to breathe [heavily]–not like this. You have to breathe very slowly, very slowly. [So] slowly that [you do] not breathe at all. It takes only [a small] space to breathe. Only this much. This is the reality of one-pointedness.[161]

JONATHAN: But Swamiji, when you do that though, sometimes in breathing, you don't get enough breath; it feels like you're not going to get enough . . .

SWAMIJI: [laughs] No, it is not suffocation. You will never become suffocated, because it is life; it is life-full at that time. You know when in my courses[162] I was not breathing. I was breathing like this [Swamiji demonstrates]. When I was out [of my courses], then I would [breathe heavily].

JONATHAN: Yes, suddenly you would breathe.

SWAMIJI: Yes, that is outside. Inside is this [Swamiji demonstrates again], i.e., when you don't breathe at all. You breathe only from here to here, *bas*! That is all. So there is no breath. It is only the glamour of *madhya nāḍi*, the central vein. You are residing in the central vein, *suṣumnā nāḍi*. It is in *suṣumnā nāḍi*. It goes in *suṣumnā nāḍi* and [breath] is finished.

JONATHAN: But from a practical point of view, you were demonstrating that to me one day when you went to Harvan, and you stopped on the side of the road and you said, "the breath must only go this much." But if a normal person sits down and makes their breath go like that, then they are short of breath, isn't it? Or does that feeling go?

SWAMIJI: No, shorter breath.

JONATHAN: But there is that feeling that you need more

---

161 "*Prāṇāpānau samau kṛtvā*, and exhaling and inhaling must remain in equal (*samatā*) move-less movement, at the state where exhaling and inhaling do not take place. *Nāsa abhyantara cāriṇau.* It must move in your *cit śakti,* in your inner consciousness. . . . And it moves only in that one point that is without movement. When you do that, in half an hours time, your breath will stop and rush in the central vein (*suṣumnā nāḍi*). If you don't do that, you may do this practice for thirty centuries, nothing will happen." *Bhagavad Gītā* (1978).

162 "Courses" refers to the time when Swamiji was becoming established in the state of Parabhairava. [*Editor's note*]

breath.

SWAMIJI: No, you don't get urge for breathing. You don't get urge for breathing. This is something different!

JOHN: My experience is though when you try to be one-pointed on watching your breath and so forth . . .

SWAMIJI: When it is one-pointed, then you don't breathe.

JOHN: Breathing slows down automatically.

SWAMIJI: Not in so much space.

JOHN: So it becomes less and less as you . . .

SWAMIJI: Huh?

JOHN: When you are breathing and you are becoming more one-pointed then your breathing becomes less and less.

SWAMIJI: Less and less, less and less. And in the end, it breathes only this much.

JOHN: But my problem is before I get to that point . . .

SWAMIJI: If it comes down from here, it goes up to this, then it returns there.

JOHN: My experience is, when I become more one-pointed and it becomes less and less and less, all of a sudden that panic comes and I go, "aaaaaaaahhhh," I take that, like I'm not breathing, I get a shock that, "no, I'm not breathing and then I take a breath."

SWAMIJI: [laughs] That is because you are not focused in that Parabhairava state. When once you are focused in the Parabhairava state then you won't breathe because you are life-full.

JOHN: So how do we get over that gap of that panic of not taking full breaths?

SWAMIJI: Yes, in both ways it is divine. Both ways. If you breathe, that is also divine; if you don't breathe, that is also divine. It is this [Swamiji demonstrates the short distance of the movement of breath]. I showed you.

JONATHAN: You showed me that day.

SWAMIJI: It is said, *nāsābhyantaracāriṇa*, only breath does not move out from *nāsa*, out from *nāsika*. It moves only this much, this much [Swamiji demonstrates]. So there is no such breathing.

You should not examine it. It is automatic. It will happen automatically some day when you are glorified with my grace.

JOHN: What do you mean, Swamiji, when you say "lengthen

the breath and make it flow longer and longer?" When we were meditating, you said we should lengthen the breath, make it slower and longer. What does that mean?

SWAMIJI: Lengthen? Lengthen, not. You should breathe very slowly.

JONATHAN: You mean length of time and less in space.

SWAMIJI: Less space.

JONATHAN: And length in time.

SWAMIJI: Yes.

JONATHAN: So it should take longer to go even that little distance.

SWAMIJI: Yes.

JONATHAN: But you shouldn't make your breath long.

SWAMIJI: Long? No [laughs].

JONATHAN: That's what I am saying. You shouldn't do that! You should only do this much. But time should be longer . . .

SWAMIJI: Yes.

JONATHAN: . . . and space should be less.

SWAMIJI: Yes.

How wonderful!

DVD 5.2 (39:20)

यतेन्द्रियमनोबुद्धिर्मुनिर्मोक्षपरायणः ।
विगतेच्छाभयक्रोधो यः सदा मुक्त एव सः ॥२८॥

yatendriyamanobuddhirmunirmokṣaparāyaṇaḥ /
vigatecchābhayakrodho yaḥ sadā mukta eva saḥ //28//
[not translated][163]

In this way, *yogī sarva vyavahārān vartayannapi* [comm.], if he does all of the activities of the world, *mukta eva*, he is Parabhairava, he is always Parabhairava.

Now last *śloka* of this chapter. 29th *śloka*.

163 "And this kind of *yogi* whose organs, mind, and intellect is controlled, and who is bent upon finding the final liberation (*mokṣa parāyaṇah*), *vigata icchā bhaya krodhaḥ*, and whose desire, *bhaya* (fear), and *krodha* (wrath) is already vanished, *yaḥ sadā mukta eva saḥ*, he is already liberated. He is liberated, there is no doubt about it." *Bhagavad Gītā* (1978).

DVD 5.2 (39:52)

भोक्तारं यज्ञतपसां सर्वलोकमहेश्वरम् ।
सुहृदं सर्वभूतानां ज्ञात्वा मां शान्तिमृच्छति ॥२९॥

bhoktāraṁ yajñatapasāṁ sarvalokamaheśvaram /
suhṛdaṁ sarvabhūtānāṁ jñātvā māṁ śāntimṛcchati //29//

[Lord Kṛṣṇa]: *Yajña tapasāṁ*, whenever some *yajña* or *havan* is offered (i.e., performed) and its fruit comes from that *havan*, [the one] who enjoys it is God, *sarva loka maheśvaram*, and who is the Lord of all the worlds (all of the one hundred and eighteen worlds) and *sarva bhūtānāṁ suhṛdaṁ* (*suhṛdaṁ* means who is the friend of all of the world). If you understand Me like that, *śāntimṛcchāte*, then you will be sentenced to the state of Parabhairava at once, without any hesitation.

Idṛśaṁ bhagavattattvaṁ vidan yathātathāsthito'pi mucyata iti śivam [comm.]. When you understand this state of Parabhairava, *yathātathāsthito'pi*, whatever you do afterwards, *mucyata eva*, you are always glorified with the Parabhairava state.

अत्र संग्रहश्लोकः

atra saṁgrahaślokaḥ

Now conclusion of this chapter.

DVD 5.2 (41:40)

सर्वाण्येवात्र भूतानि समत्वेनानुपश्यतः ।
जडवद्व्यवहारोऽपि मोक्षायैवावकल्पते ॥५॥

sarvāṇyevātra bhūtāni samatvenānupaśyataḥ /
jaḍavadvyavahāro'pi mokṣāyaivāvakalpate //5//

॥ Concluding *śloka* of 5th chapter ॥

When one, by the grace of Lord Siva, sees and observes all creatures, all human beings, everywhere from *kalāgnirudra* to *śāntātīta kāla*,[164] all of the outside worlds, if you see everywhere *samatvenā*, they are everywhere the same, *jaḍavat vyavahāro'pi*, if you roam in that ocean of glamour, of your own glamour of *śakti*, it will divert you to the state of Parabhairava. You will get entry in Parabhairava state in each and every way, [in every] respect.

I also got the state of Parabhairava when [Viresh] was [flying] this kite *tamasha* (activity).

164 *Kalāgnirudra* refers to the lowest world among the one hundred and eighteen worlds, and *śāntātīta kāla* refers to the highest world. [*Editor's note*]

Chapter 6 Part 1

अथ षष्ठोऽध्यायः

atha ṣaṣṭho'dhyāyaḥ

[Now the 6th chapter].

श्रीभगवानुवाच

śrī bhagavān uvāca

Lord Kṛṣṇa speaks to Arjuna.

DVD 6.1 (00:13)

अनाश्रितः कर्मफलं कार्यं कर्म करोति यः ।
स संन्यासी च योगी च न निरग्निर्न चाक्रियः ॥१॥

anāśritaḥ karmaphalaṁ kāryaṁ karma karoti yaḥ /
sa saṁnyāsī ca yogī ca na niragnirna cākriyaḥ //1//

Anāśritaḥ karma phalaṁ, whatever he has to do according to the capacity of his qualifications, that is *kāryaṁ*. *Kāryaṁ* means that action which he has to undergo. There are four kinds of actions. [The first] one is for brahmins.

> It is according to your qualifications, not according to your birth. I told you many times that birth does not count. If you are by birth European and you are not by birth a [brahmin], we have to see if you have got the qualifications of a brahmin.

If you want to understand and if you want to focus your mind always in *samādhi*, always in meditation, it means by qualification you are a brahmin, you are not any other caste. You are brahmin, you have qualifications, you are fit for being a brahmin.

And kṣatriya is [one] who has the tendency of fighting, i.e., warriors. It is by his nature. By birth he has got tendency of [being a warrior]. He does not like to meditate upon [Parabhairava]. He wants to fight [or] to do some mechanism [i.e. to be a mechanic] or anything . . . or go [work] in some industry. He wants that. He has got qualifications for that. He likes that. So he is fit for that [kind of activity].

No matter if he is fit for that [particular kind of work, will] he be deprived of God consciousness? He won't! He also won't be deprived of God consciousness.

And there is vaiśya. Vaiśya means [one] who does business. You know, who has got the tendency of making money.

Śūdra is [one] who has the tendency to serve the other three. To serve on the roadside, to clean utensils, to wash everything, to see that my master is quite happy with my work–that is śūdra. If he works according to [his own] qualifications, *sa saṁnyāsī yogī ca,* he will become . . . he [also has the capacity to] take the position of *saṁnyās*, *karma saṁnyās*, and he [can] take the position of *karma yoga*.

Na niragnirna cākriyaḥ.[165] It is not as other commentators have understood from this *Bhagavad Gītā* without taking help of Abhinavagupta's commentary.

DVD 6.1 (04:09)

यं संन्यासमिति प्राहुर्योगं तं विद्धि पाण्डव ।
नह्यसंन्यस्तसंकल्पो योगी भवति कश्चन ॥२॥

yaṁ saṁnyāsamiti prāhuryogaṁ taṁ viddhi pāṇḍava /
nahyasaṁnyastasaṁkalpo yogī bhavati kaścana //2//
[not recited]

They have understood this way that *karma saṁnyāsi* is that

165 "According to the sayings of *śāstras*, *saṁnyasi* should not touch fire. Not touching fire means that he should not cook. *Saṁnyasi* should not cook. He should eat ready-made food." *Bhagavad Gītā* (1978).

[person] who does not [act]. The *saṁnyās*, the renunciation of all [actions], *karma saṁnyās*, is that [person] who is *saṁnyāsi*. *Saṁnyāsi* means [one] who has got *daṇḍa* (staff) and [chants] "*harī oṁ*" and who has cut his *śikhā*[166] and has wrapped it around a stick and [walks around] wearing these dyed cloths. And he is not supposed to do any *havan* at all after he takes *saṁnyās*. Whenever he takes *saṁnyās* . . . for instance, Vyasa Deva Brahmachari took *saṁnyās* and then he was not to perform *havan*. *Havan* is prohibited for him [because] he cannot touch fire. He has discarded it for dogs. That is *karma saṁnyāsi*.

Karma yogi means who does not . . . who always does work in *yoga* (*yoga* in action). And [the *karma saṁnyāsi*] is *akriyā* (innactive). This way, it is not . . .[167]

Yoga and *saṁnyāsa* are attributable to all of these four classes. So this is . . . by these four it is said, *sve sve karmanyabhirataḥ*, if you tread according to the qualifications of your status, if you work and leave and surrender everything to God, you will, in the end, you will succeed and become one with Lord Śiva at the time of death.

Evaṁ prāktanenādhyāyagaṇena sādhitor'thaḥ ślokadvayena nigadyate [comm.]. Abhinavagupta says, "*prāktanenādhyā-yagaṇ-ena*," in all of these previous discourses . . .

How many?

Six, six discourses, from 1st to 6th.

. . . *sadhitor'thaḥ ślokadvayena nigadyate*, with these two *ślokas*, he has grazed it again.

JONATHAN: Summarized it.

SWAMIJI: No, grazed it. Because when a cow eats grass then afterwards she does . . .

JONATHAN: Chews the cud.

DENISE: She regurgitates it.

SWAMIJI: Huh?

JONATHAN: She chews the cud.

---

166 *Sikhā* is the tuft of hair at the crown of the head. [*Editor's note*]

167 "But from the sayings of Lord Kṛṣṇa, that is not the qualification of *saṁnyasi* or *yogi*. *Yogi* is not without action, *saṁnyasi* is not without touching fire. *Sāṁnyasi* and *yogi*, these both names are attributed to that person who does each and every act of this world according to the sayings of the *śāstras* and without attachment for fruits." *Bhagavad Gītā* (1978).

SWAMIJI: She chews what she has [regurgitated].

JONATHAN: . . . got inside.

SWAMIJI: That is [what is meant by] grazing.

And [Abhinavagupta] grazes this whole substance [of the first six chapters] in these two *ślokas*.

JOHN: He recapitulates.

SWAMIJI: Yes . . . what?

JOHN: Recapitulates . . . ruminates, recapitulates.

SWAMIJI: Yes.

Ata evāha, this way he explains here, *ata evāha yam saṁnyāsam taṁ yogam prāhur*, whatever is *saṁnyāsa* is *karma yoga*. *Karma yoga* and *karma saṁnyāsa* are actually one.

Yathā ca, just as, *yogamantareṇa saṁnyāso nopapadyate*, *saṁnyāsa* cannot be possible without *karma yoga*, in the same way, without *saṁnyāsa*, *karma yoga* also cannot be–they are interdependent. *Karma yoga* is dependent to *karma saṁnyāsa* and *karma saṁnyāsa* is dependent to *karma yoga*. *Tasmāt satata saṁbaddhau yoga saṁnyāsau*. *Karma yoga* and *karma saṁnyāsa* is always one body, one body of *abhyāsa* (practice of *yoga*).[168]

Na niragnirityādināyamartho dhvanyate. He is not without fire and he is not without work. That is, [one] who is *karma saṁnyāsi*, [it is not that] he has not to touch fire and he has not to adopt this *havan*. And [one] who is *karma yogi*, [it is not that] he is not to do some work.[169]

"But it is *citram*, this is a unique way of explanation of *Bhagavad Gītā*, which I have done," Abhinavagupta says.

Another *śloka*. First and second *śloka* are finished.

Now the third.

---

168 "Becoming *yogi* will not be attributed to that person who has not abandoned and renounced thoughts of mind. So, you have to renounce. Renunciation means [renouncing] thoughts. Your mind must be one-pointed, then you are *saṁnyasi*, then you are *yogi*, both." Ibid.

169 It is not by touching fire you'll lose the attribution of *saṁnyasi* and by doing actions you'll lose the name of becoming *yogi*–it is not that." Ibid.

DVD 6.1 (10:28)

आरुरुक्षोर्मुनेर्योगं कर्म कारणमुच्यते ।
योगारूढस्य तस्यैव शमः कारणमुच्यते ॥३॥

*ārurukṣormuneryogaṁ karma kāraṇamucyate /
yogārūḍhasya tasyaiva śamaḥ kāraṇamucyate //3//*

Ārurukṣormuner. Munir, that *yogi* who is *ārurukṣoḥ*, who wants to rise step by step; who wants to rise step by step and meditates by successive meditation. Successive meditation does not mean that you meditate one hour in the morning, one hour in the evening–no, it is not that. [You should] go on meditating day and night. Don't forget your meditation of thinking of the Lord with breath. Go on watching your breath, day and night. Try with all your might to watch it. If sometime you miss [a breath], that doesn't matter, but it does not mean that you meditate only one hour in the morning and one hour in the evening, and in the remaining period you will do activities [such as] *gupshup* (idle conversation) and *bakwas* (nonsense) and everything. Because that impression [of worldly activity] will be stronger, that impression will subside your *abhyāsa* (practice).
Do you understand?
So you should not work in that way. *Abhyāsa* is to start [watching your breath] just like in chain form [i.e., continuously]. Try your best [to practice] that way.

*ārurukṣormuneryogaṁ karma kāraṇamucyate /
yogārūḍhasya tasyaiva śamaḥ kāraṇamucyate //3//*

Ārurukṣormuneryogaṁ. Yogam ārurukṣor muner, the one who is trying to reside in *yoga abhyāsa*, for how long [should he practice]? Day and night. According to his capacity, he should [practice] day and night. But the balance should be of *abhyās*, i.e., [*abhyās* should be] more in weight than the daily activities of your worldly affairs. Worldly affairs should be less in balance [in] scale. Worldly activities [should be much] less, just four *anas* (16 cents) in one *rupee*, even two *annas* (8 cents) in one *rupee*. The [remaining] period of your time must be devoted to *abhyāsa*, to meditation. That is *yogam āruruksor muni*, one who wants to rise in *yoga*, who wants to step into *yoga*.

Karma kāraṇam ucyate. Karma kāraṇam ucyate, karma, abhyāsa in action. You should not sit idle, you should go on walking [etc., while] practicing *yoga*. And it is *kāraṇam*, these [worldly activities] are the means (*upāyas*) for him.[170]

Abhinavagupta has, in a unique way, translated in two ways *kāraṇam* and *kāraṇam*. There are in two places *kāraṇ* and *kāraṇ*.

JOHN: What is this *sūtra* sir?

SWAMIJI: I will show you.

āruruksormuneryogaṁ karma kāraṇamucyate /

There is *kāraṇam* first.

yogārūḍhasya tasyaiva śamaḥ kāraṇamucyate //3//

This is another *kāraṇ*, which has another meaning [than] the first *kāraṇ*, which has some other meaning. The first *kāraṇa,* for that beginner of *yoga*, [signifies] the means (*upāya*). And next [*kāraṇ* is] for *yogārūḍha*, [the one] who is established in *yoga.* [For him], *kāraṇam* means *lakṣaṇam*, these are the symptoms of a *yogi*. The symptoms of a *yogi* is that he is appeased.

Kāraṇam atra lakṣaṇam and *kāraṇam atra upāya*. No other commentator has commentated upon these two words, i.e., these separate [meanings] of [*kāraṇam*]. They couldn't understand what is the meaning of the first *kāraṇa* and what is the meaning of the second *kāraṇa*.

Second *kāraṇa* is for that [person] who is established in *yoga*; first *kāraṇa* is for that [person] who wants to become established in *yoga,* who is a beginner. For a beginner, it is the means (*upāya*) and for the one who is established in *yoga,* these are the symptoms (*lakṣaṇam*) and these are his qualifications.

[*āruruksormuneryogaṁ karma*] *kāraṇamucyate /*
yogārūḍhasya tasyaiva śamaḥ kāraṇamucyate //3//

170 The manner, the method, the way to practice *yoga.* See footnote 126 for an explanation of the *upāyas*. [*Editor's note*]

Śamaḥ, he is appeased; he has no other thoughts. He is just like a king; he becomes just like a king, i.e., the other one who is established in *yoga*.

The one who is not established in *yoga*, he has got these means (*upāya*), i.e., the way how to proceed for a beginner. And for that *yogi* who has achieved the highest state, for that it is . . .

JONATHAN: Symptoms.

SWAMIJI: Symptoms.

DVD 6.1 (17:22)

यदा हि नेन्द्रियार्थेषु न कर्मस्वनुषज्जति ।
सर्वसंकल्पसंन्यासी योगारूढस्तदोच्यते ॥४॥

yadā hi nendriyārtheṣu na karmasvanuṣajjati /
sarvasaṁkalpasaṁnyāsī yogārūḍhastadocyate //4//

Na indriyārtheṣu na karmasvanuṣajjati. He will neither get involved in worldly pleasures and *na karmasu*, nor worldly actions. When he is not involved in worldly actions, he will get rid of all *withalwuy*. *Withalwuy* [means to think], "what shall I do and what shall I not do? What can I do, what can I do? How will I achieve, how will I achieve?" This *srethasreth*; *srethasreth* means this trembling way of being.

DENISE: Insecurity.

SWAMIJI: Huh?

DENISE: Insecurity.

SWAMIJI: Insecurity.

"How I can . . . I want to become God!" You told me many times, "I want to see God." You should not get disturbed because you are yourself God.

Then *yogārūḍha*, this is *yogārūḍha*, the *yogi* who is not trembling, who thinks that I am established already in this.

JOHN: What was that number, Sir?

SWAMIJI: Number is 4th.

Asyāṁ ca buddhāvavaśyamevāvadheyam [comm.]. In this intellectual way of being, *avaśyam āvadheyam*, you should be alert in finding out this way for [yourself]. If you don't find it out, it will be lost to you.

Find out! With all of your might, find this out.
So . . .

DVD 6.1 (19:48)

उद्धरेदात्मनात्मानं नात्मानमवसादयेत् ।

uddharedātmanātmānaṁ nātmānamavasādayet /5a

You have to elevate yourself by yourself. Nobody [else] can elevate yourself; no other element can elevate yourself. You have to elevate yourself by yourself. There is no other element, which will help you to push up. You have to push [yourself up] with all of your might, because you have got that power, but that power you have ignored.

Invoke that power within [yourself]!

Find out that power that you have got!

Uddharet ātmanātmānaṁ, you have to rise with your own might. *Nātmānamavasādayet*, you should not kick yourself [down] in the depth of ignorance.

आत्मैव ह्यात्मनो बन्धुरात्मैव रिपुरात्मनः ॥५॥

ātmaiva hyātmano bandhurātmaiva ripurātmanaḥ //5//

Your own self is your friend when realized, and your own self becomes your enemy when not realized.

Have you understood?

Atra ca nānya upāya [comm.]. There is no other way of means (*upāya*); there is no other way. *Apitu ātmaiva* (*ātmaiva* means *mana eva*, your own mind), your own mind has become . . . when your mind is elevated, it takes the formation of God consciousness. When God consciousness has passed into the inferior field, that God consciousness becomes mind.

DENISE: Full of thoughts.

SWAMIJI: No, mind. Mind is the formation of *citi* (consciousness). In the upper plane, in the elevated plane, there is *citi*. In lowest plane, *citi* becomes just mind, i.e., the substance of thoughts, varieties of thoughts.

citireva cetanapadādavarūḍā cetyasaṁkocinī citram / [*Pratyabhijñāhṛdayaṁ*, *sūtra* 5]

When you are given to the objective world, [*citi*] becomes mind. If you reside in the subjective world, you become un-minded and you become consciousness. That is *citi*, consciousness.

DVD 6.1 (23:16)

बन्धुरात्मात्मनस्तस्य येनात्मैवात्मना जितः ।
अजितात्मनस्तु शत्रुत्वे वर्तेतात्मैव शत्रुवत् ॥६॥

bandhurātmātmanastasya yenātmaivātmanā jitaḥ /
ajitātmanastu śatrutve vartetātmaiva śatruvat //6//

This is another *śloka* . . . which one?

The 6th *śloka*.

Bandhurātmātmanastasya yenātmaivātmanā jitaḥ. His *ātma* is *bandhuḥ* (his *ātma* is a friend to him), his self is a friend to him who has, by his own self-treatment, conquered his mind by being un-minded. *Ajitāt manastu*, the one who has not conquered his mind by being un-minded, for him his own self behaves just like an enemy for him. [The self] becomes his enemy. Otherwise, [the self] is his friend; [the self] will push him up.[171] And otherwise [the self] will . . .

DENISE: Pull him down.

SWAMIJI: . . . kick him down.

Bandhurātmātmanastasya . . .

This is a unique [explanation] of Abhinavagupta's commentary on *Bhagavad Gītā*. I did not previously explain it to you clearly. I

171 That is, the self (*citi*) who has become the mind. Swamiji previously translated this verse: "*yenātmaivātmanā jitaḥ*, the person who has conquered one's own mind by meditation, by doing meditation, one who has conquered the position of mind, for him, his mind is his friend. And the person who has not been able to conquer his mind in going here and there (that is *ajitātmā*), who has not conquered his mind, *śatrutve vartetātmaiva*, for him, his own mind becomes his enemy, real enemy, who kicks him down in the pit of the pangs of repeated births and deaths." *Bhagavad Gītā* (1978).

have, but not in that way.[172]

Jitaṁ hi mano mitraṁ [comm.]. If the mind is conquered, he becomes your friend (*mano mitraṁ*). *Mitraṁ* means [the mind] is your friend; [the mind] is not your enemy then. *Ghoratara saṁsāroddharaṇaṁ karoti*, it will elevate you from the furious *cakra* (wheel) of repeated births and deaths. [The mind] will elevate you at once. It will become your fast friend to elevate you from that *narak*, [the hell of *saṁsāra*]. *Ajutaṁ tu*, if you don't conquer [the mind], then *tīvranirayapātanāt-chatrutvaṁ kurute*, [your mind] will kick you into hells and [it] will behave like a great enemy to you.

DVD 6.1 (26:15)

जितात्मनः प्रशान्तस्य परात्मसु समा मतिः [हितः] ।
शीतोष्णसुखदुःखेषु तथा मानावमानयोः ॥७॥

jitātmanaḥ praśāntasya parātmasu samā matiḥ [hitaḥ][173] /
śītoṣṇasukhadukheṣu tathā mānāvamānayoḥ //7//

Jitātmanaḥ praśāntasya, [the one] who is *praśānta*, who is appeased, whose mind is appeased, i.e., one-pointed (*paramātma samā hita*), *paramātma* [i.e., Parabhairava] is absolutely shaking hands with him, permanently.

On which occasions?

Śīta, when there is *śīta* (*śīta* means when there is a cold wave); *uṣṇa*, when there is a hot wave; *sukha*, when there is pleasure; *duḥkha*, when there is pain; *tathā mānā*, when there is respect and [*avamāna*], when there is disrespect. When all of these actions are there, *paramātma* is there shaking hands with you. No matter [what is happening in your life, you must] go on, go on, this is [only] the glamour of God. No matter what is good and what is bad, it is all the divine formation of Parabhairava.

How beautiful this *śloka* is.

172 Swamiji is referring to his previous translation of Abhinavagupta's *Bhagavad Gītā* recorded in the 1970's. [*Editor's note*]

173 Here, Swamiji says *paramātma samā hita* in place of *parātmasu samā matiḥ*. [*Editor's note*]

jitātmanaḥ praśāntasya paramātma samā . . .

Paramātma is there! *Paramātma*, supreme Parabhairava, remains by his side. He sits here in His lap while facing all off these ups and downs of the world. He remains with him [and says], "don't worry, this is also your glamour."

[Parabhairava] presses [i.e., massages] his body at that time. Or when he is cold, He warms him up. When he is drunk, He keeps him aware. Whatever he does, if he takes wine and is drunk, that doesn't matter. He serves him a lot.

[Abhinavagupta] has, in a unique way, explained the *Bhagavad Gītā.*

Now it is 8th verse, 8th *śloka*.

JOHN: 8th verse?

SWAMIJI: Yes.

DVD 6.1 (29:30)

ज्ञानविज्ञानतृप्तात्मा कूटस्थो विजितेन्द्रियः ।
युक्त इत्युच्यते योगी समलोष्टाश्मकाञ्चनः ॥८॥

jñānavijñānatṛptātmā kūṭastho vijitendriyaḥ /
yukta ityucyate yogī samaloṣṭāśmakāñcanaḥ //8//

Jñāna vijñāna tṛptātmā, there are two kinds of knowledge. One is *jñāna* and another is *vijñāna*. *Jñāna* is knowledge of God consciousness. *Vijñāna* means knowledge of the world's varieties.[174] These are [both existing] in one body of Parabhairava; these you will find in one body of Parabhairava. Parabhairava's pure knowledge is just one and that is *jñāna*. *Vijñāna* is varieties of knowledge. That is Parabhairava's expansion of His energies.

The person who is in both ways appeased and in both ways contented. If he is [in the internal and undifferentiated state of Parabhairava], well and good; if he is in the outside [and differentiated state of] Parabhairava, well and good, that is also His glamour.

He is just like *kūṭastho* (*kūṭastho* means that nobody can

174 "Spiritual book knowledge including [spiritual] experience is *jñāna*. *Vijñāna* is worldly knowledge." *Bhagavad Gītā* (1978).

shake him). He will not move from his one-pointedness. It [i.e., his one-pointedness] may be inside or it may be outside. If he is in the outside Parabhairava state, he holds one-pointedness there also; he [holds one-pointedness] in outside and inside also. Inside there is one-pointedness already. So he is just like *kūṭastha*, [one-pointed in *jñāna* and *vijñāna*, both of which exist] in one Being.

Vijitendriyaḥ, all of his organs, if they are appeased or if they are flickering and trembling . . .

Appeased formation is where?

When he is situated in the Parabhairava state. When these organs are trembling, it is [because he is situated in] the worldly activities.

. . . he is the same in both ways. *Yukta ityucyate yogī*, he is a *yogi*, he is a real *yogi*. *Samaloṣṭāśmakāñcanaḥ*, for him, you may give him a beating, well and good, he will laugh. You may feed him with delicious foods, he will laugh. [Eating] delicious food is the same to him as [receiving a] beating. A beating also he will enjoy because that beating will also have some glamour of God consciousness. This is the plane in which he remains.

For him, gold, jewelry, torn clothes, *dusas* (blankets), *pashminas* (shawls), or rags, or nothing, or being naked are [all] the same.

This is the 9th *śloka* now.

DVD 6.1 (34:26)

सुहृन्मित्रार्युदासीनमध्यस्थद्वेष्यबन्धुषु ।
साधुष्वपि च पापेषु समबुद्धिर्विशिष्यते ॥९॥

suhṛnmitrāryudāsīnamadhyasthadveṣyabandhuṣu /
sādhuṣvapi ca pāpeṣu samabuddhirviśiṣyate //9//

He becomes *samabuddhi*, he is a perfect *yogi*. [One] who is established in Parabhairava state is a perfect *yogi*. He remains the same . . .

In whom?

Suhṛt is the first.

I think you should note it down. Can you note it down?

JOHN: Yes.

SWAMIJI: *Suhṛt* is one class of persons with whom he is associated with in this world. There are these classes [of people with whom one is associated with in this world]. The first one is *suhṛt*. *Suhṛt* is a peculiar type of friend.

Write this down, write this down!

JOHN: Yes, *suhṛt*?

SWAMIJI: No, peculiar type of friend, the first one. And *mitra*, *mitra* is the second.

JOHN: *Mitra*?

SWAMIJI: *Mitra*, yes. Write it down! Write it down!

Why have you lost your courage?

JOHN: *Mitra*, second.

SWAMIJI: Second.

Ari. *Ari* means enemy. Enemy is third class. Enemies are also associated with you.

In the daily routine of life, there are these persons who are attached with you.

JOHN: What does the second one mean?

SWAMIJI: *Mitra*. *Mitra* means friend, a peculiar type of friend.

JOHN: What is *suhṛt*?

SWAMIJI: *Suhṛt* is that friend who does not think that he will be rewarded for this friendship.

JOHN: A selfless friend.

SWAMIJI: A selfless friend who has adopted a selfless friendship for him. There are such people, such friends also. For instance, I am your friend. I don't want any reward from you, so I am your *suhṛt*.

Mitra is that kind of friend who wants a reward also. [He says], "I have done you good so you will also, in return, help me sometime when I need." With this hope, I make friendship with you. This is another category of friendship.

Suhṛt, *mitra*, *ari*. *Ari* means enemy, the one who is an enemy.

JOHN: *Ari*.

SWAMIJI: *Ari*. *Ari* means enemy.

Udāsīnaḥ. *Udāsīnaḥ* means the one who has nothing to do with you, or your company, or what you are doing. *Udāsīnaḥ*, who has no interest in you at all. There are some associations, such people also, who do not care [to know] what you are doing, or what is your activity, what is your internal affair, what is your external affair, etc. They don't care to understand that.

JONATHAN: Detached.

SWAMIJI: What is that?

JOHN: *Udāsīnaḥ.*

SWAMIJI: *Udāsīnaḥ.*

Madhyasthaḥ. Madhyasthaḥ means *kenacidaṁśena śatru kenacid-aṁśena mitra* [comm.]. *Madhyasthaḥ* means [the person] who [is concerned with your] internal matters also asks sometimes.

"What has happened to you?

"Do you want some doctor?

"Do you want some . . . ?"

Madhyasthaḥ means [one] who comes and . . . your internal affairs also he understands, e.g., what you are doing and where you have gone. Jonathan tells me, "she has gone to the *bazaar*. She is with Viresh." That is *madhyasthaḥ.*

Dveṣa. And this is which one?

JOHN: So *madhyastha* means he is a person who is concerned with your . . .

SWAMIJI: With all of your affairs.

JOHN: Is he a friend or not a friend?

SWAMIJI: Not a friend. [*Madhyasthaḥ* is one] who is concerned with what you are doing and thinks that he will give you advice of what to do.

Dveṣa. Dveṣa means an enemy whom you hate, whom you want to kill. But you cannot kill him [because] he has got power; he won't let you kill him. That is *dveṣa. Dveṣārho dveṣṭumaśakyo*, he is worth being killed by you, but you cannot, you have no power to kill him. He has got his own strength. He won't let you kill him. That is *dveṣa, dveṣārho dveṣṭumaśakyo dveṣyaḥ.*

Suhṛnmitrāryudāsīnamadhyasthadveṣyabandhuṣu. Bandhuṣu. Bandhuṣu means who is your relative from your maternal side or paternal side.

Paternal?

JONATHAN: Yes.

SWAMIJI: Paternal side, the person who is related to you. That is *bandhau*: a relative, kith and kin–*bandhuṣu.*

Sādhuṣu. Sādhuṣu means he who is a saint. A saint also comes to you.

Pāpeṣu. Some wicked person also meets you sometime and they behave with wickedness towards you.

JOHN: What was that [word] for saint? *Sādhuṣu* means?

SWAMIJI: *Sādhuṣu*, who are saints. Saintly persons also come to you and are associated with you. Saints say, "give us food, we are hungry, give us some *praṣad*, I am hungry, I want to eat something. If you have got something, give it to me and I will go."

JOHN: What comes after that?

SWAMIJI: *Pāpeṣu*.

DENISE: Wicked.

SWAMIJI: Wicked persons who want to tease you.

For instance, he will tell you, "I will tell you one thing, John, I will tell you one thing. Denise, whom you are loving so much, has bad habits. Don't tell Denise. Don't tell her [what I am saying]. I am telling you sincerely, Denise does not have good behavior. You should leave her and marry another lady."

DENISE: Troublemakers.

SWAMIJI: Troublemakers. Those people are also associated with you . . .

DENISE: Definitely [laughs].

SWAMIJI: . . . in this world.

And the glamourous person who is residing in Parabhairava state, *sama buddhirviśiṣyate,* he thinks that all [of these persons are] the glamour of his own nature. He is not moved by these.

DENISE: Any of these associations.

SWAMIJI: Any of these things.

Good?

DVD 6.1 (43:09)

suhṛnmitrāryudāsīnamadhyasthadveṣyabandhuṣu /
sādhuṣvapi ca pāpeṣu samabuddhirviṣiṣyate //9//
[repeated]

Viṣiṣyate. Viṣiṣyate means *kramātkramaṁ saṁsārāttarati* [comm.], he rises, he rises in the end; he goes and is diluted in the Parabhairava state everywhere, in all ways.

Īdṛśaiśca vandyacaraṇaiḥ, such people who are in this Bhairava state, who have nothing to do with these associations, who are not moved by these varieties of associations, which have already been explained.

DVD 6.1 (44:28)

इहैव तैर्जितः सर्गो येषां साम्ये स्थितं मनः ।
निर्दोषं हि समं ब्रह्म तस्माद्ब्रह्मणि ते स्थिताः ॥१०॥

ihaiva tairjitaḥ sargo yeṣām sāmye sthitaṁ manaḥ /
nirdoṣaṁ hi samaṁ brahma tasmādbrahmaṇi te sthitāḥ //10

Ihaiva tairjitaḥ sargaḥ. They have, *ihaiva*, while remaining in the body also, they have *jitaḥ sarga*, they have conquered this whole universe. They have conquered this whole universe and they are Bhairava and they rule over this whole . . . not only one hundred and eighteen worlds, above that also. They rule over [everything].

Nirdoṣaṁ hi samaṁ brahma. This *brahma*, the state of Parabhairava is *nirdoṣaṁ*. *Nirdoṣaṁ* means there is not any defect, there is no leakage of any defect whatsoever. There may [appear to] be some defects but there are [actually] no defects. *Tasmāt brahmaṇi te sthitāḥ*, they are situated in Parabhairava state for good.

Chapter 6 Part 2

Now he says, Arjuṇa says, "you have told me [about] one who has conquered his mind, [but tell me] how can one conquer his mind, O Master?"

ityāśaṅkya āruruksoḥ kaścidupāyaḥ
kāyasamatvādikaścittasaṁyama upadiśyate.
[comm. intro. to 11th *śloka*]

Āruruksoḥ, one who wants to conquer his mind, who wants to start *yoga*, for him, he explains how he should act and how he should begin the practice of *yoga*.

DVD 6.2 (00:42)

योगी युञ्जीत सततमात्मानं रहसि स्थितः ।
एकाकी यतचित्तात्मा निराशीरपरिग्रहः ॥ ११ ॥

yogī yuñjīta satatamātmānaṁ rahasi sthitaḥ /
ekākī yatacittātmā nirāśīraparigrahaḥ //11//

Yogī yuñjīta satatam. *Yoga* must be done always. *Yoga* is not to be adopted for only one hour or two hours in the morning and [one or two hours in the evening], as I told you. *Yoga* is to be adopted *satatam* (always). "Always" means while you are sitting do *yoga*, while you are talking do *yoga*. Be aware!

Ātmānaṁ rahasi sthitaḥ, you should remain . . . you should keep your mind away from *bakwas*.[175] You must not keep this *bakwas* in view. You can hear *bakwas*, but don't keep it in view.

DENISE: "In one ear and out the other."

SWAMIJI: Not in one ear and another.

175 The word '*bakwas*' commonly means 'nonsense' but here it is being used in the sense of useless gossip. [*Editor's note*]

DENISE: That's an expression, not to let anything remain in your mind, just to let it go–"in one ear and out the other."

SWAMIJI: Yes.

Yogī yuñjīta satatam ātmānaṁ rahasi sthitaḥ, ekākī yatacitt-ātmā. Ekākī, remain alone, *yatacittātmā*, keep your mind under your own control, *nirāśīr*, and don't think that I should get its result soon, don't think of results also.[176] Don't commit that mistake that, "I am doing *abhyās* (practice) and just now I will enter into trance." Don't think about that.

Aparigrahaḥ. Aparigrahaḥ means you should not collect things which you don't need.

JOHN: What is that verse number, Sir?

SWAMIJI: Huh?

JOHN: Verse number?

SWAMIJI: Which number, Sir?

JOHN: The one you just did.

SWAMIJI: 11th, eleven number.

He begins with *yoga* now again. That [explanation of] Parabhairava state is over and [now] He [gives instructions] for beginners again.

Because both ways He explains the *Bhagavad Gītā*; in both ways, i.e., where we have to reach, He [explains] that, and what are the means for beginners. He [explains this] again and again. Because as long as you don't repeatedly initiate your disciples, they can't be elevated [because] they will forget. They will forget again what our master had told us about Parabhairava state. They will just get confused.

DVD 6.2 (04:31)

शुचौ देशे प्रतिष्ठाप्य स्थिरमासनमात्मनः ।
नात्युच्छ्रितं नातिनीचं चैलाजिनकुशोत्तरम् ॥१२॥
तत्रैकाग्रं मनः कृत्वा यतचित्तेन्द्रियक्रियः ।
उपविश्यासने युञ्ज्याद्योगमात्मविशुद्धये ॥१३॥

176 "You should think that it is a long course–*nirāśīr*." *Bhagavad Gītā* (1978).

śucau deśe pratiṣṭhāpya sthiramāsanamātmanaḥ /
nātyucchritaṁ natinīcaṁ cailājinakuśottaram //12//
tatraikāgraṁ manaḥ kṛtvā yatacittendriyakriyaḥ /
upaviśyāsane yuñjyādyogamātmaviśuddhaye //13//

Śucau deśe pratiṣṭāpya sthiram āsanam ātmanaḥ. You should [find a place] where people are not treading here and there; you should keep a separate place for *abhyās*. For meditation, for a beginner, it is a must. For the beginner, you have to keep a separate area where [there is no agitation, where] fighting is not done, and where temper is not lost–that room you should keep separate for meditation. No matter if you meditate collectively also, but it must be separate. *Śucau deśe*, this place must be *śuci* (*śuci* means pure).

Sthiram āsanam ātmanaḥ, your *asana* . . . you must not sit on chairs. That is not worthwhile. If you are accustomed to sitting on chairs, then you should not sit on these chairs.[177] You should sit on these chairs, where there are arms. There was one chair here with arms.

JOHN: Yes.

SWAMIJI: Because you must remain in one posture, like this [Swamiji demonstrates by sitting upright, keeping the spine erect].

Nātyucchritaṁ natinīcaṁ, it must not be with these soft cushions. It must be a hard cushion. *Caila-ajina-kuśottaram*, either there must be a little matting (*ajina* means some rug and some cloth piece) and then upon that you should sit. You must put that on the chair, and *bas*, sit like this.

Karan Singh[178] is also doing *abhyās* [upon a chair] because he is . . .

DENISE: . . . his leg is stiff.

SWAMIJI: Yes, his leg is stiff. He sits on a stool and meditates like that.

tatraikāgraṁ manaḥ kṛtvā yatacittendriyakriyaḥ /
upaviśyāsane yuñjyādyogamātmaviśuddhaye //13//

177 Swamiji indicates soft sofa type chairs. [*Editor's note*]

178 Karan Singh is a minister in the Indian Government, and also the son of Hari Singh, the last ruling Mahārāja of the princely state of Jammu and Kashmir.

Tatra, there, *ekāgraṁ manaḥ kṛtvā*, you should keep your mind one-pointed. *Yata citta indriya kriyaḥ*, the mind must be controlled and all of the organs, the activity of organs, should be kept controlled, perfectly controlled. *Upaviśya*, when you are seated on that *āsana, yuñjyāt yogam ātma viśuddhaye*, to purify your mind you should start *yoga abhyās* practice there.

It is quite true. Whatever is found in one hundred and eighteen worlds and above, you can find in this specs holder (eyeglass case)–that, everything!

DENISE: There's nowhere to go, everything is right here.

SWAMIJI: No, within these specs and within this [eyeglass case], you'll find all of the [thirty-six] elements, above one hundred and eighteen worlds also, i.e., whatever is existing above, that you will find it here [in each and every object]. One ray is equal to numberless rays.

So this is the behavior of Parabhairava, i.e., to see Parabhairava in Parabhairava, within and without.

JOHN: Everywhere and . . .

SWAMIJI: Everywhere and nowhere. I told you nowhere. Nowhere means that which is not known, unknown world also. There is unknown world also. Partly known and partly unknown, there is that world also. Absolutely unknown and different world also. And there is nothingness, there is that also. [Where] there is something, that [world] also.

God is not only on the top, God is everywhere. Everywhere he is all-pervading.

One becomes mad after thinking [about this]. I am semi-mad. I want to become mad!

JOHN: So what is this highest realization if it's more than *krama mudrā*?[179]

DENISE: If it's higher than *jagadānanda*?[180]

SWAMIJI: Huh?

DENISE: If it's higher than *jagadānanda*?

SWAMIJI: *Jagadānanda* is not limited *jagadānanda*; it is unlimited. *Jagadānanda* is the real state of Bhairava. But it is not only *jagadānanda*.

---

179 See footnote 139 for an explanation of *krama mudrā*. [*Editor's note*]

180 See footnote 139 for an explanation of *jagadānanda*. [*Editor's note*]

DENISE: It's more?

SWAMIJI: No it is . . . it is not-*jagadānanda*, no-*jagadānanda*, not-not-*jagadānanda*, yes-yes-*jagadānanda*, some-some-*jagadānanda*, everywhere-*jagadānanda*, and nowhere and everywhere, and nothing-*jagadānanda*. Whatever you can imagine, it is there. Whatever you cannot imagine, it is there.

JOHN: So *krama mudrā*, because it's some thing, it's something very limited, because it's actually some process, a practice?

SWAMIJI: It is a process. It is a process and that process is expanded in *jagadānanda*.

JOHN: So this *kuṇḍalinī* of highest *kuṇḍalinī* . . .

SWAMIJI: I had in my childhood, I had nominated Parabhairava as *badhi bodh* (greater than the greatest).

JOHN: *Badhi bodh*?

SWAMIJI: *Badhi bodh*, greater than the greatest.

[The subject] has started how [one should] begin *yoga*, again. Yesterday I [began to tell] you.

DVD 6.2 (13:21)

समं कायशिरोग्रीवं धारयन्नचलं स्थिरः ।
संपश्यन्नासिकाग्रं स्वं दिशश्चानवलोकयन् ॥१४॥

samaṁ kāyaśirogrīvaṁ dhārayannacalaṁ sthiraḥ /
saṁpaśyannāsikāgraṁ svaṁ diśaścānavalokayan //14//

Kāya means this body, *śiro* means head, *grīvaṁ* means neck, *samaṁ*, it must be like this [Swamiji demonstrates that they must be aligned]. And *dhārayan*, you must see that it is . . . *dhārayan* means, in Abhinavagupta's commentary, *dhārayan yatnena,* you must, with effort you should see that your body is just like this. This body and neck and head, it must be in one straight line. He says *dhārayan yatnena*, you have to put effort in it. *Acalaṁ*, you should not move your body, like this. *Sthiraḥ*, it should be just like a rock.

Saṁpaśyan nāsikāgraṁ svam, and you have to see your own, this [Swamiji touches the tip of his nose].

DENISE: Tip of nose.

SWAMIJI: Tip of nose.

It does not mean, Abhinavagupta says, that you have not to

look at the tip of your nose. "Tip of nose" means that you should not see on the right side and every side. You should see, *bas*. This is tip of nose. Tip of nose is, *bas*.[181] You have not to actually see the tip of nose.

JONATHAN: But is that to concentrate on one point.

SWAMIJI: Yes.

JONATHAN: Concentrate on one thing; look at one thing.

SWAMIJI: *Matparamatayā yukta āsīta*, and you should go on concentrating on your I-ness, *bas*, go on [doing it] without any break.

15th *śloka*. No, 16th *śloka* now. 14th and 15th are finished.

Acha. Oh, yes, yes!

Praśān . . . 15th now.

DVD 6.2 (16:29)

प्रशान्तात्मा विगतभीर्ब्रह्मचारिव्रते स्थितः ।
मनः संयम्य मच्चित्तो युक्त आसीत मत्परः ॥१५॥

praśāntātmā vigatabhīrbrahmacārivrate sthitaḥ /
manaḥ saṁyamya maccitto yukta āsīta matparaḥ //15//

Praśāntātmā, your mind should be appeased. Don't let your mind flicker here and there. *Vigatabhīr*, and don't have any *bhaya* (fear), any threat from outside. If there is some sound, tremendous sound outside, don't care for that, don't divert your attention to that.

Brahmacāri vrate sthitaḥ. *Brahmacāri vrate sthitaḥ*, and think it is *brahmacāri*; *brahmacāri* means you see that this whole universe is filled with God consciousness, so there is no fear.[182]

DENISE: Is filled with what? This universe is filled with?

SWAMIJI: You have to feel that the whole world is filled with

181 Swamiji demonstrates by gazing in the direction of the tip of his nose. [*Editor's note*]

182 "*Brahmacāri vrata* is not the type of being bachelor always. *Brahmacāri vrata*, from Śaiva point of view, is that you should see, you should observe in your mind, that death, life, success, fall, pain, pleasure, sadness, sorrow, happiness, joy, rise, fall, all these are expansion of His glory–that is *brahmacāri vrata*." *Bhagavad Gītā* (1978).

God consciousness, so there is no fear. If there is the sound of a plane, or sound of something, or beating of tins, don't worry about it; it should not divert your attention towards that way. Go on thinking of your own nature.

Manaḥ saṁyamya, your mind should be focused on one point. That is, between the two eyebrows. *Mat citta*, and you should divert your attention towards Me, i.e., I-consciousness. *Yukta āsīta mata paraḥ*, you should go on practicing *yoga*, i.e., watching your breath.

Now the 16th [*śloka*].

DVD 6.2 (18:38)

युञ्जन्नेवं सदात्मानं मद्भक्तोऽनन्यमानसः ।
शान्तिं निर्वाणपरमां मत्संस्थामाधिगच्छति ॥ १६ ॥

yuñjannevaṁ sadātmānaṁ madbhakto'nanyamānasaḥ /
śāntiṁ nirvāṇaparamāṁ matsaṁsthāmādhigacchati //16//

In this way, if you do this practice of *yoga* always, not only . . . I told you yesterday how much time you should devote to this. *Madbhakta*, and you should be attached to this practice; it should not [feel like a] burden. You should do it with excitement–that is *madbhakta*. You must have devotion and love for this practice, then it will work. *Ananya mānasaḥ*, don't let your mind flicker here and there. Be focused to your own one-pointedness, then you will [achieve] *śāntim* (*śānti* means peace, supreme peace).

Abhinavagupta says that this *śānti* is *nirvāṇa paramāṁ*. This *śanti* has [the capacity] to push you into the state of Bhairava. This *śānti* will push you into the state of Bhairava in a swift way, swift manner. *Matsaṁsthām*, and you will be focused in the center of Bhairava state and there your course of *yoga* will end.[183]

183 "Supreme peace of God consciousness will be the carrier. You won't hold supreme God consciousness; supreme God consciousness will hold you. When supreme God consciousness once holds you, finished, you have nothing to do. You are rising, rising, rising, rising; there is no gap then. No gap remains during one meditation and another meditation. You are in meditation always. That is *nirvāṇaparamām śāntiṁ*." Ibid.

Evam-ātmānaṁ yuñjataḥ [comm.]. *Atmānaṁ yuñjatah*, when you unite your consciousness with that supreme God consciousness, *śāntir jāyate*, the glamour of peace appears to you.

And which peace is that?

Yasyāṁ saṁsthā, when you are established in that peace, *paryantakāṣṭhā*, this is the end of your journey of *yoga*. *Matprāptiyogo asti*, and you'll have Me for good.

The 17th *śloka*.

DVD 6.2 (21:41)

योगोऽस्ति नैवात्यश्नतो न चैकान्तमनश्नतः ।
न चातिस्वप्नशीलस्य नातिजागरतोऽर्जुन ॥ १७ ॥

yogo'sti naivātyaśato na caikāntamanaśnataḥ /
na cātisvapnaśīlasya nātijāgarato'rjuna //17//

Yoga won't work, *ātyaśata*, if you fill your stomach wholeheartedly.[184] *Na caikānta manaśnataḥ*, *yoga* cannot be possible if you don't eat at all. *Na cātisvapnaśīlasya*, *yoga* cannot be possible if you only sleep day and night for twelve hours, just like a beast. *Nātijāgarato'rjuna*,[185] O Arjuna, if you are wakeful for the whole night, in that way also *yoga* is not possible.

---

184 "The process of *yoga* does not become successful to that *yogi* who eats full food. You should not eat full food. Take three fourths of your food. You should not take as much as you need, as you need in your body. There must remain slight appetite in your stomach. Slight appetite must remain. . . . Because this meditation is not [only] meant for morning hours and evening hours, this meditation is meant for always. See, watching your breath . . . cannot happen unless there is room for watching the breath." Ibid.

185 "[Vyāsa] has [written] *jāgarataḥ*, which is not correct from the viewpoint of grammar. *Jāgarataḥ* ought to have [been] written [as] *jāgrataḥ*, not *jāgarataḥ*. *Jāgarataḥ* is incorrect writing. Abhinavagupta [says], as Vyasa, Lord Kṛṣṇa, has put *jāgarataḥ* in incorrect way, [still] it is correct. It is correct because [an] elevated being has put this [word] *jāgarataḥ*. So there is no worry for grammar there. So it is just like *Vedas*, just [like] *Upaniṣad*, just [like] *Tantras*. Vyāsa, sage Vyāsa has put this reading, so it is *vedavat*, just like *Vedas* and *Tantras*. You have to accept it with great love and reverence, this incorrect word." Ibid.

Now, Abhinavagupta has commentated upon this [following] *śloka* of the *Bhagavad Gītā* in such a way that I don't accept. For this [reason], I have come to make some amendment of this commentary of Abhinavagupta here.

Do you understand?

DENISE: Yes.

JOHN: What verse? 17th?

SWAMIJI: 17th and 18th, both together.

DVD 6.2 (23:22)

युक्ताहारविहारस्य युक्तचेष्टस्य कर्मसु ।
युक्तस्वप्नावबोधस्य योगो भवति दुःखहा ॥१८॥

yuktāhāravihārasya yuktaceṣṭasya karmasu /
yuktasvapnāvabodhasya yogo bhavati duhkhahā //18//

Although this verse of the *Bhagavad Gītā* by Vyāsa is complete,[186] but Abhinavagupta has not commentated upon it as I would commentate upon this *śloka*. I will tell you his commentary, his first commentary, [which he gave] in his first life.

Āhāra means *āhriyamāṇeṣu viṣayeṣu* [comm.], when you will go here and there–this is *āhāra*. *Yuktāhāra* does not [only] mean eating. *Yuktāhāra* means *śabda* (sound), *sparśa* (touch), *rupa*

186 "Then who is the real *yogī* then? *Yuktāhāravihārasya*, you should take food in less quantity. You should do your worldly activity, [but] very little activity. Don't become victim of your business. *Yuktaceṣṭasya karmasu*, don't think too much. Think very little. Not thinking at all, anything, that is not [advisable either]–*yoga* won't take place. Think a little. Think of something, but not too much. *Yuktasvapnāvabodhasya*, and go to dreaming state also, but not always. *Yogo bhavati duhkha*, for that person, *yoga* becomes successful and very easy to be obtained. Those actions should be done in moderate way. Don't see pictures day and night, always. See pictures after a fortnight. That is good, that will lead you to *yoga*. But [if you are] not seeing pictures at all, [then] those pictures will leak in your mind then, and you will be filled with pictures in your mind. So do something, but very little, in moderation. Don't be too much attached to it [and] don't be detached to it at the same time. Detachment [and] attachment should be done moderately, in a moderate way." Ibid.

(form) . . . all of the sensual pleasures.

In sensual pleasures, what should you do?

Keep it on one side, *vihāra*. *Vihāra* means *vihāraḥ upabhogāya pravṛttiḥ*; *vihāra* means to enjoy sensual objects. This was Abhinavagupta's first commentary.

Tasyāśca yuktatvaṁ. *Yukta* means *na ātyantā saktiḥ na ātyanta parivarjanam,* you should not be a slave to those enjoyments. Neither should you become a slave nor should you renounce them. Renunciation is also not good and to be a slave to those enjoyments, that is also not good. That is *yukta*, *yuktatva*.

Evaṁ sarvatra, in this way you should commentate upon these *ślokas* of Vyāsa. This is Abhinavagupta's first commentary.

But I don't appreciate this kind of [explanation].

Yuktāhāra. *Yuktāhāra* means take food! Go on taking food, as much food as you can take, go on taking it but keep awareness in it. While taking food, offer it to your own God–that is *yuktāhāra*. *Yuktāhāra* means when you eat food, go on eating it with awareness, go on focusing on its taste. Which taste? The taste of whatever you eat . . . and there will be one-pointedness. Maintain one-pointedness while eating. Maintain one-pointedness–it is my commentary, my amendment–maintain one-pointedness in sleeping. You can sleep but maintain one-pointedness in sleeping, be aware while sleeping. If you sleep, be aware! Don't be just like a sluggish bear sleeping. Put the trick of *yoga* into it.

This is my new commentary on this *Bhagavad Gītā*.

Yuktāhāra vihārasya yuktaceṣṭasya karmasu. When you have to do activities of the daily routine of your life, do all of the daily routine of life, but don't lose your internal *yoga*. At the same time, you [should] go on practicing inside.

DENISE: You mean watching your breath.

SWAMIJI: Watching your breath and don't be taken by these activities of life, the daily routine of life.

Yukta svapnā, and when you dream, go into dreams with awareness. When you dream, you will enter into *samādhi* at the time of dreaming state; you won't go into the dreaming state. At that time, you will go into *samādhi* while dreaming.

Y*ukta svapna āvabodhasya*, and when you are awake, be awake with *yoga*. *Yogo bhavati duḥkha*, then *yoga* is very easy; everywhere *yoga* is available to you. This is my commentary, new commentary. And this is Abhinavagupta's new commentary. You should know that. So I had to [make an] amendment on this commentary.

yogo'sti naivātyaśato na caikāntamanaśnataḥ /
na cātisvapnaśīlasya nātijāgarato'rjuna //17//

Yukta means *yujaryoge.* According to Pāṇini's grammar, *yukta* means "with *yoga*". Attach *yoga* to all of your activities of the daily routine of life and *yoga* will be very easily achieved. *Yoga* cannot be achieved [by remaining] in one corner. If you lock your door from the outside and sit, you will just be wasting your time inside. You will be . . . "idles workshop is demons . . ." what?

DENISE: Idle mind is devil's workshop?

JONATHAN: Devil's playground. Idle workshop is devil's playground.

SWAMIJI: Yes.

Don't do like that. Come out in the field and see *yoga*!

Next, the 19th *śloka*.

DVD 6.2 (30:34)

यदा विनियतं चित्तमात्मन्येवावतिष्ठते ।
निःस्पृहः सर्वकामेभ्यो युक्त इत्युच्यते तदा ॥१९॥

yadā viniyataṁ cittamātmanyevāvatiṣṭhate /
niḥspṛhaḥ sarvakāmebhyo yukta ityucyate tadā //19//

The time will come when it is ripened, this *yoga* is ripened. A time will come, if you do all things with awareness, you will be filled with glamour. You will laugh.

If your disciple says, "why are you laughing, Sir?"

"Yes, I am just seeing."

He will be *bas*, excited in his own nature. He will be fond of his nature. He will be mad after his nature. He will . . .

I can't understand [i.e., express] how he will be mad after his own Self. He will be just like somebody who is attached to some lady wholeheartedly, who becomes mad after her. In the same way, a *yogi* becomes mad after himself. He cannot imagine how beautiful I am and how beautiful and glamourous . . . it is beyond my imagination.

Yukta etyucyate tadā, then you should understand that he is *yukta*, he is established in *yoga*. *Ātmani eva niyatmanāḥ*, *bas*, he enjoys in his own nature. He enjoys *his* own nature, not "in" . . . [not] "in" his own nature. He enjoys his own nature, his own being, i.e., how he is existing. This is the glamourous way of his becoming Śiva. Not becoming. *Being* Śiva.

DVD 6.2 (33:14)

यथा दीपो निवातस्थो नेङ्गते सोपमा स्मृता ।
योगिनो यतचित्तस्य युञ्जतो योगमात्मनि ॥२०॥

yathā dīpo nivātastho neṅgate sopamā smṛtā /
yogino yatacittasya yuñjato yogamātmani //20//

Just as *nivātastho dīpo*, when there is a flame and when there is no wind passing, and that flame of that candle, *neṅgate*, it does not show its trembling movement . . .

DENISE: It doesn't flicker.

SWAMIJI: It doesn't flicker.

. . . *sopamā smṛtā*, you should [understand that] this is an example of how your God consciousness is established in one point and it . . . *bheri kāmsi nirādo'pi vyutthanāya nakalpate* [comm.], if there are thunders going on, thunders of Indra are going on, "*tharrrrah, tharrrrah,*" *vyutthanāya*, he won't be moved. With those tremendous sounds also he won't be moved; he will never be moved from his peaceful state of being. He won't come out, he won't hear anything [because] he is so absorbed in his own nature. *Yogino yatacittasya yuñjato yogam ātmani*, in the same way, a *yogi*, when he is established in *yoga*, [behaves in this manner]. It is an example. A befitting example.

[Now, the fruit of *yoga* is to be explained.]

DVD 6.2 (35:10)

यत्रोपरमते चित्तं निरुद्धं योगसेवनात् ।
यत्र चैवात्मनात्मानं पश्यन्नात्मानि तुष्यति ॥२१॥
सुखमात्यन्तिकं यत्तद्बुद्धिग्राह्यमतीन्द्रियम् ।
वेत्ति यत्र न चैवायं स्थितश्चलति तत्त्वतः ॥२२॥
यं लब्ध्वा चापरं लाभं मन्यते नाधिकं ततः ।
यस्मिन् स्थितो न दुःखेन गुरुणापि विचाल्यते ॥२३॥
तं विद्याद्दुःखसंयोगवियोगं योगसंज्ञितम् ।
स निश्चयेन योक्तव्यो योगोऽनिर्विणचेतसा ॥२४॥

yatroparamate cittaṁ niruddhaṁ yogasevanāt /
yatra caivātmanātmānaṁ paśyannātmani tuṣyati //21//
sukhamātyantikaṁ yattadbuddhigrahyamatīndriyam /
vetti yatra na caivāyaṁ sthitaścalati tattvataḥ //22//
yaṁ labdhvā cāparaṁ lābhaṁ manyate nādhikaṁ tataḥ /
yasmin sthito na duḥkhena guruṇāpi vicālyate //23//
taṁ vidyādduḥkhasaṁyogaviyogaṁ yogasaṁjñitam /
sa niścayena yoktavyo yogo'nirviṇacetasā //24//

These are the 21st, 22nd, 23rd, and 24th [*ślokas*], in *kulakam*. These have got . . .

JOHN: One meaning.

SWAMIJI: . . . one meaning.

Yatra niruddhaṁ cittaṁ uparamate. *Yatra*, a stage will come when *niruddhaṁ cittaṁ*, your mind is *niruddha*, it has reached the state of *niruddha*, automatic one-pointedness. When you have not to put any effort to make it one-pointed, that is *niruddha*. We have already explained, I have already explained to you that, *niruddhāvasthā*.

By what?

Yoga sevanāt, by the constant practice of *yoga*. And there, *yatra caiva atmanātmānaṁ paśyan*, and where he experiences his own nature in a vivid way, automatically; *ātmani tuṣyati*, and he is satisfied with his own nature.

Sukham ātyantikaṁ, this is *ātyantik sukha*. *Ātyantik sukha* [means] there is no comparison to that joy, which he gets from this one-pointedness. And this joy is *buddhi grahyam*, only intellect, one's own intellect can understand it. Organs cannot . . . organs have no approach [i.e., capacity] to see that joy. It is beyond the organ's joy. Where this joy comes into his experience and *yatra na caivāyaṁ sthitaścalati tattvataḥ*, and where when once established in that joy, he is never moved from that joy.

And *yaṁ labdhvā*, and that joy, when once achieved, *aparaṁ lābhaṁ tataḥ nādhika*, then he does not believe there is something more to be got, something more to be achieved [other] than this joy. [The *yogi* feels], "this is the ultimate joy, which was to be achieved, and I have achieved that."

And in which joy, once he is established, *na guruṇāpi duḥkhena vicālyate*, tremendous waves of pains, sorrows, and sufferings do not move him from his one-pointedness. He [maintains] one-pointedness and he is always joyful. Although tides of sorrows will come to him, he does not care. [He feels] as if nothing has happened, as if there was a little scratch [on his arm], *bas,* that is all.

And that joy, *vidyād*, the *yogi* should understand that it is *duḥkha saṁyoga viyogaṁ*, it is [the condition of] being separated from all tortures. There is no torture. All tortures, all kinds of varieties of tortures, have taken their absolute end. And *yoga saṁjñitam*, this is real *yoga*. It is nominated as *yoga*, Parabhairava *yoga*.

And that *yoga* is to be practiced *niścayena* (*niścayena* is a word [that appears in the 24th *śloka* of this chapter] of the *Bhagavad Gītā*). *Niścayena* is translated by Abhinavagupta [as] *niścayena āstikatayā śraddhayā* [comm.], *niścayena* means with faith you should *yoktavyaḥ* (*yoktavyaḥ* means *abhyasanīyaḥ*), with *śraddha* (with faith) and with love you should pratice [*yoga*].[187]

And *ānirviṇa cetasā*. He has commentated upon *nirviṇa cetasā* in two ways. *Nirviṇa cetasā* means when there is *vairāgya* (*vairāgya* is detachment). *Ānirviṇa cetasā* is attachment. *Nirviṇa cetasā* is detachment, i.e., detachment for the world. *Ānirviṇa*

187 "*Niścaya* means *āstikatājanitayā śraddhayā*, [the *yogi*] knows that this is the real joy and so, his faith and devotion and love is attached to that joy only." *Bhagavad Gītā* (1978).

cetasā is attachment for joy; attachment for this joy. Both are side-by-side working. In one way, it is detachment for other joys that are seen and experienced in the outside world and, at the same time, it is attachment for the joy, which is within.

In two ways he has translated this and it is wonderful.

Yatra mano niruddhamuparamate svayameva [comm. vs. 21]. This is the commentary of Abhinavagupta. When mind is appeased, [one-pointedness is maintained] without any effort, *bas*. When the time comes when you are [continuously] one-pointed, then it becomes one-pointed altogether. You have not to make it one-pointed.

[The cook drops a glass tumbler in the kitchen]

Finished! Glass tumbler is finished [laughs]!

Ātyantikaṁ, the joy which is *ātyantikaṁ*, which has no limit of its . . . what?

JOHN: Greatness. Or its magnitude.

JONATHAN: Infinite.

SWAMIJI: Beatitude.

JOHN: Magnitude, strength.

SWAMIJI: Strength. It is more than that, something more than that. *Ātyantikam* is *viṣaya krita kāluṣyābhavāt sukhaṁ*, this is joy, where he experiences that joy. There, *aparaṁ lābha*, [he attains] another achievement of this world. What is that achievement?

Dhanadāraputrādīnām, to conquer lotteries everywhere, e.g., to get a good wife, to get good children, good faith, good status, good throne, good respect from society–these appear to him as nothing. These appear to him just . . . he spits them out. *Aparaṁ lābhaṁ veti, na adhikam tataḥ*. *Aparaṁ lābhaṁ* means all these (status, etc.), they fail there to compare with that [joy].

"*Huuuhhh*!" If there is *apara lābha*, [with] that joy which you have, [you will] terrify that *lābha* (that status, etc.) [exclaiming], "*huuuhhh*! Go! Get out! Don't appear to me! I am engaged with this joy."

DENISE: I can't understand what you are saying.

SWAMIJI: Yes [laughs].

JONATHAN: This joy has no comparison.

SWAMIJI: No [affirmative].

JONATHAN: No comparison. So it frightens away all those other enjoyments.

SWAMIJI: Yes, it frightens away *bas*, at once.

In short words, *anyatra sukhadhīr nivartate ca* [comm.], he does not find any other pleasure in any other thing. *Na vicālyate*, he is not moved. *Viśeṣeṇa na cālyate* (he has done this in a nice way, i.e., Abhinavagupta's translation), *na cālyate*, he does not move; he is not moved from tremendous tortures of the world.[188]

> *api tu saṁskāramātreṇaivāsya prathamakṣaṇamātrameva calanaṁ* [comm.]

But this kind of translation I do not accept.

[Abhinavagupta] says, "at first, he gets worried [and says], 'what has happened to all this property, my property is gone.' Then, [afterwards] he is established in his own way in that glamour of Parabhairava state."

This is not actually the meaning. *Vicālyate* [means] he does not move at all.[189] This is the real meaning in this [verse of the] *Bhagavad Gītā*.

Duḥkha saṁyogasya viyogo yataḥ, this is the absence of all tortures; this is the state where the absence of all tortures are experienced. [They are] absent, they are no longer existing. *Sa ca*, that state you should *niścayena* (*niścayena* means *āstikatā-janitayā śraddhayā sarvathā yoktavyaḥ abhyasanīyaḥ*), you should practice it with great effort and vigor and joy.

The 25th *śloka*. 25th and 26th, both together.

188 "It does not mean that he does not enjoy worldly things. He enjoys worldly things, but superficially. He does not put weight in those joys. His mind is focused to that supreme joy only, always. Whenever he takes food (good delicious food) or he embraces a woman (a beautiful woman), he does not find that [particular] joy. But his joy is focused to that joy at that time also. He does it superficially. He does not neglect these things. He does all things, *śabda*, *sparṣa*, *rūpa*, *rasa*, *gandha*, all these things he does, but without any curiosity. He has no curiosity. That curiosity is vanished altogether." *Bhagavad Gītā* (1978).

189 That is to say, a sense of worry does not arise at all. [*Editor's note*]

DVD 6.2 (48:18)

सङ्कल्पप्रभवान्कामांस्त्यक्त्वा सर्वानशेषतः ।
मनसैवेन्द्रियग्रामं विनियम्य समन्ततः ॥२५॥
शनैः शनैरुपरमेद्बुद्ध्या धृतिगृहीतया ।
आत्मसंस्थं मनः कृत्वा न किंचिदपि चिन्तयेत् ॥२६॥

saṅkalpaprabhavānkāmāṁstyaktvā sarvānaśeṣataḥ /
manasaivendriyagrāmaṁ viniyamya samantataḥ //25//
śanaiḥ śanairuparamedbuddhyā dhṛtigṛhītayā /
ātmasaṁsthaṁ manaḥ kṛtvā na kiṁcidapi cintayet //26//

Now, He starts [to speak about practicing *yoga*] again. This is [about] *yoga*. He [had finished His discussion] of *yoga*. Now, again in the *Bhagavad Gītā*, He says you should [continue to] practice it [because] there is the possibility of coming down again. Go on! Go on by starting it afresh. You should start *yoga* afresh again. Just to make it . . .

It is called *svuna nikaraṇyāya*, i.e., when you are making foundation, foundation for a big house, big logs are stuck with machinery down in . . .

JONATHAN: Ground.

SWAMIJI: . . . in the ground. If they are once stuck [into the ground, then] they are taken out again. [Then] they are stuck again with machinery, down deeper. Then they are taken out again . . .

Do you understand?

DENISE: Yes.

SWAMIJI: . . . that is done for the foundation. That is *svuna nikaraṇyāya*. In the same way, he says that you should practice [*yoga*] again afresh. [One may] leave this practice if it has taken its end, but there is the possibility of falling down again, and you should . . .

JOHN: Reinforce it.

SWAMIJI: . . . reinforce it!

What is meant by re-enforcement? [With] cement or what?

JONATHAN: Reinforce means to strengthen something.

SWAMIJI:

śanaiḥ śanairuparamedbuddhyā dhṛtigṛhītayā / 26a

Slowly and slowly, by and by, you should control your mind by [maintaining] one-pointed intellect and mind. Then when once it is established in your own nature, then you should not think about anything else. Then you should be exactly situated in that God consciousness again.[190]

JOHN: Now, this reinforcing, this re-doing meditation again, starting again.

SWAMIJI: Again.

JOHN: If the first practice of meditation has reached its fullness, then if it's already in its fullness, then you are already in that state of Parabhairava. So why would you, why would meditation come . . . ?

SWAMIJI: No, it is *yoga*. It is *yoga*. So it is not a state.

JOHN: Process.

SWAMIJI: It is a process. You reach to Parabhairava state and there is a possibility of again coming down. It is not *that* Para-

190 "*Atmasaṁsthaṁ manaḥ kṛtvā*, and in the end, you must establish your mind in one point of God consciousness. *Na kiṁcidapi cintayet*, when it is established altogether, then you should not allow any thought to leak in your mind. Any thought should not come in your mind. . . . It is to be done through mind. *Na vyāpāroparameṇa*, you have not to shun your activity. You have to act in daily routine of your way of life, *dhritim grihītvā,* just to have courage. You have to adopt courage. Without courage you cannot be successful. . . . You must not think of your worldly objects of senses that, "I will hold it, I will not hold it, this is bad, this is good." All these things you should shun from your mind. . . . There are many commentators who have translated this *śloka* of *Bhagavad Gītā*, that *na kiṁcidapi cintayet* means you should not think at all, anything. That is not right, that is not right way of explaining *na kiṁcid*. *Na kiṁcid* means you must not encourage your mind to think this is right and this is wrong. Go on doing it, go on doing it. Because, *tadasmabhyaṁ na rūcitaṁ*, this is not liked, that way of explanation is not liked by me," Abhinavagupta says. *Śūnya-vādaprasaṅgāt*, when he has to remove all his thoughts from his mind, what will remain there in mind then? God consciousness also is removed. The thought of God consciousness should prevail, should remain there." *Bhagavad Gītā* (1978).

bhairava, which is done by *śaktipāta*. [This *yoga*] is by effort.

JOHN: *Acha*. Now, then again, then this *yoga*, in this first, part this *yoga* may start in *āṇavopāya*, then by the time you reach to *śāṁbhavopāya* . . . [191]

SWAMIJI: *śāktopāya* to *śāmbhavopāya*. Then again *āṇavopāya*.

JOHN: Again *āṇavopāya*?

SWAMIJI: Yes. Again *śāktopāya,* again *śāmbhavopāya*. Then again *āṇavopāya*.

JOHN: But the second time that you start, you will immediately go to *śāktopāya* and *śāmbhavopāya*?

SWAMIJI: No, that doesn't matter. That doesn't matter; there is the possibility of . . .

JOHN: Just reinforcing.

SWAMIJI: Yes, reinforcing again and again.[192] Then it remains in *anupāya* afterwards. *Anupāya* is that fourth one.

JOHN: The *upāya* without *upāya*.

SWAMIJI: Once you are established in the fourth *upāya* (*anupāya*), then there is no fear of coming down again.

JONATHAN: So if it's through *śaktipāta*, then you go straight to *anupāya*?

SWAMIJI: Yes.

JONATHAN: You can't fall down.

SWAMIJI: There are so many varieties of *yoga*.

JOHN: But even to practice *yoga* you have to have *śaktipāta*?

SWAMIJI: Huh?

JOHN: Otherwise you won't practice?

SWAMIJI: Yes, this is *śaktipāta*. There are so many ways of *śaktipāta*. It is not one *śaktipāta*, it is about twenty-seven *śaktipātas*, twenty-seven ways of *śaktipāta*.[193] The topmost is *tīvra-tīvra-tīvra-tīvra śaktipāta,* and that is finished. Once you have achieved that, then you won't come back. Then you are

191 See footnote 126 for an explanation of the *upāyas*.

192 "When once your mind is focused on God consciousness, there you should not rest. You have not to rest. You have to go on again struggling for one-pointedness. If your mind is one-pointed and you feel it has become one-pointed, still you have to struggle for one-pointedness. This one-pointedness will fade. In next moment it will fade. So you have to be watchful and fully aware that this one-pointedness should stand." *Bhagavad Gītā* (1978).

193 See *Kashmir Shaivism–The Secret Supreme*, chapter 10.

gone. Then you are gone for good.

JONATHAN: You can't exist in this body.

SWAMIJI: No, you can't exist in this body. This body, you won't accept this body. No. The body will not accept it; the body will be shattered. What is body? Body is flesh, toothache, backache, and . . .

JONATHAN: And mucus.

SWAMIJI: . . . mucus in your nostrils.

Chapter 6 Part 3

Now, [Lord Kṛṣna] again strengthens it.

DVD 6.3 (00:08)

यतो यतो निश्चरति मनश्चञ्चलमस्थिरम् ।
ततस्ततो नियम्यैतदात्मन्येव शमं नयेत् ॥२७॥

yato yato niścarati manaścañcalamasthiram /
tatastato niyamyaitadātmanyeva śamaṁ nayet //27//

Whenever your mind goes astray, with a whip you should again pull it back to your own nature and situate it in your own nature, in your own mind, with one-pointedness. *Ātmanyeva śamaṁ nayet*, you should make it forcefully established in your own nature.

Yato yato nivartate, tat nivatranasamanantaram eva [comm.]. As soon as [your mind] goes away [to some thought], you should be so watchful that while it's going away, [when it] opens the door only, and as soon as [the mind] opens the door to go away, no, you [must] rush at once to the door and drag [it back] again into one-pointedness.

Don't let [the mind] go! Don't wait for [the mind] to go. Otherwise, [the mind] will be rash. When [the mind] goes into the field [of thoughts], then it will be very troublesome for you to get it back. You should just rush and get [your mind one-pointed].

As with those children who are just crawling [everywhere], mothers at once catch hold of their hands and keep them in one place. Motherhood is always troublesome during that period when the child begins to crawl. It is terrible because [the child] becomes just like the mind; he goes here and there.

Anyathā, if you don't do that swiftly, *apratiṣṭhaṁ cittaṁ*, this mind is fickle, *punarapi viṣayāneva*, then [the mind] won't listen to you; [the mind] will go astray.

Then what happens to your mind?

DVD 6.3 (02:42)

प्रशान्तमनसं ह्येनं योगिनं सुखमुत्तमम् ।
उपैति शान्तरजसं ब्रह्मभूतमकल्मषम् ॥२८॥

praśāntamanasaṁ hyenaṁ yoginaṁ sukhamuttamam /
upaiti śāntarajasaṁ brahmabhūtamakalmaṣam //28//

Praśānta manasaṁ hyenaṁ. This *yogi* who has un-minded his mind (*yoginaṁ*, the one who is *yogi*) . . .[194]

No other commentators have commentated upon this *śloka* in the way Abhinavagupta has commentated upon it. He says, "the *yogi* is *karma bhūtam*, the *yogi* is the object. The *yogi*, you should think, it is an object and the blissful state of Parabhairava is the subject. The blissful state of Parabhairava is subjective and the *yogi* who does *yoga* [is objective].

Actually, [according to other commentators], the *yogi* who does *yoga*, he must be subjective because he is the doer, he is the conductor of *yoga*. No, it is not that. Abhinavagupta does not explain it like that.

This way, all of the other commentators have explained that the *yogi* who is always doing the practice of *yoga* [is the subject].

[Abhinavagupta, on the other hand, says that the *yogi*] is the object. The time comes when he becomes the object and the blissful state of Parabhairava is the subject. So the blissful state of Parabhairava rushes to the *yogi*; the *yogi* does not rush to the

194 "When *praśāntamanasaṁ hyenaṁ*, when the mind of *yogi* is thus one-pointed, becomes one-pointed in God consciousness, then *sukham-uttamam upaiti śāntarājasaṁ*, then *yogi* becomes *śānta-rājasaṁ*, *rājaguṇa* disappears in the mind of *yogi* then. Only *sāttvic* attitude of *guṇa* prevails there. *Rājaguṇa* is absolutely neglected, it vanishes (*rājaguṇa* means all these activities, worldly activities). *Brahma-bhūtam*, *yogi* becomes one with Brahman. *Akalmaṣam*, he becomes fully purified and deprived of all sins. Then, what happens to *yogi*? *Sukham-uttamam upaiti*, that supreme joy of God consciousness searches for him. He does not search for God consciousness. He does not search for joy. Joy searches for him." *Bhagavad Gītā* (1978).

blissful state of Parabhairava.[195]

Have you understood?

The *yogi* does not make an effort to rush to the blissful state of Parabhairava. No. On the contrary, the blissful state of Parabhairava rushes to the *yogi*.

This is the wonderful state of *śaktipāta*.[196] *Śaktipāta* is: He comes to see you. You don't rush to see Him. You have not to see Him. The *yogi* has not to see Him.

Who has to see him?

JOHN: Parabhairava.

SWAMIJI: God has to see him! God rushes to see him. So this is the greatness of *śaktipāta*.

DVD 6.3 (05:34)

युञ्जन्नेवं सदात्मानं योगी नियतमानसः ।
सुखेन ब्रह्मसंयोगमत्यन्तमधिगच्छति ॥२९॥

yuñjannevaṁ sadātmānaṁ yogī niyatamānasaḥ /
sukhena brahmasaṁyogamatyantamadhigacchati //29//

This is the 29th *śloka*.

This way, when a *yogi* practices this *yoga*, *niyata mānasaḥ*, and his mind is one-pointed, *sukhena* (easily, without any effort), a time comes [when], without any effort, he is united in the Parabhairava state, peacefully, without any effort.[197]

---

195 "When *yogi* becomes *śāntacitta*, his mind is appeased, fully peaceful, because he is focused, his mind is focused in his own self, [then] this joy is *karta* (the doer), this joy of God consciousness takes the position of subjective case and *yogi* takes the position of objective case. He becomes object of that joy; joy comes to see him. He has not to find out joy. Joy has to find out the *yogi*. So it is grace. Through grace he achieves that state of absolute joy. This is the way how Abhinavagupta has explained this *sukhaṁ*, this joy. Joy is active, *yogi* remains passive." Ibid.

196 *Śaktipāta*, grace. See *Kashmir Shaivism–The Secret Supreme* 10.65.

197 "This is the way *yogīs* attain easily the state of God consciousness. *Natu kaṣṭayogādina*, not by *hatha yogā* or doing *sadhanā* and penance

The 30th *śloka*:

DVD 6.3 (06:41)

सर्वभूतस्थमात्मानं सर्वभूतानि चात्मनि ।
ईक्षते योगयुक्तात्मा सर्वत्र समदर्शनः ॥३०॥

sarvabhūtasthamātmānaṁ sarvabhūtāni cātmani /
īkṣate yogayuktātmā sarvatra samadarśanaḥ //30//

Then, a time comes when that *yogi* who has achieved the topmost state of *yoga* in this way, he feels that this whole universe is existing in [his] body, and [his] body is existing in the whole universe. He sees *vice versa*, "this whole universe is existing in my body and my body is–my body is not this [physical] body, [it is] my being–my being is existing in the whole universe, in the one hundred and eighteen worlds." And he becomes the same, i.e., it does not appear to him that there is any difference between inside and outside.

DVD 6.3 (08:00)

यो मां पश्यति सर्वत्र सर्वं च मयि पश्यति ।
तस्याहं न प्रणश्यामि स च मे न प्रणश्यति ॥३१॥

yo māṁ paśyati sarvatra sarvaṁ ca mayi paśyati /
tasyāhaṁ na praṇaśyāmi sa ca me na praṇaśyati //31//

Any *yogi* who perceives Me, Parabhairava, *sarvatra*, in each and every object, and who perceives each and every object in Parabhairava–who perceives Me in each and every object and who perceives each and every object in Parabhairava–*tasyāhaṁ na praṇaśyāmi*, I am not separated from him and he is not separated from Me. I am in him and he is in Me. We are both . . .

---

and all those things. They are absolutely useless. Only penance is just to become watchful and alert where your mind goes. Go on following your mind. Whenever your mind goes, wants to go astray on some worldly object, make [it] return halfway. Don't let him go to that point." *Bhagavad Gītā* (1978).

JONATHAN: Inseparable.

SWAMIJI: . . . inseparable.

Tathāhi. Now the commentary of Abhinavagupta. *Param-ātmanaḥ sarvagataṁ rupaṁ yo na paśyati, tasya paramātmā palāyitaḥ*. This *sarvagata rūpa*, the all-pervading *svarūpa*[198] of Parabhairava, [for the one] who does not experience [Parabhairava] in each and every object, from him, Parabhairava has walked out. He will never come to him. [Parabhairava] has fled away from him. Because, *svarūpa prakaṭī kārābhāvāt*, [Parabhairava] does not appear to him in His real form.

Yastu sarva gataṁ mām paśyati, tasyāhaṁ na pranaṣṭaḥ. And, on the contrary, the one who sees and experiences My nature in everybody and who experiences everybody in My nature, that is the reality of *paramātma* [i.e., Parabhairava].[199]

DVD 6.3 (10:33)

सर्वभूतस्थितं यो मां भजत्येकत्वमास्थितः ।
सर्वथा वर्तमानोऽपि स योगी मयि वर्तते ॥३२॥

sarvabhūtasthitaṁ yo māṁ bhajatyekatvamāsthitaḥ /
sarvathā vartamāno'pi sa yogī mayi vartate //32//

Yastu evam jñānāviṣṭaḥ so'vaśyamevaikatayā bhagavantaṁ sarvagataṁ vidan sarvā-vasthāgato'pi na lipyate [comm.]. In this way, any *yogi* who experiences My nature in each and every object, although he does all of the activities of the world, he acts in the state of Bhairava.[200]

---

198 Self-nature, shape, or form. [*Editor's note*]

199 "So, this is the real position when you love God. If you don't love, if you hate people, you hate God. You actually hate Him. Because God is existing in each and every being. So, if you hate people, you are taken, you are carried away from God consciousness." *Bhagavad Gītā* (1978).

200 "It is very difficult to feel oneness in each and every being because hatred comes, naturally hatred comes. Whenever a person blows [i.e., strikes] you, gives you bad names, you'll hate him, naturally you'll hate him. But you should not hate, you should embrace him on the contrary. But it is very difficult. A person who feels that God is existing in each and every being, and in each and every object, and feels and adores everybody, loves everybody, is attached to everybody–not individually,

DVD 6.3 (11:24)

आत्मौपम्येन सर्वत्र समं पश्यति योऽर्जुन ।
सुखं वा यदि वा दुःखं स योगी परमो मतः ॥३३॥

ātmaipamyena sarvatra samaṁ paśyati yo'rjuna /
sukhaṁ vā yadi vā duḥkaṁ sa yogī paramo mataḥ //33//
[not recited or translated][201]

अर्जुन उवाच
arjuna uvāca

Arjuna speaks. Arjuna puts a question.

DVD 6.3 (11:30)

योऽयं योगस्त्वया प्रोक्तः साम्येन मधुसूदन ।
एतस्याहं न पश्यामि चञ्चलत्वात्स्थितिं पराम् ॥३४॥

yo'yaṁ yogastvayā proktaḥ sāmyena madhusūdana /
etasyāhaṁ na paśyāmi cañcalatvātsthitiṁ parām //34//

This *yoga* which you have explained to me, [in which You have taught me to remain in] *sāmya* (*sāmya* means sameness, sameness outside and inside), this appears to me to be very difficult, Sir. How can I see that bad is equal to good and good is equal to bad? How can I see it? How can I believe it?

It is not believable. *Etasyāhaṁ na paśyāmi cañcalatvāt sthitiṁ parām*, because the mind is always flickering. How can it be the same in the flickering way and in the one-pointed way? If

---

universally–*sarvathā vartamāno'pi*, no matter if he does all worldly things, *sa yogī mayi vartate,* he roams and walks in My circle. In this way, who experiences in this way, *so'vaśyamevaikatayā bhagavantaṁ sarva-gataṁ vidan*, he understands that supreme God is existing [as] one with the whole universe. *Sarvāvasthāgato'pi*, if he does each and every thing of his daily life, *na lipyate*, he is not attached." Ibid.

201 "And that *yogi* who feels the pain and pleasure of others as his own pain and pleasure, he is nominated as a supreme *yogi* by Me." Ibid.

sameness is [both] flickering *and* one-pointed, how can it be understood?

He explained, Lord Kṛṣṇa explained to him that sameness is flickering in one-pointedness and is one-pointed in the flickering state–this is the sameness of *yoga*. Parabhairava *yoga* is the same; in the flickering state, it is one-pointed and in one-pointedness, it is the flickering state.

How can I believe this?

I cannot understand it. This theory is vague to me, because the mind is always *cañcala* (flickering), the mind is always going astray. It is not one-pointed at all! How can the flickering mind be one-pointed and the one-pointed mind be flickering?

This appears to me as just *bakwas* (nonsense). Because,

DVD 6.3 (13:44)

चञ्चलं हि मनः कृष्ण प्रमाथि बलवद् दृढम् ।
तस्याहं निग्रहं मन्ये वायोरिव सुदुष्करम् ॥३५॥

cañcalaṁ hi manaḥ kṛṣṇa pramāthi balavad dṛḍham /
tasyāhaṁ nigrahaṁ manye vāyoriva suduṣkaram //35//

The mind is *cañcala*, the mind is always flickering. [The mind] is *pramāthi*, he drags you anywhere he likes. For instance, I would rush and drag Viresh here, but I have got attachment of this [microphone and] it will break. And [so] it is *pramāthi* (*pramāthi* means it drags you). The mind is so *cañcala* (flickering).

JONATHAN: It is so what?

SWAMIJI: Mind.

JONATHAN: Mind is so . . . ?

SWAMIJI: *Cañcala*, flickering.

It drags you from one-pointedness at once and throws you into varieties of thoughts. How can mind be one-pointed in varieties of thoughts?

You, [O Kṛṣṇa], said, "the flickering mind is to be experienced in one-pointed thought and one-pointed thoughts are to be experienced in the flickering mind, then it is *yoga*; then it is real *yoga*."

I think either You are mad or I am mad!

No, I mean Lord Kṛṣṇa. Lord Kṛṣṇa is mad or I, [Arjuna], am mad, because I don't understand what You bark [laughs]. It is just barking! You have gone [too far]. It is too much for You to speak like this. Say sanely what is advisable [for me, something that] I can grasp. I cannot grasp this.

श्रीभगवानुवाच

śrī bhagavān uvāca

Now Śrī Bhagavān answers to this question.

DVD 6.3 (16:12)

असंशयं महाबाहो मनो दुर्निग्रहं चलम् ।
अभ्यासेन तु कौन्तेय वैराग्येण च गृह्यते ॥ ३६ ॥

asaṁśayaṁ mahābāho mano durnigrahaṁ calam /
abhyāsena tu kaunteya vairāgyeṇa ca gṛhyate //36//

It is true, O Arjuna, it is true that the mind is *durnigrahaṁ*, the mind you cannot make one-pointed easily.[202] But for this sake

202 "And it is always unsteady, it remains always unsteady; it won't remain in one point. But at the same time, *abhyāsena tu kaunteya*, it can be controlled by *abhyās*, by meditation, and by losing the charm of these universal objects, universal pleasures. All these universal pleasures, when you have no charm, when you lose all charm, in money, in your wife, in everything, in your property, when you lose the charm, you have got *vairāgya* (detachment). Detachment appears. When detachment appears, it is possible to control the mind then. . . . First you must be detached and then realization will come. And detachment won't come [until] you are fully detached, i.e., when you have no fun to live, when you feel it is useless: "why to bother, I have to die right now," finished, and detachment comes. As soon as detachment appears, mind is controlled. And at the same time, you must adjust meditation, concentration of mind. Concentration of mind becomes easier with detachment . . . So these two elements are very essential, very important. One is detachment, another is concentration. Patañjalī, the founder of *Yoga*, has also said: *ubhayādhīnaś citta vṛtti nirodhaḥ* [*Yoga Sūtras* 1.12], controlling our mind depends upon these two. What?

I told you that one-pointed mind is only [possible] when it is made one-pointed in varieties of points, then it is possible [in] varieties of points.[203] When you are not one-pointed, at that stage you should make this mind one-pointed.

DENISE: By just observing the rise of thought.

SWAMIJI: Huh?

DENISE: By just observing the rise of thought?

SWAMIJI: Not observing the rise of thought.

Just see the manifestation. In manifestation you [should] see that He is unmanifested. God consciousness is unmanifested in manifestation and God consciousness is manifested in unmanifestation.

Have you understood?

JOHN: That part I understood.

SWAMIJI: That part and [laughs]?

JOHN: That part.

SWAMIJI: That part.

He is light in darkness; He is darkness in light. This way you can understand. He is I-ness in this-ness; He is this-ness in I-ness. He is variety in oneness and oneness in varieties. In brief words, He is everywhere.

DENISE: And nowhere.

SWAMIJI: And nowhere or everywhere.

But you have to make it [your] nature; you have to make it [your] nature to think like that. *Abhyāsa* means you have to make it [your] nature. It is not "practice". Make it [your] nature. Make it the nature of your daily life.

And there must be *vairāgya* also. *Vairāgya* means love. *Vairāgya* does not mean hatred. *Vairāgya* means love; love for God.[204] Intensity of love and making it [your] nature, that will

---

Detachment and concentration." *Bhagavad Gītā* (1978).

203 "There must be triple awareness. Not two awareness' of inhaling and exhaling. There must be triple [awareness]: inhale, exhale, and junction. One step, another step, and in between. One talk, another talk, and in between that sensation of talk, i.e., in the center. When you are aware of these three centers, then you are carried to *Svacchanda* Bhairava, God consciousness." Swami Lakshmanjoo, *Shiva Sutras – The Supreme Awakening*, 3.36, p215.

204 The attachment or love of God enables one to be truly detached from the world. [*Editor's note*].

work.

Vairāgyeṇa viṣayotsukatāvināśyate [comm.]. When you adopt *vairāgya* (*vairāgya* means attachment for the Lord), *viṣayotsuka*, then *viṣayas* do not exist, they don't work.

DENISE: What doesn't work?

SWAMIJI: Worldly pleasures (*viṣayas*) don't work when there is attachment for Parabhairava; then worldly pleasures don't work. In their way, they don't work.

JOHN: How do they work?

SWAMIJI: [laughing] They work by showing you the glamour of the Parabhairava state.

JOHN: So everything carries you to that.

SWAMIJI: Yes.

Abhyāsena mokṣapakṣaḥ kramāt kramaṁ viṣayī kriyate. But by practice, *mokṣa* (liberation) becomes nearer and nearer, it comes nearer and nearer to you. The state of Parabhairava comes nearer to you by doing it, doing it, doing it.

[Swamiji sings], "everybody doing it, doing it, and doing it. Everybody doing it, doing it, and doing it . . ."

Everybody should do it.

DENISE: Do what?

SWAMIJI: This practice. This is the practice of Parabhairava.

There was one record when I was in my childhood. This was an English record. "Everybody doing it, doing it, and doing it . . ."

JONATHAN: It's a song.

SWAMIJI: Yes [laughs]. It is in my brain, knocking. I was enjoying it. When I learned this song, it was the beginning of *pralaya*.[205]

---

205 The era of destruction. [*Editor's note*]

DVD 6.3 (21:16)

असंयतात्मनो योगो दुष्प्राप इति मे मतिः ।

asaṁyatātmano yogo duṣprāpa iti me matiḥ /37a

As long as your mind is not one-pointed in varieties of points, as long as your mind is not one-pointed in varieties of points, it is very difficult to achieve. "*Asaṁyat-ātmanaḥ yogo duṣprāpa*, from My viewpoint, as far as I understand, as far as I have got understanding power," this Lord Kṛṣṇa says to Arjuna, "as long as I have got understanding power, I understand that as long as one-pointedness is not practiced in varieties of points, [then] one-pointedness is not possible to achieve. One-pointedness can be achieved only in varieties of points, not in one-pointedness [laughing]. If you become one-pointed, nothing will happen![206]

JONATHAN: So when you say variety of points, what are those points? Everywhere?

SWAMIJI: [laughs] Everywhere.

DENISE: Any points.

SWAMIJI: Every point.

DENISE: Whatever point comes to you . . .

SWAMIJI: Any point.

DENISE: . . . remain one-pointed on that point.

SWAMIJI: Yes.

DENISE: Until the next point comes to you?

SWAMIJI: Yes.

DENISE: But doesn't everybody do that naturally? Whatever comes to their mind, they are one-pointed on that point?

SWAMIJI: One-pointed, but you don't get one-pointedness.

DENISE: You don't?

SWAMIJI: You are scattered-minded. But you have not to be scattered-minded. This is the problem.

JONATHAN: Is that like that practice where it says, "wherever your mind goes and is happy, you should go with that, you should stay there?"

SWAMIJI: You should go with that and see, experience the . . .

---

206 "Without being attached to God consciousness and being detached towards worldly objects, *yoga* cannot be solved. You can't achieve *yoga*." *Bhagavad Gītā* (1978).

JONATHAN: And be one-pointed there.

SWAMIJI: Yes.

JONATHAN: And when you go to something else, you should go with that and be one-pointed.

SWAMIJI: One-pointed there, yes.

DVD 6.3 (23:24)

वश्यात्मना तु यतता शक्योऽवाप्तुमुपायतः ॥३७॥

vaśyātmanā tu yatatā śakyo'vāptumupāyataḥ //37b//

He who is *yatatā*, who is always alert, and whose organs are all under his control (under anybodies control), for him, it is no problem, it is very easy to achieve.[207]

JOHN: So this one-pointedness on various points, it seems to me to mean that you don't lose your awareness no matter what you are doing.

SWAMIJI: Yes.

JOHN: So there is always "I" there; the strength of awareness is always there in everything.

SWAMIJI: Wherever you go, you feel the presence of Parabhairava.

Now Arjuna asks again a question.

DVD 6.3 (24:15)

अर्जुन उवाच

arjuna uvāca

अयतः श्रद्धयोपेतो योगाच्चलितमानसः ।

207 "*Yoga* is possible to be achieved by means of concentration then. But first thing is detachment, detachment must be there. This is essential. This is the most important point you should possess. This is *pratijñā*, determination of Lord Kṛṣṇa. He has determined that there must be detachment and then adjustment of concentration. If you are attached to worldly pleasures and you begin to concentrate, your concentration will be useless. Your concentrating is useless, it won't bear any fruit. . . . And only being detached won't do. [There must be] detachment *and* concentration." Ibid.

लिप्समानः सतां मार्गं प्रमूढो ब्रह्मणः पथि ॥३८॥
अनेकचित्तो विभ्रान्तो मोहस्यैव वशं गतः ।
अप्राप्य योगसंसिद्धिं कां गतिं कृष्ण गच्छति ॥३९॥

ayataḥ śraddhayopeto yogāccalitamānasaḥ /
lipsamānaḥ satāṁ mārgaṁ pramūḍho brahmaṇaḥ pathi //38
anekacitto vibhrānto mohasyaiva vaśaṁ gataḥ /
aprāpya yogasaṁsiddhiṁ kāṁ gatiṁ kṛṣṇa gacchati //39//

I am so lucky that you have pointed out the reality of un-minding one's mind to me, that you can un-mind it in a mindful way and you can un-mind it in an un-mindful way. You have to un-mind it in an un-minded way and a mindful way also. I have understood this.

But as long as it is not complete, because it is a very tough task, as soon as I want to become one-pointed in varieties of points, I go astray, I go astray. I have to be careful at that time.

In the same way, life goes on, life goes on.

If I do practice, *ayataḥ*, not with whole power–because, after all, limited being is always limited being; he has not such capacity of [applying] all the force as You have (*ayataḥ*)–and *śraddhayopeta*, I want to become one-pointed.

The one who is *ayataḥ*, whose effort does not work, but who still wants to work, he has got faith in that work but his effort is low, his effort is not so powerful, *lipsamānaḥ satāṁ mārgaṁ*, and internally he wishes that I should achieve the state of Parabhairava, *pramūḍho,* but, on the contrary, *pramūḍho brahmaṇaḥ pathi*, he cannot find out the reality of Parabhairava, *aneka citta*, because he has got *aneka citta*, his mind is always astray, going here and there, but internally he is repenting, "what have I done; what sinful act in the past have I done [that] I am unluckily placed in this environment?" *Vibhrānta*, and he is *vibhrānta* (*vibhrānta*, he remains always in a fix what to do). *Mohasyaiva vaśaṁ gataḥ,* he always ignores the reality of the Lord, he does not remain one-pointed to the Lord. *Aprāpya yoga saṁsiddhiṁ*, and *yoga siddhi* (*yogic* power) he has not achieved after struggling and struggling in his lifetime [and] he passes away. What will happen to him?

He passes away; he is dead.

What will happen to him, O Lord?

Tell me what will he do afterwards when he has half-finished his work and he is dead. But his mind was craving for having that but he had not such power to un-mind his mind. What will happen to him next? [Concerning] this, I have got doubt.

He may be offered to those hell members. [They will say], "eat him!" And Yama[208] will tell the hell members, "eat him! He has not done anything."

What will happen to him, to this such creature?

Prāptādyogāt yadi calite'pi citte śraddhā na hīyate [comm.]. *Śraddhā* is not [the issue]. He has got faith. He has developed faith. He has maintained faith throughout his whole life, but he has not done [i.e., achieved] anything; he could not do [*yoga*] because of his not being capable for *yoga*.

DVD 6.3 (29:36)

कच्चिन्नोभयविभ्रंशाच्छिन्नाभ्रमिवा नश्यति ।
अप्रतिष्ठो महाबाहो विनाशं वाधिगच्छति ॥४०॥
एतन्मे संशयं कृष्ण च्छेत्तुमर्हस्यशेषतः ।
त्वदन्यः संशयस्यास्य च्छेत्ता नह्युपपद्यते ॥४१॥

kaccinnobhayavibhraṁśācchinnābhramiva naśyati /
apratiṣṭho mahābāho vināśaṁ vādhigacchati //40//
etanme saṁśayaṁ kṛṣṇa cchettumarhasyaśeṣataḥ /
tvadanyaḥ saṁśayasyāsya cchettā nahyupapadyate //41//

Kaccit, is it not that *ubhaya vibhraṁśāt*, he has been deprived in both ways? He wanted to do *yoga* [but] he couldn't do *yoga*. And he has already created hatred for *bhoga*, he has created hatred for *bhoga*, so he is not fit for *bhoga* [either].

Bhoga means what?

Enjoyment of the world.

He does not feel any pleasure in the enjoyment of the world and he has not the capacity to [achieve] that other thing also [i.e., *yoga*]. He has not achieved [*bhoga*]; he has not achieved

208 Yama is the lord of death. [*Editor's note*]

[*yoga*]. So he is in a fix, in-between. He will be deprived of both.

So his life is wasted in both ways because *apratiṣṭhaḥ mahābāho vināśaṁ vādhi*, does he not go to *vināśa*? *Vināśa* means he becomes nothing after death.

Atra nirṇayaṁ.

श्रीभगवानुवाच

śrī bhagavān uvāca

For this, [Lord Kṛṣṇa] answers and makes him understand. Whom? Arjuna.

DVD 6.3 (32:12)

पार्थ नैवेह नामुत्र विनाशस्तस्य विद्यते ।
नहि कल्याणकृत्कश्चिद्दुर्गतिं जातु गच्छति ॥४२॥

pārtha naiveha nāmutra vināśastasya vidyate /
nahi kalyāṇakṛtkaściddurgatiṁ jātu gacchatiṁ //42//

O Arjuna, neither in this *loka* (world), *na amutra*, nor in *para loka* (after death), *vināśastasya*, he is not destroyed; his soul is not destroyed. I tell you, it is granted, that he will not be destroyed!

Nahi kalyāṇa kṛtkaścit, the one who is craving for that achievement of the Parabhairava state, how can he go down in this field of the universe?

Na tasya, he is called *yoga bhraṣṭa* [comm.]. *Yoga bhraṣṭa* means that *yoga* has been done by him halfway. He did *yoga* with whatever effort he had, but it was not complete and [then] he died. So he is nominated as *yoga bhraṣṭa*. *Yoga bhraṣṭa* means he has done *yoga* not completely–incomplete *yoga*.

The 43rd *śloka*:

DVD 6.3 (33:55)

प्राप्य पुण्यकृतां लोकानुषित्वा शाश्वतीः समाः ।
शुचीनां श्रीमतां गेहे योगभ्रष्टोऽभिजायते ॥४३॥

prāpya puṇyakṛtāṁ lokānuṣitvā śāśvatīḥ samāḥ /
śucīnāṁ śrīmatāṁ gehe yogabhraṣṭo'bhijāyate //43//

Prāpya puṇya kṛtāṁ lokān, after death, what happens to him? He achieves *puṇya kṛtāṁ lokān*. After death, he is sentenced to the uppermost heavens. He is sentenced to the uppermost heavens; not those heavens where there is only enjoyment.

Do you understand?

Where there is only the enjoyment of drinking wine and dancing and [that kind] of *tamasha* (commotion), he is not sentenced to those heavens. He is sentenced to those heavens where there is Anantabhaṭṭāraka[209] and where everything is at his disposal, and where Anantabhaṭṭāraka makes him sit and practice *yoga*.

Where? In heaven.

That kind of heaven he achieves after death, i.e., this [*yoga bhraṣṭa*]. So there is no fear for him! He will rise; he will rise day-by-day. Don't worry about him. If he has not done *yoga* successfully but he had faith and couldn't succeed, [when he dies], he goes and stays there [in that heaven]. *Vaiṣṇavāni trīṇi varṣāṇi* (*vaiṣṇavāni trīṇi varṣāṇi* means Nārāyaṇa's three decades),[210] for that long he remains there for practice for [the length of] Nārāyaṇa's three days and three nights. It is a very long interval of time, say about one thousand years. For one thousand years, he does practice there under the guidance of Anantabhaṭṭāraka.

Śucīnāṁ śrīmatāṁ gehe yoga bhraṣṭo'bhijāyate, then, if he has

209 "Anantabhaṭṭāraka is that Rudra whose responsibility is to govern all these one hundred and eighteen worlds. Anantabhaṭṭāraka has to see that your *karmas* bear fruit appropriately, and that you are created, you are protected, and you are destroyed." Swami Lakshmanjoo, *Tantrāloka* 13.95 (1980).

210 *Trīṇi varṣa* can be translated as three years or three days. In his previous translation, Swamiji translated *śāśvatīḥ samāḥ* as three years. [*Editor's note*]

some agitation of society, which has [been a] hindrance in his [practice of] *yoga*, then he takes birth in that place where his home members are very pure and moneyed, where his father and mother will provide all his money for his studies.

Just as my father and mother–we had [high social status, money], and everything–my father and mother [provided] money and they didn't care if [I didn't work. They said], "let him not work, let him do his own job of *yoga*." And he spent so much money for me–not as a burden.

Or, if he has no other job, then he is born in such a family where there is no food, where there is no food, where there is only *yoga*, in a poor home.

I wanted to become like [I am], princely. I didn't want to become poor. So, I became like this. And some become like this, i.e., poor, and they do practice. But [I felt that] I must do practice when I am talking, walking, in society, and everything. I liked that, so I went there [to that kind of life].

DVD 6.3 (40:00)

अथवा योगिनामेव जायते धीमतां कुले ।
एतद्धि दुर्लबतरं लोके जन्म यदीदृशम् ॥४४॥

athvā yogināmeva jāyate dhīmatāṁ kule /
etaddhi durlabhataraṁ loke janma yadīdṛśam //44//
[not recited or translated][211]

The 45th *śloka*.

तत्र तं बुद्धिसंयोगं लभते पौर्वदैहिकम् ।
ततो भूयोऽपि यतते संसिद्धौ कुरुनन्दन ॥४५॥

211 "But this kind of *janma*, this kind of birth [in a family of *yogīs*] is very difficult [to achieve] in this Kaliyuga. This kind of birth does not take place easily. This is very difficult." *Bhagavad Gītā* (1978).

When asked if a master can organize this kind of birth for a disciple, Swamiji answered: "Master can do nothing. It depends upon your own desire." Ibid.

tatra taṁ buddhisaṁyogaṁ labhate paurvadaihikam /
tato bhūyo'pi yatate saṁsiddhau kurunandana //45//

O Arjuna, there he is united with his past achievements. There, in that life, he is united with his past achievements and he goes on practicing wholeheartedly in that [environment] where all facilities are at his disposal.

> My mother had prepared my house separated [from the family home]; my mother and father constructed a separate house for me. And they hired one servant for me to cook rice. And my mother was occasionally visiting [me to see] if there was any need for [me], to have some butter, cheese, and everything–all of these first-class dishes. And I was [eating those] dishes and practicing [*yoga*].
> Wonderful. It was a wonderful way.

DVD 6.3 (41:35)

पूर्वाभ्यासेन तेनैव ह्रियते ह्यवशोऽपि सन् ।
जिज्ञासुरपि योगस्य शब्दब्रह्मातिवर्तते ॥४६॥

pūrvābhyāsena tenaiva hriyate hyavaśo'pi san /
jijñāsurapi yogasya śabdabrahmātivartate //46//

So he rises there abruptly and gets his *yoga* complete.[212]

DVD 6.3 (42:01)

प्रयत्नाद्यतमानस्तु योगी संशुद्धकिल्विषः ।
अनेकजन्मसंसिद्धस्ततो याति परां गतिम् ॥४७॥

prayatnādyatamānastu yogī saṁśuddhakilviṣaḥ /
anekajanmasaṁsiddhastato yāti parāṁ gatim //47//

212 "Without any other distraction or obstacles he goes on with *yoga* in that life. *Jijñāsurapi yogasya śabdabrahmātivartate*, so, O Arjuna, you must not think that he will ever get destroyed or ruined, i.e., that kind of *yogi* who has not achieved *yoga* and who desires for *yoga* and has developed full faith for *yoga*. He will never be ruined." Ibid.

[incomplete translation][213]

As I did.[214] Some force came to me of doing too much effort. I told you that, in my "courses"[215] I had . . . some force had transformed my brain and I worked so intensely that I succeeded at once, and I became Parabhairava myself.

JOHN: When was that? When you were younger?

SWAMIJI: No, not younger.

DENISE: Just recently.

SWAMIJI: Just recently. A few years back.

JONATHAN: Swamiji, can I ask one question there? If you are sentenced to this sort of lifetime which you had . . .

SWAMIJI: Huh?

JONATHAN: If you are sentenced to this lifetime, after practicing for all those thousands of years under Ananta-bhaṭṭāraka, or whatever it is, then I don't understand where that experience of the reverse rise of *kuṇḍalinī*?[216]

SWAMIJI: It was *śaktipāta*. It was in-between. There was another *śaktipāta*. There was another *śaktipāta* from above.

JONATHAN: So that's also possible?

SWAMIJI: That is also possible. Yes.

JOHN: Was that the reverse rise of *kuṇḍalinī?*

SWAMIJI: Huh?

JOHN: The reverse rise of *kuṇḍalinī,* he is talking about.

JONATHAN: I am talking about, I don't understand if that, if you spend all that time with that . . .

---

213 "And *prayatnāt*, you have to use effort in fullness. And that *yogi saṁśuddhakilviṣaḥ*, all his sins are over (sins of bad thoughts, sins of various thoughts–those are sins). *Aneka janma saṁsiddha*, although it will take him many lives of practice, but in the end he will merge in Lord Śiva, in the supreme Lord. So, there is no fear of his being ruined." Ibid.

214 Swamiji is referring to his own experience. [*Editor's note*]

215 Swamiji uses the term "courses" to refer to a period of intense spiritual revelation undergone by him in the summer of 1989. [*Editor's note*]

216 This question is with reference to an earlier lecture in which Swamiji mentions that, in his childhood, he also experienced the reverse rise of *kuṇḍalinī* known as *piśācāveśaḥ*. See *Kashmir Shaivism–The Secret Supreme* 17.123. [*Editor's note*]

SWAMIJI: I was smoothly going on with my practice. Then, abruptly, *śaktipāta* came and threw all of His force in me. It was *tīvra tīvra śaktipāta.*[217] Newly reborn, I was newborn! And then it happened, and I became so great.

It is too much. I should not say this.

DENISE: No, say.

JONATHAN: I asked, Swamiji . . . what I asked was, before that though, you told me some time ago, in that interview with Mother Alice, that you had that reverse rise of *kuṇḍalinī.*

SWAMIJI: Huh?

JONATHAN: You said once that you had that reverse rise of *kuṇḍalinī.*

SWAMIJI: Yes, reverse rise, and actual rise.

JONATHAN: And then you became even more one-pointed after that.

SWAMIJI: Yes. I have had so many . . . all experiences. I had all experiences in my childhood.

JONATHAN: Everything.

SWAMIJI: Everything.

JONATHAN: Good and bad.

SWAMIJI: Good and bad.

JOHN: Up, down. Up, down–both ways?

SWAMIJI: Yes.

JONATHAN: But isn't that very rare for someone that has that?

SWAMIJI: No, I had to experience all of the states, because I had to become Bhairava. So I had to experience all of the states–the good states and bad states of *yoga.*

JONATHAN: So you understand them totally.

JOHN: What were the bad states of *yoga*?

SWAMIJI: Reverse way of *kuṇḍalinī.*

JOHN: When did that happen to you?

SWAMIJI: It was in my youth, when I was in my thirties.

JOHN: Thirties?

SWAMIJI: Twenty-five.

JOHN: Twenty-five? Why did you have that?

---

217 *Tīvra tīvra śaktipāta* means "super-supreme grace." See footnote 33. See also *Kashmir Shaivism–The Secret Supreme* 10.66. [*Editor's note*]

SWAMIJI: Huh?
JOHN: What caused that to happen?
SWAMIJI: It happened.
Not only this reverse [*kuṇḍalinī*] but everything; everything happened. Reverse way, and that way, and real way, and *cidānanda* also, *jagadānanda* also–everything happened.[218]
JOHN: In your life.
SWAMIJI: Yes.
JOHN: That's how you know that these *cakras* are not petals–they are wheels.
SWAMIJI: And those *cakras* also, going up and going down also, those *cakras* also. You can't imagine the ways of *śaktipāta*.
JONATHAN: But *you* can!
SWAMIJI: *Yogasya prādhānyamāha*, now, in the 48th *śloka*, Lord Kṛṣṇa explains to [Arjuna] what is the greatness of *yoga*.

DVD 6.3 (46:32)

तपस्विभ्योऽधिको योगी ज्ञानिभ्योऽपि मतोऽधिकः ।
कर्मिभ्यश्चाधिको योगी तस्माद्योगी भवार्जुन ॥४८॥

tapasvibhyo'dhiko yogī jñānibhyo'pi mato'dhikaḥ /
karmibhyaścādhiko yogī tasmādyogī bhavārjuna //48//

Yoga is greater than doing penance for one *crore*[219] of years on one leg. If you do that penance, *yoga* is more than that (*tapasvibhyo'dhiko yogī*).

Jñānibhyo'pi mato'dhikaḥ, one who is a *jñāni*, one who is filled with knowledge, book knowledge, *śāstras*, that also is exceeded by *yoga*. *Yoga* is more than that.

Karmibhyaścādhiko yogī, and one who is doing actions everywhere (good actions), [compared to] that person also, *yoga* is . . .
DENISE: Superior.
SWAMIJI: . . . most superior.
So I give you boons! I offer you boons. You become a *yogi*, you

218 *Cidānanda* means "the bliss of consciousness"; *jagadānanda* means "universal bliss." See footnote 139 for an explanation of *jagadānanda*. See also *Kashmir Shaivism–The Secret Supreme* 16.113-114.
219 One *crore* equals ten million. [*Editor's note*]

become a *yogi*, you become a *yogi*! Lord Kṛṣṇa speaks to Arjuna, "you become a *yogi* by My will. You have to become a *yogi*. A *yogi* is first class. There is no [other person] parallel [to a] *yogi*."

DVD 6.3 (48:20)

योगिनामपि सर्वेषां मद्गतेनान्तरात्मना ।
श्रद्धावान्भजते यो मां स मे युक्ततमो मतः ॥४९॥

yogināmapi sarveṣāṁ madgatenāntarātmanā /
śraddhāvānbhajate yo māṁ sa me yuktatamo mataḥ //49//

Between all *yogis*, the one who is filled with attachment for the Parabhairava state and who has got *śraddhā* (faith) for that, I believe, it is My feeling of belief, that he is My own heart.

And you become that! I give you boon, I give you that . . .

DENISE: Blessing.

SWAMIJI: . . . that blessing.

अत्र संग्रहश्लोकः

atra saṁgraha ślokaḥ

This is the end, the end of the 6th chapter.

भगवन्नामसंप्राप्तिमात्रात्सर्वमवाप्यते ।
फलिताः शालयः सम्यगवृष्टिमात्रेऽवलोकिते ॥६॥

bhagavannāmasaṁprāptimātrātsarvamavāpyate /
phalitāḥ śālayaḥ samyagvṛṣṭimātre'valokite //6//

॥ Concluding *śloka* of 6th chapter ॥

When there is state of Parabhairava, when Parabhairava state comes in drama . . .

What is that called? In first appearance. In screen.

. . . when Parabhairava state comes first in screen, in drama, in the hall of drama, it appears, *phalitāḥ śālayaḥ* . . .

Who is he?

. . . *phalitāḥ śālayaḥ samyag vṛṣṭi mātre'valokite*, everything is complete. Only there is need of *vṛṣṭi mātre'valokite*, there is only need of one rainfall and *bas*, it will be ripened altogether. Rainfall means sunshine.[220]

220 "If there is attachment and love for God, everything is ripened, your *yoga* has ripened, it has come to its ripening point. . . . If attachment and faith and love for God is not there and the *yogic* powers are there, you must think it is not ripe. It is ripe only when there is attachment [for God]." *Bhagavad Gītā* (1978).

Chapter 7

DVD 7 (00:00)

मय्यासक्तमनाः पार्थ योगं युञ्जन्मदाश्रितः ।
असंशयं समग्रं मां यथा ज्ञास्यसि तच्छृणु ॥ १ ॥
ज्ञानं तेऽहं सविज्ञानमिदं वक्ष्याम्यशेषतः ।
यज्ज्ञात्वा न पुनः किंचिज्ज्ञातव्यमवाशिष्यते ॥ २ ॥

mayyāsaktamanāḥ pārtha yogaṁ yuñjanmadāśritaḥ /
asaṁśayaṁ samagraṁ māṁ yathā jñāsyasi tacchṛṇu //1//
jñānaṁ te'haṁ savijñānamidaṁ vakṣyāmyaśeṣataḥ /
yajjñātvā na punaḥ kiṁcijjñātavyamavaśiṣyate //2//

O Arjuna, *mayī āsakta manāḥ*, if you are attached to Me, to My Being, and you'll perform *yoga*, and leaving all responsibilities in Me–the success of *yoga,* its responsibility you will leave, you will surrender in Me, not in your effort–*asaṁśayaṁ*, there is no doubt, *samagraṁ māṁ jñāsyasi*, you will definitely know Me and understand Me completely without any gap–completely.

By which process will you know that?

That you will hear from Me.

DVD 7 (01:25)

ज्ञानं तेऽहं सविज्ञानमिदं वक्ष्याम्यशेषतः ।
यज्ज्ञात्वा न पुनः किंचिज्ज्ञातव्यमवाशिष्यते ॥ २ ॥

jñānaṁ te'haṁ savijñānamidaṁ vakṣyāmyaśeṣataḥ /
yajjñātvā na punaḥ kiṁcijjñātavyamavaśiṣyate //2//

I will relate to you [the meaning of] *jñāna* and *vijñāna*. *Jñāna* means knowledge, supreme knowledge; *vijñāna* means other knowledge, worldly knowledge. I will explain to you both of these [kinds of] knowledge. By knowing these two [kinds of] knowledge, nothing will remain unknown; everything will be known to you.

DVD 7 (02:13)

मनुष्याणां सहस्रेषु कश्चिद्यतति सिद्धये ।
यततामपि सिद्धानां कश्चिन्मां वेत्ति तत्त्वतः ॥३॥

manuṣyāṇāṁ sahasreṣu kaścidyatati siddhaye /
yatatāmapi siddhānāṁ kaścinmāṁ vetti tattvataḥ //3//

Amongst thousands of individuals, there are very rare persons who put effort for *siddhi*, for achieving the reality. But in those [persons] also, you will find thousands of such people who try and put effort for *siddhi*. And amongst those also, there are very few–a rare one or two people–who are *siddhas*, and who have put effort. And *kaścit māṁ vetti tattvataḥ,* those are very few who realize Me in the real way.

DVD 7 (03:56)

pūjakāḥ śataśaḥ santi bhaktāḥ santi sahasraśaḥ /
prasādapātramāśvastāḥ prabhordvitrā na pañcaṣāḥ [221]

There are worshippers who worship Me, *pūjakāḥ śataśaḥ*, and there are hundreds of such worshippers who worship Me wholeheartedly. *Bhaktāḥ santi sahasraśaḥ*, there are devotees, thousands of devotees, but actually those who are blessed by Me are one or two in thousands, not [even] three. *Bhaktāḥ santi, dhī trisanti*, they are two or three . . .

JONATHAN: One or two.
SWAMIJI: One or two.
DENISE: Not even three.
SWAMIJI: Not even three.

221 This quote from *Tantrāloka* 3.288 [comm.] appears as a footnote in Swamiji's original publication of the *Bhagavad Gītā*. [*Editor's note*]

DVD 7 (05:10)

भूमिरापोऽनलो वायुः खं मनो बुद्धिरेवा च ।
अहंकार इतीयं मे भिन्ना प्रकृतिरष्टधा ॥४॥
अपरेयमितस्त्वन्यां प्रकृतिं विद्धि मे पराम् ।
जीवभूतां महाबाहो ययेदं धार्यते जगत् ॥५॥

bhūmirāpo'nalo vāyuḥ khaṁ mano buddhireva ca /
ahaṁkāra itīyaṁ me bhinnā prakṛtiraṣṭadhā //4//
apareyamitastvanyāṁ prakṛtiṁ viddhi me parām /
jīvabhūtāṁ mahābāho yayedaṁ dhāryate jagat //5//

[*Bhūmiḥ* (earth)], *āpa* (water), *anala* (fire), *vāyu* (*vāyu* means wind), *khaṁ* means ether–these are the five elements. And there are some more [included] with that: that is mind (*mana*), *buddhi* (intellect), and *ahaṁkāra* (ego).

Five elements [plus] mind, intellect, and ego. How many are there?

There are eight; eightfold *prakṛti*. *Prakṛti* means My *śakti*. But *aparā iyam*, this is *aparā*, gross. This is gross *śakti*. And there is another one which is subtle *śakti*. *Itastvanyāṁ*, that is something else. That is *parā prakṛti* (supreme *prakṛti*, supreme energy), that is *svātantrya śakti*, by which *svātantrya śakti* this whole universe is standing, is fixed [upon]. That is *svātantrya śākti*.[222] That is *parā prakṛti*. *Parā prakṛti* takes hold of the whole universe, whatever is [existing] and whatever is not existing.

Aparā prakṛti is just for inferior scale; *aparā prakṛti*, that is eightfold.

What is eightfold?

DENISE: The five elements.

SWAMIJI: Five elements and . . .

JOHN: Mind, intellect, and ego.

SWAMIJI: . . . mind, intellect, and ego. This is called *aparā prakṛti*. And *parā prakṛti* is supreme, that is *svātantrya śakti*, by which this whole universe [is existing], and in which I am also existing. That *śakti* is My personal property. And this *aparā*

222 See footnote 77 for an explanation of *svātantrya śakti*.

śakti is the property of Anantabhaṭṭāraka.[223] He has to deal with that *śakti* according to the good *karmas* (actions) and bad *karmas* of individual beings. And by that he creates them, he protects them, and he destroys them. And My great *prakṛti*, which is *svātantrya śakti*, by that *svātantrya śakti,* I conceal them and reveal My nature to them.

Pidhāna (concealing) and *anugraha* (revealing), I do with that *svātantrya śakti*. And the rest [of the five acts]–creation, protection, and destruction–are done according to your own *karmas*, and the operator is Anantabhāṭṭaraka.

This *prakṛti* is *saṁsārāvasthāyāṁ sarvajanaparidṛśyamānā* [comm. verse 4-5], this *aparā prakṛti* is held and understood by everybody, i.e., this *aparā prakṛti*, inferior *prakṛti*.

Sā ca-ekaiva satī prakārāṣṭakena bhidyate, it is *prakṛti*, [although] it is only one *prakṛti*, but it is eightfold *prakṛti* (the five elements (*mahābhūtas*) and these three [*antaḥkaraṇas*]). This [*aparā*] *prakṛti* has created this universe and protected and destroyed it from time to time.[224]

Saiva jīvatvaṁ puruṣatvaṁ prāptā parā mamaiva nānyasya [*ca*]. And then the life of this [*aparā*] *prakṛti* is separate; and the life of [*aparā*] *prakṛti* is dwelling in My *parā prakṛti*.[225]

Which is that *parā prakṛti*?

DENISE: *Svātantrya śakti.*

SWAMIJI: *Svātantrya śakti.*

Sa-ubhayarūpā vedyavedakātmakaprapañcoparacana vicitrā. These are two *prakṛtis*: one is eightfold and the other one is the

223 "Anantabhaṭṭāraka is the personal assistant to Lord Siva, the *Rudra* of Lord Śiva. He is Śiva but he is called Anantabhaṭṭāraka. Anantabhaṭṭāraka functions only in inferior creation, i.e., in creation, protection and destruction. Revealing and concealing, Lord Śiva handles Himself." Swami Lakshmanjoo, *Tantrāloka* 9.144.

224 "So one *prakṛti* has created this universe, and universe is also one. *Ekaprakṛtyārabdhatvād*, created by one *prakṛti*, this universe is also one, they are not many. . . . This whole cosmos is one, consisting of one hundred and eighteen worlds." *Bhagavad Gītā* (1978).

225 "*Svātma vimala mukuratala kalita sakala bhāva bhūmiḥ*, all states are residing in the mirror of that consciousness of that [*parā*] *prakṛti*. *Svasvabhāvātmikā*, and this is the nature of Lord Śiva. *Satatamavyabhicāriṇī prakṛtiḥ*, and this nature is always one with that Lord Śiva." Ibid.

supreme *svātantrya śakti*.

Yayedaṁ dhāryate jagat, and this is conducted, the *jagat,* this whole universe is conducted by these two *prakṛtis*. This is how creation and . . . these fivefold acts of this universe takes place. The threefold acts [i.e., creation, protection, and destruction] by inferior *prakṛti* and the other twofold acts [i.e., concealing and revealing] by the supreme *prakṛti*.

DVD 7 (11:28)

एतद्योनीनि भूतानि सर्वाणीत्युपधारय ।
अहं कृत्स्नस्य जगतः प्रभवः प्रलयस्तथा ॥६॥

etadyonīni bhūtāni sarvāṇītyupadhāraya /
ahaṁ kṛtsnasya jagataḥ prabhavaḥ pralayastathā //6//

Sarvāṇī bhūtāni etat yonīni, all individuals are *etat yonīni*, they are resting in these two *prakṛtis*, twofold *prakṛtis*. But I am the *prakṛti* holder. So you should understand, O Arjuna, *ahaṁ kṛtsnasya jagataḥ prabhavaḥ pralayastathā,* I am the creator and destroyer of this whole universe and I am the father of this *prakṛti*, I am the real father.

Who?

Lord Śiva.

DENISE: Lord Śiva or Lord Kṛṣṇa?

JONATHAN: They are one and the same, aren't they?

SWAMIJI: Śiva and Kṛṣṇa are one, i.e., Parabhairava.

Evaṁ ca tvam eva upadhāraya–yadahaṁ vāsudevī bhūtaḥ sarvasya prabhavaḥ pralayaśca [comm.]. It is not meant that I tell you that I am the creator and destroyer of the whole universe; it does not mean that. It means that *you* should also behave with this kind of behavior within your own self. You should also say, "I am the creator and destroyer of this whole universe!" You should attribute it to yourself. You should not attribute it to God, that Lord Śiva is the creator and destroyer of this whole universe. No, [you should feel that], "I am, I am the creator and destroyer of [this universe]." You should attribute these aspects to yourself. This is [the reason] the *Bhagavad Gītā* was produced.

Do you understand?

JONATHAN: Yes.

SWAMIJI: You have to attribute it to yourself.

You should not think, "O Lord, O God, my Lord who art in heaven, hallowed be Thy name, Thy kingdom come, Thy will be done in heaven and earth the same. Into the temptation lead us not, deliver us from evil, for Thine is the kingdom, Thine the power, Thine the glory still . . . " This is not this! You have not to say . . .

DENISE: It is myself.

SWAMIJI: [Swamiji points to himself] You are that!

This is the cream of Shaivism.

DVD 7 (14:47)

मत्तः परतरं नान्यत्किंचिदस्ति धनंजय ।
मयि सर्वमिदं प्रोतं सूत्रे मणिगणा इव ॥७॥

mattaḥ parataraṁ nānyatkiṁcidasti dhanañjaya /
mayi sarvamidaṁ protaṁ sūtre maṇigaṇā iva //7//

Beyond Me there is nothing. Beyond Me, beyond Myself, there is nothing greater. I am greater than the greatest. No, I am greater than the greatest. Beyond Me there is no other great being. You should attribute it to yourself, O Arjuna, that, "I am the greatest."

Mayi sarvam idaṁ protaṁ, all is interwoven within Me, *sūtra maṇigaṇā iva*, just like these beads are interwoven in that string.

JOHN: *Mala*.

SWAMIJI: *Mala*.

Now I will explain it in its vividness, clearly. Clearly I will make you understand what I mean.

DVD 7 (16:19)

रसोऽहमप्सु कौन्तेय प्रकाशः शशिसूर्ययोः ।
प्रणवः सर्ववेदेषु शब्दः खे पौरुषं नृषु ॥८॥

पुण्यः पृथिव्यां गन्धोऽस्मि तेजश्चास्मि विभावसौ ।
जीवनं सर्वभूतेषु तपश्चास्मि तपस्विषु ॥९॥

raso'hamapsu kaunteya prakāśaḥ śaśisūryayoḥ /
praṇavaḥ sarvavedeṣu śabdaḥ khe pauruṣaṁ nṛṣu //8//
puṇyaḥ pṛthivyāṁ gandho'smi tejaścāsmi vibhāvasau /
jīvanaṁ sarvabhūteṣu tapaścāsmi tapasviṣu //9//

Raso'hamapsu kaunteya. Kaunteya, O Arjuna, *raso'hamapsu*, I am *rasa* in all watery substances, I am *rasa*. In water, varieties of water, I am that *rasa*. *Rasa*–what does that *rasa* mean?

JONATHAN: Taste.

SWAMIJI: No, *rasa*, *rasa*.

DENISE: Water, liquid.

SWAMIJI: *Rasa* means liquid.

Śaśisūryayoḥ, in moon and sun I am *prakāśa*, I am light. I am light in moon and sun. I am *rasa* in all liquids.

Praṇavaḥ sarvavedeṣu, I am *oṁkāra*, *oṁkāra* in all *Vedas*. I am *oṁkara* in all *Vedas*.

Oṁkāra. There is *vaidic praṇava*[226], *śāmbhava praṇava*, and *śakti praṇava*, i.e., *oṁkāra*, *hriṁkāra*, and *huṁkāra*. *Hriṁ-kāra* is *śakti praṇava*, *oṁ-kāra* is *praṇava* of *Vedas*, and *huṁ-kāra* is *praṇava* of Shaivism. These are threefold *praṇavās*, *sarvavedeṣu*, in all *śāstras*.

I am sound in ether (*śabdaḥ khe*). And I am *pauruṣam* (*pauruṣam* means strength) in *nṛṣu* (*nṛṣu* means who is *nara*, [the limited individual]).

JONATHAN: Who is what?

SWAMIJI: Who is a real man, who has got the manner of mankind. Who is not *"whuuupp,"* [i.e., fainthearted]. Who is not just . . .

JONATHAN: Lion.

DENISE: Real men, muscle-bound.

SWAMIJI: He who is with muscles, just *pauruṣam*. In that man I am *pauruṣam* (strength). He will [make a] fist and dash down ten men to the ground. They will fall down like this. So I am that *pauruṣam*. I am not that *pauruṣam* [who] has no

226 *Praṇava*, a mystical or sacred syllable. [*Editor's note*]

strength.

Apsu, I am *rasa* in all liquids.

Sarvatra āsvādyamāno yo anudbhinna madhurādi vibhāgaḥ sāmānyaḥ so'ham [comm. verse 8]. For instance, there is Coca Cola, that is *rasa*. There is Limca, there is Thumbs . . .

JONATHAN: Thumbs up.

SWAMIJI: . . . Thumbs up–there are so many–there is lime juice, there are so many *rasas*. But I am *sāmānyaḥ rasa* in all of these liquids.[227]

Evaṁ prakāśaḥ, I am *prakāśaḥ* in *sūrya* and *candrama* (moon and sun). *Prakāśa* means I am that *prakāśa* in moon and sun, which is only light. I don't mean heat or coolness. I am not coolness of moon; I am not heat of sun. I am *prakāśa* of sun, I am *prakāśa* of moon, I am light. I am light in all of this, [whether] it is heated or if it is not heated, i.e., if it is cold.

Śabda khe, in *ākāśa* (ether) I am *śabda* (sound).

> *ākāśe yaḥ śabda iti sarvasyaiva śabdasya nabhoguṇatvād-atrāvadhāraṇam yaḥ kevalaṁ gaganaguṇatayā dhvaniḥ saṁyogavibhāgādisāmagryantrarahito['vahitahṛdayair] brahmaguhāgahanagāmī yogigaṇaiḥ saṁvedyo'nahatākhyaḥ sakalaśrutigrāmānugāmī, tadbhagavatastattvam* [comm.]

That is *śabda*. In *ākāśa*, I am *śabda*. Which *śabda*? Which sound?

I am that sound, which is produced [without] two elements.

JONATHAN: That unstruck sound.

SWAMIJI: Unstruck sound. That is the sound which a *yogi* finds at the time of *samādhi*. That is internal sound. That is called *anāhata*.

JONATHAN: Is that always the same sound?

SWAMIJI: That is always the same sound. That is *anāhata*.

JONATHAN: And that sound is silence, isn't it?

SWAMIJI: Huh?

JONATHAN: That sound is in silence?

SWAMIJI: That is silent sound.

---

227 "Where there is not sweetness nor sourness, *anudbhinna,* where it is not revealed, that sweetness is not there, only taste. That is universal. That taste can be held, can be observed in sour and sweet also, in the same way, in one level." *Bhagavad Gītā* (1978).

JONATHAN: But it is sound in silence, yes?

JOHN: Is it the sound of *oṁ*?

SWAMIJI: No. *Oṁ* is also sound [but] it is more than *oṁ*. It is *anāhata*.

I will tell you which kind of sound this is. I will try my best to explain this sound. You close your ears and see. See this [sound] there, "*mmm.*" It is not by touch, it is not produced by touch. It is just sound with bliss. It is a blissful sound. And that blissful sound you will get in *samādhi*.

JONATHAN: Only in *samādhi*.

SWAMIJI: Only in *samādhi*, yes.

JONATHAN: No other time.

SWAMIJI: I am that sound. I am, in *ākāśa,* I am that sound. I am not this sound, i.e., tremendous sound, thunder sound, [or] this skating sound. No.

JOHN: Is this sound attached to *parā vāk*?

SWAMIJI: Yes, yes, *parā vāk*.[228]

---

228 The four levels of speech are *parā*, *paśyantī*, *madhyamā*, and *vaikarī*. "[*Parā vāk*] is that soundless sound which resides in your own universal consciousness. That is supreme sound. That has no sound . . . *parā vāk* is all-pervading." Swami Lakshmanjoo, *Kashmir Shaivism–The Secret Supreme*, original audio recording (1972).

"*Parā* means supreme *vāk*, supreme word, which is *aham* ('I'). And the *camatkāra*, the taste, the *rasa*, the joy of that is there, and that is *aham*." Swami Lakshmanjoo, *Parātriśikā Vivaraṇa* (1982-85).

"*Parā* is *svātantrya śakti*, one with *svātantrya śakti*." Ibid.

See footnote 77 for an explanation of *svātantrya śakti*.

"*Parā* is supreme word, supreme word is without differentiation. . . . *Paśyantī* is when you are only looking and there is no thought in your mind, that is *paśyantī*. *Madhyamā* is when you are looking, when you don't speak, but you speak with mind [i.e., think], that is *madhyamā*. *Vaikharī* is that word when you speak with words also, with lips also. So this is inferior state of sound. Inferior state of sound is *vaikharī*, superior to that is *madhyamā*, superior to that is *paśyantī* and supreme word is *parā*. Sometimes you are established in *parā* when you are in *samādhi*. Sometimes you are established in *paśyantī* when you are about to come out from *samādhi*. That is the state of *paśyantī*. When you are only thinking in your mind and not acting with your body, that is the state of *madhyamā*. When you are acting with limbs also, that is the state of *vaikharī*. And this four-fold state of word, sound, is expanded in this universe." Swami Lakshmanjoo, *Śivastotrāvalī,* 1.13.

And *pauruṣaṁ nṛṣu. Pauruṣaṁ–yena tejasā puruṣo'hamiti sārvabhaumaṁ pratipadyate–pauruṣaṁ* means *puruṣa kāra*, the strength in men. I am strength in men.

DVD 7 (24:49)

पुण्यः पृथिव्यां गन्धोऽस्मि तेजश्चास्मि विभावसौ ।

puṇyaḥ pṛthivyāṁ gandho'smi tejaścāsmi vibhāvasau /

It is 9th *śloka* now.

जीवनं सर्वभूतेषु तपश्चास्मि तपस्विषु ॥९॥

jīvanaṁ sarvabhūteṣu tapaścāsmi tapasviṣu //9//

In earth, I am that smell (*gandha*), which is very pure, a very pure smell. That very pure smell I have noticed it many times [and wondered], "what could it be?" I am, in earth, I am that smell, which is very pure. Otherwise all other smells are mixed and they are adulterated. When you get *mitti* (soil), dry *mitti*, red *mitti* from Ishber mountains, from that side, not black *mitti* . . .

JONATHAN: No, up on the top, past your old *ashram*.

SWAMIJI: . . . and when you pour water into it and do that . . .

DENISE: Mudding.[229]

SWAMIJI: . . . mudding, and smell it. That smell is pure. When you mud [the walls] then you should smell it. That smell is [pure]. [Lord Kṛṣṇa says], "I am that smell in *pṛthvī*."

JONATHAN: Is that the same as that smell after the rain? When it rains, when you're in the field you can smell that sweetness. Is that the same or is that different?

SWAMIJI: Yes, when rain falls, [but] not on filth.

JONATHAN: No, on the grounds, on . . .

SWAMIJI: On park, on mountains when rain falls, then it is that fresh [smell].

Tejaścāsmi vibhāvasau, I am *teja* (*teja* means shining), the shining element in those which are glittering things, e.g., the

229 In parts of India, instead of painting the walls, they clean and refresh a room by plastering the walls lightly with mud. [*Editor's note*]

sun, light, all these. That *teja* I am (*prakāśa*).

Jīvanaṁ sarvabhūteṣu, I am the life in all beings–life.

Tapaścāsmi tapasviṣu, in those who are adopting penance, I am penance in them. In the adopters of penance, I am penance in them. It means, in other words, in brief words, He says, "I am the essence of everything. Whatever is and whatever is not existing in this world, I am its essence. I am everything."

Now 10th *śloka*.

DVD 7 (28:23)

बीजं मां सर्वभूतानां विद्धि पार्थ सनातनम् ।
बुद्धिर्बुद्धिमतामस्मि तेजस्तेजस्विनामहम् ॥१०॥
बलं बलवतामस्मि कामरागविवर्जितम् ।
धर्माविरुद्धो भूतेषु कामोऽस्मि भरतर्षभ ॥११॥

bījaṁ māṁ sarvabhūtānāṁ viddhi pārtha sanātanam /
buddhirbuddhimatāmasmi tejastejasvināmaham //10//
balaṁ balavatāmasmi kāmarāgavivarjitam /
dharmāviruddho bhūteṣu kāmo'smi bharatarṣabha //11//

Bījaṁ māṁ sarvabhūtānāṁ viddhi pārtha sanātanam. O Arjuna, I am the seed of everybody, [of] each and every object. [I am] the ancient, ancient seed. Ancient . . .

JOHN: Origin.

SWAMIJI: . . . originator.

Buddhir buddhi matāmasmi, those who have got topmost intellect, in those persons I am intellect, i.e., [among] those who have got topmost intellect, intellectual beings. There are some intellectual scientists, in those scientists I am intellect (*buddhir buddhi matāmasmi*).

Tejastejasvināmaham, those who are brilliant and shining, in those whose body is brilliantly shining, I am that brilliance in them.

Balaṁ balavatāmasmi kāma rāga vivarjitam, those who have got power, I am power in them. In powerful men, I am power. But not in those powerful men who have got attachment to ladies; because as soon as they are attached to ladies, to sex, they lose power. They become slaves of ladies. *That* power I am not. They become slaves, they follow them. I am not that power. I am that power which is absolutely great!

Do you understand?

Balaṁ balavatāmasmi kāma rāga vivarjitam, neither with attachment nor sex, without that I am that *bala* (strength).

Dharmāviruddho bhṛteṣu kāmo'smi bharatarṣabha, O Arjuna, I am that *kāma*, that desire, which is not against *dharma*, against duty. That desire I am. To desire, to find out the reality of Parabhairava, I am that desire.

12th *śloka*.

DVD 7 (31:52)

ये चैव सात्त्विका भावा राजसास्तामसाश्च ये ।
मत्त एवेति तान्विद्धि नत्वहं तेषु ते मयि ॥१२॥
त्रिभिर्गुणमयैर्भावैरेभिः सर्वमिदं जगत् ।
मोहितं नाभिजानाति मामेभ्यः परमव्ययम् ॥१३॥

ye caiva sāttvikā bhāvā rājasāstāmasāśca ye /
matta eveti tānviddhi natvahaṁ teṣu te mayi //12//
tribhirguṇamayairbhāvairebhiḥ sarvamidaṁ jagat /
mohitaṁ nābhijānāti māmebhyaḥ paramavyayam //13//

These are two *ślokas* in one.

Ye caiva sāttvikā bhāvā, the states of *sattvaguṇa, rājasa* states of *rājaguṇa, tāmasa* (states of *tāmaguṇa*), all these threefold states, *matta eva iti tānviddhi*, they are produced by Me. *Natu aham teṣu*, I am not existing in them, they are produced by Me. They are produced from Me. *Sattvic bhāva, rājas bhāva*, [and *tāmas bhāva*], the waves, these three kinds of threefold waves, tides, are spread, are produced by Me, but I am not in them. It means I, [Lord Kṛṣṇa], have not come into the grip of these three *guṇas*. Three *guṇas* are produced by Me, but I am not caught in the three *guṇas*. I am not in them, *te mayi,* they are existing in Me. I am not in them, I am not in the three *guṇas*. *Natvahaṁ teṣu*, I am not existing in them. On the contrary, *te mayi*, they are existing in Me.

DVD 7 (33:55)

त्रिभिर्गुणमयैर्भावैरेभिः सर्वमिदं जगत् ।
मोहितं नाभिजानाति मामेभ्यः परमव्ययम् ॥१३॥

tribhirguṇamayairbhāvairebhiḥ sarvamidaṁ jagat /
mohitaṁ nābhijānāti māmebhyaḥ paramavyayam //13//

By these threefold *guṇas*, by which this whole universe is polluted, is being crushed . . .

Sattvaguṇa also crushes people, *rajaguṇa* also crushes people, and *tamaguṇa* also crushes people. *Sattvaguṇa* crushes people and keeps them away from *rajaguṇa* and *tamaguṇa*. *Rajaguṇa* crushes people and keeps them away from *sattvaguṇa* and *tamaguṇa*.

. . . in the same way, [people] are crushed. They don't become whole, [their] wholeness is lost, [their] completion and fullness [are lost]. Fullness is not found; fullness is deprived. If you have got *sattvaguṇa,* [then] *rajaguṇa* and *tamaguṇa* are lacking in you. It can't be that you will be [experiencing] *sattvaguṇa, rajaguṇa,* and *tamaguṇa* all together. You can't be, because the behavior of these three *guṇas* are separate.

In Me, these three behaviors [i.e., *guṇas*] are existing. So this fullness shines in Me. I am *sattvaguṇa*, *rajaguṇa*, and *tamaguṇa*, but I am not separatedly in . . .

DENISE: In its grasp.

SWAMIJI: . . . in its separate grasp.

JOHN: You are not any one individual.

SWAMIJI: I am not one individual.

Commentary [verse 12-13].

Sattvādīni manmayāni natvahaṁ tanmayaḥ. *Sattvaguṇa*, *rajaguṇa*, and *tamaguṇa* are in Me, but I am not in them. *Ata eva ca bhagavanmayaḥ sarvaṁ bhagavad bhāvena saṁvedayate.* In this way, you should feel that this whole universe is filled with the state of Bhairava and the state of Bhairava is shining in each and every being.[230]

230 "It is why the background of this saying that, "they reside in me, I don't reside in them" means that this whole universe is filled with

Anenaiva cāśayena vakṣyate. In the upcoming stanzas, He will say, "*vāsudevaḥ sarvam*," everything is *vāsudevaḥ*. *Vāsudevaḥ* [*sarvam*] means it is the glamour of Lord Kṛṣṇa everywhere!

Kathaṁ khalu sattvādimātrasthitā bhagavatastattvaṁ na viduḥ? Now this is a question: Why [is it that] those who are existing in *sattvaguṇa*, those who are existing in *rajaguṇa*, and those who are existing in *tamaguṇa*, why don't they achieve the reality of Bhagavān, Lord Bhairava?

DVD 7 (38:09)

दैवी ह्येषा गुणमयी मम माया दुरत्यया ।
मामेव ये प्रपद्यन्ते मायामतितरन्ति ते ॥ १४ ॥

daivī hyeṣā guṇamayī mama māyā duratyayā /
māmeva ye prapadyante māyāmatitaranti te //14//

This *guṇamayī*[231], *guṇamayī* is filled with *sattvaguṇa*, *rajaguṇa*, [and *tamaguṇa*]–the three gunas. It is *māyā*. And it is *duratyayā*, nobody has conquered this, nobody has won [over] this *māyā*. Now there is one trick, O Arjuna, I will tell you a trick of how you can subside *māyā*.

Māmeva ye prapadyante . . .

Other commentators have commentated upon this verse [in the following way]: "those who take refuge in Me, they succeed [in conquering] *māyā*." It is the commentary, which is done by other commentators [other] than Abhinavagupta.

---

universal God consciousness. You see, universal God consciousness is everywhere found, but universal God consciousness is not found in individual state because it is universal. Individually, [universal God consciousness] won't appear. . . . In varieties of universal objects [viz., the three *guṇas*], the state of Lord Śiva does not [appear]. It [appears] in the universal way, not in individual way. In variation it does not exist. It exists in totality. . . . [the saying], "Lord Śiva does not exist in universe," it means that Lord Śiva is not *only* in universe. He is beyond that also. But universe is only in its own cycle, in its own sphere. But in that . . . that cycle of the universe exists in Lord Śiva." *Bhagavad Gītā* (1978).

231 "This is My *māyā*, My energy of illusion. O Arjuna, My energy of illusion has produced these three *guṇas*." Ibid.

Abhinavagupta has [explained], *māmeva ye prapadyante*, those persons, those elevated souls who think, "*māmeva ye prapadyante*, *māyā* is me (*māmeva*), *māyā* is the reality of Brahman"–those who attribute *māyā* in their own nature [and feel], "I am *māyā*; *māyā* is Parabhairava"–then they are free from *māyā*. You should know that *māyā* is not other than Parabhairava, then you will succeed. Otherwise there is no hope of getting rid of *māyā*, because this is *guṇamayī daivī*.[232]

tena sattvādīnāṁ vastutaḥ saṁvinmātraparabrahmān-atiriktatāyāmapi yattadatiriktatāvagamanaṁ tadeva

guṇatvaṁ–bhoktṛtattvapāratantryaṁ bhogyatvam I tacca bhedātmakaṁ-rūpaṁ saṁsāribhiranirvācyatayā, tān prati māyārūpam

And they are caught by that *māyā* . . .

ato ye paramārtha brahma prakāśa vida . . . [comm. verse 14]

Those, on the contrary, who are situated in the supreme state of Parabhairava, *tad anatiriktaṁ viśvaṁ paśyanto,* they realize that this whole universe, which is created by the *māyā* of Lord Śiva, is not separate from the Parabhairava state. For them, there is no *māyā*. They have conquered *māyā*.

15th *śloka*.

232 "*Daivī* is divine. Divine means *devaḥ krīḍākaraḥ*, *devaḥ* means who is always playful, Lord Śiva is always playful. *Māyā* and not *māyā*, illusion and not illusion, consciousness and unconsciousness–this is all His play." Ibid.

DVD 7 (41:38)

न मां दुष्कृतिनो मूढाः प्रपद्यन्ते नराधमाः ।
माययापहृतज्ञाना आसुरं भावमाश्रिताः ॥ १५ ॥

na māṁ duṣkṛtino mūḍhāḥ prapadyante narādhamāḥ /
māyayāpahṛtajñānā āsuraṁ bhāvamāśritāḥ //15//

Those who are, on the contrary, *mūḍhāḥ* (*mūḍhāḥ* means duffers), *duṣkṛtina* (who are sinners), *narādhamāḥ* (who are degraded souls), those, *na māṁ prapadyante*, they don't take refuge in Me who is Parabhairava. *Māyayāpahṛta jñānā*, on the contrary, *māyā* has extracted all the wealth from them. My *māyā* has extracted all the wealth of knowledge from them. *Āsuraṁ bhāvamāśritāḥ,* they have become *āsuras* (demons).

Ye ca māṁ satyapyadhikāriṇī kāye nādriyante [comm. verse 15]. The commentary of Abhinavagupta [says], "those who do not respect Me in [their] body–because I am illuminated, I am shining in ones own body–those persons, those unfortunate persons who do not respect Me in [their] body, who has descended into this body . . ."

DENISE: Abhinavagupta is speaking.

SWAMIJI: Abhinavagupta's commentary.

No, it is Lord Kṛṣṇa, Lord Kṛṣṇa is speaking. Abhinavagupta is the commentator.

JOHN: Commentating on Lord Kṛṣṇa's sayings.

SWAMIJI: ". . . those who do not respect Me who has stepped into [their] body . . . "

"Respect" means they must feel the presence of Parabhairava in [their] body. Body is just a golden temple, in which golden temple Lord Bhairava is existing. You have to adore Him, you have to see Him through these doors and windows, i.e., through eyes, etc. You have to see from [your own senses]. Who? Bhairava! Bhairava is seeing everything. He is enjoying this.

JOHN: So you have to see Bhairava in your own body.

SWAMIJI: Yes. Yes.

JOHN: And also in other persons?

SWAMIJI: Huh?

JOHN: Also in other people also?

SWAMIJI: Other people also.

"... *ye ca māṁ satyapyadhikāriṇī kāye nādriyante*. Those people who do not respect Me in this *adhikāri* (body), I am ..."

What is called *avatāra*?

JOHN: *Avatāra* is incarnation.

SWAMIJI: "... I am incarnated in this body, I have got incarnation in this body, I have come in this body to illuminate this whole universe. And those people who do not respect Me in this way, *te duṣkṛtina*, they are sinners, *narādhamāḥ*, they are disgusted souls, *mūḍāḥ*, they are duffers, *āsura*, they are demons, *tāmasāḥ*, and they are filled with *tamaguṇa*. *Iti māyā-mahimaivāyam*, this is the trick of *māyā* that they are misled."[233]

JONATHAN: But that's also Lord Śiva's grace also, isn't it? That He remains hidden?

SWAMIJI: Yes.

DVD 7 (46:12)

चतुर्विधा भजन्ते मां जनाः सुकृतिनः सदा ।
आर्तो जिज्ञासुरर्थार्थी ज्ञानी च भरतर्षभ ॥१६॥
तेषां ज्ञानी नित्ययुक्त एकभक्तिर्विशिष्यते ।
प्रियो हि ज्ञानिनोऽत्यर्थमहं स च मम प्रियः ॥१७॥
उदाराः सर्व एवैते ज्ञानी त्वात्मैव मे मतः ।
आस्थितःस हि युक्तात्मा मामेवानुत्तमां गतिम् ॥१८॥
बहूनां जन्मनामन्ते ज्ञानवान्मां प्रपद्यते ।
वासुदेवः सर्वमिति स महात्मा सुदुर्लभः ॥१९॥

caturvidhā bhajante māṁ janāḥ sukṛtinaḥ sadā /
ārto jijñāsurarthārthī jñānī ca bharatarṣabha //16//
teṣāṁ jñānī nityayukta ekabhaktirviśiṣyate /
priyo hi jñānino'tyarthamahaṁ sa ca mama priyaḥ //17//
udārāḥ sarva evaite jñānī tvātmaiva me mataḥ /
āsthitaḥ sa hi yuktātmā māmevānuttamāṁ gatim //18//

233 "*Mahima* means greatness. This is splendor of *māya* that they are thrown and kicked down." *Bhagavad Gītā* (1978).

bahūnāṁ janmanāmante jñānavānmāṁ prapadyate /
vāsudevaḥ sarvamiti sa mahātmā sudurlabhaḥ //19//

19th *śloka* . . .

JOHN: There are four sections of people.

SWAMIJI: There are four sections of people who take refuge in Me. O Arjuṇa, there are four sections of people who take refuge in Me, who do not take refuge in King of Nepal, who do not take refuge in Jagmohan, who do not take [refuge] in V.P. Singh, and all of these.

Who take refuge in whom?

JOHN: In You.

SWAMIJI: In Me.

These are four sections. They are *sukṛtinaḥ*, they are fortunate. Because, they are always fortunate because they take refuge in Me, Parabhairava, who is supreme.

Ārto. Ārto means [the person] who has got pain, who has got leprosy disease, or who has got some incurable disease, or who has got cancer disease . . .

DENISE: Fatal disease.

SWAMIJI: Fatal disease.

. . . and they don't go to the doctors, they don't take refuge of doctors, they don't take refuge of foreigners for pacemaker treatment . . .

They take refuge in whom?

JONATHAN: God.

SWAMIJI: God.

. . . and they are fortunate because they take refuge in Me. *Ārto.*

Jijñāsu . . .

And this [*ārto*] is one class [of people] who are not well, who are suffering.

JONATHAN: So do they take refuge only because they are suffering?

SWAMIJI: Yes. But they take refuge of Lord.

JONATHAN: Not to go to doctors.

SWAMIJI: Not doctors.

JONATHAN: So that is different than a person who has had a bad life?

SWAMIJI: Huh?

JONATHAN: That is different than that class of person who has had a bad life and is sick all the time, and then as a last resort they turn to God . . . isn't it?

SWAMIJI: No, they are fortunate. They are fortunate because they take refuge in Parabhairava. They don't take refuge in those who are also sometimes caught by these same diseases themselves.

There are four sections.

Ārto . . . jijñasu means [those people] who want to get through their [exams] in school.

JOHN: They take refuge for some result, for some purpose.

SWAMIJI: Not result. For getting through their examination. [For] getting through their examination, they don't take refuge of the registrar, they don't take refuge of masters, they don't take refuge of professors, they take refuge of Lord Śiva. [They pray], "O Lord, save me so that I become successful in my examination."

JOHN: Only exams. I mean, other business things or only . . . ?

SWAMIJI: Only exams. Only exams.

JOHN: This is only talking about people in their schooling?

SWAMIJI: Yes.

But as long as they take support of God for this, to get through their examination, they are fortunate. Because they have gone to the right person for this treatment.

Ārto, jijñasur, arthārthī, and third is *arthārthī*, who wants to earn money, who wants to have much money. [They pray], "O Lord, give me much money so that I can make my life successful, O Lord." He does not go to professors, he does not go to big kings.

He goes to whom?

JONATHAN: To Lord.

DENISE: Lord Śiva.

SWAMIJI: Lord Śiva.

These are three sections [of people] who take refuge in Lord Śiva, and they are fortunate. And the fourth one is *jñānī*, the person who wants Lord Śiva. He asks Lord Śiva, "give me your seat Sir, give me a seat at Your feet, *bas*! I want only this much." He is also fortunate.

JONATHAN: Is he most fortunate?

SWAMIJI: But He has told, in first section He has told there are four fortunate persons who take My refuge, i.e., *ārto, jijñasu, arthārthī*, and *jñānī*.

And in those four, who is the best?

DVD 7 (53:06)

तेषां ज्ञानी नित्ययुक्त एकभक्तिर्विशिष्यते ।
प्रियो हि ज्ञानिनोऽत्यर्थमहं स च मम प्रियः ॥१७॥

teṣāṁ jñānī nityayukta ekabhaktirviśiṣyate /
priyo hi jñānino'tyarthamahaṁ sa ca mama priyaḥ //17//

Teśāṁ, in those four sections, *jñānī nityayukta*, *jñānī*, the fourth one is *nityayukta*, always with Me. *Eka bhaktir,* because he has only My love, he has created only My love. He wants Me, to love Me. He does not want anything [else], e.g., wealth or knowledge or anything. *Priyo hi jñānino atyartham*, I am *priyo hi jñānino,* I am loved too much by *jñāni*. I am intensely loved by *jñāni*. I am object [of his love]. He loves Me very much. Who?

JOHN: *Jñānī.*

SWAMIJI: *Jñānī. Sa ca mama priyaḥ*, I also love him very much (*sa ca mama priyaḥ*, I also love him). He loves Me very much; I also love him very much. We are both loving each other.

But you should not say that the [others] are not fortunate. The other three are also fortunate. For this, He puts another *śloka*.

DVD 7 (54:49)

उदाराः सर्व एवैते ज्ञानी त्वात्मैव मे मतः ।
आस्थितःस हि युक्तात्मा मामेवानुत्तमां गतिम् ॥१८॥

udārāḥ sarva evaite jñānī tvātmaiva me mataḥ /
āsthitaḥ sa hi yuktātmā māmevānuttamāṁ gatim //18//

Udārāḥ sarva evaite, they are all broad-minded; all four sections are broad-minded.

But what is the history of *jñāni*, the fourth one?

He is My own life. The [other sections] are broadminded. *Jñāni* is also broadminded, but in addition, he is My life. Who?

DENISE: *Jñāni.*

SWAMIJI: *Jñāni*. Because, *āsthitaḥ sa hi yuktātmā māmevān-*

uttamāṁ gatim, he is always present to Me, and he just wants the nearness of Parabhairava and nothing else. And [holding] this kind of position is not a joke, i.e., this kind of position, this fourth position [i.e., *jñāni*] of these fortunate people.

DVD 7 (56:09)

बहूनां जन्मनामन्ते ज्ञानवान्मां प्रपद्यते ।
वासुदेवः सर्वमिति स महात्मा सुदुर्लभः ॥१९॥

bahūnāṁ janmanāmante jñānavānmāṁ prapadyate /
vāsudevaḥ sarvamiti sa mahātmā sudurlabhaḥ //19//

After numberless *janmas* (lifetimes), that *jñānavān* (that *jñānavān* means [the *jñāni*] who is [of] that fourth section), *māṁ prapadyate*, after many, many lives, he actually gets full entry in Me. When that Parabhairava state penetrates him . . . time comes [when] Parabhairava state will penetrate his whole being and he will become Parabhairava.

JONATHAN: But he must have been somewhat risen to have that state in the first place, wasn't he? To have that pure love for Bhairava, selfless love? He must have had, he must have done these things before.

SWAMIJI: Because he is not deaf, Parabhairava is not deaf [that] He will ignore him. If He sees qualifications are growing in him, growing, day-by-day growing, He embraces him and they are united. He becomes Parabhairava. What can Parabhairava do to Parabhairava? He is one, one being.

Bahūnāṁ janma, it takes place after many births. *Jñānavān-māṁ prapadyate*, *vāsudevaḥ sarvamiti*, then he realizes the whole universe is filled with Parabhairava state. *Sa mahātmā*, he is a great soul. *Sudurlabhaḥ*, he is rarely existing in this world.

Now 20th *śloka*.

DVD 7 (58:37)

कामैस्तैस्तैर्हृतज्ञानाः प्रपद्यन्तेऽन्यदेवताः ।
तं तं नियममास्थाय प्रकृत्या नियताः स्वया ॥२०॥

kāmaistaistairhṛtajñānāḥ prapadyante'nyadevatāḥ /
taṁ taṁ niyamamāsthāya prakṛtyā niyatāḥ svayā //20//

Kāmaistaistairhṛtajñānāḥ, those who are, on the contrary, those who take refuge in other gods (e.g., Brahmā, Viṣṇu, Rudra, Īśvara, Sadāśiva), they take refuge in other lords, *taistair kāmaiḥ*, by those limited askings, [they receive] limited fruits. For limited fruits, if they would have asked Me, that is another thing. But for limited fruits, to achieve those limited fruits, they ask other [gods] than Me. Do you understand?

DENISE: Other gods.

SWAMIJI: Other gods.

So they are inferior, they are not asking properly, because those fruits, I bestow to them those fruits, but it is through other channels, through other gods. [Those fruits are] supplied through other gods. But it [actually] comes from Me. I am the giver, I am the bestower of that fruit, but it comes through another channel.

So they are inferior. They don't ask for that fruit directly from Me. This is the difference.

Between those who ask for anything, whatever it is (it may be in heaven or in this world also), in this world also, if they ask for fruits directly from Me, not [from] these officers and kings and queens and all these [other gods], this makes much difference.

I have to give them fruits. I am the bestower of fruits, but that glamour is lost to them. They are, in the end, sentenced to those gods, not to Me.

DVD 7 (1:02:03)

यो यो यां यां तनुं भक्तः श्रद्धयार्चितुमिच्छति ।
तस्य तस्याचलां श्रद्धां तामेव विदधाम्यहम् ॥२१॥

yo yo yāṁ yāṁ tanuṁ bhaktaḥ śraddhayārcitumicchati /
tasya tasyācalāṁ śraddhāṁ tāmeva vidadhāmyaham //21//

Whoever it is, *yāṁ yāṁ tanuṁ bhaktaḥ*, if somebody is a devotee of Gaṇeśa or somebody is a devotee of Indra, in this way, *śraddhayā*, with faith, he wants to adore [that god], *tasya tasyā-*

calāṁ śraddhāṁ tāmeva vidadhāmyaham, I give him and I maintain this faith in him.[234]

DVD 7 (1:02:58)

स तया श्रद्धया युक्तस्तस्याराधनमीहते ।
लभते च ततः कामान् मयैव विहितान्हितान् ॥२२॥

sa tayā śraddhayā yuktastasyārādhanamīhate /
labhate ca tataḥ kāmān mayaiva vihitānhitān //22//

Although he gets fruits from Me, but that fruit has an end because they don't ask for that fruit directly from Me.

The conclusion is:

अन्तवत्तु फलं तेषां तद्भवत्यल्पमेधसाम् ।
देवान्देवयजो यान्ति मद्भक्ता यान्ति मामपि ॥२३॥

antavattu phalaṁ teṣāṁ tadbhavatyalpamedhasām /
devāndevayajo yānti madbhaktā yānti māmapi //23//

Teṣāṁ antavattu phalaṁ. *Teṣāṁ*, they have got *phalaṁ* (fruit), *anta vant*, [but] it is ending, it ends, after sometime it ends; it has not that [eternal] glamour. So in the long run they are sentenced to go to those *devas*. On the contrary, those who directly approach Me, those who have got direct approach to Me, they come to Me in the end.

Ato matta eva kāmaphalamupādadate [comm. verse 23]. They actually achieve that fruit from Me but that fruit has an end because it is through another channel. They receive that fruit from another channel, e.g., from Gaṇeśa, from Viṣṇu, from Nārāyaṇa, and others.

Nijayeiva vāsanayā parimitīkṛtatvāt. Their *vāsana*, their impression is limited. They have limited it in their own way.[235]

---

234 "So I am above all these gods." *Bhagavad Gītā* (1978).

235 "Because their *vāsana*, the understanding of their intellect has become limited, has become limited by their own desires." Ibid.

On the contrary, *matprāptiparāstu māmeva*, but, on the contrary, those who directly approach Me, they come directly to Me, I embrace them in the end.

Now there is a question.

But after all, if Bhagavān is the doer, Bhagavān is the giver and the bestower of all fruits, why are [those fruits] inferior? If Bhagavān is there, [if] Bhagavān is the fruit giver of everybody, why do they go to those other gods and not to Bhagavān who is the fruit giver of everybody?

DVD 7 (1:06:12)

अव्यक्तं व्यक्तिमापन्नं मन्यन्ते मामबुद्धयः ।
परं भावमजानन्तो ममाव्ययमनुत्तमम् ॥२४॥

avyaktaṁ vyaktimāpannaṁ manyante māmabuddhayaḥ /
paraṁ bhāvamajānanto mamāvyayamanuttamam //24//
[not translated][236]

Because they are, *matsvarūpaṁ pāramārthikamavidyamān-avyaktikaṁ* [comm.], they don't see My direct presence there

236 "Those persons, they misunderstand Me. They say that God, Lord Śiva is always *avyakta* (unmanifested), is known to nobody. And *vyaktimāpannaṁ manyante māmabuddhayaḥ*, those persons who have limited knowledge, they think that, "Lord Kṛṣṇa is manifested, He has achieved body, He has achieved power, He has achieved body, He has achieved headache, He has achieved everything whatever is due to the achievement of body, all those things." *Paraṁ bhāvamajānanto*, they don't understand My supreme state of consciousness, God consciousness, which is *avyayam* (*avyayam* is unperishable and supreme). They don't find that in Me. They think that [Lord Kṛṣṇa] is ordinary person like us, and they walk and talk and play with Me. They don't realize My real nature of God consciousness. It is why they achieve those limited fruits from other gods. They think that Lord Indra is supreme, Lord Indra is above Lord Kṛṣṇa. Lord Agni is above Lord Kṛṣṇa, because he is not manifested, he is great, greater than that person who has taken birth. In [Kṛṣṇa's] period, they believed [in this way]. Afterwards, we believe that He was not like that. In His period, everybody believed that He was not God. His mother also believed that he was not God; [she thought], 'He was my son.'" Ibid.

while receiving fruits.

Apitu nijakāmanā samucita ākāra viśiṣṭa jñāna svabhāvaṁ vyaktim evāpannaṁ vidanti nānyathā.[237] They get that limited fruit from other *devatās*. *Ata eva na nāmni ākāre vā kaścidgrahaḥ*, there is no difference,[238] but *siddhānto'yamatra–yaḥ kāmanāpari-hāreṇa yat kiṁcid devatā rūpam ālambate tasya tat śuddha-mukta bhāvena paryavasyati–viparyāttu viparyayaḥ*, the difference is only this much: [the person] who approaches Me directly, he comes to Me in the end. [The person] who indirectly approaches [Me], he goes to that person, because he has accepted another god.[239]

DVD 7 (1:07:45)

नाहं प्रकाशः सर्वस्य योगमायासमावृतः ।
मूढोऽयं नाभिजानाति लोको मामजमव्ययम् ॥२५॥
वेदाहं समतीतानि वर्तमानानि चार्जुन ।
भविष्यन्ति च भूतानि मां तु वेद न कश्चन ॥२६॥

nāhaṁ prakāśaḥ sarvasya yogamāyāsamāvṛtaḥ /
mūḍho'yaṁ nābhijānāti loko māmajamavyayam //25//
vedāhaṁ samatītāni vartamānāni cārjuna /
bhaviṣyanti ca bhūtāni māṁ tu veda na kaścana //26//

I am everywhere visible but I have this *māyā*, *yogamāyā*, *svā-*

237 "They believe that He is born in this world, *nijakāmanāsamucita*, and according to the nature of their desires, they understand him like that and ask him to help them." Ibid.

238 "*Ati eva na nāmni ākāre vā kaścidgrahaḥ*. If [God] has taken form of anybody and are named as Kṛṣṇa, you must not go in the depth of these two things, i.e., name and form, because I am beyond name and form. My name is not Kṛṣṇa, I am Śiva! I have not this formation of this body, I am formless! But they consider Me with form and with name." Ibid.

239 "That person who does not desire for any achievement, any fulfillment of his desires, *yatkiṁcit devatārūpam ālambate,* if he worships any god other than Me, [still] he will come to Me. . . . So there is only your own misunderstanding that carries you away from My reality of God consciousness." Ibid.

tantrya śakti.[240] By that, I am hidden to many people. Because *yogamāyā* is accepted by those people who are limited. *Yogamāyā* means those who have got indirect approach [to Me]. *Mūḍho'yam nābhijānāti*, those duffers do not understand what they are doing.

वेदाहं समतीतानि वर्तमानानि चार्जुन ।
भविष्यन्ति च भूतानि मां तु वेद न कश्चन ॥२६॥

240 "*Svātantrya śakti* is transformed in the form of *māyā śakti*. And *māyā śakti* is transformed in the formation of *svātantrya śakti* in the correct way of knowing. In the incorrect way of knowledge, it is transformed in the *svarūpa* of *māyā śakti*." Swami Lakshmanjoo, *Śiva Sūtra Vimarśinī*, 1.4, original audio recording (1975). See footnote 77 for an explanation of *svātantrya śakti*.

"*Puṁsaḥ prati ca sā bhogyaṁ sūte'nādīn pṛthagvidhān*. This *māyā* creates dish for this limited soul who is beginningless. She creates dish of pain, dish of pleasure, dish of illusion (ignorance). So these three dishes are created by *māyā* for this individual being." Swami Lakshmanjoo, *Tantrāloka* 13.6 (1980).

"Anantabhaṭṭāraka creates that impure class of elements, right from *māyā* to *pṛthvī* (earth). *Īśvarecchāvaśa*, by the will of Lord Śiva he creates. What is the purpose of creating this nasty universe, which has no meaning in the end? In the end, it is always painful, sad, torture, gout, diseases–filled in that. *Īśvarecchāvaśa kṣubdha bhoga lolika cidgaṇān saṁvibhaktum*. This is the will of God that, *kṣubdha bhoga lolika cidgaṇān*: *cidgaṇān*, those living beings who are *bhoga lolika,* who are fond of enjoying the worldly pleasures, who are fond of enjoying the worldly pleasures, [it is created] for them, to establish them in their own way, in the cycle of this world of repeated deaths and births, just to make them seated in their own way, in their own manner. For the person who is mad, this Anantabhaṭṭāraka puts them in this mad cycle. Each and every place, he fixes them according to their last desire." Ibid., 9.61 (1977).

"What is the purpose of my creating this whole universe? The purpose of my creating this whole universe is just to baste them with God consciousness in the end. I am creating this universe just to uplift them, just to elevate them. It is why I create. Otherwise there was no fun to create this universe." *Bhagavad Gītā* (1978).

vedāhaṁ samatītāni vartamānāni cārjuna /
bhaviṣyanti ca bhūtāni māṁ tu veda na kaścana //26//

I know what happened to people in the past, what happens to them in the present, and what will happen to them in the future. But nobody understands Me, who is omnipresent in all times (past, present, and future).

Sarveṣāṁ nāhaṁ gocaratām prāpnomi[241] [comm.]. In two words, [Abhinavagupta has given the] meaning [of this verse]: "I am not available to everybody."[242] This is the secret.

JOHN: He is not available to everyone?

SWAMIJI: He is not available to everybody in such a way; in such a way, He is not available to everybody. He is only available to those who have got direct approach to Him.

But there is another question of Arjuna.

If it is so, then in the end, [when] there is *mahāpralaya*, when all become liberated, why not then [do] they go directly to Parabhairava state at that time?

This is the question.

When there is *mahāpralaya* (*mahāpralaya* means when everything is finished), then automatically everybody will enter in the Parabhairava state.

At that moment, they are not to be blamed, they will also achieve the same state as others [i.e., *yogīs*] have achieved earlier.[243]

[Lord Kṛṣṇa] says, "no, it is not, it is not that way."

DVD 7 (1:11:10)

इच्छाद्वेषसमुत्थेन द्वन्द्वमोहेन भारत ।
सर्वभूतानि संमोहं सर्गे यान्ति परन्तप ॥२७॥

icchādveṣasamutthena dvandvamohena bhārata /
sarvabhūtāni saṁohaṁ sarge yānti parantapa //27//

---

241 Swamiji says *prāpnoti* in place of *prāpnomi*. [*Editor's note*]

242 On an earlier occasion, Swamiji translated this commentary as: "I am not *understood* by everybody." *Bhagavad Gītā* (1978).

243 "Why to worry now?" Ibid.

O Arjuna, it is not [the case] that at the time of *mahāpralaya* everybody becomes *mukta*, *jīvan mukta*–it is not that. All those who are not fit to become *jīvan mukta*, they remain in *prakṛti*, under *prakṛti*, under chloroform, in subtle bodies. In subtle bodies they are stored [at the time of] *mahāpralaya*. When this gap of *mahāpralaya* is over, then they are again created in *māyā*. So *mahāpralaya* won't make them any difference. In *mahāpralaya* state, they will remain in seed form, in larva state, in *suṣupti* (deep sleep).[244]

On the contrary . . .

DVD 7 (1:12:34)

येषां त्वन्तं गतं पापं जनानां पुण्यकर्मणाम् ।
ते द्वन्द्वमोहनिर्मुक्ता भजन्ते मां दृढव्रताः ॥२८॥
जरामरणमोक्षाय मामाश्रित्य यतन्ति ये ।
ते ब्रह्म तद्विदुः कृत्स्नमध्यात्मं कर्म चाखिलम् ॥२९॥

yeṣāṁ tvantaṁ gataṁ pāpaṁ janānāṁ puṇyakarmaṇām /
te dvandvamohanirmuktā bhajante māṁ dṛḍhavratāḥ//28//

jarāmaraṇamokṣāya māmāśritya yatanti ye /
te brahma tadviduḥ kṛtsnamadhyātmaṁ karma cākhilam //29

28th and 29th *śloka*.

Yeṣāṁ tvantaṁ gataṁ pāpaṁ janānāṁ puṇyakarmaṇām. Yeṣām puṇya karmaṇām, those who are fortunate, those who

244 "*Icchādveṣa samutthena dvandva mohena.* When there is desire and there is hatred, there is desire and there is negation of desire, when you love and when you hate in this world, when you conduct these things in this world, *dvanda mohena,* this is the illusion of *dvanda*, this is the illusion of two opposites. And [if] these two opposites are living in your mind . . . all these beings, all these souls, *saṁohaṁ sarge yānti,* are kept in great unconscious state at the time of *mahāpralaya*. They don't get liberation. They are kept in chloroform state, dead state. When *mahā-pralaya* is over, they are kicked out again in this mortality. . . . When there is only love . . . you are liberated. You are liberated from that very period." Ibid.

have always done good actions, good deeds, *antaṁ gataṁ pāpaṁ yeṣāṁ*, all sinful acts take their end to them. And the fruit of that is *te dvandva mohanirmuktā*, they come out from *samsāra*, which is always painful. *Bhajante māṁ dṛḍha vratāḥ*, they all divert their attention towards My *bhakti*, My devotion, and My meditation.

And *jarā maraṇa mokṣāya*, to escape from old age (*jarā*), to escape from death (*maraṇa*), *māmāśritya yatanti ye*, those who take refuge in Me and go on meditating upon My being, *te brahma tat viduḥ kṛtsnam adhyātmaṁ karma cākhilam*, they become, in the end, one with *brahma,* and they know what is *adhyātma* and what is *karma*, which will be explained in the 8th chapter.[245]

Ye tu vinaṣṭatāmasāḥ–the commentary–[the person] whose *tamaguṇa* and *rajaguṇa* is finished, *puṇyāpuṇyaparikṣaya-kṣemīkṛtātmānaḥ*, whose good *karmas* and bad *karmas* have ended, *vipāṭitamahāmohavitānāḥ*, whose ignorance and negligence of Parabhairava is no more existing, and *sarvameva bhagavadraśmikhacitaṁ jarā maraṇa mayatamisra srutaṁ brahma vidanti*, they, *bhagavad raśmi*, everything seems to them, *bhagavad raśmi khacitaṁ*, that everything is filled with the rays of Parabhairava, *jarā maraṇa mayatamisrasrutaṁ*, where they escape from the clutches of old age and death. And in the end, *brahma,* they achieve Parabhairava very peacefully and successfully.

Now 30th *śloka*. This is the ending *śloka*.

DVD 7 (1:16:30)

साधिभूताधिदैवं मां साधियज्ञं च ये विदुः ।
प्रयाणकालेऽपि च मां ते विदुर्युक्तचेतसः ॥३०॥

sādhibhūtādhidaivaṁ māṁ sādhiyajñaṁ ca ye viduḥ /
prayāṇakāle'pi ca māṁ te viduryuktacetasaḥ //30//

---

245 "*Adhyātmaṁ* is that element, which is residing in your heart. And *brahma,* who is handling this whole universe, it is *brahma*. They understand these three elements: *brahma, adhyātmaṁ*, and *karma. Karma* means actions." Ibid.

Those people who understand what is *sādhibhūta*,[246] those people who understand what is *sādhiyajñaṁ*,[247] these people, at the time of death, they get entry and are united in Me in the end.[248]

But he says here, *prayāṇakāle*, at the time of death, they get entry in Me. Abhinavagupta commentates upon [this that] at the time of death, you should not know that, "at the time of death, they get entry in Me." It is only when they practice this in their lifetime, then at the time of death also they will do the same thing.[249]

Kim janmāsevanayā [comm. verse 30], those people who say to people, "what is the use of thinking of Lord Śiva from your birth to death? Why should you not think of Him [only] at the time of death? At the death time we will think of Him and get *mokṣa.*" If those people who say this, what shall I tell them?

Teṣāṁ tūṣṇīṁ bhāva eva śobhana, to them, I have no words to tell them [except], "what are you barking?"

Iti śivam.

---

246 "*Adhibhūtaṁ kṣaro bhāvaḥ*, all objects which are decaying, that is called *ādhibhūtaṁ*. . . . *kṣarati sravati pariṇāmādi dharmeṇa* [comm. vs. 4], he is born, he is young, he is in childhood, he is decayed, he is old, he is nearing his death, and he has died. That is *kṣaro bhāvaḥ*, that is *ādhibhūta*. That is [the condition of the] objective world and subjective world, both." Ibid.

247 "And *ādhiyajña* is actually, in real way, I am *ādhiyajña*, found everywhere. I am residing in each and every being and who is called *ādhiyajña*; *ādhiyajña* is Myself." Ibid.

248 "[*Ādhyātmika*], *ādhibhūta*, *ādhidaiva*, and *ādhiyajña*, these names are attributed to Lord Śiva . . . He will define [these] in the [8th] chapter." Ibid.

249 "Because he has been adopting one-pointedness of God in his lifetime. If he is meditating, if he has been meditating during his lifetime continuously, then, in the end, when he leaves his body, when his consciousness has gone beyond his control, at the time when he is in coma state, he'll be meditating inside; internally he'll be meditating. If he meditates during his life period, he will meditate in that coma state also, at the time when he is going to leave this body. At that time also he will be thinking of God, internally. *Prayāṇakāle*, at the time of death, *nityaṁ bhagavad bhāvita antaḥ karaṇatvāt,* because he has *bhāvita antaḥ karaṇa,* his mind is focused in his lifetime towards God only, so, at the time of death also, his mind will be focused to Him." Ibid.

Now conclusion of this chapter.

DVD 7 (1:18:43)

स्फुटं भगवतो भक्तिराहिता कल्पमञ्जरी ।
साधकेच्छासमुचितां येनाशां परिपूरयेत् ॥७॥

sphuṭaṁ bhagavato bhaktirāhitā kalpamañjarī /
sādhakecchāsamucitāṁ yenāśāṁ paripūrayet //7//

॥ Concluding *śloka* of 7th chapter ॥

The *bhakti*, the devotion of Parabhairava, if you have possessed that devotion of Parabhairava, you understand that you have got *kalpalata*. *Kalpalata* is that *lata*, that creeper in heaven; whatever you ask, it gives, it bestows to you. It is called *pāri-jāta-mañjarī*. In heaven, in a particular heaven, there is *pāri-jāta-mañjarī* [to which] you go and ask [for whatever] you need and it will be bestowed to you. Whatever you think–if you need money, it will come, if you need anything, it will come. And if you need God consciousness, it will come. It is *kalpa mañjarī*. And in the same way, the real *kalpa mañjarī* is devotion towards Bhairava. This is the real, real *kalpa mañjarī*. It will give you the success of entering in Parabhairava state in the end.

Sādhakecchāsamucitāṁ yenāśāṁ paripūrayet, and all [worldly] desires are shunned and [*sādhakas*] are successfully taken inside the state of Parabhairava in the end.

iti śrīmahāmāheśvarācāryavaryarājānakābhinavaguptapāda-viracite śrīmadbhagavadgītārthasaṃgrahe saptamo'dhyāyaḥ

7th chapter is finished.

Chapter 8

SWAMIJI: Now it is the 8th discourse.

अर्जुन उवाच

arjuna uvāca

Arjuna asks, in his own way, [these questions] to Lord Kṛṣṇa.

DVD 8 (00:31)

किं तद्ब्रह्म किमध्यात्मं किं कर्म पुरुषोत्तम ।
अधिभूतं च किं प्रोक्तमधिदैवं किमुच्यते ॥ १ ॥
अधियज्ञः कथं कोऽत्र देहेऽस्मिन्मधुसूदन ।
प्रयाणकाले च कथं ज्ञेयोऽसि नियतात्मभिः ॥ २ ॥

kiṁ tadbrahma kimadhyātmaṁ kiṁ karma puruṣottama /
adhibhūtaṁ ca kiṁ proktamadhidaivaṁ kimucyate //1//

adhiyajñaḥ kathaṁ ko'tra dehe'sminmadhusūdana /
prayāṇakāle ca kathaṁ jñeyo'si niyatātmabhiḥ //2//

He puts these questions:
Kiṁ tat brahma, what is that *brahma*? This is first.
Kim adhyātmaṁ, what is the meaning of *adhyātma*?
Kim karma, what is the meaning of action?
Adhibhūtaṁ ca kiṁ proktam, what is *adhibhūta*? This is the fourth.

You should put these numbers. *Brahma* is first. *Adhyātmam* is second question. *Karma*, what is *karma*, that is third. *Adhibhūtaṁ ca kiṁ proktam*. *Adhibhūta*, what is *adhibhūta*, that is fourth. *Adhidaivaṁ kimucyate*. What is *adhidaiva*, that is fifth. *Adhiyajñaḥ kathaṁ*, [what is] *adhiyajñaḥ* is sixth.

Ko'tra dehe, who is inside the body, who has taken a seat inside the body? This is the seventh question.

Asmin ka tiṣṭhati, and who is [also] residing in the body in a supreme way? This is eighth.

And at the time of death, how are You understood by *yogīs*?

So these are nine ways of [questions].

Brahma (first), *adhyātmaṁ* (second), *karma* (third), *adhibhūta* (fourth), *adhidaiva* (fifth), *adhiyajña* (sixth), and who is in this body (seventh), and who is existing in this body in a supreme way (eighth), and how *yogīs* remember You at the time of death (ninth).

So these are nine questions.

श्रीभगवानुवाच

śrī bhagavān uvāca

Now Śrī Bhagavān gives the answers.

DVD 8 (03:37)

अक्षरं ब्रह्म परमं स्वभावोऽध्यात्ममुच्यते ।
भूतभावोद्भवकरो विसर्गः कर्मसंज्ञितः ॥३॥
अधिभूतं क्षरो भावः पुरुषश्चाधिदैवतम् ।
अधियज्ञोऽहमेवात्र देहे देहभृतां वर ॥४॥

akṣaraṁ brahma paramaṁ svabhāvo'dhyātmamucyate /
bhūtabhāvodbhavakaro visargaḥ karmasaṁjñitaḥ //3//
adhibhūtaṁ kṣaro bhāvaḥ puruṣaścādhidaivatam /
adhiyajño'hamevātra dehe dehabhṛtāṁ vara //4//

These are two *śloka*s in one.

Now the commentary of Abhinavagupta [comm. verse 3].

Akṣaraṁ. *Akṣaraṁ* means *bṛhatvāt bṛhakatvāt brahma*, supreme *brahma* [Parabhairava], who is Himself big and who makes others also big, broad. This is *brahma*: *akṣaraṁ brahma paramam, akṣaraṁ . . .*[250]

And His nature is *ādhyātma*–this is the answer to the second question–His nature is *ādhyātma*. *Svabhāva* means His nature is *ādhyātma*.

What is *ādhyātma*?

Yataḥ, that is *svabhāva*, His nature. *Svaḥ anivṛttadharmā caitanyākhyo bhāvaḥ*, consciousness is His own nature. That is His nature.[251]

> *tasya ca caitanyasvabhāvasyabrahmaṇo'paricchinnabāhya-lakṣaṇatayā kroḍīkṛtaviśvaśakteraiśvarya-lakṣaṇātsvātantryāt bahir-bhāvāvabhāsanātmā bahirbhūtabhāvantarāvabhāsanātmā ca yo visargaḥ krameṇa bhūtānāṁ–brahmādipramātṛṇāṁ bhāvānāṁ– jaḍānāṁ udbhavakārī–jaḍājaḍavaicitryanirbhāsakaḥ* ।

Bhūtabhāva udbhavakārī, that *visargaḥ* (*visargaḥ* means that flow, flow of His external flow), in that external flow, He is *bhūta udbhavakārī* (*bhūta* means individuals).[252] "Individuals" does not mean only individuals who are like us. *Brahmādi pramātṛṇāṁ*,

---

250 "*Akṣaraṁ brahma paramaṁ*. *Brahma* is that element which does not get destroyed, which is eternal. . . . *Bṛhatvādbriṁhakatvācca* [*paraṁ*] *brahma* [comm.], who is great and who makes everything great. *Bṛhat* [means] makes Himself great; *Bṛṁhaka* means making others great. These two qualifications are attributed to *brahma*." *Bhagavad Gītā* (1978).

251 "*Adhyātma* means that element which resides in each and every soul, that is *adhyātma*, and that is *brahma*. . . . *Svabhāva* is *adhyātma*. *Sva* means pertaining to one's own self, which is *anivṛtta dharma*, which aspect is not disconnected at all, in no case. . . . And that is *caitanyākhyo bhāvaḥ*, because it is connected with consciousness, one's own consciousness. . . . And that *caitanya* who is *brahma*, who is all-consciousness, *aparicchinna bāhya lakṣaṇatayā kroḍī kṛta viśva śakter*, that *brahma* has *kroḍī kṛta viśva śakter*, He has kept in His womb, in its Self, all energies, universal energies. So this is *svātantrya*, which is *aiśvarya*, filled with glory; glorious energy of complete independence." Ibid.

252 "*Bahir*, one flow creates the outside universe, and another flow creates the nature inside, nature residing inside, e.g., moods and various things, which are perceived by your own self. Because everybody knows that. So this two-fold creation is created by that *brahma*." Ibid.

right from Brahma to all individuals. And *bhāvānāṁ* (*bhāvānāṁ* means the objective world) is also in the same category [of "individuals"]. *Jaḍājaḍavaicitrya nirbhāsakaḥ*, so He is, in one way, creator of all [inanimate] and . . . what?

JOHN: Animate and inanimate objects.

SWAMIJI: Yes, *jaḍa* (inanimate) and *ajaḍa* (animate)–all.[253]

And it has got another meaning, internal meaning. *Bhūtabhāva udbhavakārī*. *Bhūtabhāva* means real *bhāva*. The real *bhāva* is the state of Parabhairava which is found, is existing, in the background of all of these objective worlds and subjective worlds, everywhere. He can create that *udbhava* at any moment, whenever He likes, in these *jaḍa* and *ajaḍa pramātṛbhāvas*.[254] That is His *karma*; that is His activity.

DVD 8 (07:59)

अधिभूतं क्षरो भावः पुरुषश्चाधिदैवतम् ।
अधियज्ञोऽहमेवात्र देहे देहभृतां वर ॥४॥

adhibhūtaṁ kṣaro bhāvaḥ puruṣaścādhidaivatam /
adhiyajño'hamevātra dehe dehabhṛtāṁ vara //4//

Adhibhūtaṁ kṣaro bhāvaḥ, all objects which are decaying

---

253 "And what is *karma*? Third question was, what is action? What is *bhūta bhāva udbhavakaro visargaḥ karma saṁjñitaḥ*? *Bhūta bhāva udbhavakaro visargaḥ*. That creative force (*visargaḥ*), which makes various bodies in various developments–for instance, your mood is something else, his mood is something else, and her mood is something else–in the same way, moods are created variously, faces are created variously, natures are created variously–that is [His] *karma*. Moods are created by that Brahma, and [those] moods are created by *visarga*. *Visarga* is creative energy. Creative energy which is *bhūtā bhāva udbhavakaraḥ*, which gives rise to *bhūta bhāva*. *Bhāva* means nature, moods, tendencies of people. My tendency is to find out God. Your tendency is to find out God . . . yes? Somebody's tendency is to find out a wife. In the same way, these tendencies vary. And the creator of that tendency is that creative germ of that Brahma. That is *karma* (activity)." Ibid.

254 "*Udbhava karoti* means He gives rise to God consciousness also. That is Brahma. He gives rise to God consciousness." Ibid.

(that is called *adhibhūta*), *puruṣaśca adhidaivatam*, that *puruṣa* is *adhidaivata*, he witnesses everything.

And *adhiyajña* is actually, in the real way, "I am *adhiyajña*, [I am] found everywhere. I am residing in each and every being and [I am] called *adhiyajña*; *adhiyajña* is Myself."

Kṣara means that which is perishable. *Kṣarati sravati pariṇāmādi dharmeṇa* [comm. verse 4], he is born, he is young, he is in childhood, he is decayed, he is old, he is nearing death, and he has died. That is *kṣaro bhāvaḥ*, that is *adhibhūta*. That [pertains to] the objective world and subjective world–both. And *puruṣa adhidaivata*, the *puruṣa* who does not die inside this [perishable body], who plays this drama, is *adhidaivat*; *adhidaivat* means He is witnessing this.

Because, *tatra sarvadevatānāṁ pariniṣṭhitatvāt* [comm. verse 4], all *indriyas*, all gods and goddesses, are situated in that being of His nature (*tatra sarvadevatānāṁ pariniṣṭhitatvāt*).

Ata evāśeṣayajñabhoktṛtvena yajñān–avaśyakāryāṇi karmāṇi adhikṛtya yaḥ sthitaḥ puruṣottamaḥ, so'hameva. And inside, who is *puruṣottamaḥ*, supreme *puruṣa*, side by side He is existing, and He should be considered to be Myself. I am that *puruṣa* who is always witnessing everything that is being done.

Aham eva ca dehe sthitaḥ, in each and every body, I am also existing; side by side, I am also existing and witnessing everything that is being done.

Now there is the ninth question.

How *yogīs* remember You at the time of death?

DVD 8 (11:09)

अन्तकालेऽपि मामेव स्मरन्मुक्त्वा कलेवरम् ।
यः प्रयाति स मद्भावं याति नास्त्यत्र संशयः ॥५॥
यं यं वापि स्मरन्भावं त्यजत्यन्ते कलेवरम् ।
तं तमेवैति कौन्तेय सदा तद्भावभावितः ॥६॥
तस्मात्सर्वेषु कालेषु मामनुस्मर युध्य च ।
मदर्पितमनोबुद्धिर्मामेवैष्यस्यसंशयम् ॥७॥

antakāle'pi māmeva smaranmuktvākalevaram /
yaḥ prayāti sa madbhāvaṁ yāti nāstyatra saṁśayaḥ //5//
yaṁ yaṁ vāpi smaranbhāvaṁ tyajatyante kalevaram /
taṁ tamevaiti kaunteya sadā tadbhāvabhāvitaḥ //6//
tasmātsarveṣu kāleṣu māmanusmara yudhya ca /
madarpitamanobuddhirmāmevaiṣyasyasaṁśayam //7//

Three *ślokas* in one push.

At the time of death, *antakāle'pi*, *māmeva smaran*, the one who remembers Me at the time of death, *muktvākalevaram*, and he leaves this body and dies, *yaḥ prayāti sa madbhāvaṁ yāti*, he is united in Me, *nāstyatra saṁśayaḥ*, there is no doubt about it. But you should not think that at the time of death he thinks [of Me] and so he is united in My being.

यं यं वापि स्मरन्भावं त्यजत्यन्ते कलेवरम् ।
तं तमेवैति कौन्तेय सदा तद्भावभावितः ॥ ६ ॥

yaṁ yaṁ vāpi smaranbhāvaṁ tyajatyante kalevaram /
taṁ tamevaiti kaunteya sadā tadbhāvabhāvitaḥ //6//

Kalevaram tyajati, when, at the time of leaving his body, whatever first thought comes in his mind and he possesses that thought and goes there.[255] Because he has practiced that thought in his lifetime, for his whole period of life. It is not that at the end . . . at the end only does not matter. At the end, he thinks of that thing, which he has practiced for his whole life, day and night. Then he [automatically] thinks of that at the end of [his life]. But actually, the point of death is not when . . .

When a man who is about to die calls his kith and kin at that time to his deathbed, and says you should . . . and tells them (i.e., his sons, his grandsons, his father, his wife), he gives them consolation that, "you should do this thing, you should not . . . you should remain quite happy." This is not the ending point of

255 "That state which is being remembered, anything, whatever you remember at the time of death, you go to that, you experience that, and you are united with that object [of remembrance]." *Bhagavad Gītā* (1978).

death. This is not that point when he leaves his body because he is alert at that time.

The death point is not experienced by others. He is life-full there; at that time he is life-full. Although he is weak but he is [still] life-full. He knows that this is my wife, this is my child, this is my . . . everything. But that is not the death point. People think that it is the death point and they tell him, "this is a *thali*, this is rice, this is money, you give it . . ." and they throw water on his palm and say that, "you are giving these alms to the *purohit*, your priest," and he or she sprinkles water on that money and it is given to the priest. That is not the death time.

Death time is when he is nowhere present here. He is only with hiccups and no more available in the world. That is the real death time. And death time is known by him only, not by the people who are around him at that time. They don't know that death time.

So, at the [actual] death time, he [automatically] thinks of whatever he has practiced in his whole life-period. So you should remember God lifelong and then you will automatically think [of God] at the time of death, actual death.

Na kevalaṁ svasthāvasthāyāṁ [comm. for vs. 5, 6, 7], it is not when he is quite fit. *Yāvat antakāle'pi*, in the end also, at the time of death, when he is leaving his body, at that time also he remembers God. *Māmeva, māmeva*, he thinks of Me.

Who is Me?

Vyavacchinna sakala upādhikam, who is the greatest Lord Śiva. He thinks of Me.

> *kathaṁ cāsvasthāvasthāyāṁ vinivṛttasakalendriyaceṣṭasya*
>
> *bhagavān smṛtipathamupeyāt; – ityupāyamapi upadiśati* ।
> [comm.]

But the question is *asvastha āvasthāyāṁ*. When *asvastha*, when his body is not fit, at that time, *vinivṛttasakalendriya-ceṣṭasya*, when all organs, all memories, all mind, all thoughts, all intellect, fail to function, that is the real death time.

How can he remember God?

This is the question.

For this, the answer is:

DVD 8 (18:15)

ityupāyamapi upadiśati–sarvāvasthāsu vyāvahārikīṣvapi yasya bhagavattattvaṁ na hṛdayādapayāti, tasya bhagatvayeva sakala-karma-saṁanyāsinaḥ satataṁ bhagavanmayasya-avaśyaṁ svayam–eva bhagavattattvaṁ smṛti-viṣayatāṁ I *yātīti*

For him who has practiced *yoga* for his whole lifetime when he was quite fit, at that period [of death], whatever he has done [in his lifetime], for him at the moment of death also, he automatically thinks the same thing and he is sentenced to that state of Bhairava in the end.

Sadā tadbhāvabhāvitatvaṁ cātra hetuḥ. The means [i.e., the cause] is only you should practice that when you are fit in your lifetime. You should not ignore thinking of God when you are quite fit, quite happy, quite in your wits; at that time you should think [of Him]. [Then] you will think [of Him] afterwards automatically at the time of death.

Ata evāha–yenaiva vastunā sadā bhāvitāntaḥ karaṇaḥ; tadeva maraṇasamaye smaryate–tadbhāva eva ca prāpyate.[256] And he goes automatically in that state of Parabhairava.

Iti sarvathā matparama eva matprepsuḥ syāt. So the *upadeśa*, the treatment of this is, you should always think of Lord when you are quite happy, quite in your own wits.

Natu yadevānte smaryate tattattvamevāvāpyate–iti. You should not keep this in your mind that, "whatever I think [at the time of my death] . . ." He may not think at all at that time, at that period! [Even] if he has thought of Lord Śiva in each and every breath of his daily routine of life, he may not remember God at that time. At which time?

At the time of death.

Doesn't matter, he will be sentenced to Parabhairava at

256 "*Ata evāha*, this is why he says, *yenaiva vastunā sadā bhāvitāntaḥ-karaṇaḥ*, the attachment, the one who has attachment for something in his lifetime, *tedeva maraṇasamaye smaryate*, he goes to that thought at the time of death also." *Bhagavad Gītā* (1978).

once![257]

Evaṁ hi sati jñānino'pi yāvaccharīrabhāvidhātudoṣavi-kalita-cittavṛtter-jaḍatāṁ prāptasya tāmasasyeva gatiḥ syāt. If it were so, then that [person] who is *jñāni*, who has practiced Śiva *bhāva* in his lifetime, [and when] by acute disease–when there is some acute disease, your brain has left functioning, your mind has left functioning–at that time, how can he remember God at that time? He won't remember God at that time. It doesn't matter, [still] he will be sentenced to God consciousness at the time when he leaves his body.

Abhinavagupta says, "I have written one *śloka* in *Paramārtha-sāra* regarding this."

> *tīrthe śvapacagṛhe vā naṣṭasmṛtirapi parityajanadeham* ǀ
> *jñānasamakālamuktaḥ kaivalyaṁ* [*ihādeha*] *yāti hataśokāḥ*
> [*Paramārthasāra*, 83]

Tīrthe, in Varanasi, in a great . . . *tīrtha* means that shrine. For instance, Haridwar or in Kashi, if he leaves his body in Kashi, in Benares, at the time of death, if he leaves [his body at a sacred location] . . .

Kashkak was one Vedāntist, he went to Benares to leave his body. He was particular about leaving his body at Benares. He wanted to get *mokṣa* (liberation). But that is not reality.

. . . if he leaves his body in Benares, what then?

Śvapacagṛhe vā, if he leaves his body in the house of *śvapa-cagṛhe* (*śvapacagṛhe* means that butcher who eats the flesh of dogs) or *śūdra* (low caste), in [their] house, if he leaves his body, what then? *Naṣṭa smṛtir api,* if he has not memory, if he has lost his memory at the time of death and he cannot remember God, what then? *Jñāna samakāla muktaḥ*, as soon as he has realized his nature of Parabhairava in his lifetime, from *that* period he is

257 "But this is not the main point that, "whatever you think at the time of death, you will achieve that." This is not the main point. The main point is to think of God in your lifetime, then you will think of Him. You may not think of Him, you may not be able to think of God at the time of death, [still] He will think of you, He will remember you, God will remember you at that time. If you are not capable of thinking of Him, but He will [think of you] He has to remember." Ibid.

called *mukta* (liberated). It does not matter to him the *tamaśa* (commotion) of death period–it has no meaning.

Lord Kṛṣṇa has [said], "*antakale'pi māmeva smaran* [8:5]," if *api* (*api* means "also"), if at the time of death "also" he will think [of God]. It does not mean *api*, *api* is not forcibly . . . *api* means that *if* he thinks [of God] at that [death] time also, that is also possible. That will also carry him to God consciousness in the end. But it is not necessary that he should think, at the time of death, [that] he should think [of God]. Sometimes there are such diseases in which you are not allowed to think at all at that time.

DENISE: Like in a coma.

SWAMIJI: In coma, in sleep, *bas*! Still you will go there; you will fly to that Being. That is *api* (also); "also" means it is not essential.[258]

The main point is, *sadā ca matparamo eva janaḥ sarvathā syāt* [comm. verse 5, 6, 7], you should think of My being in each and every breath in your lifetime. That is the essential thing, which you have to do.

Iti tātparyaṁ munireva prakaṭayati. And Vyāsa clears this point in this verse: '*tasmātsarveṣu kāleṣu māmanusmara.*'[259] So, O Arjuna, go on thinking in each and every moment, go on thinking of Me in each and every moment of your life, *yudhya ca,* and you can fight with them. Nothing will happen to you, nothing bad will come to you.

DVD 8 (26:29)

It is said in the *Yoga Sūtras* also:

jātideśakālavyavahitānāmapi ānantaryyam

---

258 "In *Vedas*, there are two ways of ordering, speaking. One is *vidhi* and one is *anuvāda. Anuvāda* is not predominant, *vidhi* is predominant. Predominant is here *vidhi*. What is *vidhi*? To remember God in each and every act of your life. *Anuvād* is, if by chance he remembers God at the time of death, he will also get entry in God; it is if by chance. This thing is meant for those who have no grace of God in lifetime, and at the time of death God showers grace on him and he remembers God [and] he gets entry in God consciousness. . . . always it does not work. Remembering God in each and every act of life is predominant–it is *vidhi*. So this is to be done. Don't rely on that last happening." Ibid.

259 "So it is final decision that you should remember God in each and every act of your life." Ibid.

smṛtisaṁskārayorekarūpatvād
[*Yoga Sūtra*, 4.6]

This chain is going on of *saṁskāra* (impressions); the impression of thoughts he carries with him. The chain of impressions are carried from one life to another life, from that life to another life, from that life to another life. These impressions, he carries with him.

For instance, there is a cat, one is born as a cat. At that time when it sees a rat, it jumps upon it and eats it. When, [in the next lifetime], this cat becomes a dog, at that time the dog's memory comes in him of the past when he was a dog. When he was in the life of a dog, that dog memory [becomes] visible to him. [In the same way], at the time of birth of this *billy* (cat), *billy* memory is carried by him, it appears to him. At the time of [being born as a] saint, this memory of being saintly, that memory is with him. In the same way, he carries all of these impressions with him from life to life.

JONATHAN: But there must be a first time that that cat is a cat . . . isn't there?

SWAMIJI: It is numberless, numberless times you have been a cat.

JONATHAN: But there must be a first time.

SWAMIJI: First? There is no first! There is no beginning!

JONATHAN: So you've always been a cat?

SWAMIJI: [laughing]

Yes, always [laughs], always a cat, always a rat, always everything. You have been always that.[260] There is no first, there is no beginning of this world. You can't understand that there is a beginning. If there would have been a beginning, [then] there would have been an end. It is never ending!

End is only when a *yuga*[261] changes to another *yuga*. But impressions are still there.

DENISE: That's not the real end then.

SWAMIJI: Huh?

DENISE: When the *yuga* changes, that's not an end.

260 DENISE: "Then we were all everything once?"
SWAMIJI: "Yes." Ibid.

261 An age or era. [*Editor's note*]

SWAMIJI: No.
DENISE: That's a transition, it's a change.
SWAMIJI: Yes, it is changed.
JONATHAN: So there is constantly the same amount of souls?
SWAMIJI: Yes.
JONATHAN: There are no new souls born, no souls die?
SWAMIJI: Yes. [Souls] are *ananta* (infinite), you can't imagine how many there are. In water also, in the water of this ocean you will see how many souls are there, in fish, in *magarmach* (crocodile), in everybody, in bugs, in those shells, and everything. There are so many souls and they are passing from one birth to another birth.
JOHN: Do plants have souls?
SWAMIJI: Huh?
JOHN: Plants? Do plants have souls?
JONATHAN: Trees and plants?
SWAMIJI: Trees are not born, trees are stuck. These are also souls, but they are stuck for a very long period.

For instance, there is *pahad*, there is mountain; mountain will remain for centuries and centuries. It has a very long life, until it is dashed down by some *pralaya* (destruction). Then, in that [destroyed mountain], there are some souls, they open their eyes and are created again. One who is stuck always in dreaming state, and dreaming state, and dreaming state, he becomes a rock. He becomes a rock for a million years and again he becomes a man. Time comes when he becomes a human being.

It is not [laughing] . . . one Mohammedan in Ishber was telling me, "no, no, this human being can never become an egg [laughing].
DENISE: Never become what?
SWAMIJI: [laughing] Egg. [He said], "It is bogus!"

He would tell me, "it is bogus, you will never become an egg, how can a human being become an egg?"

But everything is possible. It is infinite. Infinite into infinite, it is so much.
JONATHAN: But what happens to a soul when he becomes a saint?
SWAMIJI: Huh?
JONATHAN: What happens to that soul when he becomes a saint and becomes one with Parabhairava. Then there is no more

evolution? He doesn't go through all that?

SWAMIJI: No, he does it, he becomes Parabhairava. He will never return from that Being.

JONATHAN: So eventually there will only be Parabhairava.

SWAMIJI: [laughing]

JOHN: But there is already only Parabhairava!

JONATHAN: Yeah, well that's right.

SWAMIJI: It is already only Parabhairava. But Parabhairava is always Parabhairava. It is His manifestation that that shell is created. That shell has got the position of Parabhairava.

JONATHAN: So it's just for fun.

SWAMIJI: Yes [laughing].

From His point of view it is fun. From the point of view of the shell, it is a disgusting thing. From the point of view of that shell who has been created, for him it is terrible. But at the same time, this terrible state is tasted by Parabhairava.[262]

DENISE: And He enjoys it.

SWAMIJI: He enjoys.

Lord Kṛṣṇa was enjoying freedom with all ladies, sixteen thousand and eight hundred and eighteen. But besides that He had many more mistresses, and He was always present [with each one of them], everywhere present.

Rukmani would think, "Lord Kṛṣṇa is always with me, day and night." Radha would think, "Lord Kṛṣṇa is . . ." She would experience that Lord Kṛṣṇa was always with her, day and night.

How was He [present] day and night with everybody?

DENISE: He is omnipresent.

SWAMIJI: That is it. This is a mystery. And this mystery is unbelievable, unbelievably believable. You cannot believe it, but when you believe, you believe totally. Then you believe that everything is possible.

JOHN: So, in *Satya Yuga* . . .[263]

SWAMIJI: Huh?

JOHN: Everybody gets enlightenment in *Satya Yuga*? Every-

262 Meister Eckhart once described how "God tastes Himself and how, in this tasting, he tastes all creatures, not as creatures, but rather as God." Elizabeth Hense and Frans Maas, "Current Perspective on Spirituality in Northwestern Europe" in *Spiritus* 11.1 (2011): 69. [*Editor's note*]

263 Age or era of truth. [*Editor's note*]

body goes to the state of Parabhairava?

SWAMIJI: [laughing] No. How can everybody go to Parabhairava [state]?

JOHN: All human beings?

SWAMIJI: Human beings become human beings. It is only [due to] *śaktipāta* that [the state of] Parabhairava takes place, to whom He likes.

JOHN: So *Satya Yuga* doesn't mean that everyone gets that state of Parabhairava?

SWAMIJI: Yes, *Satya Yuga. Satya Yuga* means, yes. When *Satya Yuga* will come, all won't become Parabhairava, but all will become saintly; everybody will become saintly. Without prejudice, without hatred, without jealousy, without any false tricks–this all will be vanished. This hypocrisy will be vanished.

That is *Satya Yuga. Satya Yuga* does not mean everybody will become Parabhairava. Parabhairava is only one, and all others are millions.

DENISE: Swamiji, in *Satya Yuga* isn't it easier to evolve, to progress in *yoga*? Doesn't it become easier to progress?

SWAMIJI: Yes, yes.

DENISE: Because everything, your whole environment is supporting you.

SWAMIJI: Yes! Yes! It becomes easier.

DVD 8 (36:54)

अभ्यासयोगयुक्तेन
चेतसानन्यगामिना ।
परमं पुरुषं दिव्यं
याति पार्थानुचिन्तयन् ॥८॥

कविं पुराणमनुशासितार-
मणोरणीयांसमनुस्मरेद्यः ।
सर्वस्य धातारमचिन्त्यरूप-
मादित्यवर्णं तमसः परस्तात् ॥९॥

प्रयाणकाले मनसाचलेन
भक्त्या युक्तो योगबलेन चैव ।
भ्रुवोर्मध्ये प्राणमावेश्य सम्यक्
स तं परं पुरुषमुपैति दिव्यम् ॥१०॥

abhyāsayogayuktena
cetasānanyagāminā /
paramaṁ puruṣaṁ divyaṁ
yāti pārthānucintayan //8//
[not recited or translated][264]

kaviṁ purāṇamanuśāsitāra
maṇoraṇīyāṁsamanusmaredyaḥ /
sarvasya dhātāramacintyarūpam-
ādityavarṇaṁ tamasaḥ parastāt //9//
[note: sound missing on the last line]

prayāṇakāle manasācalena
bhaktyā yukto yogabalena caiva /
bhruvormadhye prāṇamāveśya samyak
sa taṁ paraṁ puruṣamupaiti divyam //10//

At the time of death, what should you think?

264 "*Pārtha*, O Arjuna, a *yogi* who *ananyagāminā cetāsa*, after concentrating his mind, establishing his mind in one-pointedness, by *abhyāsa yoga yuktena*, by attaching himself in meditation, he definitely attains the divine being of God consciousness and gets entry in that, *anucintayan,* by meditating on it. But this meditation, this practice is done at the time of death. When he leaves his body, this physical frame, and gets rid of the pain of body (the last pain that is the pain which one feels at the time of death, at the last movement), and he puts his mind, concentrates on God consciousness, he definitely gets entry in Him. How he has to do it? He explains it in the next *śloka*." *Bhagavad Gītā* (1978).

Kaviṁ purāṇam [verse 9]. *Kaviṁ*, who is all-knowing, *purāṇam*, who is ancient, *anuśāsitāram*, who is governing the whole kingdom of one hundred and eighteen worlds, *aṇor-aṇīyāṁsaṁ*, and who is subtler than the subtlest, *anusmared-yaḥ*, [one] who thinks of this Being [who is] *sarvasya dhātāram*, and who is the holder of everybody, who is the protector of everybody, *acintya-rūpam*, who cannot be concentrated upon, who is beyond being concentrated on, who is the concentrator and is not being concentrated on, *ādityavarṇaṁ,* whose color is glittering just like suns that [shine with] blue sparkling–you know that? That color–*tamasaḥ parastāt*, who is beyond darkness, *prayāṇakāle*, at the time of death, somebody who is lucky, he thinks of such a Being. *Bhaktyā yukto yogabalena caiva*, with devotion, with great devotion, and with the effort of *yoga,* who thinks [of that Being] at that moment, *bhruvor madhye prāṇam-āveśya samyak, bhruvor madhye,*[265] between good and bad, between one step and another step, between one breath and another breath, who establishes his breath at that moment at the time of death, *sa taṁ paraṁ puruṣamupaiti divyam*, he is at once sentenced to that state of Bhairava, at once at the time of death, and he leaves his body.

DVD 8 (40:42)

यदक्षरं वेदविदो वदन्ति
विशन्ति यद्यतयो वीतरागाः ।
यदिच्छन्तो ब्रह्मचर्यं चरन्ति
तत्ते पदं संग्रहेणाभिधास्ये ॥ ११ ॥

yadakṣaraṁ vedavido vadanti
viśanti yadyatayo vītarāgāḥ /

265 Though the literal meaning of *bhruvor madhye* is "between two eyebrows", Swamiji says, "it is not between two eyebrows . . . we have already explained that between two eyebrows means in between knowledge and action, *jñana* and *kriya*, ingoing breath and out coming breath, 'this-ness' and 'I-ness.' Between these two, he has to focus his breath. So breath will remain one-pointed. And then it will rush in that God consciousness at the time of leaving this physical frame." Ibid.

yadicchanto brahmacaryaṁ caranti
tatte padaṁ saṁgraheṇābhidhāsye //11//

Veda vidaḥ, those who are elevated in [the knowledge of the] *śāstras*, those people who are nominated as *akṣaraṁ* (*akṣaraṁ* means unperishable), *viśanti yadyatayo vītarāgāḥ*, and those who are filled with the greatest effort,[266] those *yogīs* who get entry in that Being, *vītarāgaḥ*, leaving aside all attachments of the worldly life, *yadicchanto brahmacaryaṁ caranti*, with whose desire to achieve [His presence], *yogīs* who develop *brahmacarya* (*brahmacarya* means . . . *brahmacarya* does not mean absence of sexuality. *Brahmacarya* means realizing in each and every action the existence of Parabhairava. That is *brahmacaraya*), *brahma*, Parabhairava is observed in each and every corner of your daily routine of life. *Tatte padaṁ saṁgraheṇābhidhāsye*, in brief words, I will place [i.e., explain] that state of Being before you, O Arjuna.

Now 12th *śloka*.

DVD 8 (43:28)

सर्वद्वाराणि संयम्य मनो हृदि निरुध्य च ।
मूर्ध्न्याधायात्मनः प्राणमास्थितो योगधारणाम् ॥१२॥

sarvadvārāṇi saṁyamya mano hṛdi nirudhya ca /
murdhnyādhāyātmanaḥ prāṇamāsthito yogadhāraṇām //12//

Sarvadvārāṇi saṁyamya, all organs, the openings of organs you should close at once.[267] *Sarvadvārāṇi saṁyamya mano hṛdi nirudhya ca*, you should sentence [i.e., focus] your mind in the heart. Heart means the center of the whole universe.[268] The center of the whole universe is the heart, the real heart. In that

266 "In whom those who have conducted all-round detachment get entry, after being detached from all sides, they become detached from all pleasures, pains, worldly matters . . . " Ibid.

267 "Don't see anything, don't hear anything, don't touch anything, don't smell anything." Ibid.

268 "Heart is the center of God consciousness." Ibid.

heart you should dilute your mind so there is no other thought living in your mind afterwards. *Mūrdhnyādhāyātmanaḥ prāṇam*, and your breath[269] you should take inside *suṣumnā* and make it reside in the state of *brahmarandhra*, *ūrdhva kapāla.*[270] *Āsthito yogadhāraṇām*, and you should conduct this *yoga dhāraṇā*.

DVD 8 (44:58)

ओमित्येकाक्षरं ब्रह्म व्याहरन्मामनुस्मरन् ।
यः प्रयाति त्यजन्देहं स याति परमां गतिम् ॥ १३ ॥

omityekākṣaraṁ brahma vyāharanmāmanusmaran /
yaḥ prayāti tyajandehaṁ sa yāti paramāṁ gatim //13//

Oṁ. *Oṁ* means:

antarālīnatattvaughaṁ cidānandaghanaṁ mahat /
yattattvaṁ śaivadhāmākhyaṁ tadomityabhidhīyate //[271]

Antarālīna tattvaughaṁ, where all of these differentiated thirty-six elements and one hundred and eighteen worlds are consumed inside (*antarālīna tattvaughaṁ*). And that state which is *cid-ānanda-ghanaṁ*, filled with all consciousness and all bliss. *Yat-tattvaṁ śaivadhāmākhyaṁ*, which is the reality, the abode and residence of Lord Śiva. *Tad-om-ityabhidhīyate*, that is [the meaning of] *oṁ*.

269 "That is *ātmasārathim*, this is the chariot, the chariot of your Self. Because [the breath] will carry you to God consciousness. Breath is the only ride to God consciousness." Ibid.

270 "*Icchā śaktyātmani*, just desire for God consciousness, that is, breath should be focused for God consciousness, toward God consciousness. Your breath should recite God consciousness, your breath should desire for, long for God consciousness. That is focusing your breath in *brahmarandhra,* not this skull (*urdhva kapāla*). Desire for God consciousness, that is *brahmarandhra.*" Ibid.

271 Verse from *Amriteshvara pūja*. [*Editor's note*]

And that *oṁ* you should recite inside.[272] "Recite" means you should live in that *oṁ*.

And *māmanusmaran*, at the same time, you should live in that *oṁ* and see that *oṁ* is Parabhairava; the body of Parabhairava is *oṁ*.[273]

Yaḥ prayāti tyajandehaṁ [verse 13], at that time [one] who shatters this physical body at the time of death, *sa yāti paramāṁ gatim*, he is sentenced to that supreme state of Parabhairava.[274]

DVD 8 (46:48)

अनन्यचेताः सततं यो मां स्मरति नित्यशः ।
तस्याहं सुलभः पार्थ नित्ययुक्तस्य योगिनः ॥ १४ ॥

ananyacetāḥ satataṁ yo māṁ smarati nityaśaḥ /
tasyāhaṁ sulabhaḥ pārthanityayuktasya yoginaḥ //14//

Pārtha, Hey Arjuna, O Arjuna, who in this way, *ananyacetāḥ*, being one-pointed and one-pointedly remembers Me who is Parabhairava, and remembers Me always, in each and every activity of his daily routine of life *in* his lifetime, *tasyāhaṁ sulabhaḥ pārtha*, for him, I am at his disposal, *nitya yuktasya yoginaḥ*, because that *yogi* is always a *yogi*. He has not accepted any other activity besides this *yoga*.

It is said somewhere [in a Shaivite text], he gives reference:

vyāpinyāṁ śivasattāyāmutkrāntirnāma niṣphalā /

272 "*Vāk niyamaḥ* (*vānniyamaḥ*), that is word, internal word. And that internal word must be, you must speak internal word through mind. . . . that is *parā vāk*." Ibid.

See footnote 228 for an explanation of the four levels of *vāk*.

273 "*Māmanusmaran* means you must remember Me repeatedly. Remember Me and then remember Me again, afresh. Don't put only one push of memory of God, that won't do . . . it will fade. . . . Refresh this push again and again. . . . That is *anusmarana*; repeatedly you have to remember Him." *Bhagavad Gītā* (1978).

274 Or one "who leaves this attachment for body [during their lifetime]. . . . This is *tyajan dehaṁ*, he must not be attached to this bodily existence through mind. That is a real death." Ibid.

avyāpini śive nāma notkrāntiḥ śivadāyinī ||

If Parabhairava is all-pervading, what is the meaning of throwing ones own body and entering into God consciousness? It is useless. What has he to throw and where has he to go? Wherefrom he has to go, that is Parabhairava! To which point he has to go, that is Parabhairava! That *utkrāntiḥ* means to jump. How will he jump? From which point will he jump? And to which point will he enter?

It is just a joke, it is baseless. It makes ones own self laugh. *Utkrāntiḥ* has no meaning.[275] *Avyāpini śive tattve*, [even] if Śiva is not all-pervading, still then *utkrāntiḥ* has no meaning.[276]

And Bhaṭṭanārāyaṇa, in his [*Stava*] *Cintāmaṇi* (he was a Shaivite master, one of the ancient Shaivite masters), his reference also Abhinavagupta puts in his commentary:

nimeṣamapi yadyekaṁ kṣīṇadoṣe kariṣyasi |
padaṁ citte tadā śaṁbho kiṁ na saṁpādayiṣyasi ||
[*Stava Cintāmaṇi*, *śloka* 115]

---

275 "*Utkrānti* [means] coming out from this physical body and getting entry in God consciousness–that is *utkrānti*. That is *ekadeśena*; *ekadeśena* means God consciousness is situated somewhere [else].

"This kind of teaching that is found in *Bhagavad Gītā* is absolutely incorrect. *Sāra śāstras* does not recognize this kind of *dhāraṇa*. *Sāra śāstras* say, "why to go? Where to go? What is up and what is down? Down below is Lord Śiva, up is Lord Śiva.

"Yadi sarvagato devo vadotkramya kva yāsyati. Athāsarvagatas tarhi ghaṭa-tulyastadā bhavet. If Lord Śiva is everywhere, then this body is also Lord Śiva! Why should you leave this body and go in higher level–what is there? If Lord Śiva is not everywhere, *athāsarvata,* if He is only in seventh [heaven], not in other worlds, *ghaṭa,* then He is [like] a pot, then He is just like [an inanimate object]."

Swami Lakshmanjoo, *Tantrāloka*, 14.33-34 (1980).

276 "*Avyāpini śive tattve*, if God consciousness is not pervading, even then the leaving of one thing [i.e., one's body] and holding another thing [i.e., God consciousness] has no charm. What will you leave and what will you hold if God consciousness is not there? If God consciousness *is* there, what is the fun in leaving and holding? If God consciousness is *not* there, what is the fun in leaving and holding?" *Bhagavad Gītā* (1978).

If, in the period of one twinkling of the eye, You make somebody, some fortunate soul blissful by fixing him in the state of Parabhairava, *kim na saṁpādayiṣyasi*, then what more could You do? You have done everything for him.[277] So whatever is being done in one twinkling of an eye, that is all [that is needed].[278] There is no effort, there is no [need] to insert effort. There, *tīvra tīvra śaktipāta*[279] is found and that is under your control, not under the control of Parabhairava. That *tīvra tīvra śaktipāta* is under your own control!

This is the Shaivite Philosophy.

JOHN: How is it under your control? How?

SWAMIJI: How?

JOHN: You said *tīvra tīvra śaktipāta* is under your own control.

SWAMIJI: Because you *are* Parabhairava. You have to produce *śaktipāta* for yourself. When you don't like, then don't produce it, still you are great. When you don't like, as somebody does not like to have *śaktipāta*, what then? He is always there.

This is the 15th *śloka* now.

DVD 8 (52:23)

277 "If You keep my mind, if You make my mind, only for one moment, one second, *nimeṣamapi yadyekaṁ*, *ekaṁ nimeṣa*, (*nimeṣa* means only for one twinkling of eye, that is only for one second), if You make my mind *kṣīṇadoṣe* without any blemishes, without any blemishes of variety of thoughts, i.e. variety of foreign thoughts except Your thought." Swami Lakshmanjoo, *Stava Cintāmaṇi,* 115 (1980-81).

278 "*Iti yeṣāṁ śaṅkā*. So, those people who consider, who take this for granted that, 'it does not matter if you think of God for your lifetime; if you have thought over God and concentrated on God for your lifetime, and at the time of death you don't remember Him, you will be destroyed, you will be ruined,' those people who say this, *tān vīta śaṅkānkartum,* this decision is incorrect . . . and this point is declared by this *śloka*: *ananyacetāḥ satataṁ yo māṁ smarati nityaśaḥ*, that person who remembers Me in his lifetime, always he will be with Me and he will not be destroyed at the time of death [even] if he does not think of Me." *Bhagavad Gītā* (1978).

279 *Tīvra tīvra śaktipāta* means "super-supreme grace." See footnote 33. See also *Kashmir Shaivism–The Secret Supreme* 10.66. [*Editor's note*]

मामुपेत्य पुनर्जन्म दुःखालयमशाश्वतम् ।
नाप्नुवन्ति महात्मानः संसिद्धिं परमां गताः ॥ १५ ॥

māmupetya punarjanma duḥkhālayamaśāśvatam /
nāpnuvanti mahātmānaḥ saṁsiddhiṁ paramāṁ gatāḥ //15

Māmupetya, once you achieve Me . . .

Who is Me?

JONATHAN: Parabhairava.

SWAMIJI: Parabhairava.

. . . *punar janma*, then there is no possibility of rebirth (*punar janma*). And *duḥkhālayam*, this *saṁsāra* is full of *duḥkha* (*duḥkha* means torture). *Aśāśvatam,* it is not remaining, it is not permanent. Those great souls do not experience this [suffering] at all, in any way! This *tamasha*, this drama, is closed for them for good. There is no [longer] that drama of *duḥkhālaya*; he will never experience *duḥkha* anymore. Because *saṁsiddhiṁ paramāṁ gatāḥ,* they have already resided in the supreme *siddhi* (achievement) of Parabhairava state.

The 16th *śloka*.

DVD 8 (54:03)

आब्रह्म भुवनाल्लोकाः पुनरावर्तिनोऽर्जुन ।
मामुपेत्य तु कौन्तेय पुनर्जन्म न विद्यते ॥ १६ ॥

ābrahma bhuvanāllokāḥ punarāvartino'rjuna /
māmupetya tu kaunteya punarjanma na vidyate //16//

This is the *Bhagavad Gītā* and Abhinavagupta has commentated upon it in a unique way. *Ābrahma, ābrahma* means *ābrahma bhuvanāt*, *brahma bhuvanāt* . . . other commentators have commentated [upon] this verse, *brahma bhuvanāt*, "up to Brahmā *loka*." [They say], "up to Brahmā *loka*, all [who reach] the *loka* of Brahmā, after death, if they reach to the *loka* of Brahmā, they will return again in rebirth in *saṁsāra*.

But what is that?

It means, Abhinavagupta says (he has indulged in this

explanation of other commentators), if they have accepted that up to Brahmā, if you reach the state of Brahmā, even then you have to come down again into the cycle of repeated births and deaths; [*samsāra*] is not closed for him. It means, if you reach the *loka* of Viṣṇu, even then, you have to come again and again. If you reach the *loka* of Rudra, you have to come again and again.

So this is not quite the exact befitting meaning that up to Brahmā *loka*, there is a possibility of coming again and again. It means, up to Viṣṇu *loka* there is no possibility of coming [back again]; up to Rudra *loka,* there is no possibility of coming [back again]. [They say] he is *mukta*. How can he be *mukta*?

The [real] meaning of *brahma* means the supreme Bhairava state, up to the Bhairava state. Until Bhairava state is not achieved, you have to come again and again in this world. When Bhairava state is once achieved, then this coming again in re-birth takes its end.

In this way, [Abhinavagupta] has commentated upon it.

Have you understood it?[280]

JOHN: Yes. Because the state of Bhairava is completely different.

SWAMIJI: Yes.

This was the 16th verse.

Now there are some *ślokas* regarding this *pralaya* (dissolution) in the 8th *āhnika* (chapter).

DVD 8 (57:48)

सहस्रयुगपर्यन्तमहर्यैं ब्रह्मणो विदुः ।
रात्रिं युगसहस्रान्तां तेऽहोरात्रविदो जनाः ॥१७॥
अव्यक्ताद्व्यक्तयः सर्वाः प्रभवन्त्यहरागमे ।
रात्र्यागमे प्रलीयन्ते तत्रैवाव्यक्तसंज्ञके ॥१८॥

280 "[For Abhinavagupta], *ābrahma* means the state of Brahman, the state of God consciousness. Up to the state of God consciousness, *bhuvanād,* from any world (Brahmā *loka*, Viṣṇu *loka*, etc.), you have to *punarāvartino*, you have to return again and again. *Māmupetya tu kaunteya punarjanma na vidyate*, but once you achieve the state of God consciousness, you won't return." *Bhagavad Gītā* (1978).

भूतग्रामः स एवायं भूत्वा भूत्वा प्रलीयते ।
रात्र्यागमेऽवशः पार्थ प्रभवत्यहरागमे ॥१९॥

sahasrayugaparyantamaharye brahmaṇo viduḥ /
rātriṁ yugasahasrāntāṁ te'horātravido janāḥ //17//
avyaktādvyaktayaḥ sarvāḥ prabhavantyaharāgame /
rātryāgame pralīyante tatraivāvyaktasaṁjñake //18//
bhūtagrāmaḥ sa evāyaṁ bhūtvā bhūtvā pralīyate /
rātryāgame'vaśaḥ pārtha prabhavatyaharāgame //19//

17th, 18th, and 19th.

Sahasrayuga paryantamaharye brahmaṇo viduḥ. Brahmā's span of daytime is one thousand [cycles of] four *yugas*.[281] [When] the span of one thousand [cycles of] four *yugas* passes, this much time is called one day of Brahmā.

Rātriṁ yuga sahasrāntāṁ, and his night is also one thousand [cycles of] these . . .

JOHN: Four *yugas*.

SWAMIJI: . . . four *yugas*.

JONATHAN: That's a long time.

SWAMIJI: Long time. *Te'horātravido janāḥ*, and those who are situated in the Parabhairava state, they know [the length of] his day and night also. They observe his day and night.

Whose?

DENISE: Brahmā's.

SWAMIJI: Brahmā's.

DVD 8 (1:00:00)

अव्यक्ताद्व्यक्तयः सर्वाः प्रभवन्त्यहरागमे ।
रात्र्यागमे प्रलीयन्ते तत्रैवाव्यक्तसंज्ञके ॥१८॥

avyaktādvyaktayaḥ sarvāḥ prabhavantyaharāgame /
rātryāgame pralīyante tatraivāvyaktasaṁjñake //18//

And now there is *avyakta* (i.e., *prakṛti*). *Prakṛti* is when the door is closed, i.e., *pralaya* (dissolution). From *prakṛti* all beings

281 Four *yugas* is 4,320,000 years. [*Editor's note*]

are produced [during] the time of [Brahmā's] daytime. And *rātri āgame pralīyante*, when the night time comes of Brahmā, at that time they remain in chloroform in *prakṛti*, for that period.

DVD 8 (1:00:58)

भूतग्रामः स एवायं भूत्वा भूत्वा प्रलीयते ।
रात्र्यागमेऽवशः पार्थ प्रभवत्यहरागमे ॥१९॥

bhūtagrāmaḥ sa evāyaṁ bhūtvā bhūtvā pralīyate /
rātryāgame'vaśaḥ pārtha prabhavatyaharāgame //19//

In the same way, all of these individuals, they rise and they go again into chloroform, but they never become *mukta* (liberated).[282] But those who are *dīrghadṛśvāna*, who are established in Parabhairava, they see how they are situated in *pralayas*. All *pralayas* and all *yugas* they perceive, and they are so eternal, always eternal. Their Parabhairava state never ends.

Sarvato lokebhyaḥ punar āvṛttirnatu māṁ prāpya; *iti sphuṭayati*. Now, in these *ślokas*, 20th, 21st, and 22nd *ślokas,* he, Vyāsa says, that *punarāvṛttiḥ*[283] is continuous, continuously functioning, but only *punarāvṛttiḥ* stops to function only when Parabhairava state is achieved. Then there is no *punarāvṛttiḥ*.

DVD 8 (1:03:00)

परस्तस्मात्तु भावोऽन्यो व्यक्ताव्यक्तः सनातनः ।
यः स सर्वेषु भूतेषु नश्यत्सु न विनश्यति ॥२०॥
अव्यक्तोऽक्षर इत्युक्तस्तमाहुः परमां गतिम् ।

282 "*Nānye'nye upasṛjyante* [comm.], new individuals are not born. *Apitu te eva jīvāḥ*, those individuals who are born, they die; those who die, they are born. *Kālakṛtastu cirakṣiprapratyayātmā viśeṣah*, and this is the play of the Lord of time, Lord of death, that some live for one hundred years according to their capacity. . . . Nārāyaṇa lives for one hundred years according to [his] span of time. They [i.e., the gods] have not escaped the clutches of time, death. . . . So this kind of limitation is attributed to Brahmā and all those gods also." *Bhagavad Gītā* (1978).

283 The cycle of repeated births and deaths (*saṁsāra*). [*Editor's note*]

यं प्राप्य न निवर्तन्ते तद्धाम परमं मम ॥२१॥
पुरुषः स परः पार्थ भक्त्या लभ्यस्त्वनन्यया ।
यं प्राप्य न पुनर्जन्म लभन्ते योगिनोऽर्जुन ॥२२॥
यस्यान्तःस्थानि भूतानि यत्र सर्वं प्रतिष्ठितम् ।

parastasmāttu bhāvo'nyo vyaktāvyaktaḥ sanātanaḥ /
yaḥ sa sarveṣu bhūteṣu naśyatsu na vinaśyati //20//
avyakto'kṣara ityuktastamāhuḥ paramāṁ gatim /
yaṁ prāpya na nivartante taddhāma paramaṁ mama //21//
puruṣaḥ sa paraḥ pārtha bhaktyā labhyastvananyayā /
yaṁ prāpya na punarjanma labhante yogino'rjuna //22//
yasyāntaḥsthāni bhūtāni yatra sarvaṁ pratiṣṭhitam /

This *para bhāva* (*para bhāva* means Bhairava *bhāva*) is *anyaḥ*, absolutely different from all of these [individuals].[284] *Vyaktāvyaktaḥ sanātanaḥ*, you may call it manifested or you may call it un-manifested. It is very ancient. *Yaḥ sa sarveṣu bhūteṣu naśyatsu*, if the whole world is *naśyatsu* (destroyed), *na vinaśyati*, He is not destroyed. And this is the real state of His being; *yaṁ prāpya na nivartante, taddhāma paramaṁ mama*, that is the real residence of Mine. And that *puruṣa* (individual) who is residing in Parabhairava state . . .[285]

That can be achieved. That is not impossible for anybody to achieve. Everybody can achieve Him, but with what, with what element, with what weapon?

Bhakti, devotion.

If he undergoes intense devotion towards Parabhairava, he will reach in My nature.

JOHN: So devotion is more important than *jñāna* or anything?

SWAMIJI: Devotion, yes. Nothing is . . . *jñāna* is nothing before devotion.

Yasyāntaḥsthāni bhūtāni yatra sarvaṁ pratiṣṭhitam [comm.

284 Why? "The reality of God, the reality of Siva, is *kālasaṁkalanāvivarjitaṁ*, is beyond the circle of time." *Bhagavad Gītā* (1978).

285 "*Yaṁ prāpya*, and once you achieve that supreme state of being, which is *avyakta*, which is un-manifested, *na nivartante*, you have not to come again; you will never leave that state again." Ibid.

vs. 22]. And this is the basis of all beings. What? The state of Parabhairava. And that state of Parabhairava can be achieved by anybody, any disgusted being, by *bhakti*, by devotion, by love.

You know love? What is love?

JONATHAN: What is your definition of love? What is love from your point of view?

SWAMIJI: Love is just one-pointed, love is always love, love cannot remain without love. You cannot remain without love. Love is . . . in waking state there is love, in sleeping state there is love, in walking state there is love. He can weep, at any moment he can weep, tears are always in his eyes, tears are always there when he is laughing in a dream, tears are always in him. He is filled with tears, everywhere. When he is urinating, he is filled with tears. You can't imagine what is love.

Oh, love is just blind!

And he does not know what love is. He himself does not know what is love. Love is the greatest element which is created in the body of Parabhairava.

JONATHAN: You said that in that Practice and Discipline,[286] "love is the answer and the key."

SWAMIJI: And the tea?

JONATHAN: And the key.

SWAMIJI: Yes.

JONATHAN: It is the answer and the key.

SWAMIJI: Yes.

JONATHAN: It is both things.

SWAMIJI: Yes.

DVD 8 (1:07:30)

यत्र काले त्वनावृत्तिमावृत्तिं चैव योगिनः ।
प्रयाता यान्ति तं कालं वक्ष्यामि भरतर्षभ ॥२३॥

yatra kāle tvanāvṛttimāvṛttiṁ caiva yoginaḥ /
prayātā yānti taṁ kālaṁ vakṣyāmi bharatarṣabha //23//

Now I will degrade [i.e., digress] you for a little while to come down and tell you when you should pass your body, when you should throw your body. At which time, when you throw your

286 Swami Lakshmanjoo, *Self Realization in Kashmir Shaivism*, 2.49.

body, you will return again in the cycle of repeated births [and deaths], and that particular time of throwing your body, you won't return again in rebirth.

DVD 8 (1:08:23)

अग्निज्योतिरहः शुक्लः षण्मासा उत्तरायणम् ।
तत्र प्रयाता गच्छन्ति ब्रह्म ब्रह्मविदो जनाः ॥२४॥
धूमो रात्रिस्तथा कृष्णः षण्मासा दक्षिणायनम् ।
तत्र चान्द्रमसं ज्योतिर्योगी प्राप्य निवर्तते ॥२५॥

agnijyotirahaḥ śuklaḥ ṣaṇmāsā uttarāyaṇam /
tatra prayātā gacchanti brahma brahmavido janāḥ //24//
dhūmo rātristathā kṛṣṇaḥ ṣaṇmāsā dakṣiṇāyanam /
tatra cāndramasaṁ jyotiryogī prāpya nivartate //25//

When there is *agni jyotir* (*agni jyotir* means the *prakāśa* (light) of fire), at that time, *ahaḥ*, when there is daytime, *śuklaḥ*, when there is moon period, and six months of *uttarāyaṇa*, when there is *uttarāyaṇa* (*uttarāyaṇa* means [when] days are growing [longer]), *tatra*, in this . . .

These are six. *Agni jyotir* is one . . .

JONATHAN: What does that mean, *agni joytir*?

SWAMIJI: The *prakāśa* of fire, there must be a flame at the time of death. This is the tradition. We keep a light going on. In darkness, we don't allow a dying person to leave his body. In darkness, you should not leave the body. There must be a candle.[287]

. . . *tatra prayātā gacchanti brahma brahmavido janāḥ*, there, only those who are realized souls, they go and are placed in the state of Parabhairava; those who know Parabhairava.[288]

---

287 "It is meant for *yogi,* it is not meant for everybody. This time, this period of death is meant for *yogīs*, not for each and every being. [For] each and every being [other than *yogīs*], it doesn't matter, it has no effect." *Bhagavad Gītā* (1978).

288 "[According to Abhinavagupta], the period of *agni jyotir* means *prakāśa*, internal light, where there is internal *uttarāyaṇa*. . . . Your internal moonlight, that is the period of *yogīs*. . . . It can take place at

Dhūmo rātriḥ [verse 25], when there is smoke, at the time of smoke, *rātri*, when there is night, *kṛṣṇaḥ*, when there are dark nights and six months of [*dakṣiṇāyana*] . . .

JONATHAN: Of darkened days.

SWAMIJI: Yes.

. . . *tatra cāndramasaṁ jyotiryogī prāpya*, there (this is the tradition), in that period if one dies, he *nivartate*, he comes again in *punar janma*, in rebirth.

शुक्लकृष्णे गती ह्येते जगतः शाश्वते मते ।
अनयोर्यात्यनावृत्तिमाद्ययावर्ततेऽन्यया ॥२६॥

śuklakṛṣṇe gatī hyete jagataḥ śāśvate mate /
anayoryātyanāvṛttim ādyayāvartate'nyayā //26//
[not recited or translated][289]

DVD 8 (1:11:04

नैते सृती पार्थ जानन्योगी मुह्यति कश्चन ।
तस्मात्सर्वेषु कालेषु योगयुक्तो भवार्जुन ॥२७॥

naite sṛtī pārtha jānanyogī muhyati kaścana /
tasmātsarveṣu kāleṣu yogayukto bhavārjuna //27//

O Arjuna, *naite sṛtī pārtha jānan*, the *yogi* who knows these

---

any time. In dark night also you can create light, *yogi* can create light and die." Ibid.

289 "These two pathways–one is *śukla* pathway, bright, of *uttarāyaṇa* pathway, and another is dark pathway (*kṛṣṇa*)–these two pathways, *jagataḥ śāśvate*, are established in this world eternally. And amongst these two pathways, *anayoryāti anāvṛttim ādyaya āvartate anyayā*, *ādyayā*, by first pathway of light, one achieves liberation, and by the second pathway of darkness, one achieves repeated births and deaths. So you have to create these pathways . . . through the strength of meditation and leave this body. Abhinavagupta says you can create time. You can create Varanasi shrine here in bathroom. You can create church in bathroom if you have awareness, full strength. That bathroom will be the abode of God if there is awareness." Ibid.

two ways, i.e., that these two ways have no meaning in the end, he never is deprived of his state of Parabhairava.[290] So, you should remain at ease in the state of Parabhairava; don't think of any other thing at all.[291]

Sarveṣu kāleṣu yogayukto bhavārjuna, I am giving you boons, you become *yogi*, always *yogi*, always *yogi*, here and hereafter, always be a *yogi*. *Yoga* is the most important thing. *Yoga* means union of limited in unlimited.

Now the last *śloka* of this 8th chapter.

DVD 8 (1:12:31)

वेदेषु यज्ञेषु तपःसु चैव
दानेषु यत्पुण्यफलं प्रदिष्टम् ।
अभ्येति तत्सर्वमिदं विदित्वा
योगी परं स्थानमुपैति चाद्यम् ॥२८॥

vedeṣu yajñeṣu tapaḥsu caiva
dāneṣu yatpuṇyaphalaṁ pradiṣṭam /

290 "The one who understands, who has experienced, these two pathways–how? *Abhyantareṇa krameṇa yogabhyasa svikṛtenetyarthaḥ*, internally, by *yoga abhyasa*–[to him], these two pathways have no value at all, from Abhinavagupta's point of view. He says, 'don't mind these pathways.'

"*Ābhyantara kāla kṛtam utkrānti bhedam. Utkrānti* is meant for internal time. *Utkrānti* (how to leave this body, how to leave this physical frame and achieve liberation, final liberation) is done by adopting the cycle of internal cycle of time, not external cycle of *uttarāyaṇa* and *dakṣiṇāyana* as everybody is holding this [viewpoint]." Ibid.

291 "So it is better for you to be concentrated to God consciousness every moment, each and every moment in your lifetime. Go on doing this practice of *yoga*, then there is no fear; this pathway will be selected for you. . . . The theory and the viewpoint of our masters is that *sarva anugrāhakatayā*, God bestows grace to each and every being. His grace is already there, only we have to make ourselves prepared, ready to accept it, ready to receive it, our receivers must be intact. If our receiver is defective, you can't receive this grace. This is the theory of our masters." Ibid.

abhyeti tatsarvamidaṁ viditvā
yogī paraṁ sthānamupaiti cādyam //28//

In *Vedas*, in all . . . in *yajñas*, in penances, in giving, bestowing alms to people, whatever *puṇya phalaṁ (puṇya phalaṁ* means pure fruit you can derive), *abhyeti tatsarvamidaṁ viditvā*, the *yogi,* once situated in the state of Parabhairava, all of these fruits which I have explained in other ways of good actions, *abhyeti,* he crosses that.[292] And *paraṁ sthānam upaiti cādyam*, he is always situated in that state of Parabhairava and there is no fear for him, at any cost. He is the beginning and the end of the universe.

This is the conclusion of this chapter. Twenty-eight *ślokas* of this [8th] discourse.

DVD 8 (1:15:07)

सर्वतत्त्वगतत्वेन विज्ञाते परमेश्वरे ।
अन्तर्बहिर्न सावस्था न यस्यां भासते विभुः ॥८॥

sarvatattvagatatvena vijñāte parameśvare /
antarbahirna sāvasthā na yasyāṁ bhāsate vibhuḥ //8//

|| Concluding *śloka* of 8th chapter ||

Parameśvara (Lord Śiva), if once known inside and outside, everywhere inside and outside–inside the state of Parabhairava and outside the state of Parabhairava–if once you realize this Parabhairava state inside the state of Parabhairava and outside the state of Parabhairava, *antar bahir na sāvasthā*, inside or outside, it does not matter to him. If it is inside, there is Parabhairava; *bahir*, if it is outside, there is also Parabhairava. That *avasthā* (state) is not ignored by him. [There is no state] in which he does not shine as Parabhairava. He shines as Parabhairava in Parabhairava state, and he shines as Parabhairava outside of Parabhairava state.

292 "All the impressions of your actions vanish by remembrance of the Lord. So remember the Lord everywhere, in each and every moment. This is the keynote of this chapter." Ibid.

And this is the wonder of wonders; this is the greatest wonder I have ever explained to myself. I am explaining it to myself, I don't explain it to others. I explain it to myself. You are my branches.[293]

Here ends this chapter.

Now there is the 9th chapter, then there is the 10th, and then there is 11th.

JOHN: So this inner and outer is the same as *unmīlana* and *nimīlana samādhi*?[294]

SWAMIJI: Both.

JOHN: Both. When you realize it in both, in *unmīlana* and *nimīlana*, that's . . . .

SWAMIJI: It has no difference; *unmīlana* and *nimīlana* are one. It may be *unmīlana* [or] it may be *nimīlana*, what then?[295]

JOHN: Isn't that the process of *krama mudrā* to make them one?

SWAMIJI: *Krama mudrā* [occurs] in the beginning; [it is] the sign of what will happen above. *Krama mudrā* is the sign of what will happen above. In the inferior point of world, that is *krama mudrā*. It is the signboard of that [*krama mudrā*], which will come in the end also–*krama mudrā*.[296]

JOHN: What does that mean? Explain that a little bit more, please.

SWAMIJI: [In the inferior point of world], *krama mudrā* is in its limited way. In the same way, you will find *krama mudrā* [as] broad *krama mudrā* there in the Parabhairava state. And it will be the same *krama mudrā*, but in excess.

JOHN: Excess?

SWAMIJI: Yes. [There it is] very great, very thick, very broad, and very strong.

---

293 In this paragraph, Swamiji is refering to himself. [*Editor's note*]

294 *Nimīlana samādhi* is introverted *samādhi*; *unmīlana samādhi* is extroverted *samādhi*. [*Editor's note*]

295 "*Unmīlana* and *nimīlana*, both in one is *jagadānanda. Jagadānanda* is . . . internal state of Śiva and external state of Śiva; outward and inward consciousness is *jagadānanda*." Swami Lakshmanjoo, *Tantrāloka* 13.186 (1980). See footnote 139 for an explanation of *jagadānanda,* and footnote 138 for a further explanation of *unmīlana* and *nimīlana samādhi.*

296 See footnote 140 for an explanation of *krama mudrā*.

Chapter 9

9th discourse.

DVD 9 (00:06)

श्रीभगवानुवाच

śrī bhagavān uvāca

इदं तु ते गुह्यतमं प्रवक्ष्याम्यनसूयवे ।
ज्ञानं विज्ञानसहितं यज्ज्ञात्वा मोक्ष्यसेऽशुभात् ॥ १ ॥

idaṁ tu te guhyatamaṁ pravakṣyāmyanasūyave /
jñānaṁ vijñānasahitaṁ yajjñātvā mokṣyase'śubhāt //1//

In these last chapters, I have explained to you the most secret points because you are *anasūyave*, you have got full faith in Me. I have explained to you *jñāna* and *vijñāna*, both. *Jñāna* means knowledge of Parabhairava and *vijñāna* means [knowledge] other than Parabhairava.[297] *Yad jñātvā*, by understanding these twofold knowledges, *aśubhāt mokṣyase*, you will be relieved from bad happenings.

DVD 9 (01:26)

राजविद्या राजगुह्यं पवित्रमिदमुत्तमम् ।
प्रत्यक्षावगमं धर्म्यं सुसुखं कर्तुमव्ययम् ॥ २ ॥

rājavidyā rājaguhyaṁ pavitramidamuttamam /
pratyakṣāvagamaṁ dharmyaṁ susukhaṁ kartumavyayam //2//

This is *rājavidyā* (royal knowledge). This is that kind of

297 *Jñāna* is undifferentiated internal knowledge and *vijñāna* is differentiated external knowledge. Paraphrase of *Bhagavad Gītā* (1978).

knowledge, which is . . . *rājavidyā* means it shines in all the understandings; all understandings are subsided by this supreme *vidyā* (knowledge) of Parabhairava. *Rājaguhyaṁ*, and this secret is stored in kṣatriyas (warriors), not in brahmins (priests). This secret is stored in kṣatriyas who where kings and monarchs, who had the power to divert people with force. With military rule, [they were] governing this whole universe. So this [secret] I have kept with them. This is not stored in brahmins because brahmins are cowards. If they find that they have not understood this knowledge, they fly, they hide themselves afterwards. They are just like cowards, these brahmins. Brahmins have been always cowards. If they see that they have not understood it properly, they hide themselves, they don't appear to the world.

DENISE: If they have not understood what properly? Parabhairava?

SWAMIJI: Yes. If Parabhairava is not understood by the public through their teachings, then they keep quiet and hide themselves from public. They don't want to see the public.

DENISE: Because they are ashamed?

SWAMIJI: Huh?

DENISE: Why do they hide themselves?

SWAMIJI: They have no power to divert their attention. Because they have no power, [people] will slap them, *bas*, they will go [hide]. These brahmins are vague, not courageous. The courageous [ones] are kṣatriyas.

So, I have kept this knowledge with kings and monarchs of the past, those who were absolutely elevated, and they had the power to elevate others through force, through their kingdom. If by force they wouldn't agree, [then their] troops would set them straight.

Ihaiva hyujyate–'adhyātmavidyā vidyānām' [comm.]. This is *adhyātma vidyā* (*adhyātma vidyā* is internal *vidyā*), it is the secret of all knowledges. *Rājaguhyaṁ*, and it is stored with kings.

Rājñām, what is that?

Janakādīnāmatrādhikāras teṣāṁ rahasyam. You know Janak, *rāja* (King) Janaka? Like [him], those kings had maintained this secret of *vidyā*. And this is *kṣatriyasulabhena vīrabhāvenāvikampatvāt, kartum–anuṣṭhātuṁ susukham*, it needs the power of kṣatriyas, not the power of brahmins, to work on this practice of *yoga* of Parabhairava.[298] You must have the capacity to put the greatest force [into your practice]. You must be mad after putting force. You must not be cowards like brahmins and wrap your body with *dusa* (shawl) and *paśmina* (fine Himalayan wool) and sit idle. This is not the treatment for attaining this. You have to sit with *katch* and naked with *kit*[299] and waist coat and *bas*! You have to find out the truth with vigor!

3rd [*śloka*].

DVD 9 (06:54)

अश्रद्दधानाः पुरुषा धर्मस्यास्य परन्तप ।
अप्राप्य मां निवर्तन्ते मृत्युसंसारवर्त्मानि ॥३॥

aśraddadhānāḥ puruṣā dharmasyāsya parantapa /
aprāpya māṁ nivartante mṛtyusaṁsāravartmāni //3//

Those who have not full faith, those who have not inserted full faith in this treatment of attaining the state of Parabhairava, they are not fit to achieve this [state].[300] The result is that they are caught by the constant wheel of repeated births and deaths, and they are no more available in this scene.

Nivartante means *punaḥpunarjāyante mriyante* . . .[301]

4th *śloka*.

298 "*Vīra bhavena*, because they have got *vīra bhāva*, heroic mind. Heroic mind is [possessed by] one who does not care for his life. He can kill and be killed and he doesn't mind. . . . Such people are fit to receive this kind of knowledge, who have no attachment for their bodies . . . they don't care for death, they don't care for life." *Bhagavad Gītā* (1978).

299 *Katch* means underwear, and *kit* means shorts. [*Editor's note*]

300 "What is meant by not having faith? Not having faith means [those] who have not digested this knowledge, who have not understood really this knowledge–that is not having faith. When you have no faith, you don't digest it. If you have faith, you will digest it." *Bhagavad Gītā* (1978).

301 "Those who have no faith, *nivartante*, they come again and again in this wretched field of universe, mortality. What is that? *Punaḥpunar jāyante mriyante ca*, they take repeatedly birth and repeatedly they die and die again and again." Ibid.

DVD 9 (08:00)

मया ततमिदं कृत्स्नं जगदव्यक्तमूर्तिना ।
मत्स्थानि सर्वभूतानि न चाहं तेष्ववस्थितः ॥४॥

mayā tatamidaṁ kṛtsnaṁ jagadavyaktamūrtinā /
matsthāni sarvabhūtāni na cāhaṁ teṣvavasthitaḥ //4//

Avyaktamūrtinā, I am *avyakta mūrti*, My formation is not revealed to anybody. I am formless but I work out everything. Although I am formless, I am not observed by anybody in this world.

JOHN: *Avyakta mūrti* means formless?

SWAMIJI: Huh?

JOHN: *Avyakta mūrti* means formless?

SWAMIJI: Formless, yes.

Avyakta mūrtinā, Parabhairava is not observed by anybody in this world, but Parabhairava works out and He does all of the treatment of the world; what is to be done and what is not to be done–He does it.[302] Although nobody knows who is doing it, and ignorant persons feel that, "we have done it! We have made this road clear. We have made this path. We have made this administration nicely, we have fixed this administration." People say that.

But the administrating power comes from Me, who is not observed by anybody. I am that power which is unknown to every-body, and that power works.

People say that, "we are doing this [work]." They think that, "we are maintaining this, we are working this out."

Actually, I, [Parabhairava], am working it out in disguise. I am not observed by anybody. The cause of this [activity] is Parabhairava. If He would be revealed to everybody, then there would be final destruction.[303]

302 "*Mayā tatamidaṁ kṛtsnaṁ jagad*, this whole universe is *mayā tatam*, is established by Me. You must understand this is My estab-lishment. . . . So this is a divine kingdom; divinely you should understand this world." Ibid.

303 "*Bhūtarūpabodhyātmakaprasiddhatadīyajaḍarūpapuraḥ sarīkār-eṇa tadavabhāse tadviparītabodha svabhāvatirodhānam* [comm.].

मया ततमिदं कृत्स्नं जगदव्यक्तमूर्तिना ।
मत्स्थानि सर्वभूतानि न चाहं तेष्ववस्थितः ॥४॥

mayā tatamidaṁ kṛtsnaṁ jagadavyaktamūrtinā /
matsthāni sarvabhūtāni na cāhaṁ teṣvavasthitaḥ //4//

I have created this *jagad* (this whole universe); I have created it. O Arjuna, I have created it, [I who am] not visible to anybody, who am not realized by anybody. I am just secretly creating this. *Matsthāni sarvabhūtāni*, whatever is created, all created beings are situated in My body. *Na cāhaṁ teṣvavasthitaḥ,* I am not situated in their bodies. They are only part and parcel of My body. I am not part and parcel of their body. All [beings] reside in My body, but I don't reside in their bodies.

DVD 9 (11:42)

न च मत्स्थानि भूतानि पश्य मे योगमैश्वरम् ।
भूतभृन्न च भूतस्थो ममात्मा भूतभावनः ॥५॥

na ca matsthāni bhūtāni paśya me yogamaiśvaram /
bhūtabhṛnna ca bhūtastho mamātmā bhūtabhāvanaḥ //5//

See, there is another secret, another secret that I will make you understand. Actually this whole universe is not situated in Me, because if it were actually situated in Me, then they would have become one with Myself. But they have not. They are situated in Me and they are still away from My being. They are

Because appearance, the state of being perceived is Mine. If I am not there, it won't be perceived, it will be vanished. As long as there is the question of perceiving . . . it means that it is residing in Me. Everything is residing in Me because it is perceived." Ibid.

"When He opens His eyes, it means He opens His nature. When He opens His nature, that is, in other words, the destruction of universe; destruction of differentiated universe. When He closes His eyes, that means when He ignores His nature, the universe appears [comes] into being." Swami Lakshmanjoo, *Spanda Saṁdoha* (1981).

situated in Me [but] they are away from Me. So they are not actually situated in Me.

Na ca matsthāni, this is My trick. I say they are situated in Me; in one way they are situated in Me and in another way they are not situated in Me. *Paśya me yogam aiśvaram*, this is My glamour of My trick. I only explain this kind of situation for those whom I have created, to explain that *mamātmā bhūta-bhāvanaḥ*, everyone who has been created, I have inserted in their brain the duty of remembering Me day and night. If they do not do that, they will repent. If they will try to do it, they will by and by rise. I am not responsible for their repentance when they do not actually do that.

I internally tell them [their duty].

Because there are two beings residing in each and every individual. One is the individual who is polished with limitations and another is unlimited being [who is existing] at the same time there. In each and every object, there are two beings: unlimited and limited. Because unlimited being is the life of what is and what is not. Unlimited being is life. As long as there is not unlimited being in each and every object, this whole universe will shatter to pieces, it will be no more existing in this world. So there are two opposite ghosts (Bhairava ghosts). One is the controller and another is controlled.

Because, *avidyāndhānāṁ tattva adṛṣṭeḥ* [comm. verse 5], [those] who have become blind by ignorance, *tattva adṛṣṭeḥ*, they cannot understand what is happening in [their] bodies. Although I am existing in their bodies, they don't [understand] that because they are blind.[304]

Mūḍha, those who are blind people, who are ignorant people, they have not the eyes to see what is going on in [their] bodies. [They don't know that unlimited being] who is behaving like a king in [their] bodies, as a powerful actor in [their] bodies. There is a powerful actor also, but secretly He is conducting this whole universe. And on the contrary, people say, "oh, I am feeble, I am weak, I have got headache, I have got toothache, I have got this ache, I have this ache." And they go to doctors and [say], "I have

304 "If they don't understand Me, they are not residing in Me. If they would have resided in Me, they would have understood Me. As long as . . . they don't understand Me, they don't realize Me. Without *yoga*, they don't understand Me." *Bhagavad Gītā* (1978).

created some trouble in my eye [laughing]. Now it is gone [laughing]."

DENISE: It's not really in his eye? It's in his consciousness?

SWAMIJI: Yes.

[They says such things like], "*kṛśo'ham*, I am very weak; *na vedmi*, this I don't understand; *bhūtale* [*idaṁ sthitaṁ*], this is lying here on the floor," etc. So, in this way, people think in their own limited environment.[305]

But actually, [in the] 6th and 7th *śloka*, He puts forth the reality of His being in each and every object of this world.

DVD 9 (17:26)

यथाकाशस्थितो नित्यं वायुः सर्वत्रगो महान् ।
तथा सर्वाणि भूतानि मत्स्थानीत्युपधारय ॥६॥

yathākāśasthito nityaṁ vāyuḥ sarvatrago mahān /
tathā sarvāṇi bhūtāni matsthānītyupadhāraya //6//

Just as the *vāyu* (*vāyu* means wind), the wind is actually not [blowing] at this time, it is not . . . for a kite to fly at this time, there is not enough wind, but actually wind is stored in ether.

How do you know that wind is stored in ether at this moment also when wind is not blowing?

Acha. I will give you its treatment. If you put a fan outside and go on [waving it back and forth], where does that wind come from? It is stored in *ākāśa*.

But when it does not get this treatment of *samyoga vibhāga*,[306] i.e., when both of these things do not [agitate each other], e.g., when you don't blow *ākāśa* like this, wind will [not] appear. If this wind had disappeared altogether in *ākāśa*, then how did it appear?

It appeared like this, by waving that fan.

In the same way, *tathā sarvāṇi bhūtāni matsthānī*, in the same way, all individuals are residing in Me, *iti upadhāraya*, this

305 "So they are limited, they are carried away to the limited state of perception. As long as there is establishment in the limited state of perception, one is carried away from God consciousness." Ibid.

306 *Samyoga vibhāga* means the agitation of two things, i.e., waving a fan, striking a drum, or clapping the hands. [*Editor's note*]

you should take for granted.[307]

DVD 9 (19:29)

एवं हि सर्वभावेषु चराम्यनभिलक्षितः ।
भूतप्रकृतिमास्थाय सहैव च विनैव च ॥७॥

evaṁ hi sarvabhāveṣu carāmyanabhilakṣitaḥ /
bhūtaprakṛtimāsthāya sahaiva ca vinaiva ca //7//

This was a very nice point.

Evaṁ hi sarvabhāveṣu, in the same way, *sarvabhāveṣu*, in each and every object of the world, *carāmi*, I pass on, I am appearing, *anabhilakṣitaḥ*, although nobody watches Me, nobody points Me out, nobody points out My existence in each and every action of this world. Whatever action of this world takes place, I am there, I am there, I am moving there, but I am not observed by any individual.

JONATHAN: Only someone in Parabhairava state.

SWAMIJI: No, I am existing . . . I am Parabhairava. He does not say that I am situated in Parabhairava state, I am Parabhairava also, but I pass on in each and every way of individuals, I pass on in them. *Anabhilakṣitaḥ,* they don't observe Me, they think that *they* are passing. *Bhūta prakṛtim-āsthāya sahaiva ca*, I am with them and without them. "With them" because they don't know Me; "with them" because I am with them but still they don't know Me. "Without them" because they cannot understand how He is with us. I am always with them, I am witnessing each and every [action] for instance, when you go for a walk, I hold your hands, I am there holding your hands. [Even] if you don't understand that somebody, a super-being, is holding

307 "Just as wind is existing in this great ether, in the same way, all souls are existing in Me without knowing that they are existing [in Me]. And when this wind will take its position, this wind in this ether will take its position, this is the same state where realized souls are concerned. That realizing way of God consciousness is the moment of [the rise of] that wind in ether. Otherwise, you feel there is no wind. . . . When there is blowing of wind, that is understanding; when there is blowing of *abhyāsa,* understanding through meditation, that is understanding the reality of God consciousness." *Bhagavad Gītā* (1978).

my hand [while] I am going on with my business, e.g., I am going to the optician for getting new specks (eye glasses), but I am there.

DENISE: With us.

SWAMIJI: Yes. In one way, I am there. In another way, I am not there, because I am not known by them.

JONATHAN: It is their limitation that makes You not be there.

SWAMIJI: Huh?

JONATHAN: It's our limitation that makes You not be there.

SWAMIJI: Yes.

JONATHAN: But You, You are with us.

SWAMIJI: Yes.

JOHN: Because You are our super-self.

SWAMIJI: Yes, that is what He says.

DVD 9 (22:37)

सर्वभूतानि कौन्तेय प्रकृतिं यान्ति मामिकाम् ।
कल्पक्षये पुनस्तानि कल्पादौ विसृजाम्यहम् ॥८॥

sarvabhūtāni kaunteya prakṛtiṁ yānti māmikām /
kalpakṣaye punastāni kalpādau visṛjāmyaham //8//

All individuals, Kaunteya, O Arjuna, *māmikām prakṛtiṁ yānti*, they enter in My *prakṛti* (My *māyā*), *kalpakṣaye*, at the time of *pralaya* (big *pralaya*). But *kalpādau*, at the time of the beginning of another *kalpa* (era), I create them again. They sleep for one night [of Brahmā] and then they wake up and are again caught by the repeated births and deaths in *saṁsāra*, and in this way, the whole universe goes on. It is never ending.

JONATHAN: So, do you see our actions, or other peoples actions as your own?

SWAMIJI: Huh?

JONATHAN: Do you see other peoples actions as your own?

SWAMIJI: Who?

JONATHAN: You.

SWAMIJI: Which?

JONATHAN: You said Parabhairava . . .

SWAMIJI: Yes, Parabhairava.

JONATHAN: . . . is in every action.
SWAMIJI: Yes.
JONATHAN: So do you see, I mean when you look at people, do you see they are an extension of yourself?
SWAMIJI: Don't say ["me"]; say, "does Parabhairava see?" Parabhairava sees. Parabhairava is aware. Parabhairava is aware of everything. Nothing is hidden there. All impressions are with Him. There is no need for Parabhairava to ask you, "did you do this bad act, did you do this good act?" There is nothing hidden.
DENISE: He knows.
SWAMIJI: No, it is all vivid to Him! There is no need to verify if one has done good deeds or bad deeds.
JOHN: He did them.
SWAMIJI: Who?
JOHN: Parabhairava.
SWAMIJI: [laughing]
DENISE: Didn't He do them?
SWAMIJI: You should not be so crooked to attribute your limitations to Parabhairava [laughing].
JOHN: No, but if there is only Parabhairava . . .
SWAMIJI: But you should understand Him properly, then you are Parabhairava. It is not by saying only. You must feel it, you must feel it, you must feel this position.

प्रकृतिं स्वामवष्टभ्य विसृजामि पुनः पुनः ।
भूतग्राममिमं कृत्स्नमवशं प्रकृतेर्वशात् ॥९॥

prakṛtiṁ svāmavaṣṭabhya visṛjāmi punaḥ punaḥ /
bhūtagrāmamimaṁ kṛtsnamavaśaṁ prakṛtervaśāt //9//
[not recited or translated][308]

308 "I am the creator of this whole universe. I create this whole universe [by] taking hold of My nature, *prakṛti*. I adjust [My] *prakṛti* in individuals and that [*parā*] *prakṛti* becomes *aparā prakṛti* there in individuality. But in real sense, that *aparā prakṛti* is one with that *parā prakṛti* of Mine. . . . This is why individuals have the understanding in their nature that, 'we can do anything in this world.'" *Bhagavad Gītā* (1978).

न च मां तानि कर्माणि निबध्नन्ति धनञ्जय ।
उदासीनवदासीनमसक्तं तेषु कर्मसु ॥१०॥

na ca māṁ tāni karmāṇi nibadhnanti dhanañjaya /
udāsīnavadāsīnamasaktaṁ teṣukarmasu //10//
[not recited or translated][309]

DVD 9 (25:12)

मयाध्यक्षेण प्रकृतिः सूयते सचराचरम् ।
हेतुनानेन कौन्तेय जगद्विपरिवर्तते ॥११॥

mayādhyakṣeṇa prakṛtiḥ sūyate sacarācaraṁ /
hetunānena kaunteya jagadviparivartate //11//

I am witnessing everything, O Arjuna, I am witnessing–I Parabhairava–I am witnessing everything. After I witness, I am present there. *Prakṛti*, this *māyā*, *sūyate sacarācaraṁ*, *māyā* creates *jaḍa* (insentient) and *ajaḍa* (sentient beings) in the whole universe; *viparivartate*, it goes on and goes on, entangled by creation, entangled by protection, destruction, in concealing and in revealing nature (*prakṛti*) in a limited way. It goes on like this.

Anena hetuna jagad viparivartate, this way, the movement of the whole universe, the whole ignorant surface of the universe takes place. *Viparivartate*, it goes on, sometimes there is death, sometimes there is life, sometimes there is pain, sometimes pleasure, sometimes a dog, sometimes a king, sometimes a demon, sometimes . . . it goes on like this. It has no end. But I am witnessing each and every act of this universe, but I am silent, I am not known to anybody.

309 "*Na ca māṁ tāni karmāṇi*, those actions of Mine do not bind Me. If I create them, if I destroy them, if I exclude [some people] from My God consciousness, these actions do not bind Me. Because *udāsīnava-dāsīnam*, I have not particular attachment for any individual nor I have detachment for any individual. *Asaktaṁ teṣu*, I am absolutely detached in all these actions. So these actions do not bind Me. And they bind you, they bind you because you have attachment." Ibid.

But I am always witnessing. You should not think that, "I have put off the lights and I am in a secret corner of my room, dark room, and I have put my own gas light on, I am doing business against God [and] He won't see me here." He is there also, witnessing.

DVD 9 (27:52)

अवजानन्ति मां मूढा मनुषीं तनुमास्थितम् ।
परं भावमजानन्तो ममाव्ययमनुत्तमम् ॥१२॥

avajānanti māṁ mūḍhā mānuṣīṁ tanumāsthitam /
paraṁ bhāvamajānanto mamāvyayamanuttamam //12//

Mūḍhā, those who are duffers, *avajānanti māṁ mūḍhā,* they don't care for Me. O Arjuna, people in My environment–Lord Kṛṣṇa speaks to Arjuna–that in My environment there is My father, My brother, My sister, My daughter, all of My relatives are around Me, but they don't understand actually who I am with them. They think that, "[Lord Kṛṣṇa] was created in our dynasty. He is our brother." Somebody says, "He is my cousin-brother." Somebody says, "He is my father." Somebody says . . . like that.

DENISE: He's our own.

SWAMIJI: He's our own. *Mānuṣīṁ tanumāsthitam*, they believe that He was born from Devakī Māta, Devakī, His mother. He is born from her womb, how can He be God? He is one of our own kith and kin. *Mānuṣīṁ tanumāsthitam*, they believe that, "He is also like us." *Paraṁ bhāvam ajānanto*, My supreme state of Bhairava they don't understand, that I am destroyer and . . .

JOHN: Protector and . . .

SWAMIJI: . . . creator and protector and destroyer of everything in this world–they don't understand that.

DVD 9 (29:57)

मोघाशा मोघकर्माणो मोघज्ञाना विचेतसः ।
राक्षसीं आसुरीं चैव प्रकृतिं मोहनीं श्रिताः ॥१३॥

moghāśā moghakarmāṇo moghajñānā vicetasaḥ /
rākṣasīṁ āsurīṁ caiva prakṛtiṁ mohanīṁ śritāḥ //13//

So, in this way, they understand that He is an ordinary person.

Duryodhana said, "He is a fraud."[310]

Who?

JOHN: Duryodhana said that Kṛṣṇa is . . .

SWAMIJI: "Kṛṣṇa is a fraud. You should not believe in His . . . He is treacherous, He misbehaves, He is *laphanga*, He is an adulterer. He goes, and wherever He finds a beautiful girl, He takes her into the privacy of His own room [laughing]."

Paraṁ bhāvamajānanto [verse 12], but they do not understand that I am really Parabhairava who is always omnipresent and without life and death.

DVD 9 (31:26)

महात्मानस्तु मां पार्थ दैवीं प्रकृतिमाश्रिताः ।
भजन्त्यनन्यमनसो ज्ञात्वा भूतादिमव्ययम् ॥१४॥

mahātmānastu māṁ pārtha daivīṁ prakṛtimāśritāḥ /
bhajantyananyamanaso jñātvā bhūtādimavyayam //14//

On the contrary, those who are real saints, O Arjuna, they [believe] that, "Lord Kṛṣṇa is born in our time and we are so fortunate to have Him. He is God himself, He will liberate all of us!" And in place of doing *samādhi*, they concentrate on His image. In their *pūja* rooms, they have put the image of Lord Kṛṣṇa before them, and they concentrate on Lord Kṛṣṇa's figure and they think that He will liberate us from repeated births and deaths.

And how do they behave before Me in their *pūja* rooms?

---

310 Duryodhana, a Kaurava, was the eldest son of king Dhṛtarāṣṭra, and was the chief instigator of the war. [*Editor's note*]

DVD 9 (32:38)

सततं कीर्तयन्तश्च यतन्तश्च यतव्रताः ।
नमस्यन्तश्च मां भक्तया नित्ययुक्ता उपासते ॥ १५ ॥

satatam kīrtayantaśca yatantaśca yatavratāḥ /
namasyantaśca mām bhaktyā nityayuktā upāsate //15//

Satatam kīrtayantaḥ, they always think of Me. O Arjuna, they always think of Me. They always bow their heads. As soon as they remember Me, they do, internally they do *praṇāms* [Swamiji bows with folded hands]. If they are walking on the road side, as soon as they remember My being, they bow their heads. *Namasyantaśca mām bhaktyā,* with devotion they do *praṇāms* every now and then. *Nityayuktā upāsate*, and they worship Me day and night.

The 15th *śloka* is over. Now the 16th.

DVD 9 (33:44)

ज्ञानयज्ञेन चाप्यन्ये यजन्तो मामुपासते ।
एकत्वेन पृथक्त्वेन बहुधा विश्वतोमुखम् ॥ १६ ॥

jñānayajñena cāpyanye yajanto māmupāsate /
ekatvena pṛthaktvena bahudhā viśvatomukham //16//

Just like Draupadī.[311] Draupadī was devoted to Lord Kṛṣṇa.

JOHN: Who?

DENISE: Draupadī.

SWAMIJI: Draupadī. Draupadī, that woman.

Jñānayajñena cāpyanye, some adore Me through knowledge. *Ekatvena pṛthaktvena,* some adore Me exclusively in their *pūja* rooms. Some adore Me [and] they say, "I think wherever we see

311 Draupadī was the wife of the five Pāṇḍava brothers. When the Kauravas tried to disrobe her, she prayed to Lord Kṛṣṇa to save her from such unspeakable shame. Lord Kṛṣṇa saved her by providing her with an endless amount of cloth so that she could never be disrobbed. [*Editor's note*]

people here in our country, they are just glorified by the presence of our God." They feel that, "our God has thrown light in each and every individual these days," in [Lord Kṛṣṇa's] time, in His period of life in Vṛndāvan. "All individuals are shining with His presence." They felt that.[312]

Now 17th, 18th, 19th, and 20th.[313]

DVD 9 (35:30)

अहं क्रतुरहं यज्ञः स्वधाहमहमौषधम् ।
मन्त्रोऽहमहमेवाज्यमहमग्निरहं हुतम् ॥१७॥
पिताहमस्य जगतो माता धाता पितामहः ।
वेद्यं पवित्रमोंकार ऋक्साम यजुरेव च ॥१८॥
गतिर्भर्ता प्रभुः साक्षी निवासः शरणं सुहृत् ।
प्रभवः प्रलयः स्थानं निधानं बीजमव्ययम् ॥१९॥
तपाम्यहमहं वर्षं निगृह्णाम्युत्सृजामि च ।
अमृतं चैव मृत्युश्च सदसच्चाहमर्जुन ॥२०॥

---

312 Abhinavagupta's commentary: "There is no difference in their worship because, *daivīm,* they have got nature of *satvikīm,* their nature is always filled with *sattvaguṇa.* With what substance [do] they worship Me? *Bāhyadravyādiyāgaiḥ*, some worship Me with outside materials and some worship me with internal creative offerings (internal creations). They create offerings through mind and offer it to Me. . . . *Śabda, sparśa, rūpa*, [*rasa*], and *gandha*, all these five senses, through these five senses they worship Me, by offering the nature of these five senses [to Me]. . . . The real worship is to offer whatever you have, whatever you collect for offerings, offer it to Lord Śiva direct. Don't offer it through other channels (Indra, Agni, et al.), because that offering . . . will have limited fruit. But [if you do offer to those gods], you must think Agni is another formation of Lord Śiva, Vāyu is another formation of Lord Śiva. This way you should worship." *Bhagavad Gītā* (1978).

313 *Nanu karma tāvatkārakkalāpavyāptabhedodreki kathama-bhinnaṁ bhagavat-padaṁ prāpayatīti*? [comm.]. [Abhinavagupta] puts question now. This action of the individual is *kārakakalāpa vyāpta bhedodreki,* it is always differentiated, actions are always differentiated, e.g., when you worship Māhā Gaṇapati, when you worship Sūrya, when you worship Nārāyaṇa. . . . How can it sentence you to Lord Śiva's [undifferentiated] point?" Ibid.

ahaṁ kraturahaṁ yajñah svadhāhamahamauṣadham /
mantro'hamahamevājyamahamagnirahaṁ hutam //17//
pitāhamasya jagato mātā dhātā pitāmahaḥ /
vedyaṁ pavitramoṁkāra ṛksāma yajureva ca //18//
gatirbhartā prabhuḥ sākṣī nivāsaḥ śaraṇaṁ suhṛt /
prabhavaḥ pralayaḥ sthānaṁ nidhānaṁ bījamavyayam //19
tapāmyahamahaṁ varṣaṁ nigṛhṇāmyutsṛjāmi ca /
amṛtaṁ caiva mṛtyuśca sadasaccāhamarjuna //20//

O Arjuna, I am *kratur* (external offering), I am *yajña*; I have created *yajña* and I am in *yajña*. Whatever *yajña* is conducted by people in My period here, I am that *yajña*. *Svadhāham*, I am nectar; *aham hutam*, whatever is offered in *yajña,* I am that; *mantro'ham,* I am *mantra*, whatever *mantra* is recited in *yajña* these days, in My period; *ahamevājyam*, I am that *ghee* [that is offered in *havan*]; *aham agnir*, I am fire; *ahaṁ hutam,* whatever is offered, the offering is also Myself.

Pitāhamasya jagatā, I am the father of this whole universe; *mātā*, I am mother; I am *dhātā*, I am creator; *pitāmahaḥ*, I am the forefather of this universe; *vedyaṁ pavitram oṁkāra,* I am *oṁkāra* (*oṁkāra* means all of the three *praṇavās*[314]: *vaidic praṇavās*, *śakti praṇavās*, and *śāṁbhava praṇavās*). I am all these three *oṁkāras*.

JOHN: What are those *oṁkāras*?

SWAMIJI: Huh?

JOHN: What are those *praṇavās*?

SWAMIJI: *Oṁ*, *Hrīṁ*, *Hūṁ*.[315]

I am *Ṛg Veda*, I am *Sāma Veda*, I am *Yajur Veda*, and *Atharva Veda*.

Gatir, I am the treatment of *gatiḥ*, who is diverted to unlimited *svarga* (heaven) where there is no end–*gatir*. *Bhartā*, I am the protector of this universe; *sthānaṁ*, I am the resting place of everybody; *nidhānaṁ*, I am the treasure of everybody; *bījam avyayam*, I am the seed of everything; *tampāmyaham*, in *tapasya*, in penance, I am penance; *ahaṁ varṣaṁ*, I am this rain, rainfall also; *nigṛhṇāmi*, I am [with]holding things from any-

314 Sacred or mystical syllable.

315 "*Hriṁ-kāra* is *śakti praṇava*, *oṁ-kāra* is *praṇava* of *Vedas*, and *huṁ-kāra* is *praṇava* of Shaivism. These are threefold *praṇavās*, *sarvavedeṣu*, in all *śāstras*." *Bhagavad Gītā*, 7.8.

body; *utsṛjāmi ca,* I am giving, bestowing things to somebody; *amṛtaṁ*, I am nectar; *mṛtyuśca*, I am death; I am *sat* (*sat* means truth) and I am false[hood]–everything is conducted by Me.[316]

DVD 9 (39:20)

त्रैविद्या मां सोमपाः पूतपापा
यज्ञैरिष्ट्वा स्वर्गतिं प्रार्थयन्ते ।
ते पुण्यमासाद्य सुरेन्द्रलोक-
मश्नन्ति दिव्यान्दिवि देवभोगान् ॥२१॥

traividyā māṁ somapāḥ pūtapāpā
yajñairiṣṭvā svargatiṁ prārthayante /
te puṇyamāsādya surendralokam-
aśnanti divyāndivi devabhogān //21//

316 "So, whatever deity is before you for worship, it will be My worship in the real sense. You are worshipping Me, you are not worshiping Agni. You are worshipping Me, you are not worshipping Sūrya. You are not worshipping Nārāyaṇa. . . . You are worshipping the real nature of God consciousness. *Ekasyaiva nirbhāgasya brahmatattvasya* [comm.], if the real nature of God consciousness is One, and it has created various branches of gods, but after creating various branches of gods, all those branches are [still] pointed to one point of God consciousness; they are only One.

"*Kriyāyāḥ sarvakārakātmasākṣātkāreṇāvasthāne bhagavatpada prāptiṁ pratya-vidūratvāt* [comm.]. Whatever action you do in this world, in real sense, *bhagavat pada prāptiṁ pratyavidūratvāt*, it is very near to the estabishment of God consciousness. You are established in God consciousness in whatever actions you do in this world, because the source of that is God consciousness. But only thinking makes it perfect. If you think, if you realize, that I am just worshiping God [in every act, then] you are not away from God consciousness. This way of thinking makes you perfect in this world.

"[Now, Abhinavagupta] puts another question: *Nanu evaṁ, yadi bāhyayāgādināpi brahmāptiḥ.* If it is so, that by outward external *havan* also you will become divine, you will achieve the state of divinity, then why don't they [who don't know this reality] achieve the state of divinity? Why only those persons [who know this reality] achieve this divinity? For that, Lord Kṛṣṇa puts the answer [in the following *śloka*]." *Bhagavad Gītā* (1978).

Traividyā, those who are masters in the three *Vedas* (*Ṛg*, *Yajur*, and *Sāma*[317]), they, *mām yajñairiṣṭvā*, they adore Me through, by means of adopting *havans*, and in that *Vedic* authority, they are authorized in the *Vedic* process. They take *soma rasa* (*soma rasa* means that *pān* which is left in *havan*). By that, *pūtapāpā*, all of their sins take their end altogether, for good. But in this position also they like to be sentenced to heaven, they don't want to get liberation from repeated births and deaths. They don't like it. They want to enjoy in the upper worlds, those enjoyments of the senses.

Te puṇyamāsādya surendra lokam, they, in the long run, after some period when they die, they reach that *deva loka*, and there, *aśnanti divyāndivi devabhogān*, they enjoy those enjoyments there in [heaven]. And it is *viśāla*, [it has] no end; it is for one thousand centuries, [even] more than that, they enjoy there.

DVD 9 (42:19)

ते तं भुक्त्वा स्वर्गलोकं विशालं
क्षीणे पुण्ये मर्त्यलोकं विशन्ति ।

te taṁ bhuktvā svargalokaṁ viśālaṁ
kṣīṇe puṇye martyalokaṁ viśanti /

[Their time in heaven] has got a big span [of time] and they enjoy, for that period, they enjoy whole-heartedly. *Kṣīṇe puṇye martyalokaṁ viśanti*, when that [time] is over, and then they again come for treatment of rebirths.

एवं त्रयीधर्ममनुप्रपन्ना
गतागतं कामकामा लभन्त ॥२२॥

evaṁ trayīdharmamanuprapannā

317 "*Atharva Veda* is not considered to be in that class of *Vedas* because *Atharva Veda* is just technical knowledge." *Bhagavad Gītā* (1978).

gatāgataṁ kāmakāmā labhanta[318] //22//

So, those who are given to the *Vedas*, three *Vedas*, although they get enjoyment for such a long period, even then they become again like ordinary people in the wheel of births and deaths.

But on the contrary, those who do not like this . . .

DVD 9 (43:38)

अनन्याश्चिन्तयन्तो मां ये जनाः पर्युपासते ।
तेषां नित्याभियुक्तानां योगक्षेमं वहाम्यहम् ॥२३॥

ananyāścintayanto māṁ ye janāḥ paryupāsate /
teṣāṁ nityābhiyuktānāṁ yogakṣemaṁ vahāṁyaham //23//

O Arjuna, on the contrary, those people who always focus their minds in My meditation (Parabhairava's meditation), *teṣāṁ nityābhi yuktānāṁ*, they are always one-pointedly established in My consciousness. For them, *yogakṣemaṁ vahāṁyaham*, I take care for their maintenance. They have not to worry about their maintenance, e.g., who will look after their house, who will look after their children, who will look after their gardens, etc. They are solely focused in meditation and I am looking after their gardens, I am looking after their household maintenance, I am looking after their children's maintenance (to go to school, etc.). I am doing all those jobs for them. They have to focus their minds in Me only. I do all of the other [things], e.g., their household maintaining job, etc. I take this burden on Me, on My shoulders because I have too much love for them. I have got too much love for them. I want them to be focused more and more in Me. Their other outside jobs, I take that responsibility on My shoulders.

DVD 9 (45:54)

येऽप्यन्यदेवताभक्ता यजन्ते श्रद्धयान्विताः ।
तेऽपि मामेव कौन्तेय यजन्त्यविधिपूर्वकम् ॥२४॥

318 Swamiji recites *labhante*, which appears in Abhinavagupta's commentary of this verse. [*Editor's note*]

ye'pyanyadevatābhaktā yajante śraddhayānvitāḥ /
te'pi māmeva kaunteya yajantyavidhipūrvakam //24//
[not recited]

But on the contrary, those people who concentrate on other gods, although I bestow the fruit to them through those gods, other gods, but their devotion is with blots [i.e., imperfections], it is not quite clear devotion. They also worship Me but they worship Me in a crooked way, not directly. Direct worshipping [of Me] is not done by them.

In fact . . .

DVD 9 (46:52)

अहं हि सर्वयज्ञानां भोक्ता च प्रभुरेव च ।
नतु मामभिजानन्ति तत्त्वेनातश्चलन्ति ते ॥२५॥

ahaṁ hi sarvayajñānāṁ bhoktā ca prabhureva ca /
natu māmabhijānanti tattvenātaścalanti te //25//

In fact, I am, of all activities, I am the bestower of fruit. But those people who want other sources in between, e.g., Indra, *devatās*, and all other gods. They derive fruit from them, but that fruit also is produced by Me, but it is not in a direct way. They don't get fruit [from Me] in a direct way. So they are inferior. So they are tossed down in the field of repeated births and deaths. They don't get that glamour. If they would have only thought that fruit will come from God, from Bhairava, they would have been glamorous all of the time. But only this [indirect approach to Me] makes them degraded.

JONATHAN: Impure.

SWAMIJI: So Arjuna, you should do one thing:

DVD 9 (48:23)

यान्ति देवव्रता देवान्पितृन्यान्ति पितृव्रताः ।
भूतानि यान्ति भूतेज्या यान्ति मद्याजिनोऽपि माम् २६

yānti devavratā devānpitṝnyānti pitṛvratāḥ /
bhūtāni yānti bhūtejyā yānti madyājino'pi mām //26//
[not recited or translated][319]

पत्रं पुष्पं फलं तोयं यो मे भक्त्या प्रयच्छति ।
तदहं भक्त्युपहृतमश्नामि प्रयतात्मनः ॥२७॥

patraṁ puṣpaṁ phalaṁ toyaṁ yo me bhaktyā prayacchati /
tadahaṁ bhaktyupahṛtamaśnāmi prayatātmanaḥ //27//

If you give one leaf from the garden, you pluck out one leaf from the garden and give [it to] Me directly, offer [it to] Me, or a tumbler of water, *phalaṁ*, and some fruit, *puṣpaṁ*, flowers, one flower, if you offer one flower directly to Me,[320] with all of My might, I accept it and kiss it and take it and have it and possess it.

DVD 9 (49:20)

यत्करोषि यदश्नासि यज्जुहोषि ददासि यत् ।
यत्तपस्यसि कौन्तेय तत्कुरुष्व मदर्पणम् ॥२८॥
शुभाशुभफलैरेवं मोक्ष्यसे कर्मबन्धनैः ।
संन्यासयोगयुक्तात्मा विमुक्तो मामुपैष्यसि ॥२९॥

319 "*Deva vratā*, those devotees who are bent upon worshipping other gods, they go to them, they receive, they attain their position. They don't attain My position; they are deprived from attaining My position. *Pitṝūnyānti pitṛvratāḥ*, and those who worship those who are ancestors, dead ancestors, they go to them. *Bhūtāni yānti bhūtejyā*, and those who worship ghosts for conducting black magic on others (there is that world also in this universe) . . . they go in the kingdom of devils, they reach ultimately after death in the kingdom of devils. They become devil also. *Yānti madyājino'pi mām*, and those people who adore Me in real sense, they reach Me, they are united in Me in the end." *Bhagavad Gītā* (1978).

320 ". . . with great devotion and love." Ibid.

yatkaroṣi yadaśnāsi yajjuhoṣi dadāsi yat /
yattapasyasi kaunteya tatkuruṣva madarpaṇam //28//
śubhāśubhaphalairevaṁ mokṣyase karmabandhanaiḥ /
saṁnyāsayogayuktātmā vimukto māmupaiṣyasi //29//

So whatever you do, whatever you eat, whatever you offer, whenever you give alms to people, whenever you perform penance, *tat kuruṣva madarpaṇam*, offer it to Me. Whatever you do, offer it to Me.

Then this will be the nearest and [most] hopeful trick for you to possess. [By doing] that, you will be liberated for good.[321] And you will be called *saṁnyāsa yogi* [because] you have offered everything; all of your actions, you have offered to Me. And in the long run, you will be united in Me.

This is the 29th *śloka* ending.

Now it is the 30th [*śloka*].

DVD 9 (50:32)

समोऽहं सर्वभूतेषु न मे द्वेष्योऽस्ति न प्रियः ।
ये भजन्ति तु मां भक्त्या मयि ते तेषु चाप्यहम् ॥३०॥

samo'haṁ sarvabhūteṣu na me dveṣyo'sti na priyaḥ /
ye bhajanti tu māṁ bhaktyā mayi te teṣu cāpyaham //30//

I am the same to everybody. I have not prejudice for those who don't care for Me. I love them also, but I have pity . . . on them, I have pity because they love Me indirectly, they don't love Me directly. If they love *chapals* (sandals), if they love a lady, if they love a boy, they actually love Me because I am that boy, I am that lady, I am everywhere. But they don't love Me directly. This makes Me sad.

Ye bhajanti tu māṁ bhaktyā mayi te teṣu cāpyaham, those who devote and treat Me with great devotion, they are in Me and I am in them–there is no doubt [about] it. I am he and he is Me. We are one!

321 "This way, you'll get liberated from the bondages of all *karmas* (they may be good *karmas* or bad *karmas*); you'll get rid of that and become liberated." Ibid.

DVD 9 (52:12)

अपि चेत्सुदुराचारो भजते मामनन्यभाक् ।
साधुरेव स मन्तव्यः सम्यग्व्यवसितो हि सः ॥३१॥

api cetsudurācāro bhajate māmananyabhāk /
sādhureva sa mantavyaḥ samyagvyavasito hi saḥ //31//

And it is never [too] late; again I will remind you, it is never [too] late. You just start afresh and focus all of your might in Me. Don't focus on other things of the world.

Api cetsudurācāro, if he is an adulterer and a very badly behaved person, if at all he also diverts his attention towards Me and leaves that adultery behind and adulters for the sake of Me, and makes love for the sake of Me–he does not make love for the sake of that lady–he who makes love with that lady for My sake, how divine he is! He will become divine and I will embrace him wholeheartedly and he will be united in Me in the end.

JOHN: Isn't that the point of *tantric* practice when you do sexual practice, or eating meat, when you do all those acts, those forbidden acts, for the sake of God then they all become divine?

SWAMIJI: They all become divine. But you should not . . . you should think if it is quite . . . if you are adopting it correctly. If you have just [a little] leakage of some love for that . . .

JOHN: The act itself?

SWAMIJI: . . . that lady, or . . .

DENISE: For that person.

SWAMIJI: Finished!

JOHN: Or for the taste, or anything; for eating meat for the taste rather than for the . . .

SWAMIJI: It must be divine, divinely adopted. Whatever you do, adopt it divinely and then you are Mine, then you are always Mine. I will embrace you.

What happens to him who leaves behind all of this treatment [i.e., attachment] of other things and focuses everything in Me?

DVD 9 (54:25)

क्षिप्रं भवति धर्मात्मा शश्वच्छान्तिं निगच्छति ।
कौन्तेय प्रतिजानेऽहं न मद्भक्तः प्रणश्यति ॥३२॥

kṣipraṁ bhavati dharmātmā śaśvacchāntiṁ nigacchati /
kaunteya pratijāne'haṁ na madbhaktaḥ praṇaśyati //32//

No matter, he becomes *dharmātmā* at once.[322] His all status of life changes altogether. I do that change for him and he becomes a saintly person. *Śaśvat śāntiṁ nigacchati*, and he is focused [in Me] and he enters in that peace which is an un-ending peace of Parabhairava.

Kaunteya pratijāne'haṁ, I take oath before you, O Arjuna! *Na madbhaktaḥ praṇaśyati*, once you have focused your *bhakti* (devotion) in Me, you will never decay, you will never be ruined, you are always Mine.

The 33rd *śloka*.

DVD 9 (55:23)

मां हि पार्थ व्यपाश्रित्य
येऽपि स्युः पापयोनयः ।
स्त्रियो वैश्यासतथा शूद्धरा-
स्तेऽपि यान्ति परां गतिम् ॥३३

māṁ hi pārtha vyapāśritya
ye'pi syuḥ pāpayonayaḥ /
striyo vaiśyāstathā śūddhrā-
ste'pi yānti parāṁ gatim //33//

किं पुनर्ब्रामनाः पुण्या भक्ता राजर्षयस्तथा ।
अनित्यमसुखं लोकमिमं प्राप्य भजस्व माम् ॥३४

322 "No matter if a person is debauched or a sinner, when once he directs his mind towards Me with devotion he becomes *dharmātmā*, the embodiment of purity and virtue at once." *Bhagavad Gītā* (1978).

kiṁ punarbrāhmaṇāḥ puṇyā bhaktā rājarṣayastathā /
anityamasukhaṁ lokamimaṁ prāpya bhajasva mām //34//
[not recited or translated][323]

O Arjuna, [those] who take refuge in Me, those who are called *pāpayoni* . . .

Striyo means those who are duffers, who cannot understand the philosophy, who have not that understanding power. There are so many duffers in this world. I have created duffers who do not understand what is philosophy–that is *pāpayoni*. *Pāpayoni* means they are the embodiment of sins and they have become duffers. They cannot understand . . . if you call them God, they say, "what is God?" [laughs] "I don't know what is God."

. . . and those people also, if by My grace, if they take refuge in Me, blindly (because they don't know Me), if they take blindly refuge in Me, they also come to Me in the end. I embrace them.

[If you feel], "there must be some great Being watching us," and when you focus your mind on that nothing, which is not clear to you–I mean duffer–he becomes also saint.

This is the greatness of Parabhairava!

Secretly and unknowingly, [one] who comes to My rescue [i.e. takes refuge in Me], he also becomes divine. I am so great, I cannot understand My . . . I cannot define My greatness, how great I am. I am great to those also who blindly think of Me, not knowing who I am.

So you should do one thing, O Arjuna:

DVD 9 (58:04)

मन्मना भव मद्भक्तो मद्याजी मां नमस्कुरु ।
मामेवैष्यसि युक्त्वैवमात्मानं मत्परायणः ॥ ३५ ॥

manmanā bhava madbhakto madyājī māṁ namaskuru /
māmevaiṣyasi yuktvaivamātmānaṁ matparāyaṇaḥ //35//

323 What to say when a devoted brahmin takes refuge in Me, what to speak of him? He will definitely come to Me. Paraphrase of *Bhagavad Gītā* (1978).

Manmanā bhava, keep your mind always within Me; *mad-bhakta*, be My devotee; *mat yāji*, be My worshipper; *māṁ namaskuru*, do *praṇām* (prostrate) to Me; *māmevaiṣyasi*, you will reach near Me when your [mind] is *matparāyaṇaḥ*, focused in My nature.[324]

This is the end of the chapter.

JOHN: What verse is that?

SWAMIJI: This verse is the 35th *śloka*. Now the conclusion of this [chapter].

DVD 9 (59:19)

अत्र संग्रहश्लोकः
अद्वैते ब्रह्मणि परा सर्वानुग्रहशालिनी ।
शक्तिर्विजृम्भते तेन यतनीयं तदाप्तये ॥९॥

advaite brahmaṇi parā sarvānugrahaśālinī /
śaktirvijṛmbhate tena yatanīyaṁ tadāptaye //9//

॥ Concluding *śloka* for the 9th chapter ॥

You should know, everybody should know, that the gracious, divine, that *śaktipāta*, is everywhere glittering for those who are deprived of that and for those who are fit for having that. But this *śaktipāta* is available to everybody! This *śaktipāta* is not locked [from] anybody. It is open. *Śaktipāta* is always at your disposal. *Śaktipāta* of Parabhairava is at your disposal, always. So you have to just divert your attention towards that and you will have it. It is nothing, you have not to *seek* for that. You have to divert your attention towards that and it is there, I have given [it to] you!

This is the conclusion of this chapter, 9th chapter.

Bas.

324 "When you put your mind bent upon finding Me." *Bhagavad Gītā* (1978).

Chapter 10

DVD 10 (00:01)

श्रीभगवानुवाच

śrī bhagavān uvāca

भूय एव महाबाहो श्रृणु मे परमं वचः ।
यत्तेऽहं प्रीयमाणाय वक्ष्यामि हितकाम्यया ॥१॥

bhūya eva mahābāho śr̥ṇu me paramaṁ vacaḥ /
yatte'haṁ prīyamāṇāya vakṣyāmi hitakāmyayā //1//

O Arjuna, I will again repeat the same substance, which I have already told you in these [previous] discourses.

Yatte'haṁ prīyamāṇāya, because I love you very much, so, for your *hitakāmyayā*, for your being . . .

DENISE: Upliftment.

SWAMIJI: . . . upliftment, I will again repeat the same substance to you.

DVD 10 (00:59)

न मे विदुः सुरगणाः प्रभवं न महर्षयः ।
अहमादिर्हि देवानां महर्षीणां च सर्वशः ॥२॥

na me viduḥ suragaṇāḥ prabhavaṁ na maharṣayaḥ /
ahamādirhi devānāṁ maharṣīṇāṁ ca sarvaśaḥ / /2//

Neither *devas* (gods) nor *r̥ṣis* (saints) can understand really, in the real sense, My being. Because *aham ādirhi devānāṁ*, I am the source of all *devas* and I am the producer of all *r̥ṣis* and *munis*.

DVD 10 (01:43)

यो मामजमनादिं च वेत्ति लोकमहेश्वरम् ।
असंमूढः स मर्त्येषु सर्वपापैः प्रमुच्यते ॥३॥

yo māmajamanadiṁ ca vetti lokamaheśvaram /
asaṁmūḍhaḥ sa martyeṣu sarvapāpaiḥ pramucyate //3//

Anybody who understands Me, that I am *ajama*, that I am without birth, *anadiṁ*, I am endless, I am the lord of the whole universe, without any doubt, that person is freed from all of his sins. He will be deprived of all sins if he only understands Me.

DVD 10 (02:37)

बुद्धिर्ज्ञानमसंमोहः क्षमा सत्यं दमः शमः ।
सुखं दुःखं भवो भावो भयं चाभयमेव च ॥४॥
अहिंसा समता तुष्टिस्तपो दानं यशोऽयशः ।
भवन्ति भावा भूतानां मत्त एव पृथग्विधाः ॥५॥

buddhirjñānamasaṁmohaḥ kṣamā satyaṁ damaḥ śamaḥ /
sukhaṁ duḥkham bhavo bhāvo bhayaṁ cābhayameva ca //4
ahiṁsā samatā tuṣṭistapo dānaṁ yaśo'yaśaḥ /
bhavanti bhāvā bhūtānāṁ matta eva pṛthagvidhāḥ //5//

He explains it in the 3rd, 4th, and 5th *ślokas* together.

Buddhir jñānam asaṁmohaḥ. Bhuddhir (intellect), *jñānam* (knowledge), *asaṁmohaḥ* (awareness of God consciousness), *kṣamā* (to be compassionate to everybody), *satyaṁ* (be truthful), *damaḥ* (control your breath), *śamaḥ* (control your mind), and pleasure (*sukham*), pain (*duḥkham*), creation, position (being born and being established), *bhayaṁ* (threat) and [*abhaya*], absence of threat,[325] *bhavanti bhāvā bhūtānāṁ*, these are the

325 ". . . and *ahiṁsā* (non-violence), *samatā* (becoming same to everybody, same attitude for everybody), *tuṣṭi* (contentment in whatever you have), *tapa* (mode of doing penance), *dānaṁ* (giving alms), *yaśa* (fame), *ayaśaḥ* (defame)." *Bhagavad Gītā* (1978).

moods, which I have created in each and every object.[326] Sometimes they are with threat, sometimes they are without threat, sometimes they are peaceful, sometimes they are painful, sometimes they are well established, sometimes they are not established at all, i.e., flickering.

DVD 10 (04:40)

महर्षयः सप्त पूर्वे चत्वारो मनवस्तथा ।
मद्भावा मानसा जाता येषां लोक इमाः प्रजाः ॥६॥

maharṣayaḥ sapta pūrve catvāro manavastathā /
madbhāvā mānasā jātā yeṣāṁ loka imāḥ prajāḥ //6//

The ancient seven *ṛṣis* (*sapta ṛṣis*) . . .

You know those are the seven stars on the North side. When we locate *dhruva* (polar star), there are seven *ṛṣis* (four and three). Those are ancient *ṛṣis.*

. . . and four *manu prajāpati*,[327] and *madbhāvā mānasā jātā*, they are My creations, and they are created by My mind, they are not created by wombs.[328] From them, all of creation is produced.

DVD 10 (05:55)

एतां विभूतिं योगं च मम यो वेत्ति तत्त्वतः ।
सोऽविकम्पेन योगेन युज्यते नात्र संशयः ॥७॥

etāṁ vibhūtiṁ yogaṁ ca mama yo vetti tattvataḥ /
so'vikampena yogena yujyate nātra saṁśayaḥ //7//

This kind of . . . My *aiśvari* (glory), My Kingdom, and *yoga*, whoever understands [these] in the real sense, he, without any

326 The limited subject is also considered to be an object. [*Editor's note*]
327 "In the beginning of this creation of this universe, there were seven *mahāṛṣis* (seven saints) and four *manus,* four great kings: king for Satya Yuga, king for Treta Yuga, king for Dvāpara Yuga and king for Kali Yuga." *Bhagavad Gītā* (1978).
328 "They were not created through sex." Ibid.

doubt, he is united in *yoga* and union with My supreme state of Bhairava.[329]

JOHN: What number?

SWAMIJI: 7th *śloka*.

DVD 10 (06:43)

अयं सर्वस्य प्रभव इतः सर्वं प्रवर्तते ।
इति मत्वा भजन्ते मां बुधा भावसमन्विताः ॥८॥

ayaṁ sarvasya prabhava itaḥ sarvaṁ pravartate /
iti matvā bhajante māṁ budhā bhāvasamanvitāḥ //8//

I am the creator of everybody, *itaḥ sarvaṁ,* I am the producer of everybody.[330] This way, whoever knows Me, he is really a realized soul and he has got full faith in Me.

How [does] he act in this remaining period of [his] life?

DVD 10 (07:24)

मच्चित्ता मद्गतप्राणा बोधयन्तः परस्परम् ।
कथयन्तश्च मां नित्यं तुष्यन्ति रमयन्ति च ॥९॥

maccittā madgataprāṇā bodhayantaḥ parasparam /
kathayantaśca māṁ nityaṁ tuṣyanti ramayanti ca //9//

Mat cittā, they focus their minds towards Me; *madgataprāṇā,* their life is, their breath is in Me, situated in Me; *bodhayantaḥ parasparam,* they discuss and sing the glory of Me with each other, i.e., they are situated collectively and they discuss the glory of Parabhairava together; *kathay-antaśca māṁ nityaṁ,* and they are always explaining My history, everywhere; *tyuṣyanti*

329 "One who understands this is His *yoga*, this is His kingdom, he is united in the end in *yoga* of God consciousness. There may be black magic, there may be anything. It is His kingdom. Nobody has any power to interfere in His kingdom." Ibid.

330 "Lord Śiva is the creator of everything and this is created from Lord Śiva. He does not create it in differentiated way; He creates this universe in His own nature." Ibid.

ramayanti, and they are quite happy and they make others also happy; their presence makes others also happy.

Now the 10th and 11th [*ślokas*].

DVD 10 (08:39)

तेषां सततयुक्तानां भजतां प्रीतिपूर्वकम् ।
ददामि बुद्धियोगं तं येन मां प्रापयन्ति ते ॥१०॥
तेषामेवानुकम्पार्थमहमज्ञानजं तमः ।
नाशयाम्यात्मभावस्थो ज्ञानदीपेन भास्वता ॥११॥

teṣāṁ satatayuktānāṁ bhajatāṁ prītipūrvakam /
dadāmi buddhiyogaṁ taṁ yena māṁ prāpayanti te //10//
teṣāmevānukampārthamahamajñānajaṁ tamaḥ /
nāśayāmyātmabhāvastho jñānadīpena bhāsvatā //11//

Those who are *satatayuktānāṁ*, always present in Me, their wits are focused always in Me, I bestow to them, without any hesitation, that *buddhi yoga*, that *jñāna yoga*, by which they not only get freedom themselves, they make the whole universe freed from repeated births and deaths–they achieve *that* power. I don't leave them that way, I still [bestow] them [with] more force [of *jñāna yoga*].[331]

Teṣām evānu kampārtham, for them again, again and again, by My free will, *aham ajñānajaṁ tama,* whatever gap is there leaking–a gap of their position of Parabhairava and My position of Parabhairava–if there is the slightest gap existing, that gap also I remove so that they become one with Me. *Teṣām evānu kampārtham aham ajñānajaṁ tamaḥ nāśayāmyātma*, I destroy that leakage also. By [what]?

By the torch of Bhairava knowledge–this is a torch. I put that torch on and illuminate them.

Now Arjuna . . . as [Lord Kṛṣṇa] has explained His greatness to Arjuna, now Arjuna asks again. He has come to [his] senses now that actually Lord Kṛṣṇa is very great.

331 "*Prītipūrvakam*, I bestow to them, not by pressure of their devotion [to Me]. I give them with open heart that wisdom and that unification of God consciousness." Ibid.

[Arjuna]: "I was thinking He was my playmate, however, it was not that way."

DVD 10 (11:25)

अर्जुन उवाच

arjuna uvāca

परं ब्रह्म परं धाम पवित्रं परमं भवान् ।
पुरुषं शाश्वतं दिव्यमादिदेवमजं विभुम् ॥१२॥

paraṁ brahma paraṁ dhāma pavitraṁ paramaṁ bhavān /
puruṣaṁ śāśvataṁ divyamādidevamajaṁ vibhum //12//

O *paraṁ brahma,* O my Lord! *Paraṁ dhāma,* O supreme abode of universality! *Bhavān*, You are *pavitraṁ*, the purest element than the pure; *paramaṁ*, You are great; *śāśvataṁ puruṣaṁ*, You are that ancient being; *divyam*, You are a divine being; *ādidevam*, You are the source of all *devas*; *ajaṁ*, You are without birth and without death; *vibhum*, You are all-pervading.

DVD 10 (12:27)

आहुस्त्वामृषयः सर्वे देवर्षिर्नारदस्तथा ।
असितो देवलो व्यासः स्वयं चैव ब्रवीषि माम् ॥१३॥

āhustvāmṛṣayaḥ sarve devarṣirnāradastathā /
asito devalo vyāsaḥ svayaṁ caiva bravīṣi mām //13//

All *ṛṣis* sing Your glory always. Vyāsa also himself sings Your glory. *Devarṣi* Nārada, Nārada *muni* also sings Your glory. *Svayaṁ caiva bravīśi,* and You are Yourself singing Your own glory (*svayaṁ caiva bravīṣi mām*).

DVD 10 (13:09)

सर्वमेतदृतं मन्ये यन्मे वदसि केशव ।
नहि ते भगवन्व्यक्तिं विदुर्देवा महर्षयः ॥१४॥

sarvametadṛtaṁ manye yanme vadasi keśava /
nahi te bhagavanvyaktiṁ vidurdevā maharṣayaḥ //14//

I believe it is quite true. Whatever You have spoken to me with Your divine lips, that is true, that is one thousand percent true. *Nahi te bhagavan vyaktiṁ vidurdevā maharṣayaḥ*, Your rise, neither *devas* nor *ṛṣis*, nobody knows wherefrom You have appeared. You are so great, nobody knows Your rise. You are ancient.

DVD 10 (13:58)

स्वयमेवात्मनात्मानं वेत्थ त्वं पुरुषोत्तम ।
भूतभावन भूतेश देवदेव जगत्पते ॥१५॥

svayamevātmanātmānaṁ vettha tvaṁ puruṣottama /
bhūtabhāvana bhūteśa devadeva jagatpate //15//

O Puruṣottama, O great Being! O Parabhairava! You explain Your nature with Your own lips. *Bhūta bhāvana*, O Being who is adored by everybody (You are adored by everybody); *bhūteśa*, You are master of everybody; *devadeva*, You are Lord of Lords; *jagatpate*, You are the ruler of the whole one hundred and eighteen worlds.

DVD 10 (15:02)

वक्तुमर्हस्यशेषेण विभूतीरात्मनः शुभाः ।
याभिर्विभूतिभिर्लोकानिमांस्त्वं व्याप्य तिष्ठसि ॥१६॥

vaktumarhasyaśeṣeṇa vibhūtīrātmanaḥ śubhāḥ /
yābhirvibhūtibhirlokānimāṁstvaṁ vyāpya tiṣṭhasi //16//

I would like to know from Your lips what are Your glories, which are existing in this universe, which You have created. Where will I concentrate on Your glory? On which point I will concentrate on Your glory? I would like to know that.

DVD 10 (15:42)

कथं विद्यां महायोगिंस्त्वामहं परिचिन्तयन् ।
केषु केषु च भावेषु चिन्त्योऽसि भगवन्मया ॥ १७॥

kathaṁ vidyāṁ mahāyogiṁstvāṁahaṁ paricintayan /
keṣu keṣu ca bhāveṣu cintyo'si bhagavanmayā //17//

O Lord, *kathaṁ vidyāṁ mahā*, O great *yogi* (he calls Him great *yogi*), how can I concentrate on Your being? Which way I will concentrate on Your being? In which object, whatever object You have created in this world, where shall I concentrate on Your glory? Where in this outward world, where is Your glory existing? I want to concentrate on that glory in outside world also.

DVD 10 (16:43)

विस्तरेणात्मनो योगं विभूतिं च जनार्दन ।
भूयः कथय तृप्तिर्हि श्रृण्वतो नास्ति मेऽमृतम् ॥ १८॥

vistareṇātmano yogaṁ vibhūtiṁ ca janārdana /
bhūyaḥ kathaya tṛptirhi śṛṇvato nāsto me'mṛtam //18//

Please explain to me Your glory. *Bhūyaḥ kathaya*, You have already explained to me this glory but still I want to know again and again. I am not satisfied. I want to know again and again. I want to think of You and think of Your glory. Please explain where is Your glory to be concentrated on?

Now Śrī Bhagavān *uvāca*. Now Lord Kṛṣṇa explains to him His glory.

DVD 10 (17:43)

हन्त ते कथयिष्यामि विभूतीरात्मनः शुभाः ।
प्राधान्यतः कुरुश्रेष्ठ नास्त्यन्तो विस्तरस्य मे ॥ १९॥

hanta te kathayiṣyāmi vibhūtīrātmanaḥ śubhāḥ /
prādhānyataḥ kuruśreṣṭha nāstyanto vistarasya me //19//
[not recited]

I will relate to you [My glory]. *Kuruśreṣṭha*, you are great [amongst the] Kauravas and Pāṇḍavās; you are very great in the dynasty of your Kauravas and Pāṇḍavās. I will explain to you My glories, which are worth explaining, worth nominating. I will tell you My glory. There is no end of My glory. Actually there is no end of My glory [but] still I will tell you some predominant points of My glory. Because there is no end of [it] if I begin to explain to you My glory, there will be no end. If I explain to you for an unlimited period of time, [even then] the explanation of [My] glory will not end. It is so vast. My glory is inexpressible.

DVD 10 (19:04)

अहमात्मा गुडाकेश सर्वभूताशयस्थितः ।
अहमादिश्च मध्यं च भूतानामन्त एव च ॥२०॥

ahamātmā guḍākeśa sarvabhutāśayasthitaḥ /
ahamādiśca madhyaṁ ca bhūtānāmanta eva ca //20//

I am the soul, O Guḍākeśa, O Arjuna!

Guḍākeśa means Arjuna who has conquered sleep, who never slept. Arjuna never slept. He was always thinking of the Lord. He had control on his senses. He never slept.

O Arjuna, I am the soul, *sarvabhutāśayasthitaḥ*, situated in each and every heart of individuals. I am the beginning, I am the center, and I am the end, the last end of all living beings.

DVD 10 (20:15)

आदित्यानामहं विष्णुर्ज्योतिषां रविरंशुमान् ।
मरीचिर्मरुतामस्मि नक्षत्राणामहं शशी ॥२१॥

ādityānāmahaṁ viṣṇurjyotiṣāṁ raviraṁśumān /
marīcirmarutāmasmi nakṣatrāṇāmahaṁ śaśī //21//

In twelve suns, I am Viṣṇu Digambar,[332] I am Viṣṇu. In [twelve] suns, I am Nārāyaṇa. Nārāyaṇa is the predominant

332 Viṣṇu was the name of the cook in Nepal whom Swamiji playfully called "Viṣṇu Digambar." [*Editor's note*].

[deity] in the classes of sun. There are twelve suns, in twelve suns, the twelfth is Nārāyaṇa. I am Nārāyaṇa in suns. Although I am all suns, but in predominance I am Nārāyaṇa [amongst] suns (*ādityānāmahaṁ viṣṇur*).

Jyotiṣāṁ raviraṁśumān, those which are illuminating powers existing in this universe, i.e., the light giving, light producing powers, in those light producing powers, I am the sun who gives light. It is the brightness of light.

When the sun produces its light, where is the moon? The moon does not shine, stars do not shine, all are subsided. So in light producing powers, I am the sun.

Marīcir marutāmasmi nakṣatrāṇāmahaṁ śaśī. Marīciḥ, Marīciḥ *ṛṣi*. I am, in *maruta gaṇas*,[333] I am Marīciḥ *ṛṣi.* Marīciḥ was the topmost *ṛṣi* who produced that power in which all *vāyu* (wind), *jala* (water), *agni* (fire) could not survive, could not tolerate. He is Marīciḥ. Marīciḥ I am in all of those powers of these universal powers, which are controlling this whole universe. Where there is wind, where there is storm, where there is thunder, where there is . . . and these producing elements, in these producing elements, I am Marīciḥ.

Nakṣatrāṇāmahaṁ śaśī, in stars I am the moon because [amongst] the stars, the moon is also brilliant.

DVD 10 (23:16)

वेदानां सामवेदोऽहं देवानामस्मि वासवः ।
इन्द्रियाणां मनश्चास्मि भूतानामस्मि चेतना ॥२२॥

vedānāṁ sāmavedo'haṁ devānāmasmi vāsavaḥ /
indriyāṇāṁ manaścāsmi bhutānāmasmi cetanā //22//

Vedānāṁ sāmavedo'smi, in *Vedas,* I am *Sāma Veda.* [Among] *Ṛg Veda*, *Yajur Veda, Atharva Veda*, and *Sāma Veda*, I am *Sāma Veda* in all the four *Vedas. Sāma Veda* means song. Song diverts you, makes you enter into Parabhairava state.

It is well said in *Tantrāloka* in the third *āhnika* in the end,

333 "Eight gods deputed for producing powerful wind, i.e., storms." *Bhagavad Gītā* (1978).

by Abhinavagupta. When there is song, not song by mouth . . .

JOHN: By sitar, by string sitar.

SWAMIJI: . . . by string, string instrument, that string instrument will divert you and push you into Parabhairava state in no time. But there are some people–he has put a question in [his] commentary of *Tantrāloka*, i.e., Jayaratha–[he says], "but there are those [people] who hear this instrumental song and they don't realize God consciousness." Abhinavagupta says, "well, if they don't realize God consciousness, then they are duffers. They have no right to live in this world, they are duffers. *Teśaṁ hṛdaya*, they have no heart. They are heartless. They are just like footballs, without any understanding [laughs]."

Vedānāṁ sāmavedo'haṁ devānāmasmi vāsavaḥ. In *devas*, I am Indra. Indra is the topmost head of the *devas*. *Indriyāṇāṁ manaścāsmi*, in all organs, I am *mana*. Mind is the controller of all organs. If your eyes see somebody and if mind is not there, you won't see. Although you see . . . somebody tells you, "you were looking at him, did you see him?" You tell him in answer, "no, I have not seen him," because your mind must have been somewhere else. When there is not mind in organs, the organs do not function. So, [Lord Kṛṣṇa says], "in *indriyās* (in organs), I am mind." *Bhutānāmasmi cetanā*, in living beings, I am intellect, I am intellect.[334]

---

334 Swamiji translated *cetanā* as "intellect" in both the audio and video translations of the *Bhagavad Gītā*. *Cetanā* is generally translated as "consciousness," however, Kashmir Shaivism does make a distinction between two kinds of consciousness, which are conveyed by the terms *cetanā* and *caitanya*. [*Editor's note*]

In the *Śiva Sūtras*, for example, it is said: "The one and the only aspect of Lord Śiva is complete independence (*svātantrya*). *Anyā-saṁbhavinaḥ*, and that complete independence is found nowhere except in Lord Śiva, in the state of Lord Śiva. So, the complete independence, the state of complete independence is shown here with full effort. So, [he uses] *caitanyam*, the word *caitanyam*, not the word *cetanā*." Swami Lakshmanjoo, *Śiva Sūtra Vimarśinī*, 1.1, orig. audio recording (1975).

"That consciousness of *caitanya* is reflected in intellect." Swami Lakshmanjoo, *Tantrāloka* 9.195 (1977).

DVD 10 (26:50)

रुद्राणां शङ्करश्चास्मि वित्तेशो यक्षरक्षसाम् ।
वसूनां पावकश्चास्मि मेरुः शिखरिणामहम् ॥२३॥

rudrāṇāṁ śaṁkaraścāsmi vitteśo yakṣarakṣasām /
vasūnāṁ pāvakaścāsmi meruḥ śikhariṇāmaham //23//

In *rudras*, in eleven *rudras*, I am Śaṅkara, i.e., I am Mahādeva. In *rudras* (there are eleven *rudras*), in eleven *rudras*, Mahādeva is the topmost.

JOHN: What are these *rudras*?

SWAMIJI: *Ekādaśa rudras*, there are eleven *rudras*, eleven *rudras* in Śiva's category. There is Śiva . . . it is very [much] lower than that Parabhairava state. There are some . . . there is one planet of *rudras* [where] there are eleven *rudras*. In eleven *rudras,* Śaṅkara is the topmost *rudra* (Śaṅkara is Mahādeva), but this Mahādeva is just . . . He plays the part of Mahādeva there in that small handful section of *rudras*.

This universe is very great, you cannot imagine how great it is.

Vitteśo yakṣarakṣasām, those *yakṣas* (*yakṣas* means those . . .)[335] [The supreme *yakṣa*] is in this northern side (the topmost northern side), he is residing there. His name is Kubera. He is the treasury officer [amongst the] *devas*. He has got this money, he is money keeper, treasurer.

In all *yakṣas* and *rākṣasas,* I am treasurer. Because he produces this pay to those *rākṣasas* and demons and everything, he gives it, he produces it. He is also a fraud, i.e., Kubera.

DENISE: Why?

SWAMIJI: Huh?

DENISE: Why is he a fraud?

SWAMIJI: Because he is treasury officer of all these *devas* who create fuss in this upper world. They get help from him.

Vasūnāṁ pāvakaścāsmi meruḥ śikhariṇām aham. In *vasū*

"*Cetanā* means *dṛk śaktiḥ puruṣaḥ. Cetanā* is the director inside, who directs [whether or not] you should do it or you should not do it." *Bhagavad Gītā* (1978).

335 "*Yakṣasas* and *rākṣasas* are the treasury holders of heaven." Ibid.

guṇa . . . there are eight *vasūs*. Those also are one collection of *devas*, eightfold *devas*, there are eight. In those *devas*, I am Agni *devatā*. Agni *devatā* is the topmost *devatā* in those [*vasūs*].

Meruḥ śikhariṇām aham, and in all mounts, I am Sumeruḥ *paravat*. Sumeruḥ *paravat* is that golden mount. I am [that] mount [amongst] all mounts in the Himalayan range.

DVD 10 (30:28)

परोधसां च मुख्यं मां विद्धि पार्थ बृहस्पतिम् ।
सेनान्यामप्यहं स्कन्दः सरसामस्मि सागरः ॥२४॥

parodhasāṁ ca mukhyaṁ māṁ viddhi pārtha bṛhaspatim /
senānyāmapyahaṁ skandaḥ sarasāmasmi sāgaraḥ //24//

In the priests of *devas,* I am Bṛhaspati. Bṛhaspati means just as we have Śāṁlal, our priest. In the same way, [amongst] priests, I am Bṛhaspati. Bṛhaspati means priest of all *devas*, not demons. I am *guru* of all *devas*, Bṛhaspati. Bṛhaspati is [the priest] who is the king of all Thursdays. Thursday is Bṛhaspati.

Senānyāmapyahaṁ skandaḥ sarasāmasmi sāgaraḥ, *senānyām, senānyām* in warriors I am Kumar; I am Kumar in warriors. Because Kumar is the only person who can conquer the whole world–Kumar. [He] is produced, he is a womb-born son [of Lord Śiva]–Kumar.

> *Kumar sambhava* [was born] when *devas* and *asuras* had become just like demons, and *asuras* [and *devas*] were fighting with each other in the upper worlds. Then they went to Brahmā, all *devas* went to Brahmā with this request that, "these demons are giving us trouble every now and then, how should we conquer them?" He said, "there is no other way [to conquer them except] only from the *vīrya* of Mahādeva. [A warrior] must be produced, a son."
>
> Because as Mahādeva has no son, he is without a child. He has son, he has a son, that adopted son. He had adopted a son and that is Gaṇeśa. He is his doorkeeper; Gaṇeśa is [Mahādeva's] doorkeeper and he is very furious. He is an

adopted son but he does not care for fighting. He knows that he is very powerful, but he has not those guts to destroy demons and protect *devas*.

So they implored Brahmā, and Brahmā told them, "no, we will all go to Nārāyaṇa and request [his assistance]." Nārāyaṇa also told the same thing that, "I have no guts. Let us go to Mahādeva and ask him that, 'your production [i.e., offspring] is needed to destroy all of the demons.'"

Pārvatī, [Mahādeva's wife], said, "but what do you think of me? Once I am in courses with Lord Śiva, nobody can tell me that [you must stop because] your courses are going on, going on, going on, for centuries and centuries. There is no end to that flow of that *vīrya*." And it was so [much] flow that . . .

JOHN: *Vīrya* is semen?

SWAMIJI: Yes.

. . . and all *devas* were terrified what will happen to this world [and exclaimed], "this will all get burnt; this whole universe, it will be burnt [by] the fire of this . . . "

JOHN: *Vīrya*.

SWAMIJI: Yes. And there was a big [mountain] thrown [i.e., produced] with that [*vīrya*] and it became that mercury. And this is the way how mercury [was created]; that is *pārada* (quicksilver, mercury). These are old ancient happenings from the past. You should not disbelieve it. It is believable.

And [Pārvatī] said, "you have disturbed my peace, so Kumar will be produced, Kumar will be produced with a handful of that [*vīrya*]. But what about that [the remaining] *vīrya*, who will digest it? You will get burnt by this."

Then Lord Śiva said, "no, it will be a mount, it will be just a big mount of silver, a silver mount, and it will be nominated as silver mount, Mahādeva mount." [That mount is] still being adored by people there, by *devas*, not in Kashmir!

DENISE: Oh, where?

SWAMIJI: In *devas*, up [in heaven].

Sarasāmasmi sāgaraḥ, I am the ocean in all small streams, small flows. Flows?

JOHN: Rivers.
SWAMIJI: Rivers.

DVD 10 (37:44)

महर्षीणां भृगुरहं गिरामप्येकमक्षरम् ।
यज्ञानां जपयज्ञोऽस्मि स्थावराणां हिमालयः ॥२५॥

maharṣīṇāṁ bhṛguraham girāmapyekamakṣaram /
yajñānāṁ japayajño'smi sthāvarāṇāṁ himālayaḥ //25//

In *maharṣīs*, I am Bhṛguḥ, Bhṛguḥ *ṛṣi*.
Sarasāmasmi sāgaraḥ [verse 24], in all small oceans, I am *sāgara*, *kṣira sāgara* (ocean of milk). *Maharṣīṇāṁ bhṛgur ahaṁ*, I am Bhṛguḥ in all *maharṣīs*. *Girāmapyekamakṣaram*, in sounds I am *ekamakṣaram*, i.e., *oṁkara*. *Yajñānāṁ japayajño'smi*, in all *havans*, I am *japa yajña*, which is internally done with . . .
DENISE: *Mālā* (prayer beads)?
SWAMIJI: . . . with *mālā*.[336] *Sthāvarāṇāṁ himālayaḥ*, in those big mountains, I am Himālayaḥ, Himachal.

DVD 10 (39:00)

अश्वत्थः सर्ववृक्षाणां देवर्षीणां च नारदः ।
गन्धर्वाणां चित्ररथः सिद्धानां कपिलो मुनिः ॥२६॥

aśvatthaḥ sarvavṛkṣāṇāṁ devarṣīṇāṁ ca nāradaḥ /
gandharvāṇāṁ citrarathaḥ siddhānāṁ kapilo muniḥ //26//

I am *aśvatthaḥ*, *aśvatthaḥ* in all trees. *Aśvatthaḥ* is a tree existing in heaven and that tree gives you, bestows you, anything you want. That is *pārijāta*. I have nominated it many times to you.
DENISE: Wish-fulfilling tree.
SWAMIJI: Yes, wish, yes.
Devarṣīṇāṁ ca nāradaḥ (you have to help me in explaining).

336 "*Japa yajña* means when you are reciting silently and doing that offering in fire; recite mantras silently and offer." *Bhagavad Gītā* (1978).

Devarṣīṇāṁ ca nāradaḥ, Nārada I am in *deva ṛṣi*; Nārada *ṛṣi* I am [amongst] *deva ṛṣīs*.

Gandharvāṇāṁ citrarathaḥ, in *gandharvās* I am Citrarathaḥ. *Gandharvās* are the most beautiful *devas*. And that Citrarathaḥ is the most beautiful person. And he is the topmost in producing those . . . not songs, but *rāgas, rāgas*.

You know *rāgas*?

Rāgas, e.g., *Bhairavī rāga*, *Malkosa rāga*, and [those other] *rāgas*. [One] who is the topmost in that *rāga*, producing that *rāga*, that is *gandharva*. And he is himself also very beautiful because of this *rāga*. *Rāga*, this *rāga* has made him beautiful.

Siddhānāṁ kapilo muniḥ, in those who are achieved *ṛṣīs*, in those achieved *ṛṣīs*, topmost *ṛṣīs*, I am Kapila *deva*. Kapila *deva* is [the one] who is the producer of the Sāṁkhya *śāstra*, [which explains] *puruṣa* and *prakṛti*.

DVD 10 (41:22)

उच्चैःश्रवसमश्वानां विद्धि माममृतोद्भवम् ।
ऐरावतं गजेन्द्राणां नराणां च नराधिपम् ॥२७॥

uccaiḥśravasamaśvānāṁ viddhi māmamṛtodbhavam /
airāvataṁ gajendrāṇāṁ narāṇāṁ ca narādhipam //27//

In *aśvās*, in those . . .

What are *aśvās* called?

JOHN: Ponies.

SWAMIJI: Ponies, ponies.

. . . in ponies, I am *uccaiḥśravas. Uccaiḥśravas* is a pony, that very big pony, white colored pony–*uccaiḥśravas.*

Viddhi māmamṛtodbhavam, [*uccaiḥśravas* have] come from *kṣira sāgara* (the milky ocean); they have been produced by *kṣira sāgara–uccaiḥśravas*, those ponies–when *kṣira sāgara* was churned.

Airāvataṁ gajendrāṇāṁ, and Airāvata, this elephant is *gajendrāṇāṁ.*[337] In *dikgaja*, in great elephants, I am Airāvata. Airā-

337 The elephant that carries Indra. "Airāvata is that Airāvata who was liberated by offering flowers on Lakṣmi when he was caught by that *makarmaccha* (alligator)." *Bhagavad Gītā* (1978).

vata has also been produced from *kṣira sāgara*.

Narāṇāṁ ca narādhipam, in individuals, I am king.

DVD 10 (42:49)

आयुधानामहं वज्रं धेनूनामस्मि कामधुक् ।
प्रजनश्चास्मि कन्दर्पः सर्पाणामस्मि वासुकिः ॥२८॥

āyudhānāmahaṁ vajraṁ dhenūnāmasmi kāmadhuk /
prajanaścāsmi kandarpaḥ sarpāṇāmasmi vāsukiḥ //28//

Āyudhānāmahaṁ vajraṁ, in weapons I am thunder, the thunder of Indra. There is no other parallel weapon to Indra's weapon, that thunder.

JOHN: Thunderbolt.

SWAMIJI: Thunderbolt.

Dhenūnāmasmi kāmadhuk, I am *kāmadhuk* in all cows, milk-producing cows. *Kāmadhuk* means [the cow] which is found in heavens. Whatever you think, it will give you. Which *kāmadhuk* was . . . you have been explained *kāmadhuk* of . . . [sage] Vasiṣṭha had this *kāmadhuk*.

Prajanaścāsmi kandarpaḥ, the one who is creating, the creating force, in these creators, I am Kandarpa, I am the Lord of love (*prajanaścāsmi kandarpaḥ*).[338] *Sarpāṇāmasmi vāsukiḥ*, in snakes, I am Vāsuki snake; Vāsuki snake, which is ornamented around the neck of Mahādeva.

DVD 10 (44:15)

अनन्तश्चास्मि नागानां वरुणो यादसामहम् ।
पितृणामर्यमा चास्मि यमः संयमतामहाम् ॥२९॥

anantaścāsmi nāgānāṁ varuṇo yādasāmaham /
pitṝṇāmaryamā cāsmi yamaḥ saṁyamatāmaham //29//

---

338 "Because it is said in Shaivism, creation does not come out from woman, creation does not come out from this man, creation does not come with their sexual act. Creation comes from that bliss that takes place there. That is *ānando'chalam*, the flowing out of that bliss, that is creative." Ibid.

Ananta, I am . . . in *nāgas*, I am *ananta nāga*.[339] Not this Anantanag in Srinagar.[340]

Varuṇo yādasāmaham. Varuṇa *devatā*. Varuṇa *devatā* means the *devatā* of water. In *yādas* (*yādas* means those who are the *devas* existing in water), amongst those *devas*, I am Varuṇa *deva*, Varuṇa, God Varuṇa.

Pitṝṇāmaryamā cāsmi yamaḥ saṁyamatāmaham. In *pitṝ*, *pitṝṇām*, in those who are dead, Aryamā, in those dead people,[341] I am Aryamā. Aryamā is the controller of all dead [people]. There is a dead circle [in heaven]; there is a class of all dead persons and Aryamā is taking care of all of those until they get another life. [Until then], they are on a waiting list. It is also one scale of heaven.

JOHN: Heaven. This is one kind of heaven?

SWAMIJI: One kind of heaven where all are on waiting list.

JOHN: Pending.

SWAMIJI: Pending. To get . . .

JOHN: So what, are they in a coma state while they are pending?

SWAMIJI: *Pitṝs,* those who are dead.

JOHN: So when they are pending . . .

SWAMIJI: Pending?

JOHN: . . . means?

SWAMIJI: For getting another birth.

JOHN: So during that time what, are they enjoying or they . . . what are they doing?

DENISE: Are they born?

SWAMIJI: No, they are not born, they are waiting. They are on a waiting list.

JONATHAN: On standby.

SWAMIJI: When time comes, they will be produced one by one.

JOHN: So they are not in that heaven where they enjoy?

SWAMIJI: They are also enjoying in their own way there. But they cannot rise; they cannot rise there. They are only enjoying in their own way because they want to rise. They want to rise

339 "There are classes of snakes: one is dry snakes, one is wet snakes. Wherever there is wet snake, it will produce a spring. *Ananta* [*nāga*] is this chief producer of spring, that snake." Ibid.

340 Anantanag is a place on the outskirts of Srinagar, Kashmir.

341 "Dead *supreme* souls." *Bhagavad Gītā* (1978).

so . . .

JOHN: They can't rise.

SWAMIJI: They can't rise.

DVD 10 (46:51)

प्रह्लादश्चास्मि दैत्यानां कालः कलयतामहम् ।
मृगाणां च मृगेन्द्रोऽहं वैनतेयश्च पक्षिणाम् ॥३०॥

prahlādaścāsmi daityānāṁ kālaḥ kalayatāmaham /
mṛgāṇāṁ ca mṛgendro'haṁ vainateyaśca pakṣiṇām //30//

In *daityās* (demons), I am Prahlāda.

You know Prahlāda of Hiraṇyakaśipu? Hiraṇyakaśipu was a *daityā*, he was a demon. [Lord Kṛṣṇa says], "in demons, I am Prahlāda, who was a devotee of Mine." He killed his father afterwards. Prahlāda killed him, killed his father. Prahlāda's [father] wanted him to be a demon but he didn't [want to be a demon]. In the demon dynasty, he was just an incarnate of Lord Bhairava, and his name was Prahlāda.

And Prahlāda I am [amongst] demons. In demons also I have created My being.

JOHN: Nothing is outside of the Lord.

SWAMIJI: *Kālaḥ kalayatāmaham*, Mahākāla, Lord of death. I am *kalayatām*, with calculators. Those calculators, in all calculators, topmost calculators, I am the Lord of death. He is the [topmost] calculator. He calculates [when] there is [time for] death, e.g., this point, this second, this moment, they will be dead, and it acts. Calculator, [Mahākāla is] the best calculator. [In comparison], these [mechanical] calculators do not mean any-thing.

Mṛgāṇāṁ ca mṛgendro'haṁ vainateyaśca pakṣiṇām. In *mṛgas*, those who are residing in dense forests, all *mṛgas*, all of those deers and all of those beings, in those, I am *mṛgendra*, I am a tiger. *Vainateyaśca pakṣiṇām*, I am Garuḍa in all *pakṣis*, in all . . .

JONATHAN: Birds.

SWAMIJI: Birds, big birds. I am Garuḍa.

DVD 10 (49:26)

पवनः पवतामस्मि रामः शस्त्रभृतामहम् ।
झषाणां मकरश्चास्मि स्रोतसामस्मि जाह्नवी ॥३१॥

pavanaḥ pavatāmasmi rāmaḥ śastrabhṛtāmaham /
jhaṣāṇāṁ makaraścāsmi strotasāmasmi jāhnavī //31//
[not recited]

[sound and video missing]

. . . in purest element. There is no other purest [element] purer than this *vāyu*. *Vāyu* is the purest element, i.e., breath. Breath is the purest element in the body also. And the purest element, through this purest element, we can find out this position of Parabhairava, when we go on following our breath, in and out. This is the purest element in the body.

Which?

DENISE: Breath.

SWAMIJI: Breath.

Rāmaḥ śastrabhṛtāmaham. Rāma in *śastrabhṛt*. I am Rāma in warriors.

Jhaṣāṇāṁ makaraścāsmi srotasāmasmi jāhnavī. Jhaṣāṇāṁ means those creatures which are found in the ocean. There are so many creatures [in the ocean]. In those, I am *makar*, *makaramaccha*, that big one . . .

DENISE: Alligator?

SWAMIJI: Yes, who destroys ships also.

JONATHAN: That's a whale?

SWAMIJI: Whale . . . ship.[342]

Strotasāmasmi jāhnavī in flows, in flows I am the purest element. That is, I am Gaṅga. I am Gaṅga [among] flowing [waters].

JOHN: What verse Sir?

SWAMIJI: 31st.

342 In mythology, Makara was half animal, half fish, but most commonly associated with a crocodile. [*Editor's note*]

DVD 10 (51:36)

सर्गाणामादिरन्तश्च मध्यं चैवाहमर्जुन ।
अध्यात्मविद्या विद्यानां वादः प्रवदतामहम् ॥३२॥

sargāṇāmādirantaśca madhyaṁ caivāhamarjuna /
adhyātmavidyā vidyānāṁ vādaḥ pravadatāmaham //32//

I am the beginning, center, and the end of all creation. *Adhyātma vidyā vidyānāṁ*, I am, in knowledge, I am the knowledge of Parabhairava, *adhyātma vidyā*, by which knowledge you understand and you realize your real position of your being. *Vādaḥ pravadatāmaham*, I am *vādaḥ,* discussion in those discussing communities. Where there is discussion, discussion I am. I am the discussion existing there. Because those who are discussing with each other, "this must be done, this must be done, this must be done," and they put cross-questions with each other, and [then] nothing is solved. And the solution which is solved afterwards, I am that discussion by which they come to a conclusion.[343]

DVD 10 (53:09)

अक्षाराणामकारोऽस्मि द्वन्द्वः सामासिकस्य च ।
अहमेवाक्षयः कालो धाताहं विश्वतोमुखः ॥३३॥

akṣarāṇāmakāro'smi dvandvaḥ sāmāsikasya ca /
ahamevākṣayaḥ kālo dhātāhaṁ viśvatomukhaḥ //33//

In *akṣarās*, [amongst] all [letters of the alphabet], I am "*a*", the first *akṣarā*. In *sāmāsa*, in combinations, I am *dvandva*. Where there are . . . *dvandvaḥ sāmāsa* is[344] . . . there are so many *sāmāsas*. In *sāmāsa*, I am *dvandvaḥ samāsa*. *Dvandvaḥ sāmāsa* is where, [for example], "*rāmasca kṛṣṇasca*" [conjugates into] "*rāma-kṛṣṇau.*" *Rām prayaśca ubhipradano dvandvaḥ*. *Dvandva*

343 "*Vādaḥ pravadatāmaham*, I am, in those who are given to logic, logical world, in those, I am *vādaḥ*, I am that logic itself. I am the embodiment of logic in logicians." *Bhagavad Gītā* (1978).

344 *Dvandha* is a grammatical term meaning a copulative compound. [*Editor's note*]

sāmāsa [signifies] predominance in both [terms].[345]

> For instance, John and Denise-*au*; we will put John and Denise [as a *dvandva sāmāsa* compound]. John is also predominant, and Denise is also predominant. It is *dvandva sāmāsa* where both [terms] are in predominance. It does not mean John is only topmost and Denise is inferior. Where both parties are on the same level, that is *dvandva* [*sāmāsa*].

I am, in combinations, I am *dvandva*. *Dvandvaḥ sāmāsikasya ca*, the main point of this discussion is where[ever] there is predominance, there you should think of Me. Otherwise, I am that [i.e., other things] also, everything. There is no end of My glory, which I will discuss with you. I'll make you understand what is the the wealth of everything–that I am there.

Ahamevākṣayaḥ kālo dhātāhaṁ viśvatomukhaḥ. I am the time which has no beginning and no end and no center. I am that time. I am timeless in time. I am, in other words, in time, I am timeless, I am beyond time.

DVD 10 (55:54)

मृत्युः सर्वहरश्चाहमुद्भवश्च भविष्यताम् ।
कीर्तिः श्रीर्वाक् च नारीणां स्मृतिर्मेधा धृतिः क्षमा ३४

mṛtyuḥ sarvaharaścāhamudbhavaśca bhaviṣyatām /
kīrtiḥ śrīrvāk ca nārīṇāṁ smṛtirmedhā dhṛtiḥ kṣamā //34//

I am death in smashing [i.e., destructive] way of conduct. When I am going to smash [someone or thing], there you will find Me as death. I won't scare anybody without death. At that time, I won't scare anybody without death. They will die. When I am going to smash, there you should find Me as death in predominance.[346]

---

345 "In compound words I am *dvandva*. Not *tatpuruṣa*, not *bahuvrīhi*." *Bhagavad Gītā* (1978).

346 "I am death winding up the whole universe. When I want to wind up the whole universe, you [should] consider Me as death (*mṛtyu*). *Udbhavaśca bhaviṣyatām*, I am the creation in being created. In created beings, I am creation." Ibid.

Kīrtiḥ śrīrvāk ca nārīṇāṁ smṛtirmedhā dhṛtiḥ kṣamā. In divine ladies, in ladies who are divine, I am behavior, good behavior, good conduct, and soft words, not harsh words.[347] I am, in those who are good-conducted ladies, in good-conducted ladies, I am those soft words and good behavior, which will make your husband rise in the flow of joy.

Not when, [for example], he is cooking food and you slap him [and say], "you don't know how to cook it!" Not this way. If you behave like, treat him as a real wife [should], then you are . . . that wife I am. I am that kind of wife. Lord Śiva says, "I am that wife." I am not that wife who comes and grabs her husband and eats him, and he also remains in another corner repenting, "what have I done?"

This way I explain it.

DVD 10 (58:30)

बृहत्साम तथा साम्नां गयत्री छन्दसामहम् ।
मासानां मार्गशीर्षोऽहमृतूनां कुसुमाकरः ॥३५॥

bṛhatsāma tathā sāmnāṁ gāyatrī chandasāmaham /
māsānāṁ mārgaśīrṣo'hamṛtūnāṁ kusumākaraḥ //35//

Bṛhatsāma tathā sāmnāṁ. In *sāmnāṁ*, in that . . . there is *rathantara* (*rathantara* means when you are singing *rāgas*). *Rāgas* means not by words; [*rāgas* are like], "*a, a, a, a, a, a, a, a, a . . . aah, aah*," like this. In these [*rāgas*], I am *bṛhatsāma*. *Bṛhatsāma* is where there is a pause, which will carry you to God consciousness at once. This kind of . . . [348]

Do you understand?

I am that in *sāmnāṁ*. In that, I am that *rathantara*. *Rathantara* is topmost [melody] where you'll just be carried into God consciousness at once without any question. You will be situated

347 "In female class, I am fame (good fame), I am *śrī* (I am *śrī* means wealth), *vāk*, I am speech, I am memory, I am tolerance. These things generally appear in woman class." Ibid.

348 "*Bṛhatsāma* is when you get, "*nadara-tum-dara-drīm-drīm-tanu-met-dhare-dhare*." [There is] no meaning from that, [just rhythm]. I am *bṛhatsāma* in all those steps of music." Ibid.

in Parabhairava state. This is *rathantara*. I am *bṛhatsāma tathā sāmnāṁ*.

Gāyatrī chandasāmaham, and *chanda* is *gāyatrī*. *Gāyatrī* is the topmost *chanda*. *Chanda* means the meters. *Gāyatrī* meter is the topmost meter, where you are directed to the state of Bhairava when *gāyatrī* is conducted.

Māsānāṁ mārgaśīrṣo'ham. In months, I am *mārga*. *Mārga* means *magar* . . . *magar* you know?

Mārga means when the whole [crop] production is ripe.[349]

JONATHAN: *Acha*, August, in autumn.

SWAMIJI: August, yes.

JONATHAN: August or autumn?

SWAMIJI: Autumn, autumn. I am autumn in all months. In [all] months, I am autumn.

Ṛitūnāṁ kusumākaraḥ, I am, in seasons, I am spring. In seasons I am spring, when there is my birthday. My birthday is in springtime.[350] I am the season [of] spring.

DVD 10 (1:02:05)

द्यूतं छलयतामस्मि तेजस्तेजस्विनामहम् ।
जयोऽस्मि व्यवसायोऽस्मि सत्त्वं सत्त्ववतामहम् ॥ ३६ ॥

dyūtaṁ chalayatāmasmi tejastejasvināmaham /
jayo'smi vyavasāyo'smi sattvaṁ sattvavatāmaham //36//

Dyūtaṁ chalayatāmasmi, [in] those who are tricky, I am the trick in them. Those who are . . . for instance, you are conducting with cards . . .

JONATHAN: Playing cards.

SWAMIJI: . . . playing cards, and you are [dealing to] those four people. *Chalayatām*, there is some trick, when you play some trick [and your opponents] lose, [they] lose the game; at that time [they] lose the game. That trick is [Me]. In tricks, I am trick in that game. It means I am tricky.

349 *Mārgaśīrṣa* means the months when flowers abound; generally the lunar month spanning November to December. [*Editor's note*]

350 Here Swamiji is referring to his own birthday, which falls in spring (May 9th).

JOHN: You win the game or lose the game?

SWAMIJI: Huh?

JOHN: When you play this trick you win the game or lose the game?

SWAMIJI: You win the game. Although you have got some kings and queens and two, ten . . . what are those in playing cards?

JOHN: Aces, etc.

SWAMIJI: Yes.

DVD 10 (1:03:46)

जयोऽस्मि व्यवसायोऽस्मि सत्त्वं सत्त्ववतामहम् ॥३६॥
वृष्णीनां वासुदेवोऽस्मि पाण्डवानां धनञ्जयः ।
मुनीनामप्यहं व्यासः कवीनामुशना कविः ॥३७॥

jayo'smi vyavasāyo'smi sattvaṁ sattvavatāmaham //36//
vṛṣṇīnāṁ vāsudevo'smi pāṇḍavānāṁ dhanañjayaḥ /
munīnāmapyahaṁ vyāsaḥ kavīnāmuśanā kaviḥ //37//

In Yadavas [i.e., Vṛṣṇī], I am Lord Kṛṣṇa. In Yadavas, I am Lord Kṛṣṇa, O Arjuna! In Yadavas, I am Lord Kṛṣṇa in Yadavas.[351]

Pāṇḍavānāṁ dhanañjayaḥ. In Pāṇḍavās, I am Arjuna. [Understand] that I am Arjuna in Pāṇḍavās. So I am you!

Munīnāmapyahaṁ vyāsaḥ. In *ṛṣi munīs*, I am Vyāsa who has conducted [i.e., composed] the *Mahābhārata*.

Kavīnāmuśanā kaviḥ. In *kavis* (*kavis* means who is the adviser of demons), He is Śukra, Śukra *devatā*.[352] Fridays.[353]

---

351 Among the Yadavas was a clan known as Vṛṣṇī from which Lord Kṛṣṇa came. [*Editor's note*].

352 "Śukra is the *guru* of demons. He was a realized soul." *Bhagavad Gītā* (1978).

353 Śukra is the presiding deity over Friday's. Friday is also called *Śukravār.* [*Editor's note*]

DVD 10 (1:05:00)

दण्डो दमयतामस्मि नीतिरस्मि जिगीषताम् ।
मौनं चैवास्मि गुह्यानां ज्ञानं ज्ञानवतामहम् ॥३८॥

daṇḍo damayatāmasmi nītirasmi jigīṣatām /
maunaṁ caivāsmi guhyānāṁ jñānaṁ jñānavatāmaham //38//

In *damayatām*, those who are *damayatām*, those who are behaving [with] proper treatment to those who are sinners. That is *daṇḍa*.[354] That *daṇḍa* punishment, I am. I am punishment in those. I am existing in punishment, which is given to those who deserve that punishment.

Nītirasmi jigīṣatām, [among] those who are supposed to win the victory, I am the trick of how to win the victory there. I behave [as] that trick, i.e., how to get victory in that section.

Maunaṁ caivāsmi guhyānāṁ. If you want to keep a secret, in all secrets I am *bas*, I don't talk. If I don't talk, the secret won't be out. I am *maun*. *Maun* means . . .

What is *maun*?

JOHN: Silence.

SWAMIJI: Silence.

I am silence in secrets. A secret will never remain secret until there is silence. [Even] if you beat him, whatever you do, he will remain secret [i.e., silent]. It won't be exposed.

DVD 10 (1:07:02)

यच्चापि सर्वभूतानां बीजं तदहमर्जुन ।
न तदस्ति विना यत्स्यान्मया भूतं चराचरम् ॥३९॥

yaccāpi sarvabhūtānāṁ bījaṁ tadahamarjuna /
na tadasti vināyatsyānmayā bhūtaṁ carācaram //39//

O Arjuna, whatever is the seed of everything existing in each and every object, I am that seed. There is nothing excluded, whatever is and whatever is not existing. Nothing is excluded

354 The word *daṇḍa* is generally translated as a stick, but it also means chastisement or imprisonment. [*Editor's note*]

[from] Me. I have not excluded anything; I have included everything.

DVD 10 (1:07:50)

नान्तोऽस्ति मम दिव्यानां विभूतीनां परन्तप ।
एष तूद्देशतः प्रोक्तो विभूतेर्विस्तरो मया ॥४०॥

nānto'sti mama divyānām vibhūtīnāṁ parantapa /
eṣa tūddeśataḥ prokto vibhūtervistaro mayā //40//

The glories of Mine are not . . . you cannot describe My glories. They are endless.

यद्यद्विभूतिमत्सत्त्वं श्रीमदूर्जितमेव वा ।
तत्तदेवावगच्छ त्वं मम तेजोंशसंभवम् ॥४१॥

yadyadvibhūttimatsattvaṁ śrīmadūrjitameva vā /
tattadevāvagaccha tvaṁ mama tejoṁśasaṁbhavam //41//
[not recited]

So, in a brief way, you should understand [that] whatever is too much glorified, whatever you see [to be] too much glorified in this world and hereafter, that is My being, that is Me. You should understand that is My existence there. I am the glory of all glories.[355]

DVD 10 (1:08:54)

अथवा बहुनैतेन किं ज्ञानेन तवार्जुन ।
विष्टभ्याहमिदं कृत्स्नमेकांशेन जगत्स्थितः ॥४२॥

athavā bahunaitena kiṁ jñānena tavārjuna /
viṣṭabhyāhamidaṁ kṛtsnamekāṁśena jagatsthitaḥ //42//

Athavā, in brief words . . . what can you understand if I go on

355 "You [should] think, whatever is fine, whatever is beautiful, whatever is delicious, whatever is fragrant, that is Mine. My being is all-round best. So whatever you find, whenever you find all-round best in anything, think that I am that thing." *Bhagavad Gītā* (1978).

speaking to you and explaining to you My greatness? In brief words, you should conclude that I am the glory of the whole universe and one ray of My glory is existing in one hundred and eighteen worlds. One ray. The other rays are kept, protected in My Being. It is only one ray, the glory of one ray, which is existing in one hundred and eighteen worlds. It is the glory of My one ray. The remaining store [of rays] is stored in My own nature.

So I am here, I am conducting this, not wholly; it is only one ray of Mine that is conducting this behavior here and . . .[356]

This is the end of [this chapter of the] *Bhagavad Gītā*; this is the end of the 10th chapter.

JOHN: What verse is that Sir?

SWAMIJI: This is 42nd verse.

In Vedānta also it is said, Abhinavagupta says, "in Vedānta [it is said]:"

pādo'sya viśvā bhūtāni tripādasyāmṛtaṁ divi |[357]

He is . . . actually, Parabhairava is just like a horse. He is a horse. Parabhairava is a horse.

Viresh, you also understand!

Parabhairava is a horse who has four legs. Horse has got four legs. Has he got? Four legs. *Pādo'sya viśvā bhūtāni*, Parabhairava is . . . and this one hundred and eighteen worlds, in one hundred and eighteen worlds, His one leg is conducting the whole kingdom; and three legs are reserved in Reserve Bank of India [laughs], there in His abode of consciousness above one hundred and eighteen worlds.

DVD 10 (1:12:14)

अत्र संग्रहश्लोकः

atra saṅgraha ślokaḥ

356 "It is only for beginners that He has spoken, "I am beautiful things, I am fragrant things, etc." It is only for beginners, just to begin with. Otherwise, in disgusted things, in wretched things also [He] is existing. But that lesson is for those who are advanced, advanced in that awareness." Ibid.

357 *Puruṣa Sukta*, vs. 3.

इच्छयामिन्द्रिये वापि यदेवायाति गोचरम् ।
हठाद्विलापयंस्तत्तत्प्रशान्तं ब्रह्म भावयेत् ॥१०॥

icchayāmindriye vāpi yadevāyāti gocaram /
haṭhādvilāpayaṁstattatpraśāntaṁ brahma bhāvayet //10//

|| Concluding *śloka* of 10th chapter ||

Whatever comes in your will, whatever comes in your organs, you dismantle all of this, you smash it altogether, and you see that *brahma* is appeased, the Parabhairava is appeased, existing in appeased condition. Appeased condition is [where] there is no agitation at all. Agitation cannot exist in His presence. In His presence, no agitation can exist. If it exists, it will be smashed; there and then, it will be smashed.

Chapter 11

Arjuna speaks to Lord Kṛṣṇa.

DVD 11 (00:08)

अर्जुन उवाच

arjuna uvāca

मदनुग्रहाय परमं गुह्यमध्यात्मसंज्ञितम् ।
यत्त्वयोक्तं वचस्तेन मोहोऽयं विगतो मम ॥१॥

madanugrahāya paramaṁ guhyamadhyātmasaṁjñitam /
yattvayoktaṁ vacastena moho'yaṁ vigato mama //1//

To elevate me, O Lord, You have placed before me the secret of secrets and You have revealed to me that secret, and by that secret, *moho'yaṁ vigato mama*, all ignorance is shattered to pieces from my mind.

DVD 11 (00:54)

भवाप्ययौ हि भूतानां श्रुतौ विस्तरतो मया ।
त्वत्तः कमलपत्राक्ष माहात्म्यमपि चाव्ययम् ॥२॥

bhavāpyayau hi bhūtānāṁ śrutau vistarato mayā /
tvattaḥ kamalapatrākṣa māhātmyamapi cāvyayam //2//

How this whole universe rises from Your nature and how this whole universe again melts in Your nature, that I have heard and that I have accepted. Your eyes are beautiful, Your eyes are shining just like lotuses, and Your greatness also You have revealed with Your own words to me.

DVD 11 (01:47)

एवमेतद्यथात्थ त्वमात्मानं परमेश्वरम् ।
द्रष्टुमिच्छाम्यहं रूपमैश्वरं पुरुषोत्तम ॥३॥

evametadyathāttha tvamātmānaṁ parameśvaram /
draṣṭumicchāmyahaṁ rūpamaiśvaraṁ puruṣottama //3//

This is quite correct what You have revealed to me. It is quite correct. I cannot deny this. And the greatness, which You have revealed to me of Your Self, that is quite correct. I would like to see that greatest form of Thee, if You [think that I] deserve it, that I am fit to observe that *rūpa* (form), the universal *rūpa* of Thee.

DVD 11 (02:46)

मन्यसे यदि तच्छक्यं मया द्रष्टुमिति प्रभो ।
योगीश्वर ततो मे त्वं दर्शयात्मानमव्ययम् ॥४॥

manyase yadi tacchakyaṁ mayā draṣṭumiti prabho /
yogīśvara tato me tvaṁ darśayātmānamavyayam //4//

I don't stress on Thee, if I am not fit to see Your nature (i.e., how You are universal). If You don't think that I am fit for that, then I won't stress on it.

श्रीभगवानुवाच
śrī bhagavān uvāca

Now Lord Kṛṣṇa speaks in return.

DVD 11 (03:26)

पश्य मे पार्थ रूपाणि शतशोऽथ सहस्रशः ।
नानाविधानि दिव्यानि नानावर्णाकृतीनि चा ॥५॥

paśya me pārtha rūpāṇi śataśo'tha sahasraśaḥ /
nānāvidhāni divyāni nānāvarṇākṛtīni ca //5//

O Arjuna, see in My body, *śataśo*, in one hundred ways, *sahasraśa*, in one thousand ways, see in My body, *nānāvidhāni divyāni nānāvarṇākṛtīni ca*, divine things and divine images you will see in My body. Go on seeing, and whatever you think to see, you can see those also. I am revealing it to you.

DVD 11 (04:22)

पश्यादित्यान्वसून् रुद्रानश्विनौ मरुतस्तथा ।
बहून्यदृष्टपूर्वाणि पश्याश्चर्याणि पाण्डव ॥ ६ ॥

paśyādityānvasūnrudrānaśvinau marutastathā /
bahūnyadṛṣṭapūrvāṇi paśyāścaryāṇi pāṇḍava //6//

All [twelve] suns you see in My body. *Vasūn*,[358] all *devas*, all gods, *rudrān*, all [eleven] *rudras*, *maruta*, all *marut gaṇas*,[359] all *devas*, and those [things] which you have not seen before, those also see in My body. And you will see everything delightful and everything amazing in My body.

DVD 11 (05:12)

इहैकस्थं जगत्कृत्स्नं पश्याद्य सचराचरम् ।
मम देहे गुडाकेश यच्चान्यद् द्रष्टुमिच्छसि ॥ ७ ॥

ihaikasthaṁ jagatkṛtsnaṁ paśyādya sacarācaram /
mama dehe guḍākeśa yaccānyad draṣṭumicchasi //7//

In this body of Mine, this whole universe you will see in this body of Mine. I am so great, you will see the whole universe from *kālāgnirudra* up to *śāntātīta kalā*.[360] This whole universe is residing in My body.

Mama dehe, in My body, in this big body you will see. And

---

358 "*Vasūs* are eight gods concerned with jewelry, gold, rubies, etc. They are the producer of these." *Bhagavad Gītā* (1978).

359 "*Marutas* are gods concerned with winds, wind producers." Ibid.

360 Kashmir Shaivism recognizes this universe to be made up of 118 worlds, of which *kālāgnirudra* is the lowest, and *śāntātīta kalā* is the highest. [*Editor's note*]

yaccānyad draṣṭum, whatever you think, you will see in that body also.

DVD 11 (06:01)

नतु मां शक्यसे द्रष्टुमनेनैव स्वचक्षुषा ।
दिव्यं ददामि ते चक्षुः पश्य मे रूपमैश्वरम् ॥८॥

natu māṁ śakyase draṣṭumanenaiva svacakṣuṣā /
divyaṁ dadāmi te cakṣuḥ paśya me rūpamaiśvaram //8//

You cannot tolerate to face this scene in My body because your eyes are not so developed and so divine. So I bestow divine eyes to you! O Arjuna, see whatever you think, see in My body, everything you will see. This is the greatness of Lord Kṛṣṇa, what He says . . .

Now Sañjaya speaks to Dhṛtarāṣṭra.

DVD 11 (06:51)

सञ्जय उवाच
sañjaya uvāca

एवमुक्त्वा ततो राजन् महायोगीश्वरो हरिः ।
दर्शयामास पार्थाय परमं रूपमैश्वरम् ॥९॥
अनेकवक्त्रनयनमनेकाद्भुतदर्शनम् ।
अनेकदिव्याभरणं दिव्यानेकोद्यतायुधम् ॥१०॥
दिव्यमाल्याम्बरधरं दिव्यगन्धानुलेपनम् ।
सर्वाश्चर्यमयं देवमनन्तं विश्वतोमुखम् ॥११॥
दिवि सूर्यसहस्रस्य भवेद्युगपदुत्थिता ।
यदि भाःसदृशी सा स्याद्भासस्तस्य महात्मनः ॥१२॥
तत्रैकस्थं जगत्कृत्स्नं प्रविभक्तमनेकधा ।
अपश्यद्देवदेवस्य शरीरे पाण्डवस्तदा ॥१३॥

evamuktvā tato rājan mahāyogīśvaro hariḥ /
darśayāmāsa pārthāya paramaṁ rūpamaiśvaram //9//
anekavaktranayanamanekādbhutadarśanam /
anekadivyābharaṇaṁ divyānekodyatāyudham //10//
divyamālāmbaradharaṁ divyagandhānulepanam /
sarvāścaryamayaṁ devamanantaṁ viśvatomukham //11//
divi sūryasahasrasya bhavedyugapadutthitā /
yadi bhāḥ sadṛśī sā syādbhāsastasya mahātmanaḥ //12//
tatraikasthaṁ jagatkṛtsnaṁ pravibhaktamanekadhā /
apaśyaddevadevasya śarīre pāṇḍavastadā //13//

[verses recited but not translated][361]

361 Verse 9: "[Sañjaya]: O Dhṛtarāṣṭra, when Lord Kṛṣṇa spoke to Arjuna this way, then He began to show him the supreme glorified nature of His God consciousness in His own body."

Verse 10: "*Aneka vaktra nayanam,* he found in [His] body many mouths, many faces, many eyes, *anekāt bhuta darśanam*, many various figures, various shapes, in His own body, *aneka divya bharaṇaṁ*, various divine dresses, *divya aneka udyatāyudham*, and various divine instruments, weapons."

Verse 11: "*Divya mālāmbara dharaṁ*, and divine garlands, *divya gandhā*, divine fragrance, divine scent, *sarvāścaryamayaṁ*, it was all amazing, whatever he saw in His body. *Anantaṁ*, it was numberless, it was without end what he saw in His body. It was, *viśvatomukham*, it was just universal body. It became universal body, everything he perceived in His body."

Verse 12: "Just imagine when in heaven, *sūrya sahasrasya bhaved yugapad utthitā*, when simultaneously, one thousand suns will rise in the field of heavens. You can imagine the same divinity and glamour of light was produced in that body. Just the glamour of one thousand suns. It was shining, His body was shining totally."

Verse 13: "Then Arjuna, at that moment, perceived the whole universe existing only in one body of Lord Kṛṣṇa. *Pravibhaktam-anekadhā*, he didn't perceive that world gathered. No! He perceived that the whole universe was residing in its own nature, in its own time, space . . . space also he found in that body. For instance, miles and miles, millions of miles in His body. At various points, he perceived that, those things, those divine things in His body."

Bhagavad Gītā (1978).

Tataḥ sa vismayāviṣṭo. He was amazed and drowned in amazement [of] what [he was] seeing.

"Do I really see this? What is this?"

He couldn't understand what he was seeing in the body of Lord Kṛṣṇa.

DVD 11 (08:28)

ततः स विस्मयाविष्टो हृष्टरोमा धनञ्जयः ।
प्रणम्य शिरसा देवं कृताञ्जलिरभाषत ॥१४॥

tataḥ sa vismayāviṣṭo hṛṣṭaromā dhanañjayaḥ /
praṇamya śirasā devaṁ kṛtāñjalirabhāṣata //14//

Then, you know that *romānch*?

Romānch means his, all his [pores in his] body, these . . .

JONATHAN: Pores.

SWAMIJI: . . . pores, they were standing, they were . . .

JOHN: His hair stood on end.

SWAMIJI: . . . and he bowed his head before Him and *abhāṣata. Abhāṣata* means he prayed and spoke to Lord Kṛṣṇa.

अर्जुन उवाच
पश्यामि देवांस्तव देव देहे
सर्वांस्तथा भूतविशेषसङ्घान् ।
ब्रह्माणमीशं कमलासनस्थ-
मृषींश्च सर्वानुरगांश्च दीप्तान् ॥१५॥
अनेकबाहूदरवक्त्रनेत्रं
पश्यामि त्वां सर्वतोऽनन्तरूपम् ।
नान्तं न मध्यं न पुनस्तवादिं
पश्यामि विश्वेश्वर विश्वरूप ॥१६॥
किरीटिनं गदिनं चक्रिणं च

तेजोराशिं सर्वतो दीप्तिमन्तम् ।
पश्यामि त्वां दुर्निरीक्ष्यं समन्ता-
दीप्तानलार्कद्युतिमप्रमेयम् ॥ १७ ॥
त्वमक्षरं परमं वेदितव्यं
त्वमस्य विश्वस्य परं निधानम् ।
त्वमव्ययः शाश्वतधर्मगोप्ता
सनातनस्त्वं पुरुषो मतो मे ॥ १८ ॥
अनादिमध्यान्तमनन्तवीर्य-
मनन्तबाहुं शशिसूर्यनेत्रम् ।
पश्यामि त्वां दीप्तहुताशवक्त्रं
स्वतेजसा विश्वमिदं तपन्तम् ॥ १९ ॥
द्यावापृथिव्योरिदमन्तरं हि
व्याप्तं त्वयैकेन दिशश्च सर्वाः ।
दृष्ट्वाद्भुतं रूपमिदं तवेदं-
ग्लोकत्रयं प्रव्यथितं महात्मन् ॥ २० ॥

arjuna ucāca.
paśyāmi devāṁstavadeva dehe /
sarvāṁstathā bhūtaviśeṣasaṅghān /
brahmāṇamīśaṁ kamalāsanastham-
ṛṣīṁśca sarvānuragāṁśca dīptān //15//
anekabāhūdaravaktranetraṁ
paśyāmi tvāṁ sarvato'nantarūpam /
nāntaṁ na madhyaṁ na punastavādiṁ
paśyāmi viśveśvara viśvarūpa //16//
kirīṭinaṁ gadinaṁ cakriṇaṁ ca
tejorāśiṁ sarvato dīptimantam /
paśyāmi tvāṁ durnirīkṣaṁ samantād-
dīptānalārkadyutimaprameyam //17//
tvamakṣaraṁ paramaṁ veditavyaṁ

tvamasya viśvasya paraṁ nidhānam /
tvamavyayaḥ sāttvatadharmagoptā
sanātanastvaṁ puruṣo mato me //18//
anādimadhyāntamanantavīrya-
manatabāhuṁ śaśisūryanetram /
paśyāmi tvāṁ dīptahutāśavaktraṁ
svatejasā viśvamidaṁ tapantam //19//
dyāvāpṛthivyoridamantaraṁ hi
vyāptaṁ tvayaikena diśaśca sarvāḥ /
dṛṣṭvādbhutaṁ rūpamidaṁ tavedṛg-
lokatrayaṁ pravyathitaṁ mahātman //20//

[verses not recited or translated][362]

---

362 Verse 15: "O Lord, I am seeing in Your body all Lords, all gods. *Sarvāṁ stathā bhūta viśeṣa*, all ghosts, all *bhūtas*, all *rakṣasas* I am perceiving in Your body. I am perceiving in Your body Brahmā, I am perceiving in Your body Lord Śiva, I am perceiving in Your body *kamalāsanastham*, Brahmā residing on the seat of lotus."

Verse 16: "I am perceiving in Your body [numberless] arms. I perceive in Your body thousands and thousands of bellies [i.e., stomachs]. I perceive in Your body *netraṁ*, thousands and thousands of eyes. *Paśyāmi tvāṁ sarvato'nantarūpam*, I perceive nothing except Your body everywhere. Wherever I put my sight, Your body is there. If I run away from my point where I am standing, I run away in Your body. . . . Where can I go? I have no space to get rid [of Your] body. I am caught by this body because it is *ananta*, it is [endless]. *Nāntaṁ na madhyaṁ*, there is no end, there is no center, there is no source. There is no beginning wherefrom [Your] body has begun to rise [or] where it ends. Everywhere I find Your body. You are exactly universal body."

Verse 17: "*Kirīṭinaṁ gadinaṁ cakriṇaṁ ca*. [Your innumerable faces] are with *kirīṭ* (*kirīṭs* are crowns), all Your faces are crowned. *Gadinaṁ*, there is *gada*, [maces are held by Your innumerable arms]. *Cakra*, *sudarśana cakra*, wherever I feel, I feel that *cakra* in Your hands. *Tejorāśiṁ*, and there is effulgent light flowing from Your body. *Tejorāśiṁ sarvato dīptimantam*, it is all-round shining body. *Paśyāmi tvām durnirīkṣaṁ*, I can't look at Your body because it is so delightful and so . . . it is burning, burning and delighting, delightful burning, delightful sensation of burning. [I am drawn to Your body] just as that [moth is drawn to a light. The moth] burns delightfully. Doesn't he burn delightfully? *Paśyāmi tvām durnirīkṣaṁ samantādṝptāna-lārkadyutim-aprameyam*, it is *aprameya,* you can't measure Your body. *Dīptāna-*

lārka, it is just like shining sun or shining fire, flame of fire."

Verse 18: "You are *akṣara*, You are unperishable. *Paramaṁ*, You are supreme. You are to be known, You are worth knowing. *Tvamasya viśvasya paraṁ*, You are the treasure of this whole universe. *Tvam-avyayaḥ*, You are unperishable. *Sāttvata dharma goptā*, You are protecting the supreme aspect of Yourself. *Sanātanastvaṁ puruṣo mata*, I have understood that You are the ancient *puruṣa*, ancient being. *Sāttvata dharma goptā* [comm.], what is that ancient aspect? *Satyaṁ kriyā jñānayor ubhayorapi bheda apratibhāsātmakaṁ*, where differentiatedness and undifferentiatedness does not shine. Differentiatedness is also divine. Undifferentiatedness is also divine. That is the real aspect of nature of Thy body. So that aspect is actually *prakāśat makaṁ tattvaṁ vidyate yeṣāṁ te sāttvatāḥ*. . . . Real light is that which pervades in light and darkness, both. That I have found in Your body. This is *grahaṇa* and *saṁnyās*, taking and abandoning. . . . For instance, you look at this [object, then] you look at another object. . . . Taking and discarding is *sṛṣṭi* and *saṁhāra*, creation and destruction. So the aspect of creation and destruction is found in Your body. There is the aspect of creative energy [and] there is the aspect of destructive energy also. That I found in Your body."

Verse 19: "Arjuna relates, explains, to Lord Kṛṣṇa what he experiences in His body. *Anādi madhyāntam ananta vīryam*, I see You as *anādi*, without the source, without the beginning. You are beginningless, You have not center, You have no end. *Ananta vīryam*, Your power is unending power. You have got unending power. *Anata bāhuṁ*, I see in You hundreds and thousands of arms. *Śaśi sūrya netram*, and Your eyes are just like *śaśi* and *sūrya* (*śaśi* means moon and [*sūrya* means] sun), shining. *Paśyāmi tvāṁ*, I experience, I see You, *dīta hutāśa vaktraṁ*, as Your mouths, Your various mouths are *dīpta hutāśa*, just like burning fire. *Svatejasā viśvamidaṁ tapantam*, by Your own light and flame, I feel that this whole universe is not peaceful . . . because it is about to burn, about to be crushed at once, it will get destroyed."

Verse 20: "*Dyāvāpṛthvyoridamantaraṁ hi*, now I observe that Your body is *vyāptaṁ tvayaikena diśaśca sarvāḥ*, right from the earth up to the sky, the whole space is occupied by Your body. I see only Your body, right from earth to *ākāśa*, that ether. *Diśaśca sarvāḥ*, [every direction is] occupied by Your body, with Your body. Everywhere I see Your body. This is *adbhutaṁ* (*adbhutaṁ* means wonderful form of Your body), everybody is seeing [Your body] and after seeing this wonderful form, *lokatrayaṁ pravyathitaṁ mahātman*, O great Lord, all the three worlds are terrified. They are restless [at the sight of You]."
Bhagavad Gītā (1978).

DVD 11 (09:20)

अमी हि त्वा सुरसङ्घा विशन्ति
केचिद्भीताः प्राञ्जलयो गृणन्ति ।
स्वस्तीति चोक्त्वैव महर्षिसङ्घाः

amī hi tvā surasaṅghā viśanti
kecidbhītāḥ prāñjalayo gṛṇanti / 21a
svastīti coktvaiva maharṣisaṅghāḥ

I see all *devas* run, rush and enter into Your body and they are finished, all *devas*. *Amī hi tvā surasaṅghā viśanti kecidbhītāḥ prāñjalayo gṛṇanti.* And some *devas* are *bhītāḥ*, they are afraid of this huge body. *Prāñjalayo gṛṇanti*, "O Lord, save us, save us, save us," they were shouting before that Lord.[363]

स्तुवन्ति त्वां स्तुतिभिः पुष्कलाभिः ॥२१॥

stuvanti tvāṁ stutibhiḥ puṣkalābhiḥ //21//
[not translated][364]

DVD 11 (10:25)

रुद्रादित्या वसवो ये च साध्या
विश्वेऽश्विनौ मरुतश्चोष्मपाश्च ।
गन्धर्वयक्षासुरसिद्धसङ्घा
वीक्षन्ते त्वां विस्मिताश्चैव सर्वे ॥२२॥
रूपं महत्ते बहुवक्त्रनेत्रं
महाबाहो बहुबाहूरुपादम् ।

363 "*Svastīti coktvaiva maharṣisaṅghāḥ*, and there are saints, many saints I see that they say, "let You be peaceful to all, let You be kind to all, don't destroy us all." Ibid.

364 "*Stuvanti tvāṁ stutibhiḥ puṣkalābhiḥ*, and they worship You wholeheartedly." Ibid.

बहूदरं बहुदंष्ट्राकरालं
दृष्ट्वालोकाः प्रव्यथितास्तथाहम् ॥२३॥

rudrādityā vasavo ye ca sādhyā
viśve'śvinau marutaścoṣmapāśca /
gandharvayakṣāsurasiddhasaṅghā
vīkṣante tvāṁ vismitāścaiva sarve //22//[365]

rūpaṁ mahatte bahuvaktranetraṁ
mahābāho bahubāhūrupādam /
bahūdaraṁ bahūdaṁṣṭrākarālaṁ
dṛṣṭvā lokāḥ pravyathitāstathāham //23//[366]

O Lord, everybody is afraid in seeing Your huge body; everybody is afraid and I am also afraid, I am squeezed with fear.

DVD 11 (11:30)

नभःस्पृशं दीप्तमनेकवर्णं
nabhaḥspṛśaṁ dīptamanekavarṇaṁ / 24a

This whole body of Yours, there is no *ākāśa*, i.e., *ākāśa* is also in Your body, ether is also in Your body, one hundred and eight-

365 "Eleven *rudras*, *ādityā* (*ādityā* means suns), *vasuva* (eight *vasus*), and *sādhyā* (*sādhyā* means those gods who are worshiped by worshipers), *viśve aśvinau*, and all *aśvini* and *kumar*, *marutaḥ*, all gods of wind, *oṣmapāśca* and those who are dead (*pitṛs*), *gandharva*, all *gandharvas* (*gandharvas* are gods of music, experts in music), *yakṣa* (*yakṣa* means those gods who are treasury officers), *sura siddha saṅghā*, and *siddhas* and gods, all those *vīkṣante tvāṁ vismitāścaiva sarve,* they just observe Your body, this tremendous, great body, just, they are all wonder struck (*vismitāścaiva sarve*)." Ibid.

366 "*Rūpaṁ mahatre bahu vaktra netraṁ*. I also perceive that Your formation of this body is very great because *bahu vaktra netraṁ*, I feel so many mouths, so many eyes in this, *mahābāho bahu bāhūr*, so many abdomens, *upādam*, so many feet, *bahūdaraṁ bahūdaṁ ṣtrākarālaṁ,* so many jaws, and *karālaṁ*, with terrible jaws. *Dṛṣṭvā lokāḥ*, and after seeing such a body of Yours, *lokāḥ pravyathitāḥ*, everybody is terrified. In the same way, I am also terrified. I don't know where to go, where to fly." Ibid.

een worlds are in Your body. I cannot find out where is the beginning and where is the end of Your body.

Nabhaḥspṛśaṁ dīptam anekavarṇaṁ, vyāttānanaṁ. And You are [with open mouths], "*aaaaaaaaaahhhhhh,*" like this. You are opening Your mouth, "*aaaaaaaaaahhhhhh.*"

DVD 11 (12:16)

नभःस्पृशं दीप्तमनेकवर्णं
व्यात्ताननं दीप्तविशालनेत्रम् ।
दृष्ट्वा हि त्वां प्रव्यथितान्तरात्मा
धृतिं न विन्दामि शमं च विष्णो ॥२४॥

nabhaḥspṛśaṁ dīptamanekavarṇaṁ
vyāttānanaṁ dīptaviśālanetram /
dṛṣṭvāhi tvāṁ pravyathitāntarātmā
dhṛtiṁ na vindāmi śamaṁ ca viṣṇo //24//

Those who have entered in *samādhi*, those also are scattered; their mind is scattered and they have come out from *samādhi* and they are stuck in fear [and wonder], "what has happened outside?"

Dhṛtiṁ na vindāmi śamaṁ, I cannot tolerate Your *rūpa* (form). O Lord Kṛṣṇa, I cannot tolerate it, I cannot bear [it]. What I am seeing?[367]

DVD 11 (13:10)

दंष्ट्राकरालानि च ते मुखानि

daṁṣṭrākarālāni ca te mukhāni / 25a

367 "I, after seeing Your body, which is *nabhāspṛśaṁ*, which is touching sky (so long, so great), *dīptam*, delightful, *anekavarṇaṁ*, with so many colors, *vyāttānanaṁ*, with open mouths, *dīpta viśāla netram*, and with long eyes, *dṛṣṭvāhi tvāṁ*, after observing You, *pravyathitāntarātma*, my internal consciousness is trembling. *Dhṛtiṁ na vindāmi*, I can't maintain courage. *Śamaṁ ca viṣṇo*, and neither there is peace in me. I am not peaceful." Ibid.

Your mouths are, "*aaaaaaaaahhhhhh*," like that, and You are eating everybody. You are eating Kauravas, Pāṇḍavās, whatever it is, all go inside Your body and [You] digest it.

दंष्ट्राकरालानि च ते मुखानि
दृष्ट्वैव कालानलसन्निभानि ।

daṁṣṭrākarālāni ca te mukhāni
dṛṣṭvaiva kālānalasannibhāni

[Your] mouths are just like *kalāgnirudras*, only fire. *Dhṛtiṁ na vindāmi* [verse 24], I cannot exist, I cannot stand, I cannot live, I cannot breathe, I cannot stop my breath. What have I to do?

दिशो न जाने न लभे च शर्म
diśo na jāne na labhe ca śarma /

I cannot find out where to escape, because wherever I am going to escape, You are there. If I am going to escape this way, You are there. *Śamaṁ ca viṣṇo* [verse 24], I am not in my wits.

O Lord, save me! What have You shown me! I was not expecting this kind of tremendous greatness.

प्रसीद देवेश जगन्निवास ॥२५॥
prasīda deveśa jagannivāsa //25//

Please, please take pity on me. Save me from this terrifying way of seeing [You].

DVD 11 (14:54)

अमी सर्वे धृतराष्ट्रस्य पुत्राः
सर्वे सहैवावनिपालसङ्घैः ।

amīsarve dhṛtarāṣṭrasya putrāḥ
sarve sahaivāvanipālasaṅghaiḥ

Amīsarve dhṛtarāṣṭrasya putrāḥ, these all Kauravas, *sarve sahaivā-vanipālasaṅghaiḥ*, all with their kings and . . .

भीष्मो द्रोणः सूतपुत्रस्तथासौ
सहास्मदीयैरपि योधमुख्यैः ॥२६॥

bhīṣmo droṇaḥ sūtaputrastathāsau
sahāsmadīyairapi yodhamukhyaiḥ //26//

. . . along with our class, our kith and kin–Arjuna says–along with Pāṇḍavās . . .

DVD 11 (15:36)

वक्त्राणि ते त्वरमाणा विशन्ति
दंष्ट्राकरालानि भयानकानि ।

vaktrāṇi te tvaramāṇā viśanti
daṁṣṭrākarālāni bhayānakāni /

. . . they [all] enter into Your open mouths, *tvaramāṇā,* with haste as if they have got a very [great] urge to go there. *Daṁṣṭrā-karālāni,* and these are with open teeth and open mouths, "*haaa-aaaaaaahhhhhh,*" and they are rushing inside.

केचिद्विलग्ना दशनान्तरेषु
सन्दृश्यन्ते चूर्णितैरुत्तमा . . .

kecidvilagnā daśanāntareṣu
sandṛśyante cūrṇitairuttamāṅgaiḥ //27//

Some Kauravas and Pāṇḍavās have entered into Your mouth and they are stuck in Your, those gums, and they are seeing that their heads are all cut and they are . . . those fall down. Pieces of their heads, they fall down from Your mouth on the ground where they . . . on the ground, which is [also] Your body.

DVD 11 (17:20)

नानारूपैः पुरुषैर्बाध्यमाना
  विशन्ति ते वक्त्रमचिन्त्यरूपम् ।
यौधिष्ठिरा धार्तराष्ट्राश्च योधाः
  शस्त्रैः कृत्ता विविधैः सर्व एव ॥२८॥

nānārūpaiḥ puruṣairbādhyamānā
  viśanti te vaktramacintyarūpam /
yaudhiṣṭhirā dhārtarāṣṭrāśca yodhāḥ
  śastraiḥ kṛttā vividhaiḥ sarva eva //28//

All those *yama kiṅkaras*,[368] those *yama kiṅkaras*, those who are *yama kiṅkaras*, they are . . . just after, I see that they are just [going] after the Kauravas and Pāṇḍavās, beating them [and telling them], "go on, go on, rush, into these mouths!" And they are pushing them into Your mouths.[369]

त्वत्तेजसा निहता नूनमेते
  तथाहीमे त्वच्छरीरे प्रविष्टाः ।

tvattejasā nihatā nūnamete
  tathāhīme tvaccharīre praviṣṭāḥ /
[not recited or translated][370]

368 *Yama kiṅkara's* are the punishers in hell. [*Editor's note*]

369 "And outside, in Your outside body, by Your arms also, everybody, *yaudhiṣṭā dhārtarāṣṭraśca*, and all those warriors are being slaughtered at once by Your arms, by Your weapons. I see them. Where shall I go? Where shall I hide now?" *Bhagavad Gītā* (1978).

370 "By Your great flame of Your splendor, *nihatā*, they are all dead, they are all destroyed, i.e., the Kauravas and Pāṇḍavās. *Tathāhīme tvaccharīre praviṣṭāḥ*, and they get entry in Your body in this way." Ibid.

DVD 11 (18:20)

यथा नदीनां बहवोऽम्बुवेगाः
 समुद्रमेवाभिमुखा व्रजन्ति ॥२९॥
तथा तवामी नरलोकवीरा
 विशन्ति वक्त्राण्यभितो ज्वलन्ति ।

yathā nadīnāṁ bahavo'mbuvegāḥ
samudramevābhimukhā vrajanti //29//
tathā tavāmī naralokavīrā
viśanti vaktrāṇyabhito jvalanti / 30a

Just as *nadīnāṁ bahavaḥ*, those various streams, with great force they are rushing and entering into the ocean, in the same way, everybody is rushing into Your body and they are calmed down, they are finished. There is no sign of their lives or anything, or existence.

He puts another example.

DVD 11 (29:18)

यथा प्रदीप्तं ज्वलनं पतङ्गा
 विशन्ति नाशाय समृद्धवेगाः ।
तथैव नाशाय विशन्ति लोका-
 स्तवापि वक्त्राणि समृद्धवेगाः ॥३०॥

yathā pradīptaṁ jvalanaṁ pataṅgā
viśanti nāśāya samṛddhavegāḥ /
tathaiva nāśāya viśanti lokā-
stavāpi vaktrāṇi samṛddhavegāḥ //30//

Just as *pradīptaṁ jvalanaṁ*, when there is flame, just as *pataṅgā* (*pataṅgā* means that [moth] who dies and burns in that flame) . . .

Who is that?

DENISE: Corpse?

SWAMIJI: Corpse? No, *pataṅgā, pataṅgā* means that . . .
JONATHAN: That moth.
SWAMIJI: . . . moth.
JONATHAN: That flies into that flame.
SWAMIJI: Yes.

. . . it rushes to that fire and he is finished. In the same way, everybody rushes into Your flame and they are, "*purrrrrrr*," finished.

DVD 11 (20:34)

लेलिह्यसे ग्रसमानः समन्ता-
ल्लोकान्समग्रान्वदनैर्ज्वलद्भिः ॥ ३१ ॥

lelihyase grasamānaḥ samantāt
lokānsamagrānvadanairjvaladbhiḥ //31//

Lelihyase grasamānaḥ samantāt, You just lick them like this, with furious mouths, *lokān samagrānvadanair jvaladbhiḥ*, by Your big mouths, [You swallow all these *lokās* (worlds)].

तेजोभिरापूर्य जगत्समग्रं
भासस्तवोग्राः प्रतपन्ति विष्णो ।

tejobhirāpūrya jagatsamagraṁ
bhāsastavogrāḥ paratapanti viṣṇo /
[not recited or translated][371]

DVD 11 (20:58)

आख्याहि मे को भवानुग्ररूपो
नमोऽस्तु ते देववर प्रसीद॥ ३२ ॥

371 "O Lord, *tejobhir āpūrya jagatsamagraṁ*, this whole universe is filled with the delight of Your body. *Stavogrāḥ bhāsa*, and Your shining, shining light, *pratapanti* (*paratapanti* [means] fires everything), burns everything." *Bhagavad Gītā* (1978).

ākhyāhi me ko bhavānugrarūpo
namo'stu te devavara prasīda / 32a

Ākhyāhi me ko bhavānugrarūpo, please tell me who You are.
Are you Lord Kṛṣṇa?
You are not Lord Kṛṣṇa!
You are something else, You are . . .
Please tell me who You are?
Am I dreaming?
Am I going to die?
O Lord Kṛṣṇa, tell me who You are in front of me?
Namo namaste, I bow to You one hundred times; one thousand times I bow to You, before You.

विज्ञातुमिच्छामि भवन्तमाद्यं
नहि प्रजानामि तव प्रवृत्तिम्

vijñātumicchāmi bhavantamādyaṁ
nahi prajānāmi tava pravṛttim //32//
[not recited]

Vijñātumicchāmi, I wanted to know what is Your greatness, but I cannot find out the beginning of Your greatness [nor] the end of Your greatness. There is neither beginning nor end.

What have I . . . am I dreaming or I am going to die?
Now Śrī Bhagavān says in the same mood.

DVD 11 (21:53)

श्रीभगवानुवाच

śrī bhagavān uvāca

कालोऽस्मि लोकक्षयकृत्प्रवृद्धो-
ल्लोकान्समाहर्तुमिह प्रवृत्तः ।

kālo'smi lokakṣayakṛtpravṛddhān-
llokānsamāhartumiha pravṛttaḥ /

I am the Lord of Death! O Arjuna, I am the Lord of death, I am not Kṛṣṇa. I am the Lord of death. I have come here to finish everybody. *Lokān samāhartum,* I have come here to finish each and every being.

ऋतेऽपि त्वा न भविष्यन्ति सर्वे
  येऽवस्थिताः प्रत्यनीकेषु योधाः ॥३३॥

ṛte'pi tvā nabhaviṣyanti sarve
  ye'vasthitāḥ pratyanīkeṣu yodhāḥ //33//
[not recited]

[Except for] thee, nobody will live. And your kith and kin whom you love, those will also live. Those who are your wellwishers and who were associated with you and were friendly [to you], they will also live. Others won't live. They will get finished.

DVD 11 (22:58)

तस्मात्त्वमुत्तिष्ठ यशो लभस्व
  जित्वा शत्रून्भुङ्क्ष्व राज्यं समृद्धम् ।

tasmāttvamuttiṣṭha yaśo labhasva
  jitvā śatrūnbhuṅkṣva rājyaṁ samṛddham /

So, stand up! *Jitvā śatrūn*, you [must] kill these Kauravas. *Jitvā śatrūn bhuṅkṣva rājyaṁ samṛddham*, you enjoy the kingdom of this whole universe.

DVD 11 (23:38)

मयैवैते निहताः पूर्वमेव
  निमित्तमात्रं भव सव्यसाचिन् ॥३४॥

mayaivaite nihatāḥ pūrvameva
  nimittamātraṁ bhava savyasācin //34//

Mayaivaite nihatāḥ pūrvameva, I have already killed them before. If you don't kill them, [still] they are killed.[372]

DVD 11 (23:50)

द्रोणं च भीष्मं च जयद्रथं च
कर्णं तथान्यानपि लोकवीरान् ।
मया हतांस्त्वं जहि मा व्यथिष्ठा
युध्यस्व जेतासि रणे सपत्नान् ॥३५॥

droṇaṁ ca bhīṣmaṁ ca jayadrathaṁ ca
karṇaṁ tathānyānapi lokavīrān /
mayā hatāṁstvaṁ jahi mā vyathiṣṭhā
yuddhyasva jetāsi raṇe sapatnān //35//

Droṇacari, Bhīṣma, Jayadratha, Karṇa, and all others, *mayā hatān,* I have already killed. You have only to just touch them and they will die–they are [already] dead. *Yuddhyasva*, you fight with them, *cetāsi raṇe sapatnān*, you will achieve the kingdom and you will become the king of kings.

सञ्जय उवाच

sañjaya uvāca

Now Sañjaya speaks to Dhṛtarāṣṭra:

DVD 11 (24:53)

एतच्छ्रुत्वा वचनं केशवस्य
कृताञ्जलिर्वेपमानः किरीटी ।
नमस्कृत्वा भूय एवाह कृष्णं
सगद्गदं भीतभीतः प्रणम्य ॥३६॥

372 ". . . as you saw how they were destroyed in My body. *Nimittamātraṁ*, just only you have to stand and fight with them and they'll get their end." *Bhagavad Gītā* (1978).

etacchrutvā vacanaṁ keśavasya
kṛtāñjalirvepamānaḥ kirīṭī /
namaskṛtvābhūya evāha kṛṣṇaṁ
sagadgadaṁ bhītabhītaḥ praṇamya //36//

This way, when [Arjuna] heard these words from Lord Kṛṣṇa in the formation of that *viśvarūpa* (universal form), *kṛtāñjalir*, he was standing before Him and he found himself also in the body of Lord Kṛṣṇa, as he was standing before Him with hands folded. *Vepamānaḥ,* his body was shaking with fear. *Namaskṛtvābhūya evāḥa kṛṣṇaṁ*, he prostrated before that great Being. *Sagad-gadaṁ*, with hiccups he tried to reveal his views regarding that great Master.

Arjuna speaks to Lord Kṛṣṇa:

DVD 11 (26:27)

अर्जुन उवाच

arjuna uvāca

स्थाने हृषीकेश तव प्रकीर्त्या
जगत्प्रहृष्यत्यनुरज्यते च

sthāne hṛṣīkeśa tava prakīrtyā
jagatprahṛṣyatyanurajyate ca /

Sthāne hṛṣīkeśa tava prakīrtyā, it is quite correct what You have spoken to me. O Lord, it is quite correct. I cannot deny [it] and neither is it incorrect. *Jagatprahṛṣyatyanurajyate*, this whole universe is full of joy and it seems to be peaceful.

रक्षांसि भीतानि दिशो द्रवन्ति
सर्वे नमस्यन्ति च सिद्धसङ्घाः ॥ ३७ ॥

rakṣāṁsi bhītāni diśo dravanti
sarve namasyanti ca siddhasaṅghāḥ //37//

All demons are running from one corner to another and finding no rescue and they just dash their heads and are finished. They finish themselves by fear. Not . . . You don't touch them. They finish their [own] bodies with fear and they are finished.

DVD 11 (27:28)

सर्वे नमस्यन्ति च सिद्धसङ्घाः ॥३७॥
कस्माच्चैते न नमेयुर्महात्मन्
गरीयसे ब्रह्मणोऽप्यादिकर्त्रे ।
अनन्त देवेश जगन्निवास
त्वमक्षरं सदसत्तत्परं यत् ॥३८॥

sarve namasyanti ca siddhasaṅghāḥ //37//
kasmāccaite na nameyurmahātman
garīyase brahmaṇo'pyādikartre /
ananta deveśa jagannivāsa
tvamakṣaraṁ sadasattatparaṁ yat //38//
[not recited in full]

Kasmāccaite na nameyurmahātman, who else cannot bow before You, O *mahātmā*, O great soul! There is no way out; everybody has to bow before You. *Garīyase*, You are greater than the greatest. *Brahmaṇo'pyādikartre*, You are the creator of Parabhairava, You have created Parabhairava.[373] I cannot under-stand who You are. *Ananta*, You are endless; *deveśa*, You are Lord of Lords; *jagat nivāsa*, You are omnipresent every-where. You are *akṣaram*, You are existing, You are not existent, and You are above that also.

DVD 11 (28:31)

त्वमादिदेवः पुरुषः पुराण-
स्त्वमस्य विश्वस्य परं निधानम् ।

373 "You are *brahmaṇo'pyādikartre*, You are the producer of all five great *kāraṇas*, i.e., Brahmā, Viṣṇu, Rudra, Īśvara, and Sadāśiva. These five *kāraṇas* are produced by You. Why should everybody not bow before You?" *Bhagavad Gītā* (1978).

वेत्तासि वेद्यं च परं च धाम
त्वयाततं विश्वमनन्तरूपम् ॥३९॥

tvamādi devaḥ puruṣaḥ purāṇas-
tvamasya viśvasya paraṁ nidhānam /
vettāsi vedyaṁ ca paraṁ ca dhāma
tvayātataṁ viśvamanantarūpam //39//

You are *ādi devaḥ*, You are the eternal Lord. You are [that] ancient Being. You are the treasure of this whole universe. You are the knower, You are the known, and You are the supreme seat of Bhairava. *Tvayātataṁ viśvamananta*, You have created this numberless and *ananta* (endless) universe.

DVD 11 (29:36)

वायुर्यमोऽग्निर्वरुणः शशाङ्कः
प्रजापतिस्त्वं प्रपितामहश्च ।
अनादिमानप्रतिमप्रभावः
सर्वेश्वरः सर्वमहाविभूते ॥४०॥

vāyuryamo'gnirvaruṇaḥ śaśāṅkaḥ
prajāpatistvaṁ prapitāmahaśca /
anādimānapratimaprabhāvaḥ
sarveśvaraḥ sarvamahāvibhūte //40//
[not recited in full]

Vāyuryamo'gnirvaruṇaḥ śaśāṅkaḥ, You are Vāyu, You are Yama, You are Agni, You are Varuṇa, You are the moon, You are Brahmā, you are the Lord of Brahmā. *Anādimānapratima prabhāvaḥ*, You are endless, You are beginningless. *Aprabhāvaḥ*, Your greatness is unparalleled, incomparable to anybody, it cannot be compared. *Sarveśvaraḥ*, You are Lord of all Lords, and You are the glory of everybody.

DVD 11 (30:26)

नमो नमस्तेऽस्तु सहस्रकृत्वः
पुनश्च भूयोऽपि नमो नमस्ते ।
नमः पुरस्तादथ पृष्ठतस्ते
नमोऽस्तु ते सर्वत एव सर्व ॥४१॥

namo namaste'stu sahasrakṛtvaḥ
punaśca bhūyo'pi namo namaste /
namaḥ purastādatha pṛṣṭhataste
namo'stu te sarvata eva sarva //41//
[not recited in full]

Namo namaste'stu sahasrakṛtvaḥ, I bow before You; one thousand times I bow before You. After that, *punaśca bhūyo'pi namo*, I bow before You again another one thousand times.

How can I end my bowing before You?

You are great! I have not understood You! *Namaḥ purastād*, I bow before You in front, I bow before You on the right side, I bow before You on the [left] side, You are . . . [I bow before you] on the backside also [because] You are existing [everywhere].

How can I bow before You? You are everywhere.

DVD 11 (31:13)

नहि त्वदन्यः कश्चिदपीह देव
लोकत्रये दृश्यतेऽचिन्त्यकर्मा ।
अनन्तवीर्योऽमितविक्रमस्त्वं
सर्वं समाप्नोषि ततोऽसि सर्वः ॥४२॥

nahi tvadanyaḥ kaścidapīha deva
lokatraye dṛśyate'cintyakarmā /
anantavīryo'mitavikramastvaṁ
sarvaṁ samāpnoṣi tato'si sarvaḥ //42//

O Lord, there is no parallel to You in this world.[374]

Ananta vīrya, Your power is endless, *amitavikrama*, and Your strength is not exhausted; Your strength never exhausts. *Sarvaṁ samāpnoṣi*, You have covered the topmost existence everywhere. So You are everything!

DVD 11 (32:25)

सखेति मत्वा प्रसभं यदुक्तो
हे कृष्ण हे यादव हे सखे च ।
अजानता महिमानं तवेमं
मया प्रमादात्प्रणयेन वापि ॥४३॥

sakheti matvā prasabhaṁ yadukto
he kṛṣṇa he yādava he sakhe ca /
ajānatā mahimānaṁ tavemaṁ
mayā pramādātpraṇayena vāpi //43//

In old age [and] in young age, I was thinking that You were my friend. And whatever I have [done], *prasabhaṁ yadukto*, I have slapped You. O my Lord, I have slapped You!

Whom I have slapped, I cannot imagine!

Why I slapped You? I was behaving [with] You just like an ordinary person. *Ajānatā mahimānaṁ tavemaṁ*, this greatness, I was not knowing that You are so great to me and You are doing the work of being my charioteer. And at the same time, I have done [this] great blunder to You.

DVD 11 (33:36)

यच्चावहासार्थमसत्कृतोऽसि
विहारशय्यासनभोजनेषु ।
एकोऽथवाप्यच्युत तत्समक्षं
तत्क्षामये त्वामहमप्रमेयम् ॥४४॥

374 "*Deva*, O Lord, there is nobody parallel to You in these worlds, in these three worlds, *dṛṣyate acintyakarmā*, who does this divine action as You do?" *Bhagavad Gītā* (1978).

yaccāvahāsārthamasatkṛto'si
vihāraśyyāsanabhojaneṣu /
eko'thavāpyacyuta tatsamakṣaṁ
tatkṣāmaye tvāmahamaprameyam //44//

By cutting jokes with You, I was cutting jokes with You.
O Lord, I was cutting jokes with You!
I ought not to have cut jokes with You. And I was giving You bad names in everybody's presence. What blunder I have created. I ask *kṣāma*. *Kṣāma* means, "please forgive me for all of these past actions [because] I didn't know that You are so great."

DVD 11 (34:38)

पितासि लोकस्य चराचरस्य
त्वमस्य विश्वस्य गुरुर्गरीयान् ।
न त्वत्समोऽस्त्यभ्यधिकः कुतोऽन्यो
लोकत्रयेऽप्यप्रतिमप्रभावः ॥४५॥

pitāsi lokasya carācarasya
tvamasya viśvasya gururgarīyān /
na tvatsamo'styabhyadhikaḥ kuto'nyo
lokatraye'pyapratimaprabhāvaḥ //45//
[not recited in full]

Pitāsi lokasya carācarasya, You are the Father of the whole universe. *Tvamasya viśvasya gururgarīyān*, You are adored, You are to be adored, worth adoration [from] everybody. *Na tvatsamo'sti*, there is no parallel to Thee. How can anybody become greater than You? It is impossible!

DVD 11 (35:14)

तस्मात्प्रणम्य प्रणिधाय कायं

tasmātpraṇamya praṇidhāya kāyaṁ

So, I bow before You again. I surrender my body to Thee (*praṇidhāya kayāṁ*). *Prasādaye tvām*, I beg forgiveness from You.

DVD 11 (35:34)

प्रसादये त्वामहमीशमीड्यम् ।
पितेव पुत्रस्य सखेव सख्युः
प्रियः प्रियस्यार्हसि देव सोढुम् ॥४६॥
दिव्यानि कर्माणि तवाद्भुतानि
पूर्वाणि पूर्वे ऋषयः स्मरन्ति ।
नान्योऽस्ति कर्ता जगतस्त्वमेको
धाता विधाता च विभुर्भवश्च ॥४७॥

prasādaye tvāmahamīśamīḍhyam /
piteva putrasya sakheva sakhyuḥ
priyaḥ priyasyāthasi deva soḍhum //46//
[incomplete translation][375]

divyāni karmāṇi tavādbhutāni
pūrvāṇi pūrve ṛṣayaḥ smaranti /
nānyo'sti kartā jagatastvameko
dhātā vidhātā ca vibhurbhavaśca //47//

You are the Lord. Your all actions are highly great. You are the controller of this whole universe. You are omnipresent. You are all-pervading. *Bhavaśca*, You are universal, and You are Yourself the universe.[376]

---

375 "You are praised by everybody. So You should forgive my sins, which I have committed beforehand, just as a father forgives the sins of his child, just as a friend forgives mistakes of his friend, just as a devoted husband forgives mistakes of his wife. In the same way, You should forgive my faults." *Bhagavad Gītā* (1978).

376 "Ancient *ṛṣis* and those sages who have come in this universe, those ancient sages sing the glory of Your divine actions . . . and [You are] filled with divine and wonderful actions. *Nānyo'sti kartā jagatastvam-eko*, nobody can create this universe without Thee. You are the only one who creates this universe, who protects this universe, who holds this universe, and who pervades this universe." Ibid.

तवाद्भुतं किं नु भवेदसह्यं
किं वा शक्यं परतः कीर्तयिष्ये ।
कर्तासि सर्वस्य यतः स्वयं वै
विभो ततः सर्वमिदं त्वमेव ॥४८॥
अत्यद्भुतं कर्म न दुष्करं ते
कर्मोपमानं नहि विद्यते ते ।
न ते गुणानां परिमाणमस्ति
न तेजसो नापि बलस्य नर्द्धेः ॥४९॥

tavādbhutaṁ kiṁ nu bhavedasahyaṁ
kiṁ vā śakyaṁ parataḥ kīrtayiṣye /
kartāsi sarvasya yataḥ svayaṁ vai
vibho tataḥ sarvamidaṁ svameva //48//
atyadbhutaṁ karma na duṣkaraṁ te
karmopamānaṁ nahi vidyate te /
na te guṇānāṁ parumāṇamasti
natejaso nāpi balasya narddheḥ //49//
[verses not translated][377]

---

377 Verse 48: "Thy wonderful actions are to be tolerated by us. We have to tolerate Thy wonderful actions. *Tavadbhutaṁ kiṁ nu bhaveda-sahyaṁ*, everybody has to tolerate Your actions. *Kiṁ vā śakyaṁ parataḥ kīrtayiṣye*, there is no way out [except] just to tolerate Your wonderful actions. I would, *parataḥ kīrtayiṣye,* I would announce [this] with open heart and with arms like this [Swamii demonstrates], I would announce like this in this universe, *kartāsi sarvasya yataḥ svayaṁ vai*, because You are the creator of this universe, You are the pervader of this universe, and You are the universe itself."

Verse 49: "Whatever You act, it may be super-wonderful actions. You know super-wonderful actions? Those wonderful actions which no one can do. Your supreme-wonderful actions [are] very easy for You to do. *Karma upamānaṁ nahi*, there is no comparison in activities with You. Nobody can act as You act. *Na te guṇānāṁ parimāṇamasti*, there is no measure, you can't measure, one cannot measure the weight of Your qualities. One cannot measure the weight of Your brightness. One cannot measure the weight of Your strength. One cannot measure the

DVD 11 (36:38)

अदृष्टपूर्वं हृषितोऽस्मि दृष्ट्वा
भयेन च प्रव्यथितं मनो मे ।
तदेव मे दर्शय देव रूपं
प्रसीद देवेश जगन्निवास ॥५०॥

adṛṣṭapūrvaṁ hṛṣito'smi dṛṣṭvā
bhayena ca pravyathitaṁ mano me /
tadeva me darśaya deva rūpaṁ
prasīda deveśa jagannivāsa //50//

In fact, I am very happy that I have seen You in this amazing, big, highest form. But I feel [within] myself that I am so fortunate that I was with You, [that] I was playing with You; I was playing with You, the greatest of the greatest. But at the same time, side by side, *bhayena ca pravyathitaṁ*, I am trembling with fear. I am trembling with fear [that] You may dash me down at once because You have got all powers.

Tadeva me darśaya deva rūpaṁ, please reveal Your [previous] formation as before You were with me, with four arms and . . . four arms (*catur bujaḥ*).[378] *Tadeva me darśaya deva rūpaṁ, prasīda deveśa jagat nivāsa.*

DVD 11 (38:08)

किरीटिनं गदिनं चक्रहस्त-
मिच्छामि त्वां द्रष्टुमहं तथैव ।
तेनैव रूपेणचतुर्भुजेन
सहस्रबाहो भव विश्वमूर्ते ॥५१॥

---

weight of Your glory. It is beyond measurement." *Bhagavad Gītā* (1978).

378 "He had four arms because He was divine. And sometimes He had two arms. His devotees would see Him [with four arms] and with two arms the ordinary class would see Him. He would appear in two ways: with four arms and with two arms. With four arms He would appear to Arjuna, to His mother, father, and all His devotees." Ibid.

kirīṭinaṁ gadinaṁ cakrahasta-
micchāmi tvāṁ draṣṭumahaṁ tathaiva /
tenaiva rūpeṇa caturbhujena
sahasrabāho bhava viśvamūrte //51//
[not recited]

Kirīṭinaṁ, You had that *mukuṭa* (crown), *cakranam* (discus), *gada* (mace), *śāṅka* (conch shell), *cakra*, and *gada*, and *padam*, You were four-handed (*catur bujaḥ*). You were always dancing and playing with me. I want to see You in that formation. This [universal] formation, I don't . . . I cannot tolerate.

Prasīda deveśa jagat, nivāsa [verse 50], please forgive me and show me Your own formation with which I was used to.

O *Sahasrabāho*, You have got thousands and millions of arms; I don't want to see this tremendous form of Thee.

Now Śri Bhagavān speaks and consoles him and He responds to his request. But He does not reveal to him those four arms yet. He is only still in this *viśvarūpa* (universal form).

DVD 11 (39:41)

श्रीभगवानुवाच

śrī bhagavān uvāca

मया प्रसन्नेन तवार्जुनेदं
रूपं परं दर्शितमात्मयोगात् ।
तेजोमयं विश्वमनन्तमाद्यं
यन्मे त्वदन्येन न दृष्टपूर्वम् ॥५२॥

mayā prasannena tavārjunedaṁ
rūpaṁ paraṁ darśitamātmayogāt /
tejomayaṁ viśvamanantamādyaṁ
yanme tvadanyena na dṛṣṭapūrvam //52//

I was so happy and so pleased with you that I have revealed to you My formation, this actual formation of My *viśvarūpa*. Don't get afraid. *Tejomayaṁ*, this is full of glamour. *Viśvaṁ*, this is the universal form of Mine, and nobody has seen this universal formation of Mine except you.

DVD 11 (40:40)

न वेदयज्ञाधिगमैर्न दानै-
र्न च क्रियाभिर्न तपोभिरुग्रैः ।
एवं रूपं शक्यमहं नृलोके
द्रष्टुं त्वदन्येन कुरुप्रवीर ॥५३॥

na vedayajñādhigamairna dānair-
na ca kriyābhirna tapobhirugraiḥ /
evaṁ rūpaṁ śakyamahaṁ nṛloke
draṣṭuṁ tvadanyena kurupravīra //53//

[Even] by studying the *Vedas*, by performing *yajñas*, by giving alms to the universe, and by penance also, and by austerities also, this *rūpa* cannot be shown to anybody except you.

DVD 11 (41:32)

मा ते व्यथा मा च विमूढता भूद
दृष्ट्वा रूपं घोरमुग्रं ममेदम् ।
व्यपेतभीः प्रीतमनाः पुनस्त्वं
तदेव मे रूपमिदं प्रपश्य ॥५४॥

mā te vyathā mā ca vimūḍhatā bhūda
dṛṣṭvā rūpaṁ ghoramugraṁ mamedam /
vyapetabhīḥ prītamanāḥ punastvaṁ
tadeva me rūpamidaṁ prapaśya //54//
[not recited in full]

Mā te vyathā mā ca vimūḍhatā bhūda. Don't fear, O Arjuna, don't fear. See Me, see Me wholeheartedly. This kind of *rūpa* is not very easily observed. You see, you see [My form] without fear. *Dṛṣṭvā rūpaṁ,* this [form] is *ghoram* (*ghoram* means furious and universal). *Vyapetabhīḥ,* discard all of your fear from your mind.

Prītamanāḥ, be happy, be one-pointed, and console yourself and then you will see Me in that old fashion of My *rūpa* with four arms.

सञ्जय उवाच

sañjaya uvāca

Sañjaya says now and reveals [what has happened] to that Dhṛtarāṣṭra.

DVD 11 (42:34)

इत्यर्जुनं वासुदेवस्तथोक्त्वा
स्वकं रूपं दर्शयामास भूयः ।
आश्वासयामास च भीतमेनं
भूत्वा पुनः सौम्यवपुर्महात्मा ॥५५॥

ityarjunaṁ vāsudevastathoktvā
svakaṁ rūpaṁ darśayāmāsa bhūyaḥ /
āśvāsayāmāsa ca bhītamenaṁ
bhūtvā punaḥ saumyavapurmahātmā //55//

This way, Vāsudeva (Lord Kṛṣṇa), after this way of explaining to [Arjuna], He revealed to him His own formation with four arms.

Āśvāsayāmāsa ca bhītamevaṁ, still he was trembling with fear. He had seen Him with four [arms] but still he was trembling with fear from the first threat [i.e., vision]. And [Lord Kṛṣṇa] was consoling him, "don't fear, don't fear! You are Mine. You are Mine. Don't fear! Be bold!"

अर्जुन उवाच

arjuna uvāca

Then, Arjuna sighs, "*ahhhh*," when he was already crushed.

DVD 11 (44:00)

दृष्ट्वेदं मानुषं रूपं तव सौम्यं जनार्दन ।
इदानीमस्मि संवृत्तः सचेताः प्रकृतिं गतः ॥५६॥

dṛṣṭvedaṁ mānuṣaṁ rūpaṁ tava saumyaṁ janārdana
idānīmasmi saṁvṛttaḥ sacetāḥ prakṛtiṁ gataḥ //56//

O Lord Kṛṣṇa, I have seen Your nature with [the human form that] I was accustomed to seeing. All my senses are finding the period of resting and I am fully alert. *Sa*[*cetāḥ*] *prakṛtiṁ gataḥ*, I have known my reality.

Now Śrī Bhagavān says:

DVD 11 (44:52)

श्रीभगवानुवाच

śrī bhagavān uvāca

सुदुर्दर्शमिदं रूपं दृष्टवानसि यन्मम ।
देवा अप्यस्य रूपस्य नित्यं दर्शनकाङ्क्षिणः ॥५७॥

sudurdarśamidaṁ rūpaṁ
dṛṣṭavānasi yanmama /
devā apyasya rūpasya
nityaṁ darśanakāṅkṣiṇaḥ //57//

This *rūpa* which you were observing of Mine–that *viśvarūpa*, universal [form]–*devas* also crave for seeing this *rūpa*, and nobody has seen this *rūpa* except for you.

DVD 11 (45:20)

नाहं वेदैर्न तपसा न दानेन न चेज्यया ।
शक्य एवंविधो द्रष्टुं दृष्टवानसि मां यथा ॥५८॥

nāhaṁ vedairna tapasā na dānena na cejyayā /
śakya evaṁvidho draṣṭuṁ dṛṣṭavānasi māṁ yathā //58//

Neither with penance, nor [by] giving alms, nor [by] adopting *havans*, nor with *pūja*, nor with universal . . . this universal *japa*, I am not possible to be seen in this way, in which way you were seeing Me.

भक्त्या त्वनन्यया शक्यो ह्यहमेवंविधोऽर्जुन ।
ज्ञातुं द्रष्टुं च तत्त्वेन प्रवेष्टुं च परन्तप ॥५९॥

bhaktyā tvananyayā śakyo hyahamevaṁviddho'rjuna /
jñātuṁ draṣṭuṁ ca tattvena praveṣṭuṁ ca parantapa //59//
[not recited or translated][379]

DVD 11 (46:06)

मत्कर्मकृन्मत्परमो मद्भक्तः सङ्गवर्जितः ।
निर्वैरः सर्वभूतेषु यः स मामेति पाण्डव ॥६०॥

matkarmakṛnmatparamo madbhaktaḥ saṅgavarjitaḥ
nirvairaḥ sarvabhūteṣu yaḥ sa māmeti pāṇḍava //60//

Matkarmakṛt, you do whatever action you do [and] you surrender it to Me. *Matparama*, you remain just after Me, just after [i.e., intent upon] finding the glamour of Me. *Matparama*, you remain just after Me, just don't be absent for even one second, half a second.[380] Don't be attached to the world. *Nirvairaḥ sarva-*

379 "Only there is one way how you can experience it. *Bhaktyā tvananyayā*, if you [have] one-pointed devotion for Me, then you can experience again. If you develop attachment and devotion for Me wholeheartedly, then you can experience this formation of Mine again. *Jñātuṁ*, you won't experience it, you will know it, you will feel it, and you will touch it, and you will get entry in it in the end. So I would order you to . . . [see verse 60]." *Bhagavad Gītā* (1978).

380 "Those who have adopted devotion for Me, which is *avidyamāna anyajñeyaramaṇīyā*, that devotion which does not accept, which does not recognize any other attachment. All [other] attachments are absolutely discarded. Where all attachment for other things is discarded, only you are attached to that God consciousness, that is *bhaktiḥ*. When

bhūteṣu, and love everybody, love everybody who is in the state of Bhairava and outside of the state of Bhairava–love them all. *Māmetu pāṇḍava*, he will come to Me in the end.

Here ends the 11th chapter. This is the conclusion of this.

DVD 11 (47:28)

अत्र संग्रहश्लोकः

atra saṅgraha ślokaḥ

शुद्धाशुद्धविमिश्रोत्थसंविदैक्यविमर्शनात् ।
भूर्भुवःस्वस्त्रयं पश्यन्समत्वेन समो मुनिः ॥११॥

śuddhāśuddhavimiśrotthasaṁvidaikyavimarśanāt
bhūrbhuvaḥ svastrayaṁ paśyansamatvena samo muniḥ //11//

॥ Concluding *śloka* of 11th chapter ॥

If you see that all of the three *lokas* (pure *loka*, pure and impure *loka*, and impure *loka*; *bhūḥ*, *bhuvaḥ*, and *svaḥ*), see them in one stage [i.e., level]. Nothing is pure, nothing is impure, and nothing is pure and impure mixed, and it is only the glamour of Parabhairava. Then you are existing for good in the state of Parabhairava.

Here ends the 11th chapter.

Bas!

[they] adopt that kind of devotion, for them, *māṁ prapadyate*, they are actually bowing to Me. They have come, they have taken refuge in Me. *Vāsudevaḥ sarvam'iti*, they have understood what is the real state of Lord Kṛṣṇa; they have understood it really, in real sense." Ibid.

Chapter 12

DVD 12 (00:00)

अर्जुन उवाच

arjuna uvāca

Arjuna puts a question.

एवं सततयुक्ता ये भक्तास्त्वां पर्युपासते ।
ये चाप्यक्षरमव्यक्तं तेषां के योगवित्तमाः ॥ १ ॥

evaṁ satatayuktā ye bhaktāstvāṁ paryupāsate /
ye cāpyakṣaramavyaktaṁ teṣāṁ ke yogavittamāḥ //1//

In this way, there are some devotees of Thee who remain Your devotees [with] devotion and love You very much. And they are [Your] devotees and always they think of You as their master. And there are some devotees who think of [You as] formless, Your formless image.

O Lord, whom [do] you nominate [as] the highest ones?

श्रीभगवानुवाच

śrī bhagavān uvāca

Śri Bhagavān answers.

DVD 12 (01:32)

मय्यावेश्य मनो ये मां नित्ययुक्ता उपासते ।
श्रद्धया परयोपेतास्ते मे युक्ततमा मताः ॥२॥

mayyāveśya mano ye māṁ nityayuktā upāsate /
śraddhayā parayopetāste me yuktatamā matāḥ //2//

Those who have focused their minds in Me, and *nityayuktā,* always are present, and *upāsate,* and think of [Me] and concentrate on [Me] . . . concentrate on Me, *śraddhayā parayopeta,* and they have got extreme devotion for [Me] . . . extreme devotion for Me (this is Lord Kṛṣṇa saying), *te me yuktatamā matāḥ*, I think I have considered them [to be] the most fortunate devotees of Mine.[381]

DVD 12 (03:02)

ये त्वक्षरमनिर्देश्यमव्यक्तं पर्युपासते ।
सर्वत्रगमचिन्त्यं च कूटस्थमचलं ध्रुवम् ॥३॥
सन्नियम्येन्द्रियग्रामं सर्वत्र समबुद्धयः ।
ते प्राप्नुवन्ति मामेव सर्वभूतहिते रताः ॥४॥

ye tvakṣaramanirdeśyamavyaktaṁ paryupāsate /
sarvatragamacintyaṁ ca kūṭasthamacalaṁ dhruvam //3//
sanniyamyendriyagrāmaṁ sarvatra samabuddhayaḥ /
te prāpnuvanti māmeva sarvabhūtahite ratāḥ //4//

2nd, 3rd, and 4th *śloka* in one.

There are some devotees of Mine, O Arjuna, those people who concentrate on My formless being, and they focus their minds in

381 "So, you must perceive this whole state of the world as one with God; see Śiva and Śakti residing everywhere. Oh, that hateful Śiva, this loveful Śiva, or hateful Śakti, just bow before them. I don't mean with your body. Mentally you should feel [that] . . . because if you bow before them with body, [ignorant people] will take undue advantage of that. So you should conceal [this] treasure [of devotion] in your own self." *Bhagavad Gītā* (1978).

one-pointedness and feel the presence of the formless God everywhere, those also are My devotees. But they think, they concentrate on My form in each and every object; and those also are My devotees, those also come into Me.

So there are three categories of My devotees.

One who has My devotion, who loves Me, who has got *bhakti*, and who thinks that I am their master and they focus all their activities in Me. I have the greatest degree [of love] for them. They are very near devotees of Mine.

And there are some [devotees] who concentrate on My formless being everywhere, and devote all of their activity in feeding people and concentrating that, "this whole universe is His creation. If we are serving him, if [we] are serving these souls, we are serving actually Lord Kṛṣṇa." They also reach at My feet.

But there are some people who concentrate on My formless state, but from my view point I think that [My] formless state is not possible to concentrate upon as long as they are residing in [their] bodies.

So there are three categories.

One is devotion (*bhakta*, devoted), and they think that [I am] their master and they are [My] servants, they are [My] *sevakas*–they are the topmost.

And there are some who think that Lord Śiva is above this cycle and He is omnipresent and all-pervading. They also reach Me because they see the presence of Me in each and every living being. They also attain Me.

DVD 12 (07:59)

क्लेशोऽधिकतरस्तेषामव्यक्तासक्तचेतसाम् ।
अव्यक्ता हि गतिर्दुःखं देहभृद्भिरवाप्यते ॥५॥

kleśo'dhikatarasteṣāmavyaktāsaktacetasām /
avyaktā hi gatirdūḥkhaṁ dehabhṛdbhiravāpyate //5//
[not recited]

And there are some [devotees] who, while living in [their] body, they concentrate upon the formless state of Mine. That does not work. I would not recommend that kind of meditation as long as the body is there. Because, in the body it is not possible to concentrate on the formless state.[382] The formless state can be concentrated [upon] when there is death, when body is not there.

DVD 12 (08:47)

ये तु सर्वाणि कर्माणि मयि संन्यस्य मत्पराः ।
अनन्येनैव योगेन मां ध्यायन्त उपासते ॥६॥

ye tu sarvāṇi karmāṇi mayi saṁnyasya matparāḥ /
ananyenaiva yogena māṁ dhyāyanta upāsate //6//

There are some devotees of Mine who surrender all of their activities to Me and always think of My being, of supreme Parabhairava.[383]

DVD 12 (09:31)

तेषामहं समुद्धर्ता मृत्युसंसारसागरात् ।
भवामि न चिरात्पार्थ मय्यावेशितचेतसाम् ॥७॥

teṣāmahaṁ samuddhartā mṛtyusaṁsārasāgarāt /
bhavāmi na cirātpārtha mayyāveśitacetasām //7//

As they have focused their body, mind, and intellect and everything in Me, I elevate them from repeated births and deaths, the cycle of repeated births and deaths. And without any hesitation I elevate them, because they have focused all of their

382 "To meditate in one corner and find out the center of God consciousness within, it is a very difficult path. Because *avyaktāsakta*, they have got to find out what is not found. They have to find out [that which is] unfound. They have to see [that] which is unperceived. They have to think [that] which is not thought, which has not become the object of thought, any thinking. They have to point out [that] which is not pointed out at all, i.e., un-pointed thing. So it is very difficult for them to tread on this path." Ibid.

383 "*Ananyenaiva yogena māṁ dhyāyanta upāsate*. Meditate on Me everywhere. See the glamour of God residing in each and every object, each and every sound, each and every word, each and every touch, sensation, anything." Ibid.

activities in Me.

Arjuna sees that He is so great.

O Arjuna, you should do one thing:

DVD 12 (10:31)

मय्येव मन आधत्स्व मयि बुद्धिं निवेशय ।
निवत्स्यसि त्वं मय्येव योगमुत्तममास्थितः ॥८॥

mayyeva mana ādhatsva mayi buddhiṁ niveśaya /
nivatsyasi tvaṁ mayyeva yogamuttamamāsthitaḥ //8//

Surrender your mind in Me, surrender your intellect in Me, [then] you will reside in Me and you will be considered situated in *uttama yoga*, supreme *yoga*.

Abhinavagupta says, "I have conducted [i.e., described] this state of Lord Kṛṣṇa's devotees in these *ślokas*. I have penned down this *śloka* in my *stotra*.

> *viśiṣṭakaraṇāsanasthitisamādhisaṁbhāvanā-*
> *vibhāvitatayā yadā kamapi bodhamullāsayet /*
> *na sā tava sadoditā svarasavāhinī yā citir-*
> *yatastritayasaṁnidhau sphuṭamihāpi saṁvedyate //*
> [comm. verse 8, *Devīstrotra* by Abhinavagupta]

Viśiṣṭa karaṇāsana sthiti samādhi saṁbhāvanā. To sit in *padmāsana*[384] and concentrate on You, O Devī . . .

It is *Devīstotra* penned down by Abhinavagupta. He says, "in *Devīstotra*, I have conducted this point, I have touched this point there."

. . . O Devī, O *Svātantrya śakti*[385] of Lord Śiva, *viśiṣṭa karaṇāsana sthiti samādhi saṁbhāvanā*, when one is situated, placed, in the *pūja* room, seated in *padmāsana* and concentrates upon *svātantrya śakti*, and realizes the knowledge of *svātantrya śakti* in *samādhi*, *na sā tava sadoditā*, O *Svātantrya śakti*, the person who observes and sees You in that state, that is not Your actual state. [Because] to us, You appear to us not only in *samā-*

384 Lotus posture.

385 See footnote 77 for an explanation of *svātantrya śakti*.

dhi; You appear to us in *samādhi* and in *yoga*, and in worldly activities also. So, that *samādhi* is not real *samādhi*.[386]

JOHN: Where we only see You in *samādhi* in one way.

SWAMIJI: Yes. That is not the real *svarūpa* (actual form) of Thine.

DVD 12 (14:55)

> *yadā tu vigatendhanaḥ svavaśavartitāṁ saṁśrayann-*
> *akṛtrimasamullasatpulakakampabāṣpānugaḥ* /
> *śarīranirapekṣatāṁ sphuṭamupādadānaścitaḥ*
> *svayaṁ jhagiti budhyate yugapadeva bodhānalaḥ* //
> [comm. verse 8, *Devīstrotra* by Abhinavagupta]

Yadā tu vigatendhanaḥ, when there is no agitation of this kind of agitation[387], *svavaśavartitām saṁśrayan*, and one is focused in concentrating upon Your universal nature of Bhairava, *akṛtrima samullasat pulaka kampabāṣpānugaḥ*, he observes that he is shivering, he has got *kampa* (trembling), he has got tears dripping down from his eyes, and he has got hiccups; and he is trembling, he is weeping, he is crying, he is laughing, laughing loudly, and at the same time he is crying loudly, and weeping, crying. *Śarīranirapekṣatāṁ sphuṭamupādadānaścitaḥ*, he does not know in which way [he is] existing: "am I really weeping or laughing?"

---

386 "Because, *yata stritaya saṁnidhau sphuṭam ihāpi,* there are such people also in this world who feel the presence of Your Self in wakefulness, in dreaming, and in dreamless state also–not only in *turya* (fourth state). Whenever you feel the presence of God in *turya* [only], that is not the way. . . . You must feel this state [of God consciousness] in the other three states also: wakefulness, dreaming, and dreamless state also–that is *turyātīta*." *Bhagavad Gītā* (1978). See footnote 138 for a further explanation of *turyātīta*.

387 "Agitation in which sense? [When] you make your mind controlled, under your control. That is not the real way. You should not control your mind. When your mind is controlled in some particular way, that is not the real way of God consciousness. It won't shine in its *svātantrya bhāva* (actual state of freedom). . . . You must leave it open. Let [your mind] go wherever it goes, and watch. Wherever it goes, there is the glamour of God. You watch the position of God consciousness everywhere." *Bhagavad Gītā* (1978).

He does not know that.[388]

tadaiva tava devi tadvapuruṣāśrayairvarjitaṁ
maheśamavabudhyate vivaśapāśasaṁkṣobhakam //
[*Devīstrotra* by Abhinavagupta]

O *Svātantrya śakti*, there and then that *yogi* realizes the real nature of Your *svātantrya śakti*, when he is . . . in one way he is laughing, in one way he is weeping, in one way he is crying. He does not know what [he is] doing. He is just mad after You! And that is the real realization of Thee, O *Svātantrya śakti*.

So this is what I mean, O Arjuna, this is what I mean, how you should devote everything to Me.

JOHN: What verse is that, Sir?

SWAMIJI: That is the 8th *śloka*.

DVD 12 (18:23)

अथावेशयितुं चित्तं न शक्नोषि मयि स्थिरम् ।
अभ्यासयोगेन ततो मामिच्छाप्तुं धनञ्जय ॥९॥

athāveśayituṁ cittaṁ na śaknoṣi mayi sthiraṁ /
abhyāsayogena tato māmicchāptuṁ dhanañjaya //9//

If you cannot do this, this kind of *sādhanā* (practice) . . .

Which *sādhanā*? When you are absolutely . . . when you have focused all of your might and all of your desires and all of your thoughts and ambitions and desires and cravings and longings towards Me, [asking], "how should I achieve that?" in madness, in sanity, in . . . in each and every action he does that.

. . . if you cannot do that, if you have not that kind of strength, *abhyāsa yogena tato māmicchāptuṁ dhanañjaya*, go on meditating then between two breaths. Go on meditating. In the course of time, this will lead you to that state where you will die [i.e., crave] after that Bhairava.

So there is . . . all ways are His. Some are a bit longer, and

388 "Because he finds the glamour of God without any control. Glamour of God you find in *samādhi* under control [but] when you are outside, you will lose that [control]." Ibid.

some are shorter, and some are just . . . just they start and the starting point is the ending point for them. As soon as they start, they end. Their *sādhanā* ends there and then, when they start [with an] intense desire. That is *tīvra tīvra śaktipāta*.[389]

DVD 12 [20:43)

अभ्यासेऽप्यसमर्थः सन्मत्कर्मपरमो भव ।
मदर्थमपि कर्माणि कुर्वन्सिद्धिमवाप्स्यसि ॥१०॥

abhyāse'pyasamarthaḥ sanmatkarmaparamo bhava /
madarthamapi karmāṇi kurvansiddhimavāpsyasi //10//

If you cannot do this meditation, if you are not capable of doing meditation because of your environment, e.g., of your being householder . . .

You have not that much time that you could do practice, because as soon as you do practice, your kith and kin want something and they give you blows, "give us tea, give us *chai*, give us toast!"

. . . if you cannot do *abhyāsa*, never mind. Then *mat karma paramo*, then feed your children! Feed your children but think these children are created by Me, Lord Śiva, Parabhairava (I mean Lord Kṛṣṇa). They are created by Me! [Think, "when] I serve them, I serve Lord Kṛṣṇa."

[So] feed Viresh, feed Shanna, feed everybody, feed your husband, feed your *guru*, feed your master, *madarthamapi karmaṇi kurvan siddhim*, you will reach [Me], you will reach there, don't worry.

DVD 12 (22:32)

अथैतदप्यशक्तोऽसि कर्तुं मद्योगमास्थितः ।
सर्वकर्मफलत्यागं ततः कुरु यतात्मवान् ॥११॥

389 *Tīvra tīvra śaktipāta* means "super-supreme grace." See footnote 33. See also *Kashmir Shaivism–The Secret Supreme* 10.66. [*Editor's note*]

athaitadapyaśakto'si kartuṁ madyogamāsthitaḥ /
sarvakarmaphalatyāgaṁ tataḥ kuru yatātmavān //11//

If you cannot do this also, because of too much children, too many children, too much society, you cannot do, you cannot think that, "I am serving God," because the time does not remain for you to think of God. Nevermind! Then surrender everything to Him. Whatever you do, whatever you think, think of the Lord: "O Lord, I cannot serve You, I cannot think of You, I have surrendered [everything] to You." But surrender with awareness. Go on surrendering: "*acha* (okay), this is for Him, this is for the Lord." Go on doing everything, doing *chapatti* for the Lord, making *chapatti* for Lord, like that. That is also a way that you will rise. It will take some time, but you will rise.

Amumevāśayamāśritya laghuprakriyāyāṁ mayaivoktam [comm. verse 11], "I have, regarding this *śloka* of Lord Kṛṣṇa," Abhinavagupta says that, "I have in my *stotra* of Bhairava, in my *stotra* of Lord, I have penned down these *ślokas*:"

ūnādhikamavijñātaṁ paurvāparyavivarjitam /
yaccāvadhānarahitaṁ buddherviskhalitam ca yat //
tatsarvaṁ mama sarveśa bhaktasyārtasya durmateḥ /
kṣantavyaṁ kripayā śambho yatastvaṁ karuṇāparaḥ //
anena stotrayogena tavātmānaṁ nivedaye /
punarniṣkāraṇamahaṁ duḥkhānāṁ naimi pātratāṁ //

Ūnādhikamavijñātaṁ, I don't know what is to be done and what is not to be done. *Paurvāparya vivarjitam*, I don't know what is to be done first and what is to be done afterwards. *Yaccāvadhānarahitaṁ*, and I have lost my awareness; I cannot put [my] awareness on one point. *Buddher viskhalitam ca yat*, I am always fickle-minded.[390]

"O God, please forgive me for this, not remembering You!"

You should think like that, you should, after doing all of this nonsense from morning to evening, then in the end [of the day], while resting you should pray, you should call God at the time of

390 *Tatsarvaṁ mama sarveśa* because I am Your devotee, I am filled with torture of this world; *durmate*, I have no intellect, *kṣantavyaṁ* you should forgive me for that. [Because] *yatastvaṁ karūṇāparaḥ* . . . You are embodiment of forgiveness. *Bhagavad Gītā* (1978).

sleeping: "God I have not been able to think of You and I am sleeping now, I leave everything to You, and I will sleep now because I am tired."[391]

This way also you will rise, in the course of time.

Now the conclusion of all of these treatments for entering into God consciousness sooner or later.

DVD 12 (27:18)

श्रेयो हि ज्ञानमभ्यासाज्ज्ञानाद्ध्यानं विशिष्यते ।
ध्यानात्कर्मफलत्यागस्त्यागाच्छान्तिरनन्तरा ॥ १२ ॥

śreyo hi jñānamabhyāsājjñānāddhyānaṁ viśiṣyate /
dhyānātkarmaphalatyāgastyāgācchāntiranantarā //12//

Knowledge is better than doing practice.[392] *Jñānāt dhyānaṁ viśiṣyate*, if there is knowledge, *dhyāna* (meditation) becomes successful, and by *dhyāna karma phalatyāga*, you can leave [aside] all of the asking of fruits from your actions. And then, in the long run, you will achieve peace of mind. So then it is never [too] late to mend.

391 "*Anena stotrayogena*, by this way, *tavātmānaṁ nivedaye*, I surrender my everything before You, *punarniṣkāraṇamahaṁ duḥkhānāṁ naimi pātratāṁ*, and then I won't be the victim of torture and crisis in this world." Ibid.

392 "*Jñānam* (knowledge) is *āveśātma*, just entry in God consciousness, i.e., fixing your mind on the point of God consciousness. *Abhyāsācchreyaḥ*, it is better than practice. It is why in Shaivism it is said that *yoga* in action is divine. *Yoga* in meditative mood is not so divine, as *yoga* in action is divine. The more you work, and at the same time you are aware of your breath, you are aware of your center of meditation, you will become divine . . . very quickly. . . . One days practice in this way will be as good as one thousand [days] practice in your meditation room. It is why, because of that *āveśa* (absorption), *dhyāna* (meditation) becomes purified, *dhyāna* becomes strong. *Viśeṣatvaṁ yāti*, *abhimataprāptyā*, because it fills your desire of getting entry in God consciousness." Ibid.

For '*Yoga* in Action' see also *Kashmir Shaivism–The Secret Supreme* 15.101-103.

DVD 12 (28:21)

अद्वेष्टा सर्वभूतानां मैत्रःकरुण एव च ।
निर्ममो निरहंकारः समदुःखसुखः क्षमी ॥१३॥
सन्तुष्टः सततं योगी यतात्मा दृढनिश्चयः ।
मय्यर्पितमनोबुद्धिर्यो मद्भक्तः स मे प्रियः ॥१४॥

adveṣṭā sarvabhūtānāṁ maitraḥ karūṇa eva ca /
nirmamo nirahaṁkāraḥ samaduḥkhasukhaḥ kṣamī //13//
santuṣṭaḥ satataṁ yogī yatātmā dṛḍhaniścayaḥ /
mayyarpitamanobuddhiryo madbhaktaḥ sa me priyaḥ //14//

The 13th and 14th *śloka*.

The main thing for you is, if you cannot do anything [i.e., meditate], the main thing for you [to do] is don't hate anybody. In this world, don't hate anybody. Serve everybody, good or bad people. *Maitraḥ,* be friendly to everybody. *Karūṇa*, be compassionate to everybody. *Nirmamaḥ*, don't behave as your own . . . I mean your own *nirmamaḥ*, that, "[because] I am doing this, it will bestow some fruit, God will bestow some fruit [to me]." Don't think of any fruit! Go on remaining friendly with everybody. *Nirahaṁkāraḥ,* leave your ego away; keep your ego away and be very humble to people. *Samaduḥkha sukhaḥ kṣamī*, when there is pain, when there is pleasure, remain the same. And tolerate whatever comes before you in the long run in this world. Whatever comes [to you], good or bad, tolerate [it], don't cry.

DVD 12 (30:30)

सन्तुष्टः सततं योगी यतात्मा दृढनिश्चयः ।
मय्यर्पितमनोबुद्धिर्यो मद्भक्तः स मे प्रियः ॥१४॥

santuṣaḥ satataṁ yogī yatātmā dṛḍhaniścayaḥ /
mayyarpitamanobuddhiryo madbhaktaḥ sa me priyaḥ //14//

The *yogi* who is always peaceful, who is always happy, *dṛḍha niścayaḥ*, who believes in his own mind that God will never kick me because I have surrendered to Him, *mayyarpita mano buddhir*, the one who offers, who surrenders his mind, his intellect, and his ego in Me, *sa me priyaḥ,* he is My devotee, he is . . . I love him. Don't think that he will be at a loss in the end. If you feel [Me in] the presence of the universe and love each and everybody, that will work tremendously for you, He says.

DVD 12 (32:02)

यस्मान्नोद्विजते लोको लोकान्नोद्विजते च यः ।
हर्षामर्षभयोद्वेगैर्मुक्तो यः स च मे प्रियः ॥ १५ ॥

yasmānnodvijate loko lokānnodvijate ca yaḥ /
harṣāmarṣabhayodvegairmukto yaḥ sa ca me priyaḥ //15//

From whom *lokas* (people) are not fed up. For instance, this is the sign of My devotees, O Arjuna, this is the sign of My devotees: whenever My devotees are seated [and] when anybody who comes to him, neither he gets worried from people who come for his *darśan*, nor people get worried from his *darśan*.[393] They are not fed up from [seeing] him. They want to see him again and again. And he is not himself also worried [or disturbed] about people coming to him for *darśan*. He behaves and surrenders to them. Because he has to think that, "anybody who has come to me for *darśan* is sent by God."

DVD 12 (33:34)

अनपेक्षः शुचिर्दक्ष उदासीनो गतव्यथः ।
सर्वारम्भफलत्यागी यो मद्भक्तः स मे प्रियः ॥ १६ ॥

anapekṣaḥ śucirdakṣa udāsīno gatavyathaḥ //
sarvārambhaphalatyāgī yo madbhaktaḥ sa me priyaḥ //16//

Who has no other thoughts (*anapekṣa*), who is always pure (*śuci*), who is witty inside, he is alert always (*dakṣa*), *udāsīna*, who does not indulge in [worldly] discussions, *gatavyathaḥ*, who

393 Traditionally, *darśana* means the "sight" or "vision" of a deity or master, which confers a blessing. In this case, *darśana* means "audience." [*Editor's note*]

has no anxiety, *sarva ārambha phala tyāgī*, who does not ask for any fruit from his actions, he is My [devotee]. I love him.

DVD 12 (34:22)

योन हृष्यति न द्वेष्टि न शोचति न कांक्षति ।
शुभाशुभफलत्यागी भक्तिमान्यः स मे प्रियः ॥ १७ ॥

yo na hṛṣyati na dveṣṭi na śocati na kāṁkṣati /
śubhāśubhaphalatyāgī bhaktimānyaḥ sa me priyaḥ //17//

That person who does not get excited when achieving some good thing, who does not get sad when not achieving anything, *na śocati*, who does not accept . . . who is not grieved . . .

You know grieved?

. . . by bad happenings, *na kaṁkṣati*, and who does not desire for good results, *śubhāśubha phalatyāgī*, good and bad [actions], who has avoided [desire for their fruits], that kind of devotee is My own. I love him.

DVD 12 (35:33)

समः शत्रौ च मित्रे च तथा मानावमानयोः ।
शीतोष्णसुखदुःखेषु समः सङ्गविवर्जितः ॥ १८ ॥

samaḥ śatrau ca mitre ca tathā mānāvamānayoḥ /
śītoṣṇasukhaduḥkheṣu samaḥ saṅgavivarjitaḥ //18//

That person who is the same to his enemy and to his friend, who remains the same in respect and disrespect, who remains the same in coolness and hotness, who remains the same in pain and pleasure, and who has no attachment, he is [Mine]. I love him.

DVD 12 (36:19)

तुल्यनिन्दास्तुतिर्मौनी सन्तुष्टो येनकेनचित् ।
अनिकेतः स्थिरमतिर्भक्तिमान्मे प्रियो नरः ॥ १९ ॥

tulyanindāstutirmaunī santuṣṭo yenakenacit /
aniketaḥ sthiramatirbhaktimānme priyo naraḥ //19//

If he is given bad names, he remains the same; if he is praised by people, he remains the same. *Aniketaḥ*, who has not particular state of living (e.g., that "I will live only in Kathmandu," "I will live only in the United States," "I will live only in Srinagar"), he is My devotee. Wherever he is seated, well and good, he remains fine.

DVD 12 (37:20)

ये तु धर्मामृतमिदं यथोक्तं पर्युपासते ।
श्रद्दधाना मत्परमा भक्तास्तेऽतीव मे प्रियाः ॥२०॥

ye tu dharmāmṛtamidaṁ yathoktaṁ paryupāsate /
śraddadhānā matparamā bhaktāste'tīva me priyāḥ //20//

Those who taste this nectar of My wisdom and they conduct *śradda* . . .

Śradda means faith in My *upadeśa*; *upadeśa* means . . .

JOHN: Teachings.

SWAMIJI: Teachings.

. . . and who are bent upon thinking of Me, those are very much the topmost of My beloveds.

20th *śloka*. There ends the 12th chapter and this [following *śloka* is the] conclusion.

DVD 12 (38:32)

परमानन्दवैवश्यसञ्जातावेशासंपदः ।
स्वयं सर्वास्ववस्थासु ब्रह्मसत्ता ह्ययत्नतः ॥१२॥

paramānandavaivaśyasañjātāveśasaṁpadaḥ /
svayaṁ sarvāsvavasthāsu brahmasattā hyayatnataḥ //12//

|| Concluding *śloka* of 12th chapter ||

If, when *paramānanda vaivaśya*, when the supreme bliss of the state of Parabhairava, the achievement of the state of Parabhairava, the supreme bliss of that achievement of Parabhairava, one who once realizes it, and *vaivaśya*, he loses his wits, he loses his wits for good . . .

Wits, what are wits?

JONATHAN: Senses.

SWAMIJI: . . . he cannot remain in his [normal] position. He becomes . . . sometimes he is mad, sometimes he is sane, sometimes he is laughing, sometimes he is crying, sometimes he is weeping, sometimes he is . . .

DENISE: He seems kind of unbalanced [laughs].

SWAMIJI: [laughs]

JONATHAN: So he's not tied to any convention.

SWAMIJI: . . . and his *brahma sattā* (the *brahma sattā* means the presence of the state of Parabhairava) is always at his disposal, at that man's personal disposal.[394]

Bas, there ends our lesson for tonight.

394 "Because of that supreme bliss, *svayaṁ sarvāsvavasthāsu brahma sattā*, for him the state of [God] consciousness is everywhere present." *Bhagavad Gītā* (1978).

Chapter 13

Arjuna asks questions.

DVD 13 (00:05)

अर्जुन उवाच

arjuna uvāca.

प्रकृतिं पुरुषं चैव क्षेत्रं क्षेत्रज्ञमेव च ।
एतद्वेदितुमिच्छामि ज्ञानं ज्ञेयं च केशव ॥ १ ॥

prakṛtiṁ puruṣaṁ caiva kṣetraṁ kṣetrajñameva ca /
etadveditumicchāmi jñānaṁ jñeyaṁ ca keśava //1//

O Lord Kṛṣṇa, what is *prakṛti* and what is *puruṣa*? What is *kṣetra* and what is *kṣetrajña*? And what is *jñāna* and what is *jñeyaṁ*? *Prakṛti* and *puruṣa*, *kṣetra* and *kṣetrajña*, and *jñāna* and *jñeyaṁ*.

श्रीभगवानुवाच

śrī bhagavān uvāca

Śrī Bhagavān answers his questions.

DVD 13 (00:54)

इदं शरीरं कौन्तेय क्षेत्रमित्यभिधीयते ।
एतद्यो वेद तं प्राहुः क्षेत्रज्ञ इति तद्विदः ॥ २ ॥

idaṁ śarīraṁ kaunteya kṣetramityabhidhīyate /
etadyo veda taṁ prāhuḥ kṣetrajña iti tadvidaḥ //2//

This body, O Arjuna, this body is called *kṣetra*. *Kṣetra* means [the field] where your actions are stored for getting [their] fruits. [The knower of] this body is *kṣetrajña*. *Kṣetrajña* means this body is the field for sowing the seeds of *karma*.

Etadyo veda, and the person who indulges [i.e., is conscious of] this body, he is *kṣetrajña*. *Kṣetrajña* means he is *jīva*, a limited soul. This body is *kṣetra* (*kṣetra* means the field in which you sow your *karmas*), and *kṣetrajña* is the limited soul who is entangled in actions and he gets its fruits. But at the same time, you should know, O Arjuna:

DVD 13 (02:39)

क्षेत्रज्ञं चापि मां विद्धि सर्वक्षेत्रेषु भारत ।

kṣetrajñaṁ cāpi māṁ viddhi sarvakṣetreṣu bhārata /

Kṣetrajñaṁ cāpi māṁ viddhi sarvakṣetreṣu bhārata. I am also, side by side, I am [also] *kṣetrajña*, because the fruit is produced by Me also. So there are two beings: one is the limited soul and another is the unlimited soul. The limited soul is handling the seeds [of action] and I am the producer of its fruit.

क्षेत्रक्षेत्रज्ञयोर्ज्ञानं यत्तज्ज्ञानं मतं मम ॥३॥

kṣetrakṣetrajñayorjñānaṁ yattajjñānaṁ mataṁ mama //3//

And if you know, by the grace of God, by the grace of Me, if you know what is limited being and what is unlimited being, if you know both of these, that both are present in one body, then you are fully illuminated. Then you know the giver of fruits is inside–that is God.[395]

395 "For worldly people, this *śarīraṁ* (this body) is *kṣetra*, the field in which seeds of our actions are sown. *Karmabīja* are the seeds of action. They grow in this body and they give you fruit accordingly. For instance, you perceive something, good or bad, and its [seed/impression] is sown there in your body. And *āgantuka kālupyarūṣitaḥ*, and it is

DVD 13 (04:06)

तत्क्षेत्रं यच्च यादृक्च यद्विकारि यतश्च यत् ।
स च यो यत्स्वभावश्च तत्समासेन मे शृणु ॥४॥

tatkṣetraṁ yacca yādṛkca yadvikāri yataśca yat /
sa ca yo yatsvabhāvaśca tatsamāsena me śṛṇu //4//

That *kṣetra*, this body, *yat vikāri*, the changes which take place in this body, e.g., sometimes this *kṣetra* becomes invalid [i.e., debilitated]; you cannot work out this *kṣetra*, it becomes invalid by some disease, by some old age, by some . . .

JONATHAN: Accident.

SWAMIJI: . . . accident, by some pain, pleasure, sorrow; then this *kṣetra* becomes invalid and this *kṣetra* is shattered to pieces. And the one who is taking care of [i.e., inhabits] this *kṣetra*, he moves into another *kṣetra*.

DENISE: The limited soul moves into another body.

SWAMIJI: Yes, into another body. And that soul who is passing from one *kṣetra* to another *kṣetra*, if one *kṣetra* is finished (it has no water, it has no rain, it has nothing, all is *bakwas* (rubbish), it becomes invalid), then he moves to another *kṣetra*, which is well

---

polluted by the *mala* (impurity) of your attachment. When there is attachment, when you do action with attachment, that action is polluted. That seed is polluted and it will grow and give you polluted fruits, not pure fruit. For those who are elevated souls also, this body is [also a] field. *Anvarthamedastu*, but there is difference for elevated souls and not elevated souls in sowing. *Kṣiṇoti karma bandham upabhogena*, because the attachment of your actions is destroyed by enjoying it for those who are elevated. For those who are elevated, they enjoy, they do act accordingly in this body, but by that action they get liberation. And *trāyate janma maraṇa bhayāt*, and they are protected from the threat of repeated births and deaths and get liberation. For them, the knower of the field (*kṣetrajña*) would be universal God, not limited soul. When limited soul sows this seed of action, he gets limited fruit. And for un-limited soul, he gets liberation, it will give you liberation. So for him who is knower of that field, knower of the field is, for elevated soul, God Himself. Because he does act godly. Who? Elevated soul." *Bhagavad Gītā* (1978).

looked after, a young *kṣetra*, and there he puts his actions and its fruits also are maintained properly. But the *kṣetrajña* who is handling this, He is immortal, He never dies, He never is torn. And that *kṣetrajña*, I will tell you who He is.

DVD 13 (06:37)

ऋषिभिर्बहुधा गीतं छन्दोभिर्विविधैः पृथक् ।
ब्रह्मसूत्रपदैश्चैव हेतुमद्भिर्विनिश्चितम् ॥५॥

ṛṣibhirbahudhā gītaṁ chandobhirvividhaiḥ pṛthak /
brahmasūtrapadaiścaiva hetumadbhirviniścitam //5//

Old *ṛṣis* have sung the glory of that *kṣetrajña*, [the one] who is the real *kṣetrajña*. *Chandobhir*, the *Vedas* have nominated its glory in various ways of the *Vedas*. *Brahmasūtra padaiścaiva*, and in this *Brahmasūtra* of Vyāsa, Vyāsa has explained the glamorous position of this *kṣetrajña*. This is *kṣetrajña* in the real sense.

Now that *kṣetra*.[396] *Kṣetra* is [that] which is handled by this [immortal] *kṣetrajña*, from one life to another life, from another life to another life. And it has got some elements in *kṣetra* in which you sow *karmas*.[397]

DVD 13 (08:12)

महाभूतान्यहंकारो बुद्धिरव्यक्तमेव च ।
इन्द्रियाणि दशैकं च पञ्च चेन्द्रियगोचराः ॥६॥
इच्छा द्वेषः सुखं दुःखं सङ्घातश्चेतना धृतिः ।
एतत्क्षेत्रं समासेन सविकारमुदाहृतम् ॥७॥

mahābhūtānyahaṁkāro buddhiravyaktameva ca /
idriyāṇi daśaikaṁ ca pañca cendriyagocarāḥ //6//

396 The field or the body.

397 "And this body gets changed by sowing seeds, various seeds. You sow seed of sex, it will give you that kind of [physical] reaction. You sow seed of wrath or joy or excitement, it will give you fruit like that." *Bhagavad Gītā* (1978).

icchā dveṣaḥ sukhaṁ duḥkhaṁ saṅghātaścetanā dhṛtiḥ /
etatkṣetraṁ samāsena savikāramudāhṛtaṁ //7//

The five great elements. This *kṣetra* is derived from the five great elements: *pṛthvī* (earth), *jala* (water), *agni* (fire), *vāyu* (air), and *ākāśa* (ether), [and] *ahaṁkāra* (ego), *buddhiḥ* (intellect), *avyaktameva ca*, and *prakṛti*. *Prakṛti* means the undifferentiated form of the three *guṇas*, i.e., when the three *guṇas* are not differentiatedly existing, where the three *guṇas* are residing in seed form. That is *prakṛti*.

And the ten *indrīyas*: the organs of action (*karmendriyas*) and organs of knowledge (*jñānendriyas*); *ekaṁ ca*, and the mind (*ekaṁ ca* means that one, the mind); and *indriya gocarāḥ*: *śabda* (sound), *sparśa* (touch), *rūpa* (form), *rasa* (taste) and *gandha* (smell). These are the productions of organs: *śabda, sparśa, rūpa, rasa* and *gandha* (sound, touch, form, taste, and smell).

Icchā dveṣaḥ, and in that [*kṣetra*] also there is another [set of aspects]: *icchā* (desire), *dveṣaḥ* (hatred), *sukhaṁ* (pleasure), *duḥkhaṁ* (pain), *saṅghāta* (agitation). Sometimes agitating state in your body [takes place]. *Etat kṣetraṁ samāsena*, this is *kṣetra*, which is derived by, which is handled by that *kṣetrajña* who is the Lord. *Savikāram*, [the *kṣetra*] has got changes, changes come to it. And the great change is death. The great change is death and this *kṣetra* is finished. And then *kṣetrajña* derives [produces] another *kṣetra* for conducting *karmas*.

This is what is being done by Me, O Arjuna.

Now, I will tell you what is knowledge. *Jñānam* . . .

[Arjuna] had asked this [question]: what is knowledge and what is known? What is knowledge and what is known? That was also one question in the beginning from Arjuna.

amānitvam . . .

Now, what is knowledge?

amānitvamadambhitvamahiṁsā kṣāntirā . . .

(You should put the number of *jñāna*.)

Jñāna is a big totality of things. *Jñāna* is not only knowledge *bas*, that is all, knowledge of God or knowledge of yourself.[398]

DVD 13 (12:10)

अमानित्वमदम्भित्वमहिंसा क्षान्तिरार्जवम् ।
आचार्योपासनं शौचं स्थैर्यमात्मविनिग्रहः ॥८॥
इन्द्रियार्थेषु वैराग्यमनहंकार एव च ।
जन्ममृत्युजराव्याधिदुःखदोषानुदर्शनम् ॥९॥
असक्तिरनभिष्वङ्गः पुत्रदारागृहादिषु ।
नित्यं च समचित्तत्वमिष्टानिष्टोपपत्तिषु ॥१०॥
मयि चानन्ययोगेन भक्तिरव्यभिचारिणी ।
विविक्तदेशसेवित्वमरतिर्जनसंसदि ॥११॥
अध्यात्मज्ञाननिष्ठत्वं तत्त्वज्ञानार्थदर्शनम् ।
एतज्ज्ञानमिति प्रोक्तमज्ञानं यदतोऽन्यथा ॥१२॥

amānitvamadambhitvamahiṁsā kṣāntirārjavam
ācāryopāsanaṁ śaucaṁ sthairyamātmavinigrahaḥ //8//
indriyārtheṣu vairāgyamanahaṁkāra eva ca /
janmamṛtyujarāvyādhiduḥkhadoṣānudarśanam //9//
asaktiranabhiṣvaṅgaḥ putradāragṛhādiṣu /
nityaṁ ca samacittatvamiṣṭāniṣṭopapattiṣu //10//
mayi cānanyayogena bhaktiravyabicāriṇī /
viviktadeśasevitvamaratirjanasaṁsadi //11//
adhyātmajñānaniṣṭhatvaṁ tattvajñānārthadarśanam /
etajjñānamiti proktamajñānaṁ yadato'nyathā //12//

This is knowledge, these things. Where these things are combined and shining, that is knowledge.

Note it down.

Amānitvam, this is first, [this] knoweldge is the first one. *Amānitvam* means where there is no ego, where there is no ego of "I am." Where there is no ego, that is *amānitvam*. That is the

398 "Kṛṣṇa explains knowledge in many ways, collectively." *Bhagavad Gītā* (1978).

first part of knowledge.

Adambhitvam is second, *adambhitvam*. *Adambhitvam* means *dambha*. *Dambha* means fraud, fraudness of behavior. The absence of fraudness (*adambha*) in behavior is knowledge.[399] Second.

Ahiṁsā, not *hiṁsā*. *Hiṁsā* means [violence].

DENISE: Non-violence.

JOHN: Non-violence.

SWAMIJI: [*Ahiṁsā* means] non-violence. Non-violence is the third knowledge. Non-violence, when you are not violent to anybody in this world.

JONATHAN: Subtle and predominant.

SWAMIJI: Huh?

JONATHAN: Subtle and predominant. Like no killing, but also not giving bad names, not upsetting anybody.

SWAMIJI: Yes.

DENISE: By thoughts, words, and action.

SWAMIJI: Yes.

DENISE: Non-violent.

SWAMIJI: *Amānitvam adambhitvam*, *ahiṁsā*. That is *ahiṁsā*.

Kṣāntir (tolerance), tolerance is the fourth knowledge. This is the fourth knowledge, tolerance. Tolerate, don't lose your temper at all. Tolerate whatever bad comes to you, just have tolerance, don't grumble.

This is which one?

JOHN: The fourth one, tolerance. But what's the name of it?

SWAMIJI: *Kṣāntir*.

Ārjavam. *Ārjavam* means *āgopi viṣaya rijitaḥ* (*ārjavam* means straightforwardness). It is not that straightforwardness which is [like the] straight-forwardness of that Pyarelal.

You know Pyarelal?

DENISE: Yes. The one [devotee] that's a little mad?

SWAMIJI: Which Pyarelal?

DENISE: Yes.

SWAMIJI: Not that straightforwardness. Straightforwardness when there is not madness. Straightforwardness. You must be straightforward just like gods [who are] straightforward. You

---

399 "Whatever you think and whatever you say, it must be one, it must not differ." Ibid.

must be humble to everybody, straightforward. You must not be mad. That is straight-forwardness, that is *ārjavam, āgopi viṣaya rijitaḥ*.

In Kashmiri you call it *sadardapaza*, when you are not internally crooked. Or teasing, when teasing element is not there, i.e., teasing others. Mad person also does not tease, but that [kind of] teasing is not counted in *jñāna*, i.e., that not-teasing of mad people just like Pyarelal. No, it must be wise not-teasing, the wisdom of not teasing.

Ācāryopāsanaṁ, which one?

JOHN: *Ācāryopāsanaṁ*.

SWAMIJI: *Ācāryopāsanaṁ*.

JOHN: Number six.

SWAMIJI: Six. *Amānitvam* is one, *adambhitvam* is second . . .

JOHN: *Ahiṁsā* is three.

SWAMIJI: *Ahiṁsā* is three.

JOHN: *Kṣāntir* is four.

SWAMIJI: *Kṣāntir* is four.

JOHN: *Ārjavam*.

SWAMIJI: *Ārjavam*, *ārjavam* is fifth, *ācāryopāsanaṁ* is sixth. *Ācārya upāsanaṁ* means to serve with [your] whole, total surrender to your master. Serving with total surrender to your master. Not serving for [gaining something in] return [from your] master, from the masters hand. Without [expecting any] return, you serve your master without thinking of [any return].

Śaucaṁ. *Śaucaṁ* means purity, purity of mind, body, and soul. Not purity of shaving and putting on good dresses and then being in mind filthy, with filthy thoughts. [*Śaucaṁ* is] the purity of mind, body, and soul.

JOHN: That is another one?

SWAMIJI: Yes.

JOHN: *Śaucaṁ*.

SWAMIJI: *Śaucaṁ*. *Śaucaṁ* is seventh, huh?

Sthairyam is eighth. *Sthairyam*.

JOHN: *Śaucaṁ* is purity?

SWAMIJI: Huh?

JOHN: *Śaucaṁ* is purity?

SWAMIJI: *Śaucaṁ* is, yes, purity of mind, body, and soul. *Śaucaṁ* does not mean to fit [i.e., wear] the best clothes and put on scents, perfumes–that is not *śaucaṁ*.

Sthairyam. Sthairyam means not being fickle-minded, the absence of being fickle-minded, absence of being . . . *sthairyam. Sthairyam* means [the one] who has got tolerance. Not tolerance, [*sthairyam* means one] who does not shake.

JONATHAN: Waver.

SWAMIJI: Huh?

JONATHAN: Who doesn't waver.

SWAMIJI: Waver. Whose mind does not waver, that is *jñāna* (knowledge).

Ātmavinigrahaḥ is ninth.

JOHN: What is that one?

SWAMIJI: Possessing controlled mind.

JOHN: What was that word again.

SWAMIJI: *Ātmavinigrahaḥ*. And tenth is . . . tenth is . . .

DVD 13 (20:23)

Indriyārtheṣu vairāgyam [verse 9], detachment for sensual objects, not to be given to them. Detachment for sensual objects, that is *indriyārtheṣu vairāgya*. It is knowledge (*jñāna*). Tenth.

JOHN: What's that one?

SWAMIJI: *Indriyārtheṣu vairāgyam*.

Anahaṁkāra eva ca. Anahaṁkāra means [not thinking], "I am qualified." This kind of ego [that feels], "I am qualified. I am behaved [i.e., respected] by everybody as great. I am behaved by everybody who comes around me. They behave me as great." Thinking of this [is to be avoided]. Not thinking of this is *jñāna* (knowledge).

That rise of . . . it is a kind of ego when you see that, "so many great people are respecting me highly, and they have got high opinion of me." This you should not have. Because this will toss you down from your real position of knowledge.

Do you understand?

Janma mṛtyu jarā vyādhi duḥkha doṣānudarśanam. And this is all, all are combined [in the] 12th [verse]. [One] who keeps in his mind, in view, [that] there is birth, in this world there is birth, there is death, there is old age, there are *vyādhi* (*vyādhi* means diseases), there are pains, and there are all *doṣās* (*doṣās* means leakages, leakages of torture), and [when] you keep all of these in view, that is knowledge. Keep all of these in view in this world. Otherwise [i.e., in this way], they won't give you trouble afterwards if you keep them in view, these things, [that] they are always existing in this world.

This is the twelfth [knowledge].

DVD 13 (23:47)

असक्तिरनभिष्वङ्गः पुत्रदारागृहादिषु ।
नित्यं च समचित्तत्वमिष्टानिष्टोपपत्तिषु ॥१०॥

asaktiranabhiṣvaṅgaḥ putradārāgṛhādiṣu /
nityaṁ ca samacittatvamiṣṭāniṣṭopapattiṣu //10//
[repeated]

Asaktir (non-attachment) and *anabhiṣvaṅgaḥ*. Non-attachment is one and *anabhiṣvaṅgaḥ* is not to be a slave of your kith and kin–slave.

Do you know what a slave is?

Asaktir anabhiṣvaṅgaḥ–to whom?–*putra*, to your son, to your wife, to your household, and to your property, *asaktir. Asaktir* means not to be given to, not to be slave of these. So, in the course of time, when [these people and things are] dashed down, you will be brave. *Asaktir anabhuṣvaṅgaḥ putra dāra gṛhādiṣu*.

Which one is this?

JOHN: Thirteenth I believe.

SWAMIJI: Thirteenth.

Nityaṁ ca samacittatvamiṣṭāniṣṭopapattiṣu . . .

This line is the fourteenth [knowledge].

. . . when good results come to you and when bad results come to you from your past actions, [you should] remain the same, remain unmoved–that is also knowledge. You [should] remain unmoved. You know what this is?

This is the fourteenth [knowledge]. And the fifteenth [knowledge] is in another, one sentence [of the next verse].

DVD 13 (25:55)

मयि चानन्ययोगेन भक्तिरव्यभिचारिणी ।

mayi cānanyayogena bhaktiravyabhicāriṇī /

[verse repeated][400]

And *mayi*–Lord Kṛṣṇa says to Arjuna–*mayi*, in Me, in Me, [continue] focusing devotional attachment; devotional attachment which is not moved by so many tests.

DVD 13 (26:30)

विविक्तदेशसेवित्वमरतिर्जनसंसदि ॥ ११ ॥
अध्यात्मज्ञाननिष्ठत्वं तत्त्वज्ञानार्थदर्शनम् ।
एतज्ज्ञानमिति प्रोक्तमज्ञानं यदतोऽन्यथा ॥ १२ ॥

viviktadeśasevitvamaratirjanasaṁsadi //11//
adhyātmajñānaniṣṭhatvaṁ tattvajñānārthadarśanam /
etajjñānamiti proktamajñānaṁ yadato'nyathā //12//
[repeated]

Viviktadeśasevitvam, the tendency of remaining aloof from society–this is *jñāna*. *Vivikta deśa sevitvam*, always, [having] the tendency of always being aloof from kith and kin, and parties, and people, and associations, and *gupshups* (idle conversations), and all of this. *Vivikta deśa sevitvam,* this tendency, where this tendency is found, it is *jñāna*.

Which one?

JOHN: Remaining aloof, that's number sixteen.

SWAMIJI: Sixteenth.

And *aratirjanasaṁsadi*. *Janasaṁsadi aratir*, although you are situated in society . . . [for example], there is a party of society and people have come and you have to entertain them with tea, etc. And you give them a cup of tea and they laugh; while taking tea they laugh and they drink and you also laugh, you also laugh, but unwillingly. Internally you are unwillingly laughing with them, just to keep the status of your being a householder intact. Otherwise, you have not choice [i.e., desire] of that. This kind, this is knowledge. Although you laugh with society . . . it is not when society is there, you tell John, "no, no, no, I won't [participate], I want to meditate." This way you should not do.

400 "Be attached devotedly to My point of meditation–that is knowledge." *Bhagavad Gītā* (1978).

You should indulge in that but internally you must not be . . .

JOHN: Immersed in that. You must keep yourself . . .

SWAMIJI: Away, away from that.

JOHN: How is this different from the sixteenth [knowledge]? Sixteenth was the tendency to be aloof from society.

SWAMIJI: No, that is *vivikta deśa sevitvam*, always [having this] tendency, e.g., when everybody is gone, her husband is gone to work, Viresh, he has gone to school, she will meditate. She will meditate. She will not do gardening, and she will tell Vishnu (the cook), "take care of [preparing the meals] and I will rest in my room," and you do your practice.

Aratir means when you are forced to indulge, that is [in] society.

JOHN: What was that one?

SWAMIJI: *Aratir janasaṁsadi.*

Vivikta deśa sevitvam is sixteenth [knowledge]. *Aratir janasaṁsadi* is seventeenth [knowledge]. *Aratir* means you indulge in everything, you do everything, but externally you laugh also when they tease you or . . .

JONATHAN: Tell jokes.

SWAMIJI: "Oh, yes . . . " You will also laugh with them. But internally you are weeping; in your own heart you are weeping. You think, "but I have to do it. It is my duty."

JONATHAN: But doesn't there come a time when you just think, "I can't be bothered with that any more."

SWAMIJI: No [laughs]. It is just *playa* and *paka*, it is making others sad. Others are affected. And in that, Lord Bhairava is affected. You must not be so cruel to anybody.

JONATHAN: No, but you said–if I can give an example–when we were in Srinagar, so many people, they say, "you must come out to dinner with us. You know, like Inderji invites me out for dinner two or three times in a week, "you must come to meet these people, these people would like to see you." But I don't go because I just think it's a waste of time.

DENISE: I think it's more like with family.

SWAMIJI: Huh?

DENISE: I really feel it's our duty to keep my family happy. They are living near us, you know. I mean, you know, to celebrate their birthdays, and do all that.

SWAMIJI: Yes.

JONATHAN: But this other thing, like going out for dinner and stuff, just casual acquaintances?

SWAMIJI: But actually it is not good. Because this is the manifestation of Parabhairava everywhere, so you should not make them depressed, I mean disappointed.

JONATHAN: So you should go?

SWAMIJI: You should indulge. You should indulge but with a hollow heart.

JONATHAN: But that's what I do. Thats why I don't go. Because when I go to these things, I sit down and I don't want to be there. I sit there and I just think, "it's a waste of time."

SWAMIJI: [laughs] No, no, you should not think that it is a waste of time.

DENISE: You should think that you are doing it for others.

SWAMIJI: Yes.

DENISE: But internally you want to be with your master.

SWAMIJI: Yes.

DENISE: That's where the real joy is, but that doesn't matter. You can't be with Him at night time anyway . . . sometimes you can't [laughs]!

SWAMIJI:

DVD 13 (32:46)

अध्यात्मज्ञाननिष्ठत्वं तत्त्वज्ञानार्थदर्शनम् ।
एतज्ज्ञानमिति प्रोक्तमज्ञानं यदतोऽन्यथा ॥१२॥

adhyātmajñānaniṣṭhatvaṁ tattvajñānārthadarśanam /
etajjñānamiti proktamajñānaṁ yadato'nyathā //12//
[repeated]

Adhyātma jñāna niṣṭhatvaṁ [means] to be focused in *adhyātma jñāna*, knowlege within, the knowledge of Parabhairava, *tattva jñānārtha darśanam*, and to conduct all means for this. This is *tattvajñānā. Niṣṭhatvaṁ* is eighteenth [knowledge]. *Adhyātma jñāna niṣṭhatvaṁ* is eighteenth. [It is] when you are situated in *adhyātma jñāna* (*jñāna*, knowledge, of your Parabhairava Self), *tattva jñānārtha darśanam*, and [use] all of your might for maintaining this *tattva jñāna. Etat jñānamiti*, this whole nineteen-fold is knowledge.

JOHN: What is nineteenth?

SWAMIJI: *Tattva jñānārtha darśanam*, [to use] all of your might to maintain this, maintain the knowledge of Parabhairava in each and every respect. And this is *jñāna* and opposite to this is *ajñāna* (ignorance). Opposite to this is *ajñānaṁ. Ajñānaṁ yadato'nyathā*, it is just absolutely opposite to this.

DENISE: Ignoring it.

JOHN: Is this number seventeen?

SWAMIJI: Huh?

JOHN: To engage but to remain aloof, is that also the same thing as compassion?

SWAMIJI: What?

JOHN: Number seventeen?

SWAMIJI: *Aratir janasaṁsadī*, aloof.

JOHN: Is that the same as compassion, to care for others.

SWAMIJI: No, *aratir* is *jana saṁsadi.*

JOHN: It's not compassion.

SWAMIJI: Yes, [it is] not liking to remain in society.

JOHN: But yet still . . .

SWAMIJI: But in society you should not show disliking. That will mar the state of Parabhairava. Because Parabhairava is also there; in those brutes Parabhairava is existing. So Parabhairava should not get . . .

JONATHAN: Squeezed.

SWAMIJI: Not squeezed. It is something else. Huh?

DENISE: Saddened?

SWAMIJI: Saddened, saddened, yes.

JOHN: Is this what it says in *Bhagavad Gītā* also, where it says you must love everyone everywhere . . .

SWAMIJI: Yes.

JOHN: . . . no matter whether they are high or low or different?

SWAMIJI: Yes. But you must love and you must not be given to love. You must not be a slave to love afterwards.

Now from 13th [*śloka*]. 13th, 14th, 15th, 16th, 17th, and 18th.

What is knowable (*jñeya*). *Jñānam* . . . because [Arjuna's] question was, "what is knowledge and what is known, what is to be known?" Through knowledge something is known. This knowledge, which is nineteen-fold, nineteen-fold knowledge, by this nineteen-fold knowledge, that which is known is explained now in these verses, in these beginning from 13th *śloka* to 18th *śloka*.

DVD 13 (36:56)

ज्ञेयं यत्तत्प्रवक्ष्यामि यज्ज्ञात्वामृतमश्नुते ।
अनादिमत्परं ब्रह्म न सत्तन्नासदुच्यते ॥१३॥
सर्वतः पाणिपादं तत्सर्वतोऽक्षिशिरोमुखम् ।
सर्वतः श्रुतिमल्लोके सर्वमावृत्य तिष्ठति ॥१४॥
सर्वेन्द्रियगुणाभासं सर्वेन्द्रियविवर्जितम् ।
असक्तं सर्वभृच्चैव निर्गुणं गुणभोक्तृच ॥१५॥
बहिरन्तश्च भूतानामचरं चरमेव च ।
सूक्ष्मत्वात्तदविज्ञेयं दूरस्थं चान्तिके च तत् ॥१६॥
अविभक्तं विभक्तेषु विभक्तमिव च स्थितम् ।
भूतभर्तृ च तज्ज्ञेयं ग्रसिष्णु प्रभविष्णु च ॥१७॥
ज्योतिषामपि तज्ज्योतिस्तमसः परमुच्यते ।
ज्ञानज्ञेयं ज्ञानगम्यं हृदि सर्वस्य विष्ठितम् ॥१८॥

jñeyaṁ yattatpravakṣāmi yajjñātvāmṛtamaśnute /
anādimatparaṁ brahma na sattannāsaducyate //13//
sarvataḥ pāṇipādaṁ tatsarvato'kṣiśiromukham /
sarvataḥ śrutimalloke sarvamāvṛtya tiṣṭhati //14//
sarvendriyaguṇābhāsaṁ sarvendriyavivarjitam /
asaktaṁ sarvabhṛccaiva nirguṇaṁ guṇabhoktṛ ca //15//
bahirantaśca bhūtānāmacaraṁ carameva ca /
sūkṣmatvāttadavijñeyaṁ dūrasthaṁ cāntike ca tat //16//
avibhaktaṁ vibhakteṣu vibhaktamiva ca sthitam /
bhūtabhartṛ ca tajjñeyaṁ grasiṣṇu prabhaviṣṇu ca //17//
jyotiṣāmapi tajjyotistamasaḥ paramucyate /
jñānajñeyaṁ jñānagamyaṁ hṛdi sarvasya viṣṭhitam //18//

This is *jñeya*, this is what is to be known. *Jñeyaṁ yat tat pravajñāmi*, now I will explain to you, O Arjuna, I will explain to you *jñeya*, what is to be known by this knowledge. This knowledge, nineteen-fold knowledge, by this nineteen-fold knowledge, [that] which is to be known, I will explain to you that. By knowing that [which] is to be known, you will become Parabhairava only by knowing [that]. If you know this knowledge, this knowledge is capable to make you the known. You will become that Parabhairava.

Anādimatparaṁ brahma, this Parabhairava is *anādimat*, without beginning. *Na sat*, it is not existing; *na asat*, it is not non-existing. *Sarvataḥ pāṇi pādaṁ tat*, all-around, [Parabhairava] has got hands. You have to know that His hands are everywhere present. His feet are everywhere present, stepping. It is not that you will do secretly some mischief and say that . . . under your curtains of your room, you will do some mischief.

No, it is not that.

He has got all hands; everywhere His hands are pervading. And His steps are there, he is stepping outside and inside–everywhere! *Sarvata akṣi,* He has got eyes everywhere, He sees everywhere (*akṣi, sarvata akṣi*). *Śiro*, He has got heads everywhere. He has not only [one] head in the one hundred and eighteenth world. He has got heads everywhere. He is seeing [everything]. *Śiro*, *mukham*, and He has got [innumerable] mouths also. He will talk to you and punish you at that very moment.

Sarvataḥ śrutimat loke, and He has got hearing power from all sides. He hears whatever nonsense or good words we utter–He hears that. *Sarvataḥ śrutimat loke sarvamātvṛtya tiṣṭhati*, He covers everything. He covers everything but He is silent, He is silent everywhere. It is why He is everywhere.

Sarvendriyaguṇābhāsaṁ sarvendriya vivarjitam . . . sarvataḥ śruti mat loke sarvamāvṛtya tiṣṭhati [repeated verse 14]. *Sarvendriya guṇābhāsaṁ* [verse 15], He is hearing [through] all organs. [Though] He has no organs, but He hears from all organs. All organic sounds He hears. *Sarvendriya-vivarjitam*, He has no organs, but He has the capacity to hear, He has the capacity to touch, He has capacity to see, and He can do anything.[401]

---

401 "*Sarva indriya guṇābhāsaṁ*, He is the light of all organs but He is not included in organs. He is the light giver of organs but He is not organs." *Bhagavad Gītā* (1978).

Asaktaṁ sarvabhṛt, He is detached from the world and He is attached to the world also. He is detached, because if you say [some] nonsense, if you act in a nonsense way, He won't kill you at that time, He won't curse you at that time, you will be saved. But He knows what [you have spoken or done]. He has come to know your weakness. He knows your weakness; your weakness of your . . . He knows [laughs] and it is wonderful. You can't escape.

Bahirantaśca bhūtānām acaraṁ carameva ca [verse 16]. He is inside and outside of everybody. *Acaraṁ* (*acaraṁ* means He is one-pointed), *carameva ca*, and He is all-pointed. He is one-pointed and, at the same time, His points are numberless.[402] *Sūkṣmatvāttadavijñeyaṁ dūrasthaṁ cāntike ca tat*. Because He is too much subtle, so He is not known. *Dūrasthaṁ*, He is very far away from you, but He is very near to you (*āntika ca tat*).

Avibhaktaṁ vibhakteṣu vibhaktamiva ca sthitam [verse 17]. *Avibhaktaṁ*, He is unmanifested in [that which is] manifested. *Vibhaktam*, He is just as [if] manifested [although] He is unmanifested. He looks as if He is manifested.[403]

Bhūtabhartṛ ca tajjñeyaṁ, He is the basis of all beings. *Grasiṣṇu*, He is digesting everybody; He has got the power to digest everybody. *Prabhaviṣṇu*, He has got the power to rule over everybody.

Jyotiṣām api tat jyotiḥ [verse 18], He is the illuminator of all illuminating beings, e.g., the sun, moon, stars, fire, and all of these illuminators. He is the illuminator of all of those illuminating [beings]. *Tamasaḥ paramucyate*, He is beyond darkness.

Jñānajñeyaṁ jñānagamyaṁ hṛdi sarvasya. He is understood by knowledge and He is situated in each and every heart of individuals.

Now the 19th *śloka*.

DVD 13 (45:56)

एतत्क्षेत्रं तथा ज्ञानं ज्ञेयं चोक्तं समासतः ।
मद्भक्त एतद्विज्ञाय मद्भावायोपपद्यते ॥ १९ ॥

402 "*Acaraṁ*, He is not moving, *carameva ca*, He is moving also." Ibid.
403 "*Avibhaktaṁ vibhakteṣu*, in universe, He is *avibhaktaṁ*, He is one. He is one in everything. *Vibhaktam iva ca*, He appears to be just away from [everything], but He is not away from the universe." Ibid.

etatkṣetraṁ tathā jñānaṁ jñeyaṁ coktaṁ samāsataḥ /
madbhakta etadvijñāya madbhāvāyopapadyate //19//

This is *kṣetra* (the field/body). I have explained to you what is *kṣetra*, what is knowledge (*jñāna*), what is to be known (*jñeya*). In brief words, I have explained to you these things. That *puruṣa* who is My devotee, he, after knowing this, *madbhāvāyopa-padyate*, he is likely to get dissolved in the state of Parabhairava.

Etat lakṣaṇaṁ kṛtvā parīkṣā kriyate [comm.]. He has related that, what is *prakṛti*, what is *puruṣa*, what are *guṇas*–all that He has already explained–and *jñāna* and *jñeya*, whatever . . .

> ["Now He explains *parīkṣā*. *Parīkṣā* means the conclusion of these three, i.e., *kṣetra*, *jñāna*, and *jñeya*."][404]

DVD 13 (47:10)

प्रकृतिं पुरुषं चैव विद्ध्यनादी उभावपि ।
विकारांश्च गुणांश्चैव विद्धि प्रकृतिसंभवान् ॥ १० ॥

prakṛtiṁ puruṣaṁ caiva viddhyanādī ubhāvapi /
vikārāṁśca guṇāṁścaiva viddhi prakṛtisaṁbhavān //20//

Prakṛti and *puruṣa* both are beginningless and endless. *Prakṛti* is endless and beginningless and *puruṣa* is endless and beginningless. Both are endless and beginningless, but *vikārāṁśca guṇāṁścaiva viddhi prakṛti saṁbhavān*, the three *guṇas* and the *ghaṭa padādi*, all of the objective world is produced by *prakṛti*. *Prakṛti* has produced these flowers and plants and everything, whatever [is found in creation]. This is *prakṛti's* creation, production. This is all *prakṛti*, i.e., these houses, plants, motorcars, all other things, they are produced by *prakṛti*. And *prakṛti* has nothing to do with this production.[405]

Prakṛti has made this for *puruṣa* to taste so that he will be entangled in the wheel of repeated births and deaths. *Prakṛti* is

404 *Bhagavad Gītā* (1978).

405 "These are changes of *prakṛti* . . . these are ending and these have rise also. But *prakṛti* is unending and unchanged, and without beginning." *Bhagavad Gītā* (1978).

dumb, quiet, she is *jaḍa* (inert). She creates this. She creates this for *puruṣa*. As soon as *puruṣa* gets awareness of *prakṛti* that, "*prakṛti* is dancing on me," he will become *mukta*. At once he becomes *mukta* and he remains aloof from *prakṛti*. Then he enters into the state of Parabhairava and he is *mukta*, *jīvan mukta* (liberated while embodied).

As long as *prakṛti* is not aware that he knows me–who? *Puruṣa*–she dances, she kicks him, she plays him, from one birth to another birth, from another birth to another birth, whatever she likes. But, as soon as he is aware of *prakṛti*, i.e., "*prakṛti* is playing with me," he becomes *jīvan mukta* at once. That is the knowledge. That is the . . . when you are established in *samādhi*, then you will become *jīvan mukta*.

DVD 13 (50:08)

कार्यकारणकर्तृत्वे हेतुः प्रकृतिरुच्यते ।
पुरुषः सुखदुःखानां भोक्तृत्वे हेतुरुच्यते ॥२१॥

kāryakāraṇakartṛtve hetuḥ prakṛtir ucyate /
puruṣaḥ sukhaduḥkhānāṁ bhoktṛtve heturucyate //21//

Kārya means effect, *kāraṇa* means cause, *kartṛtve* means doer (doer, done and effect, doing). *Prakṛti* is adopting this, *prakṛti* is conducting these three things: *kārya*, *kāraṇa*, *kartṛ bhāva*.[406] And

406 "*Prakṛti* is the cause of your actions in this world. Whatever you act in this world, [be it] *śabda* (hearing), *sparśa* (touch), *rūpa* (form), *rasa* (taste), and *gandha* (smell), in all these five ways, whatever you act, the cause of that action is your *prakṛti*. According to your *prakṛti*, you act. Somebody is compassionate, somebody is full of passion, somebody is always attached, somebody is moody–this is due to *prakṛti*. *prakṛtis* are many, *puruṣa* is one. Your nature is something else, his nature is something else, my nature is something else–but the Self is the same. It is polluted by our way of nature. You know, when once your *puruṣa*, your state of *puruṣa*, will get entry in God consciousness, there will be no difference in *prakṛti*. *Prakṛti* will be one there with *puruṣa*. That is the situation of union of Śakti and Śiva. Śakti and Śiva are united there. As long as *prakṛti* is differentiated, the union will never take place, i.e., the union of Śiva and Śakti will never take place. *Prakṛti* must not be differentiated." *Bhagavad Gītā* (1978).

puruṣa is just for tasting this and to be, to get entangled in repeated births and deaths.

DVD 13 (51:11)

पुरुषः प्रकृतिस्थो हि भुङ्क्ते प्रकृतिजान्गुणान् ।
कारणं गुणसङ्गोऽस्य सदसद्योनिजन्मसु ॥२२॥

puruṣaḥ prakṛtistho hi bhuṅkte prakṛtijānguṇān /
kāraṇaṁ guṇasaṅgo'sya sadasadyonijanmasu //22//

Puruṣa, actually *puruṣa* is dependent on *prakṛti,* and *bhuṅkte prakṛti jānguṇān*, he enjoys the three *guṇas* (three *guṇas* means just that worldly creation) and he just goes on enjoying the worldly creation. Sometimes with *sattva guṇa,* sometimes with *rāja guṇa*, and sometimes [with *tāma guṇa*], and he is sometimes happy, sometimes painful, sometimes . . .

DENISE: Unconscious.

SWAMIJI: . . . unconscious. *Sukha, duḥkha,* and *moha*, these are the three *guṇas*: *sukha* is from *sattvic, duḥkha* is from *rājas*, *moha* is from *tāmas*.

Moha means, "*zzzzzz* [snoring]." This is *moha*.

Duḥkha is activity, e.g., going to the cinema, going to play ball, baseball, whatever ball he plays, that is *rājas*.

And *sukha* is *sāttvic*, e.g., when he is seated and prays to God, at that time it is *sāttvic*.

And as long as *puruṣa* is attached to the *guṇas*, the three *guṇas*, it conducts for him *sadasad yoni janmasu*, *aneke* (*aneke* means numberless births and deaths), numberless births and deaths are produced for him because he deserves that. And he never gets away from this, this grabbing [i.e., attachment by which] he is caught.[407]

Upadraṣṭānumantāca, and in the long run, there is another being, that is Parabhairava . . .

---

407 "*Kāraṇaṁ guṇa saṇgo'sya*, the cause of enjoyment, enjoying the three dishes [i.e., three *guṇas*], is only the attachment for those enjoyments. This attachment for enjoyments becomes the cause of his enjoying these dishes, *sat asat yoni janmasu,* by which he goes either to hell or to heaven, or to liberation, or to higher worlds." Ibid.

DVD 13 (53:54)

उपद्रष्टानुमन्ता च भर्ता भोक्ता महेश्वरः ।
परमात्मेति चाप्युक्तो देहेऽस्मिन्पुरुषः परः ॥२३॥

upadraṣṭānumantā ca bhartā bhoktā maheśvaraḥ /
paramātmeti cāpyukto dehe'sminpuruṣaḥ paraḥ //23//

Upadraṣṭā, [the one] who is witnessing, what is going on, what is this damn thing going on, [i.e. happening] to *puruṣa,* and he is tossed [around] with *prakṛti*, *upadraṣṭā*, He sees, He observes, He witnesses, *anumantā ca*, and He thinks how far [*puruṣa*] is entangled by *prakṛti*, and He is Himself Maheśvara, Parabhairava, *paramātma*. *Paramātma* means supreme being. *Deha asmin puruṣaḥ,* and He is also existing in *deha* (body) and observing what is happening to that [*puruṣa*]. Both are [there]; one is above that and one is entangled in *prakṛti*.

Now, there are some, a few, who are, who have been graced by the *śaktipāta* of Parabhairava.

DVD 13 (55:12)

य एवं वेत्ति पुरुषं प्रकृतिं च गुणैः सह ।
सर्वथा वर्तमानोऽपि न स भूयोऽभिजायते ॥१४॥

ya evaṁ vetti puruṣaṁ prakṛtiṁ ca guṇaiḥ saha /
sarvathā vartamāno'pi na sa bhūyo'bhijāyate //24//

Anyone who fortunately understands what is *puruṣa* and what is *prakṛti* and what are these *guṇas* by which I was kicked by, played by *prakṛti*, *sarvathā,* if he knows, if he comes to this understanding, then he remains away, he remains aloof from *prakṛti*. He does not allow *prakṛti* to touch him!

Sarvathā vartamāno'pi na sa bhūyo'bhijāyate, he is established in the state of Parabhairava and he is *mukta*.

JONATHAN: So he can only become aware of that in *samādhi* though?

SWAMIJI: Yes.

So there are such people . . . it is not meant that only by/in *samādhi* they will understand Him.

DVD 13 (56:26)

ध्यानेनात्मनि पश्यन्ति केचिदात्मानमात्मना ।
अन्ये सांख्येन योगेन कर्मयोगेन चापरे ॥२५॥
अन्ये त्वेवमजानन्तः श्रुत्वान्येभ्य उपासते ।
तेऽपि चातितरन्त्येव मृत्युं श्रुतिपरायणाः ॥२६॥

dhyānenātmani paśyanti kecidātmānamātmanā /
anye sāṁkhyena yogena karmayogena cāpare //25//
anye tvevamajānantaḥ śrutvānyebhya upāsate /
te'pi cātitarantyeva mṛtyuṁ śrutiparāyaṇāḥ //26//

Everybody is behaving . . . when [an aspirant] has become *pāta*, [graced with] *śaktipāta* . . .

Śaktipāta is in various ways conducting everybody. It is not *śaktipāta* in [only] one way that he is in *samādhi*.

. . . some sing the glory of Lord Śiva day and night. Some go on doing service for mankind everywhere without any reward. *Dhyānenātmani paśyanti*, some people concentrate in the heart and see Him. *Kecidātmānamātmanā*, some people by mind, they focus their minds and they enter into *samādhi*. *Annye sāṁkhyena yogena*, some people, by hearing the *śāstras* from masters lips, by that they rise. *Karma yogena cāpare*, some in adopting *karma yoga* (*karma yoga* [means] *yoga* in action), they go on [acting] and thinking of Lord Śiva.

And they have got friends, and his friend is seated before his master. Although he does not understand the philosophy of his friends' master, he asks his friend, "what has he said, what has he said to you?" He in reply says, "he has said like this," and he goes on deriving that [knowledge] and *bas*, he also rises. *Śrutvānyebhya,* from friends they hear the reality of generalizing [i.e., explanation] in this Parabhairava state. All are rising. All rise!

JOHN: Which number sir?

SWAMIJI: Number 26th.

DVD 13 (59:17)

यावत्किञ्चित्संभवति सत्त्वं स्थावरजङ्गमम् ।
क्षेत्रक्षेत्रज्ञसंयोगात्तद्विद्धि भरतर्षभ ॥२७॥

yāvatkiñcitsaṁbhavati sattvaṁ sthāvarajaṅgamam /
kṣetrakṣetrajñasaṁyogāttadviddhi bharatarṣabha //27//

Whatever happens in this world, *kṣetra* and *kṣetrajña* is conducting in each and every respect. *Kṣetra* means this body, *kṣetrajña* is soul.

Which soul? Limited soul (*puruṣa*).

And limited soul is conducted by unlimited soul side by side in the body. [The unlimited soul] also whips [the limited soul]; He takes the whip and sees if he has some capacity for learning [saying], "let him rise, let him rise." [The unlimited soul] pushes him and he rises.

Kṣetra kṣetrajña saṁyogāt tat viddhi bharatarṣabha.[408] All is done automatically. It is an automatic machine. This is a computer, real computer. He rises.[409]

---

408 "That creation takes place by the union of *kṣetra* and *kṣetrajña*. When there is *kṣetra* (*kṣetra* is the field) and the plougher of field, that is *kṣetrajñā*. Plougher of field is *puruṣa*, who is governed by *prakṛti*." *Bhagavad Gītā* (1978).

409 " . . . if you don't become slave of *prakṛti*. If you become slave of *prakṛti*, you are gone. When you follow these, follow the movements of these five senses of organs, i.e., five senses of cognition and five senses of action, along with the touch of these three *guṇas*, you are just sheep, you are just carried by *prakṛti*. And this is that individual being who is governed by *prakṛti*. He creates this, he creates this universe. Because everybody has his own universe in his mind; you have your own world, you have your own world, you have your own world. And that world you have created by the combination of these . . . by following your nature. When you command *prakṛti*, then you don't create your world. Once you have not created your world, you are free, you have no rebirth. You won't come . . . you won't be entangled in the repeated births and deaths." Ibid.

DVD 13 (1:00:40)

समं सर्वेषु भूतेषु तिष्ठन्तं परमेश्वरम् ।
विनश्यत्स्वविनश्यन्तं यः पश्यति स पश्यति ॥२८॥

samaṁ sarveṣu bhūteṣu tiṣṭhantaṁ parameśvaram /
vinaśyatsvavinaśyantaṁ yaḥ paśyati sa paśyati //28//

And Parameśvaraḥ who is existing in each and every body, not only in human beings but in insects also (in insects also that Parabhairava is existing), *vinaśyatsu,* if this body holder (body holder means that limited body holder), if he dies, that next one[410] does not die. He carries him into another fresh body and goes on, goes on, goes on carrying him with new improvements, a new increment.

Everybody increases, everybody increases. There is no doubt that he is [not] lost. He is never lost! [One] who sees this, who understands this, he is understanding, he is understanding it in real sense, and he is filled with wisdom and he is likely to become, sooner or later, one with Parabhairava.[411]

समं पश्यन् हि सर्वत्र समवस्थितमीश्वरम् ।
न हिनस्त्यात्मनात्मानं ततो याति परां गतिम् ॥२९॥

samaṁ paśyan hi sarvatra samavasthitamīśvaram /
na hinastyātmanātmānaṁ tato yāti parāṁ gatim //29//
[not recited or translated][412]

410 That is, the unlimited soul, Parabhairava. [*Editor's note*]

411 "That person who believes and perceives that this whole universe along with *prakṛti* and *puruṣa* takes place by the free will of Lord Śiva and that *puruṣa*, that individual never dies (though he leaves his body, but he never dies, he is always alive), by that understanding he becomes *jīvan mukta.*" *Bhagavad Gītā* (1978).

412 "And that person who sees everything in sameness, in equal state–pain and pleasure, happiness and absence of happiness–everything he experiences in the same attitude. There is no difference between pain

DVD 13 (1:02:26)

प्रकृत्यैव हि कर्माणि क्रियमाणानि सर्वशः ।
यः पश्यति तथात्मानमकर्तारं स पश्यति ॥३०॥

prakṛtyaiva hi karmāṇi kriyamāṇāni sarvaśaḥ /
yaḥ paśyati tathātmānamakartāraṁ sa paśyati //30//

Prakṛti does everything, *prakṛti* conducts whatever is good and bad or . . . good, bad, or?

JOHN: Indifferent . . . good bad or neutral?

SWAMIJI: No, the three *guṇas*. Good, bad and . . .

JOHN: Illusion or what?

SWAMIJI: . . . illusion. Good, bad, and illusion (*māya*).

All of these three-fold acts are conducted by *prakṛti*. The one who observes this, the one, that limited soul who observes this, he observes the reality that [there is] another observer is inside . . .

Do you understand?

. . . the one who observes that, "*prakṛti* is doing this nonsense with me, *prakṛti* is doing this play . . . "

DENISE: Nonsense play with me.

SWAMIJI: ". . . with me," [one] who understands this [play] of *prakṛti*,[413] he understands that other Person who is there with

and pleasure for that person who is realized. Pain is adjusted to body; pleasure is adjusted to body and senses. And pain and pleasures, all these things, are not adjusted to *ātman*, the soul. Soul is absolutely above this cycle. . . . So when you serve a cup of tea to [your wife], you should serve the same, in the same scale, that tea to some other person, thinking that God is same existing in each and every being. If there is differentiation, then that means you are tamed by *prakṛti*. You have become sheep. You are entangled in some limited cycle." Ibid.

413 "*Yaḥ paśyati tathātmānam akartāraṁ sa paśyati*. Now what you have to do? What do you have to perceive? You have to perceive that this is the adjustment of *prakṛti*, what to me? I am just detached from *prakṛti* and so he remains *akartāra*, absolute detached from the clutches of *prakṛti*. . . . So he is *akarṭritvam*, he is beyond, he has risen beyond the cycle of doing, doer-ship. He does not do anything. Although he does everything, but he understands that I am not doing it, it is *prakṛti* who does." *Bhagavad Gītā* (1978).

him in the body.

DENISE: Parabhairava.

SWAMIJI: Bhairava, yes. He understand Him. At once he understands Him. So He gives him a patting, "yes, you have found, you have found the truth."

So it is never [too] late!

O Arjuna, I am just open-heartedly waiting for everybody to come and embrace Me and become one with Me. [There is] no fear, nothing, don't worry about anything. It will come in its place as soon as possible, as soon as you like [to have] it. It is your liking. If you don't like it, don't like it.[414] Still you are with Me.

DVD 13 (1:04:57)

यदा भूतपृथग्भावमेकस्थमनुपश्यति ।
तत एव च विस्तारं ब्रह्म संपद्यते तदा ॥ ३१ ॥
अनादित्वान्निर्गुणत्वात्परमात्मायमव्ययः ।
शरीरस्थोऽपि कौन्तेय न करोति न लिप्यते ॥ ३२ ॥
यथा सर्वगतं सौक्ष्म्यादाकाशं नोपलिप्यते ।
सर्वत्रावस्थितो देहे तथात्मा नोपलिप्यते ॥ ३३ ॥

yadā bhūtapṛthagbhāvamekasthamanupaśyati /
tata eva ca vistāraṁ brahma saṁpadyate tadā //31//
anāditvānnirguṇatvātparamātmāyamavyayaḥ /
śarīrastho'pi kaunteya na karoti na lipyate //32//
yathā sarvagataṁ saukṣmyādākāśaṁ nopalipyate /
sarvatrāvasthito dehe tathātmā nopalipyate //33//

These three *ślokas*: 31st, 32nd, and 33rd in one.

414 "*Saktipāta* means you have to maintain your vigor, you have to maintain your will. There must be firm will. That is *śaktipāta*. *Śaktipāta* is not derived from other sources. You have got *śaktipāta*, you have got the power of *śaktipāta*, to have it. You possess it with vigor, with force, because you have got that power. But you don't like it [laughs]! *Śaktipāta* comes from within. From within! *Śaktipāta* does not come from without. It is not [from] without. It is there!" *Bhagavad Gītā*, 2.65.

When a person sees *bhūta pṛthag bhāvam*, all *pañca* (five) *bhūtas* (five elements), organs of action, organs of cognition, mind, intellect and ego, when this limited soul understands [that] they are–all of these organs, mind, etc.–are residing in some super-being; in some super-being they are residing, they are life-full in a super-being (that is the second person who is [residing] in your body), *akarthāraṁ paśyati* [verse 30], then he is likely to get dissolved in that. There is cent-per-cent hope of him to get absorbed in the Parabhairava state.[415]

So Parabhairava state is not far away from you!

DVD 13 (1:07:14)

अनादित्वान्निर्गुणत्वात्परमात्मायमव्ययः ।
शरीरस्थोऽपि कौन्तेय न करोति न लिप्यते ॥३२॥
यथा सर्वगतं सौक्ष्म्यादाकाशं नोपलिप्यते ।
सर्वत्रावस्थितो देहे तथात्मा नोपलिप्यते ॥३३॥

anāditvānnirguṇatvātparamātmāyamavyayaḥ /
śarīrastho'pi kaunteya na karoti na lipyate //32//
yathā sarvagataṁ saukṣmyādākāśaṁ nopalipyate /
sarvatrāvasthito dehe tathātmā nopalipyate //33//
[repeated]

Anāditvāt, being endless, *nirguṇatvāt*, above *guṇas*, *param-ātma* is *avyaya*, unperishable. Although He is existing in the body, *na karoti na lipyate*, He does not do anything, anything wrong, and neither He gets impression of anything bad. He is just like *ākāśa*, i.e., everywhere, all-pervading, and without any

415 "When a *yogi* perceives that this expansion of this universe is centered in my own consciousness, in the consciousness of the state of Lord Śiva, and perceives that it is created from me–"this creation also takes place from me, and this destruction of all this universe takes place in me"–he does not become entangled by doing and not doing, in vice and virtue. Because he is God himself. Although he is situated in body, *na lipyate ākāśavat*, he becomes just like *ākāśa* (ether), he is not touched by anything, whatever he does. He is just above it. He does everything divine." *Bhagavad Gītā* (1978).

dust, without any smell, bad smell, without anything which is derived from *pṛthvī*, *jala*, *agni*–all of those [*mahābhūtas*]. He becomes just [like] *ākāśa*. *Ākāśa* is great. In *ākāśa*, there is nothing . . . dust won't remain there. In the same way, his *ātma* does not get dusty, does not get . . .

JONATHAN: Tarnished.

SWAMIJI: What? Tarnished?

JONATHAN: Dirty.

SWAMIJI: Dirty, yes, yes.

DVD 13 (1:09:00)

यथा प्रकाशयत्येकः कृत्स्नं लोकमिमं रविः ।
क्षेत्रं क्षेत्री तथा कृत्स्नं प्रकाशयति भारत ॥३४॥

yathā prakāśayatyekaḥ kṛtsnaṁ lokamimaṁ raviḥ /
kṣetraṁ kṣetrī tathā kṛtsnaṁ prakāśayati bhārata //34//

O Arjuna, just as the sun glorifies this whole world (only one sun), in the same way, *kṣetraṁ kṣetrī tathā kṛtsnaṁ prakāśayati bhārata*, this body (this body means the totality of body, not only one body), all the bodies from *śāntātītā kalā* to down below,[416] all of these bodies are shining with that glamour of God consciousness.

DVD 13 (1:10:02)

क्षेत्रक्षेत्रज्ञयोरेवमन्तरं ज्ञानचक्षुषा ।
भूतप्रकृतिमोक्षं च ये विदुर्यान्ति ते परम् ॥३५॥

kṣetrakṣetrajñayorevamantaraṁ jñānacakṣuṣā /
bhūtaprakṛtimokṣaṁ ca ye viduryānti te param //35//

How *kṣetra* and *kṣetrajña* can be conducted? What is the secret of *kṣetra* and *kṣetrajña* (body and body holder)? What is meant by

416 "*Kālāgnirudra bhuvana* is the lowest *bhuvana* (lowest world). *Kālāgnirudra bhuvana* is the territory of that *rudra* who is the embodiment of fire. His body is made of fire, only fire with consciousness." Swami Lakshmanjoo, *Tantrāloka* 9.3 (1977).

[there being] another being in the body?

If, by opening their eyes of knowledge (the supreme Parabhairava knowledge), they understand the reality of this process, *yānti te param*, [then] they are focused to that Parabhairava state in the end.

[13th chapter is] finished.

Pumānprakṛtirityeṣa . . . this is the conclusion. This is the 35th *śloka*.

Now, the conclusion of Abhinavagupta.

DVD 13 (1:11:08)

पुमान्प्रकृतिरित्येष भेदः संमूढचेतसाम् ।
परिपूर्णास्तु मन्यन्ते निर्मलात्ममयं जगत् ॥

pumānprakṛtirityeṣa bhedaḥ saṁmūḍhacetasām /
paripūrṇāstu manyante nirmalātmamayaṁ jagat //13//

॥ Concluding *śloka* of 13th chapter ॥

Pumān prakṛtirityeṣa bhedaḥ saṁmūḍha cetasām. "This is *puruṣa*, this is *prakṛti*, this is *buddhiḥ*, this is *ahaṁkāra*, this is that, this is . . . these are these varieties," this kind of differentiated perception is meant for *saṁmūḍha cetasām*, those who are not actually God-realized.

Paripūrṇāstu, those who are God-realized, they see all of this *tamāsha* [i.e., the differentiated world], *nirmalātmamayaṁ,* it is quite pure and quite . . . this is only the substance of Parabhairava and nothing else.

So enjoy this state of Parabhairava.

This is the conclusion of this [13th chapter].

Chapter 14

SWAMIJI: This is the 14th chapter.

DVD 14 (00:08)

श्रीभगवानुवाच
śrī bhagavān uvāca

परं भूयः प्रवक्ष्यमि ज्ञानानां ज्ञानमुत्तमम् ।
यज्ज्ञात्वा मुनयः सर्वे परां सिद्धिमितो गताः ॥१॥

paraṁ bhūyaḥ pravakṣyami jñānānāṁ jñānamuttamam /
yajjñātvā munayaḥ sarve parāṁ siddhimito gatāḥ //1//

[Lord Kṛṣṇa]: I will again tell you [about] the supreme knowledge, which is the topmost-supreme, in the same way. I have already told you [about] this supreme knowledge. I will tell you again the most supreme knowledge [that is even greater] than this.

Yat jñātvā, when you are residing in that [supreme knowledge], *yat jñātvā munayaḥ sarve*, all *ṛṣis* and *devas*, and individuals, and everybody, *parāṁ siddhimito gatāḥ*, they have achieved the greatest *siddhi*, the greatest power of being manifested, of being united, united in the Parabhairava state, *ito*, here and hereafter (*ito gatāḥ* means here and hereafter). Not [only] after [leaving] this body; here, here also in body, in [this] existing body and after throwing this body also.

DVD 14 (01:23)

इदं ज्ञानमुपाश्रित्य मम साधर्म्यमागताः ।
सर्गेऽपि नोपजायन्ते प्रलये न व्यथन्ति च ॥२॥

idaṁ jñānamupāśritya mama sādharmyamāgatāḥ /
sarge'pi nopajāyante pralaye na vyathanti ca //2//

[Those] who possesses this kind of knowledge, O Arjuna, they *mama sādharmyamāgatāḥ*, they are qualified just like Me; they become qualified, fully qualified just like Me. All qualifications which I have, they [also] have, not [even] this much less [Swamiji demonstrates]; [not even] this much difference of qualifications between Me and them.

Do you understand?

Sarge'pi nopajāyante, at the time of the new creation of this world, when one *yuga* changes and another *yuga* comes, at the time of the new *yuga, nopajāyante*, they are not born [again]. *Pralaye na vyathanti ca*, and at the stage of *saṁhāra* (destruction), *na vyathanti*, they are not killed; they are not killed, they are just living.

[In the next *śloka*], first He says how *saṁsāra* takes place, how *saṁsāra* is conducted in the state of Parabhairava. *Saṁsāra* means this world.

DVD 14 (03:19)

मम योनिर्महद्ब्रह्म तस्मिन्गर्भं दधाम्यहम् ।
संभवः सर्वभूतानां ततो भवति भारत ॥ ३ ॥

mama yonirmahadbrahma tasmingarbhaṁ dadāmyaham /
saṁbhavaḥ sarvabhūtānāṁ tato bhavati bhārata //3//

My seed form, *mama yonir* means My *yoni*, My great *śakti* is *brahma* (*tasmin brahma* means that *svātantrya śakti*[417]). *Tasmingarbhaṁ dadāmyaham*, in that, I insert [My] seed. I, Lord Śiva, insert [My] seed in that . . .

JOHN: Like womb?

SWAMIJI: Yes.

. . . in that womb of *brahma* (universal divine *śakti*, *svātantrya śakti*, of Lord Śiva). That is the universal womb. In that universal womb, I insert [My] seed, *saṁbhavaḥ sarvabhūtānāṁ*, so that all *jaḍa* (insentient), *cetana* (sentient), good, bad, all are created.

417 See footnote 77 for an explanation of *svātantrya śakti*.

DVD 14 (04:44)

सर्वयोनिषु कौन्तेय मूर्तयः संभवन्ति याः ।
तासां ब्रह्म महद्योनिरहं बीजप्रदः पिता ॥४॥

sarvayoniṣu kaunteya mūrtayaḥ saṁbhavanti yāḥ /
tāsāṁ brahma mahadyoniraham̐ bījapradaḥ pitā //4//

In all *yonīs*, in all births and deaths, in all *yonīs*[418] (say in human beings, insects, snakes, serpents, whatever creation is seen in this world), in all created beings, those *mūrtis* (forms) which appear after this creation, *tāsāṁ brahma mahat yonir*, in these creations this also functions, this sex. That is individual sex. [And] that is universal sex, i.e., Mine is universal sex. The sex played in the world is individual sex. And in those *yonis* . . .

JOHN: Individual *yonis*.

SWAMIJI: . . . individual *yonis, svātantrya śakti* is a big *yoni*, and I am the father. I am the father of everybody. Father means grand-grandfather who is the creator.[419]

DVD 14 (06:37)

सत्त्वं रजस्तम इति गुणाः प्रकृतिसंभवाः ।
निबध्नन्ति महाबाहो देहे देहिनमव्ययम् ॥५॥

sattvaṁ rajastama iti guṇāḥ prakṛtisaṁbhavāḥ /
nibadhnanti mahābāho dehe dehinamavyayam //5//

Sattvaguṇa, *rajaguṇa*, and *tamaguṇa*, these three *guṇas* which are, which come out from *prakṛti*, which are created by *prakṛti*, they bind the individual who is *avyayam*, who is un-

418 *Yoni* means the womb, female organ of generation. [*Editor's note*]

419 "So that *brahma* [i.e., *svātantrya śakti*] with that universal sexual organ is the mother of this universe. [She] is the great mother, *sakala saṁsāra vamana svabhāvā,* because She creates the whole universe. One hundred and eighteen worlds are created by that *śakti* and without change. She produces this whole universe without any change in Her nature. I am universal father and My energy is universal mother of this whole universe." *Bhagavad Gītā* (1978).

perishable.[420]

Tatra sattvaṁ . . . 6th, 7th [*ślokas*].

DVD 14 (07:28)

तत्र सत्त्वं निर्मलत्वात्प्रकाशकमनामयम् ।
सुखसङ्गेन बध्नाति ज्ञानसङ्गेन चानघ ॥६॥
रजो रागात्मकं विद्धि तृष्णासङ्गसमुद्भवम् ।
तन्निबध्नाति कौन्तेय कर्मसङ्गेन देहिनम् ॥७॥

tatra sattvaṁ nirmalatvātprakāśakamanāmayam /
sukhasaṅgena badhnāti jñānasaṅgena cānagha //6//
rajo rāgātmakaṁ viddhi tṛṣṇāsaṅgasamudbhavam /
tannibadhnāti kaunteya karmasaṅgena dehinam //7//

In that, in the three *guṇas*, this *sattvaguṇa* is *nirmalatvāt*, it is *nirmala*, it is pure, and *prakāśakam*, it gives light, it throws light in individuals. *Sukha saṅgena badhnāti*, but it entangles a human being with joy. Joy is also bondage. And *jñāna saṅgena cānagha*, by remembering God, remembering God also binds him to one [limited] point–that *sattvaguṇa*.[421]

Rajo rāgātmakaṁ viddhi tṛṣṇāsaṅga samudbhavam. And *raja-*

420 "Now, why this family of universal father and universal mother is put to torture? Why they are kept in the field of being tortured everywhere, crisis? The nature of that mother is *prakṛti* and from *prakṛti* three *guṇas* are produced, which are held by universal mother. *Dehi*, the possessor of body, who is in fact immortal, *ātmatayā sattvarajastamobhir*, he believes that 'I am body' because of these *guṇas*; three *guṇas* make him understand that 'you are body, you are not immortal.'" Ibid.

421 "This kind of knowledge binds you because when you confirm in your brain that you are joy, [then] you are discarding pain, you are discarding sadness. . . . We possess *sattvaguṇa* in the beginning just to get fitness in meditation. When you get fitness in meditation through *sattvaguṇa*, then in the end you realize that *sattvaguṇa, rajaguṇa*, and *tamaguṇa* is only the expansion of Lord Śiva. It is nothing other than Lord Śiva. . . . God consciousness does not recognize only *sattvaguṇa* and discards *rajaguṇa* and *tamaguṇa*. God consciousness is filled in all the three *guṇas*." Ibid.

guṇa is attachment, it is *rāga*. It comes from *triṣṅā*, from thirst, from the thirst for worldly affairs. *Tat nibadhnāti kaunteya karma saṅgena*, by the activity of worldly activities, it binds the individual.

Now is *tamaguṇa*.

DVD 14 (09:35)

तमस्त्वज्ञानजं विद्धि मोहनं सर्वदेहिनाम् ।
प्रमादालस्यनिद्राभिस्तन्निबध्नाति भारत ॥८॥

tamastva jñānajaṁ viddhi mohanaṁ sarvadehinām /
pramādālasyanidrābhistannibadhnāti bhārata //8//

O Arjuna, *tamaguṇa* is *ajñānajaṁ*, it rises, it gets its force through ignorance, and it is *mohanaṁ* (*mohanaṁ* means it keeps you away from remembering God). And it binds you by *pramāda* (*pramāda* means forgetfulness), *ālasya*, by *ālasya* (*ālasya* means [one] who is very slow in action), and by sleeping.[422] These three make him entangled in the way, in the circle of *tamaguṇa*.[423]

422 "*Nidrā* is just negligence; *nidrā* is not sleeping. *Nidrā* does not mean here sleep. *Nidrā* is just negligence." Ibid.

423 "*Pramāda* (by forgetfulness), *ālasya* (by sluggishness), *nidrābhi* (and by sleeping, drowsiness), Abhinavagupta explains, after doing thousands and *lakhs* (100,000) of good actions, you have gained this body, which is the only way to reach the state of God consciousness and final liberation; and [to] just waste it in other ways is *pramādaḥ*, is negligence. . . . You must realize that this body is meant to meditate and to get liberated. This body cannot be repeatedly bestowed to you. It is very difficult to get this body of a human being.

"For instance, one breath is gone, one breath you have exhaled . . . while exhaling, you were not aware of watching your breath, and that is one *kṣaṇa* (one moment) of that life. *Sarvaratnairna*, if you will try and spend all your money to get that moment back, it will never come. That moment is gone, wasted. *Sa vṛthā nīyate yena*, and the person who wastes their whole life in this way, *sa pramādī*, he is filled with negligence, *narādhamaḥ*, and he is to be pitied.

"*Ālasyaṁ śubha karaṇīyeṣu*, find out! Don't waste your time of this precious life. This precious life, it won't be repeated to you every now and then. You have got it by I don't know how many good actions of your past lives." Ibid.

DVD 14 (10:48)

सत्त्वं सुखे सञ्जयति रजः कर्मणि भारत ।
ज्ञानमावृत्य तु तमः प्रमादे सञ्जयत्युत ॥९॥

sattvaṁ sukhe sañjayati rajaḥ karmaṇi bhārata /
jñānamāvṛtya tu tamaḥ pramāde saṅjayatyuta //9//

Sattvaguṇa actually unites the individual in *sukha*, in peace of mind. *Rajaguṇa* unites the individual in the activities of the world and *tamaguṇa* covers his knowledge of *sukha* and unites him in [the state of] forgetfulness so that he goes on sleeping.

Now, again He clarifies these activities of *sattvaguṇa*, *rajaguṇa*, and *tamaguṇa*.

DVD 14 (11:55)

रजस्तमश्चाभिभूय सत्त्वं भारत वर्धते ।

rajastamaścābhibhūya sattvaṁ bhārata vardhate / 10a

And in the same way, *rajaguṇa* and *tamaguṇa,* after subsiding *rajaguṇa* and *tamaguṇa, sattvaṁ* gets rise, *sattvaguṇa* [comes into] force. *Sattvaguṇa* gets into force after . . . although there are all of the three *guṇas* always (always they are existing in one's body, all the three *guṇas*), but in all the three *guṇas*, *rajaguṇa* and *tamaguṇa* are subsided, they get subsided, and *sattvaguṇa* remains in predominance and it rises, *sattvaguṇa* rises.

And it is [correct] behavior for *sādhaka* (a *yogi*), how he should take hold of *sattvaguṇa* when it rises, when it goes on rising, make it, give it span of length in its force of rising so that you don't lose [it]. God consciousness will be helpful [i.e., available] to you at the time when *sattvaguṇa* is in force. Because, at the time when *sattvaguṇa* is in force, *rajaguṇa* and *tamaguṇa* are naturally subsided, [but] you must not think that *rajaguṇa* or *tamaguṇa* are finished; they are in a depressed [i.e., subsided] state.

So *sādhaka* should be watchful at that time when *sattvaguṇa* rises. He should prolong it, prolong it with effort, so that *sattva-*

guṇa rises for a long time and he can be, his *abyāsa* (practice) will be fruitful.

And at the same time . . .

DVD 14 (14:06)

रजः सत्त्वं तमश्चैव तमः सत्त्वं रजस्तथा ॥१०॥

rajaḥ sattvaṁ tamaścaiva tamaḥ sattvaṁ rajastathā //10//

. . . *rajaḥ*, *rajaguṇa* gets in force; when, at that same time, *sattvaguṇa* and *tamaguṇa* are subsided, *sattvaguṇa* and *tamaguṇa* are subsided and *rajaguṇa* gets into force, at that time you should not do any action, you should leave this [activity] because this is a hindrance for *sādhaka*. Because *rajaguṇa* is, at that time, *rajaguṇa* is in force and *sattvaguṇa* and *tamaguṇa* are subsided. So you should remain [like a] eunuch, i.e., you should not do any activity for maintaining this [*rajaguṇa*]. You should keep absent from that, from this force of *rajaguṇa*.

DENISE: Not to feed it, so it [doesn't] get stronger.

SWAMIJI: Yes.

And *tamaguṇa* gets in force sometimes [when] *sattvaguṇa* and *rajaguṇa* are subsided. At that time, *tamaguṇa* just wants to [carry you] to neglectfullness and [makes you want to] go to sleep, and you [feel that you] have no other duty. There you should be alert and not be given to that *tamaguṇa*, because *rajaguṇa* and *sattvaguṇa* have no power [at that time].

Another way of clearing [i.e., explaining] this *sattvaguṇa* . . .

DVD 14 (15:48)

सर्वद्वारेषु देहेऽस्मिन्प्रकाशमुपजायते ।
ज्ञानं यदा तदा विद्याद्विवृद्धं सत्त्वमित्युत ॥११॥

sarvadvāreṣu dehe'sminprakāśamupajāyate /
jñānaṁ yadātadāvidyādvivṛddhaṁ sattvamityuta //11//

This is the 11th *śloka*, and 12th *śloka*, and 13th *śloka*.

DVD 14 (16:06)

लोभः प्रवृत्तिरारम्भः कर्मणामशमश्च तृट् ।
रजस्येतानि जायन्ते विवृद्धे भरतर्षभ ॥१२॥
अप्रकाशोऽप्रवृत्तिश्च प्रमादो मोह एव च ।
तमस्येतानि जायन्ते विवृद्धे कुरुनन्दन ॥१३॥

lobhaḥ pravṛttirārambhaḥ karmaṇāmaśamaśca tṛṭ /
rajasyetāni jāyante vivṛddhe bharatarṣabha //12//

aprakāśo'pravṛttiśca pramādo moha eva ca /
tamasyetāni jāyante vivṛddhe kurunandana //13//

When an individual finds that in all [his] organs, in all senses (in mind, in the state of mind, in the state of *ahaṁkāra*, in the state of ego, in the state of intellect, in the state of organic field), *prakāśam upajāyate*, something illuminating rises and you are forced to do *abhyāsa* (practice) at that time; your organs all become divine, your mind becomes divine, your intellect becomes divine (these are the tides going on of the three *guṇas*). This is . . . [at this time], you should know that *sattvaguṇa* is in force. This is the kingdom of *sattvaguṇa* at this time. At that time, you should make good purpose of this and do *abhyāsa*, do *abhyāsa*. Do *abyāsa* and that *abhyāsa* will have much more effect. At that time, you should know that *vivṛddhaṁ sattvamityuta*, that *sattvaguṇa* is in force, it is the kingdom of *sattvaguṇa*. You should not neglect that point.[424]

DVD 14 (17:51)

लोभः प्रवृत्तिरारम्भः कर्मणामशमश्च तृट् ।
रजस्येतानि जायन्ते विवृद्धे भरतर्षभ ॥१२॥

424 "You have to get rid of the kingdom of these two first (*rajaguṇa* and *tamaguṇa*) . . . and then you get entry in the kingdom of *sattvaguṇa*. And *sattvaguṇa* will also be shattered afterwards when you get entry in the *guṇātīta* state. *Guṇātīta* is where these three *guṇas* are just one with God consciousness." *Bhagavad Gītā* (1978).

lobhaḥ pravṛttirārambhaḥ karmaṇāmaśamaśca tṛṭ /
rajasyetāni jāyante vivṛddhe bharatarṣabha //12//
[repeated]

And another thing is when *lobha*, there is the rise of *lobha* (*lobha* means greed, *lobha*), *pravṛttir*, to do work, *ārambhaḥ*, to start new work, new project, *karmaṇāmaśamaśca*, and activity of . . . your activity has no end, it rises, at that time, you should know that *rajaguṇa* is in force; it is the kingdom of *rajaguṇa*. You should try do avoid it, you should try to avoid it. Because it won't be effective for your *abhyāsa* (practice). Although you do *abhyāsa*, it will take you to activities of behavior, outward behavior.[425]

DVD 14 (19:06)

अप्रकाशोऽप्रवृत्तिश्च प्रमादो मोह एव च ।
तमस्येतानि जायन्ते विवृद्धे कुरुनन्दन ॥ १३ ॥

aprakāśo'pravṛttiśca pramādo moha eva ca /
tamasyetāni jāyante vivṛddhe kurunandana //13//
[repeated]

O beloved to Kauravas, Arjuna,[426] when there is *aprakāśa*,[427] you cannot know how to get out from this forgetfulness, *apravṛttiśca*, you have no liking for doing anything, *pramāda*, you forget everything, *moha eva ca*, and you are caught by *moha* (*moha* means negligence of the Lord), you don't want to think of the Lord also; you hate the Lord at that time. *Tamasyetāni jāyante vivṛddhe*, you must know that *tamaguṇa* is in [force]; this is the kingdom of *tamaguṇa*, so you should remain, you should about turn from this drama.

DENISE: Swamiji, when people are in depression, they are in *tamoguṇa*?

SWAMIJI: Yes.

---

425 That is, even while meditating, your mind will remain involved in worldly activities. [*Editor's note*]

426 "[Arjuna] didn't want to kill Kauravas, so Lord Kṛṣṇa addresses him as the lover of the Kauravas." *Bhagavad Gītā* (1978).

427 *Aprakāśa* means the absence of light, i.e., *tamaguṇa*. [*Editor's note*]

Now He clears [i.e., explains] again what will happen at the time of death.

DVD 14 (20:39)

यदा सत्त्वे विवृद्धे तु प्रलयं याति देहभृत् ।
तदोत्तमविदां लोकानमलान्प्रतिपद्यते ॥१४॥
रजसि प्रलयं गत्वा कर्मसङ्गिषु जायते ।
तथा प्रलीनस्तमसि मूढयोनिषु जायते ॥१५॥

yadā sattve vivṛddhe tu pralayaṁ yāti dehabhṛt /
tadottamavidāṁ lokānamalānpratipadyate //14//
rajasi pralayaṁ gatvā karmasaṅgiṣu jāyate /
tathā pralīnastamasi mūḍhayoniṣujāyate //15//

And there is also another point to be observed, to be noted. If by chance, at the time of death, *sattvaguṇa* is in force–at the time of death, this is the last moment of his [life], at that time [if] *sattvaguṇa* is in force and *pralayaṁ yāti*, he dies, he leaves his body–*tadottamavidāṁ lokānamalān-pratipadyate*, then he is pushed to those *lokas*, those worlds of Anantabhaṭṭāraka where he does *abhyāsa*.[428] He is forcefully pushed in *śaktipāta* of Lord Śiva. When, at the time of [death], by chance–by chance it is the will of God, will of Parabhairava–by chance, at that moment of death, he . . .

What?

JONATHAN: He's in that cycle of *sattvaguṇa*.

SWAMIJI: What?

JOHN: At the moment of death, he's in *sattvaguṇa*.

SWAMIJI: Yes.

. . . *sattvaguṇa* rises all around and he passes away, [then] he is pushed to that state of upper worlds and he does practice [there]. And from there he goes and is united in the Parabhairava state.

428 "*Yadā sattve vivṛddhe tu* [comm.], *sattvaguṇa* must be conducted in your whole lifetime. When you conduct the nature of *sattvaguṇa* in your lifetime, your nature becomes *sāttvic*, then you will rise to heaven, otherwise not." *Bhagavad Gītā* (1978). See also *Bhagavad Gītā*, 6.43.

JOHN: So he doesn't have to return to this world?

SWAMIJI: No, he has not to return. It is *śaktipāta* working; *śaktipāta* is actually working everywhere.

DVD 14 (22:58)

रजसि प्रलयं गत्वा कर्मसङ्गिषु जायते ।
तथा प्रलीनस्तमसि मूढयोनिषु जायते ॥ १५ ॥

rajasi pralayaṁ gatvā karmasaṅgiṣu jāyate /
tathā pralīnastamasi mūḍhayoniṣujāyate //15//
[repeated]

When *rajasi* (*rajaguṇa*) is in force and he leaves his body, *karma saṅgiśu jāyate*, he becomes a warrior, he becomes *kṣatriya* [in his next life].

And at the time when *tāmaguṇa* is in force and he unfortunately leaves his body at that very moment, *mūḍha yoniṣujāyate*, he becomes a rock [in his next life]. This is also the will of Parabhairava. This is His play: He becomes rock, He becomes warrior, and He becomes *mukta* (liberated). So, all of the three ways are enjoyed by Parabhairava.

DVD 14 (24:09)

कर्मणः सुकृतस्याहुः सात्त्विकं निर्मलं फलम् ।
रजसस्तु फलं दुःखमज्ञानं तमसः फलम् ॥ १६ ॥

karmaṇaḥ sukṛtasyāhuḥ sāttvikaṁ nirmalaṁ phalam /
rajasastu phalaṁ duḥkhamajñānaṁ tamasaḥ phalam //16//

This is the 16th *śloka*. *Sukṛtasya karmaṇaḥ*, when you are doing good actions and you get its fruit, *sāttvic* fruit, and it is without any impurity, it is *nirmalaṁ*, it is quite clean.

Rajasastu phalaṁ duhkham. *Rajaguṇa's* fruit is *duḥkham* (pain), being tired, always tired [because of excessive activity]. The tiring element is still in force and still there is another call, another telephone call to him: "you have got another project to do, you have to come and sit here from tomorrow." And he has to rush and [make] arrangement for another work, because he gets money, he earns money here and there. It is painful always.

सत्त्वात्सञ्जायते ज्ञानं रजसो लोभ एव च ।

sattvātsañjāyate jñānaṁ rajaso lobha eva ca /
[not recited or translated][429]

DVD 14 (25:36)

प्रमादमोहौ जायेते तमसोऽज्ञानमेव च ॥ १७॥

pramādamohau jāyete tamaso'jñānameva ca //17//

By the *tamaguṇa*, *pramāda* and *moha* (*pramāda* means negligence and *moha* means *ajñāna* (ignorance) of not remembering God). This is the fruit of *tamaguṇa*.

Another way of explaining these *guṇas*:

DVD 14 (26:08)

ऊर्ध्वं गच्छन्ति सत्त्वस्था मध्ये तिष्ठन्ति राजसाः ।
जघन्यगुणवृत्तिस्था अधो गच्छन्ति तामसाः ॥ १८॥

urdhvaṁ gacchanti sattvasthā madhye tiṣṭhanti rājasāḥ /
jaghanyaguṇavṛttisthā adho gacchanti tāmasāḥ *//18//*

Those who have the nature of being *sattvic*, they rise, they rise up [to the heavens]. *Madhye tiṣṭhanti rājasāḥ*, [those who have the nature of] *rājasāḥ* remain on waiting list; they neither rise nor go down.[430]

Jaghanyaguṇavṛttisthā adho gacchanti tāma[*saḥ*], those who are given to *tamaguṇa* always, they always go down and down,

429 "*Sattvātsañjāyate jñānaṁ*, again, in another way, He explains what fruit is derived from these *guṇas*. *Sattvātsañjāyate jñānaṁ*, by conducting *sattvaguṇa* knowledge rises. *Rajaso lobha eva ca*, by conducting the *rajaguṇa lobha eva ca*, desire rises." *Bhagavad Gītā* (1978).

430 "They reside in the this field of mortality. They come again and again in this world, in this mortal world." Ibid.

down and down, down, down, down, down, down, and down . . . there is no end.

JOHN: So, some of those . . . so those attached to *sattvaguṇa*, they have *aghora śaktis*?

SWAMIJI: Yes.

JOHN: *Ghorāghora śaktis* are others . . .

SWAMIJI: Yes, and *ghoratarī śakti*.[431]

DVD 14 (27:10)

नान्यं गुणेभ्यः कर्तारं यदा द्रष्टानुपश्यति ।
गुणेभ्यश्च परं वेत्ति मद्भावं सोऽधिगच्छति ॥ १९ ॥

nānyaṁ guṇebhyaḥ kartāraṁ yadā draṣṭānupaśyati /
guṇebhyaśca paraṁ vetti madbhāvaṁ so'dhigacchati //19//

Now there is one [person] in *lakhs* (100,000) of people, there is some fortunate person who always observes that I am above the cycle of three *guṇas* and I am situated . . . I am not touched or painted, whitewashed, whitewashed by the three *guṇas*. *Madbhāvaṁ so'dhigacchati*, fortunately he enters into the state of Parabhairava.[432]

---

431 "There are three classes of energies of Lord Siva. There is *aghora śakti*, *ghora śakti*, and *ghoratarī śakti*. *Aghora śakti* is at the time when you find meditation quite clear for you. At times you find that your meditation works nicely. Sometimes you find that your meditation . . . it gives good result. That is due to *aghora*; *aghoras* are adjusted with you. When *ghora* [*śaktis*] are adjusted with you, you are stuck in meditation, you can't find out the clearance of meditation. And *ghoratarī* [*śakti* is] when you are pushed, pulled, kicked down . . . but for those who are already enlightened, *aghora śaktis* push them up, *ghora śaktis* push them up, and *ghoratarī śaktis* push them up." Swami Lakshmanjoo, *Parātriśikā Vivaraṇa* (1982-85).

432 "Now, a *yogi* who knows, who practices, and comes to this understanding, *nānyaṁ guṇebhyaḥ kartāraṁ yadā draṣṭānupaśyati*, the doer and life giver of these three *guṇas* is that Being who is above these *guṇas* . . . he is cautious of that Being in each and every act of this world, and he, in the end, where he goes? He just merges into that Being. He becomes *guṇātīta* himself, that *sādhaka*." *Bhagavad Gītā* (1978).

So what is the conclusion of the three *guṇas,* and escaping from the three *guṇas*?

DVD 14 (28:27)

गुणानेतानतीत्य त्रीन्देही देहसमुद्भवान् ।
जन्ममृत्युजरादुःखैर्विमुक्तोऽमृतमश्नुते ॥२०॥

guṇānetānatītya trīndehī dehasamudbhavān /
janmamṛtyujarāduḥkhairvimukto'mṛtamaśnute //20//

Etān trīn guṇān atītya. Dehī, any individual who rises from the boundary of these three *guṇas*, which are created by this body, *janma mṛtyu jarā duḥkhair vimukta*, he is liberated from repeated births, repeated deaths, repeated old age, repeated pains and pleasures in old age; he is liberated once and for all from these tortures, and *amṛtamaśnute*, he becomes a *jīvan mukta,* and *amṛtamaśnute*, he is united for good in Parabhairava state.

[Arjuna asks a] question now, before his master:

DVD 14 (29:50)

अर्जुन उवाच
arjuna uvāca

कैर्लिङ्गैस्त्रीन्गुणानेतानतीतो भवति प्रभो ।
किमाचारः कथं चैतांस्त्रीन्गुणानतिवर्तते ॥२१॥

kairliṅgaistrīnguṇānetānatīto bhavati prabho /
kimācāraḥ kathaṁ caitāṁstrīnguṇānativartate //21//

O Prabho, O my Master, what are the symptoms by which you can understand that an individual has risen from these three *guṇas* on the higher scale, i.e., that an individual has crossed the environment of these three *guṇas*?

Kimācāraḥ, what is his action afterwards when he is above the three *guṇas*? *Kathaṁ caitāṁstrīnguṇā*, how [does] he rise above these three *guṇas*? [From] this encircling of the three *guṇas*, how [does] he rise?[433]

श्रीभगवानुवाच

śrī bhagavān uvāca

Now Śrī Bhagavān gives him, puts answer before his disciple, Arjuna.

DVD 14 (30:53)

प्रकाशं च प्रवृत्तिं च मोहमेव च पाण्डव ।
न द्वेष्टि संप्रवृत्तानि न निवृत्तानि काङ्क्षति ॥२२॥
उदासीनवदासीनो गुणैर्यो न विचाल्यते ।
गुणा वर्तन्त इत्येव योऽवतिष्ठति नेङ्गते ॥२३॥
समदुःखसुखस्वस्थः समलोष्टाश्मकाञ्चनः ।
तुल्यप्रियाप्रियो धीरस्तुल्यनिन्दात्मसंस्तुतिः ॥२४॥
मानावमानयोस्तुल्यस्तुल्यो मित्रारिपक्षयोः ।
सर्वारम्भपरित्यागी गुणातीतः स उच्यते ॥२५॥

prakāśaṁ ca pravṛttiṁ ca mohameva ca pāṇḍava /
na dveṣṭi saṁpravṛttāni na nivṛttāni kāṅkṣati //22//

433 "Now, as long, as far as there is connection with this body, with this limited body, *tatkathaṁ guṇātīto*, how can a person come across the level of three *guṇas*? As far as the connection with this body is concerned, he can't be *guṇātīta*. He won't leave the level of three *guṇas*. Because as long as the maintenance of this body is concerned with that being, with that soul, with that individual, he has to breathe, breathing, the action of breathing is through *guṇas*, action of thinking is through *guṇas*, action of this rise of loosing your temper is three *guṇas*, wrath is three *guṇas*, anger is three *guṇas*, appetite is three *guṇas*, headache is three *guṇas*–they are all combined in the cycle of three *guṇas*. How can he come across the level of three *guṇas* as long as the body is concerned? As long as body is concerned, as long as he is living in this body, he can't be *guṇātīta*. This is the question of Arjuna." Ibid.

udāsīnavadāsīno guṇairyo na vicālyate /
guṇā vartanta ityeva yo'jñastiṣṭhati neṅgate //23//
samaduḥkhasukhasvapnaḥ samaloṣṭāśmakāñcanaḥ /
tulyapriyāpriyo dhīrastulyanindātmasaṁstutiḥ //24//
mānāvamānayostulyastulyo mitrāripakṣayoḥ /
sarvārambhaphalatyāgī guṇātītaḥ sa ucyate //25//

How many *ślokas*?

Up to the 25th ending.

Kairliṅgaistrīṇguṇānetānatīto bhavati prabho [verse 21]. What are the symptoms by which one can feel . . . what are the symptoms of that person who rises above the cycle of the three *guṇas*?

Kimācāraḥ, what is his behavior afterwards? What behavior [does] he conduct afterwards, after he has risen above the cycle of the three *guṇas*? *Kathaṁ caitāṁ* [*strīn*]*guṇān ativar-tate*, how can he cross this *māyā*, this cycle of these three *guṇas*? How can he cross that?

This is my question.

Now Śrī Bhagavān [answers]:

Prakāśaṁ ca pravṛttiṁ ca mohameva ca pāṇḍava [verse 22]. If *prakāśa* comes, if *sattvaguṇa* comes in force to him, *pravṛttiṁ ca*, if *rajaguṇa* comes in force to him, *mohameva ca*, if *tamaguṇa* comes in force to him, *na dveṣṭi saṁ pravṛttāni*, he does not neglect them, he does not get afraid from them, he remains the same. He says, "what are they, they are nothing, they are also the state of Parabhairava."

Na dveṣṭi saṁpravṛttāni, when they are in force, he does not get worried [and ask], "why are they in force? Why are they acting in force, i.e., *sattvaguṇa*, *rajaguṇa*, and *tamaguṇa*?" *Na nivṛttāni*, when these three *guṇas* leave, take leave for good, he does not mind at that time also. He remains the same, unmoved by the three *guṇas*.

How [does] he remain like that?

Udāsīnavadāsīno guṇairyo na vicālyate [verse 23]. *Udāsīna vadāsīno*, just as I am *udāsīna* (*udāsīna* means neither have I indulged in friendship [with] these three *guṇas*, nor have I hatred for these *guṇas*), [he says], "they are . . . let them do their work, I have nothing to do with them. *Guṇā vartanta*, let them do their work. What to me? I am above this." *Yo'jñastiṣṭhati*, he becomes absolutely ignorant of these . . . ignorant not. *Ajña* means he does not come into their grip.

JONATHAN: He is not entangled.

SWAMIJI: Huh?

JONATHAN: He doesn't get tangled up in them.

SWAMIJI: And how he remains [afterwards]?

DVD 14 (35:19)

समदुःखसुखस्वप्नः समलोष्टाश्मकाञ्चनः ।
तुल्यप्रियाप्रियो धीरस्तुल्यनिन्दात्मसंस्तुतिः ॥२४॥

samaduḥkhasukhasvapnaḥ samaloṣṭāśmakāñcanaḥ /
tulyapriyāpriyo dhīrastulyanindātmasaṁstutiḥ //24//
[repeated]

Samaduḥkhasukhasvapnaḥ. Sukha, duḥkha, and *svapnah,*[434] the fruit of these three *guṇas*, he remains the same in [receiving] these fruits. *Sama loṣṭāśmakāñcanaḥ. Loṣṭāśma*, if there is a ball of clay, if there is a ball of stone, if there is a ball of gold, he remains the same for them. He has no valuation for these, [no] different valuation for these.

Tulya priyāpriya, one who is dear to him, one who is not dear to him, he remains the same to both classes. *Dhīra*, [he is] unmovable. *Stulya nindātma saṁstutiḥ*, when people give bad names to him, he remains the same; [when] people praise him, he remains the same. [He says], "what then? I am not moved. I am what I am. I don't care for these behaviors of ants."

DVD 14 (36:54)

मानावमानयोस्तुल्यस्तुल्यो मित्रारिपक्षयोः ।
सर्वारम्भफलत्यागी गुणातीतः स उच्यते ॥२५॥

mānāvamānayostulyastulyo mitrāripakṣayoḥ /
sarvārambhaphalatyāgī guṇātītaḥ sa ucyate //25// [repeated]

434 *Sukha* (joy) means *sattvaguṇa*, *duḥkha* (pain) means *rajaguṇa*, and *svapnaḥ* (dreaming) means *tamaguṇa*. [*Editor's note*]

Mānāvamānayostulyastulya, if he is praised, well and good; if he is hated by people, well and good. *Tulya mitrāri pakṣayoḥ*, if his friends also come to save him, well and good, and [if] his enemies come to tease him, well and good. *Sarvārambha phalatyāgī*, he does not do anything; he does not indulge in any matter. *Guṇātītaḥ sa*, he is above these *guṇas*. You should understand that he is the person who is above the *guṇas;* [he is] in *guṇas* and without, above them.

At the same time, what is his behavior inside?

DVD 14 (38:04)

मां च योऽव्यभिचारेण भक्तियोगेन सेवते ।
स गुणान्समतीत्यैतान्ब्रह्मभूयाय कल्पते ॥२६॥

māṁ ca yo'vyabhicāreṇa bhaktiyogena sevate /
sa guṇānsamatītyaitānbrahmabhūyāya kalpate //26//

And who only does this work, *mām* (*mām* means Parabhairava), who is always beloved, remains beloved to Parabhairava, and Parabhairava loves him and he loves Parabhairava. And he has adopted *bhakti* [for] Parabhairava. *Bhakti* means [he is] always aware of Parabhairava.[435]

He is likely . . . he is . . . no matter, there is no doubt that he is united in Parabhairava.

Once he is united in Parabhairava . . .

---

435 "And that person . . . who has got intense desire to find out the reality of Lord Śiva, intense desire, he does not hear, he does not see. Although he sees, he does not see; although he smells, he does not smell; [although] he touches, he does not touch. And if everybody asks him, begins to ask him, "what are you doing? Why are you dumb? Why don't you speak to others? Why are you not jolly? Why are you not happy? Why don't you talk?" He answers to them, he answers to them only with tears in his eyes. Because he puts deaf ear to all other things. He has got deafless ear only to find out the truth, that intense desire. That is the intensity of that desire. That is what Abhinavagupta says. He is purified by the divinity of great attachment for Lord Śiva and he is glorified by that state." *Bhagavad Gītā* (1978).

DVD 14 (39:02)

ब्रह्मणो हि प्रतिष्ठाहममृतस्याव्ययस्य च ।
शाश्वतस्य च धर्मस्य सुखस्यैकान्तिकस्य च ॥२७॥

brahmaṇo hi pratiṣṭhāhamamṛtasyāvyayasya ca /
śāśvatasya ca dharmasya sukhasyaikāntikasya ca //27//

And Parabhairava state is "I". [He understands that], "I am situated in Parabhairava state, and I am *pratiṣṭha* of Parabhairava state, i.e., I am the seat on which I am seated in Parabhairava state."[436] And it is *amṛta*, nectar, intense nectar; *avyayasya*, unfading nectar. It rises, it gives more and more, more and more it grows. It does not fade by spending. When you spend this [physical] nectar by drinking [alcohol], it does not last. [The nectar of the Parabhairava state] is everlasting.

Śāśvatasya ca dharmasya. This *dharma* of nectar, this aspect of *dharma* is *śāśva* (*śāśva* is eternal), always remaining the same (*aikāntikasya sukhasya*).

This is the end of chapter 14th . . . 15th.

JONATHAN: 14th.

SWAMIJI: 14th, yes, 14th.

Atra saṁgraha ślokaḥ, this is the conclusion. This [was] the 27th *śloka*. This is now the conclusion.

DVD 14 (40:45)

लसद्भक्तिरसावेशहीनाहंकारविभ्रमः ।
स्थितेऽपि गुणसंमर्दे गुणातीतः समो यतिः ॥१४॥

lasadbhaktirasāveśahīnāhaṁkāravibhramaḥ /
sthite'pi guṇasaṁmarde guṇātītaḥ samo yatiḥ //14//

---

436 "I am the basis of *brahma*, I am the basis of supreme nectar, I am the basis of eternity, I am the basis of the eternal aspect of Lord Śiva, and I am the basis of the one-pointedness of bliss. . . . Whoever is attached to Me, he becomes Brahman. Otherwise, if you [try to] cultivate the state of Brahman [through sources] other than Me, that will carry you only to the voidness of *śūnya pramātṛ bhāva* (deep sleep)." Ibid.

॥ Concluding *śloka* of 14th chapter ॥

When one has intense love for Parabhairava, *hīnāhaṁkāra vibhramaḥ*, the one who has lost the ego of himself and has been united in the Parabhairava state by intense love, *sthite'pi guṇa saṁmarde*, although he is crushed by the three *guṇas*, *guṇātītaḥ*, he is above these *guṇas*. Nobody can crush him, he remains uncrushed, he remains untouched, he remains unmoved by the three *guṇas*.

So he is one with Parabhairava. *Bas*.

Chapter 15

DVD 15 (00:01)

श्रीभगवानुवाच

śrī bhagavān uvāca

ऊर्ध्वमूलमधः शाखमश्वत्थं प्राहुरव्ययम् ।
छन्दांसि यस्य पर्णानि यस्तं वेद स वेदवित् ॥ १ ॥

ūrdhvamūlamadhaḥ śākhamaśvatthaṁ prāhuravyayam /
chandāṁsi yasya parṇāni yastaṁ veda sa vedavit //1//

Śrī Bhagavān explains to Arjuna that there is a *aśvattha* tree. The *aśvattha* tree is existing here in this universe. It has got *ūrdhva mūlam*; *ūrdhva mūlam* [means] it has got roots in the Parabhairava state, roots [up] in *śantātītā kalā*, there are roots of this tree.[437] *Adhaḥ śākham*, the branches of this tree are spread down below in *kālāgnirūdra*, down below. And this *aśvattha* [tree] is *prāhur*, said to be *avyayam*, unperishable.

So *aśvattha* is a tree, which is imperishable. It is not . . . in one

437 "*Urdhva mūlam*, it is singular case. It has only one root upwards; it has only one root. That is *praśāntaṁ rūpam*–it is Abhinavagupta's commentary–*praśāntaṁ rūpam*, that peaceful state of Lord Śiva is the root of this tree.

"Why upwards? *Sarvato hi nivṛttasya tadāptiḥ.* You will never achieve the state of that root unless you shun all the stuff of that tree downwards. As long as you are residing in the center, or in the trunk of that tree, you will never achieve that root. That root is achieved only when you shun all those and keep them down below. Branches, trunks, leaves, everything, you have to keep them down, downwards. Then you'll achieve the state of that root."
Bhagavad Gītā (1978).

way it is *aśvattha*, i.e., this [tree] is *saṁsāra* (*saṁsāra* means this world), and this has no beginning, neither any beginning nor any end. But it grows from above to down below. And it is *avyayam* (*avyayam* [means] it never perishes, it is unperishable).

So this [tree] is *saṁsāra*. *Saṁsāra* is this manifestation of Parabhairava. *Saṁsāra* is the manifestation of Parabhairava. You have to cut the branches of this *saṁsāra* down below and keep only the roots above. Branches are varieties of its manifestation down below in the world.

Chandāṁsi yasya parṇāni, it has got leaves. "Leaves" are all *śāstras*, all *advaita* (non-dual) *śāstras*; all [*śāstras* of] Shaivism are the leaves of this tree. Because by [observing] the leaves, you can understand what, which . . .

DENISE: Which branch?

SWAMIJI: No, [not] which branch.

. . . which tree this is. By [observing the] leaves, you can calculate this is . . . for instance, there are [mango] leaves, [so] this must be a mango tree. By leaves you can recognize [which tree it is].

DENISE: Different varieties.

SWAMIJI: Huh?

DENISE: Different varieties.

SWAMIJI: Different varieties.

And all *śāstras–sāṁkyam yogam pañcarātram vedānścaiva na nindayet*–you should not discard Sāṁkya *śāstra*; *yogam*, you should not discard Yoga *śāstra*, you should not disbelieve Yoga *śāstra*; *pañcarātram*, you should not disbelieve Pañcarātram *śāstra–sāṁkyam yogam pañcarātram–vedānścaiva*, you should not discard the three *Vedas*, i.e., *Ṛig Veda*, *Yajur Veda*, *Sāma Veda*, and *Ātharva Veda*. All four *Vedas*, you should not discard [them].

Why?

Yada śivabodhabhavasarveśivadhāmaphala, all have been manifested in this world from Parabhairava and they are ultimately pushed in Parabhairava state, no matter [if it's] later or afterwards, sooner or later, they all go there.

This is the first *śloka* [of this 15th chapter].

DVD 15 (05:28)

अधश्चोर्ध्वं प्रसृता यस्य शाखा
गुणप्रवृद्धा विषयप्रवालाः ।
अधश्च मूलान्यनुसन्ततानि
कर्मानुबन्धीनि मनुष्यलोके ॥२॥

adhaścordhvaṁ prasṛtā yasya śākhā
guṇapravṛddhā viṣayapravālāḥ /
adhaśca mūlānyanusantatāni
karmānubandhīni manuṣyaloke //2//

Adhaśca urdhvaṁ ca. Adhaśca, towards downwards and towards upwards, *prasṛtā yasya śākhā*, the branches have grown towards [upward] and downward also.

Karmānubandhīni . . . guṇapravṛddhā viṣayapravālāḥ. Sattvaguṇa, *rajaguṇa*, and *tamaguṇa* have created leaves in this [tree]. *Sattvaguṇa* is found in this tree, *rajaguṇa* is found in this tree, *tamaguṇa* is found in this tree. [All three *guṇas* are] perceived in this tree. And all varieties of these *guṇas*, which I have already explained to you in previous discourses . . .

What we are doing?

JOHN: 14th chapter.

SWAMIJI: 14th, 13th chapter, these were all [concerning] *guṇas*; these are all the leaves of this [tree].

Adhaśca mūlānyanusantatāni, karmānubandhīni manuṣya-loke, downwards there are, downwards also there are roots, upwards also there are roots. Upwards also there are branches, downwards also there are branches. [There are] roots and branches [on] both sides, they grow.

Adhaśca mūlānyanusantatāni, downwards, those roots . . .

Which are those?

. . . *karmānubandhīni manuṣyaloke*, those roots which are down below, they entangle, their work is to entangle the individual by the grip of *karmas*, past actions. They entangle them; those are also roots. Those roots are found downwards.

DVD 15 (08:35)

न रूपमस्येह तथोपलभ्यते
नान्तो न चादिर्न च संप्रतिष्ठा ।

na rūpamasyeha tathopalabhyate
nānto na cādirna ca saṁpratiṣṭhā / 3a
[not recited in full]

Nānto na . . . go on, this is also that.

Na rūpamasyeha tathopalabhyate, you should not try to understand the formation of this tree because *nānto na cādirna ca saṁpratiṣṭhā*, neither there is [an] end of this tree [with] roots and branches upwards, nor is there an end of this tree [with] roots and branches downwards. Because there is no end and there is no beginning.

So . . .

DVD 15 (09:39)

अश्वत्थमेनं सुविरूढमूल-
मसङ्गशस्त्रेण शितेन च्छित्त्वा ॥ ३ ॥

aśvatthamenaṁ suvirūḍhamūlam-
asaṅgaśastreṇa śitena chittvā //3//

. . . this *aśvattha*, you have to do a great job in [dealing with] this [tree]; you have to act bravely, just like Parabhairava. *Aśvattham-enaṁ suvirūḍha-mūlam*, those roots, upwards which have grown, and [those roots] downwards which have grown (roots, not branches), *asaṅgaśastreṇa śitena chittvā*, you should handle that push-saw . . .

What saw?

JONATHAN: Bow-saw.

JOHN: For sawing trees?

JONATHAN: Bow-saw.

SWAMIJI: Push-saw and pull-saw, huh? Pull-saw and push-saw, there are two saws. With both the push-saw and pull-saw, *asaṅga śastreṇa*, that is *asaṅga śastreṇa*, don't be attached to this tree. Don't be afraid of this tree and don't be attached to this tree that, "it is a great tree, how can it be . . . how can one get rid of this tree?" This [tree] is endless and beginningless. But when you are detached, be detached [from] it altogether. Think only, "this is the glamour of Parabhairava and nothing else. It is nothing! It is only appearing, it only appears. It does not exist."

When you cut all of the roots of this tree with detachment of axe or these saws . . .[438]

DVD 15 (11:53)

ततः पदं तत्परिमार्गितव्यं
यस्मिन्गतो न निवर्तंत भूयः ।

tataḥ padaṁ tatparimārgitavyaṁ
yasmingato na nivarteta bhūyaḥ /

O Arjuna, then afterwards, *tataḥ padaṁ tatparim*, then afterwards, *tat padaṁ*, that state of Parabhairava, *param ārgitavyaṁ*, you should find out, you should search where is the basis of this, where is the basis of that [tree].[439] And you will find that basis in the formation of Parabhairava, supreme universal con-

438 "Many commentators have commented on this *śloka*: *aśvattamenaṁ suvirūdha mūlam*, this strong, firm [tree] with its roots, this *aśvattha* tree is to be cut down. This is not the proper commentary of this *śloka*. The proper commentary of this *śloka* is: the roots are to be cut, not *aśvattha*. *Aśvattha* is the universal truth. *Aśvattha* itself is the universal truth of God. The roots, which have grown down below [must be cut], not the roots upwards. *Asaṅga śastreṇa śitena chittvā*, and there must be one sword of detachment, absolute detachment. By the hatchet of absolute detachment, you have to cut these roots. You have not to cut the tree. You have to cut the roots of down below, which are entangling the individual every now and then." *Bhagavad Gītā* (1978).

439 "So all roots situated down below should be cut altogether by the hatchet of detachment. Then you should long for that root, *tataḥ padaṁ tat*, that supreme state of God consciousness which is the real root; you have to *parimārgitavyaṁ*, you have to search for [the real root] . . . . Not before that, not before cutting these roots. You have to cut these roots first and then desire for achieving that supreme state of God consciousness." Ibid.

sciousness, and glamorous. *Yasmingato na nirvateta bhūyaḥ*, once you enter in that, you will never come out of it. You will be established in it for eternity.

DVD 15 (13:04)

तमेव चाद्यं पुरुषं प्रपद्ये-
यतः प्रवृत्तिः प्रसृता पुराणी ॥४॥

tameva cādyaṁ puruṣaṁ prapadyed-
yataḥ pravṛttiḥ prasṛtā purāṇī //4//

O Arjuna, *tameva cādyaṁ puruṣaṁ prapadyet*, you should bow your head. Bow your head, bow your mind, bow your everything, whatever you have achieved in maintaining this *aśvattha* in the past, in maintaining this *aśvattha* tree; what you have achieved in the past, you surrender all of your achievements, previous achievements, to this Parabhairava, *yataḥ pravṛttiḥ prasṛtā purāṇī*, wherefrom this ancient *pravṛttiḥ* (manifestation) flows out.[440]

Now this *śloka*, 5th *śloka*.

DVD 15 (14:16)

निर्मानमोहा जितसङ्गदोषा
अध्यात्मनित्या विनिवृत्तकामाः ।
द्वन्द्वैर्विमुक्ताः सुखदुःखसंज्ञै-
र्गच्छन्त्यमूढाः पदमव्ययं तत् ॥५॥

nirmānamohā jitasaṅgadoṣā
adhyātmanityā vinivṛttakāmāḥ .
dvandvairvimuktāḥ sukhaduḥkhasaṁjñair-
gacchantyamūḍhāḥ padamavyayaṁ tat //5//

Nirmānamohā, those who are fortunate to see the ultimate glory of this tree, which is residing behind this . . .

---

440 "*Yataḥ pravṛttiḥ prasṛtā*, and that is that root from which the whole trunk and body and branches of this *aśvattha* tree have grown." Ibid.

What was that?

The state of Parabhairava!

. . . *nirmānamohā*, they have no ego, they have no forgetfulness of the Self, *jitasaṅgadoṣā*, and they are absolutely detached. *Adhyātmanityā*, they are eternally established in *adhyātma* (*adhyātma* means internal Parabhairava state). *Vinivṛttakāmāḥ*, they have no desires. *Dvandvair vimuktāḥ*, they are free from *dvandvas*, the two opposites which are existing in this *aśvattha* (two opposites: *sukha* and *dukha*, bad and good).

DENISE: Love and hate.

SWAMIJI: Yes. Everything. *Sukhaduḥkhasaṁjñair*, which are called *sukha*, *duḥkha*, etc.

Gacchantyamūḍhāḥ padamavyayaṁ tat. And *amūḍhāḥ*, those who are alert, they are pushed into that Parabhairava [state] for good.

Five *ślokas* are finished.

DVD 15 (16:36)

न तद्भासयते सूर्यो न शशाङ्को न पावकः ।
यद्गत्वा न निवर्तन्ते तद्धाम परमं मम ॥६॥

na tadbhāsayate sūryo na śaśāṅko na pāvakaḥ /
yadgatvā na nivartante taddhāma paramaṁ mama //6//

O Arjuna, I will explain to you which is My real residence, where I am living, where I am established.

Na tadbhāsayate sūryo. Sūrya (the sun) cannot show that residence (*na tadbhāsayate sūryo*); *na śaśāṅko na pāvakaḥ*, the moon cannot show that residence of Mine; *na pāvakaḥ*, fire cannot show the residence of Mine. In the long run, the meaning of these three inwardly is: the objective world cannot show Me, subjective world cannot show Me, and cognitive world cannot show Me. I am beyond object, subject, and cognition.[441]

---

441 "That personal state [of Mine] cannot be created by the light of the sun means, at the time of breathing out that personal state won't shine. At the time of breathing in [i.e., the light of the moon], that personal state [of Mine] won't shine. At the time of junction, putting your awareness on junction of the two, My personal state won't shine. My personal state will shine when all these three aspects are vanished. That is at

the time of entering in the central vein, when *prāṇa*, *apāna*, and *samāna* sink, get absorbed in that central vein. That is the reality of that root. That is the supreme state of Mine. Have you heard my poem?

There is the point between sleep and waking
where thou shalt be alert without any shaking
enter into the new world where forms so hideous pass
they are passing, endure, do not be taken by the dross
then the pulls and the pushes about the throttle
all those shalt thou tolerate
close all ingress and egress

You have to shun this breathing in and out.

yawnings there may be . . .

There may be yawning's so that you'll come out again.

shed tears, crave, implore
thou wilt not prostrate
a thrill passes, that goes down to the bottom
it riseth, may it flow
that is bliss, that is bliss, that is bliss
O blessed Being, greetings be to Thee!

And that is the real state of that root. *Suryādīnāṁ tatrānavakāśaḥ* [comm.], there is no room for these three movements: breathing in, breathing out, and centering–there is not room for these there. They have no room as long as that supreme state is concerened. As long as you are breathing in and out, there is no possibility of achieving that state of God consciousness. That state of God consciousness is achieved only when they come to their end. There is no room for these three movements because *teṣāṁ kālādyavecchedāt* [comm.], they have finite aspects attached to them because of limitation of time, *vedyatvāt*, *karaṇopakārakatvāt*, because of being [in the] residence of the objective world, and because of nourishing the aspects of the five senses. *Tasya tu dikkālādyanavacchedāt*, there is no time, space, and form existing before that state of God consciousness because *vedakatvāt*, He is the knower, He is not known. *Karaṇapravartakatvāt*, He is the producer of organs, [but] He is not residing in the organs. As long as you are breathing, there is no hope of realizing that God consciousness." *Bhagavad Gītā* (1978).

JOHN: *Pramiti*?

SWAMIJI: *Pramiti* [i.e., *pramātṛ*], *pramāna*, and *prameya*; *sṛṣṭi, sthiti,* and *saṁhāra*. All of these three-fold elements, which are seen in this universe, in this manifestation of Parabhairava, [cannot show you My residence].

JOHN: So *pramiti* can show it.

SWAMIJI: Huh?

JOHN: *Pramiti*.

SWAMIJI: *Pramiti* . . . yes, *pramiti*.

He is *pukka* (first class) Shaivite.

Pramiti is, for instance Viresh knows his lessons. Viresh is *pramātā* then when he takes his books in his hand and goes on reading; [at that time], he is *pramātṛ*.[442] And when he explains it to his friends, school friends, schoolboys, then he is *pramāṇa* (cognition). When he works on that masters work and he writes it down, that is the work of *prameya* (objectivity). In the same, way he is residing in [the differentiated field of] *pramāṇa*, *prameya*, and *pramātṛ bhāva*.

But at the time when he has no books, when his master Swami Lakṣmanjoo asks him sometime, "what do you read, in which class do you read?" He does not get books at that time, he does not collect books, he does not collect pencils. He says verbally, "I am reading in the eighth class, I am reading in the ninth class, Sir." So he knows, he knows everything without . . .

JOHN: Taking support of some other thing.

SWAMIJI: That is *pramiti* . . . that is *pramiti*.

---

442 That is, a subject standing in relation to an object. "The state of *pramātṛ* is found when a person is lecturing some points, and he is full of those objects that he explains; but when the same *pramātṛ* is without the agitation of lectures and there is no objective world before him, that is the state of *pramiti*. You see the state of *pramiti* is without any object at all. In other words, when he is in his own nature, residing in his own nature that subjective consciousness is called the state of *pramiti*. And this state of *pramiti* is found in the kingdom of *turya*. This state of *turya* is said to be the penetration of all energies simultaneously, not one by one. Simultaneous penetration of all energies is called *turya*. All energies are there residing, although not in manifestation. All the energies together without any distinction." Swami Lakshmanjoo, *Kashmir Shaivism–The Secret Supreme* (1972).
See footnote 138 for a further explanation of *turya*.

DENISE: Is that memory?
SWAMIJI: Huh?
DENISE: Is that memory?
SWAMIJI: No, that is *pramiti*. *Pramiti* means above *pramātṛ*. *Pramātṛ* is when he explains a book in class to the master. He reads and the master hears it well. He gives him good marks, "you have done good work, sit down." But when he sits down, still he is knowing without books. Without books he has that capacity of understanding–that is *pramiti*.
DENISE: Stored knowledge.
JOHN: No, it's more than that.
SWAMIJI: Stored knowledge in *nirvikalpa* state, where there are no *vikalpas*, that is *pramiti*.
JOHN: It is like creative intelligence, it's something flowing out from him.
SWAMIJI: Yes.
JONATHAN: It's understanding then, isn't it?
SWAMIJI: *Na tadbhāsayate . . .*
Understanding that is intellect. [*Pramiti* is] when there is no intellect, it is stored undifferentiatedly (*nirvikalpa*).[443]
For instance, I am a teacher, when I am sleeping, "*zzzzzzz-zzzzzz*," [and when I wake], somebody asks me, "what is the definition of Parabhairava state?" I don't collect books at that time. I just explain it to him, *bas*. That is *pramiti*.[444]
JOHN: It flows from within.
SWAMIJI: Yes.

DVD 15 (22:04)

न तद्भासयते सूर्यो न शशाङ्को न पावकः ।
यद्गत्वा न निवर्तन्ते तद्धाम परमं मम ॥ ६ ॥

na tadbhāsayate sūryo na śaśāṅko na pāvakaḥ /
yadgatvā na nivartante taddhāma paramaṁ mama //6//
[repeated]

Yadgatvā na nivartante, when once you enter . . . when you get entry into that, *na nivartante,* you never come out again from

443 See footnote 61 for a further explanation of *nirvikalpa*.
444 See footnote 44 for a further explanation of *pramiti bhāva*.

that state. *Taddhāma paramaṁ,* that is My real residence, O Arjuna! There I live, that is My glamorous residence.

DVD 15 (22:42)

ममैवांशो जीवलोके जीवभूतः सनातनः ।
मनः षष्ठानीन्द्रियाणि प्रकृतिस्थानि कर्षति ॥७॥

mamaivāṁśo jīvaloke jīvabhūtaḥ sanātanaḥ /
manaḥ ṣaṣṭhānīndriyāṇi prakṛtisthāni karṣati //7//

And at the same time, *mamaivāṁśa*, My ray, My one ray, has spread in the universe and He has become numberless individuals; He has become numberless individuals. And on the contrary, I, what is the number of Me? *Bas*! One.

And what is the number of My manifestation?

JONATHAN: Endless.

SWAMIJI: Numberless. Numberless individuals are created and that is [produced by] My *aṁśa* (one ray). *Jīvaloke*, in the individual world, *jīva bhūtaḥ*, and He has become an individual–pitiable, trodden down, worth to be pitied on.

Manaḥ ṣaṣṭhānīndriyāṇi, and [the limited individual] collects with him his bag, his money bag [laughing]. Yes, he has got money bag. That is *manas*, *buddhiḥ*, and *ahaṁkāra*, and five organs (eight: [three *antaḥkaraṇas* and] five organs of knowledge).[445]

---

445 In this translation, Swamiji has listed the eight elements of the *sūkṣma śarīra*, or subtle body, also known as the *puryaṣṭaka* (lit. the city of eight). Among the fourfold bodies (i.e., *deha*, *prāṇa*, *puryaṣṭaka*, and *śūnya**) that are possessed by the limited individual, the *puryaṣṭaka* (i.e., three *antaḥkaraṇas*: *manas*, *buddhiḥ,* and *ahaṁkāra*, and the five *tanmātras*) make up the eight elements of the subtle body that carries the soul's impressions from one life to another. [*Editor's note*]

"*Puryaṣṭaka* carries the impressions again and again, extracts impressions. Otherwise, if *puryaṣṭaka* is not existing, at the time of death, you'll be united with God automatically, without doing anything. *Puryaṣṭaka* is the trouble-maker." Swami Lakshmanjoo, *Parātriśikā Vivaraṇa* (1982-85).

"You know *puryaṣṭaka*? *Puryaṣṭaka* is that body which is found in dreaming state–that is *puryaṣṭaka*, that body. And he enters in that

It is *sūkṣma śarīra* (*sūkṣma śarīra* means subtle body). With subtle body he goes on [transmigrating]. This is his money bag [with which] he goes on from one life to another, one life to another, one life to another. And it never ends, this *tamasha* (commotion) never ends.

[For Parabhairava], it is on the contrary. [Lord Kṛṣṇa says], "this is the condition of My ray, which is also existing side by side." *Prakṛti sthāni karṣati*, and *prakṛti* is holding . . .

What is that?

JONATHAN: Reins.

SWAMIJI: *Nadam lākam*, when you ride on a pony.

DENISE: Reins

SWAMIJI: Yes. *Prakṛti* is holding reins and, "*ga-ga-ga-ga . . .*"

DENISE: Riding.

SWAMIJI: Yes. This is the pitiable condition of *bicchāra* (Kashmiri word), that trodden man [i.e., *puruṣa*], side by side, although that is also Parabhairava.

This way I had not explained to you [previously].

---

puryaṣṭaka body and he takes the journey in each and every womb in this universe. Thus he is called *antarātmā*, he is really *antarātmā*, the interior self." Swami Lakshmanjoo, *Śiva Sūtra Vimarśinī*, 3.10 (1975).

In his previous translation, Swamiji explained: "*manaḥ ṣaṣṭān-īndriyāṇi prakṛti sthāni karṣati. Prakṛti* (nature), and in nature are situated six more aspects. . . . Five organs of senses and mind are situated in the boundary, in the circle of *prakṛti* in each and every individual. And in that, this ray is functioning . . . and tossing you, kicking you here and there according to your choices." *Bhagavad Gītā* (1978).

* "*Deha* is this gross body [existing in the waking state], *puryaṣṭaka* is the body existing in dreaming state, *prāṇa* is body existing in dreamless state, *śunya* is body existing in *pralayakalā* (deep sleep). These four-fold bodies are called *kulā*. From these four classes you have to achieve something. What is that achievement (siddhi)? All this discrimination, ascertainment. When you ascertain this is tape recorder, this is book, etc. You ascertain it in the world of *jagrat* (wakefulness), in the world of *svapna* (dreaming), in the world of *suṣupti* (dreamless sleep) and in the world of voidness (*pralayakalā*). And that is also attributed to God consciousness." Swami Lakshmanjoo, *Parātriśikā Vivaraṇa* (1982-85).

DVD 15 (25:54)

शरीरं यदवाप्नोति यच्चाप्युत्क्रामतीश्वरः ।
गृहीत्वैतानि संयाति वायुर्गन्धानिवाशयात् ॥८॥

śarīraṁ yadavāpnoti yaccāpyutkrāmatīśvaraḥ /
gṛhītvaitāni saṁyāti vāyurgandhānivāśayāt //8//

Whatever body, *śarīraṁ yadavāpnoti*, whatever body he possesses (Īśvara or *shikas* Īśvara[446]). . .

He is also Īśvara, but *shikas*. Who?

JOHN: Individual.

SWAMIJI: Individual. That is, [Lord Kṛṣṇa] puts the name of Īśvara [to indicate the limited individual] because he is not separate from Īśvara [although] he is *shikas lad* Īśvara [laughs].

. . . whatever body he achieves, and whenever he leaves that body at the time when that Lord of death tells him, whispers to him that, "you have to leave this body," *gṛhītvaitāni*, and he carries this money bag [i.e., the subtle body] with him and goes on, goes on from one life to another life, that life to another life, that life . . . and goes on, goes on, goes on . . . and it never ends.

DVD 15 (27:27)

श्रोत्रं चक्षुः स्पर्शनं च रसनं घ्राणमेव च ।
अधिष्ठाय मनश्चायं विषयानुपसेवते ॥९॥

śrotraṁ cakṣuḥ sparśanaṁ ca rasanaṁ ghrāṇameva ca /
adhiṣṭhāya manaścāyaṁ viṣayānupasevate //9//

Śrotraṁ, śrotraṁ means eyes (*śrotraṁ cakṣuḥ*). No, *śrotraṁ* means this [ear].

DENISE: Ears.

SWAMIJI: *Cakṣuḥ* means eyes. *Śrotraṁ cakṣuḥ sparśanaṁ, sparśanaṁ* is touch, the organ of touch. *Cakṣuḥ sparśanaṁ ca, rasanaṁ* [Swamiji shows his tongue]

JONATHAN: Taste.

---

446 *Shikas lad Iśvara* means that Lord (*Iśvara*) who is *shikas lad* (ill-fated). [*Editor's note*]

SWAMIJI: Taste. *Ghrāṇameva ca* [Swamiji sniffs to indicate the nose].

JONATHAN: Smell.

SWAMIJI: *Adhiṣṭhāya manaścāyaṁ*, and along with the mind, *viṣayānupasevate*, he goes on enjoying this life, this *shikas lad* life.[447]

DVD 15 (28:29)

तिष्ठन्तमुत्क्रामन्तं वा भुञ्जानं वा गुणान्वितम् ।
विमूढा नानुपश्यन्ति पश्यन्ति ज्ञानचक्षुषः ॥ १० ॥

tiṣṭhantamutkrāmantaṁ vā bhuñjānaṁ vā guṇānvitam /
vimūḍhā nānupaśyanti paśyanti jñānacakṣuṣaḥ //10//

And on the contrary, [the one] who is actually residing in the body, and who is coming out from body at the time of death, *bhuñjānaṁ*, who is taking food at the time of dinner and lunch, and bed tea and daytime tea, *vimūḍhā nānupaśyanti*, those ignorant people cannot understand Him, who He is actually. *Paśyanti jñāna cakṣuṣaḥ,* those who have opened their eyes, whose eyes of knowledge are opened by the *śaktipāta* of Parabhairava, they can see with their divine eyes actually who is there. He is a great prince who is eating, drinking, etc., but he has ignored that state and he has become *shikas lad* (ill-fated).

Now, actually [the one] who is residing in the body, and who is coming out from the body at the time of death, and who eats in this body, and *guṇānvitam*, who has got three *guṇas*, actually [he ßis] Parabhairava. *Vimūḍhā nānupaśyanti*, those ignorant people cannot understand who is in the body doing all of this. Only those with eyes of divine knowledge understand that He is divine, otherwise they think He is just like an ordinary soul, [that] He is just *shikas lad* (ill-fated) at that time. But those who are with divine eyes, they feel at that time also, "I am [Parabhairava]." Because I [Parabhairava] am also like individuals, eating, drinking, and playing.

DVD 15 (31:20)

447 "As long as I am traveling with these, I am individual. If I don't travel with them, I am universal." *Bhagavad Gītā* (1978).

यतन्तो योगिनश्चैनं पश्यन्त्यात्मन्यवस्थितम् ।
यतन्तोऽप्यकृतात्मानो नैनं पश्यन्त्यचेतसः ॥ ११ ॥

yatanto yoginaścainaṁ paśyantyātmanyavasthitam /
yatanto'pyakṛtātmāno nainaṁ paśyantyacetasaḥ //11//

Yatanto, those who are bent [upon] finding out the actual position of that Being who has become *jīva* in the body–the actual position of being is Parabhairava–and they, by their effort of *yoga*, *paśyanti ātmanyavasthitam*, they perceive Him as Parabhairava in the body, but [only] those who [practice *yoga*] with effort. But those who have not focused their mind one-pointedly, *nainaṁ paśyanti*, they cannot find [Him]. They are in a fix to calculate [their actual position]; they think, "[I am an] individual, I am worth nothing, I am worth nothing."

If somebody asks him, "what is your position of understanding?"

[He responds], "no, I am nothing! I am defeated in this world. I have gained nothing."

DVD 15 (32:54)

यदादित्यगतं तेजो जगद्भासयतेऽखिलम् ।
यच्चन्द्रमसि यच्चाग्नौ तत्तेजो विद्धि मामकम् ॥ १२ ॥
गामाविश्य च भूतानि धारयाम्यहमोजसा ।
पुष्णामि चौषधीः सर्वाः सोमो भूत्वा रसात्मकः ॥ १३ ॥
अहं वैश्वानरो भूत्वा प्राणिनां देहमास्थितः ।
प्राणापानसमायुक्तः पचाम्यन्नं चतुर्विधम् ॥ १४ ॥

yadādityagataṁ tejo jagadbhāsayate'khilam /
yaccandramasi yaccāgnau tattejo viddhi māmakam //12//
gāmāviśya ca bhūtāni dhārayāmyahamojasā /
puṣṇāmi cauṣadhīḥ sarvāḥ somo bhūtvā rasātmakaḥ //13//
ahaṁ vaiśvānaro bhūtvā prāṇinām dehamāsthitaḥ /
prāṇāpānasamāyuktaḥ pacāmyannaṁ caturvidham //14//

Three *ślokas* in one: 12th, 13th, and 14th.

Yadādityagataṁ tejo, O Arjuna, whatever *teja* (light) is residing in the sun, *jagat bhāsayate'khilam*, and that illuminating power which is existing in the sun, and by that this sun illuminates the whole world (*jagat bhāsayate akhilam*). Everybody is wakeful and goes on working, goes on [with their] duties, goes on [working at] offices and everybody works on.

Yat candram asi, whatever light is felt in the moon, *yat cāgnau*, whatever light is felt in fire, *tat tejo viddhi māmakam*, O Arjuna, you should actually understand that this is not their [own] light.

Whose light?

JONATHAN: Moon or sun or . . .

SWAMIJI: Sun, moon, or fire.

It is My light. I have bestowed this light to them–Parabhairava says to Arjuna.

DVD 15 (35:10)

गामाविश्य च भूतानि धारयाम्यहमोजसा ।
पुष्णामि चौषधीः सर्वाः सोमो भूत्वा रसात्मकः ॥१३॥

gāmāviśya ca bhūtāni dhārayāmyahamojasā /
puṣṇāmi cauṣadhīḥ sarvāḥ somo bhūtvā rasātmakaḥ //13//
[repeated]

I am that Being who enters in *gāma* (*gāma* means this earth); I enter in this *pṛthvī*, in earth. *Bhūtāni dhārayāmyaham ojasā*, I make all individuals shine on this earth by My glamour, and I create herbs and eatable things from this earth.

Puṣṇāmi cauṣadhīḥ sarvāḥ somo bhūtvārasātmakaḥ. I become *soma* and give *somarasa*, [I] spread *somarasa* in *pṛthvī* by which everybody becomes shining with glamour, and they get good food, good *rasa* (taste), good *nashikar*, good *nutri-nugget* (soy-based meal); whatever it is, they get good things, eatable.

DVD 15 (36:40)

अहं वैश्वानरो भूत्वा प्राणिनां देहमास्थितः ।
प्राणापानसमायुक्तः पचाम्यन्नं चतुर्विधम् ॥१४॥

ahaṁ vaiśvānaro bhūtvā prāṇinām dehamāsthitaḥ /
prāṇāpānasamāyuktaḥ pacāmyannaṁ caturvidham //14
[repeated]

I am that Being who enters into the body of individuals and go on breathing in and breathing out in this body. And there is fire, in the body there is fire, there is pulse, there is circulation of blood, circulation of blood goes on, and heart also beats in one round everywhere, and all of the food that is being chewed by individuals is digested by Me! I am the digester, I am digesting that food. They are not [capable of digesting]; they have no guts to digest it. I am, I am existing in those bodies also.

Conclusion of Myself:

DVD 15 (38:01)

सर्वस्य चाहं हृदि संनिविष्टो
मत्तः स्मृतिर्ज्ञानमपोहनं च ।
वेदैश्च सर्वैरहमेव वेद्यो
वेदान्तकृद्वेदविदेव चाहम् ॥ १५ ॥

sarvasya cāhaṁ hṛdi saṁniviṣṭo
mattaḥ smṛtirjñānamapohanaṁ ca /
vedaiśca sarvairahameva vedyo
vedāntakṛdvedavideva cāham //15//

Sarvasya cāhaṁ hṛdi saṁniviṣṭa, O Arjuna, I am situated in each and every heart of individuals; not only men [i.e., humans], even mosquitoes also, worms also. Whatever life-full or life-less thing that exists, I am existing in their hearts. *Mattaḥ smṛtir jñānam apohanaṁ ca*, from Me, knowledge (*jñānam*), memory (*smṛti*), and forgetfulness (*apohanaṁ*) are produced.

Knowledge. Knowledge means that which you have . . . knowledge of your past when you were [living] in Mahārājganj, when you where in Mahārājganj situated. It is knowledge of your past, that is past knowledge. Now you have got its memory, now memory is present of that.

Don't you remember?

That is memory. Memory also comes from Me. And *apohanaṁ*, when you forget [something], that forgetfulness also comes from Me. If there was not forgetfulness, then everybody would become mad. Forgetfulness gives you a rest, it gives your consciousness (*cit*) rest. You are appeased, you forget everything. When you try to remember, you do like this [scratching your head], "O, I have found it. This was that."

Vedaiśca sarvairahameva vedyo, by all *śāstras* I am realized. *Vedāntakṛt*, I am the producer of *śāstras* and I am the knower of *śāstras*. I am the only [one existing]; there is nobody [else] in this drama.

Again He goes down [i.e., digresses] now.

DVD 15 (41:20)

द्वाविमौ पुरुषौ लोके क्षरश्चाक्षर एव च ।
क्षरः सर्वाणि भूतानि कूटस्थोऽक्षर उच्यते ॥१६॥
उत्तमः पुरुषस्त्वन्यः परमात्मेत्युदाहृतः ।
यो लोकत्रयमाविश्य बिभर्त्यव्यय ईश्वरः ॥१७॥
यस्मात्क्षरमतीतोऽहमक्षरादपि चोत्तमः ।
अतोऽस्मि लोके वेदे च प्रथितः पुरुषोत्तमः ॥१८॥

dvāvimau puruṣau loke kṣaraścākṣara eva ca /
kṣaraḥ sarvāṇi bhūtāni kūṭastho'kṣara ucyate //16//
uttamaḥ puruṣastvanyaḥ paramātametyudāhṛtaḥ /
yo lokatrayamāviśya bibhartyavyaya īśvaraḥ //17//
yasmātkṣaramatīto'hamakṣarādapi cottamaḥ /
ato'smi loke vede ca prathitaḥ puruṣottamaḥ //18//

Sixteenth, 17th and 18th in one.

There are two classes of *puruṣas* (conscious beings) existing in this world, in this kingdom of Mine. In this kingdom of Mine, there are two *puruṣas* existing. *Kṣaraścā*, one *puruṣa* is side by side [existing with the other], which is perishable, and another *puruṣa* is that who is . . .

JOHN: Imperishable.

SWAMIJI: . . . eternal. *Kṣaraḥ sarvāṇi bhūtāni*, that *puruṣa* who is perishable, *sarvāṇi bhūtāni*, all individuals are like that–they are all [mortal]. *Kūṭastho'kṣara ucyate*, and one is *akṣara* (*akṣara* means He does not get perished). That is I, O Arjuna.

DVD 15 (43:02)

उत्तमः पुरुषस्त्वन्यः परमातमेत्युदाहृतः ।
यो लोकत्रयमाविश्य विभर्त्यव्यय ईश्वरः ॥१७॥

uttamaḥ puruṣastvanyaḥ paramātametyudāhṛtaḥ /
yo lokatrayamāviśya vibhartyavyaya īśvaraḥ //17//

There is one *uttama puruṣa*. *Uttama puruṣa* is that [being] who is *kṣara* and *akṣara* both. *Uttama puruṣa* is *kṣara* and *akṣara*, perishable and not perishable–that is *uttama puruṣa*. First He explained there are two *puruṣas*: one is *kṣara*, another is imperishable (*akṣara*). And there is *uttam puruṣa* also. *Uttam puruṣa* is perishable and unperishable, both.

Yo lokatrayamāviśya vibhartyavyaya, who does not decay, who does not decay in any way. Although He has come into the inferior world and [has] become *shikas lad,* still in *shikas lad* (ill-fated) state He is glamorous. He feels that, "I am glamorous," He Himself. So there is whole [existing] in parts also. So you cannot understand what is what.

This is the kingdom of one Being.

DVD 15 (44:44)

यो मामेवमसंमूढो जानाति पुरुषोत्तमम् ।
स सर्वविद्भजति मां सर्वभावेन भारत ॥१९॥

yo māmevamasaṁmūḍho jānāti puruṣottamam /
sa sarvavidbhajati māṁ sarvabhāvena bhārata //19//

That person who understands and exists, and understands fully well this kind of [existence of] My being, *sa sarvavit*, he knows everything, *bhajati māṁ*, and he is devoted to Me with full devotion, *sarvabhāvena*, wholeheartedly, *bhārata*, O Arjuna.

Tathā ca mayaiva śivaśaktyavinābhāva stotre [comm. verse19].

I, [Abhinavagupta], have also somewhere in the *Siva Sakti Avinābhāva Stotra*, I have penned down *ślokas* for Devī.

Who is Devī?

JOHN: *Svātantrya śakti.*

SWAMIJI: *Svātantrya śakti*, which is existing where? In manifestation, not above manifestation. Huh?

JONATHAN: In outside world.

SWAMIJI: Huh?

DVD 15 (46:18)

तव च काचन न स्तुतिरम्बिके
सकलशब्दमयी किल ते तनुः ।
निखिलमूर्तिषु मे भवदन्वयो
मनसिजासु बहिष्प्रसरासु च ॥

tava ca kācana na stutirambike
sakalaśabdamayī kila te tanuḥ /
nikhilamūrtiṣu me bhavadanvayo
manasijāsu bahiṣprasarāsu ca //

It is *Devī Stotra* by Abhinavagupta.

Tava ca kācana na stutir ambike. O Mother, O Mother, *tava ca kācana stutir na*, by going, by sitting in meditation room aloof, leaving all activities aside and thinking of You, [reciting], "*oṁ parā vāk devī namaḥ, oṁ parā vāk devī namaḥ, oṁ parā vāk devī namaḥ . . . parabhairavāya namaḥ, parabhairavāya namaḥ . . .* ," like this, and reciting [Your] name, that is not Your *stuti* (hymn)–Abhinavagupta says–that is actually not Your *stuti*, i.e., the one who sings [Your] glory in the secluded corner of *pūja* room with all of the doors shut.

Why? Why is it not that?

Sakala śabdamayī kila te tanuḥ. O Mother, O great Mother *svātantrya śakti*, "this is jug, this is paneer, this is lime juice, this is ghee, this is parātha," *sakala śabda mayī*, this is also Your *stuti*. When I perceive [these things], this is also Your *stuti* (hymn). *Sakalaśabda*, You are not excluded there! *Sakala śabda mayī kila te tanuḥ*, this [objective world] is existing in Your universal body, O Mother.

So, *nikhila mūrtiṣu me bhavad anvayo*, and [Your] *mūrti* (form), You have got four arms and eighteen heads, like this–this is not Your body. *Nikhila mūrtiṣu me bhavad anvayo*, when I see Viresh, I see Mother; when I see Jonathan, I see Mother; when I see George, I see Mother; when I see that *shikas*, that mad [person], I see Mother. *Nikhila mūrtiṣu me bhavad anvayo*, I am united in Thee, O Mother! *Manasijāsu bahiṣ prasarāsu ca*, and while thinking thoughts, in those thoughts also You are existing for me!

DVD 15 (50:54)

इति विचिन्त्य शिवे शमिताशिवे
जगति जातमयत्नवशादिदम् ।

iti vicintya śive śamitāśive
jagati jātamayatnavaśādidam /

Going into the depth . . . myself, after going into the depth of this secret of Thee, *jagati jātamayatna vaśādidam*, I find that in this universe, it has happened automatically!

What?

स्तुतिजपार्चनचिन्तनवार्जिता
न खलु काचन कालकलापि मे ॥

stutijapārcanacintanavarjitā
na khalu kācana kālakalāpi me //

Each and every moment I am adoring You, thinking of You, O divine Mother! I have no one [else] in view, only You. You are existing [for] me in each and every *mūrti* (form), in each and every step, in each and every movement of this world.

So, this way you should think [about] this state of Parabhairava, not only in the individual *shikas* (ill-fated) way.

DVD 15 (52:24)

इति गुह्यतमं शास्त्रमिदमुक्तं मयानघ ।
एतद्बुद्ध्वा बुद्धिमान्स्यात्कृतकृत्यश्च भारत ॥२०॥

iti guhyatamaṁ śāstramidamuktaṁ mayānagha /
etadbuddvā buddhimānsyātkṛtakṛtyaśca bhārata //20//

This is the last *śloka* of this chapter.

This way, *guhyatamaṁ śāstram*, this secret of secrets I have placed before you, O Arjuna. *Idamuktaṁ mayā*, I have explained to you [because] *anagha*, you are blameless, you have no blame, you have no blemishes, you have no dots [i.e., imperfections] of any sort.

Etat buddvā buddhi mānsyāt kṛta-kṛtyaśca bhārata. If you go into the depth of this chapter, if you are wise, you will become the possessor of the wisdom of Parabhairava.

Bas, [we have] finished this *adhyāya* (chapter).

DVD 15 (53:33)

हृत्वा द्वैतमहामोहं कृत्वा ब्रह्ममयीं चितिम् ।
लौकिके व्यवहारेऽपि मुनिर्नित्यं समाविशेत् ॥१५॥

hṛtvā dvaitamahāmohaṁ kṛtvā brahmamayīṁ citim /
laukike vyavahāre'pi munirnityaṁ samāviśet //15//

॥ Concluding *śloka* of 15th chapter ॥

Munir, who is always focused in the thought of Parabhairava, he has [driven] all thoughts, all thoughts, all *dvaita. Dvaita* means . . .

JOHN: Duality.

SWAMIJI: Duality. Duality of thoughts, he has [driven] all away, and who is established in Parabhairava state, *laukike vyavahāre'pi*, in each and every action of his daily actions of daily life, he gets *samāveśa* (absorption) in Parabhairava, always; he is getting that, he sinks always into that [Parabhairava state]. He sinks and [returns] with glamour, sinks and [returns] with the glamour [of that state].[448]

448 "See that in your mind, all this ignorance and illusion of being separated from God consciousness, separated from the memory of God consciousness is carried away, is smashed, is vanished. You must see that. And *hṛtvā brahmamayīṁ citim*, and focus your mind to Brahman, to Lord Śiva, in each and every action of this universe. *Laukike vyavahāre'pi*, no matter whatever you do in this world, everything will become divine." *Bhagavad Gītā* (1978).

Chapter 16

DVD 16 (00:01)

अभयः सत्त्वसंशुद्धिर्ज्ञानयोगव्यवस्थितिः ।
दानं दमश्च यज्ञश्च स्वाध्यायस्तप आर्जवम् ॥१॥
अहिंसा सत्यमक्रोधस्त्यागोऽसक्तिरपैशुनम् ।
दया भूतेष्वलौल्यं च मार्दवं ह्रीरचापलम् ॥२॥
तेजः क्षमा धृतिस्तुष्टिरद्रोहो नातिमानिता ।
भवन्ति संपदं दैवीमभिजातस्य भारत ॥३॥
दम्भो दर्पोऽभिमानश्च क्रोधः पारुष्यमेव च ।
अज्ञानं चाभिजातस्य पार्थ संपदमासुरिम् ॥४॥
दैवी संपद्विमोक्षाय निबन्धायासुरी मता ।
मा शुचः संपदं दैवीमभिजातोऽसि पाण्डव ॥५॥

abhayaṁ sattvasaṁśuddhirjñānayogavyavasthitiḥ /
dānaṁ damaśca yajñaśca svādhyāyastapa ārjavam //1//
āhiṁsā satyamakrodhastyāgo'saktirapaiśunam /
dayā bhūteṣvalaulyaṁ ca mārdavaṁ hrīracāpalam //2//
tejaḥ kṣamā dhṛtistuṣṭiradroho nātimānitā /
bhavanti saṁpadaṁ daivīmabhijātasya bhārata //3//
dambho darpo'bhimānaśca krodhaḥ pāruṣyameva ca /
ajñānaṁ cābhijātasya pārtha saṁpadamāsurīm //4//
daivī saṁpadvimokṣāya nibandhāyāsurī matā /
mā śucaḥ saṁpadaṁ daivīmabhijāto'si pāṇḍava //5//

[Now, Lord Śiva (Lord Kṛṣṇa) says that there are two kinds of glories: one is divine glory, one is not divine glory. Divine glory shines in those who are blessed and the symptoms of divine glory is what He says now.][449]

Abhayaṁ, the absence of fear, when there is absence of fear in some person; this is first, absence of fear. He does not get afraid because he is pure, purely situated in devotion of God. *Sattva saṁśuddhir*, and he has purified behavior, the purest behavior. *Jñāna yoga vyavasthitiḥ,* and he is established in *jñāna* and *yoga*, i.e., in the knowledge of God and in being united with His nature–that is *yoga*.

Dānaṁ, he has got tendency to give alms to the poor who [are in] need. *Damaśca*. *Damaśca* means he has got power to keep his organs controlled. *Yajñaśca*, he performs *yajñas* (*yajñas* means offerings). He offers to the gods and to the poor and to those who [are in] need. *Svādhyāya*, he is always absorbed in singing the glory of Lord Śiva in books, in Shaivite books. *Tapa*, he has got penance. *Tapa* means [the person] who has got penance in mind, in body, and in soul (*tapasya*, tolerance). *Ārjavam*, he has got . . . *ārjavam* means *rujita*, he is simple, [he has] simple behavior. Simple behavior does not mean that he is dull or he is a duffer. No. "Simple" means he is alert in [being] concentrated upon God consciousness. But he is not duffer, he is not that simple. But he has got all behaviors [that] are simple, without crookedness.

Āhimsā [verse 2], he does not want to hurt anybody. *Satyam*, and he speaks the truth. *Akrodha*, he is not given to wrath. *Tyāga*, he has the power of detachment. *Asaktir*, he is not slave to . . . he has not become slave to this . . . *asaktir* means he has not become slave to his desires. He controls his desires, which [means that] he understands what is a good desire [and] he possesses that. [That] which is a bad [desire], he does not allow that [to enter] into his mind. *Apaiśunam*. *Apaiśunam* means *chugalkhor*, he is not *chugalkhor*.

Chugalkhor means the [person who speaks] absolute falsehoods [about] others to his nearly attached persons [i.e., friends or relatives]. For instance, if I have got *āsurī saṁpat* (demonic behavior), I will tell you a falsehood, a falsehood about your wife, a falsehood about your kith and kin, e.g., [I will tell you], "they are not behaving [with] good character [towards] you. And afterwards, when [they are] face to face [with you], they behave

449 *Bhagavad Gītā* (1978).

with good actions; but, when you are out [of their presence], they talk about you with bad manners [amongst] your kith and kin." [I say this] so that your kith and kin will get wrath and will [develop] hatred for you for nothing. This is the act of *āsurīs* (demons).

But he has not this [demonic behavior]. He does not do this *chugalkhor. Chugalkhor* means to speak [of] false behavior . . .

JOHN: Gossiping.

SWAMIJI: Bad opinion.

JONATHAN: Behind somebody's back.

SWAMIJI: Behind somebody's back.

JOHN: Caviling.

SWAMIJI: Huh?

JOHN: Caviling? To cavil somebody means to say bad things about them, and make rumors . . .

SWAMIJI: Yes. So that they don't behave [with] you as they ought to behave [with] you. They want to separate . . . two beloved ones, they want to separate [them]. But those who have not [*āsuri saṁpat*], they want to join [them]. Those who have got *daivī saṁpat* (godly behavior), they want to join the two, one couple, with each other. They don't want to separate them. That is *apaiśunam*, absence of *chugalkhor. Chugalkhor* means that.

Do you understand *chugalkhor*?[450]

Dayā bhūteṣu [verse 2], and they have got *dayā* (*dayā* means compassion for all living beings). *Alaulyaṁ ca*, they have got no selfish motive [in their dealings with] others. *Mārdavaṁ*, they use only soft words. *Hrīr*, they are ashamed [of] bad behavior, conducting bad behavior. They don't conduct bad behavior. They are ashamed of that. They don't like to indulge in bad behavior. Who? Those who have got . . .

DENISE: The ones who have wealth of spiritual knowledge.

SWAMIJI: Yes.

Acāpalam, who are not moved easily from that one-pointedness.

Tejaḥ [verse 3], who have got *tejaḥ* (*tejaḥ* means who have got brightness, brightness of mind, brightness of being). *Kṣamā*, who have got *kṣamā* (*kṣamā* means tolerance), they don't lose their

450 The literal meaning of *chugalkhor* is backbitting, or scandal-mongering. [*Editor's note*]

wits.[451] *Dhṛti*, they have got *dhairya* (*dhairya* means tolerance).[452] *Tuṣṭiḥ*, they have got satisfaction, they are always satisfied with what they have, [with what] they possess. *Adroha*, they don't hate anybody; they don't hate anybody [whether they are] good or bad. *Nātimānitā*, and they don't think they are [more] well-off than others. They think everybody is fine; everybody should rise. [They feel], "if I rise, that is also well, but everybody should rise along with me." They don't say that, "I must only rise and all [others] must become subsided."

This is the wealth of spiritual wealth and this I have found in you, O Arjuna.

> [And, on the contrary, there is another glory, which is undivine, which is not divine. That I will explain to you.][453]

Dambha [verse 4], *dambha* means *kapaṭ*.[454] *Dambha* means *ahaṁkāra*, it is a kind of ego. And with that ego he says, "I am, I am a great person," although he is not great. *Darpaḥ*. *Darpaḥ* means I-ness, uncontrolled I-ness. *Abhimānaśca*. *Abhimānaśca* means *abhimāna* (arrogance), e.g., "I am such and such person." *Krodha*, wrath, always conducting [himself] with wrath. *Pāruṣyam*, harsh words, he [uses] harsh words with everybody. *Ajñānaṁ*, and negligence and forgetfulness of God. These behaviors are found in those who have got *rākṣasa* (demonic) behavior.

And *daivī* (godly) behavior is supposed to sentence you in *mokṣa*, Parabhairava, in the union of Parabhairava. And *āsurī saṁpat* (demonic behavior) is for entangling [you] in the wheel of repeated births and deaths.

Mā śucaḥ, don't get afraid. You have got . . . I feel there is the rise of *daivī saṁpat* in you, [O Arjuna].

Now 6th, 7th, 8th, 9th, 10th, 11th, all of these.

---

451 "Forgive! Forget and forgive. Don't look on the drawbacks of people. Forgive them. There must be tendency of forgiving."
Bhagavad Gītā (1978).

452 "*Dhṛti* means courage. You must have courage. When you come in contact with crisis, torture, pain, sadness, have courage. Develop courage at that moment." Ibid.

453 *Bhagavad Gītā* (1978).

454 *Kapaṭ* is a Hindi word meaning "fraud". [*Editor's note*]

DVD 16 (12:00)

द्वौ भूतसर्गौ लोकेऽस्मिन्दैव आसुर एव च ।
दैवो विस्तरतः प्रोक्त आसुरं पार्थ मे श्रृणु ॥ ६ ॥

dvau bhūtasargau loke'smindaiva āsura eva ca /
daivo vistarataḥ prokta āsuraṁ pārtha me śṛṇu //6//

Dvau bhūta sargau. There are two ways of creation. One creation is of that class who have possessed that wealth of divine wealth and there are other persons who have got *rākṣasa* wealth, wealth of *rākṣasas*. *Daivo vistarataḥ prokta,* I have related to you the divine wealth; *āsuraṁ pārtha me śṛṇu*, now I will explain to you *rākṣasas* wealth in detail.

DVD 16 (13:01)

प्रवृत्तिं च निवृत्तिं च जना न विदुरासुराः ।
न शौचं नापि चाचारो न सत्यं तेषु विद्यते ॥ ७ ॥

pravṛttiṁ ca nivṛttiṁ ca janā na vidurāsurāḥ /
na śaucaṁ nāpi cācāro na satyaṁ teṣu vidyate //7//

Pravṛttiṁ, [that work] which I have to do, which work I should do and from which work I should withdraw, these things those *rākṣasas* do not understand. These discriminations: from which work I should behave with and from which I should . . .

DENISE: Not behave in.

SWAMIJI: Yes.

Na śaucaṁ nāpi cācāro, na satyaṁ teṣu vidyate. In addition, in those [*rākṣasas*], there is no cleanliness of mind, body, and soul. *Ācāra*, they have not good behavior. *Na satyaṁ,* they have not truth in them. They are always fraud people; there is no truth in their words.

DVD 16 (14:21)

असत्यमप्रतिष्ठं ते जगदाहुरनीश्वरम् ।
अपरस्परसंभूतमकिंचित्कमहेतुकम् ॥ ८ ॥

asatyamapratiṣṭhaṁ te jagadāhuranīśvaram /
aparasparasaṁbhūtamakiṁcitkamahetukam //8//

Those people see, realize [i.e., believe] that this universe is *asatya*, it has no basis; in the long run, it has no basis wherefrom it has appeared, [that] there is nothing known about that. And it is not existing; the basis of this world is not existing–it has [just] appeared like this. *Apratiṣṭhaṁ te*, and it is not conducted by some power. There is no power which is handling [it], who handles this position of world. *Jagat āhur anīśvaram*, they say that this world is *anīśvaram*, it has no god, no god in the background.

Aparaspara saṁbhūtam, [they believe] it is created by each other, i.e., by union with each other.[455] *Akiṁcitkam*, it has no basis in the end. *Ahetukam*, there is no cause of this universe being created.

JOHN: Cārvākas.

SWAMIJI: Just like Cārvākas (atheists), [but more] degraded than that.

JOHN: Atheists, worse than atheists.

SWAMIJI: Cārvākas are . . .

DENISE: Devil worshippers? People who . . .

SWAMIJI: Devil worshippers. Cārvākas are still better than this.[456] They say, "*saṁdigdehe paraloke*." It is true that Cārvākas . . . this is the behavior of the philosophy of Cārvāka's, those who are atheists, they say, "this world is not based on some handler; there is no *paraloka* (heaven), there is no . . . after death, there is nothing." *Saṁdigdehe paraloke*, although [they believe] it is a fact that there is no *paraloka*, there is no hereafter, there is nothing existing in the background hereafter, *tyājam eva śubhabuddhayaḥ*, [still they believe] it is worthwhile to do good actions in this world. [They say], "although there is no other world but suppose there is *paraloka*? *Nāsti gohatha*, [one] who has acted in a bad way in this life, he will be killed, he will be put to task [in this life], and we will be free. So it is better, it

455 "*Apara spara saṁbhūtam* . . . only mother and father are responsible for its creation. That is all they know." *Bhagavad Gītā* (1978).

456 Here, Swamiji is saying that the Cārvāka's are still better than the *rākṣasas* mentioned in verse 7.

is worthwhile, to do good actions in this *loka* (world) although there is no *paraloka* (heaven)."

So Cārvākas are better than these [*rākṣasas*].

DVD 16 (17:42)

एतां दृष्टिमवष्टभ्य नष्टात्मानोऽल्पबुद्धयः ।
प्रभवन्त्युग्रकर्माणः क्षयाय जगतोऽशुभाः ॥९॥

etāṁ dṛṣṭimavaṣṭabhya naṣṭātmāno'lpabuddhayaḥ /
prabhavantyugrakarmāṇaḥ kṣayāya jagato'śubhāḥ //9//

This viewpoint they occupy, those *rākṣasas*.[457] *Naṣṭātmānaḥ,* their internal consciousness, which is knocking at their door in disguise, they have killed that, killed that *ātma* inside who is knocking in the background of their [consciousness saying], "oh don't act like this. I warn you, don't act like this!" But he acts. He does not care for that sound which comes [from] within him from God's side. That is *naṣṭātmāna. Alpabuddhayaḥ*, because their intellect, power of understanding, is totally finished.

Prabhavantyugrakarmāṇaḥ, they go on behaving with bad actions. What for? *Kṣayāya jagato aśubhāḥ*, just to destroy the whole universe. They want to destroy the whole universe and become sovereign and adopt and attain sovereignty over it.

DVD 16 (19:34)

काममाश्रित्य दुष्पूरं दम्भलोभमदान्विताः ।
असद्ग्रहाश्रिताः क्रूराः प्रचरन्त्यशुचिव्रताः ॥१०॥

kāmamāśritya duṣpūraṁ dambhalobhamadānvitāḥ /
asadgrahāśritāḥ krūrāḥ pracarantyaśucivratāḥ //10//

This is the 10th [*śloka*].

Kāmamāśritya duṣpūraṁ, they have got desires which have no

457 "They don't understand wherefrom this universe has come and to which place it will get absorption in the end. They don't care for that. They care to eat, drink, and be merry, that is all."
Bhagavad Gītā (1978).

end. [They say],"I will do this, and I will do this, and I . . ." They have got this detail in their so-called future of their behavior. They go on and they are absorbed in those details, "I will do this, and I will do this, and I will do . . ." And while thinking [about these things], they are smashed down by Parabhairava.

Dambha lobha madānvitāḥ. They have got *dambha*, they have got *lobha*, and they have got *mada*. *Dambha* means *kapaṭ* (fraud). *Lobha* means greed. *Mada* means [thinking], "I am such and such person, I am the greatest man in this world." *Asat grahāśritāḥ*, and they have got *asadgraha* (*asadgraha* means that which has no basis).[458] And that behavior they possess. *Krūrāḥ*, they are very *krūra* (*krūra* means cruel to everybody). *Pracaranti aśucivratāḥ*, and they behave with dirty behavior.

Now the 11th [*śloka*].

DVD 16 (21:15)

चिन्तामपरिमेयां च प्रलयान्तामुपाश्रिताः ।
कामोपभोगपरमा एतावदिति निश्चिताः ॥११॥

cintāmaparimeyāṁ ca pralayāntāmupāśritāḥ /
kāmopabhogaparamā etāvaditi niścitāḥ //11//

Cintām aparim eyāṁ ca, and they have got . . . in Kashmiri it is called '*czerts*'. What do you call *czerts*? *Czerts* is . . . I will give you one example of *czerts*.

There was one black bee, a black bee sucking the nectar of some lotus, in lotus . . .
JONATHAN: Pond.
SWAMIJI: . . . lotus pond. He was sucking this nectar of lotus. And you know that lotus, when sun sets down, lotus . . .
Huh?
DENISE: Closes.
SWAMIJI: . . . closes. And [the black bee] didn't know that sun setting was possible and so I should get out from this

458 That is, they hold on to false beliefs, e.g., thinking that they are their body. [*Editor's note*]

[lotus] and go to my nest–that black bee. He was enjoying the nectar, sucking the nectar. And by ill luck, the lotus closed and he thinks now [about] tomorrow.

This is one *kavi*. *Kavi* means [poet]. There was one poet, he was a great poet, Kālidāsa, he was a great poet [named] Kālidāsa, he [composed] this story. He has created this story of his own.

This is called '*czerts*', i.e., he does this, he thinks of what will come in the future.

[The trapped bee thought], "*rātrirgamiśyati bhavaṣyati sūprabhātam*, there are nine hours to rest in this [lotus]. After all, this night will *gamiśyati*, will expire, *bhavaṣyati sūprabhātam*, and [then] there will be dawn."

"*Bhāsvānudeṣyati haśisyati paṅkajaśrī*, *bhāsvan*, the sun will rise, *haśisyati paṅkajaśrī*, this lotus will laugh and get opened and I will fly. I will fly to the nest. So I have to wait only for a few hours [during the] night."

"*Hā hanta hanta nalinīm gaja ujjahārā*, the torture is," Kālidāsa says, "*hā hant*, it is very sad news for you, which I handle, [which I] pass on to you people in this world. 'In this world, everything, every bad thing is possible.'" Although he was thinking of the future. Who?
JONATHAN: Bee. Black bee.
SWAMIJI: Bee. *Hā hanta hanta*, it was a great misery, miserable condition, that one elephant came [during the night], and he went for bathing in that [lotus] pool, and he smashed all of those flowers and lotuses along with that bee also. The bee also was finished along with this. This is the way of the world. What is this called?
JOHN: This is tragedy.
SWAMIJI: No, what he was thinking.
JOHN: Before.
SWAMIJI: What the bee was, black bee was thinking. That is called '*czerts*' in Kashmiri.
JOHN: It means he thinks a better side is going to happen.

SWAMIJI: Yes.
JOHN: That's optimism.
JONATHAN: But really, I mean, you shouldn't think about the future at all, should you?
SWAMIJI: You should not think [about the future].
JONATHAN: Good or bad, whatever comes you should accept that.
SWAMIJI: Yes.
DENISE: But the point is that if you are stuck in a position you are uncomfortable in, you are naturally going to think of the future because . . .
SWAMIJI: Yes. You know . . .
DENISE: . . . you want to get out of that position.
JOHN: So some people see the negative side, "oh, I'm done . . ."
SWAMIJI: But all bad things are possible in this world. It is not known [what will happen].

So in the same way, those *āsuris*, those demons, who have got demons wealth, they think of the future, e.g., "this will come, this will come, this will come", and while thinking [about the future], Parabhairava smashes them just like the elephant [smashed the bee in the lotus], and they are no more existing in this world.[459]

So Parabhairava does not . . . Parabhairava is the topmost element who is watching all of your activities. It does not mean that you will think of [doing] this and that and it will happen.

This is the 11th *śloka* finished.

DVD 16 (27:15)

आशापाशशतैर्बद्धाः कामक्रोधपरायणाः ।
ईहन्ते कामभोगार्थानन्यायेनार्थसञ्चयान् ॥१२॥

459 "And their desires shine up to the point of death, death time, death period. They are only desiring, "this will happen, and this . . . and you should do this." And at the time of death also they teach their kith and kin to take care of cows, to take care of *ashram*, to take care of money, to take care of. . . . What to him? But they do not understand what they are barking and talking nonsense. Because they are dying, they won't be any more in this world." *Bhagavad Gītā* (1978).

āśāpāśaśatairbaddhāḥ kāmakrodhaparāyaṇāḥ /
īhante kāmabhogārthānanyāyenārthasañcayān //12//

Āśāpāśa śatair baddhāḥ, they have got *pāśas* (*pāśaś* means bindings), bindings of so many desires, hundreds and thousands of desires, and [those desires] bind their behavior–those *rākṣasas. Kāma krodha parāyaṇāḥ*, because they are bent upon indulging with *kāma* (lust) and *krodha* (anger).

Īhante kāmabhogārthān, and for *kāma* and *bhoga* (enjoyment), they behave *anyāyenārthasañcayān,* with not . . . they collect money with bad behavior. It is impure collection.

Now the 13th and 14th and 15th in one.

DVD 16 (28:26)

इदमद्य मया लब्धमिदं प्राप्स्ये मनोरथम् ।
इदमस्तीदमपि मे भविष्यति पुनर्धनम् ॥१३॥
असौ मया हतः शत्रुर्हनिष्ये चापरानपि ।
ईश्वरोऽहमहं भोगी सिद्धोऽहं बलवान्सुखी ॥१४॥
आढ्योऽभिजनवानस्मि कोऽन्योऽस्ति सदृशो मया ।
यक्ष्ये दास्यामि मोदिष्ये इत्यज्ञानविमोहिताः ॥१५॥
अनेकचित्ता विभ्रान्ता मोहस्यैव वशं गताः ।
प्रसक्ताः कामभोगेषु पतन्ति निरयेऽशुचौ ॥१६॥

idamadya mayā labdhamidaṁ prāpsye manoratham /
idamastīdamapi me bhaviṣyati punardhanam //13//
asau mayā hataḥ śatrurhaniṣye cāparānapi /
īśvaro'hamahaṁ bhogī siddho'haṁ balavānsukhī //14//
āḍhyo'bhijanavānasmi ko'nyo'sti sadṛśo mayā /
yakṣye dāsyāmi modiṣye ityajñānavimohitāḥ //15//
anekacittā vibhrāntā mohasyaiva vaśaṁ gatāḥ /
prasaktāḥ kāmabhogeṣu patanti niraye'śucau //16//

[*Rākṣasas* think], "*idamadya mayā labdham*, this money I have stored today. *Idaṁ prāpsye manoratham*, and this money I will get very soon in the future. *Idam asti*, this is my bank balance at present. *Idam api bhavaṣyati punardhanam*, and more wealth will come in a few days, in the near future. *Asau mayā hataḥ śatrur* [verse 14], I have killed one enemy, so many enemies I have killed so far. *Haniṣye cāparānapi*, more enemies I will kill in the near future. *Īśvaro'ham*, I will become God. *Ahaṁ bhogī*, I will become enjoyer of this world. *Siddho'ham*, I will become the greatest person, personality in this world. *Balavān*, I will become powerful in this world. *Sukhī*, I will become peaceful in this world."

DVD 16 (30:33)

आढ्योऽभिजनवानस्मि कोऽन्योऽस्ति सदृशो मया ।
यक्ष्ये दास्यामि मोदिष्ये इत्यज्ञानविमोहिताः ॥१५॥

āḍhyo'bhijanavānasmi ko'nyo'sti sadṛśo mayā /
yakṣye dāsyāmi modiṣye ityajñānavimohitāḥ //15//
[repeated]

"*Āḍhya abhijanavānasmi*, I am praised by all in which society I am seated. All are with folded hands praising me because they are likely to praise me. They have no way out. They can't remain outside that. They have to praise me because I am great. *Ko'nyo 'sti sadṛśo mayā*, who is parallel to me in this world? Nobody! God, shod, this is all *bakwas* (nonsense). *Yakṣye*, I spend [my] wealth, I'll spend my wealth, *dāsyāmi*, I'll bestow this wealth to those who think of me as Lord, *modiṣye*, and I will remain peaceful." *Iti ajñāna vimohitāḥ*, in this way, they are deluded altogether.

DVD 16 (32:08)

अनेकचित्ता विभ्रान्ता मोहस्यैव वशं गताः ।
प्रसक्ताः कामभोगेषु पतन्ति निरयेऽशुचौ ॥१६॥

anekacittā vibhrāntā mohasyaiva vaśaṁ gatāḥ /
prasaktāḥ kāmabhogeṣu patanti niraye'śucau //16//
[repeated]

Anekacittā, they have got so many thoughts, various thoughts. *Vibhrāntā*, they are just playing in the ether, baselessly. They construct houses and bungalows in ether, which has no basis. *Prasaktāḥ kāmabhogeṣu*, and they are bent upon using these sensual pleasures day and night. *Patanti niraye'śucau*, in the long run they are tossed by Me into dirty hells wherefrom they have no hope of coming out.

The 17th and 18th together now.

DVD 16 (33:30)

आत्मसंभाविताः स्तब्धा धनमानमदान्विताः ।
यजन्ते नामयज्ञैस्ते दम्भेनाविधिपूर्वकम् ॥१७॥
अहंकारं बलं दर्पं कामं क्रोधं च संश्रिताः ।
मामात्मपरदेहेषु प्रद्विषन्तोऽभ्यसूयकाः ॥१८॥

ātmasaṁbhāvitāḥ stabdhā dhanamānamadānvitāḥ /
yajante nāmayajñaiste dambhenāvidhipūrvakaṁ //17//
ahaṁkāraṁ balaṁ darpaṁ kāmaṁ krodhaṁ ca saṁśritāḥ /
māmātmaparadeheṣu pradviṣanto'bhyasūyakāḥ //18//

Ātmasaṁbhāvitāḥ, their *ātmasaṁbhāvitāḥ* means wherever they go, they watch people, they watch people from a distance, [and] if people don't attend [to] him, [even though] they think that he is great, but [because of] negligence, it is possible that people who walk around him, they may not watch [i.e., acknowledge] him . . .

DENISE: They may ignore him.

SWAMIJI: Huh?

DENISE: They may ignore him?

SWAMIJI: They may ignore him. At that time, he gets furious and he orders military *walla*, "shoot him! He has [improper] behavior, he does not do *praṇāms* (obeisance). Because I was here standing and he ignored me. Shoot him!" And he is shot. This is *ātmasaṁbhāvitāḥ*.

So, *stabdhā* (*stabdha* means they are rigid), *dhanamāna madānvitāḥ*, they have got *mada* (pride) because of [having] lots of money. They don't . . . they know no boundaries [with] money. Money is just rolling before those people.

Yajante nāma yajñaiste, they conduct some meeting in public, and public is forced to think [of his] glory, to say and sing glory of him.[460] Whom? "You are our God, you are [our] everything, you are everything, you can kill us, you can have us, you can . . . whatever you like you can do. You can kill God also for us."

DENISE: We adore you.

SWAMIJI: "We adore you wholeheartedly."

So in this way, *ahaṁkāra* [verse 18] (*ahaṁkāra* means I-ness), *balaṁ* (strength), *darpaṁ* (ego, topmost ego), *kāma* (lust) and *krodha* (anger), they possess.

And O Arjuna, they actually, those people actually hate Me and [they hate] those who are residing in My meditation; they hate those. They hate those who meditate on Me and [they] hate Me also.

Now what happens to them in the end?

That He says [now]. This is the 19th and 20th *śloka*.

DVD 16 (37:21)

तानहं द्विषतः क्रूरान्संसारेषु नराधमान् ।
क्षिपाम्यजस्रमशुभास्वासुरीष्वेव योनिषु ॥१९॥
आसुरीं योनिमापन्ना मूढा जन्मनि जन्मनि ।
मामप्राप्यैव कौन्तेय ततो यान्त्यधमां गतिम् ॥२०॥

tānahaṁ dviṣataḥ krūrānsaṁsāreṣu narādhamān /
kṣipāmyajasramaśubhāsvāsurīṣveva yoniṣu //19//
āsurīṁ yonimāpannā mūḍhā janmani janmani /
māmaprāpyaiva kaunteya tato yāntyadhamāṁ gatim //20//

Tānahaṁ (those), *aham* (I); *dviṣata*, [those] who hate Me, *krūrān*, who are possessing that bad behavior, *narādhamān*, who are degraded beings, *kṣipāmi ajasram*, I at once *kṣipāmi*, kick them. *Āsurīṣveva yoniṣu*, [they get rebirth in] those *yonīs* (wombs) which [are of] *āsurīs* (demons); they become more

460 "*Yajante nāma yajñaiste,* and they perform *havan* also for the sake of fame. Not for the sake of gods." *Bhagavad Gītā* (1978).

rākṣasas, more *rākṣasas* . . . where other *rākṣasas* eat them and grab them. I have prepared hells for these people, [which are full] of *rākṣasas*, and those *rākṣasas* are more furious than him. Wherever . . . if they are thrown there, and they [scream] "*aaa-aaah* . . .", and they kill them at once!

Āsurīṁ yonimāpannā mūḍhā janmani janmani [verse 20]. And when they become *āsura* (demon), they become *āsura*, that person becomes *āsura* in that [hell where there are] great *āsuras* who grab them, who kill them, who . . .

DENISE: Torture them.

SWAMIJI: . . . torture them.

DVD 16 (39:34)

आसुरीं योनिमापन्ना मूढा जन्मनि जन्मनि ।
मामप्राप्यैव कौन्तेय ततो यान्त्यधमां गतिम् ॥२०॥

āsurīṁ yonimāpannā mūḍhā janmani janmani /
māmaprāpyaiva kaunteya tato yāntyadhamāṁ gatim //20//
[repeated]

O Arjuna, when they are kept away from My state of Bhairava, *tato yāntyadhamāṁ gatim*, they are tossed down [even further]. I have got more demons in My other . . . I have created other, [more furious] hells also than that. Because in those [more furious] hells, there are more demons, which . . . those demons, which eat that person, they eat those demons also there. What to speak of that poor fellow who is alone, caught in those [hells]? So there is no hope for his rise again in this world. He is gone.

But, actually, time will come he will become Bhairava, when he does this [Swamiji beats his head], always [asking himself], "what has happened to me"?

Trividhaṁ narakasyedaṁ . . . this is now the 21st *śloka*.

DVD 16 (41:06)

त्रिविधं नरकस्येदं द्वारं नाशनमात्मनः ।
कामः क्रोधस्तथा लोभस्तस्मादेतत्त्रयं त्यजेत् ॥२१॥

trividhaṁ narakasyedaṁ dvāraṁ nāśanamātmanaḥ /
kāmaḥ krodhastathā lobhas-tasmādetattrayaṁ tyajet //21//

Trividhaṁ narakasyedaṁ dvāraṁ. O Arjuna, there are three doors, three entries of hells. One entry is sex (*kāma*), one entry is *krodha* (anger) . . . undistinctive sex.

DENISE: Indiscriminate sex?

SWAMIJI: In . . . ?

DENISE: Indiscriminate, with anybody?

SWAMIJI: [With] anybody whom he grabs, *bas*, it is his choice. This is . . . there are three entries of *naraka* (hell): *kāma* (lust/desire), *krodha* (anger), and *lobha* (greed). *Tasmāt etat trayaṁ tyajet*, O Arjuna, you should discard these three, and you have to discard these three.

DENISE: *Kāma*, *krodha*, and what?

JONATHAN: What was the third one?

SWAMIJI: *Kāmaḥ krodhastathā lobha. Lobha* (*lobha* means greed). *Kāma*, *krodha*, and greed, greed of money.

What for do you collect money? You should not [do that].

Tasmādetattrayaṁ tyajet.

DVD 16 (42:44)

एतैर्वियुक्तः कौन्तेय तमोद्वारैस्त्रिभिर्नरः ।
आचरत्यात्मनः श्रेयस्ततो याति परां गतिम् ॥२२॥

etairviyuktaḥ kaunteya tamodvāraistribhirnaraḥ /
ācaratyātmanaḥ śreyastato yāti parāṁ gatim //22//

If you collect money for rising in God consciousness, that is not greed. That is not greed! I tell you again and again, that is not greed, sir. If you collect money for rising in God consciousness, i.e., to do things to throw light on society, in everybody, that is not greed. In this way, you can collect money. But not collecting money for [committing] bad behavior.

So this is the entry for going into hells. Three, there are three entries: *kāma*, *krodha*, and *lobha. Tasmād etat trayaṁ tyajet*, so you should keep away from these three things.

DVD 16 (43:58)

यः शास्त्रविधिमुत्सृज्य वर्तते कामकारतः ।
न स सिद्धिमवाप्नोति न सुखं न परां गतिम् ॥२३॥

yaḥ śāstravidhimutsṛjya vartate kāmakārataḥ /
na sa siddhimavāpnoti na sukhaṁ na parāṁ gatim //23//

The 23rd *śloka.*

Whoever . . . *śāstras vidhimutsṛjya*. The *vidhi* (this is the 23rd *ślokai*), *śāstra vidhim*, the *vidhi* means the behavior which has been thrown [i.e., decreed] by *śāstras* (*śāstras* means those *śāstras* (scriptures) which are Shaivite *śāstras*, Advaita *śāstras*, i.e., monistic *śāstras*), and [the person] who does not behave like that,[461] *na sa siddhim avāpnoti*, neither he achieves any *siddhi*, any power, *na sukhaṁ*, he does not achieve any peace, *na parāṁ gatim*, and he does not achieve any *mokṣa* (liberation).

So you should tread according to the teachings of *śāstras*, the highest *śāstras*.[462]

DVD 16 (45:12)

तस्माच्छास्त्रं प्रमाणं ते कार्याकार्यव्यवस्थितौ ।
ज्ञात्वा शास्त्रविधानोक्तं कर्म कर्तुमिहार्हसि ॥२४॥

tasmācchāstraṁ pramāṇaṁ te kāryākāryavyavasthitau /
jñātvā śāstravidhānoktaṁ karma kartumihārhasi //24//

So, the conclusion of this, My saying is, *śāstraṁ pramāṇaṁ te*, those Shaivite *śāstras* are *pramāṇaṁ*, the torch for you, [which prescribe] what to do and what not to do.

Jñātvā śāstra vidhānoktaṁ, when you know that, i.e., what is told [to] you in *śāstras*, *karma kartumihārhasi*, go on indulging in activities of the world in your own way and find out the reality of Parabhairava in the end.

Finished. 16th chapter is finished.

Now conclusion of this:

461 In accordance with these *śāstras*. [*Editor's note*]
462 That is, monistic *śāstras*. [*Editor's note*]

DVD 16 (46:22)

अबोधे स्वात्मबुद्ध्यैव कार्यं नैव विचारयेत् ।
किन्तु शास्त्रोक्तविधिना शास्त्रं बोधविवर्धनम् ॥१६॥

abodhe svātmabuddhyaiva kāryaṁ naiva vicārayet /
kintu śāstroktavidhinā śāstraṁ bodhavivardhanam //16//

॥ Concluding *śloka* of 16th chapter ॥

In ignorant people also, in ignorant people, you should not insert this kind of knowledge into them that, "[you should act in accordance with] whatever you feel [is] good and whatever you feel [is] bad." You should not do that. You should not say that [to them] just like . . . who was that? Jai Kṛṣṇamurti told everybody, "whatever comes in your mind that [feels] good, [you should act upon that]; whatever comes into your mind [that feels] bad, don't act [upon] that." But [this understanding] is not fact. You should depend upon the sayings of *śāstras* (*śāstras* means Shaivite *śāstras*). *Karma kartumihārhasi,* then you should act accordingly.

Śāstraṁ bodha vivardhanam. Śāstras will illuminate you in the end. Because your power of intellect is very undeveloped, it is undeveloped for the time being. As long as it is not developed totally, you should not use your own way of thinking. You should depend upon the sayings of *śāstras.*

Bas. This is the end of this chapter.

Now there is the 17th and 18th chapter.

Chapter 17

DVD 17 (00:01)

अर्जुन उवाच
arjuna uvāca

ये शास्त्रविधिमुत्सृज्य वर्तन्ते श्रद्धयान्विताः ।
तेषां निष्ठा तु का कृष्ण सत्त्वमाहो रजस्तमः ॥ १ ॥

ye śāstravidhimutsṛjya vartante śraddhayānvitāḥ /
teṣāṁ niṣṭhā tu kā kṛṣṇa sattvamāho rajastamaḥ //1//
[not recited]

[Arjuna]: I have got one doubt in me. You have already explained in the previous discourse, previous chapter, that whatever the Shaivite *śāstras* will tell you, that you should behave according to the sayings of that. You should not behave in your own way.

But [Arjuna] puts this kind of question:

If, suppose there are some people who have got *śraddha*, they have got faith, by *śraddha*, they act with good faith, they act. In their own way, they [have] some viewpoint, they understand some viewpoint of behavior themselves with faith. As far as I know, there are some people who have got only faith, who have not indulged in [reading] the Shaivite *śāstras* because they have not that kind of extreme knowledge to understand the Shaivite *śāstras*. They behave according to their *śraddha* (faith). Are they situated in *sattvaguṇa*, or are they situated in *rajaguṇa*, or are they situated in *tamaguṇa*? This is my question.

If they do [actions] with faith, commit their behavior, tread on the path of behavior according to their faith (not *śāstras* because *śāstras* they don't understand properly), are they doing [actions] according to *sattvaguṇa*, are they doing according to *rajaguṇa*, or are they doing that according to *tamaguṇa*?

Now, in [response to] that, Śrī Bhagavān explains to Arjuna:

DVD 17 (02:50)

श्रीभगवानुवाच

śrī bhagavān uvāca

त्रिविधा भवति श्रद्धा देहिनां सा स्वभावजा ।
सात्त्विकी राजसी चैव तामसी चेति ताः श्रृणु ॥२॥

trividhābhavati śraddhā dehināṁ sā svabhāvajā /
sāttvikī rājasī caiva tāmasī ceti tāḥ śṛṇu //2//
[not recited]

Śraddha is . . . this faith, faith grows in people in three varieties. Some people are those who have got faith in *sattva-guṇa*, some people are those who have got faith in *rajaguṇa*, and some people have got faith in *tamaguṇa*. How do they behave in this world?

Now Lord Kṛṣṇa explains to him, you should know that faith also is automatic . . . if one has [*sāttvic*] faith, with good faith he indulges in behavior, his behavior is always *sāttvic*, automatically.[463] [If a person has faith in *sattvaguṇa*], his behavior will never remain in the field of *rājas* or in the field of *tāmas*. His behavior will be always existing in *sāttvic* state, because whatever he does, he does according to *śāstras*, automatically. Automatically he does according to *śāstras*, which are taught in Shaivism.[464] That is what He says.

---

463 "Faith means trust. [*Rājasic* faith means], 'I believe in amusement. If you ask me, I believe in amusement.' [*Sāttvic* faith means], 'if you ask me, I believe in meditation, doing prayers always.' [*Tāmasic* faith means], 'if you ask me, I want to lie down.' This is *śraddha*, this is attachment, a kind of attachment. *Śraddha* means not faith, it is just attachment." *Bhagavad Gītā* (1978).

464 "The first thing you must understand, without *śāstra* nothing can happen. *Śāstra* is the only way, and only torch to get you, to put you on the straight path of life. *Śāstra* will get you adjusted. If you are living in

DVD 17 (04:42)

श्रीभगवानुवाच
śrī bhagavān uvāca

त्रिविधा भवति श्रद्धा देहिनां सा स्वभावजा ।
सात्त्विकी राजसी चैव तामसी चेति ताः शृणु ॥२॥

trividhābhavati śraddhā dehināṁ sā svabhāvajā /
sāttvikī rājasī caiva tāmasī ceti tāḥ śṛṇu //2//

This is the *svabhāva*, *svabhāvajā śraddhā*, this faith is according to the nature of your own *prakṛti*, and this is three-fold [faith, which] rises in human beings. There is *sāttvikī śraddhā*, there is *rājasī śraddhā*, and there is *tāmasī śraddhā*. *Tāḥ śṛṇu*, I will explain it to you in detail.

---

your own way of *tāmasic* way, *śāstra* will adjust you to the right way. *Śāstra* is very important in these matters. This is Abhinavagupta's commentary. What *śāstra* does? First thing you should know that the greatness of *sāśtra* is, it has no *pakṣapāt* (no partiality). . . . *Śāstra* will rule out the ways and regulations of human life in sameness [for] poor and rich. . . . then, if you accept those rules and regulations of *śāstras*, then it will become fruitful to you. Otherwise, if you don't accept, if you accept only because of curiosity, then it is useless. Don't read *śāstras* with curiosity! Read *śāstras* for understanding, for some guidance, getting some information. Not for curiosity sake. Then it becomes fruitful. . . . And at the same time, the greatness of *śāstra* is that, whenever it is accepted, whenever it is conducted by the person who hears that *śāstra*, it will direct him to the ultimate state of God consciousness. . . . When, [by the instructions of *śāśtras*], you withdraw all your activities, you are centralized in God consciousness, and the greatness of that God consciousness is that it will give you again push into universal manifestation. And when it gives push again in universal manifestation, it is just for that purpose that you should see the shining of God consciousness everywhere, in each and every action of the world. This is done by *śāstras*. . . . When once *śāstra* is infused in a person, then there is no need to guide him. When once *śāstra* is [infused] in your thought, then okay, then master [doesn't need to] guide you. It is you who will guide yourself. You have to adjust your guidance yourself." Ibid.

DVD 17 (05:27)

सत्त्वानुरूपा सर्वस्य श्रद्धा भवति भारत ।
श्रद्धामयोऽयं पुरुषो यो यच्छ्रद्धः स एव सः ॥३॥

sattvānurūpā sarvasya śraddhā bhavati bhārata /
śraddhāmayo'yaṁ puruṣo yo yacchraddhaḥ sa eva saḥ //3//

Sattvānurūpā, according to their capacity of behavior and understanding of those three classes: those who are residing in the environment of *sāttvic*, those who are residing in the environment of *rājas,* and those who are residing in the environment of *tāmas*. With the exception of *rājas* and *tāmas*, those who are residing in the environment of *sāttvic,* their behavior is automatically according to the *śāstras*. They do, whatever they do, they act according to the Shaivite *śāstras* by nature, it is their nature. Their *ācāran* (conduct) is just like *śāstras*. And the *ācāran* of the other two is not according to the *śāstras*. That behavior is *rājas* and [the other] behavior is *tāmas*; [for them, *śāśtras*] have no fruit, it does not bear fruit.[465]

So, it [happens] automatically when you have [*sāttvic*] faith and you have got full faith and your behavior . . . if you are residing in the *sāttvic* field, you behave according to the *śāstras* automatically, without knowing [or hearing *śāstras*] from the lips of your master. Your nature becomes like that.

Because He says, *yajante sāttvikā devān* . . . this is the 4th *śloka*.

DVD 17 (07:37)

यजन्ते सात्त्विका देवान्यक्षरक्षांसि राजसाः ।
भूतप्रेतपिशाचांश्च यजन्ते तामसा जनाः ॥४॥

465 "*Sastraṁ hi sattvavatāmeva phalavad iti śāstramevāha* [comm. verse 2]. *Śāstras* will give, bear fruit only to *sāttvic* people, not *rājasic* and not *tāmasic*. Because if you are *rājasic*, if [your] life is staying in the *rājasic* way, if I teach you *śāstras*, you won't understand it properly, you will just while away the period." Ibid.

yajante sāttvikā devānyakṣarakṣāṁsi rājasāḥ /
bhūtapretapiśācāṁśca yajante tāmasā janāḥ //4//

Sāttvikā, those who have got *sāttvic* wave in, residing, i.e., those who are living in the *sāttvic* tide, they automatically worship the *devas* (gods).

Rājasā, those who have got *rājas* wave, *rājas* tide, those who are living in the *rājas* tide, they automatically worship *yakṣas* (ghosts) and *rākṣasas* (demons).

And those who are residing in *tāmas* tide, they automatically worship *bhūta* (ghosts), *preta* (spirits), and *piśācā* (devils), and *rākṣasas* (demons).[466] They automatically run that way [i.e., follow that path].

And those who are *rājas*, they are also no good. *Sāttvic* wave is . . . *sāttvikās* are truly acting like the behavior which is explained in the *śāstras*. *Tena ācharitaṁ śāstritam eva* [comm.], whatever is explained in the *śāstras*, they do that automatically. So their behavior stands good.

DVD 17 (09:27)

अशास्त्रविहितं घोरं तपस्तप्यन्ति ये जनाः ।
दम्भाहंकारसंयुक्ताः कामरागबलान्विताः ॥५॥
कर्षयन्तः शरीरस्थं भूतग्राममचेतनम् ।
मां चैवान्तःशरीरस्थं तान्विद्ध्यासुरनिश्चयान् ॥६॥

aśāstravihitaṁ ghoraṁ tapastapyanti ye janāḥ /
dambhāhaṁkārasaṁyuktāḥ kāmarāgabalānvitāḥ //5//
karṣayantaḥ śarīrasthaṁ bhūtagrāmamacetanam /
māṁ caivāntaḥśarīrasthaṁ tānviddhyāsuraniścayān //6//

The 5th *śloka* and 6th *śloka*.

Aśāstravihitaṁ, that [penitential] action, which is not explained in the *śāstras*, in Shaivite *śāstras* (i.e., that kind of *tapasya*, that kind of penance, [which is] *ghoraṁ*, fearful *tapas-*

466 ". . . who govern sluggishness, who govern sleep, who govern forgetfulness, all these things." Ibid.

ya[467]), [they] who work out [their penance] with *dambha*, *āhaṁkāra* (*dambha ahaṁkāra saṁyuktāḥ*, with *dumbha* and *āhaṁkāra*, i.e., ego and fraud-mindedness), *kāma rāga balāni-vitāḥ*, they have got *kāma* (lust), and *rāga* (attachment), and greed for enjoyments.

And the fruit of their penance is:

DVD 17 (10:50)

कर्षयन्तः शरीरस्थं भूतग्राममचेतनम् ।
मां चैवान्तःशरीरस्थं तान्विद्ध्यासुरनिश्चयान् ॥ ६ ॥

karṣayantaḥ śarīrasthaṁ bhūtagrāmamacetanam /
māṁ caivāntaḥśarīrasthaṁ tānviddhyāsuraniścayān //6//
[repeated]

They *karṣayantaḥ*, they are troublesome, they are understood as troublesome people for . . . [their] *bhūtagrāma* (*bhūtagrāma* are organs, activities of organs, activities of touch, sound (*śabda*), *sparśa* (touch), *rūpa* (form), *rasa* (taste), and *gandha* (smell), whatever exists in the body), that behaves in that body in an absolutely wrong way. They behave [i.e., use] their organs and [conduct] all activities in the wrong way.

And *māṁ caivāntaḥ śarīrasthaṁ*, and I am Parabhairava who is residing in their body also; they misbehave with Me also in that *śarīrastham* (body). *Tāt viddhi āsura niścayān*, those [people] you should consider to be *rākṣasas* (demons). They are no good at all.

Now I will tell you [about] *āhāra* also. *Āhāra* means those [particular] likings of taking food. That also is automatic according to the three tides, three *guṇas*. It is also according to *śraddhā* (faith).

467 "Terrible penance as Rāvana did, as Kumbhakarṇa did. Not as Viveśana did [these are characters from Valmiki's epic, *Rāmāyana*]. Viveśana performed *sāttvic tapasya*. Rāvana performed *tapasya* of *rajaguṇa*, and Kumbhakarṇa performed *tapasya* of *tamaguṇa* . . . and there are some people who want to destroy other people, enemies, and they have got *dambha ahaṁkāra*. And *kāma rāga balānivitāḥ*, they want to take, snatch [other people's] wives, beautiful wives, and possess them and destroy them. For that reason they perform penance." Ibid.

If there is . . . with good faith, some person residing in *sāttvic* wave, he does, he eats food according to the statements, according to the directions of the *śāstras*. Whatever Shaivite *śāstras* have ordered that you should take this [particular] kind of food, they eat this kind of food automatically by faith, i.e., those who are residing in the *sāttvic* mood.

DVD 17 (13:22)

आहारस्त्वपि सर्वस्य त्रिविधो भवति प्रियः ।
यज्ञस्तपस्तथा दानं तेषां भेदमिमं शृणु ॥७॥

āhārastvapi sarvasya trividho bhavati priyaḥ /
yajñastapastathā dānaṁ teṣāṁ bhedamimaṁ śṛṇu //7//

Āhārastvapu sarvasya trividho bhavati priyaḥ. So *āhara* (food preference) is also threefold for everybody. [People] like [food in] threefold [ways]; this [is] *trividho*, it is threefold (you should put the number three, *trividha*, on the top of [the word] *trividha*).

Yajñastapastathā dānaṁ. *Yajña* (worship) is threefold; *tapaḥ* (penance) is threefold; *dānaṁ* (alms giving) is threefold; *teṣāṁ bhedamimaṁ śṛṇu*, that I will explain to you one by one.

First *āhāra* (food preference). *Āhāra* is automatically threefold: *sāttvic āhāra*, *rājas āhāra*, and *tāmas āhāra*.[468] And that comes according to the *śāstras* and according to no *śāstras*. [For example], that [person] who is residing in the *sāttvic* wave, he does eat according to the directions of the *śāstras*.

DVD 17 (14:54)

आयुःसत्त्वबलारोग्यसुखप्रीतिविवर्धनाः ।
रस्याः स्निग्धाः स्थिरा हृद्या आहाराः सत्त्विकप्रियाः ॥८

āyuḥsattvabalārogyasukhaprītivivardhanāḥ /
rasyāḥ snigdhāḥ sthirā hṛdyā āhārāḥ sattvikapriyāḥ //8//

468 "According to your own nature you act like this. If your nature is *sāttvic*, you will act like that. If your nature is *rājasic*, you will act like that, and if your nature is *tāmasic*, you will act like that." Ibid.

These kinds of *āhāra* [are *sāttvic*], these kinds of taking food: those foods which [are] *āyu*, which increase one's span of life, *sattva*, increases a good mood (*sāttvic* mood), *balā*, increases strength for doing *ābhyāsa* (*yoga* practice), *ārogya*, and it keeps you healthy always, *sukha*, and keeps you peaceful always, and *prīti*, bestows you [with a] good mood for [maintaining] good behavior with others also (he does not lose his temper by [eating] that *āhāra*), *rasyāḥ*, and you [eat] that which has got a good taste, *snigdhāḥ*, and which has got, which is good, not in quantity, but in quality. For instance, there is ghee, there is butter, there is all good things are in that [food]. You automatically like that kind of *āhāra*.

Who?

One who resides in the *sāttvika* state.

Sthirā, and that [food], which is digested slowly, slowly; it gives you strength for the day, the full day. You don't need any other varieties of intaking [food].

Āhārāḥ sattvikapriyāḥ, these kinds of *āhāra* is automatically [desired] by those *sāttvikas* according to the statements of the *śāstras*. They behave with [i.e., eat] that *āhāra*.

And there is *rājas āhāra*, and there is another one [called] *tāmas āhāra*.

DVD 17 (17:31)

कट्वम्ललवणात्युष्णतीक्ष्णरूक्षविदाहिनः ।
आहारा राजसस्येष्टा दुःखशोकामयप्रदाः ॥९॥

kaṭvamlalavaṇātyuṣṇatīkṣṇarūkṣavidāhinaḥ /
āhārā rājasasyeṣṭā duḥkhaśokāmayapradāḥ //9//

Another thing, this 9th *śloka* [explains] *āhāra*, which is automatically liked by those who are existing in *rājas* wave. *Kaṭu. Kaṭu* means . . .

What is *kaṭu*?

Kaṭu means . . .

DENISE: Spicy.

SWAMIJI: No, *kaṭu* means not with chilis, not hot, not hot actually, *kaṭu*.[469]

469 *Kaṭu* means pungent-sharp taste like *amla*. [*Editor's note*]

Amla means . . .

DENISE: Sour.

SWAMIJI: . . . *amla* means sour; *lavaṇa* means with too much of salt (*lavaṇa*); *atyuṣna*, very hot; *tīkṣṇa*, and with chilies; *rūkṣa*, [dry] and with no substance in it, i.e., not ghee, not butter, just *rasa* (juice) and *matsa vanghan* (chili powder) dust.

And you take [this hot food and] afterwards you go on putting that [handkerchief on your nose] to [catch the] drips afterwards.

JONATHAN: When your nose is running because it's so hot.

SWAMIJI: Yes.

Rūkṣa . . . vidāhinaḥ, and [food that] burns your heart; your heart is just palpitating with a burning sensation. This kind of *āhāra* is liked by those who are established in *rājas* wave.

Now *āhāra* for those which is liked [by people] who are residing in the *tāmas* wave.

DVD 17 (19:48)

यातयामं गतरसं पूति पर्युषितं च यत् ।
उच्छिष्टमपि चामेध्यं भोजनं तामसप्रियम् ॥१०॥

yātayāmaṁ gatarasaṁ pūti paryuṣitaṁ ca yat /
ucchiṣṭamapi cāmedhyaṁ bhojanaṁ tāmasapriyam //10//

Yātayāmaṁ, [that food] which has passed overnight; that food which has been cooked and it has remained overnight and then you warm it up again and eat it. That kind of *āhāra* is eaten by those who are residing in the *tāmas* wave. It is *tāmas* liking (i.e., *yātayāmaṁ*).

Gatarasaṁ, without any taste, *pūti*, and it gives the smell of being rotten (*pūti*), *paryuṣitaṁ*, and it is just gone, i.e., without any substance in it, *ucchiṣṭam*, and it is very impurely handled, *āmedhyaṁ*, and *āmedhyaṁ*, not pure. This kind of *bhojan* (food) is automatically liked by those who are residing in the *tāmas* wave.[470]

470 "*Pūti* (impure), *paryuṣitaṁ*, they take from ground also, dirty things, *ucchiṣṭam*, and they take from other mouths, e.g., you put something in your mouth [and then] you throw it away, and he will take that; he won't mind that it is impure." *Bhagavad Gītā* (1978).

Now, *havan* (*yajña*). *Havan* is threefold. *Havan* conducted by *sāttvikas*, *havan* conducted by *rājasas*, and *havan* conducted by *tāmasas* is different, He says.

DVD 17 (21:36)

अफलाकाङ्क्षिभिर्यज्ञो विधिदृष्टो य इज्यते ।
यष्टव्यमित्येव मनः समाधाय स सात्त्विकः ॥११॥

aphalākāṅkṣibhiryajño vidhidṛṣṭo ya ijyate /
yaṣṭavyamityeva manaḥ samādhāya sa sāttvikaḥ //11//

Sāttvika havan is that, which, when adopted by a person with faith, he does not keep in mind its reward from gods; *aphalākāṅkṣibhir*, without asking for its fruit from the gods of whom he is worshipping and conducting this *havan*. And *vidhidṛṣta*, according to the *śāstras*; automatically he does [*havan*] according to the *śāstras*. Whatever the *śāstras* have directed [for performing a] *havan* [in a certain] way, he [automatically] does [it that] way, but he does not ask for any fruit out of its [performance].

Vidhidṛṣṭa ya ijyate, yaṣtavyam ityeva manaḥ. [He thinks], "it is my duty to do it. It is not for satisfying my gods. No, I am not pleasing my gods by conducting this *havan*. It is my duty to do it. Gods may be pleased or gods may not be pleased, I don't care about that. I care that it is my duty and I must do it."

And I have forgotten to give you this [information] to you that at the time of *sāttvic havan*, when the *sāttvic havan* is being conducted, he does the *havan* one-pointedly. He does not do *havan* where he offers that *sāmagrī* into [the fire] and [at the same time he] asks his devotees to get tea for such and such people: "give him tea, get potatoes [for him/her]."

No, on the [contrary], he is just focused in doing this *havan*. He does not care for who has come and who is to be honored.

Because, [contrarily, the one who performs a *rājas havan*] keeps an eye [out for] who has given me one hundred rupees and who has given me ten rupees only.[471] For ten rupees worth

471 In terms of donations for the performance of the *havan*. [*Editor's note*]

devotee, he does not care to ask [his devotees] to give tea to him, [and] for him [who gave one hundred rupees], he asks his devotees to give him two *parāthas*, two *puris*, and [laughs], and like that. This should not [happen].

DENISE: He's absorbed in his devotion.

SWAMIJI: Yes. So he is not doing, he is not [performing the *havan* for the sake of] satisfying *devas*.[472] He is with his own [i.e., introverted] environment. This is *sāttvika havan*; this is done automatically by those who are residing in the *sāttvic* wave.

Now those who are residing in the *rājas* wave, they also do *havan*, they also conduct *havan* [in a particular way].

DVD 17 (24:59)

अभिसन्धाय तु फलं दम्भार्थमपि चैव यः ।
इज्यते विद्धि तं यज्ञं राजसं चलमध्रुवम् ॥१२॥

abhisandhāya tu phalaṁ dambhārthamapi caiva yaḥ /
ijyate viddhi taṁ yajñaṁ rājasaṁ calamadhruvam //12//

[The one] who thinks that, "some fruit will come by conducting this kind of *havan*. I am conducting this *havan* [so that] people will come and offer money, contribute some money, I will have some money, and I will be respected by people [who will say], 'he is doing such and such action.'" *Dambhārtham*, it is a kind of . . . just a show; with show he conducts this *havan*. And [one who] does this [kind of] *havan*, that *havan* you should understand [that] it is done by those who have got faith in *rājas* tide. And it is *calam*, it is not established and *adhruvam*, it is not permanent. It does not remain for always because some leakage comes out in the public and they say, "it was all fraud, he was collecting his money and saving some money, and putting that in the bank."

Do you understand?

This is *rājas* havan.

472 Here, Swamiji is using the term "*devas*" in terms of external entities to whom one prays to gain favor. See *Bhagavad Gītā,* 3.11 for a discussion on the actual meaning of *devas* and what it means to satisfy them. [*Editor's note*]

And now that [*havan* performed by one] who is residing in *tāmas* wave. It is the 13th *śloka*.

DVD 17 (26:51)

विधिहीनमसृष्टान्नं मन्त्रहीनमदक्षिणम् ।
श्रद्धाविरहितं यज्ञं तामसं परिचक्षते ॥ १३ ॥

vidhihīnamasṛṣṭānnaṁ mantrahīnamadakṣiṇam /
śraddhāvirahitaṁ yajñam tāmasaṁ paricakṣate //13//

He does not . . . [for instance], if Shamlal[473] tells him that you should get *sāmagrī* for one hundred rupees, he says, "Shamlal does not know, Shamlal, they are priests, they are all rogues. It is not worthwhile to purchase *sāmagrī* for one hundred rupees. We can purchase it for ten rupees; ten rupees is enough. We'll offer a little bit, little bit [at a time]. And [the purpose] will be served." That is *tāmas*; that is doing *tāmas havan*.

Vidhi hīnam asṛṣṭānnaṁ mantrahīnam. And *mantras* also, when [the priests] try to [recite] in long verses, at ease they recite *ślokas* with prayer, with love, with devotion, he [tells] them, "no, no, no, it is too late, we have to finish soon. Go hurriedly! Don't keep wasting my time because I have so much engagement afterwards." He stops that [devotional recitation of *mantras*]. So he has no faith in that. Whatever he is doing, he does it faithlessly.

Āhāras . . . this is *yajña*, this is *havan* threefold.

Now there is *tapa* (penance).

Tapasya, He will explain threefold *tapasya*: *sāttvic tapasya*, *rājas tapasya*, and *tāmas tapasya*.

Now *sāttvic tapasya*. *Sāttvic tapasya* is conducted in the 14th *śloka*.

DVD 17 (29:22)

देवद्विजगुरुप्राज्ञपूजनं शौचमार्जवम् ।
ब्रह्मचर्यमहिंसा च शारीरं तप उच्यते ॥ १४ ॥

473 Swamiji's priest.

devadvijaguruprājñapūjanaṁ śaucamārjavam /
brahmacaryamahiṁsā ca śārīraṁ tapa ucyate //14//

This is *tapasya* conducted with your body; the penance conducted with your body. [If it] is *sāttvic* penance, [it will be] according to, it is according to the *śāstras*. He does it . . . the penance of body, he does it according to the *śāstras* because he is residing in the *sāttvic* tide.

What he does?

Devadvijaguruprājña. Deva (gods), *dvija* (priests), *guru* (masters), *prājña–prājña* means those who are . . . *prājña* means those who are intelligent in the *śāstras*, who are extremely *prājña. Prājña* means . . .

DENISE: Learned.

SWAMIJI: Huh?

DENISE: Learned in *śāstras*.

SWAMIJI: . . . learned in *śāstras*–these people, *devadvijaguru-prājñapūjanaṁ*, he adores them. He adores them, it is his nature to adore them with his body; this is *tapasya* with body. He adores them. He does not care if his body is shattered [by] doing their service.

Who?

Gods, *dvija* (priests), *guru* (masters), *prājña* means scholars. He worships them with his body, with all of his might.

And he has got *ārjavam* (*ārjavam* means *rijutā*, straight-forwardness). He is not . . . his manners are not worshipping these elders with hypocrisy, [for] show; it is his nature, not with show. He does not worship them [for] show.

Brahmacaryam, and he conducts *brahmacarya vrata*.[474] *Ahiṁsā ca*, and he does not put anybody in trouble with his body. *Śārīraṁ tapa ucyate*, this is the penance derived from the body of that person who has got *sāttvic* wave, who is residing in *sāttvic*

474 "You must think of all other girls as your sisters and mothers; not have sexual desires for other girls than your own [wife], not have sexual desire for other men than your own [husband]. That is *brahmacarya.* There are two kinds of *brahmacarya vrata*. One is sexual desire for only your wife, only your husband, [and] *naiṣṭika brahmacarya* is no sexual desire. Lord Kṛṣṇa was a *naiṣṭika brahmacarya*, he had no sexual desires." *Bhagavad Gītā* (1978).

wave. His bodily penance is like that. This is *śārīraṁ tapaḥ*. This is *tapasya* of the body. Now *tapasya* of word, behavior, body.

JOHN: For *sāttvic* person?

SWAMIJI: *Sāttvic*, yes.

DVD 17 (33:04)

अनुद्वेगकरं वाक्यं सत्यं प्रियहितं च यत् ।
स्वाध्यायाभ्यसनं चैव वाङ्मयं तप उच्यते ॥१५॥

anudvegakaraṁ vākyaṁ satyaṁ priyahitaṁ ca yat /
svādhyāyābhyasanaṁ caiva vāṅmayaṁ tapa ucyate //15//
[not recited]

Anudvegakaraṁ vākyaṁ, He behaves, he conducts [his speech] with that sentence, which is *anudvegakaraṁ*, by which you won't get disturbed, i.e., another person does not get disturbed by that behavior of his talk. His talk is so mild, so soft (*anudvegakaraṁ vākyaṁ*). *Satyaṁ*, and his words are *satyaṁ*, just truthful. *Priya,* and [his words are] just liked [by those to] whom he talks; there is liking [of his words]. [The person to whom he speaks] does not get worried [by his words]. *Hitaṁ ca*, and his words are *hitaṁ*, ultimately good for his future, i.e., [for the person] with whom he [talks].

Svādhyāyābhyasanaṁ, and his behavior of speech in seclusion is that of *svādhyāya abhyasanaṁ*: either he goes on understanding his books of *śāstras* or he does the practice of *yoga*. *Vāṅmayaṁ tapa ucyate*, this is *tapasya* of his sound. His sound is like that *tapasya*, *sāttvic*.

Then there is *tapasya* of mind also, *sāttvic*.

Manaḥprasādaḥ . . . this is another one, 16th *śloka*.

DVD 17 (35:02)

मनःप्रसादः सौम्यत्वं मौनमात्मविनिग्रहः ।
भावसंशुद्धिरित्येतत्तपो मानसमुच्यते ॥१६॥

manaḥprasādaḥ saumyatvaṁ maunamātmavinigrahaḥ /
bhāvasaṁśuddhirityetattapo mānasamucyate //16//

Manaḥ prasādaḥ, his *manaḥ* (his mind) is *prasāda*; his *manaḥ* . . . [he] removes all hypocrisy in his mind, from his mind. *Saumyatvaṁ*, he keeps in his mind just straightforwardness. And he has got in his mind *ātma vinigrahaḥ*, to conduct [all his dealings] with one-pointedness. *Maunam ātma vinigrahaḥ*, and he does not talk too much. His mind . . . he does not talk useless talks; he does not indulge in useless talks, i.e., *gupshup* (gossip) and all of that.

Bhāva saṁśuddhir, and he has got, internally he remains good-hearted in his mind for everybody. *Tapo mānasamucyate*, this is the penance of mind for that person who is residing in the *sāttvic* wave.

DVD 17 (36:45)

श्रद्धया परयोपेतं तपस्तत्त्रिविधं नरैः ।
अफलाकङ्क्षिभिर्युक्तैः सात्त्विकं परिचक्षते ॥१७॥
सत्कारमानपूजार्थं तपो दम्भेन चैव यत् ।
क्रियते तदिह प्रोक्तं राजसं चलमध्रुवम् ॥१८॥
मूढग्रहेणात्मनो यत्पीडया क्रियते तपः ।
परस्योत्सादनार्थं वा तत्तामसमुदाहृतम् ॥१९॥

śraddhayā parayopetaṁ tapastattrividhaṁ naraiḥ /
aphalākaṅkṣibhiryuktaiḥ sāttvikaṁ paricakṣate //17//
satkāramānapūjārthaṁ tapo dambhena caiva yat /
kriyate tadiha proktaṁ rājasaṁ calamadhruvam //18//
mūḍhagraheṇātmano yatpīḍayā kriyate tapaḥ /
parasyotsādanārthaṁ vā tattāmasmudāhṛtam //19//

Now 17th, 18th, and 19th [*ślokas*].

DVD 17 (36:46)

श्रद्धया परयोपेतं तपस्तत्त्रिविधं नरैः ।
अफलाकङ्क्षिभिर्युक्तैः सात्त्विकं परिचक्षते ॥१७॥

śraddhayā parayopetaṁ tapastattrividhaṁ naraiḥ /
aphalākaṅkṣibhiryuktaiḥ sāttvikaṁ paricakṣate //17//

Tapasya also I will explain to you threefold. When you do *tapasya*, when you undergo in penance without asking any fruit out of it and you are always concentrating your mind one-pointedly in your behavior of *ābhyāsa* (practice), that is *sāttvic tapasya* (*sāttvic* penance).

DVD 17 (38:12)

सत्कारमानपूजार्थं तपो दम्भेन चैव यत् ।
क्रियते तदिह प्रोक्तं राजसं चलमध्रुवम् ॥ १८ ॥

satkāramānapūjārthaṁ tapo dambhena caiva yat /
kriyate tadiha proktaṁ rājasaṁ calamadhruvam //18//

[*Rājas tapasya* is done] for getting honor from people (*satkāra*). And *māna* (*māna* means good humor [i.e., respect]). People will . . . he [tells] people, "I am doing this, I am undergoing this *tapasya*." He asks his disciples to publish this that, "Swami Lakṣmanānanda Sarasvatī is undergoing *tapasya* from this date to this date." So, afterwards, when he comes out from this *tapasya*, everybody is requested to take the privilege of [his] *darśana* when he comes out from this *tapasya*. He [announces] it in advance.

JONATHAN: To glorify himself.

SWAMIJI: Yes.

Satkāra māna, for honor. *Pūjārthaṁ*, and they come with flower bunches and keep them at his feet when he comes out from *tapasya*.

I was doing *mauna vrat* for fifteen days.

DENISE: You were doing what?

SWAMIJI: I was observing silence for fifteen days.

DENISE: When was this?

SWAMIJI: In my old ashram. You had not come yet. After every fifteen days I would see people. And at that time, people would come in a rush, but it kept me [at a] loss, losing some of the vigor of *ābhyās* (practice). So, I stopped that. I said, "no, this *tamasha* (commotion) is not good." There was a huge crowd that would gather on every fortnight to have my *darśan*. I was young and I was . . . I kept increasing . . . it gave me some excitement [thinking] that, "I am so great that people respect me." Then I shunned that. I said, "no, I will undergo my silence [without people] knowing when I will come out. I will come out just by my own will and don't . . . I will not . . . nobody will know when I have come out. After I have come out, after eight days, fifteen days, then you will know afterwards."[475] That was a good procedure. I didn't get that [inflated] ego. That is what I told you.

DENISE: But it was your *sāttvic* nature that made you do that, made you make that change.

SWAMIJI: Yes, it was *sāttvic* nature.

That is *tapasya* done in *rājas* wave.

And *tapasya* done in *tāmas* wave, what is that?

DVD 17 (42:14)

मूढग्रहेणात्मनो यत्पीडया क्रियते तपः ।
परस्योतसादनार्थं वा तत्तामसमुदाहृतम् ॥१९॥

mūḍhagraheṇātmano yatpīḍayā kriyate tapaḥ /
parasyotasādanārthaṁ vā tattāmasamudāhṛtam //19//

Mūḍhagraheṇa, without undergoing *tapasya* . . . *mūḍha graha*, *mūḍha graha* means doing *tapasya* on one leg, *bas* [Swamiji stands on one leg]. Like that. *Mūḍhagraheṇa ātmano yatpīḍayā*, to give one's own body trouble and then when the body, after undergoing that *tapasya* is over, his leg becomes . . .

JONATHAN: Withered and thin.

SWAMIJI: Yes, very thin. Like this he does *tapasya*. He gives trouble to his body in which I am existing, O Arjuna! Parabhairava is [inside his body] and he gives trouble to that body.

---

475 During that time, Swamiji would spend two to three months in seclusion. [*Editor's note*]

Parasya utasādanārthaṁ, and the ambition [i.e., purpose] of that *tapasya* is just to destroy his enemies.

DENISE: What's the purpose of it?

SWAMIJI: Purpose.

JOHN: To get power.

DENISE: Oh, power.

SWAMIJI: Power, to get power and to destroy his enemies. *Tat tāmasam*, this is *tapasya* [conducted] in *tāmas* wave, *tāmas* tide. It has no success.

DENISE: It doesn't work?

SWAMIJI: It doesn't work.

DENISE: It doesn't work to destroy ones enemies?

SWAMIJI: Yes.

DENISE: It does?

SWAMIJI: It does not destroy. How can it destroy?

JOHN: Why do they say in these *śāstras* so many times that, if somebody did some *tapasya* and stood on his [one] leg for so many years, and then by that he could destroy this kingdom and so forth . . . he did something, he didn't eat anything, or starved himself.

SWAMIJI: No, if it is with good conduct, e.g., to give trouble to body for the sake of [gaining] a good result from Lord, that is good. That has got good effect. But not for . . .

JOHN: Harming others.

SWAMIJI: . . . harming others.

Now there is *dāna*, bestowing alms to people. And bestowing alms to people is threefold: *rājas* way . . . *sāttvic* way, *rājas* way, and *tāmas* way.

DVD 17 (45:06)

दातव्यमिति यद्दानं दीयतेऽनुपकारिणे ।
देशे कले च पात्रे च तद्दानं सात्त्विकं स्मृतम् ॥२०॥

dātavyamiti yaddānaṁ dīyate'nupakāriṇe /
deśe kale ca pātre ca taddānaṁ sāttvikaṁ smṛtam //20//

That *dāna*, that alms giving is *sāttvic*, which is given to people who need it, that *dāna*; who need it and with this intention of the giver that *anupakāriṇe*, I don't want any return from him, any return service from him [for] this.

Deśe kale ca pātre ca. And [alms are given] in a good *deśa* (place) and [at] a good time; and *pātre ca*, and he gives alms to that [person] who deserves that. Not giving alms to [someone] who plays gambling afterwards with that money. Not that. He should think that I am bestowing this money to that person who will [make] good purpose of this. He will feed his kith and kin, he won't go and do gambling with that money and go to [prostitutes] and conduct that such bad behavior. To that [person] you should not give any alms. You should think that you must give alms to that [person] who deserves it. *Tat dānaṁ sāttvikaṁ samṛtam*, that *dāna* is really *sāttvic* way of giving.

DVD 17 (47:15)

यत्तु प्रत्युपकारार्थं फलमुद्दिश्य वा पुनः ।
दीयते च परिक्लिष्टं तद्राजसमिति स्मृतम् ॥२१॥

yattu pratyupakārārthaṁ phalamuddiśya vā punaḥ /
dīyate ca parikliṣṭaṁ tadrājasamiti smṛtam //21//

Yattū pratyupakārārthaṁ, that *dāna,* those alms which are given to people just for the sake of that, "he will serve me some time when I call him," and he gives him [alms], not willingly also. He gives that to him with this hope that he will be of some service [to me]. In spite of that also, he gives him unwillingly. *Dīyate ca parikliṣṭaṁ,* that kind of giving is *rājas* [way] of giving. It has no fruit, it is useless. It is better not to give anything to anybody.

Now giving in *tāmas* way.

DVD 17 (48:24)

अदेशकाले यद्दानमपात्रेभ्यश्च दीयते ।
असत्कृतमवज्ञातं तत्तामसमुदाहृतम् ॥२२॥

adeśakāle yaddānamapātrebhyaśca dīyate /
asatkṛtamavajñātaṁ tattāmasamudāhṛtam //22//

Adeśakāle [means] not in good time, not at a good moment, not in a good way, e.g., whatever [money] is given to people for uprooting others. And he gives them [money and tells them], "there are so many enemies of mine. One is residing in Fatakadal, one is residing in Habakadal,[476] one is residing [some-where else]." He gives him that list [and tells him], "I will give you money, but you [have to] burn [down] his house at night, [then] I will give you money." This way of giving is *tāmas* giving. It has no fruit. He gives [alms] to destroy others.

Bas, this *sāttvic*, [*rājas*, and *tāmas*] system is finished.

Now [Abinavagupta] says, "*idānīṁ ye guṇatritayasaṁkaṭottīrṇadhiyaste kriyāṁ kathamācarantīti tādṛk prakāra ucyate*" [comm. verse 22]. Now He explains–Lord Kṛṣṇa explains to Arjuna–those who are above the environment of the three *guṇas*, they are *guṇātītas*. How they behave in this world, He explains that way.

DVD 17 (50:10)

ओं तत्सदिति निर्देशो ब्रह्मणस्त्रिविधः स्मृतः ।
ब्राह्मणास्तेन वेदाश्च यज्ञाश्च विहिताः पुरा ॥२३॥
तस्मादोमित्युदाहृत्य यज्ञदानतपःक्रियाः ।
प्रवर्तन्ते विधानोक्ताः सततं ब्रह्मवादिनाम् ॥२४॥
तदित्यनभिसन्धाय फलं यज्ञतपःक्रियाः ।
दानक्रियाश्च विविधाः क्रियन्ते मोक्षकाङ्क्षिभिः ॥२५॥
सद्भावे साधुभावे च सदित्येतत्प्रयुज्यते ।
प्रशस्ते कर्मणि तथा सच्छब्दः पार्थ गीयते ॥२६॥
यज्ञे तपसि दाने च स्थितिः सदिति चोच्यते ।
कर्म चैव तदर्थीयं सदित्येवाभिधीयते ॥२७॥

oṁ tatsaditi nirdeśo brahmaṇastrividhaḥ smṛtaḥ /
brāhmaṇāstena vedāśca yajñāśca vihitāḥ purā //23//

476 These are areas in Srinagar, Kashmir.

tasmādomityudāhṛtya yajñadānatapaḥkriyāḥ /
pravartante vidhānoktāḥ satataṁ brahmavādinām //24
tadityanabhisandhāya phalaṁ yajñatapaḥkriyāḥ /
dānakriyāśca vividhāḥ kriyante mokṣakāṅkṣibhiḥ //25//
sadbhāve sādhubhāve ca sadityetatprayujyate /
praśaste karmaṇi tathā sacchabdaḥ pārtha gīyate //26//
yajñe tapasi dāne ca sthitiḥ saditi cocyate /
karma caiva tadarthīyaṁ sadityevābhidhīyate //27//

23rd, 24th, 25th, 26th, and 27th together.
Oṁ, *tat*, and *sat*. These are the names, threefold names of supreme Parabhairava (*oṁ*, *tat*, and *sat*).
What is the meaning of *oṁ*? What is the meaning of *tat*? And what is the meaning of *sat*?

DVD 17 (51:36)

तस्मादोमित्युदाहृत्य यज्ञदानतपःक्रियाः ।
प्रवर्तन्ते विधानोक्ताः सततं ब्रह्मवादिनाम् ॥२४॥

tasmādomityudāhṛtya yajñadānatapaḥkriyāḥ /
pravartante vidhānoktāḥ satataṁ brahmavādinām //24//
[repeated]

Whatever *havan* is produced by . . . the *havan* [which] is conducted by those who are *guṇātītas*, they internally recite *oṁ*. *Oṁ iti udāhṛtya, oṁ* is the producer of all *yajñas,* all *tapasyas*, all alms giving–*oṁ* is that. *Oṁ* is that [which] is residing in the state of Parabhairava; all behaviors of *yajñas*, of *tapasyas*, of alms giving, all these behaviors reside in the state of Parabhairava in actual way.
What is *tat*?
Tat. It is whenever you conduct these things: *yajñas, tapasya, dāna*, etc.

DVD 17 (53:06)

तदित्यनभिसन्धाय फलं यज्ञतपःक्रियाः ।
दानक्रियाश्च विविधाः क्रियन्ते मोक्षकाङ्क्षिभिः ॥२५॥

सद्भावे साधुभावे च सदित्येतत्प्रयुज्यते
प्रशस्ते कर्मणि तथा सच्छब्दः पार्थ गीयते ॥२६॥
यज्ञे तपसि दाने च स्थितिः सदिति चोच्यते ।
कर्म चैव तदर्थीयं सदित्येवाभिधीयते ॥२७॥

tadityanabhisandhāya phalaṁ yajñatapaḥkriyāḥ /
dānakriyāśca vividhāḥ kriyante mokṣakāṅkṣibhiḥ //25//
[repeated]

sadbhāve sādhubhāve ca sadityetatprayujyate /
praśaste karmaṇi tathā sacchabdaḥ pārtha gīyate //26//
yajñe tapasi dāne ca sthitiḥ saditi cocyate /
karma caiva tadarthīyaṁ sadityevābhidhīyate //27//
[verses not recited][477]

Tat iti. Tat iti means *oṁ*; *oṁ* is this whole universe. *Tat iti* is just to realize God; just to realize God is *tapasya*. Whatever you [do] in this world, you should think that it is [done in] the king-

477 Verse 26: "Arjuna, this *sadbhāva* (*sadbhāva* means the state of *sat*), what does that explain? The state of *sat* explains that this is *sadbhāva*, this is the reality. . . . Feeding [your son] is not reality. [When] you are feeding [your son], you are feeding Lord Śiva, this is the reality in feeding [your son]. This is *sādhubhāva.* And *sat iti etat prayujyate* . . . this *sat* is adopted in this way by those who have gone above the surface of three *guṇas. . . . Praśaste karmaṇi tathā sat śabdaḥ pārtha*, O Arjuna, this is *praśaste karma*, this is glorified action, this action is glorified action."

Verse 27: "Now He says in conclusion: in *yajñas*, in *tapasya*, in performing penance, and in the action of giving, the establishment is of *sat*. . . . That thing is existing which is always existing. And what is that thing? That is the only element which is existing–that is Lord Śiva. *Karma caiva tadarthīyaṁ sadityevābhidhīyate*, and the real action should be done in a real way, not in a wrong way. Whatever action is done [it] must be done for the sake of *sat,* for the sake of Lord Śiva, not for the sake of individuality. When this action, any action, is done for the sake of individuality it is wrong. Do all actions for the sake of Śiva then everything is fine."
Bhagavad Gītā (1978).

dom of God–*tat* . . . or *oṁ*.[478] *Tat* [means] it is residing for Him, it is residing for Him; it is not for me, it is not for others. It is for Him, for the state of Bhairava, Parabhairava.[479]

[When you understand this, then your activities] will be fruitful; if you will conduct *yajñā* and *dāna* and whatever you conduct, it will direct, it will push you into the state of Parabhairava in the end–*oṁ*, *tat*, and *sat*.

JOHN: This is the meaning of *sat* again . . . that's the fruit?

SWAMIJI: Huh?

JOHN: Whatever you do will be successful, that's the meaning of *sat*?

SWAMIJI: *Sat. Sat* means this [universe] is *sat* (*sat* is existing), existing in Parabhairava state.[480]

And in *Parātriśikā*, yes it is *Parātriśikā*, it is written:

caturdaśayutaṁ bhadre tithīśāntasamanvitam /
tṛtīyaṁ brahma suśroṇi hṛdayaṁ bhairavātmanaḥ //

478 "*Oṁ* is acceptance, i.e., I accept *tat,* that element (Lord Siva), is existing (*sat*)." Ibid.

479 "*Tat* means, [for example], "I am feeding [my son] for the sake of *tat*, not for the sake of [my son]." *Tat* means "that." [What is] that? *Sat*, who is existing, who is the only [one] existing. Śiva is the only [one] existing everywhere and that you have to believe, that you have to know . . . whatever is done is done in the cycle of Lord Śiva, in Śiva's kingdom." Ibid.

480 "When you believe that whatever is existing in this universe (in all these one hundred and eighteen worlds), whatever is existing is for the sake of Lord Śiva, who is only existing, when this is done, then there won't be *viśeṣa phala*, there won't be particularity of fruits. When there is *viśiṣṭaphala* (*viśiṣṭaphala* is particularity of your action), when you are attached to particular actions, then that is wrong, then you are wrongly attached. When there is no particularity, you are attached to that in each and every respect, then that is the right way of acting. So you must act in this world thinking that you have to act. You have to feed [your son], but in actual position. Actual position is that you are feeding Lord Śiva. Then there is no bondage. If you do that way, if you act that way, then there is no bondage. Bondage is when you think, you believe, that you are doing [i.e. acting] in individual way. When you do all these things in universal way, thinking that you are only moving in the cycle of Lord Śiva's kingdom, then there is no bondage." Ibid.

[*Parātriśikā śloka* 9]

It will be united with this. This is from *Parātriśikā Vivaraṇa*. *Parātriśikā* is of [*Rudrayāmala*] *tantras*, and he has, Abhinavagupta has, translated this *Parātriśikā Vivaraṇa*.

Om, *tat*, *sat*, this is *brahmaṇa trividha smṛtam*, the threefold state of Parabhairava (*tṛtīyaṁ*).[481] For instance, *catur*

---

481 "*Oṁ* is first *brahma*, *tat* is second *brahma*, and *sat* is third *brahma* (*oṁ*, *tat*, *sat*). *Śa* is first *brahma*, and after that, *murdhanya ṣa* (*murdhanya*, [the lingual letter] *ṣa* is second *brahma*), then *sa* is third *brahma*." Swami Lakshmanjoo, *Parātriśikā Vivaraṇa* (1982-85).

"*Śa* is first *brahma*, *ṣa* is second *brahma*, *sa* is third *brahma*, *ha* is fourth *brahma*, and *kṣa* is fifth *brahma*. This is called *brahma pañcakam*, fivefold state of five *brahmas*. And this flow of creation is with the root of [the vowel] *a* (*amūla*) and *kṣāntā*, ending in *kṣa*. Beginning from *a* ending in *kṣa*. This *sṛṣṭi*, the flow of creation is *udāhṛtā*, explained in *trika śāstras*. *Kramājjñeya*, and this flow of creation is the cause–*iyam yoniḥ samākhyātā*–this flow of creation is the cause of all *mantras*, all knowledge, and all letters in each and every *tantra* concerned with Shaivism." Swami Lakshmanjoo, *Parātriśikā Laghuvṛtti* (1982).

"These are nominated as five *brahmans*, i.e., *anāśritaśiva*, *śakti*, *sadāśiva*, *īśvara*, and *śuddhavidyā*. *Anāśritaśiva* is the first element (*kṣa*), *śakti* is the second element (*ha*), third element is *sadāśiva* (*sa*), fourth element is *īśvara* (*ṣa*), and fifth element is *śuddhavidyā* (*śa*)." Swami Lakshmanjoo, *Parātriśikā Vivaraṇa* (1982-85).

"Why are they called *brahmans,* these five states? *Bṛhattvat bṛṁhakatvat ca brahma*, who is himself great and who makes others great is *brahma*. *Bṛhattvaṁ* is being great, *bṛṁhakatvaṁ* is making others great. *Prāyo*, qualification is there existing because *bhedasamuttīrṇatvāt*, because they are above the cycle of differentiated world. And *saṁsārasūtikartṛtvāt ca*, and they create this whole universe. *Bhedasamuttīrṇatvāt*, because they are above this level of differentiatedness, so they are themselves great. And *saṁsāra-sūti-kartṛtvāt ca,* because they create this whole universe, they make others also great." Ibid.

"Why it is called Brahman? Because it is full with subjectivity, and these five *brahmans* are represented by five letters: *śa*, *ṣa*, *sa*, *ha*, and *kṣa*. In its originated state, these five states are called respectively: *śuddhavidyā*, *īśvara*, *sadāśiva*, *śakti* and *śiva*, i.e. *śa*, *ṣa*, *sa*, *ha*, and *kṣa*. And in its subtle formation of *svarūpā*, you get respectively the state of *pṛthvī*, (earth), water (*jala*), *agni* (fire), *vāyu* (air), and *ākāśa*

daśa yutaṁ bhadre, the fourteenth [vowel]. What is fourteenth [vowel]? Fourteenth [vowel] is *au*, fourteenth is *au* vowel (*a*, *ā*, *i*, *ī*, *u*, *ū*, *ṛ*, *ṝ*, *li*, *lī*, *e*, *ai*, *o*, *au*). You calculate. You see on your fingertips: *a*, *ā*, *i*, *ī*, *u*, *ū*, *ṛ*, *ṝ*, *li*, *lī*, *e*, *ai*, *o*, *au*.

JOHN: Fourteen.

SWAMIJI: Fourteenth. *Caturdaśayutaṁ*, this is the fourteenth [vowel], it is *au*. It is called *triśulabija*; *triśulabīja* [is]

(ether). And in its five acts, the representers are respectively: *sadyojāta*, *vāmadeva*, *aghora*, *tatpuruṣa*, and *īśāna*. *Sadyojāta* for *śa*, *vāmadeva* for *ṣa*, *aghora* for *sa*, *tatpuruṣa* for *ha*, and *īśāna* for *kṣa*." Swami Lakshmanjoo, *Parātriśikā Laghuvṛtti* (1982).

"These are five *brahmans*, they are just close to the state of Śiva, they are very near to the Śiva state, which are created just in the end. . . . Those elements which were very far away from Śiva, those were created in the beginning; first they were created. So it seems nothing is created. Because, how it could be done that He would create the lowest thing first and the nearest thing in the end? So there is no near, there is no end, there is no first, there is no last." Swami Lakshmanjoo, *Parātriśikā Vivaraṇa* (1982-85).

"These four-fold letters (*śa*, *ṣa*, *sa*, and *ha*) are called *ūṣma*. They are nominated by Bhairava as *ūṣma akṣaras* (*ūṣma* letters). *Ūṣma* means where there is warmth, heat, heat of your own nature. What is your nature? Nature is all-consciousness (*cit*) and all-bliss (*ānanda*). . . . *Śa* is that warmth which carries you to the state of *śuddhavidya*. And next *ṣa* is that warmth which carries you to the state of *īśvara*. And the third [*sa*] is carrying you to *śadāśiva*. And the fourth [*ha*] is carrying you to *śakti–śa*, *ṣa*, *sa*, and *ha*." Swami Lakshmanjoo, *Tantrāloka* 3.79 (1973).

"*Ka* is the first consonant produced by a vowel, and *sa* is the last consonant produced by the vowel. Vowel is Śiva and consonant is Śakti. So the first consonant is *ka* and the last consonant is *sa*. Afterwards there is *ha*. *Ha* is *śakti*. So *ha* is not counted in consonants, it is separate. Now what happens? This first consonant is united with the last consonant. This first consonant, first female (*ka*), is united with last female (*sa*) in a sexual way and they produce another word, another letter–that is *kṣa*. . . . It is call *kūṭabīja*. . . . So from Śaiva point of view, from subjective point of view [i.e., Śiva's point of view], the *mantra* is *a* and *ha*, the combination of *a* and *ha* [i.e., *ahaṁ*]. And from Śakti point of view, the *mantra* of *ahaṁ* is the combination of *ka* and *sa*. So *kṣa* is also one *mantra*. As you find in *ahaṁ*, so you find in *kṣa* also. *Kṣa* is *mantra* produced by *yonīs*. *Ahaṁ* is *mantra* produced by vowels and consonants." Ibid.

where there is *īccha*, *jñāna*, and *kriyā* together in force (*īccha, jñāna and kriyā*).[482] *Caturdaśayutaṁ*, fourteenth, the fourteenth vowel (*a*, *ā*, *i*, *ī*, *u*, *ū*, *ṛ*, *ṝ*, *li*, *lī*, *e*, *ai*, *o*, *au*).

Tithī śānta samanvitam. Tithī śānta samanvitam means [the vowels] *aṁ* and *aḥ* (*tithī śānta samanvitam*). *Caturdaśayutaṁ bhadre tithīśānta-samanvitam. Tṛtīyaṁ brahma suśroṇi. Tṛtīyaṁ brahma* means [the letter] *sa*. *Tṛtīyaṁ brahma* is *sa*. *Tithīśānta* means *aṁ* and *aḥ*. *Tṛtīyaṁ brahma* means *sa*. *Sa* means *pārabīja*; *sa* means *amṛta bīja*.[483] In [the letter] *sa* you will find the existence of thirty-one elements, from *pṛthvī* to *māyā*. From *pṛthvī* to *māyā*, there are thirty-one elements that are residing in *sa*.[484] That is *tṛtīyaṁ brahma*, third *brahma*. Third *brahma* is [de-scribed] in *Bhagavad Gītā* also: *oṁ*, *tat*, *sat*. It is *brahmana tṛtīyaṁ smṛta*. *Brahma* is threefold, it is third *brahma*. What is third *brahma*? *Sat*, [which is the letter] *sa*. *Sa* is third *brahma* because *sat* is . . . this [affix] after *sa* . . . there is [the affix] *at* according to grammarians; that [affix] has no value, that gives no indication. Only there is *sa* without *a*, and *sa* is *parabīja*, *sa*. So it becomes *sauḥ*, i.e., *sa*, *au*, and *visarga*

482 Lord Siva's energies of will, knowledge, and action. [*Editor's note*]

483 "*Amṛtaṁ ca paraṁ dhāma*, this is nominated as *amṛta bīja*. This [letter] *sa*, it is *amṛta,* because it is filled with internal nectar of Lord Śiva. And this is the real state of Lord Śiva, *paraṁ dhāma*, supreme state. *Yoginas tat pracakṣate*, *yogīs* have nominated this state as *amṛta*, and as *param*, supreme state. Because only *yogīs* only experience this state of being. *Yogīs* do not experience the state of being as Paramaśiva. Paramaśiva is not experienced because there you will find Paramaśiva [as the] experiencer. He is never experienced. These three states are experienced by *yogīs*. Which three states? *Śuddhavidyā*, *īśvara*, and *sadāśiva*, i.e. *śa*, *ṣa*, and *sa*." Swami Lakshmanjoo, *Tantrāloka* 3.164 (1973).

484 "And the last state of his being outside in his own warmth is *sa*; *sa* is that [letter] which represents the state of *śadāśiva*. It is why in this state of *sakāra*, in the state of the last letter *sa*, this whole universe is found in the warmth of His, that blissful state. The whole *sphuṭaṁ viśvaṁ prakāśate*, [the appearance of this universe is perceived] not in differentiated way, [it is perceived] in an undifferentiated way. This whole universe is found in an undifferentiated way. It is why the *parāmarśa* of this state is *ahaṁ-idaṁ*." Ibid.

(*aḥ*).[485] This is *hṛdayaṁ bhairavātmanaḥ*, the heart of Parabhairava.[486] [Introduction to verse 28.][487]

485 "*Sa* is third *brahma*. Third *brahma* represent from earth to *māyā*, i.e. thirty-one elements of *tattvas*. Afterwards there are another three elements above *māyā*. Above *māyā* are three elements, *śuddhavidyā*, *īśvara*, and *sadāśiva* [which are represented by the vowel *au*]. And above *sadāśiva* are two elements, *Śakti* and *Śiva* [which are represented by the vowel *aḥ*]. There ends this whole elementary movement of Lord Śiva. That is *sauḥ*." Swami Lakshmanjoo, *Parātrīśikā Laghuvṛtti* (1982).

"Cognitive world of consciousness is represented by *au*, the fourteenth movement of Lord Śiva. And subjective movement of consciousness is represented by *visarga* (*aḥ*). And this *aḥ* is representing two elements, *Śiva* and *Śakti*. So you have to unite this subjective consciousness with objective consciousness through cognitive consciousness. *Tṛtīyaṁ brahma* means objective consciousness (*sa*), *caturdaśayutam* means cognitive consciousness (*au*), *tithīśānta* means subjective consciousness (*aḥ*)." Ibid.

486 "As you find that individual being is adjusted in this body which is made of thirty-six elements, in the same way, Bhairavanātha is also adjusted in that universal body, in which body all these thirty-six elements are found, which are represented by fifty letters beginning from *a* to ending in *kṣa*. And this is the essence of this whole universe. This whole universe is the essence of Bhairava. The whole universe is the essence of Bhairava and Bhairava is the essence of universe. There is not at all the slightest difference between Bhairava and this world. This is the philosophy of Trika system.

"Trika philosophy teaches us to realize what is already in front of you. You have not to realize what is not in front of you. You have to realize this pencil, this tape recorder, this stove, this money, this specks, etc., you have to realize it, what it is actually. To realize it actually is the essence of Shaivism. You have not to realize God who is situated in seventh heaven. That is not to be realized. You have to realize what is already before you." Ibid.

487 "Now, the most important point is to have faith in whatever is spoken to you by your master. Whatever is spoken to you, taught to you by your master, you must have full faith in that. Don't put your intellect there. Have faith, *bas*! Whatever has come from his lips, believe that is true. If some logician will tell you, "no that is not true, I will prove that." [Tell him], "please, don't prove [that]! I don't want this botheration." You must not put any doubt in that. That is what [Abhinavagupta] says." *Bhagavad Gītā* (1978).

DVD 17 (59:50)

अश्रद्धया हुतं दत्तं तपस्तप्तं कृतं च यत् ।
असदित्युच्यते पार्थ न च तत्प्रेत्य नो इह ॥२८॥

aśraddhayā hutaṁ dattaṁ tapastaptaṁ kṛtaṁ ca yat /
asadityucyate pārtha na ca tatpretya no iha //28//

Whatever *tapasya* is done, whatever alms are given, whatever action is being done without *śraddhā* (faith), i.e., not [with] *sāttvic* mood, *asat iti ucyate*, that [action] is *asat* (false/useless). *Na ca tat pretya*, after death there is no whereabouts of [the fruit of] that action and *no iha*, and in this lifetime there is no whereabouts of [the fruit of] that action, i.e., it is useless [action] which is done with a *rājas* mood and *tāmas* mood.

Whatever is done in a *sāttvic* mood, that will remain, that will live for centuries and centuries and it will [direct] you and make you exist in the state of Parabhairava in the end.

Sa ev kāra . . .

Now the conclusion of this chapter.

DVD 17 (1:01:20)

स एव कारकावेशः क्रिया सैवाविशेषिणी ।
तथापि विज्ञानवतां मोक्षार्थे पर्यवस्यति ॥

sa ev kārakāveśaḥ kriyā saivāviśeṣiṇī /
tathāpi vijñānavatāṁ mokṣārthe paryavasyati //17//

॥ Concluding *śloka* of 17th chapter ॥

The conduct is the same but there is that trick for those who are residing in a *sāttvic* wave. *Mokṣārthe prayavasyati*, by this trick of remaining in a *sāttvic* wave, he [is successful] to this extent that he resides for eternity in the state of Parabhairava.[488]

488 "If there is truth in action, if there is reality in action, all your acts will lead you, will carry you, to Lord Śiva, not that other person. He does the same thing, he eats, you eat. I eat in such a way I go there. He

eats in such a way he doesn't go. So *vijñānavatāṁ*, this is *vijñānavatāṁ*, those who are realized they are divine. But they do the same actions as ignorant persons do. They are doing [actions] in the same way, but they are divine. This you should understand." Ibid.

Chapter 18 Part 1

Aṣṭādaśo'dhyāyaḥ. Now there is the 18th chapter.

DVD 18a (00:15)

अर्जुन उवाच

arjuna uvāca

Arjuna asks Lord Kṛṣṇa:

संन्यासस्य महाबाहो तत्त्वमिच्छामि वेदितुम् ।
त्यागस्य च हृषीकेश पृथक्केशिनिषूदन ॥ १ ॥

saṁnyāsasya mahābāho tattvamicchāmi veditum /
tyāgasya ca hṛṣīkeśa pṛthakkeśiniṣūdana //1//

Mahābāho, hey [One] with great arms, O Lord Kṛṣṇa, I want to know the reality of what is *saṁnyāsa* and *tyāgasya ca hṛṣīkeśa*, and what is *tyāga*. What is *saṁnyāsa* (*karma saṁnyāsa*) and what is *tyāga*? I want to know separately, what do You mean by *tyāga* and what do You mean by *saṁnyāsa*? *Saṁnyāsa* means *karma saṁnyāsa*.

There are two [kinds] of *yogīs*: one is *yogi* and one is *saṁnyāsi*. *Saṁnyāsi* [is one] who does not do any actions; *yogi* is [one] who does action in *yoga*. What is the behavior in these? What is the difference between these two [kinds of *yogīs*]? I want to know separately, O Lord Kṛṣṇa.

श्रीभगवानुवाच

śrī bhagavān uvāca

Srī Bhagavān puts before him this answer:

DVD 18a (01:56)

काम्यानां कर्मणां न्यासं
संन्यासं कवयो विदुः ।
सर्वकर्मफलत्यागं
प्राहुस्त्यागं विचक्षणाः ॥२॥

kāmyānām karmaṇāṁ nyāsaṁ
saṁnyāsaṁ kavayo viduḥ /
sarvakarmaphalatyāgaṁ
prāhustyāgaṁ vicakṣaṇāḥ //2//

Kāmyānām karmaṇāṁ nyāsaṁ, saṁnyāsaṁ kavayo viduḥ. Kavayo, ancient *ṛṣis* and *munis* (this is the viewpoint of ancient *ṛṣis* and *munis;* this is not only the viewpoint of Mine), there have been *ṛṣis* and *munis* in the past generations, they understood that *kāmyānām karmaṇāṁ nyāsaṁ saṁnyāsaṁ*, *saṁnyāsa* [means] you should abandon those actions which have got [your desire for] fruit in the background. So, if you do [those] actions without asking for its fruit . . .[489]

काम्यानां कर्मणां न्यासं
संन्यासं कवयो विदुः ।

489 "Renunciation is not to abandon all the actions. Renouncing all actions is not renunciation in real sense. Renouncing those actions which are with fruit, which are done with the desire of some achievement of fruit. Those actions should be avoided and that is *saṁnyāsa*, that is renunciation. . . . Do only those actions which bear no fruit. For instance, watching your breath, it won't bear any fruit. Meditating on some center, it won't bear any fruit. These actions should be done. All other actions should be avoided. This is in real sense *saṁnyāsa* accepted by some scholars, by some elevated souls." *Bhagavad Gītā* (1978).

सर्वकर्मफलत्यागं
प्राहुस्त्यागं विचक्षणाः ॥२॥

kāmyānām karmaṇāṁ nyāsaṁ
saṁnyāsaṁ kavayo viduḥ /
sarvakarmaphalatyāgaṁ
prāhustyāgaṁ vicakṣaṇāḥ //2//
[repeated]

Sarvakarmaphalatyāgaṁ prāhustyāgaṁ vicakṣaṇām, and there are some great souls, great wise people of the past generations, they say *tyāga* (*tyāga* is *sarva karma phala tyāgaṁ*), go on doing your actions, *yoga* in actions, [and] don't ask for its fruit.

And [now] He says what is the behavior of other ancient masters, i.e., what is *tyāga* from their viewpoint and what is *saṁnyāsa* from their viewpoint.

DVD 18a (04:36)

त्याज्यं दोषवदित्येके कर्म प्राहुर्मनीषिणः ।
यज्ञदानतपःकर्म न त्याज्यमिति चापरे ॥३॥

tyājyaṁ doṣavadityeke karma prāhurmanīṣiṇaḥ /
yajñadānatapaḥkarma na tyājyamiti cāpare //3//

Some ancient *ṛṣis* and *munis*, their viewpoint is that, *tyājyaṁ doṣavadityeke*, *doṣavad karma tyājyaṁ*. That *havan* . . . you should not perform [that *havan*] where, in *havan,* there is a sacrifice of living beings. You know living beings? Sacrifice, when they sacrifice living beings and [they first] adore that living being and [then] offer [its] blood in *āhuti*[490] in *havan*.

My father also did *havan*, performed this *havan*, in

490 *Ahuti* means any offering to the deities in a *havan*. [*Editor's note*]

> Khrew. You know Khrew?[491] They would get that sheep and cut his throat and place that blood in clay pots for offering it to Devī. This was done with great effort by priests. In those days our priest was Shamlal Jhatu's father. Shamlal Jhatu's father was the priest of . . . our priest, and he performed this. And he was doing it with great faith, i.e., my father. I was also thinking, "what they are doing? This is not a good action."

Some *ṛṣis* and *munis* of the past say that, "this kind of *havan* you should not perform; this is against the will of Parabhairava to cut the throat [of a living being] for the sake of pleasing gods and goddesses.

Yajña dāna tapaḥ karma, na tyājyam iti cāpare. Otherwise, *yajñas* [performed] without this *bakwas* (nonsense), e.g., *dāna* (alms giving), and penance (*tapaḥ*), and all austerities, you should perform. You should not abandon [those austerities] for the sake of [abandoning] this, i.e., if [animal sacrifices] are not done. This should not be done. It is the viewpoint of some other masters.

DVD 18a (08:06)

निश्चयं श्रृणु मे तत्र त्यागे भरतसत्तम ।
त्यागो हि पुरुषव्याघ्र त्रिविधः संप्रकीर्तितः ॥४॥
यज्ञदानतपःकर्म न त्याज्यं कार्यमेव तत् ।
यज्ञो दानं तपश्चैव पावनानि मनीषिणाम् ॥५॥
एतान्यपि च कर्माणि सङ्गं त्यक्त्वा फलानि च ।
कर्तव्यानीति मे पार्थ निश्चितं मतमुत्तमम् ॥६॥

niścayaṁ śṛṇu me tatra tyāge bharatasattama /
tyāgo hi puruṣavyāghra trividhaḥ saṁprakīrtitaḥ //4//
yajñadānatapaḥkarma na tyājyaṁ kāryameva tat /
yajño dānaṁ tapaścaiva pāvanāni manīṣiṇām //5//
etānyapi ca karmāṇi saṅgaṁ tyaktvā phalāni ca /
kartavyānīti me pārtha niścitaṁ matamuttamam //6//

491 Khrew is a particular shrine in Kashmir. [*Editor's note*]

This is *śloka* 4th, 5th, and 6th in one.

He says, "now, what is My opinion [about] this?" Who [gives] his opinion? Lord Kṛṣṇa [says] before Arjuṇa, "what is My opinion of these ancient traditions of the past?" But they are all good because they have already nominated that you should not do those *havans* where the throats are cut of sheep. They are all good but My viewpoint is this *tyāga*, this renunciation, renunciation is–*puruṣa vyāghra*, O great being, O Arjuṇa–*trividhaḥ,* it is in three ways explained; it is [from] My viewpoint. I would explain it in three ways: *sāttvic tyāga (tyāga* means *karma saṁnyāsa*), *sāttvic karma saṁnyāsa, rājas karma saṁnyāsa*, and *tāmas karma saṁnyāsa.*

DVD 18a (10:22)

यज्ञदानतपःकर्म न त्याज्यं कार्यमेव तत् ।
यज्ञो दानं तपश्चैव पावनानि मनीषिणाम् ॥५॥

yajñadānatapaḥkarma na tyājyaṁ kāryameva tat /
yajño dānaṁ tapaścaiva pāvanāni manīṣiṇām //5//
[repeated]

Yajña, austerity, penance, and all *karmas*, according to the statement of the *śāstras, na tyājyaṁ*, you should not abandon [them]; *kāryameva tat*, you should do that, you should perform them with great faith. Because the performance of *yajña*, performance of austerity, performance of penance, these [actions are] *manīṣaṇām pāvanāni*, even the *ṛṣis* and *munis* also get purified by these actions.

DVD 18a (11:18)

एतान्यपि च कर्माणि सङ्गं त्यक्त्वा फलानि च ।
कर्तव्यानीति मे पार्थ निश्चितं मतमुत्तमम् ॥६॥

etānyapi ca karmāṇi saṅgaṁ tyaktvā phalāni ca /
kartavyānīti me pārtha niścitaṁ matamuttamam //6//
[repeated]

O Arjuna, all these *karmas* you should do, you should act, [but] one should act without being attached to [these actions]. And don't think of [receiving] any fruit out of it. *Kartavyāni*, you [should] think that, "it is my duty to do it." [Lord Kṛṣṇa says], "this is My viewpoint, what I have understood Myself."

DVD 18a (12:07)

नियतस्य च संन्यासः कर्मणो नोपपद्यते ।
मोहात्तस्य परित्यागस्तामसः परिकीर्तितः ॥७॥
दुःखमित्येव यः कर्म कायक्लेशभयात्त्यजेत् ।
स कृत्वा राजसं त्यागं नैव त्यागफलं लभेत् ॥८॥
कार्यमित्येव यत्कर्म नियतं क्रियतेऽर्जुन ।
सङ्गं त्यक्त्वा फलं चैव स त्यागः सात्त्विको मतः ॥९

niyatasya ca saṁnyāsaḥ karmaṇo nopapadyate /
mohāttasya parityāgastāmasaḥ parikīrtitaḥ //7//
duḥkhamityeva yaḥ karma kāyakleśabhayāttyajet /
sa kṛtvā rājasaṁ tyāgaṁ naiva tyāgaphalaṁ labhet //8//
kāryamityeva yatkarma niyataṁ kriyate'rjuna /
saṅgaṁ tyaktvā phalaṁ caiva sa tyāgaḥ sāttviko mataḥ 9

And now in these, 7th *śloka*, 8th *śloka*, and 9th *śloka* (three in one), in these He explains:

DVD 18a (13:09)

नियतस्य च संन्यासः कर्मणो नोपपद्यते ।
मोहात्तस्य परित्यागस्तामसः परिकीर्तितः ॥७॥

niyatasya ca saṁnyāsaḥ karmaṇo nopapadyate /
mohāttasya parityāgastāmasaḥ parikīrtitaḥ //7//
[repeated]

Whatever is ordered by the *śāstras,* you should do that. You should not sleep at the time of early in the morning. At dawn time you should not sleep; you should leave your bedding and do your *abhyāsa* (practice). That is *niyat*; it is the *śāstras* ruling for everybody to conduct. It is not good behavior to not tread on this path of the *śāstras*. You will think that, "let me sleep for another half an hour and then I will rise, then I will get up and do my *abhyāsa*." You should not do that.

Mohāttasya parityāga, because if he does that, if he waits for another one hours rest, to conduct another one hours rest, [then] this is *tyāga* (renunciation) of that [which] is done by, committed by *tāmas*, by those who are entangled by *tamaguṇa*. This is *tamaguṇa's* action. That you should not do. Whatever the *śāstras* have ordered [you] to do, you should act upon that. Don't be sluggish at that moment.

> When I was a child and my father and mother would say that, "it is *sandhyā* (junction) between the day, [which] is all finished, and the night [that] is beginning, it is *sandhyā samaya* (dusk). At this moment, Lord Śiva is dancing. You should think of Lord Śiva at this moment. You should not think . . . you should not . . . don't play." She, [my mother], would deny us [from playing]. She would ask Bhagavan Das, Nilakāntha,[492] and myself, "not to do . . . don't play like this; it is *sandhyā samaya*, sit and do prayers. Because Lord Śiva is . . . at this time, Lord Śiva is dancing, you should do your prayers." This was our tradition.
>
> **DENISE:** Everyday she did that?
>
> **SWAMIJI:** Huh?
>
> **DENISE:** At night when it started to get dark?
>
> **SWAMIJI:** Huh?
>
> **DENISE:** She did that continuiously?
>
> **SWAMIJI:** And in the morning also.

So that kind of *tyāga* is *tyāga* committed by *tāmasis*.

492 Bhagavan Das and Nilakantha were Swamiji's younger brothers. [*Editor's note*]

DVD 18a (16:50)

दुःखमित्येव यः कर्म कायक्लेशभयात्त्यजेत् ।
स कृत्वा राजसं त्यागं नैव त्यागफलं लभेत् ॥८॥

duḥkhamityeva yaḥ karma kāyakleśabhayāttyajet /
sa kṛtvā rājasaṁ tyāgaṁ naiva tyāgaphalaṁ labhet //8//
[repeated]

And there are some people who say, "I have got a headache; at this moment I have got a headache. I must rest a little. It is not worthwhile to do *abhyās* (practice) at this time, at this critical moment of dawn or this critical moment of *sandhyā* in the evening. I want to take rest because I have a headache. I am not feeling well."

That [behavior] also is incorrect!

At that time you should sit! Don't do anything [else], but sit. Do like this [rubbing your head], but sit. Don't stretch your legs in bed just like a fool. That is *rājas tyāga*. That is *rājas tyāga* that is conducted by *rajaguṇa*.

Now, what is conducted by *sattvaguṇa*?

DVD 18a (18:07)

कार्यमित्येव यत्कर्म नियतं क्रियतेऽर्जुन ।
सङ्गं त्यक्त्वा फलं चैव स त्यागः सात्त्विको मतः ॥९

kāryamityeva yatkarma niyataṁ kriyate'rjuna /
saṅgaṁ tyaktvā phalaṁ caiva sa tyāgaḥ sāttviko mataḥ //9
[repeated]

[The one residing in *sattvaguṇa* feels], "I have to do [*abhyāsa*]! Let this body fall and [die], I don't care. I have not been created for this kind of easiness, i.e., being an easy-loving person. This is my duty." *Niyataṁ kriyate'rjuna*, and he does [*abhyās*] from time to time [as] it is [prescribed] by the *śāstras*. Say in the morning, at midnight, and in the evening time when there is *sandhyā*.[493] And some people say that at midnight also, and midday also, there is some equality. At twelve o'clock when sun comes in the center, when there is no shadow, shadow is finished, that is [the time of] oneness. Oneness shines there of the whole cosmos in the universe. So you should be alert there. Maybe sometime you will get elevated and get established in the state of Parabhairava.

DVD 18a (19:57)

न द्वेष्ट्यकुशलं कर्म कुशले नानुषज्जति ।
त्यागी सत्त्वसमाविष्टो मेधावी छिन्नसंशयः ॥१०॥
नहि देहभृता शक्यं त्यक्तुं कर्माण्यशेषतः ।
यस्तु कर्म फलत्यागी स त्यागीत्यभिधीयते ॥११॥

na dveṣṭyakuśalaṁ karma kuśale nānuṣajjati /
tyāgī sattvasamāviṣṭo medhāvī chinnasaṁśayaḥ //10//
nahi dehabhṛtā śakyaṁ tyaktuṁ karmāṇyaśeṣataḥ /
yastu karma phalatyāgī sa tyāgītyabhidhīyate //11//

In addition, this is also My viewpoint of understanding. This way I have understood what you should do and what you should not do; what one should do and what one should not do.

Na dveṣṭyakuśalaṁ karma. Akuśalaṁ karma means that behavior of acting, that behavior of acting, which comes into force automatically into [you]. You should tolerate that. You should tolerate that if you have to act that way, according to

493 "*Sandhyā* means the junction of two [movements]. There are four junctions [to be observed] in breathing in and out. These are four junctions to be marked with awareness. One junction is *prābātikī sandhyā*, in the morning, in the dawn. In midday sun, when sun is in the center, that is *mādhyānikī sandhyā*. There you have to adopt another *sandhyā*, that is another junction. And at the time of sun-setting, that is *sāyaṁ sandhyā*. And at the time of midnight there is *ardha rātrī sandhyā*. So these *sandhyās* are to be observed by *sādhakās*." Swami Lakshmanjoo, *Tantrāloka* 6.24 (1974).

your past *karmas*.[494] You should not [renounce that activity], you should accept that and tolerate that. *Kuśale nānuṣajjati*, and at that time you should not try to [change] your behavior and strive for *kuśal kāra* [i.e., *sāttvic* behavior] because [when] that wave is finished, that *sāttvic* wave is finished, [then] there [may be] *rājas* wave there. So you should accept *rājas* wave with tolerance and think of the Lord at that time.

Tyāgī, you should be *tyāgī*, you should be . . . you should abandon everything.[495] *Tyāgī* means the one who has surrendered everything to Lord Śiva, *sattva samāviṣṭa*, who is alert, always alert and concentrated, whose mind is concentrated and focused in the state of Parabhairava (*sattva samāviṣṭa*), *medhāvī*, and who is filled with wisdom, *chinna saṁśayaḥ*, and whose all doubts have vanished.

DVD 18a (22:22)

नहि देहभृता शक्यं त्यक्तुं कर्माण्यशेषतः ।
यस्तु कर्म फलत्यागी स त्यागीत्यभिधीयते ॥११॥

nahi dehabhṛtā śakyaṁ tyaktuṁ karmāṇyaśeṣataḥ /
yastu karma phalatyāgī sa tyāgītyabhidhīyate //11//

It is not possible for that person who is existing in the body, that he can leave, he can abandon all actions. He cannot abandon all actions as long as the body is there. So, you should do your actions, [but] don't ask for its fruit. Think that

494 "*Dehabhṛtā*, as long as you are attached with this body, you can't renounce everything. You can't be detached from each and every action in this world. . . . So renunciation is that, *yastu karma phalatyāgī*, go on doing actions, [just] don't ask for its fruit, good or bad. If bad fruit comes, welcome that; if good fruit comes, welcome that. That is renunciation!" *Bhagavad Gītā* (1978).

495 "Detachment is not the renunciation of all action. . . . Attachment and detachment should be avoided. Don't be attached to good fruit; don't be detached to bad fruit of your actions. If your actions bear bad fruit, don't be detached to it. If they bear good fruits, don't be attached to it. . . . Be brave in this field of mortality! That is *tyāga*." Ibid.

you have to do . . .[496]

DVD 18a (23:06)

अनिष्टमिष्टं मिश्रं च त्रिविधं कर्मणः फलम् ।
भवत्यत्यागिनां प्रेत्य नतु संन्यासिनां क्वचित् ॥१२॥

aniṣṭamiṣṭaṁ miśraṁ ca trividhaṁ karmaṇaḥ phalam /
bhavatyatyāgināṁ pretya natu saṁnyāsināṁ kvacit //12//

Aniṣṭam (bad fruits of your actions), *miśraṁ* (*miśraṁ* means united [i.e., mixed] fruits of actions), *aniṣṭam*, and *iṣṭam* (good fruits of your actions). Good fruits of your actions, bad fruits of your actions, and united fruits of your actions (i.e., in one way good and in another way bad), these fruits appear before you in your lifetime in three ways. One is good, one is bad, and one is . . .

JONATHAN: Mixture.

SWAMIJI: Mixture, partially good and partially bad.[497]

Bhavati atyāgināṁ pretya. Pretya, after you leave this body, this fruit of actions takes place after leaving your body,[498] *natu saṁnyāsināṁ kvacit*, not by leaving [i.e., renouncing] that body.[499] As long as the body is there, you have to do this, you have to indulge in these, you have to tolerate these threefold fruits of actions.

DVD 18a (24:56)

पञ्चेमानि महाबाहो कारणानि निबोध मे ।
सांख्ये कृतान्ते प्रोक्तानि सिद्धये सर्वकर्मणाम् ॥१३॥

496 "[Think that you have to do] each and every action in this world, which are to be done, but don't ask for its fruit. That is *tyāga*." Ibid.

497 "*Sāttvic* [action] bears good fruit, *rājasa* action bears mixed fruit, and *tāmas* [action] bears bad fruit." Ibid.

498 "This fruit appears to those who are *atyāginā*, who are attached to their actions." Ibid.

499 "*Natu saṁnyāsināṁ kvacit*, but those who are *saṁnyāsins*, those who are detached from the very beginning, their actions bear fruit at that very moment." Ibid.

अधिष्ठानं तथा कर्ता करणं च पृथग्विधम् ।
विविधा च पृथक्चेष्टा दैवमेवात्र पञ्चमम् ॥१४॥
शरीरवाङ्मनोभिर्हि यत्कर्मारभतेऽर्जुन ।
न्याय्यं वा विपरीतं वा पञ्चैते तस्य हेतवः ॥१५॥
तत्रैवंसति कर्तारमात्मानं केवलं तु यः ।
पश्यत्यकृतबुद्धित्वान्न स पश्यति दुर्मतिः ॥१६॥
यस्य नाहं कृतो भावो बुद्धिर्यस्य न लिप्यते ।
हत्वापि स इमाँल्लोकान्न हन्ति न निबध्यते ॥१७॥

pañcemāni mahābāho kāraṇāni nibodha me /
sāṁkhye kṛtānte proktāni siddhaye sarvakarmaṇām //13
adhiṣṭhānaṁ tathā kartā karaṇaṁ ca pṛthagvidham /
vividhā ca pṛthakceṣṭā daivamevātra pañcamam //14//
śarīravāṅmanobhirhi yatkarmārabhate'rjuna /
nyāyyaṁ vā viparītaṁ vā pañcaite tasya hetavaḥ //15//
tatraivaṁsati kartāramātmānaṁ kevalaṁ tu yaḥ /
paśyatyakṛtabuddhitvānna sa paśyati durmatiḥ //16//
yasya nāhaṁkṛto bhāvo buddhiryasya na lipyate /
hatvāpi sa imāṁllokānna hanti na nibaddhyate //17//

Now [13th], 14th, 15th, 16th, and 17th [*ślokas*].

In these *ślokas*, He says there are five great causes. Whatever is being done, whatever action is being committed in this world, there are, for [all actions], five great causes are responsible, not only one cause. Five great causes are responsible for that.

The first [cause] is *adhiṣṭānaṁ* [verse 14], on which basis we have to do some action. That is *adhiṣṭānaṁ*. *Adhiṣṭānaṁ* means on which basis, i.e., which desire [is in] the background [of your mind]; you keep some desire in the background before you start some action. [That] basis is first. The first responsibility is the basis, on which basis you commit this action. That is *adhiṣṭānaṁ*.[500]

And the second responsibility goes to the behavior [of *puruṣa*], the [individual] who acts, the actor of that action. The basis [i.e., *adhiṣṭānam*] for what he acts, this is also responsible, and the [individual] actor also he is responsible. It is not only the [individual] actor who is responsible. This is the second responsibility, which goes to [individual] actor.

Karaṇaṁ, the means [by which one] acts. Third responsibility goes to the means, i.e., how to act that, how to do/act that action, through which sources. And those sources are different for each and every action; [for] each and every action, the sources are [different].

For instance, you have to cut this wood, cut this tree. *Adhiṣṭānaṁ* is first, i.e., the tree is to be cut. Who is cutting [it]? That is *kartā*. *Kartā* is the [individual actor] who has to cut this tree. That is the second behaving agent. And the third is *karanāṇi–adhiṣṭānaṁ tathā kartā karaṇaṁ–karaṇaṁ* means the third is the means. Means are not only one, means are *pṛthag vidham*, [there are] varieties of means. For instance, for cutting branches you need a hatchet; for cutting trunk you need a big saw; for cutting roots you need a hammer, hammer and those . . .

JONATHAN: *Gyanti*.

SWAMIJI: Not *gyanti* (pick axe), those, which are . . .

JONATHAN: *Sambal*.

SWAMIJI: *Sambal*, and which are stuck in that.

So this is the variety of means. These [means] are also responsible for cutting this tree. If, for example, I say for instance, there is cutting of a tree. In the same way, there is the construction of a house. *Adhiṣṭāni* is the main [cause], i.e., construction of the house is to be done. [*Adhiṣṭāni*] is responsible for one way [of this activity]. And there is the one who is constructing. That is *kartā*. *Karaṇaṁ* means how he has to do it, how he has to construct house. He has to call masons, he has to call carpenters, he has to call sawers, he has to call *coolies* (unskilled laborers), he has to call [for]

500 "Basis is just the state of Lord Siva. Action is done on the basis of Lord Śiva. That is the chief actor, chief player . . . when there is not the state of Lord Śiva, no action will take place." Ibid.

cement, he has to call [for all] varieties [of things]. That is the means.

JONATHAN: Can there be a joint person? Like if say John and Denise, when they built their house in Kashmir, there were two people acting, or can it be only one person?

SWAMIJI: One person cannot [build a house]. John and Denise cannot do [this by themselves]. There are five [actors].

JONATHAN: No, the means are many.

SWAMIJI: The means [i.e., causes] are five. There are five means responsible for [any given] action. *Adhiṣṭānaṁ* is first, *kartā* (doer) is second, *karaṇaṁ* is the means, varieties of means, this is third, *vividhā ca pṛthak ceṣṭā*, and the activity of going here [and there] to the market, to get hasps and bolts and hinges, and whatever [you need]. You have to do that! You cannot do it yourself, you cannot create [those] yourself, i.e., hinges, etc. You have to ask for hinges from the market. You have to go there [to acquire them]. That is *vividhā ca pṛthakceṣṭā*.[501]

And *daivamevātra pañcamam*, and God's will is the fifth. God's will is the fifth, fifth [cause]. For instance, you construct a house and it is [completed]. [Then] afterwards there is an earthquake and it is smashed down. This is the fifth [cause]. God's will is also responsible for this. If it is not God's will [for it to stand], it will be dashed down, smashed down, it will not stand.

Now there is one ego, the ego that crushes that individual and makes him weep, makes him cry, makes him pound his chest [and say], "I have lost all of my money. What shall I do? It is gone in an earthquake, it is buried down in the ground."

DVD 18a (33:44)

शरीरवाङ्मनोभिर्हि यत्कर्मारभतेऽर्जुन ।
न्याय्यं वा विपरीतं वा पञ्चैते तस्य हेतवः ॥१५॥

śarīravāṅmanobhirhi yatkarmārabhate'rjuna /
nyāyyaṁ vā viparītaṁ vā pañcaite tasya hetavaḥ //15//

---

501 "*Vividhā ca pṛthakceṣṭā,* and ambitions, various ambitions in your mind–that is the fourth actor." *Bhagavad Gītā* (1978).

With ones own body (*śarīra*); *vāk*, with ones own . . . *vāk* means by talk, by talking. He has to talk, for this [activity], he has to talk with [others]. For what? For doing some construction.

Śarīra (body) is also needed; *vāk* means talking; *mano*, thinking how [to construct it], i.e., planning. *Bhirhi yat-karma*, whatever action, *arabhate'rjuna*, [that] one does, O Arjuna, *nyāyyaṁ vā*, it may be with black money or it may be with clean money,[502] *pañcaite tasya hetavaḥ*, jointly these five [causes] are behaving [i.e., are responsible for] this action.

If it is [done] with black money or if it is [done with clean money], that does not matter. That is seen everywhere, i.e., some people use black money, some people use clean money.

Now what one should do in [light of] these five responsibilities, where there are five responsibilities?

DVD 18a (35:33)

तत्रैवंसति कर्तारमात्मानं केवलं तुयः ।
पश्यत्यकृतबुद्धित्वान्न स पश्यति दुर्मतिः ॥ १६ ॥

tatraivaṁsati kartāramātmānaṁ kevalaṁ tuyaḥ /
paśyatyakṛtabuddhitvānna sa paśyati durmatiḥ //16//

Evaṁsati, when this is a fact, what I have placed before you, O Arjuna, and the person who thinks, "I have constructed this house; only I have constructed this house with money, with everything [else], and with everything I have done this, it is my doing," he understands this and he attributes this [activity] to his own person, but he attributes this with ignorance. He ought not to have attributed this to his own person, this kind of doing. *Na sa paśyati*, he has no eyes, he is blind. He is not seeing properly. He thinks that, "I have done it." He should not have thought like this.

Do you understand?

Now, on the contrary, *yasya nāhaṁkṛto bhāva*, the one who

502 "[Whatever] good action or bad action is to be adopted [in any given action] . . . " Ibid.

is Bhairava, who does this [activity] and who behaves *yasya nāhaṁkṛto bhāvo buddhiryasya . . .*

17th, huh?

Do you go through it?

JOHN: Yes.

SWAMIJI: Good.

DVD 18a (37:18)

यस्य नाहंकृतो भावो बुद्धिर्यस्य न लिप्यते ।
हत्वापि स इमाँल्लोकान्न हन्ति न निबध्यते ॥१७॥

yasya nāhaṁkṛto bhāvo buddhiryasya na lipyate /
hatvāpi sa imāṁllokānna hanti na nibaddhyate //17//

The one who has *na ahaṁkṛto bhāva* (*ahaṁkṛto bhāva* means *ahaṁ karomi bhāva*, [feeling that], "I have done it."), this kind of understanding, [the one] who has abandoned this . . .

Which kind of understanding?

DENISE: That I have done something.

SWAMIJI: "I have done this." *Buddhiryasya na lipyate*, and in the end, what happens to him who has got his *ahaṁkṛto bhāva*, [the feeling that], "I have done it"? His intellect gets involved in grief in the end. When, [for example], he has used black money and after he has used too much black money in this connection, in this construction, and the government comes and stops construction altogether. [They tell him], "no, you have no right [to continue this construction]." You are asked to show wherefrom you got this money. [They say], "you are a pauper. How did you construct this house worth fifty crores? Wherefrom you got this money? So stop this construction and give us the details of what you have done, wherefrom your money has come."

So he has to repent at that time. Has he not?

JOHN: This ownership of doing, is this *kārmamala* or *mayīyamala*?

SWAMIJI: No, these are all three *malas*.

JOHN: All three.

SWAMIJI: All three *malas*.[503]

Those who have not this kind of treatment in their understanding, in their actions, *hatvāpi sa imāṁllokān* [verse 17], if he kills the whole country, *na hanti*, he has not killed anybody. *Na lipyate*, nobody will catch him, nobody will put him into imprisonment, because he is God, i.e., [one] who has not this I-ness, I-doing activity (*ahaṁkṛto bhāva*).

This is what you should do, O Arjuna.

---

503 "*Apūrṇaṁ manyatā*, [considering oneself incomplete] is *āṇavamala*." Swami Lakshmanjoo, *Tantrāloka* 9.62 (1977).

"*Āṇavamala* is just a gap, desire, appearance of desire in one's mind." Ibid., 9:96.

"*Āṇavamala* is the cause of differentiated perception." Ibid., 9.88.

"*Āṇavamala* is the root of the other two impurities. Which are those other two impurities? *Māyīyamala* and *kārmamala*. *Kārmamala* is that impurity [that makes you feel], "I am joyous," "oh, I am nothing, I am dead, I am no more existing," "I am sad," "I am beautiful," "I am ugly," "I am healthy," "oh, I am filled with illness, I am sick." This is *kārmamala*. What is *māyīyamala*? "Denise is mine," "this girl is not mine," "this husband is mine," "that man is not mine." What is that? *Māyīyamala*. The root of these two impurities is *āṇavamala*. *Āṇavamala* is just ignorance, pure ignorance of God consciousness." Swami Lakshmanjoo, *Parātriśikā Vivaraṇa* (1982-85).

"When you are shrunk, you are in *āṇavamala*. That state of being shrunk is *āṇavamala*. That is the only definition of *āṇavamala*. Otherwise, *āṇavamala* is created by *svātantrya* of Lord Śiva and *kārmamala* too is created by the *svātantrya* of Lord Śiva. Only *āṇavamala* acts as support, i.e., support that *kārmamala* functions rightly, in its proper way. When a man or human being is shrunk with these two *malas*, [he feels], "this is good fruit," "this is bad fruit," "this good fruit has come for me," "this bad fruit has come for me," and in this way, he enjoys the fruit of his actions (good or bad). And, by that experiencing of these states, he is thrown in many lives, unlimited repeated births and deaths. . . . And so he attributes all this happiness, joy, and pain to his own nature. And by this way, he is thrown in the field of universe." Swami Lakshmanjoo, *Tantrāloka* 9.99-100 (1977). See also *Kashmir Shaivism–The* Secret Supreme 7.47.

DVD 18a (40:07)

ज्ञानं ज्ञेयं परिज्ञाता त्रिविधा कर्मचोदना ।
करणं कर्म कर्तेति त्रिविधः कर्मसंग्रहः ॥१८॥
ज्ञानं कर्म च कर्ता च त्रिधैव गुणभेदतः ।
प्रोच्यते गुणसंख्याने यथावच्छृणु तान्यपि ॥१९॥

jñānaṁ jñeyaṁ parijñātā trividhā karmacodanā /
karaṇaṁ karma karteti trividhaḥ karmasaṁgrahaḥ //18
jñānaṁ karma ca kartā ca tridhaiva guṇabhedataḥ /
procyate guṇasaṁkhyāne yathāvacchṛṇu tānyapi //19//

Now two *ślokas* in one, 18th and 19th.

One is *jñāna* (knowledge).

This *karma codanā* is threefold [and] *karma saṁgrahaḥ* is threefold: *sāttvic*, *rājas*, and *tāmas*. The behavior of action (*karma codanā*) is threefold and the completion of behavior [*karma saṁgrahaḥ*] is threefold: *sāttvic*, *rājas*, and *tāmas*.[504] *Jñānaṁ jñeyaṁ parijñātā*: *jñānaṁ* means knowledge, *jñeyaṁ* means known, *parijñātā* means knower.

So there is *jñāna* threefold: *sāttvic*, *rājas*, and *tāmas*. There is known [which] is also threefold (*jñeya*): *sāttvic*, *rājas*, and *tāmas*. And knower (*parijñātā*) is also threefold: *sāttvic*, *rājas*, and *tāmas*.

And *karaṇa*, *karma*, and *kartā*. *Karaṇaṁ* means the means of action, *karma* means action, *kartā* means doer. These are also threefold: *sāttvic*, *rājas*, and *tāmas*.

And now these: *jñānaṁ*, *jñeyaṁ*, and *parijñātā*, and *karaṇaṁ*, *karma*, and *kartā*. These are explained in three ways.

[First, Lord Kṛṣṇa explains] what is *sāttvic jñāna* (knowledge), what is *sāttvic* known (*jñeyaṁ*), what is *sāttvic* knower (*parijñātā*). [Then He will explain] what is *sāttvic* means (*karaṇaṁ*), what is *sāttvic* action (*karma*), and what is *sāttvic* doer, actor (*kartā*).

504 "*Karma codanā* is just desire, just thinking, [for example], "I'll go to movie; we are planning to go to movie." When you start going that is *karma saṁgrahaḥ*, that is actual, it takes actual shape afterwards." *Bhagavad Gītā* (1978).

DVD 18a (42:51)

ज्ञानं कर्म च कर्ता च त्रिधैव गुणभेदतः ।
प्रोच्यते गुणसंख्याने यथावच्छृणु तान्यपि ॥१९॥

jñānaṁ karma ca kartā ca tridhaiva guṇabhedataḥ /
procyate guṇasaṁkhyāne yathāvacchṛṇu tānyapi //19//
[repeated]

So, this is explained in *guṇa saṁkhyāne*, in the category of the three *guṇas*. I will explain this to you one by one now in the following *ślokas*.

This is the 20th, 21st, and 22nd.

DVD 18a (43:43)

सर्वभूतेषु येनैकं भावमव्ययमीक्षते ।
अविभक्तं विभक्तेषु तज्ज्ञानं विद्धि सात्त्विकम् ॥२०॥

sarvabhūteṣu yenaikaṁ bhāvamavyayamīkṣate /
avibhaktaṁ vibhakteṣu tajjñānaṁ viddhi sāttvikam //20

That knowledge (*jñāna*) is *sāttvic* knowledge, O Arjuna, when [by] this knowledge one understands the same[ness] in each and every individual. *Sarva bhūteṣu yena ekaṁ bhāvam. Īkṣate*, the one who perceives that there is only one mode of knowledge (that knowledge, *avibhaktaṁ vibhakteṣu*), although there are hundreds of individuals and they have [all] got knowledge, but the one who perceives that the knowledge [of] all of these hundreds and thousands of individuals is [only] one [knowledge] arising from God, this is one knowledge arising from one God (*avibhaktaṁ vibhakteṣu*, it is undifferentiated [knowledge] in the differentiated [knowledge of] souls), this knowledge he perceives . . . actually, that knowledge [of] various souls is differentiated, but the *sāttvic* knowledge is that when one perceives that knowledge, although it is differentiated, he sees that this is differentiated knowledge in undifferentiated . . . it is actually undifferentiated [knowledge]. Because all individuals are manifestations of the one Parabhairava, so there is only one knowledge residing everywhere.[505]

JONATHAN: Is that the same as seeing it as coming from one source?

SWAMIJI: One source, yes. So it is *sāttvic* knowledge; it is *sāttvic* knowledge.

DVD 18a (46:18)

पृथक्त्वेन तु यज्ज्ञानं नानाभावान् पृथग्विधान् ।
वेत्ति सर्वेषु भूतेषु तद्राजसमिति स्मृतम् ॥२१॥

pṛthaktvena tu yajjñānaṁ nānābhāvān pṛthagvidhān /
vetti sarveṣu bhūteṣu tadrājasamiti smṛtam //21//

Now, that person who behaves, who sees, who understands this knowledge differentiatedly, who perceives knowledge differentiatedly, this *jñāna* differentiatedly in all beings–*nānābhāvān pṛthak vidhān*, *vetti sarveṣu bhūteṣu*, in each and every individual, he perceives that this knowledge is differentiated, altogether differentiated–that knowledge is called *rājas* knowledge and it has no value. It is not correct knowledge. Correct knowledge is knowledge which is observed in a *sāttvic* mood, *sāttvic* behavior. *Sāttvic* behavior is [when] he sees knowledge as differentiated in undifferentiatedness. The one who sees differentiated knowledge in all different beings, it is incorrect knowledge. So it has no value.

Now the knowledge which is derived from *tamaguṇa*. What is that?

DVD 18a (48:04)

यत्तु कृत्स्नवदेकस्मिन्कार्ये सक्तमहेतुकम् ।
अतत्त्वार्थवदल्पं च तत्तामसमुदाहृतम् ॥२२॥

505 "You must understand, you'll know that *avyayam bhāvam*, that imperishable state of God consciousness is residing in each and every being. . . . In that way you won't hate anybody. If you hate anybody, it means you don't find the state of God consciousness in that person. If you ever found that the state of God consciousness is in that person, you'd never hate him." Ibid.

yattu kṛtsnavadekasminkārye saktamahetukam /
atattvārthavadalpaṁ ca tattāmasamudāhṛtam //22//

Yattu kṛtsnavad ekasmin kārye, and that knowledge which he puts in one point, *ekasmin kārye*, in one thing to be done, e.g., "this is to be done, this is to be fixed, this watch is to be fixed," and he sees . . . he goes on opening it and fixing it but with no results. He goes on . . . he calls another watchmaker and asks for his opinion: "what to do with this watch? It is a very costly watch but it cannot be fixed. I cannot fix it. Can you understand how you can fix it?"

"No, I have no knowledge." He says, "no, I have no knowledge of fixing this."

So they do this job uselessly, uselessly trying, and this is a waste of time. It is a waste of time. And they give it [back] to Jonathan [and say], "return this [watch], no it cannot be [repaired]." And then [Jonathan] gives this watch to S.P. Dhar [saying], "it is nice but [laughs] it cannot be fixed. If it is [so] nice, why don't you fix it?"

That is *tāmas*. That is the *tāmas* action and that has no value.[506]

DVD 18a (50:06)

नियतं सङ्गरहितमरागद्वेषतः कृतम् ।
अफलप्रेप्सुना कर्म यत्तत्सात्त्विकमुच्यते ॥२३॥

niyataṁ saṅgarahitamarāgadveṣataḥ kṛtam /
aphalaprepsunā karma yattatsāttvikamucyate //23//

[Whatever] the *śāstras* have [prescribed] . . .

This is the 23rd *śloka*?

JOHN: Yes, Sir.

SWAMIJI: Whatever the *śāstras* have ordered us [how] to

506 "That is *kṛtsnavat ekasmin kārye*, he will give all his power to one [job], which his master has told him to do . . . and he will neglect all other things. . . . This kind of knowledge which he utilizes, is called *tamaguṇa*." *Bhagavad Gītā* (1978).

behave, you should do that action, *saṅgarahitam*, without being attached to that action. *Arāgadveṣataḥ kṛtam*, and *rāga* and *dveṣa*, attachment and hatred, you should discard while doing this action. *Aphalaprepsunā*, and you should not behave [i.e., seek] how to get fruits out of it. You should not think of fruits, any [fruits from] this action. That action is *sāttvic* action.

Yattu kāmepsunā karma . . . now *rājas* action.

DVD 18a (51:14)

यत्तु कामेप्सुना कर्म साहंकारेण वा पुनः ।
क्रियते क्लेशबहुलं तद्राजसमिति स्मृतम् ॥२४॥

yattu kāmepsunā karma sāhaṁkāreṇa vā punaḥ /
kriyate kleśabahulaṁ tadrājasamiti smṛtam //24//

Yattu kāmepsunā, that action which is done with desires, various desires and thoughts and ambitions, *sāhaṁ kāreṇa*, and putting I-ness in that that, "I am doing this job for such and such profit," *kriyate kleśa bahulaṁ*, and he puts all [kinds] of effort in that [desire for achieving] success [in] doing that computer's work . . .

> How much you tried your best to do it, but it was, in the long run, it was for realizing the truth of God, so it was divine.[507] Otherwise, if it would have been for satisfying [your] nature with songs and dancing, then it would have been *rājas* [action].

JONATHAN: But Swamiji, can I ask one question here? If you do some work, sometime, but you have the desire to get money to be able to live . . .

SWAMIJI: Huh?

JONATHAN: Sometimes if you do work, you have some desire to get a reward for that. Because you are doing some employment because you need money to live.

---

507 Swamiji is referring to the computer business which John had started in the USA. [*Editor's note*]

SWAMIJI: Yes. That is fine.
JONATHAN: That could be *sāttvic*?
SWAMIJI: Yes, that is accepted. That is accepted.
JONATHAN: Or to look after your family, that's okay?
SWAMIJI: Yes.
JONATHAN: The desire is there to make your family comfortable.
SWAMIJI: Yes, that is good, that is good.
JOHN: Because that's *dharma*?
SWAMIJI: Then that is *dharma*, yes. That is your duty. [But] not collecting more money for nothing, to just . . . just to keep in the World Bank. What for?
JONATHAN: Because you said, "to possess more than you need in this lifetime is a sin."
SWAMIJI: Yes.
Twenty-fifth.

DVD 18a (53:46)

अनुबन्धं क्षयं हिंसामनवेक्ष्य च पौरुषम् ।
मोहादारभ्यते कर्म यत्तत्तामसमुच्यते ॥२५॥

anubandhaṁ kṣayaṁ hiṁsāmanavekṣya ca pauruṣam /
mohādārabhyate karma yattattāmasamucyate //25//

[*Anubandhaṁ*], what will be the fruit of this action? *Kṣayaṁ*, [will] anybody get harmed by this action? *Hiṁsām anavekṣya*, and [will] anybody get slaughtered by this action? And [*anavekṣya ca pauruṣam*], are you capable of doing this [action]?

While asking [him these questions], he [replies], "I am capable of doing this!" And he thrusts–without understanding–he thrusts into that job.[508] *Yattat tāmasam ucyate*, to indulge in that job [in this manner] is *tāmas*.

This was the 25th *śloka*.

From the 26th *śloka*, there is [explanation of] *kartā*, which means the doer: *sāttvic* doer, *rājas* doer, and *tāmas* doer.

---

508 Without understanding the job itself nor its effects. [*Editor's note*]

DVD 18a (55:16)

मुक्तसङ्गोऽनहंवादी धृत्युत्साहसमन्वितः ।
सिद्ध्यसिद्ध्योर्निर्विकारः कर्ता सात्त्विक उच्यते ॥२६॥

muktasaṅgo'nahaṁvādī dhṛtyutsāhasamanvitaḥ /
siddhyasiddhyornirvikāraḥ kartā sāttvika ucyate //26//

Muktasaṅga, who is not attached to whatever action he does, he is not attached to it. *Anahaṁ vādī*, and he does not believe that, "I have done this" [or] "I am doing this." *Dhṛti utsāha samanvitaḥ*, he has got courage, he has got tolerance and courage. He does his work with tolerance and courage. And he is not moved if that work is fulfilled or if that work remains unfulfilled. In these both ways, he remains the same. And this way of doer is called *sāttvic* doer. And he is on the right path; this way of doing is the right way of doing.

DVD 18a (56:42)

रागी कर्मफलप्रेप्सुर्लुब्धो हिंसात्मकोऽशुचिः ।
हर्षशोकान्वितः कर्ता राजसः परिकीर्त्यते ॥२७॥

rāgī karmaphalaprepsurlubdho hiṁsātmako'śuciḥ /
harṣaśokānvitaḥ kartā rājasaḥ parikīrtyate //27//

[The *rājas* doer is] *rāgī*, who has got attachment for that work; *karma phala-prepsur*, who always craves and longs for its fruit; *lubdho*, he has too much greed; *hiṁsātmaka*, he does not mind if somebody is harmed by [his] doing. [He feels], "let him be harmed. I must get its fruit." *Aśuciḥ*, and his behavior is dirty [i.e., impure]; *harṣaśokānvitaḥ*, he is always with *harṣa* means happiness and *śoka* is grief; happiness and grief are absolutely at his disposal. If he has done . . . if he is successful in his doing [something], he is happy; if he is not successful, he is filled with grief. This way of doer is called *rājas* doer and it has no value.

Now the doer of action in *tāmasa* state.

DVD 18a (58:14)

अयुक्तः प्राकृतः स्तब्धः शठो नैकृतिकोऽलसः ।
विषादी दीर्घसूत्रश्च कर्ता तामस उच्यते ॥२८॥

ayuktaḥ prākṛtaḥ stabdhaḥ śaṭho naikṛtiko'lasaḥ /
viṣādī dīrghasūtraśca kartā tāmasa ucyate //28//

Ayuktaḥ, who does not know how to do this action [and] who is not truly doing actions with good behavior. *Prākṛtaḥ*, he does not listen to anybody's suggestion that, "this way you should do it." [He replies], "no, no, no, I don't like your suggestion, I know how to do it." That is *prākṛtaḥ*, he depends upon his own [limited] understanding. *Stabdhaḥ* (*stabdhaḥ* means he is unmoved by others suggestions). *Śaṭha*, he is *śaṭha* (*śaṭha* means he is internally rigid[509]). *Naikṛtika* (*naikṛtika* [means] he has no compassion for others[510]). *Alasaḥ* (*alasaḥ* means he is always sluggish). *Viṣādī*, he is always repenting [afterwards], "I have done it wrongly." *Dīrgha sūtraśca*, and his [activity] takes more [time] than anything in this world, more time. [If] he can do that work of half an hour, it will take him at least fifteen days to complete it.

This way of doer is called *tāmas* doer.

This [was] the 28th *śloka*.

DVD 18a (1:00:30)

बुद्धेर्भेदं धृतेश्चैव गुणतस्त्रिविधं शृणु ।
प्रोच्यमानमशेषेण पृथक्त्वेन धनञ्जय ॥२९॥

buddherbhedaṁ dhṛteścaiva guṇatastrividhaṁ śṛṇu /
procyamānamaśeṣeṇa pṛthaktvena dhanañjaya //29//

Buddher bhedaṁ, the three ways of intellectual under-

509 "*Saṭha* is just centered in his own way of action." *Bhagavad Gītā* (1978).

510 "*Naikṛtika* means he has no humility. He has no humility for others." Ibid.

standing, three ways [are]: the *sāttvic* way of intellectual understanding, the *rājas* way of intellectual understanding, and the *tāmas* way of intellectual understanding. And *dhṛteś*, courage also [is threefold]: *tāmas* courage, *sāttvic* courage and . . . *sāttvic* courage, *rājas* courage, and *tāmas* courage. Courage also is threefold, *guṇata*, according to the three *guṇas*. *Śṛṇu*, you hear from Me.

Procyamānamaśeṣeṇa pṛthaktvena dhanañjaya.

It is the 29th *śloka* ending.

Now He will relate three intellectual ways and three courages.

JOHN: Ways of courage.

SWAMIJI: Huh?

JOHN: Kinds of courage.

SWAMIJI: Kinds of courage. Courage of three kinds and intellectual understanding of three kinds. *Pravṛttiṁ*, that He explains in the 30th *śloka*, 31st *śloka*, and 32nd *śloka*. This is the intellectual understanding of three kinds and courage of three kinds. In the 33rd *śloka* is the *sāttvic* courage, in 34th *śloka* is the *rājas* courage, and in 35th *śloka* is the *tāmas* courage.

Bas.

Up to 35th [*śloka*], I will explain it.

What was the first?

JOHN: *Pravṛttiṁ* . . .

SWAMIJI:

DVD 18a (1:03:05)

प्रवृत्तिं च निवृत्तिं च कार्याकार्ये भयाभये ।
बन्धं मोक्षं च या बुद्धिर्वेद सा सात्त्विकी मता ॥३०॥

pravṛttiṁ ca nivṛttiṁ ca kāryākārye bhayābhaye /
bandhaṁ mokṣaṁ ca yā buddhirveda sā sāttvikī matā //30

O Arjuna, *pravrittiṁ*, wherefrom I should . . . what I should act, on which [task] should I act? *Nivṛttiṁ ca*, from which [action] I should walk out, I should leave? *Kāryākārye*, what is worth doing and what is not worth doing? *Bhayābhaye*, in which doing [i.e., activity] is there fear and in which doing is there not fear? Where is bondage and where is liberation? This way, the intellectual understanding, that intellectual understanding is called *sāttvika*, the *sāttvic* way of understanding, intellectual understanding.

Do you understand?

JONATHAN: Not clearly.

SWAMIJI: No, the *sāttvic* intellectual understanding discriminates [between] all of these things. Before going into this, before jumping into [action, this] intellectual understanding, this *sāttvic* understanding . . .

[gap in recording]

. . . [discriminates between] which [action] I should do and which [action] I should not do. What is worth doing and what is not worth doing? Where is the bondage, i.e., where I will be bound and where I will be free? This way of understanding, that *buddhi* (intellect) makes him understand. That is *sāttvika buddhiḥ*.

Now there is the *rājas* intellectual understanding. *Rājas* intellectual understanding:

DVD 18a (1:05:22)

यया धर्ममधर्मं च कार्यं चाकार्यमेव च ।
अयथावत् प्रजानाति बुद्धिः सा पार्थ राजसी ॥३१॥

yayā dharmamadharmaṁ ca kāryaṁ cākāryameva ca /
ayathāvat prajānāti buddhiḥ sā pārtha rājasī //31//

O Arjuna, that intellectual understanding is called *rājasī* understanding, by which understanding he comes to this conclusion, he understands *dharma* as *adharma*.[511] In fact, [for him], that [*adharma*] is *dharma*; in fact, it is *dharma*. What is *dharma*? [What] he understands as *dharma*, it is not *dharma*, it is opposite to that [i.e., *adharma*].

What is worth doing and what is not worth doing?

What is worth doing, he understands by this intellectual,

511 *Dharma* means virtue and *adharma* means sin. [*Editor's note*]

rājas intellectual power, [the thing that] is worth doing [i.e., *dharma*], he thinks by his *buddhi* (intellect) that it is not worth doing [i.e., *adharma*]. And that which is actually worth doing . . . that actually which is not worth doing, he [comes to the] conclusion that it is worth doing. [That which is] not worth doing is opposite [for him] . . . he understands this in an opposite way. And it is a sin, it is a sinful act. It will be a sinful act, and [he thinks that] it is a pure act. Pure act he understands, it as a sinful act, and sinful act he understands, it as a pure act. This kind of understanding is called *rājas* understanding.

And now the *tāmas* understanding.

DVD 18a (1:07:26)

अधर्मं धर्ममिति या बुध्यते तमसान्विता ।
सर्वार्थान्विपरीतांश्च बुद्धिः सा तामसी मता ॥३२॥

adharmaṁ dharmamiti yā buddhyate tamasānvitā /
sarvārthānviparītāmśca buddhiḥ sā tāmasī matā //32//

But he . . . *tāmasī* understanding is [that] he cannot understand what is wrong and what is right. His intellect cannot understand, cannot conclude anything. *Bas*, he jumps [into activity] without any understanding, and he is ruined.

JONATHAN: Is that also the person that can't make up his mind about anything?

SWAMIJI: No, he has nothing [i.e., no understanding].

JONATHAN: But if you ask him something, he says, "I don't know."

SWAMIJI: Yes, he is stuck.

Now is courage now, threefold courage. First is *sāttvic* courage, second is *rājas* courage, and the third is *tāmas* courage.

DVD 18a (1:08:28)

धृत्या यया धारयते मनः प्राणेन्द्रियक्रियाः ।
योगेनाव्यभिचारिण्या धृतिः सा सात्त्विकी मता ॥३३

dhṛtyā yayā dhārayate manaḥ prāṇendriyakriyāḥ /
yogenāvyabhicāriṇyā dhṛtiḥ sā sāttvikī matā //33//

O Arjuna, that courage is *sāttvikī* courage by which courage he controls his mind, he controls his breath, and he controls all of his senses, and by adopting one-pointed *yoga*. That courage is called *sāttvikī* courage. It is always successful.

Now *rājasi* courage is defined in the 34th *śloka*. And *tāmas* courage is defined in 35th *śloka*.

DVD 18a (1:09:22)

यया तु धर्मकामार्थान्धृत्या धारयतेऽर्जुन ।
प्रसङ्गेन फलाकाङ्क्षी धृतिः सा पार्थ राजसी ॥३४॥

yayā tu dharmakāmārthāndhṛtyā dhārayate'rjuna /
prasaṅgena phalākāṅkṣī dhṛtiḥ sā pārtha rājasī //34//

O Arjuna, that courage is called *rājasī* courage, by which courage, *dharma*, *kāma*, *artha* . . . he does everything, he has got courage only to make money, to do good deeds for [making] money, and for [the sake of] pleasures, and this is his courage, and that courage is called *rājasī* courage and it has no value.

And *tāmasī* courage. *Tāmasī* courage is that courage by which courage one cannot . . .

DVD 18a (1:10:30)

यया स्वप्नं भयं शोकं विषादं मोहमेव च ।
न विमुञ्चति दुर्मेधा धृतिः सा तामसी मता ॥३५॥

yayā svapnaṁ bhayaṁ śokaṁ viṣādaṁ mohaneva ca /
na vimuñcati durmedhā dhṛtiḥ sā tāmasī matā //35//

. . . by which courage he cannot remain away from dreams, he cannot remain away from fear, he cannot remain away from grief, *śokam viṣādaṁ*, and he cannot remain away from *mohaṁ* (ignorance). So he wants to indulge in dreaming state and [remain in] ignorance and yawning and everything. This is his courage. He has courage only to have this. He does not care for anything else in this world. That courage is called *tāmasī* courage. He will never come out from dreams. He will sleep this way . . . if he is called by his mother or father, "get up! it is time for tea," [he responds lazily], "*ahhh*" [laughs], and he will lie down [again] in another way, and [then in] another way. And [after] all have taken tea, he is [still] stuck there [sleeping].

This way is this courage which is called *tāmas* courage, and it has no sense.

JOHN: Is daydreaming the same thing, daydreaming?

SWAMIJI: Huh?

JOHN: Daydreaming, when you are just sitting with your eyes open, and dreaming this, dreaming that. There are people who daydream a lot.

SWAMIJI: No. Daydreaming is . . . it has nothing to do with daydreaming.

DENISE: So they dream, they keep sleeping and dreaming to escape their life, don't they? It's an escape.

SWAMIJI: Yes, they escape . . . they escape. They think that this is very tasty. What is tasty?

JOHN: This dream.

DENISE: This dream.

SWAMIJI: Yes, to sleep is tastier than having tea.

DENISE: Isn't that true also with people who drink alcohol and take drugs?

SWAMIJI: Yes, yes.

DENISE: They do that because they can't tolerate life. They are escaping.

SWAMIJI: Yes, they also remain . . . they are escaping.

DENISE: And they are enjoying in their own way.

Chapter 18 Part 2

SWAMIJI:

DVD 18b (00:01)

सुखं त्विदानीं त्रिविधं श्रृणु मे भरतर्षभ ।
अभ्यासाद्रमते यत्र दुःखान्तं च नियच्छति ॥ ३६ ॥

sukhaṁ tvidānīṁ trividhaṁ śṛṇu me bharatarṣabha /
abhyāsādramate yatra duḥkhāntaṁ ca niyacchati //36//

I will tell you now *sukha*, what is *sukha*. *Sukha* is also three fold: *sāttvic sukha*, *rājas sukha*, and *tāmas sukha*. I mean happiness, joy.

Now the 37th *śloka* is explaining *sukha* of *sāttvic* [kind].

DVD 18b (00:39)

यत्तदात्वे विषमिव परिणामेऽमृतोपमम् ।
तत्सुखं सात्त्विकं विद्यादात्मबुद्धिप्रसादजम् ॥ ३७ ॥

yattadātve viṣamiva pariṇāme'mṛtopamam /
tatsukhaṁ sāttvikaṁ vidyādātmabuddhiprasādajam //37

Yattadātve, that *sukha* (joy) which, in the beginning, seems to be *viṣamiva*, just like poison; in the beginning it seems just poisonous.

For instance, when mother wakes him, wakes Viresh up with force, and asks Viresh (after [all], Viresh is also in my circle, he has come into my circle) that, "Swamiji is calling you. He wants that you should sit for meditation." At first, he thinks *viṣamiva*, it is very dreadful . . .

DENISE: [laughs]

SWAMIJI: . . . it is very dreadful to wake up [early to

meditate]. And when once he is awake, at that time, at the time of doing practice afterwards when he is [meditating] in front of me, *pariṇāme amṛta upamam*, at that time he feels the blissful state, at that time.

That *sukha* is *sāttvic sukha*, you should understand that is *sāttvic sukha*. In the first beginning, [*abhyāsa*] seems very dreadful, it seems poisonous.

JOHN: *Sāttvic sukha*?

SWAMIJI: *Sāttvic sukha*. At first it seems poisonous, but when he has conducted this *sāttvic sukha* of *abhyāsa* and meditation, he feels just blissful.

DENISE: Why is that? Is that because he feels so much sweetness within himself that he doesn't want to go out and get some other sweetness?

SWAMIJI: No. It is just an examination for him, if he wakes up or not.

DENISE: Aha!

SWAMIJI: If you are fortunate, you'll wake up; you will wake up and you will throw [the bedding off] just like it's *shikas* (rubbish), and [you will] be situated in God consciousness, and you will remain blissful. That is *sāttvic sukha*.

JOHN: So, in the first instance, spirituality seems to be really . . .

SWAMIJI: Yes, really not good.

DENISE: Undesirable.

SWAMIJI: Undesirable. It is very painful.

DENISE: Painful.

SWAMIJI: Painful.

JOHN: Frightening also?

SWAMIJI: Yes. That is *sāttvic sukha* (joy).

DENISE: So Swamiji, you're talking about spiritual joy? You're not talking about pleasures in the world? You're talking about spiritual joy?

SWAMIJI: Yes, spiritual joy.

Tadātve means *abhyāsakāle* [comm. verse 37], at that time, [*abhyāsa*] seems very fearful.[512]

512 "For instance, I am meditating, I meditate for half an hour. After half an hours time, I want to lean, I want to lean and medi-

kṣurasya dhārā viṣamā duratyayā /
durgaṁpadhastat kavayo vadanti [513]

[Abhinavagupta] has given [this] example in his commentary. *Kṣurasya dhārā viṣamā duratyayā*, this pathway of spiritual bliss, blissful pathway, is to tread on the swords edge; to walk [the spiritual path], this is *viṣamā duratyayā*, it is not easily conducted. *Durgaṁ paddhas tat kavayo*, it is very difficult to tread on, but once you are on it, then it is filled with spiritual joy.

Now the joy of *rājas* joy, *rājas sukha*.

DVD 18b (05:14)

षियेन्द्रियसंयोगाद्यत्तदात्वेऽमृतोपमम् ।
परिणामे विषमिव तद्राजसमिति स्मृतम् ॥३८॥

viṣayendriyasaṁyogādyattadātve'mṛtopamam /
pariṇāme viṣamiva tadrājasamiti smṛtam //38//

When *viṣaya* (*viṣaya* means sensual objects and your organs), [when] your organs are behaving [i.e., in contact] with sensual objects, at the time, at the beginning of [that] time when your sensual objects are behaving with . . . [when] your organs are behaving with sensual objects, it seems very peaceful, very joyous. For instance, you have to go to some picture and you are so happy. Viresh also dresses himself nicely, you also dress, everybody dresses, and you go and arrange for a car, arrange for a taxi and you go there. And then Viresh says after half an hour, "Daddy, we want to go, we are tired [laughs]. We want to go home."

---

tate. After half an hours time I will sit in easy chair and meditate. It means it is poisonous. It [feels] like poison to you. At the time it [feels like] poison, not leaning against a wall or not relaxing in easy chair is poisonous for you. You don't want to sit [erect]. If you just have courage to sit for some [longer] period without leaning against wall, you'll see what kind of joy you'll achieve. That is *sāttvic sukha*." *Bhagavad Gītā* (1978).

513 Verse from the *Kaṭha Upaniṣad*.

DENISE: Go home, again.

SWAMIJI: Yes, go home again. You only [see] half . . . the picture is only halfway finished and you then [return home] and you come [to see me] and I ask you, "why have you returned so [soon]?"

"Oh, it was *bakwas* [laughs]. It was *bakwas*, it had no understanding. It was only a waste of time."

This is the joy of . . .

DENISE: *Rājas.*

SWAMIJI: . . . *rājas*, *rājas* joy.

JOHN: What does that mean? It means it's fleeting joy? This *rājas* joy means fleeting joy, temporary joy?

SWAMIJI: Temporary joy.

DENISE: This is very common in children. They get so excited about doing something and it's almost always a disappointment once they do it.

SWAMIJI: Yes. [Afterwards they say], "I don't like it."

DENISE: Yes.

SWAMIJI: "Mommy, I don't like it, I will go. I have to do schoolwork."

Now *sukha*, *tāmas sukha*.

DVD 18b (07:49)

यदग्रे चानुबन्धे च सुखं मोहनमात्मनः ।
निद्रालस्यप्रमादोत्थं तत्तामसमुदाहृतम् ॥३९॥

yadagre cānubandhe ca sukhaṁ mohanamātmanaḥ /
nidrālasyapramādotthaṁ tattāmasamudāhṛtam //39

[*Tāmas sukha*] is the *sukha* (joy), which, in the beginning and in the end and in the center, puts you in an unconscious state; *mohanam ātmanaḥ,* you forget all of your activities and it is derived from *nidrā* (*nidrā* means sleeping), *alasya* means sluggishness, [and] *pramāda* is forgetfulness. This kind of *sukha* is called *tāmas sukha*.

DVD 18b (08:50)

न तदस्ति पृथिव्यां वा दिवि देवेषु वा पुनः ।
सत्त्वं प्रकृतिजैर्मुक्तं यदेभिः स्यात्त्रिभिर्गुणैः ॥४०॥

na tadasti pṛthivyāṁ vā divi deveṣu vā punaḥ /
sattvaṁ prakṛtijairmuktaṁ yadebhiḥ syāttribhirguṇaiḥ 40

You cannot find any living being in this world, in this gross world of earth, earthly world (for instance, in this so called world, *divi),* in *deveṣu*, [nor] in heavens also, you cannot find any individual, either in this world or in heavens, who has escaped from the *guṇas* of *prakṛti*, from these *guṇas* of *prakṛti*, who is not entangled by the *guṇas* of *prakṛti*. Everybody is entangled by the *guṇas* of *prakṛti*! Neither will you find [anybody] liberated from these pangs of the jaws of *prakṛti* in this world or in the upper worlds.

Ā brahmaṇaśca kīṭāntaṁ . . .

He says in this commentary, Abhinavagupta, [in] that small *śloka*:

ā brahmaṇaśca kīṭāntaṁ na kaścittattvataḥ sukhī /
karoti vikṛtistāstāḥ sarva eva jijīviṣuḥ //

Right from Brahmā up to *kīṭāntaṁ*, up to a worm, a neglected worm, *na kaścit tattvataḥ sukhī*, nobody will you see [who is] established in a peaceful state. *Karoti tāstāḥ vikṛti*, and you will see everybody is striving and [going] this way and that way to escape from death, from old age, and from repeated births and deaths. Everybody is striving for that. And nobody has escaped [this struggle] in this world or in the upper worlds also. These three *guṇas* have caught them through their *prakṛti*, through the *śakti*, *māya śakti*, that is *svātantrya śakti* of Parabhairava.

DVD 18b (12:00)

ब्राह्मणक्षत्रियविशां शूद्राणां च परन्तप ।
कर्माणि प्रविभक्तानि स्वभावप्रभवैर्गुणैः ॥४१॥
शमो दमस्तथा शौचं क्षान्तिरार्जवमेव च ।
ज्ञानं विज्ञानमास्तिक्यं ब्राह्मं कर्म स्वभावजम् ॥४२॥

शौर्यं तेजो धृतिर्दाक्ष्यं युद्धे चाप्यपलायनम् ।
दानमीश्वरभावश्च क्षात्रं कर्म स्वभावजम् ॥४३॥
कृषिगोरक्ष्यवाणिज्यं वैश्यकर्म स्वभावजम् ।
पर्युत्थानात्मकं कर्म शूद्रस्यापि स्वभावजम् ॥४४॥

brāhmaṇakṣatriyaviśāṁ śūdrāṇāṁ ca parantapa /
karmāṇi pravibhaktāni svabhāvaprabhavairguṇaiḥ //41//
śamo damastathā śaucaṁ kṣāntirārjavameva ca /
jñānaṁ vijñānamāstikyaṁ brāhmaṁ karma svabhāvajam 42
śauryaṁ tejo dhṛtirdākṣyaṁ yuddhe cāpyapalāyanam /
dānamīśvarabhāvaśca kṣātraṁ karma svabhāvajam //43//
kṛṣigorakṣyavāṇijyaṁ vaiśyakarma svabhāvajam /
paryutthānātmakaṁ karma śūdrasyāpi svabhāvajam //44

Bas, these four, up to the 44th *śloka*: 41st, 42nd, 43rd, and 44th. In these four *ślokas*, He says, "*brāhmaṇa kṣatriya viśāṁ śūdrāṇāṁ ca parantapa.*" There are four classes of living beings: one class is of brahmin, second class is of kṣatriya, *viśāṁ* means third class is vaiśyas, and fourth class is śūdrās. *Karmāṇi pravibhaktāni*, they have . . . their [manner] of doing actions is *pravibhaktāni*, differentiated according to their qualifications; according to their qualifications, not according to their birth.

Now He says what is the qualification of being a brahmin; what is the qualification of a brahmin, and what is the qualification of a kṣatriya, what is the qualification of a vaiśya, and what is the qualification of śūdrās. It is not qualification through birth. It is qualification through qualities; the qualities, which you will find . . . qualities of brahmin you can find in Mohammedans, [so] he is brahmin. This way.

DVD 18b (14:32)

शमो दमस्तथा शौचं क्षान्तिरार्जवमेव च ।
ज्ञानं विज्ञानमास्तिक्यं ब्राह्मं कर्म स्वभावजम् ॥४२॥

śamo damastathā śaucaṁ kṣāntirārjavameva ca /
jñānaṁ vijñānamāstikyaṁ brāhmaṁ karma svabhāvajam 42

This is the *prakṛti* (nature) of brahmin. *Prakṛti* of *brāhmaṇa* [is] *śama* (*śama* means to control sensual senses), *dama*, to control breath (controlling of breath), *śaucaṁ*, to be purified (always to be pure in actions), *kṣāntir*, to have tolerance, *ārjavam*, to be very straightforward (being straightforward), *jñānaṁ*, [having] knowledge of books [i.e., *śāstras*], *vijñānam*, to have knowledge of Self, *astikyaṁ*, and being *astikyaṁ*, [one] who is God-fearing (being God-fearing).

Brāhmaṁ karma svabhāvajam. This is, according to qualifications, this is called brahmin *karma*. He is actually a brahmin. [Even] if he is from another cast [and he posseses these qualities], he is a brahmin.

Now, who is kṣatriya?

DVD 18b (16:00)

शौर्यं तेजो धृतिर्दाक्ष्यं युद्धे चाप्यपलायनम् ।
दानमीश्वरभावश्च क्षात्रं कर्म स्वभावजम् ॥४३॥

śauryaṁ tejo dhṛtirdākṣyaṁ yuddhe cāpyapalāyanam /
dānamīśvarabhāvaśca kṣātraṁ karma svabhāvajam //43//

Śauryaṁ, who has got *śurita* (*śurita* means [one] who is strong), who has got the strength of becoming robust (*śauryaṁ*)[514], *tejas*, who has got brilliant power of light[515], *dhṛtir*, who has got courage, *dākṣyaṁ* means who has got wits (who never loses his wits)[516], *yuddhe cāpyapalāyanam*, and who does not walk out from war (who is not afraid of war), *dānam*, who has got the nature to give (to feed people), *īśvara bhāvaśca*, and who has got tendency of thinking of God, believing that God is great, He has created us. *Kṣātraṁ*

514 Swamiji previously translated *śauryaṁ* as heroic. [*Editor's note*]
515 Swamiji previously translated *teja* as the splendor of being heroic. [*Editor's note*]
516 Swamiji previously translated *dakṣyaṁ* as skill or cleverness. [*Editor's note*]

karma svabhāvajam, this is naturally the *karma* of kṣatriyas. It is their nature.

DVD 18b (17:33)

कृषिगोरक्ष्यवाणिज्यं वैश्यकर्म स्वभावजम् ।
पर्युत्थानात्मकं कर्म शूद्रस्यापि स्वभावजम् ॥ ४४ ॥

kṛṣigorakṣyavāṇijyaṁ vaiśyakarma svabhāvajam /
paryutthānātmakaṁ karma śūdrasyāpi svabhāvajam //44

Vaiśyas. Vaiśyas action is *kṛṣi gorakṣya vāṇijyaṁ*, to keep cows, to make lands (i.e., to be landlords), and *vāṇijyaṁ*, to indulge in trade, business. *Vaiśya karma svabhāvajam*, this is the nature of vaiśyas. He is also the same in doing things in the same category [as brahmins and kṣatriyas], i.e., he is not away from the God-fearing state.

Paryutthānātmakaṁ karma śūdrasyāpi svabhāvajam. And *paryutthāna ātmakaṁ karma* means to serve all of the [above] three [classes], all of these three. The serving tendency to serve all of these three is by nature, by *prakṛti*, the nature of śūdras.

Sve sve karmaṇyabhirataḥ . . .

Now 45th *śloka*, 46th *śloka*, 47th *śloka*, and onwards.

DVD 18b (19:14)

स्वे स्वे कर्मण्यभिरतः संसिद्धिं लभते नरः ।
स्वकर्मनिरतः सिद्धिं यथा विन्दति तच्छृणु ॥ ४५ ॥
यतः प्रवृत्तिर्भूतानां येन विश्वमिदं ततम् ।
स्वकर्मणा तमभ्यर्च्य सिद्धिं विन्दति मानवः ॥ ४६ ॥

sve sve karmaṇyabhirataḥ saṁsiddhiṁ labhate naraḥ /
svakarmanirataḥ siddhiṁ yathā vindati tacchṛṇu //45//
yataḥ pravṛttirbhūtānāṁ yena viśvamidaṁ tatam /
svakarmaṇā tamabhyarcya siddhiṁ vindati mānavaḥ 46

Sve sve karmaṇya abhirataḥ, you should always go on

doing your own work in which you are situated. If you are brahmin, you are a brahmin, you have to do brahmin *karmas* (actions) and you will be successful in the end.

Svakarmanirataḥ siddhiṁ, so everybody should do [their] own way of acting [according to their qualities]. If he is kṣatriya (warrior), he should do kṣatriyas work; if he is vaiśya (industry, business), he should do vaiśyas work; if he is śūdrā (servant), he should do śūdrās work. All of these four sections are God-fearing sections. You should not think that I am inferior to brahmins. Kṣatriya should not think that I am inferior to brahmins; vaiśya should not think that I am inferior to kṣatriyas; śūdra should not think that I am inferior to vaiśyas. You should think that, "I am God's creation, I am fine, I am fine in my own way, and I will become *jīvan mukta* (liberated) in this way."

DENISE: Also, Swamiji, not to think that you are superior, e.g., if you are a brahmin, that you are superior to the rest.

SWAMIJI: [shakes head in affirmation]

DVD 18b (21:08)

यतः प्रवृत्तिर्भूतानां येन विश्वमिदं ततम् ।
स्वकर्मणा तमभ्यर्च्य सिद्धिं विन्दति मानवः ॥४६॥

yataḥ pravṛttirbhūtānāṁ yena viśvamidaṁ tatam /
svakarmaṇā tamabhyarcya siddhiṁ vindati mānavaḥ 46

All of these four sections of people should think that the One who has created us, the One (Parabhairava) who has created us, *yena viśvam idaṁ tattam*, and who has established this manifestation in its glamorous way . . .[517]

Svakarmaṇā tamabhyarcya, by doing, by indulging in your own efforts [according to] your own environment, you will rise, you will reach at the feet of your Lord Parabhairava.

517 "No matter if you are placed as brahmin or kṣatriya or vaiśya or śūdra, you must adore Him. You must adore that Lord who has created this whole universe and who has pervaded this whole universe. And then you will achieve the perfection of God consciousness." *Bhagavad Gītā* (1978).

DVD 18b (22:08)

श्रेयान्स्वधर्मो विगुणः परधर्मात्स्वनुष्ठितात् ।
स्वभावनियतं कर्म कुर्वन्नाप्नोति किल्विषम् ॥४७॥

śreyānsvadharmo viguṇaḥ paradharmātsvanuṣṭhitāt /
svabhāvaniyataṁ karma kurvannāpnoti kilviṣaṁ //47//

It is best to live in your own way of *dharma*. If you are kṣatriya [by qualities], do as kṣatriya has to do work. Don't crave for doing *brāhmaṇas* work at that point. You have been posted on this seat of kṣatriya, [or] you have been posted on vaiśya, [or] you have been posted on śūdrā. But the posting managing committee has come from Parabhairava. You should indulge in your own work and *tamabhyarcya* [verse 46], you should think of Parabhairava in [your activities] always. *Siddhiṁ vindati mānavaḥ*, you will get its reward in the long run; in its proper time, you will get its reward, you will achieve its reward.

DVD 18b (23:22)

श्रेयान्स्वधर्मो विगुणः परधर्मात्स्वनुष्ठितात् ।
स्वभावनियतं कर्म कुर्वन्नाप्नोति किल्विषम् ॥४७॥
सहजं कर्म कौन्तेय सदोषमपि न त्यजेत् ।
सर्वारम्भा हि दोषेण धूमेनाग्निरिवावृताः ॥४८॥

śreyānsvadharmo viguṇaḥ paradharmātsvanuṣṭhitāt /
svabhāvaniyataṁ karma kurvannāpnoti kilviṣaṁ //47//
[repeated verse]

sahajaṁ karma kaunteya sadoṣamapi na tyajet /
sarvārambhā hi doṣeṇa dhūmenāgnirivāvṛtāḥ //48//

If it is that *sahaja karma* (*sahaja karma* means *svabhāva karma*, [those *karmas*] which you have to do), if you are *brāhmaṇa* in your qualities, do your *brāhmaṇas* work. Don't indulge that [feeling] that, "I am a westerner. Why should I not do the western work?" Don't do that. Do *brāhmaṇas* work [if you are qualified as such]. *Sadoṣamapi na tyajet*, if [that work] seems [to] you, appears to you [to be] defective, don't call it defective, don't leave it aside. Do that. Indulge in that *karma*. *Sarvārambhā hi doṣeṇa dhūmenāgnirivāvṛtāḥ*, because all . . .

You see . . . what is that?

To indulge with that whitewash, to whitewash it in a [supposed] better way, you should not do that. You should not whitewash your business. Whatever . . . in [whatever] business you are [situated]. . .

JONATHAN: You shouldn't disguise it.

SWAMIJI: . . . you should not disguise it. You should not [disguise] it in another way, e.g., according to your [status of] birth.

DENISE: Why would anyone do that?

SWAMIJI: [Your status] according to your birth, you should not indulge in it. You should let [your natural qualities and tendencies] remain [as they are]. [For example], by birth you are a westerner . . .

DENISE: Right.

SWAMIJI: . . . don't think that you are a westerner and that you should give westerner's shape to your [natural] position. Keep it as brahmin because in qualification you are a brahmin.[518]

DVD 18b (25:42)

असक्तबुद्धिः सर्वत्र जितात्मा विगतस्पृहः ।
नैष्कर्म्यसिद्धिं परमां संन्यासेनाधिगच्छति ॥४९॥

asaktabuddhiḥ sarvatra jitātmā vigataspṛhaḥ /
naiṣkarmyasiddhiṁ paramāṁ saṁnyāsenādhigacchati 49

518 "*Sahajaṁ karma* is whatever is destined to you, on which cycle you are placed, you should do like that. You should act like that. If you are a brahmin, you should not [try to] act as a kṣatriya. If you are a kṣatriya, you should not act as vaiśya or śūdra. Stick to your own nature of *dharma*." Ibid.

When you feel, in your own way, by the supreme way of *śaktipāta*, if He has blessed you in that way, *asakta buddhiḥ sarvatra*, when you are detached from all sides, *jitātmā*, when your mind is under your control, *vigataspṛhaḥ*, all of your desires are finished, they are completed, there is no desire now, there is no leakage of any desire in your mind, it does not remain. This time comes, in the way you are acting upon (e.g., if you are brahmin, in the way you are acting as brahmin), time will come, naturally time will come when you will become *asakta buddhiḥ*, detached from all sides.[519] *Jitātma*, your mind [becomes] under your control [and] *vigatspṛhaḥ*, all desires are gone from your impressions of mind. *Naiṣkarmya siddhiṁ paramāṁ saṁnyāsen*, then you throw, you surrender all of your actions to Parabhairava, and *saṁnyāsenādhigacchati*, then you can do *karma saṁnyāsa*; *karma saṁnyāsa* you can do. *Bas*, you will reside in that [state of] doing nothing. That will be the supreme state of Parabhairava. [You will be] only waiting for the period when you will throw your body. Your body is just already finished. You are only moving with glamour [in the world]. Just as I am moving with glamour. I have no body.

JONATHAN: You said to me once, just recently, you said, "the only difference between me and Parabhairava at the moment is this bag [i.e., this body]."

SWAMIJI: Yes.

JONATHAN: "Once that bag is gone, then there will be no difference at all."

---

519 "*Asakta buddhiḥ sarvatra* . . . when time comes you feel that there is no attachment for any pleasure in this life, *jitātmā*, your mind becomes one-pointed, *vigataspṛhaḥ*, there is no desire in your mind, *naiṣkarmya siddhiṁ paramāṁ saṁnyā*, then you must renounce the world and become a *saṁnyāsin*. Then that *saṁnyāsin* will prove successful.

"Otherwise, if you just go and become *saṁnyāsin* and you put [on] your dyed clothes, you are lost, you are ruining yourself. You must become a *saṁnyāsi* when you have achieved detachment throughout, and no desire for worldly pleasures, then *saṁnyāsa* will prove successful for you." Ibid.

SWAMIJI: Yes. *Naiṣkarmya.*[520] I am waiting for that period.

DVD 18b (28:14)

सिद्धिं प्राप्तो यथा ब्रह्म तथाप्नोति निबोध मे ।
समासेन तु कौन्तेय निष्ठा ज्ञानस्य या परा ॥५०॥

siddhiṁ prāpto yathā brahma tathāpnoti nibodha me /
samāsena tu kaunteya niṣṭhā jñānasya yā parā //50//

O Arjuna, when you have come to this state of achievement in this very life, and by which trick you will achieve the state of Parabhairava; there is a trick there in that, at that moment. I will tell you that trick, *samāsena*, in brief words, *niṣṭhā jñāna*, which is the actual supreme state of Parabhairava.

DVD 18b (29:12)

बुध्या विशुद्धया युक्तो धृत्यात्मानं नियम्य च ।
शब्दादीन्विषयांस्त्यक्त्वा रागद्वेषौ व्युदस्य च ॥५१॥
विविक्तसेवी लघ्वाशी यतवाक्कायमानसः ।
ध्यानयोगपरो नित्यं वैराग्यं समुपाश्रितः ॥५२॥
अहंकारं बलं दर्पं कामं क्रोधं परिग्रहम् ।
विमुच्य निर्ममः शान्तो ब्रह्मभूयाय कल्पते ॥५३॥

buddhyā viśuddhayā yukto dhṛtyātmānaṁ niyamya ca /
śabdādīnviṣayāṁstyaktvā rāgadveṣau vyudasya ca //51//
viviktasevī laghvāśī yatavākkāyamānasaḥ /
dhyānayogaparo nityaṁ vairāgyaṁ samupāśritaḥ //52//
ahaṁkāraṁ balaṁ darpaṁ kāmaṁ krodhaṁ parigraham /
vimucya nirmamaḥ śānto brahmabhūyāya kalpate //53//

[Lord Kṛṣṇa] asks him to come down again: "You come

520 Freedom from limited acts and their consequences. [*Editor's note*]

down again in this field as long as you have a body."[521]

Buddhyā viśuddhayā yukto, your intellect is very pure, it has become very pure. When you are having that, possessing that kind of intellect, by courage, *ātmānaṁ niyamya ca,* you [should] focus your mind in one-pointedness. *Śabdādīn viṣayāṁstyaktvā, śabda, sparśa, rūpa, rasa* and *gandha*, all of these sensual objects you should discard, not by discarding [them externally], you should discard them internally. If you see, don't see; if you hear, don't hear; if you touch, don't touch; if you have got attachment, don't be attached; if you have got detachment, don't be detached. *Dhyāna yogaparo nityaṁ*, be united in that *dhyāna* (meditation) of Parabhairava. *Vairāgyaṁ samupāśritaḥ*, be attached to Parabhairava. *Vairāgya* means attachment. *Vairāgya* here does not mean detachment. *Vairāgya* means [having] too much attachment for Parabhairava.[522]

DVD 18b (31:12)

अहंकारं बलं दर्पं कामं क्रोधं परिग्रहम् ।
विमुच्य निर्ममः शान्तो ब्रह्मभूयाय कल्पते ॥५३॥

ahaṁkāraṁ balaṁ darpaṁ kāmaṁ krodhaṁ parigraham /
vimucya nirmamaḥ śānto brahmabhūyāya kalpate //53//

---

521 Verse 50: "When you have achieved that power of that purity, how you will attain the state of Brahman or God consciousness, you hear from Me! I will explain to you in brief words [that] which is the supreme truth of knowledge (*jñānasya, parā niṣṭhā*)." *Bhagavad Gītā* (1978).

522 "In Shaivism, non-attachment is not recognized. Attachment for Lord Śiva is recognized. . . . When you believe that this whole, whatever is existing in this universe, in all these one hundred and eighteen worlds, whatever is existing is for the sake of Lord Śiva, who is only existing, when this is done, then there won't be *viśeṣa phala*, there won't be particularity of fruits. For instance, you love [your wife]. If you love [your wife] and believe that this loving [your wife] is loving Lord Śiva, who is only existing, then there won't be any trouble. If she dies, if she is trodden down, what to you? Lord Śiva won't be ruined. So this way you have to act in this world, then everything is divine." Ibid.

When there is no ego (*ahaṁkāra*), when there is no *bala* (strength),[523] when there is no *darpa* (arrogance), when there is no *kāma* (desire), when there is no *krodha* (anger), when there is no collecting [i.e., possessing] tendency (*parigraha*), *vimucya nirmamaḥ*, without [the sense of] I-ness and without [the sense of] my-ness (without I-ness and without my-ness and without this-ness), *brahma bhūyāya*, it is likely, it is likely the time has come that you will become, you will be united in Parabhairava very soon.

DVD 18b (32:05)

ब्रह्मभूतः प्रसन्नात्मा न शोचति न हृष्यति ।
समः सर्वेषु भूतेषु मद्भक्तिं लभते पराम् ॥५४॥

brahmabhūtaḥ prasannātmā na śocati na [kaṅkhyatim] hṛṣyati /
samaḥ sarveṣu bhūteṣu madbhaktiṁ labhate parām //54

Brahma bhūtaḥ, when you are actually one with *brahma, parabrahma* (that is Parabhairava), *prasannātmā*, your *ātma*, your soul is always happy, filled with bliss. *Na śocati na kaṅkhyati*, you will never . . . neither you will accept grief or accept any desire. *Samaḥ sarveṣu bhūteṣu*, you will be the same to everybody; [in the company of] rascals also you will be the same. *Madbhaktiṁ labhate parām*, you will abruptly undergo [i.e., achieve] My entire devotion, entire oneness.

DVD 18b (33:15)

भक्त्या मामभिजानाति योऽहं यश्चास्मि तत्त्वतः ।
ततो मां तत्त्वतो ज्ञात्वा विशते तदनन्तरम् ॥५५॥

bhaktyā māmabhijānāti yo'haṁ yaścāsmi tattvataḥ /
tato māṁ tattvato jñātvā viśate tadanantaram //55//

523 "*Balaṁ* [means the] strength that, 'I am! I will tell him, I will make him understand who I am.'" Ibid.

By that *bhakti* (devotion), by that supreme *bhakti*, which is real *bhakti,* you will understand Me, who I am, how much I am and how long I am, how great I am, how broad I am, and how I am broad, and [even] more than that actually. *Tato mām tattvato jñātvā*, then you will get entry in that union with Me. *Viśate tada*, you will undergo, you will melt in that oneness.

Now, He indulges [Arjuna] again how you should do that, again in another way, from the beginning.

DVD 18b (34:27)

सर्वकर्माण्यपि सदा कुर्वाणो मद्व्यपाश्रयः ।
मत्प्रसादादवाप्नोति शाश्वतं पदमव्ययम् ॥५६॥
चेतसा सर्वकर्माणि मयि संन्यस्य भारत ।
बुद्धियोगं समाश्रित्य मच्चित्तः सततं भव ॥५७॥
मच्चित्तः सर्वदुर्गाणि मत्प्रसादात्तरिष्यसि ।
अथ चेत्त्वमहंकारं न मोक्ष्यसि विनङ्क्ष्यसि ॥५८॥

sarvakarmāṇyapi sadā kurvāṇo madvyapāśrayaḥ /
matprasādādavāpnoti śāśvataṁ padamavyayam //56//
cetasā sarvakarmāṇi mayi saṁnyasya bhārata /
buddhiyogaṁ samāśritya maccittaḥ satataṁ bhava //57//
maccittaḥ sarvadurgāṇi matprasādāttariṣyasi /
atha cettvamahaṁkāraṁ na mokṣyasi vinaṅkṣyasi //58//

58th. Up to the 58th [*śloka*] in one push again.

सर्वकर्माण्यपि सदा कुर्वाणो मद्व्यपाश्रयः ।
मत्प्रसादादवाप्नोति शाश्वतं पदमव्ययम् ॥५६॥

sarvakarmāṇyapi sadā kurvāṇo madvyapāśrayaḥ /
matprasādādavāpnoti śāśvataṁ padamavyayam //56//
[repeated]

Sarva karmāṇyapi sadā, whatever action you do, do it and

surrender it to Me, *mat vyapāśrayaḥ*, and go on doing it. *Mat prasādāt,* by My grace, *avāpnoti* (achieve)–he does not say that [only] if *you* do; anybody who does all actions and surrenders all of his actions unto Me–*mat prasādāt*, by My grace, by My divine grace, he achieves *śāśvataṁ padam avyayam* (*śāśvataṁ padam* means the undecayed seat of Myself, which is imperishable, which never ends).

Now 57th [*śloka*]:

DVD 18b (36:36)

चेतसा सर्वकर्माणि मयि संन्यस्य भारत ।
बुद्धियोगं समाश्रित्य मच्चित्तः सततं भव ॥५७॥
मच्चित्तः सर्वदुर्गाणि मत्प्रसादात्तरिष्यसि ।
अथ चेत्त्वमहंकारं न मोक्ष्यसि विनङ्क्ष्यसि ॥५८॥

cetasā sarvakarmāṇi mayi saṁnyasya bhārata /
buddhiyogaṁ samāśritya maccittaḥ satataṁ bhava //57//
maccittaḥ sarvadurgāṇi matprasādāttariṣyasi /
atha cettvamahaṁkāraṁ na mokṣyasi vinaṅkṣyasi //58//
[repeated]

So Bhārata, O Arjuna, this is the general "light-throwing" of Mine, which I throw on [i.e., teach] anybody who does this [practice].

Now you, how you should do [this practice]. Bhārata, O Arjuna, *sarva karmāṇi cetasā mayi saṁnyasya*, all actions, whatever you do, through your mind you should surrender it to Me, *buddhi yogaṁ samāśritya*, and be united in *buddhi yoga. Buddhi yoga* means *jñāna yoga.*[524] *Mat cittaḥ satataṁ bhava*, always focus your mind in Me.

Mat cittaḥ sarva durgāṇi mat prasādāt tariṣyasi (58th *śloka*). *Mat citta*, when you focus your mind in Me, in Me the

524 "*Buddhi yoga* (or *jñāna yoga*) is nature or awareness. Awareness means just to remember Lord in each and every action of this world. Whatever actions you do, remember Lord; remember, don't go astray from that point. Always think of Him. Always remember Him. . . . Through mind, you must remember Him and go on doing whatever you do." *Bhagavad Gītā* (1978).

supreme Bhairava, *sarva durgāṇi*, all *durg* (*durga* means those mounts which are very difficult to climb up, very difficult to cross over), all of those difficult processes you'll *tariṣyasi*, you will conquer.[525]

Atha cet, otherwise, if you *ahaṁkāraṁ na mokṣyasi*, if you still [think] in your mind that, "I am . . . I have to do this, I am doing this by the grace of God." You should not [think] that, "*I* am doing this by the grace of Lord." God is doing it! You should think like that. *Ahaṁkāraṁ*, if you put I, I-ness in that, *vinaṅkṣyasi,* you will be destroyed; you'll be destroyed altogether, nothing will remain of you. And I will be so cruel to you at that time. *Vinaṅkṣyasi*, you will vanish altogether. You'll be no more in this world.

DVD 18b (39:27)

यदहंकारमाश्रित्य न योत्स्य इति मन्यसे ।
मिथ्यैव व्यवसायस्ते प्रकृतिस्त्वां नियोक्ष्यते ॥५९॥

yadahaṁkāramāśritya na yotsya iti manyase /
mithyaiva vyavasāyaste prakṛtistvāṁ niyokṣyate //59//

Yadahaṁkāramāśritya na, and because you have got *ahaṁkāra* (ego) still existing, I feel that in your mind there is *ahaṁkāra* (*ahaṁkāra* means [you still feel that], "I have to indulge in this war!"), *yat ahaṁkāram āśritya na yotsya iti manyase*, you have made up your mind, in your own mind, in your own way, [you think], "I won't indulge in this war," *mithyaiva vyavasāyaste*, and this way of your behavior with Me[526] even [though] I revealed to you My nature of being the whole Bhairava in the 11th chapter (*mithyaiva vyavasāyaste*, this conclusion which you had derived from that chapter of

525 "And when you have diverted your mind towards Me always, in each and every action of the world, *sarva durgāṇi matprasādā*, all your difficulty will be vanished altogether by My grace, not by your action. By My grace, all your difficulties will be over, finished." Ibid.

526 "This understanding is wrong understanding. This understanding is wrong notion. It has appeared in you that, "I will do it" [or] "I won't do it." Don't say "I". Who are you to say [that]? Surrender in Me!" Ibid.

Mine, from the 11th [chapter], i.e., [My] *viśvarūpa* [universal form]), *prakṛtistvāṁ niyokṣyate*, but keep in your mind that *prakṛti*, My power of *svātantrya śakti*, will make you [fight in] this war. You will be no more . . . you have no value in doing or not doing. You are not the doer [and] you are not not-doing. I am the doer! I will make you do [it]!

DVD 18b (41:14)

स्वभावजेन कौन्तेय निबद्धः स्वेन कर्मणा ।
कर्तुं नेच्छसि यन्मोहात्करिष्यस्यवशोऽपि तत् ॥६०

svabhāvajena kaunteya nibaddhaḥ svena karmaṇā /
kartuṁ necchasi yanmohātkariṣyasyavaśo'pi tat //60//

By your *svabhāva*, your nature is [that] of being warrior, you are a *kṣatriya*. *Nibaddhaḥ svena karmaṇā*, you have to do your . . . you have to act according to your work [i.e., nature]. *Kartuṁ necchasi yanmohāt*, this indulgence of war, doing and indulging in this war, you don't like. *Kariṣyasyavaśo'pi tat*, [but] you will have to do it. You will have to do it.

How you will have to do it? I will explain that to you in the next *śloka*. That is 61st *śloka*.

DVD 18b (42:08)

ईश्वरः सर्वभूतानां हृद्येष वसतेऽर्जुन ।
भ्रामयन्सर्वभूतानि यन्त्रारूढानि मायया ॥६१॥

īśvaraḥ sarvabhūtānāṁ hṛdyeṣa vasate'rjuna /
bhrāmayansarvabhūtāni yantrārūḍhāni māyayā //61//

Īśvaraḥ, I, think [of] Me. I am Īśvaraḥ, I am Parabhairava, I am residing in each and every heart of everybody, every soul. *Bhrāmayan*, I am playing with them with My own will.

Who are you to [say] that you will not [engage in this war]? Who are you? You are not existing at all; your will is a failure!

Bhrāmayan sarva bhūtāni yantrārūḍhāni māyayā. By My *svātantrya śakti*, they are going here and there, and I am indulging [in] that way.[527]

So, what you should do?

DVD 18b (43:08)

तमेव शरणं गच्छ सर्वभावेन भारत ।
मत्प्रसादात्परां सिद्धिं स्थानं प्राप्स्यसि शाश्वतम् ॥ ६२ ॥

tameva śaraṇaṁ gaccha sarvabhāvena bhārata /
matprasādātparāṁ siddhiṁ sthānaṁ prāpsyasi śāśvatam 62

Tameva śaraṇaṁ gaccha, bow before [Me], to that Being of Mine! Prostrate yourself and surrender everything that you have achieved, surrender everything to Him who . . . I am that Being. *Tameva śaraṇaṁ gaccha sarva bhāvena*, with all of your might and with all your soul, you surrender in Him and you just throw your I-ness into pieces, away from your existence.

Then, *mat prasādāt avāpnoti*[528] . . . *sthānaṁ prāpsyasi śāśvatam, mat prasādātparāṁ siddhiṁ sthānaṁ prāp* . . . then I'll be glad on you, I'll be satisfied with you, [only] then, if you surrender wholeheartedly to Me, and then you will be established in the eternal, divine residence of the Kingdom of Mine.

I have to indulge the commentary of Abhinavagupta.

yatha, īśvaraḥ paramātmāvaśyaṁ . . . eṣa īśvaraḥ
paramātmāvaśyaṁ śaraṇatvena grāhyaḥ /

This *Īśvaraḥ paramātmā, avaśyaṁ śaraṇatvena grāhyaḥ*, you should bow your head, bow your body, bow your mind before Him. Be prostrate, surrender everything to Him. Because, *yatha* . . .

[tatra hi]-adhiṣṭhātari kartari boddhari svātmamaye

527 *Bhrāmayan*, He handles it; whatever you do, it is handled by Him, not by you. There is only ignorance in you that you say, "I am doing it, I am doing it." He is doing it. He is handling it." Ibid.

528 Here, Swamiji recites the second line of verse 56. [*Editor's note*]

vimṛṣṭe, na karmāṇi sthitibhāñji bhavanti /

Tatra hi, when here, *adhiṣṭātari*, the whole Being who has lifted and who has maintained this whole universe here and hereafter, *kartari*, who is the doer, *boddhari*, who is the knower, *svātmamaye*, who is residing in each and every I-ness of beings, *na karmāṇi sthitibhāñji bhavanti*, these, your *karmas*, your actions, your actions have no guts to stand. Your actions, they have no guts to stand. They won't exist. They will be shattered into pieces before Me.[529] I will give you an example of that.

Nahi! If you say [*nahi*,[530] then] I will [give you an] example of this:

niśitataranakharakoṭi-vidārita-samadakarikaraṭa-galita muktā-phala-nikara-parikara-prakāśitapratāpamahasi siṁhakiśorake guhām-adhitiṣṭhati sati,

When, *niśitatara*, with very sharp *nakharakoṭi* (*nakhara* means nails, very sharp nails of his hand [i.e., paw]), the lion, the lion with the sharp nails of his hand, who has *nakhara-koṭi vidārita samadakarikaraṭa, vidārita,* who has cut the [neck] near the trunk of that *samada* (a great elephant) . . .

[The lion] who jumps on that great elephant on the top and [with its claws] opens up [the elephant's] neck, and all of the blood [flows out in a] stream, and the blood also is soaked in [the lion's] hands.

. . . *galita muktāphala nikara*, and that [jewelry falls out] . . .

It is said that the great elephant has jewels; jewelry also is [in the elephants neck]. [The lion] has done that. He has cut it with [his claws], and jewelry has [scattered everywhere].

529 *Svātmamaye*, he is one with you. . . . but you wrongly understand that, "I am doing it." He is handling internally. . . . each and every action is based on his supreme state, who is residing in your heart." *Bhagavad Gītā* (1978).

530 In this context, *nahi* means "surely not" or "certainly not!" [*Editor's note*]

. . . [then], while going, while watching . . .[531]

Because [the lion] has nothing to do with the flesh of that elephant. He has only sucked his . . . what?

JOHN: Blood.

SWAMIJI: Blood only. He wants blood. He has taken that blood of [the elephant] and his [paws] are soaked with blood and the jewelry has fallen down on the pathway of this lion to his cave, and he is existing in cave, furious, like this.

. . . when he is furiously [seated] in that cave, when *siṁha kiśorake guhām adhitiṣṭhati*, and that young lion, *guhām adhitiṣṭhati*, when he is seated in his cave, furiously, *capala manaso vidravaṇamātra balaśālino hiraṇapotakāḥ,* by that way, by chance, if those deers, which are *capala manasa* (deers, they have got *capala manasa*, their mind is always fickle), *vidravaṇa mātra balaśālina*, they'll . . . as soon as they see this kind of furious [young lion] in that cave, as they automatically [i.e., happen to] see that young, this *kiśora* of this . . .

JONATHAN: The young one is called a cub.

SWAMIJI: Yes.

. . . *capala manaso vidravaṇa mātrabala śālina. Capala manasa vidravaṇa mātra*, [these deer] are always . . . whenever they see this lion, they will run with such velocity, you cannot understand how fast they will run. But, when they see *this* kind of scene, will they [be able to] run? They [will lose their] guts [to run]. They will just die.

DENISE: Frozen in fear.

SWAMIJI: Frozen with fear. They [will] have no guts to act.

In the same way, you have no guts to act against My behavior. I am that, I am that [lion] in the cave, and I am watching, witnessing your actions. Will you do your action? Your action will fail just like those deer. All action of running far away will fail. You can't do anything.[532]

Have you understood now?

531 Referring to the deers who are watching the young lion. [*Editor's note*]

532 "So, [if] I tell you to fight, you will fight. If you say, "I won't fight," you will still fight because I am the handler. So you must take refuge in Me." *Bhagavad Gītā* (1978).

DVD 18b (51:30)

इति ते ज्ञानमाख्यातं गुह्याद्गुह्यतरं मया ।
विमृश्यैतदशेषेण यथेच्छसि तथा कुरु ॥६३॥

iti te jñānamākhyātaṁ guhyādguhyataraṁ mayā /
vimṛśyaitadaśeṣeṇa yathecchasi tathā kuru //63//

This knowledge [which] I have revealed to you, which is the secret of secrets, *guhyāt guhyataraṁ,* which I have revealed to you (this knowledge, it is the secret of secrets[533]), *vimṛśya etat aśeṣeṇa*, you [should] undergo [i.e., reflect upon] My knowledge, which I have delivered to you, *yathecchasi tathā kuru*, then whatever you like, you can do. You can indulge as you [like] because you will be one with Me. Your doing is My doing afterwards.

DVD 18b (52:22)

सर्वगुह्यतमं भूयः शृणु मे परमं वचः ।
इष्टोऽसि मे दृढमतिस्ततो वक्ष्यामि ते हितम् ॥६४॥

sarvaguhyatamaṁ bhūyaḥ śṛṇu me paramaṁ vacaḥ /
iṣṭo'si me dṛḍhamatistato vakṣyāmi te hitam //64//

Again I will repeat [that which is] more secret than [even] this secret, i.e., *sarva guhyatamaṁ,* which is the secret of all secrets. I will again repeat this secret to you, which is the secret of all secrets, *iṣṭo'si me*, because you are [My] beloved, *dṛḍhamati*, and you have got understanding power also by My grace. So I will reveal this secret to you, which is just elevating for you, i.e., which will elevate you for good.

---

533 "Secret of secrets means it is above Vedānta. This knowledge is above Vedānta. This is knowledge of Shaivism–this is Abhinavagupta's commentary–this is knowledge of Shaivism. *Paramādvaitaprakāśanāt*, because this knowledge reveals to you the supreme monistic state of consciousness." Ibid.

DVD 18b (53:20)

मन्मना भव मद्भक्तो मद्याजी मां नमस्कुरु ।
मामेवैष्यसि सत्यं ते प्रतिजाने प्रियोऽसि मे ॥६५॥

manmanā bhava madbhakto madyājī māṁ namaskuru /
māmevaiṣyasi satyaṁ te pratijāne priyo'si me //65//

Manamanā bhava, focus your mind in Me, *mad bhakta*, be My devotee, *madyājī*, be My worshipper, *māṁ namaskuru*, prostrate before Me, *māmevaiṣyasi*, you will become Me. *Satyaṁ*, this is one hundred, one thousand percent correct; *pratijāne*, I take oath that it is quite one hundred percent correct. *Priyo'si me*, you are My dear; after all, you are My dear.

What is that, that supreme [secret]?

DVD 18b (54:28)

सर्वधर्मान्परित्यज्य मामेकं शरणं व्रज ।
अहं त्वां सर्वपापेभ्यो मोक्षयिष्यामि मा शुचः ॥६६॥

sarvadharmānparityajya māmekaṁ śaraṇaṁ vraja /
ahaṁ tvāṁ sarvapāpebhyo mokṣayiṣyāmi mā śucaḥ //66//

Leave all, surrender all acts, good and bad, to Me (*sarva dharmān parityajya*). *Māmekaṁ śaraṇaṁ vraja*, get entry in Me for good. *Ahaṁ tvāṁ sarva pāpebhyo*, because good actions are also bad, bad actions are also bad in this world. [Whenever] you do good actions, those also have a bad effect. [Whenever] you do bad actions, those also have a bad effect. Surrender all of these both actions to Me, and surrender everything in Me. I have taken responsibility to save you from all diseases of good and bad. This is a disease; this is an incurable disease.

What is an incurable disease?

Doing good actions and doing bad actions, or doing good actions and not doing bad actions. This is an incurable disease; this is just like a cancer disease.[534]

And this secret . . .

Idaṁ te nātapaskāya nābhaktāya kadācana . . . 67th [*śloka*].

DVD 18b (56:10)

इदं ते नातपस्काय नाभक्ताय कदाचन ।
न चाशुश्रूषवे वाच्यं न च मां योऽभ्यसूयति ॥६७॥

idaṁ te nātapaskāya nābhaktāya kadācana /
na cāśuśrūṣave vācyaṁ na ca māṁ yo'bhyasūyati //67//

This secret of secrets you should never disclose to that person who has not undergone the *tapasya* of *sāttvic tapasya*; who has not undergone *tapasya* of *sāttvic tapasya* (*tapasya* of the mind, *tapasya* of *buddhi*, *tapasya* of the intellect), which has been already explained to you, i.e., *sāttvic tapasya* of all kinds of *tapasyas*.

That [person] who has undergone this [*sāttvic*] *tapasya*, you should [only] tell [this secret to him]. [But the one] who has not undergone this [*sāttvic*] *tapasya,* you should not disclose this secret to him. *Nābhaktāya*, and [one] who is not My devotee, you should not disclose this [secret to him].

Na cāśuśrūṣave vācyaṁ, [the one] who has not the desire to hear [this], you should not reveal this secret to him. *Na ca māṁ yo'bhyasūyati*, [the one] who hates Me, who is just like a *rākṣasa* (demon) and hates Me, you should not disclose this secret to that [person] also.

DVD 18b (57:37)

य इदं परमं गुह्यं मद्भक्तेष्वभिधास्यति ।
भक्तिं मयि परां कृत्वा स मामेष्यत्यसंशयः ॥६८॥

534 "Because virtues will carry you to heaven and sin will carry you to hell, and you will be entangled in hell and entangled in heaven. With the world of senses, you will be entangled in heaven and with cruel action over your senses, you will be entangled in hell. I will be [the one] who liberates you, but only when you bow before Me and leave everything before Me." Ibid.

ya idaṁ paramaṁ guhyaṁ madbhakteṣvabhidhāsyati /
bhaktiṁ mayi parāṁ kṛtvā sa māmeṣyatyasaṁśayaḥ //68

And [the one] who discloses this supreme secret to My devotees, in My devotees, and indulges in My devotion himself also, *sa māmeṣyatya-saṁśayaḥ*, he will definitely come unto Me.

DVD 18b (58:12)

न च तस्मान्मनुष्येषु कश्चिन्मे प्रियकृत्तमः ।
भविता न च मे तस्मादन्यः प्रियतरो भुवि ॥६९॥
अध्येष्यते च य इमं धर्म्यं संवादमावयोः ।
ज्ञानयज्ञेन तेनाहमिष्टः स्यामिति मे मतिः ॥७०॥
श्रद्धावाननसूयश्च शृणुयादपि यो नरः ।
सोऽपि मुक्तः शुभांल्लोकान्प्राप्नुयात्पुण्यकर्मणाम् ॥७१॥

na ca tasmānmanuṣyeṣu kaścinme priyakṛttamaḥ /
bhavitā na ca me tasmādanyaḥ priyataro bhuvi //69//
adhyeṣyate ca ya imaṁ dharmyaṁ saṁvādamāvayoḥ /
jñānayajñena tenāhamiṣṭaḥ syāmiti me matiḥ //70//
śraddhāvānanasūyaśca śṛṇuyādapi yo naraḥ /
so'pi muktaḥ śubhāṁllokānprāpnuyātpuṇyakarmaṇāṁ 71

Na ca tasmāt manuṣyeṣu kaścit me priya kṛttamaḥ [verse 69]. *Tasmāt*, [apart] from that person, no one is greater [than that person] who has done greatness to Me, and no one will become greater [than that person]. And the person who, *adhyeṣyate ca ya imaṁ dharmyaṁ saṁvādam* [verse 70], [by] this conversation between you and Me (between Lord Kṛṣṇa and Arjuna), [that person] who will *adhyeṣyate*, who will read this conversation of Mine, i.e., our conversation (of Lord Kṛṣṇa and Arjuna), *jñāna yajñena tenāham iṣṭaḥ syām*, My understanding is [that] he has adored Me by *jñāna yajña*.[535]

535 "He has worshipped Me through supreme knowledge. This is My understanding." Ibid.

Śraddhāvānanasūyaśca śr̥ṇuyādapi yo naraḥ [verse 71]. [The one] who has got faith and *anasūyaśca*, who has no hatred [for] Me, if that person, that being also, hears [My words] from someone else, *so'pi muktaḥ*, he is also, he will also become one with Bhairava. And *śubhāṁ lokān prāpnuyāt puṇya karmaṇāṁ*, he will go, after death he will go and reside in Anantabhaṭṭāraka's heaven[536], and be elevated from that way, and he will never come in this wretched world [again].

DVD 18b (1:00:38)

कच्चिदेतच्छ्रुतं पार्थ त्वयैकाग्रेण चेतसा ।
कच्चिदज्ञानसंमोहः प्रनष्टस्ते धनञ्जय ॥७२॥

kaccidetacchrutaṁ pārtha tvayaikāgreṇa cetasā /
kaccidajñānasaṁmohaḥ pranaṣṭaste dhanañjaya //72//

Now, you tell me sincerely, O Arjuna, have you understood something which I have told you [concerning] that secret? Have you understood something? *Kat cit ajñāna saṁmohaḥ,* has some ignorance and *mohaḥ* ([which] means ignorance, forgetfulness of the Lord) been removed from your mind?

Arjuna says:

DVD 18b (1:01:21)

अर्जुन उवाच

arjuna uvāca

नष्टो मोहः स्मृतिर्लब्धा त्वत्प्रसादान्मयाच्युत ।
स्थितोऽस्मि गतसन्देहः करिष्ये वचनं तव ॥७३॥

naṣṭo mohaḥ smr̥tirlabdhā tvatprasādānmayācyuta /
sthito'smi gatasandehaḥ kariṣye vacanaṁ [samam] *tava 73*

536 See *Bhagavad Gītā*, 6.43.

Naṣṭo mohaḥ, all of my ignorance is shattered to pieces, O Lord! *Smṛtir labdhā*, I have got the recollection of what I am by Your grace. *Tvat prasādāt*, by Your grace, Maheśvara, *acyuta*, O unmoved person, *sthito'smi gata sandehaḥ*, I am existing here in my own wits. *Kariṣye vacanaṁ tava*, I will stand and fight with [them] according to Your orders.

Now Sañjaya says to Dhṛtarāṣṭra:

DVD 18b (1:02:18)

सञ्जय उवाच

sañjaya uvāca

इत्यहं वासुदेवस्य पार्थस्य च महात्मनः ।
संवादमिममश्रौषमद्भुतं रोमहर्षणम् ॥७४॥

ityahaṁ vāsudevasya pārthasya ca mahātmanaḥ /
saṁvādamimamaśrauṣamadbhutaṁ romaharṣaṇam //74

O Dhṛtarāṣṭra, this way I was hearing the conversation between Lord Kṛṣṇa and Arjuna, which was *adbhutaṁ,* it was divine, a divine conversation. *Roma harṣaṇam*, all of my *romas* (hairs) were standing [on end].

DVD 18b (1:03:02)

व्यासप्रसादाच्छ्रुतवानेतद्गुह्यतरं महत् ।
योगं योगीश्वरात्कृष्णात्साक्षात्कथयतः स्वयम् ॥७५

vyāsaprasādācchrutavānetadguhyataraṁ mahat /
yogaṁ yogīśvarātkṛṣṇātsākṣātkathayataḥ svayam //75//

By the *anugraha* (grace) of Vyāsa, who has composed this Mahābhārata, by his grace, I was hearing this conversation. *Yogaṁ yogīśvarā kṛṣṇāt*, this *yoga*, *sākṣātkathayataḥ*, [Lord Kṛṣṇa] was expressing this secret of *yoga* with His own lips (divine lips) to Arjuna.

DVD 18b (1:03:52)

राजन् संस्मृत्य संस्मृत्य संवादमिममद्भुतम् ।
केशवार्जुनयोः पुण्यं हृष्यामि च पुनः पुनः ॥७६॥

rājan saṁsmṛtya saṁsmṛtya saṁvādamimamadbhutam /
keśavārjunayoḥ puṇyaṁ hṛṣyāmi ca punaḥ punaḥ //76//

O Dhṛtarāṣṭra, whenever I remember what I have heard by [the grace of] Vyāsa, this *saṁvāda*, this conversation, *keśavārjunagoḥ,* between, Keśava and Arjuna (Lord Kṛṣṇa and Arjuna), *hṛṣyāmi ca punaḥ punaḥ*, I am elevated; again and again I get elevation. I don't know any wits, i.e., I am not residing in my own wits.[537]

DVD 18b (1:04:48)

तच्च संस्मृत्य परमं रूपमत्यद्भुतं हरेः ।
विस्मयो मे महाराज प्रहृष्ये च पुनः पुनः ॥७७॥

tacca saṁsmṛtya paramaṁ rūpamatyadbhutaṁ hareḥ /
vismayo me mahārāja prahṛṣye ca punaḥ punaḥ //77//

And that *rūpa* of *viśvarūpa* (universal form) of Lord Kṛṣṇa, which He was revealing to Arjuna, I am lost in that, in that scene. *Prahṛṣye ca punaḥ punaḥ*, I am, again and again, I get soaked in extreme joy.

DVD 18b (1:05:32)

यत्र योगीश्वरः कृष्णो यत्र पार्थो धनुर्धरः ।
तत्र श्रिर्विजयो भूतिर्ध्रुवा नीतिर्मतिर्मम ॥७८॥

yatra yogīśvaraḥ kṛṣṇo yatra pārtho dhanurdharaḥ /
tatra śrīrvijayo bhūtirdhruvā nītirmatirmama //78//

You recite it [for] ten times.

---

537 "Excitement comes in my mind as soon as I remember this conversation." *Bhagavad Gītā* (1978).

yatra yogīśvaraḥ kṛṣṇo yatra pārtho dhanurdharaḥ /
tatra śrīrvijayo bhūtirdhruvā nītirmatirmama //78//
[repeated]

Yatra yogīśvaraḥ kṛṣṇo, where there is *yogīśvaraḥ kṛṣṇo,* [Lord Kṛṣṇa] existing, *yatra pārtho dhanur dharaḥ*, where Arjuna, this warrior is holding his bow with arrow, *tatra*, there you will find *śrī*, the wealth of supreme wealth, divine wealth, *bhūtir*, divine *aiśvari* (glory) and *nītir*, all of the tricks how to destroy this whole disgusting universe with all of those *rākṣasas* (demons). This is my understanding, O Dhṛtarāṣṭra![538]

DVD 18b (1:07:00)

भङ्क्त्वा ज्ञानविमोहमन्थरमयीं सत्त्वादिभिन्नां धियं
प्राप्य स्वात्मविभूतसुन्दरतया विष्णुं विकल्पातिगम् ।
यत्किंचित्स्वरसोद्यदिन्द्रियनिजव्यापारमात्रस्थिते-
हेलातः कुरुते तदस्य सकलं संपद्यते शङ्करम् ॥

bhaṅktvā jñānavimohamantharamayīṁ
sattvādibhinnāṁ dhiyaṁ
prāpya svātmavibūtasundaratayā
viṣṇuṁ vikalpātigam /
yatkiṁcitsvarasodyadindriyanija-
vyāpāramātrasthiter-
helātaḥ kurute tadasya sakalaṁ
saṁpadyate śaṅkaram //18//

॥ Concluding *śloka* of 18th chapter ॥

538 "Sañjaya has indicated this memory, "as soon as I remember, it gives me excitement." So, it means he has adjusted this memory of Shaivism. . . . Memory is the only element by which you can rise in God consciousness. When memory is lost, everything is lost. . . . Memory means adjustment of awareness, i.e., when you adjust awareness in continuity, in chain-like state." Ibid.

This is the conclusion of this 18th chapter.

Bhaṅktvā jñāna vimoha mantharamayīṁ. Jñāna vimoha manthara mayīṁ, when the negligence, the absence of real knowledge[539], when it is *bhaṅktvā*, when it is uprooted (i.e., negligence of real knowledge), *prāpya svātma vibhūta sundaratayā viṣṇuṁ vikalpātigam*, when you reside in that allpervading Lord Kṛṣṇa, who is *vikalpātigam,* who is *nirvikalpa* always[540], *yatkiṁcit svarasodyad indriyanija vyāpāramātra sthite*, after that, after understanding that, whatever exists in this . . . whatever action he does in this world, whatever bad actions he indulges in this world, whatever good actions he indulges in this world, whatever nasty actions he indulges in the world, whatever outcast[-like] actions he indulges in this world, it will be his play, and by this play he will be focused in Parabhairava in the end. There will be no fear of any actions afterwards.[541]

Now, [Abhinavagupta] says, "who was my master for this, for commentating upon this [*Bhagavad Gītā*]?"

DVD 18b (1:09:18)

श्रीमान्कात्यायनोऽभूद्वररुचिसदृशः
प्रस्फुरद्बोधतृप्त-
स्तद्वंशालङ्कृतो यःस्थिरमतिरभवत्
सौशुकाख्योऽतिविद्वान् ।

---

539 "When your intellect, which is *sattvādibhinnaṁ*, which is sometimes adjusted with *sattvaguṇa*, sometimes adjusted with *rajaguṇa*, and sometimes adjusted with *tamaguṇā*, [when] it makes you rooted in ignorance, in the absence of knowledge, pure knowledge." Ibid.

540 See footnote 61 for an explanation of *nirvikalpa*.

541 "[When] this threefold intellect is shattered to pieces [then] you have not to control your senses afterwards. Don't control your senses, let them do whatever they want to do, *tadasya sakalaṁ saṁpadyate*, [because] they will only [divert you] towards the entry of Lord Śiva, state of Lord Śiva. You will get entry in that state by this doing also. Then! Not before that! Before that, you have to control [your senses and actions]." *Bhagavad Gītā* (1978).

विप्रः श्रीभूतिराजस्तदनु समभवत्
तस्य सूनुर्महात्मा
येनामी सर्वलोकास्तमसि निपतिताः
प्रोद्धृता भानुनेव ॥ १ ॥

śrīmānkātyāyano'bhūdvararucisadṛśaḥ
prasphuradbodhatṛpta-
stadvaṁśālaṅkṛto yaḥ sthiramatirabhavat
sauśukākhyo'tividvān /
vipraḥ śrībhūtirājastadanu samabhavat-
tasya sūnurmahātmā
yenāmī sarvalokāstamasi nipatitāḥ
proddhṛtā bhānuneva //1//

Kātyāyana was one person, *vararuci sadṛśaḥ,* who was just like the sun; just like the midday sun, he was shining. *Prasphurat bodha tṛpta*, he was appeased [by] Parabhairava knowledge. *Tat vaṁśālaṅkṛta*, in [Kātyāyana's] dynasty, one person appeared *sthiramatir*, whose mind was focused in one-pointedness. His name was Sauśuk and he was *vidvān* (*ati-vidvān* means possessing Parabhairava knowledge).

Vipraḥ śrībhūtirājastadanu samabhavat, and afterwards, from [Sauśuk] was born Bhūtirāja. He was a brahmin; he was a brahmin by birth and by action also he was a brahmin. *Tasya sūnurmahātmā*, he was [Sauśuk's] son, *yenāmī sarvalokāstamasi nipatitāḥ proddhṛtā bhānuneva*, who uplifted all living beings who were drowned in intense ignorance; he elevated them all, one-by-one.

DVD 18b (1:11:28)

तच्चरणकमलमधुपो
भगवद्गीतार्थसंग्रहं व्यदधात् ।
अभिनवगुप्तः सद्विज-
लोटककृतचोदनावशतः ॥ २ ॥

taccaraṇakamalamadhupo
bhagavadgītārthasaṁgrahaṁ vyadadhāt /
abhinavaguptaḥ sadvija-
loṭakakṛtacodanāvaśataḥ //2//

Tat-caraṇa-kamala-madhupa, and for his . . . the nectar of [Bhūtirāja's] feet like lotuses, from his lotus-feet, the black bee was Abhinavagupta. The black bee would taste the nectar of his lotus-feet. Bhūtirāja was his master of the *Bhagavad Gītā*, this *Bhagavad Gītā*. Bhūtirāja was his direct master. Whose? Abhinavagupta's.

And Abhinavagupta was the black bee. He was mad after sucking the nectar of the lotus feet, of his master. He, *bhagavad gītārtha saṁgrahaḥ vyadadhāt*, and he has placed [i.e., revealed] this secret of the *Bhagavad Gītā*, the essence of the *Bhagavad Gītā*, and the truth of the *Bhagavad Gītā*, i.e., what is the real meaning of the *Bhagavad Gītā*.

Sadvija-loṭakakṛta-codanāvaśataḥ, I had one friend, he was my friend [and] his name was Loṭaka. His name was Loṭaka and he was not actually a learned scholar, but I liked him because he was filled with the *bhakti* of Parabhairava. He had lost everything for Parabhairava's sake, and he requested me to [disclose] some secret: "please, reveal some secret of the *Bhagavad Gītā* and I will also be benefited." And I did it for his sake.

DVD 18b (1:14:06)

अत इदमयथार्थं वा यथार्थमपि सर्वथा नैव ।
विदुषामसूयनीयं कृत्यमिदं बान्धवार्थं हि ॥३॥

ata idamayathārthaṁ vā yathārthamapi sarvathā naiva /
viduṣāmasūyanīyaṁ kṛtyamidaṁ bāndhavārthaṁ hi //3

Whatever it is, I have not commentated upon *Bhagavad Gītā* as other commentators have done, word by word; I have not done word by word. Because these were just a few points [that I] revealed to Loṭaka, my friend, because he was my associated friend.[542]

DVD 18b (1:14:40)

अभिनवरूपा शक्तिस्तद्गुप्तो यो महेश्वरो देवः ।
तदुभययामलरूपमभिनवगुप्तं शिवं वन्दे ॥४॥

abhinavarūpā śaktistadgupto yo maheśvaro devaḥ /
tadubhayayāmalarūpamabhinavaguptaṁ śivaṁ vande //4

The *Śakti* is *abhinava*, it is always new, and *Śakti* has concealed that *gupta* (*gupta* means [Lord Śiva who is] protected [by His unexhaustive energy). *Tadubhayayāmalarūpam*, *Śakti* and *Śiva*, the combination of both *Śakti* and *Śiva* (*saṁgata* of *Śakti* and *Śiva*) is Abhinavagupta, and he is *Śiva*. I bow before Abhinavagupta. Abhinavagupta says, "I bow before me; I get entry, final entry in Abhinavagupta."[543]

Sāṁkhyayogādiśāstrajñaḥ pāṇinīye . . . my *ślokas*, my *ślokas* are in the end.

[Swamiji's concluding *ślokas*]:

542 "So, this commentary of mine, if *ayathārthaṁ*, if it is just like Shaivism, well and good; if it is not just like Shaivism, well and good. *Sarvathā naiva viduṣāmasūyanīyaṁ*, Shaivite masters should not blame me for this, for doing this commentary of *Bhagavad Gītā* because, *kṛtyamidaṁ bāndhavārthaṁ*, this was done for the benefit of my friends, not my disciples." *Bhagavad Gītā* (1978).

543 "*Abhinava* means 'always new'. What is always new? Always new is the energy of Lord Śiva. Energy of Lord Śiva is never exhausted, inexhaustible energy, that is *abhinavarūpā śakti*. And that which is protected by that inexhaustible energy is Śiva. . . . That person who is protected by the always new, inexhaustible energy, that is Abhinavagupta. And Abhinavagupta is, in other words, not only me; Abhinavagupta says it is the combination of Śiva and Śakti. Abhinavagupta is *tad ubhaya yāmala rūpam*, Abhinavagupta is the connective formation of Śiva and Śakti. So Abhinavagupta is *Śivaṁ*, Lord Śiva Himself." Ibid.

DVD 18b (1:15:43)

ॐ

सांख्ययोगादिशास्त्रज्ञः पाणिनीये कृतश्रमः
शिवार्करश्मिसंपातव्याकोशहृदयाम्बुजः ।
महामाहेश्वरः श्रीमान्राजानकमहेश्वरः
शैवशास्त्रगुरुः स मे वाग्पुष्पैरस्तु पूजितः ॥

sāṁkhyayogādiśāstrajñaḥ pāṇinīye kṛtaśramaḥ /
śivārkaraśmisaṁpātavyākośahṛdayāmbujaḥ //
mahāmāheśvaraḥ śrīmānrājānakamaheśvaraḥ /
śaivaśāstraguruḥ sa me vāgpuṣpairastu pūjitaḥ //

Sāṁkhya yogādi śāstrajñaḥ. Sāṁkhya-Yoga, this *śāstra,* [my *guru*, Maheśvara Rāzdan] had fully undergone [i.e., he was fully informed in the] understanding of Sāṁkhya *śāstra* and Yoga *śāstra*, all *yoga śāstras. Pāṇinīye kṛta śramaḥ*, he had undergone in [the study of] Pāṇinī's *āṣṭadhyayi* (grammar), which was commentated upon [by] Patañjalī [who composed the] *Yoga Sūtras*. He was also elevated in that [knowledge], i.e., my Shaivite *guru*.

Śivārkaraśmisaṁpātavyākośahṛdayāmbujaḥ, whose lotus-heart, heart of lotus, [his] heart-lotus had been bloomed out by the *tīvra śaktipāta* of Parabhairava; or who had *śaktipāta* also, who had *tīvra śaktipāta* of Lord Śiva also.

Who?

My . . .

JOHN: Your *vidya guru*.

SWAMIJI: . . . *Śaiva Śāstra guru*, my *vidyā guru*, Mahā Māheśvaraḥ. He was . . . actually he was devoted to Parabhairava. Rājānaka Maheśvaraḥ, his name was Maheśvaraḥ Rāzdan. *Śaivaśāstra guruḥ sa me vākpuṣpair astu pujitaḥ*, I give him thanks, wholeheartedly.

Now, who I am now [Swamiji points towards himself]?

DVD 18b (1:17:56)

शिवभक्त्यमृतास्वादात्तृणीकृतरसान्तरः
राजानलक्ष्मणाभिख्यः सुधीर्नारायणात्मजः ।
हृदन्तर्वर्त्तिना साक्षाच्छ्रीरामेण प्रचोदितः
प्राकाश्यमनयद् गीताव्याख्यामभिनवोदिताम् ॥

[śivabhakty]amṛtāsvādāttṛṇīkṛtarasāntaraḥ /
rājānalakṣmaṇābhikhyaḥ sudhīrnārāyaṇātmajaḥ //
hṛdantarvarttinā sākṣācchrīrāmeṇa pracoditaḥ /
prākāśyamanayad gītāvyākhyāmabhinavoditām //

Śivabhakti amṛtāsvādāt, by tasting the nectar of *śiva bhakti* (the devotion of Lord Śiva), *tṛṇīkṛta rasāntaraḥ,* who had lost all craving for sensual enjoyments. Who was that? *Rājāna lakṣmaṇābhikhyaḥ*, his name was Lakṣmana Rājāna. Me.

Sudhīr, he was a scholar, *nārāyaṇātmaja*, he was the son of Nārāyaṇa Dass, *hṛdantar vartinā sākṣāt*, and in his heart there was residing his grandmaster, Swami Rām. *Śrī Rāmeṇa pracoditaḥ*, he had put this, a kind of request or behavior into my intellect.[544] *Prākāśyamanayad*, so I have published and revealed this in publicity, the *gītā vyākhyām*, the commentary of the *Bhagavad Gītā*, *abhinavoditām*, which is commentated upon by Abhinavagupta himself.

|| Here ends the *Bhagavad Gītā* ||

इति निवेदयति शिवभक्तानुचरः
राजानकलक्ष्मणः ।

———O———

544 It was Swamiji's grand master, Swami Rām, who requested Swamiji to edit and publish Abhinavagupta's commentary of the *Bhagavad Gītā*. [*Editor's note*]

Bibliography

Publications:

Srimad Bhagavad Gita With Commentary By Mahāmāheshvara Rājānaka Abhinava Gupta, Edited with notes by Pandit Lakshman Raina Brahmachārī (Swami Laksmanjoo), Kashmir Pratap Steam Press, Srinagar, Kashmir, 1933.

Kashmir Shaivism, The Secret Supreme, Swami Lakshmanjoo, ed. John Hughes, Universal Shaiva Fellowship, Los Angeles, 1985-2003.

Self Realization in Kashmir Shaivism – The Oral Teachings of Swami Lakshmanjoo, ed. John Hughes, State University of New York Press, Albany, 1995.

Shiva Sutras, The Supreme Awakening, Swami Lakshmanjoo, ed. John Hughes, Universal Shaiva Fellowship, Los Angeles, 2002.

Vijñāna Bhairava – The Manual for Self-Realization, revealed by Swami Lakshmanjoo, Universal Shaiva Fellowship, Los Angeles, 2007.

Current Perspective on Spirituality in Northwestern Europe, Elizabeth Hense and Frans Maas, from Spiritus: A Journal of Christian Spirituality. Volume 11, Number 1, pp. 67-83. Spring 2011.

Original Audio Recordings:

Bhagavad Gītā of Abhinavagupta: Swami Lakshmanjoo, original audio recording (1978) Universal Shaiva Fellowship archive, Los Angeles.

The Tantrāloka of Abhinavagupta, chapters 1 to 18, Swami Lakshmanjoo, original audio recordings (1972-1981), USF archive, Los Angeles.

Parāprāveśikā by Kṣemarāja, Swami Lakshmanjoo, original audio recording (1980), USF archive, Los Angeles.

Parātriśikā Laghuvṛtti with commentary of Abhinavagupta, Swami Lakshmanjoo, original audio recording (1982), USF archive, Los Angeles.

Parātriśikā Vivaraṇa with commentary of Abhinavagupta, Swami Lakshmanjoo, original audio recordings (1982-85), USF archive, Los Angeles.

Dehasthadevatācakrastotram of Abhinavagupta, Swami Lakshmanjoo, original audio recordings (1980), USF archive, Los Angeles.

Śiva Sūtras of Vasugupta, with the Vimarśinī (commentary) of Kṣemarāja, Swami Lakshmanjoo, original audio recording (1975), USF archive, Los Angeles.

Spanda Kārikā of Vasugupta, with Nirṇaya (commentary) of Kṣemarāja, Swami Lakshmanjoo, original audio recording (1975), USF archive, Los Angeles.

Spanda Saṁdoha of Kṣemarāja, Swami Lakshmanjoo, original audio recording (1981), USF archive, Los Angeles.

Kashmir Shaivism, The Secret Supreme, Swami Lakshmanjoo, original audio recording (1972), USF archive, Los Angeles.

Bodhapañcadaśikā of Abhinavagupta, Swami Lakshmanjoo, original audio recording (1980), USF archive, Los Angeles.

Paramārthasāra of Abhinavagupta, with commentary of Yogarāja, Swami Lakshmanjoo, original DVD recording (1990), USF archive, Los Angeles.

Bhagavad Gītā in a Nutshell, Abhinavagupta's concluding ślokas for each chapter, Swami Lakshmanjoo, original audio recording (1978), USF archive, Los Angeles.

Śivastotrāvalī of Utpaladeva, Swami Lakshmanjoo, original audio recording (1975-80), USF archive, Los Angeles.

Stava Cintāmaṇi of Bhaṭṭanārāyaṇa, Swami Lakshmanjoo, original audio recording (1980-81), USF archive, Los Angeles.

abhimāna 235, 562
Abhinavagupta 1–2, 6, 10–11, 13, 37, 45–46, 48, 53, 61, 64, 69, 73, 76, 81, 87–88, 96–97, 102, 113–116, 119–121, 123, 134, 151, 154–155, 161, 170, 175–176, 178–179, 182, 184, 186, 188, 196, 198, 205, 208, 228, 237, 253–254, 256, 261, 273, 275–277, 282–284, 286, 290, 293, 326–328, 339, 342, 346, 353, 364, 366–367, 372–373, 391, 393, 413, 430, 473–475, 477, 513, 519, 532, 554, 600, 639, 641, 656, 667, 669–670, 672
abhyāsa 74, 91, 254–256, 359, 384, 475–476, 522–524, 613–614, 638
absorption 101, 215, 478, 556, 565
actor 123, 175, 228, 382, 619–620, 624
adharma 35
advaita 536
aghora 527, 601
agitation 271, 305, 383, 431, 474, 489, 543
agni 194, 372, 412, 489, 512, 601
aham 99, 144, 151, 153, 160, 321, 324, 392, 403, 407, 414–415, 572
ahaṁkāra 144, 151, 315, 489, 513, 522, 545, 562, 572, 582, 651, 654
ahiṁsā 404, 491
ajñāna 211, 234, 498, 526, 570, 663
ākāśa 164, 320–321, 383, 441, 443, 489, 511–512, 601
anāhata 320–321
anāmayā 216
ānanda 14, 94, 125, 180, 198, 216, 273, 309, 362, 376, 601
ānanda śakti 14, 125
ananta 15, 158, 356, 420, 440–441, 454–455
āṇava 623
āṇavamala 623
āṇavopāya 101, 190, 201, 287
anger 149, 529, 569, 572, 574, 651
antarātmā 546
anupāya 201, 287
apāna 196, 542
aparā 315–316, 386
aparā śakti 315
Arjuna 18
arrogance 236, 562, 651
āsana 217, 272
aspirant 73, 95, 143–144, 202, 506
atheists 564
ātmā 41, 50, 53, 55, 229, 270
ātman 228, 509
attachment 15, 74, 84, 89, 101, 112–114, 135, 138–139, 160, 173, 203, 243, 253, 277, 282–283, 295, 297–298, 310–311, 323–324, 352, 363, 379, 387, 399, 466, 481, 487, 494–495, 504, 519, 532, 578, 582, 628, 630, 648, 650
attention 234, 274–275, 341, 378, 399, 402
avatār 51
avidyā 11
avyakta 336, 368, 370, 380

awareness 4, 56, 64, 69, 71, 75, 91, 95, 101, 118, 189, 204, 206, 208, 210, 212, 278–279, 297, 300, 373, 404, 430, 477, 503, 615, 653, 666
bhakti 203, 217, 341, 343, 370, 400, 471, 532, 652, 669, 672
Bhaṭṭanārāyaṇa 364
bheda 441
bhidyate 316
Bhīṣma 19
bhūta 243, 347–348, 382, 440, 511, 563, 581
Bhūtirāja 669
bhuvana 512
bija 602
bindu 4
bliss 4, 14, 77, 94, 125, 216, 309, 321, 362, 419, 483, 533, 542, 601, 639, 651
bondage 67, 518, 599, 633
brahma 102, 119–121, 124–125, 127, 154, 177–181, 183–184, 186, 198–199, 219, 238, 243–245, 267, 327, 340–341, 345–347, 361–362, 366–367, 372, 408, 431, 483, 499–500, 510, 516–517, 533, 600, 602–603, 649, 651
brahmacarya 361, 589
brāhmaṇa 86, 163, 642, 646
brahmānanda 198
brahmarandhra 362
breath 29–30, 61, 74–75, 194, 196, 212, 219, 246–248, 255, 275–276, 278, 352, 354, 360, 362, 404, 406, 422, 445, 478, 519, 529, 608, 635, 643
buddhi 76–77, 79, 150–151, 234, 238, 282, 315, 323, 407, 556, 633–634, 653, 661
caitanya 347, 413
cakra 1, 127, 260, 440, 462
cakṣuḥ 436, 547
camatkāra 126, 321
caturdaśa 603
center 29, 60, 109, 162, 187, 212, 275, 297, 361, 411, 423–424, 440–441, 472, 478, 535, 608, 615, 640
central vein 246, 542
cetanā 412–413
cidānanda 198, 216, 309
cit śakti 14, 125
cleanliness 563
cognition 122, 193, 507, 511, 541, 543
cognitive 75, 541, 603
cognitive consciousness 603
cognitive world 541
complete essence of everything 3
completion 325, 624
concentration 201, 296–297, 300
contemplation 30
contentment 404
craving 116, 302–303, 672
creation 3, 11, 114, 120, 170, 180, 229–230, 316–317, 347, 387, 404–405, 419, 423–424, 441, 471, 502, 504, 507, 511, 516–517, 563–564, 600, 645
creation and destruction 230, 441
creative energy 348, 441
cycle of repeated births and deaths 366, 369, 472

darśana 480, 592
death 29–30, 41–42, 45, 47–50, 52, 58–59, 63, 102, 139, 164, 224, 253, 274, 302–304, 341–342, 346, 349–354, 359–360, 363, 365–366, 369, 372, 379, 387, 389, 393, 397, 408, 421, 424, 451, 472, 489, 493, 524, 545, 547–548, 564, 568, 604, 641, 663
deep sleep 340, 533, 546
deha 50, 505, 545
depression 523
desire 5–7, 71, 73, 77, 89, 112, 135, 141, 143, 147, 151, 163–164, 212, 215, 229, 240, 244, 248, 305, 324, 337–338, 340, 361–362, 476, 478, 481, 489, 495, 526, 532, 539, 560, 574, 589, 608, 618, 623–624, 628–629, 648, 651, 661
destruction 46, 120, 229–230, 298, 316–317, 356, 380–381, 387, 441, 511
devatā 116, 337, 415, 420, 427
devotion 154, 203, 205, 217, 275, 282, 341, 343, 360, 370, 390, 396–398, 400, 407, 466, 469–471, 553, 560, 587–588, 651–652, 662, 672
dhāraṇā 362
dharma 35
Dhṛtarāṣṭra 31
dhyāna 478, 650
differentiated knowledge 625–626
disciples 61, 110, 197–198, 203–204, 224, 270, 592, 670
doer 136, 290–291, 336, 503, 510, 527, 620, 624, 629–631, 655, 657
drama 127, 167, 178, 191, 194, 211, 239, 310, 349, 366, 523, 552
dreaming state 31, 74, 109, 215, 277–278, 356, 546, 636
dreamless 215, 474, 546
dualistic 86
duḥkha 67, 260, 278, 282, 366, 493, 504, 531, 541
dvaita 556
dveṣa 139, 264, 628
ear 124, 204, 269–270, 532, 547
earth 23, 28, 100, 114, 123, 125, 240, 315, 318, 322, 338, 441, 489, 550, 601, 603, 641
eating 87, 117–119, 121–122, 125, 185, 189, 231, 278, 306, 399, 445, 548, 584
ego 101, 108–109, 136, 144–145, 236, 315, 479–480, 489–490, 493, 511, 522, 534, 541, 562, 572, 582, 593, 620, 651, 654
ekāgra 92–93, 187
elementary 603
elements 123, 209, 218, 272, 296, 315–316, 320, 338, 341, 362, 412, 488–489, 511, 543, 545, 601–603
elevate 51, 109, 135, 258, 260, 338, 378, 433, 472, 659
elevation 665
embodiment 3, 14, 146, 400–401, 423, 477, 512

energy 14, 125–126, 158, 201, 215–216, 242, 245, 315, 326, 347–348, 441, 517, 670
energy of action 14, 125, 201
energy of bliss 125
energy of consciousness 14, 125
energy of knowledge 14, 125
energy of will 14, 125
enjoyer 121–124, 190, 570
enjoying 89–90, 94, 122, 164, 188, 190, 239, 328, 338, 357, 420, 487, 504, 548, 567, 636
enjoyment 6, 71, 89–90, 114–116, 122, 124, 162, 188, 190, 198, 239, 302, 304, 395, 504, 569
enjoys 101, 249, 280, 284, 357, 504, 623
enlightenment 82, 357
entangled 32, 123, 174–175, 227, 387, 486, 502, 504–505, 507, 509, 511, 519, 531, 613, 641, 661
entangles 518
entangling 539, 562
essence 3, 8, 52, 86, 126, 150, 182, 196, 323, 603, 669
ether 164, 217, 315, 319–320, 383–384, 441, 443, 489, 511, 571, 601
eunuch 521
evil 318
excitement 275, 488, 593, 666
existence 49–50, 69, 84, 111, 114, 125, 151, 216, 361, 363, 384, 429, 448, 457, 553, 602, 656
expansion 87, 164, 182, 244, 261, 274, 511, 518
experiencer 2, 602
experiencing 2, 5, 15, 83, 325, 623
extroverted 376
eyes 33, 39, 110, 148–150, 184, 203, 222, 241, 328, 356, 371, 381–382, 413, 433, 436–437, 440–441, 443–444, 474, 500, 513, 532, 547–548, 621, 636
faith 62, 138, 204, 210, 282–283, 301–302, 304, 306, 310–311, 334–335, 377, 379, 406, 482, 577–580, 582–583, 586–588, 603–604, 610–611, 663
fallen 50, 133, 658
falsehood 560
fear 34, 65–66, 68, 86–87, 102, 131, 151, 160, 163, 248, 274–275, 287, 304, 307, 374–375, 443–444, 453–454, 461, 463–464, 510, 560, 632–633, 635, 658, 667
final liberation 248, 374, 519
fire 3, 26, 49, 55, 147–148, 175, 180–181, 183–184, 187, 194, 208, 252–254, 315, 372, 392, 412, 416–417, 441, 445, 449, 489, 501, 512, 541, 550–551, 586, 601
five tanmātras 545
form 8, 84–85, 88, 99, 123, 176, 179, 185, 216, 255, 278, 293, 337–338, 340, 434, 441, 444, 453, 461–463, 465, 471, 474, 489, 503, 516, 542, 555, 582, 655, 665
fourth state 474
freedom 123, 125–126, 188, 357, 407, 474

fullness 127, 216, 286, 307, 325
gāḍha 74
gandha 123, 179–180, 284, 322, 391, 489, 503, 582, 650
gap 100, 186, 247, 275, 313, 340, 407, 623, 633
Garuḍa 421
ghoratarī 527
God Consciousness 41, 77
grace 2, 8–10, 60, 71, 78, 135, 142–143, 245, 247, 250, 291, 308, 329, 354, 365, 374, 401, 476, 486, 653–654, 659, 664–665
grace of Lord Śiva 8, 250
grammar 155, 176, 185, 276, 279, 671
grammarian 179, 185
greed 36, 523, 566, 574, 582, 630
gross body 546
guṇas 72, 324–326, 489, 502, 504–505, 507, 509, 511, 517–518, 520, 522, 526–532, 534, 537, 548, 582, 596, 598, 625, 632, 641
guru 8, 20, 36, 154–155, 415, 427, 476, 589, 671
ha 39, 600–601
harṣa 144–145, 630
haviḥ 179–180, 183
hearing 61, 78, 83, 181, 194, 500, 503, 506, 580, 664
hell 31, 132, 135, 260, 302, 447, 504, 573–574, 661
hero 194
icchā 7, 14, 125, 248, 489
idam 99
impurities 623
independence 3–4, 347, 413
Indra 134, 280, 334, 336, 391, 396, 413, 418–419
inference 49
inferior 30, 92, 106, 120, 136, 215, 258, 315–317, 321, 334, 336, 376, 396, 424, 553, 645
initiate 203, 270
initiation 196, 199, 203–204
insentient 175, 387, 516
intellect 77, 79, 94–95, 108, 144, 148–151, 173–176, 182, 220, 226–227, 231, 238, 240, 248, 282, 286, 315, 323, 335, 351, 404, 413, 472–473, 477, 480, 489, 511, 522, 544, 565, 576, 603, 622, 633–634, 650, 661, 667, 672
īśāna 601
jaḍa 68, 175, 348, 387, 503, 516
jagad-ānanda 216, 273, 309
jagadānanda 198, 202, 216–217, 272–273, 309, 376
jagrat 546
jāgrat 215–216
jala 412, 489, 512, 601
japa 417, 466
jealousy 358
jīva 486, 545, 549
jñāna 7, 14, 67, 107, 109, 125, 147, 149, 194, 196, 201, 208, 210, 234, 261–262, 314, 337, 370, 377, 407, 485, 489, 492–493, 495, 497–498, 502, 518, 548, 560, 602, 624–626, 649, 653, 662, 667
jñāna śakti 14, 125
jñānendriyas 489
joyful 45, 282

joyous 623, 639
junction 297, 541, 613, 615
kalā 114, 123, 435, 512, 535
kāla 98, 123, 250, 374
kāma 5–6, 141, 143, 147–152, 240, 244, 323–324, 569, 572, 574, 582, 635, 651
karaṇa 212, 221, 342, 624
karma 37, 71, 74, 76, 107–109, 111–112, 119–121, 123–124, 132–136, 153, 159–160, 162, 165–168, 170, 173–176, 178, 181, 208, 211–215, 218–222, 225–229, 231, 233, 251–256, 290, 340–341, 345–346, 348, 352, 391, 460, 476, 478, 486–487, 506, 519, 525, 575, 597–598, 607, 609–612, 614–616, 624–625, 627–630, 642–644, 646–648
kārmamala 622–623
karmendriyas 489
Kaṭha Upaniṣad 639
Kauravas 20
kleśa 628
knowledge 154
krama 182, 201–202, 216–217, 272–273, 376
kriyā śakti 14, 125
krodha 151
Kṣatriya 154
Kṣemarāja 4, 230
kula 31
kuṇḍalinī 224–225, 273, 307–309
kūṭabīja 601
laya 7
liberation 6
Liberation 7
limited being 41, 301, 486
loka 145, 162, 190, 249, 303, 366–367, 394, 405, 467, 565
Lord of death 369, 421, 451, 547
Loṭaka 669
madhyamā 321
Mahābhārata 6
mahābhūtas 316, 512
Mahākāla 421
mahānanda 198
mala 487, 623
manas 545
mantra 117, 201, 204–205, 225, 392, 601
manuṣya 162, 537
māyā 87–88, 92, 97, 120, 123–126, 135, 169, 242, 326–329, 337–338, 340, 385, 387, 530, 602–603
māyā śakti 126, 338
māyīyamala 623
meat 399
meditation 16, 79, 92, 110, 169, 210–211, 252, 255–256, 259, 271, 275–276, 286, 296, 341, 359, 373, 384, 395, 471, 476, 478, 495, 518, 527, 554, 572, 578, 637–638, 650
medium energy 215
merge 242, 307
misery 567
moha 41, 98, 504, 522–523, 526
mokṣa 5–7, 15, 115, 124, 127, 146, 162, 243, 248, 298, 342, 353, 562, 575
monistic 575, 659
muktaḥ 353, 662–663
mystical 319, 392
nara 53, 319

nibodha 618, 649
nimeṣa 365
nimīlana 215, 376
nimīlana samādhi 215, 376
nirānanda 198
nirmala 518
niruddha 92, 94, 187, 281
nirvāṇa 243, 275
nirvikalpa 75, 98–101, 111, 544, 667
niyati 123
non-violence 404, 491
nose 184, 222, 273–274, 548, 585
nothingness 217, 272
objective consciousness 603
objectivity 203, 231, 543
offerings 118–119, 176, 180, 199, 391, 560
oṁ 204, 253, 319, 321, 362–363, 392, 554, 596–597, 599–600, 602
one-pointed 93, 173, 190–191, 198, 238, 247, 254, 260, 262, 272, 278, 281, 283, 286–287, 289–291, 294–297, 299–301, 308, 360, 363, 371, 463, 466, 501, 561, 635, 648
one-pointedness 93, 98, 180, 187–188, 194, 201, 219, 246, 262, 275, 278, 281–283, 287, 289, 295, 299–300, 342, 359, 471, 533, 591, 650, 668
organ of generation 517
organs of action 110, 489, 511
padmāsana 473
Pāṇḍavās 19
pāṇi 500
Pāṇini 185
para 15, 145, 303, 370, 460
parā 4, 150, 153, 215, 315–316, 321, 362, 386, 402, 554, 649–650
parā vāk 321, 362, 554
paraloka 564–565
parāmarśa 602
Paramaśiva 602
parameśvara 232
Parāprāveśikā 4, 230
parāvāk 3
Pārvatī 30
patience 15
peace 15, 27, 29, 95, 146, 275–276, 400, 416, 444, 478, 520, 575
perfect independence 3
power of acting 3
power of existing 3
prakāśa 3–4, 14, 126, 319–320, 323, 327, 372, 530
pralaya 340, 356, 367–368, 385
pramāṇa 75, 122, 193, 543
pramātā 543
pramātṛ bhāva 75
prameya 50, 75, 122, 193, 543
pramiti 75, 190, 204–205, 216, 543–544
pramiti bhāva 75, 190, 204–205, 216, 544
prāṇa 198, 542, 545–546
prāṇāyāma 196–197
prārabdha karma 233
prayer 113, 417, 588
predominent glory of supreme Śiva 3
priest 177, 184, 351, 415, 588, 610
property 152, 284, 296, 315–316, 494

punishment 428
pure ignorance 623
pure knowledge 261, 667
purification 209
purity 14, 31, 95, 209–210, 400, 492, 650
puruṣa 9, 11, 47, 52, 322, 349, 370, 418, 441, 485, 502–505, 507–508, 513, 546, 552–553, 611, 619
puryaṣṭaka 545–546
rāga 15, 84, 123, 139, 323–324, 418, 519, 582, 628
Rāma 422
rasa 89, 123, 179–180, 284, 319–321, 391, 394, 489, 503, 550, 582, 585, 650
rasa (taste) 123, 489, 503, 550, 582
realization 99–100, 272, 296, 475
reflection 147
Renunciation 75
rudras 414, 435, 443
rūpa 74, 123, 179–180, 216, 284, 293, 391, 434, 444, 463–465, 489, 503, 582, 650, 665
rūpa (form) 123, 434, 444, 489, 503, 582
śabda 88, 123, 179–180, 185, 278, 284, 320, 489, 503, 554, 582, 650
sacred 319, 353
sacrifice 19, 121, 609
sadāśiva 600–603
sādhaka 73, 201, 520–521, 527
sādhanā 475–476
sakala 7, 198, 316, 351–352, 517, 554
sākṣāt 672
śakti 3–4, 14–15, 75, 120, 125–126, 157–159, 242, 245, 250, 315–317, 319, 321, 338, 392, 473, 475, 516–517, 527, 554, 600–601, 641, 655, 670
śakti tattva 120
śaktipāta 2
samādhi 8, 71, 81, 110, 178, 181, 187, 189, 202, 215–217, 252, 278, 320–321, 376, 389, 444, 473–475, 503, 505–506
samāveśa 101, 217, 556
śāmbhavopāya 101, 201–202, 287
sameness 46, 294–295, 509, 579
saṁghaṭṭa 31
saṁnyāsin 648
saṁsāra 5, 227, 260, 366, 369, 385, 516–517, 536, 600
saṁskāra 92, 209, 355
saṁvit 14, 100, 123–124
sand 357, 456
Sañjaya 31
Śaṅkara 414
śāntātītā kalā 512
sāra 3, 29, 353
śarīra 47, 158, 545–546, 621
śāstra 5, 116, 193, 418, 536, 575, 578–579, 671
sat 33, 393, 500, 504, 597–600, 602–603
sattva guṇa 231, 504
sāttvika 584, 587, 630, 633
sauḥ 603
savikalpa 100
scriptures 575
seat 3, 31, 33, 148, 161, 178, 211, 331, 346, 440, 455, 533, 646, 653

semen 416
sensations 46
sex 141, 323–324, 405, 488, 517, 574
sexual 6
sexual act 419
siddha 443
siddhas 314, 443
sin 30–31, 67, 119, 183, 211, 223, 629, 633–634, 661
śiva 15, 601, 672
Śiva Sūtra Vimarśinī 338, 413, 546
Śiva Sūtras 216, 413
śiva tattva 15
skin 184, 222, 241
smell 123, 179, 184, 188, 322, 361, 489, 503, 512, 532, 582, 585
soma 394, 550
soul 34, 43, 46, 50–53, 55–57, 63, 71, 73, 91, 126, 148, 150, 159, 169–171, 196, 205, 207, 217, 303, 333, 338, 347, 356, 364, 406, 411, 427, 454, 486–487, 492, 507–509, 511, 529, 548, 560, 563, 651, 655–656
sound 21, 23, 123, 183, 188, 274–275, 278, 319–321, 359, 422, 472, 489, 565, 582, 590
soundless 321
space 99, 164, 208, 246–248, 437, 440–441, 542
spanda 4
sparśa 46–47, 67, 123, 179–180, 238, 278, 391, 489, 503, 582, 650
sparśa (touch) 67, 123, 278, 489, 503, 582
speech 321, 425, 590
sphurattā 3
spirituality 638
sthiti 158, 229, 473, 543
strength of consciousness 3
subject 122, 139, 190, 193, 200, 210, 273, 290, 405, 541, 543
subjective consciousness 75, 190, 543, 603
subjectivity 231, 600
subtle 47–50, 144, 183, 315, 340, 501, 545–547, 601
subtle body 545–547
śuddha 16, 337
śuddhavidyā 16, 600–601, 603
śūdra 161, 252, 353, 645, 647
sūkṣma 545–546
sūkṣma śarīra 545–546
supreme grace 308, 365, 476
supreme secret 154
supreme word 3, 321
surrender 62, 253, 313, 458, 472–473, 477, 492, 540, 648, 653, 656, 660
sūrya 153, 320, 437, 441
suṣumnā 246, 362
suṣupti 215–216, 340, 546
svādhyāya 196–197, 590
svapna 215–216, 278, 546
svātantrya 4, 75, 123–127, 157, 159, 202, 242, 315–317, 321, 338, 347, 413, 473–475, 516–517, 554, 623, 641, 655
svātantrya śakti 4, 75, 125–126, 157, 159, 242, 315–317, 321, 338, 473, 475, 516–517, 554, 641, 655
Swami Lakshmanjoo 3–4, 15, 30, 32, 60, 75, 86, 94, 99–101, 120, 125–127, 161, 163, 170,

190, 200–202, 204, 215–217, 230, 242, 297, 304, 316, 321, 338, 364–365, 371, 376, 381, 413, 512, 527, 543, 545–546, 600–603, 615, 623
Swami Ram 195
sword 539
tāmas 324, 504, 578, 580–581, 583–585, 588, 593–596, 604, 611, 613, 617, 624, 627, 629, 631–632, 634–637, 640
tanmātras 545
tantra 600
Tantrāloka 3–4, 30, 75, 86, 100–101, 120, 125–126, 163, 170, 182, 188, 201–202, 204, 215–217, 242, 304, 314, 316, 338, 364, 376, 412–413, 512, 601–602, 615, 623
tantras 4, 600
taste 89, 116, 123, 179, 184, 228, 239, 278, 320–321, 399, 482, 489, 502–503, 550, 582, 584–585, 669
tatpuruṣa 424, 601
tattva 15, 114, 120, 123, 382, 497
tattvas 123, 603
thoughtless 75
three guṇas 72, 324–326, 489, 502, 504, 507, 509, 517–518, 520, 522, 527–531, 534, 537, 548, 582, 596, 598, 625, 632, 641
tirodhāna 245
tolerance 46, 425, 491, 493, 560–562, 616, 630
tongue 184, 547
touch 10, 31, 67, 69, 75, 115, 123, 135, 145, 179, 183–184, 188–189, 223–224, 252–254, 278, 321, 361, 444, 452, 454, 466, 472, 489, 500, 503, 505, 507, 532, 547, 582, 650
trance 116, 142, 270
transcendental 202
trika 600
Trika system 603
truth 6, 65, 69–70, 94, 143–144, 201, 205, 225, 357, 379, 393, 510, 532, 539, 560, 563, 605, 628, 650, 669
turya 215–217, 474, 543
turyātīta 215–217, 474
tyāga 75
unawareness 97
universal 4, 64, 115, 120, 126, 151–152, 160–161, 168, 176, 178, 182, 203, 207–208, 215–216, 296, 309, 320–321, 326, 347, 412, 434, 437, 440, 453, 459, 462–463, 465–466, 474, 487, 516–518, 539, 548, 579, 599, 603, 655, 665
universal God consciousness 151
universal heart 4
universal movement 4
universal-I conscious-ness 151
universality 151–152, 206, 408
ūṣma 601
Utpaladeva 57
vacaḥ 40, 403, 659
vacuum 164
vaiśya 252, 642, 645–647
vāk 321, 362, 425, 554, 621
varṇa 31
Vāsudeva 464
vāyu 315, 383, 412, 422, 489, 601

vāyu (air) 489, 601
Vedas 70, 72–73, 200, 276, 319, 354, 375, 392, 394–395, 412, 463, 488, 536
vega 240
vidhi 233, 354, 575
vidyā 9, 123, 235, 378, 423, 671
vijñāna 149, 261–262, 314, 377
vikalpa 15, 99, 101, 126
vimarśa 3–4, 126
violence 404, 491
vīrya 415–416, 457
visarga 4, 348–348, 603
viśiṣṭa 337, 473
Viṣṇu 82, 334–335, 367, 411, 454
viśva 347
viśvam 15, 645
void 217
voidness 533, 546
vowels 601–602
waking state 31, 371, 546
water 26, 55, 62, 72, 89, 177, 223, 315, 319, 322, 351, 356, 397, 412, 420, 487, 489, 601
wind 55, 280, 315, 383–384, 412, 424, 435, 443
woman 41, 284, 390, 419, 425
womb 147, 347, 388, 415, 516–517, 546
worship 201, 217, 220, 314, 390–391, 393, 396–397, 442–443, 581, 583, 589
Yājñavalkya 14
yoga 30, 74, 76–77, 79, 88, 90–94, 107, 153–154, 156, 185, 187, 205, 210, 213–215, 218–221, 225–227, 252–257, 269–270, 272–273, 275–282, 285–287, 290–292, 294–295, 299, 301–306, 308–309, 311, 313, 352, 358–360, 362–363, 374, 379, 382, 405–407, 473–474, 478, 506, 549, 560, 584, 590, 607, 609, 635, 653, 664, 671
yogī 96, 240, 248, 251–252, 261–262, 269, 277, 291, 293–294, 306, 309, 374, 479
yoni 504, 516–517
yuga 158, 355, 368, 516

Lakshmanjoo ACADEMY

The teachings of Swami Lakshmanjoo are a response to the urgent need of our time: the transformation of consciousness and the evolution of a more enlightened humanity.

The Universal Shaiva Fellowship and its educational branch, The Lakshmanjoo Academy, a fully accredited non-profit organization, was established under Swamij's direct inspiration, for the purpose of realizing Swamiji's vision of making Kashmir Shaivism available to the whole world. It was Swamiji's wish that his teachings be made available without the restriction of caste, creed or color. The Universal Shaiva Fellowship and the Lakshmanjoo Academy have preserved Swamiji's original teachings and are progressively making these teachings available in book, audio and video formats.

This knowledge is extremely valuable and uplifting for all of humankind. It offers humanity a clear and certain vision in a time of uncertainty. It shows us the way home and gives us the means for its attainment.

For information on Kashmir Shaivism or to support the work of The Universal Shaiva Fellowship and the Lakshmanjoo Academy and its profound consciousness work,

visit the Lakshmanjoo Academy website or
email us at info@LakshmanjooAcademy.org.

www.LakshmanjooAcademy.org

Instructions to download audio files

1. Open this link to download the free audio . . .
   https://www.universalshaivafellowship.org/BhagavadGita

   It will **direct** you to "**Bhagavad Gita - Audio**".

2. Select "**Add to basket** " which will send you to the next page.

3. Copy "**Gita**" into the "**Add Gift Certificate or Coupon**" box

4. Click "**Checkout**" and fill in your details to process the free downloads.

If you have any difficulties please contact us at:
www.LakshmanjooAcademy.org/contact

www.ingramcontent.com/pod-product-compliance
Lightning Source LLC
Chambersburg PA
CBHW052008290426
44112CB00014B/2159
* 9 7 8 0 9 8 1 6 2 2 8 7 3 *